W9-CRP-022

LEADERS IN AMERICAN EDUCATION

Officers of the Society

1970-71

(Term of office expires March 1 of the year indicated.)

EDGAR DALE
(1971)
Ohio State University, Columbus, Ohio

N. L. GAGE
(1972)
Stanford University, Stanford, California

JOHN I. GOODLAD
(1973)
University of California, Los Angeles, California

ROBERT J. HAVIGHURST
(1971)
University of Chicago, Chicago, Illinois

HERMAN G. RICHEY
(Ex-officio)
University of Chicago, Chicago Illinois

HAROLD G. SHANE
(1972)
Indiana University, Bloomington, Indiana

RALPH W. TYLER
(1973)
Director Emeritus, Center for Advanced Study in the Behavioral Sciences
Stanford, California

Secretary-Treasurer

HERMAN G. RICHEY
5835 Kimbark Avenue, Chicago, Illinois 60637

LEADERS IN AMERICAN EDUCATION

The Seventieth Yearbook of the National Society for the Study of Education

PART II

By

THE YEARBOOK COMMITTEE
and
ASSOCIATED CONTRIBUTORS

Edited by

ROBERT J. HAVIGHURST

Editor for the Society

HERMAN G. RICHEY

1 9  *7 1*

Distributed by THE UNIVERSITY OF CHICAGO PRESS • CHICAGO, ILLINOIS *60637*

The responsibilities of the Board of Directors of the National Society for the Study of Education in the case of yearbooks prepared by the Society's committees are (1) to select the subjects to be investigated, (2) to appoint committees calculated in their personnel to insure consideration of all significant points of view, (3) to provide appropriate subsidies for necessary expenses, (4) to publish and distribute the committees' reports, and (5) to arrange for their discussion at the annual meeting.

The responsibility of the Society's editor is to prepare the submitted manuscripts for publication in accordance with the principles and regulations approved by the Board of Directors.

Neither the Board of Directors, nor the Society's editor, nor the Society is responsible for the conclusions reached or the opinions expressed by the Society's yearbook committees.

Library of Congress Catalog Number: 6-16938

Published 1971 by

THE NATIONAL SOCIETY FOR THE STUDY OF EDUCATION

5835 Kimbark Avenue, Chicago, Illinois 60637

First Printing, 10,000 Copies

Printed in the United States of America

The Society's Committee on Leaders in American Education

ROBERT J. HAVIGHURST
(Chairman)
Professor of Education
University of Chicago
Chicago, Illinois

CHARLES BURGESS
Professor of History of Education
University of Washington
Seattle, Washington

ROBERT L. MC CAUL
Associate Professor of Education
University of Chicago
Chicago, Illinois

JONATHAN MESSERLI
Dean of the School of Education, Professor of Education
Hofstra University
Hempstead, New York

ANNE ROE
Professor of Education and Director of
Center for Research in Careers Emeritus
Harvard University
Cambridge, Massachusetts

PAUL WOODRING
Distinguished Service Professor of the College
Western Washington State College
Bellingham, Washington

Associated Contributors

JOHN S. BRUBACHER
Professor of History and Philosophy of Education Emeritus
Yale University
New Haven, Connecticut
Professor of Education Emeritus
University of Michigan
Ann Arbor, Michigan

RAYMOND E. CALLAHAN
Professor of Education
Washington University
St. Louis, Missouri

WILLIAM G. CARR
President, World Confederation of Organizations of the Teaching Profession
Washington, D.C.

GERALDINE JONÇICH CLIFFORD
Associate Professor of Education
University of California
Berkeley, California

JAMES BRYANT CONANT
President Emeritus
Harvard University
Cambridge, Massachusetts

GEORGE S. COUNTS
Professor of Education Emeritus
Teachers College, Columbia University
New York, New York
Distinguished Visiting Professor
Southern Illinois University
Carbondale, Illinois

ARTHUR I. GATES
Professor of Educational Psychology Emeritus
Teachers College, Columbia University
New York, New York

PATRICIA ALBJERG GRAHAM
Associate Professor of History and Education
Barnard College and Teachers, Columbia University
New York, New York

MAXINE GREENE
Professor of English
Teachers College, Columbia University
New York, New York

J. STEPHEN HAZLETT

Assistant Professor of Education
University of Chicago
Chicago, Illinois

VINCENT P. LANNIE

Associate Professor of Education
University of Notre Dame
Notre Dame, Indiana

SIDNEY LEAVITT PRESSEY

Professor of Psychology Emeritus
Ohio State University
Columbus, Ohio

GEORGE N. SHUSTER

President Emeritus
Hunter College,
New York, New York
Assistant to the President
University of Notre Dame
Notre Dame, Indiana

GEORGE D. STODDARD

Distinguished Professor of Education Emeritus
New York University
New York, New York
Chancellor
Long Island University
Greenvale, New York

RUTH M. STRANG

Professor of Education Emeritus
Teachers College, Columbia University
New York, New York

ROBERT E. TOSTBERG

Associate Professor of Education
University of Washington
Seattle, Washington

ROBERT ULICH

Professor of Philosophy and History of Education
and Comparative Education Emeritus
Harvard University
Cambridge, Massachusetts

CARLETON WOLSEY WASHBURNE

(Deceased)

Table of Contents

CHAPTER I

Origin and Development of the Yearbook

ROBERT J. HAVIGHURST

Preliminary Planning

This yearbook has evolved out of discussions and experiments carried on by the Board of Directors of the National Society for the Study of Education, beginning in 1964.[1] Nothing like it had been done before, and the board had to explore a number of questions before it could actually approve the yearbook project.

The first proposal was for a set of biographical sketches of a selected group of leaders, supplemented by brief autobiographies. The board agreed to think about it and to ask the advice of a leading historian of education. A year later, in February 1965, the subject was brought up again at a meeting of the board, and the minutes read as follows:

> Mr. Tyler read a letter from Professor ——— in which he pointed out the problems and difficulties in producing a good yearbook of the type under discussion. In Mr. ———'s judgment, both the collection of autobiographies that were to be sought and an adequate biographical treatment of the selected subjects involved almost insurmountable difficulties.
>
> It was agreed that the problems cited were real ones but it was not agreed that the proposal need be entirely abandoned.
>
> It was suggested that the Society might undertake to collect ten or more autobiographies with the declared intention of using them some ten years after their preparation. There would be no guarantee that any autobiography would be used but assurance would be given that the Society was committed to a publication that would make use of such material.
>
> It was agreed that Mr. Havighurst would discuss the proposal with others and keep it before the Board until it was better informed con-

1. This chapter gives a rather detailed account of the development of the yearbook on the assumption that it may have some historical value.

cerning the problems and issues involved in preparing such a yearbook.

It was agreed that the Society would provide funds in modest amount, if needed, for further exploration of the proposal.

Before proceeding with a yearbook, the NSSE Board considered the possibility of a more ambitious project. At that time there was a growing interest in the history of science and medicine. The American Institute of Physics was developing a project on the history of physics in the twentieth century, including the collection of autobiographical and biographical material on a number of prominent American physicists. The *History of Psychology in Autobiography* was being continued in a fifth volume edited by Edwin G. Boring and Gardner Lindzey. The University of Akron was setting up the Archives of Psychology and soliciting papers, letters, and other biographical material from psychologists. The Oral History Project at Columbia University was interviewing people who had taken part in important twentieth-century developments in various fields of work.

Mr. Havighurst proposed that the NSSE set up a committee on the study of educational leaders, which might work for a period of five to ten years, and that this committee should operate with a good deal of autonomy but make annual reports to the NSSE Board and take no major step without board approval.

It was further proposed that this committee would consist of experts in the history of education, biographers with an interest in American biography, and social scientists who have a broad acquaintance with contemporary American society. This committee would work on the production of *biographies* of leaders in American education and would be encouraged to get out a series of publications independent of the Society's yearbook series.

This proposal was more ambitious than the board was prepared to undertake, but Mr. Havighurst was authorized to call together a small committee to discuss the preparation of a yearbook and present a plan to the board. A preliminary plan was prepared between February 1966 and July 1967. Mr. Havighurst consulted first with Dr. Ruth Eckert of the University of Minnesota, Dr. Ann Heiss of the Center for the Study of Higher Education at the University of California–Berkeley, and Dr. Robert L. McCaul of the University of Chicago.

Mr. Havighurst worked out an extended outline of an autobiographical sketch and then approached George S. Counts and Ruth Strang with the proposal that they should prepare autobiographical sketches along the lines of the outline. Both cooperated fully and graciously. Miss Strang wrote her autobiography quite fully. Mr. Counts supplied some earlier biographical sketches and then dictated on tape at some length in response to the outline.

Meanwhile a yearbook committee was being formed. The first committee meeting took place on July 21-22, 1967, with Paul Woodring, Jonathan Messerli, Robert McCaul, and Robert J. Havighurst in attendance. They met with the NSSE Board on July 22 and proposed a yearbook to be published in 1971 which would be essentially an autobiography-biography combination on about ten people in the age range of seventy to eighty. This was approved by the NSSE Board, with the comment that the more ambitious project might emerge in manageable form out of experience with the yearbook.

Another committee meeting was held in December to develop more definite plans for the yearbook, and these plans were approved by the NSSE Board in February 1968. The committee was enlarged to include Dr. Anne Roe of Tucson, Arizona, and Professor Charles Burgess of the School of Education of the University of Washington.

Among memoranda prepared for the December 1967 meeting was the following by Dr. Robert L. McCaul.

Some of the chief values to be derived from the study of educational history are the following:

1. The study of the educational past may enable us to learn from the experience of men who have faced educational problems similar to our own and have developed solutions appropriate to their times and perhaps with some adjustments to ours.

2. The study of the educational past may enable us to reach some understanding of how and why the institution within which we work and the profession of which we are members have come to possess their present characteristics.

3. The study of the educational past necessarily concerns the actions of men and women; some of these persons may serve as career models for contemporary members of the profession or for those persons who are contemplating entering the profession.

4. The study of the educational past may enable us to escape from the provincialism and exclusiveness of our own ego and our own milieu.

The committee had moved toward an emphasis on autobiography in the yearbook, with supporting biographical essays. It was therefore necessary to select the subjects who would be asked to write their autobiographies and also the people who would be asked to write biographical essays about the subjects.

Selection of the Subjects of the Yearbook

Three categories of educational leaders were defined and the committee nominated approximately ten people in each category—scholars, creative administrators, and leaders through the force of ideas. The committee took responsibility for the original list of thirty-one persons that were nominated. But it was decided that the committee should name a panel of electors, men and women with wide experience and a wide acquaintance in the field of education. To these people—twenty-five in number—the following letter was sent in the spring of 1968.

Dear Colleague: *Confidential*

This letter is going to a specially selected Panel of about 25 Consultants whom we are asking to help us select a dozen living leaders to become the Subjects of a *Yearbook on Leaders in American Education.* We hope you will assist the project by casting a preference ballot for 12 people from the attached list of nominees.

The Yearbook is planned as follows: Each Subject who is selected will be asked to write an autobiography of 5 to 10 thousand words, following a general scheme or outline that we will provide. Then a competent historian-biographer will be assigned, a separate Biographer to each Subject, to write a biographical sketch of 3 to 8 thousand words on the Subject.

The Subjects must all have been born before 1902, so that they will be 70 or over in 1971, when the Yearbook will be published.

Everyone has his own ideas about who was and is important in the field of education, and we want you to apply your ideas. We suggest the criterion of *impact on American education.* How much impact has this person's activity, writing, teaching, etc., had on American education? We are thinking of the entire range of institutionalized education from elementary school through adult education. The person should have done most of his work in America.

In order to get a variety of styles of leadership represented, we have selected nominees from three categories: scholars, creative administrators, and leaders through ideas. While each category does not have to be equally represented with each other one in the Yearbook, we hope to get some representation from each category. You might keep that in mind in casting your ballot.

Three Subjects have already been selected by the Committee, partly in order to gain experience in the process of soliciting autobiographies. They have agreed to participate. These three are: James B. Conant; George S. Counts; Ruth Strang.

You may think of other people who should be nominated whose names are not on the list. If so, will you write their names at the bottom of the Ballot. If several Consultants name the same person, this will cause us to consider this person as a possible candidate. It will also help us in selecting a second group of Subjects for a possible second Yearbook.

I hope this interests you enough to cause you to respond immediately with your Ballot.

Please rank 12 from the total list, numbering them from 1 to 12 in order of your preference.

Robert J. Havighurst

The members of the Panel of Electors were the following:

James E. Allen
Melvin W. Barnes
Harry S. Broudy
Norman Burns
William W. Brickman
Aaron Brown
R. Freeman Butts
Lee J. Cronbach
Ruth E. Eckert
John H. Fischer
John I. Goodlad
Maxine Greene
Herold C. Hunt
Cyril O. Houle
Lawrence D. Haskew
H. Thomas James
Ann Keppel
William C. Kvaraceus
Neil McCluskey, S.J.,
Frederick L. Redefer
P.C. Reinert, S.J.
Helen M. Robinson
Harold G. Shane
Lindley J. Stiles
Ralph W. Tyler

None of these panel members was born earlier than 1902. Nearly all of them voted, anonymously. Seven of them added names, but none was mentioned repeatedly. In fact, the majority of the names they mentioned were born after 1901 and therefore not eligible.

It turned out that the bulk of the votes went to *scholars* and to *leaders through ideas*. Very few of those in our category of *creative administrators* were selected in the preference ballot. This writer's judgment is that it would have been better to set up several categories in advance and elect a certain quota of persons in each category. In addition to the categories named, there might have been categories for women, Negroes, college presidents, etc. This would have given us a wider spread of types of leaders, though some would have made the list who were not so well and popularly known as some who would not be elected under those arrangements.

It was desired to have ten to twelve subjects in the yearbook, and the committee took the top fifteen names, assuming that some would decline or otherwise be unable to participate. Actually three people declined, and another (Harold Benjamin) died after accepting the invitation but before he could write his autobiography. Carleton Washburne mailed his autobiography to the chairman just a few days before he suffered the stroke that ended his life.

The age range of the eleven subjects extends from seventy (in the year 1971) to eighty-two.

Directions to Yearbook Subjects

A letter was written to each person elected, describing the yearbook briefly and telling him that he had been chosen. The names of others on the list, chosen or not chosen, were not divulged to him until later. He was given the three-page "outline for an autobiographical sketch" as a suggestion. (Some followed this carefully; others appeared to ignore it.) He was asked to sign the attached agreement, which was also to be signed by the chairman of the yearbook committee and the author of the biographical sketch. He was told that the combined autobiography-biographical sketch could go to thirteen thousand words (exclusive of bibliography). He was advised that the author of the biographical sketch would be asked to write from three thousand to five thousand words, thus leaving eight thousand to ten thousand words for the autobiography. There were some complaints about these limits from several people, but they all proved to be "good soldiers." No subject exceeded ten thousand words, and a few went under that mark, leaving the biographers more than three thousand words, which they were glad to have.

Choice of Authors of Biographical Essays

The committee concluded that it would try to match subjects with biographers so as to secure mutual satisfaction, but that it would have to take the final responsibility. The committee drew up a list of thirty possible biographers, most of them teachers of the history of education. These were matched to subjects as the committee thought wise, and a letter was sent to each subject giving him the name of the suggested biographer and asking whether he approved. In two cases the subject expressed some doubt, and another person was nominated and accepted. The acceptable biographers then received letters asking them to write biographical essays, and all but one accepted. The one who did not accept explained that he was too busy completing a book to do justice to another assignment. The list of biographers is presented at the end of this chapter.

The arrangement between the subject of the autobiography and his biographer was defined in three possible ways, as follows: The biographer could:

1. Help the subject amplify and improve his autobiography and add only a minimum of supporting material. The biographer would serve mainly as a catalyst and an editor. This would maximize the value of the autobiography and make it a better source of data for future historical work.

2. Accept the autobiography with whatever amplification seemed clearly necessary. The biographer would write a kind of vignette that would supply other kinds of information about the subject.

3. Accept the autobiography with little or no amplification and add to it about 50 percent as much wordage in the nature of a critical evaluation of the subject. The additional material would be regarded as *very* important, supplying information that the subject did not or could not provide in his autobiography. Possibly the biographer might ask four or five people who knew the subject well to write brief evaluations from several points of view.

All three procedures were used, together with variations on them. Some biographers entered into active correspondence with their subjects and paid them one or more visits. Others sought very little personal contact. In one case (Carleton Washburne) Patricia Albjerg Graham received the autobiography after his death, but she had known him in connection with his leadership in the Progressive education movement, of which she had written a history.

The yearbook committee read the autobiographies as they came in and also the biographical sketches. A final meeting in Seattle in September 1969 gave the committee members opportunity to discuss critically almost the entire yearbook in first draft form. As a result of this meeting the chairman wrote to the subjects and biographers, reporting the committee's suggestions for possible improvement of their pieces. The final drafts came in shortly thereafter, though most of the autobiographies were little changed after the first revision. The subjects were informed that they would see the biographical sketches in their final form and would not be encouraged to write rejoinders, even if they wished to do so. However, if they found actual errors in fact, they should report these to the chairman.

Everybody played his role in this process pleasantly, and it appeared that the process was reasonably satisfactory to everybody involved.

Final Chapter

The concluding chapter by Paul Woodring and Robert L. McCaul had been anticipated from the start. Mr. Woodring had written a memorandum in 1967 suggesting that the yearbook serve as a basis for "an inquiry into the nature and origins of educational leadership," and the committee accepted this suggestion with alacrity. However, there was not time to do this in any systematic manner, and the eleven autobiographies might not be an adequate sample for an inductive study.

Mr. Woodring and Mr. McCaul were asked to write a concluding chapter commenting on the yearbook as a source of systematic information on the nature and origins of educational leadership. They read the entire text of the yearbook as a basis for this chapter.

Finances

Like all NSSE yearbooks, this one has been prepared on the proverbial "shoestring." Authors were not paid. Committee members were not paid, though their expenses were paid for attending committee meetings. The NSSE Board was especially generous in the case of this yearbook, however, and offered to pay the cost of one visit of each biographer to his subject and also the cost of securing photocopies of journal articles, of typing manuscripts, etc. Each biographer was guaranteed up to two hundred dollars for these purposes. Most of them did not report any such expenses, though all of them went to a great deal of trouble.

At an early meeting, it was proposed that more money be invested in the yearbook. It was thought that an average of five hundred dollars might be allocated to each biographer, thus totaling fifty-five hundred dollars for eleven biographers. In addition, the NSSE Board would pay the usual expenses of committee meetings. The board authorized Mr. Havighurst to request up to ten thousand dollars from a foundation for the extra expense of this yearbook and for committee work on the larger continuing biography project which was mentioned at the beginning of this chapter. Mr. Havighurst wrote to one of the larger foundations proposing a grant of ten thousand dollars, but received a declination.

Supporting Documents

The subjects and their biographers were given a limited amount of guidance by the yearbook committee, and the relevant documents are reprinted here.

The following outline was prepared by Mr. Havighurst with the aid of suggestions and criticisms especially from Ruth Eckert, Ann Heiss, and Robert McCaul. It was mailed in June 1968. The reader will note that several of the subjects referred explicitly to this outline and used it to structure their autobiographies. Others made little or no use of it.

Outline for an Autobiographical Essay

Suggestions for using this outline

Try to use this outline in your own way. You may want to make notes on cards, or write several essays on various aspects of the outline. In length, try to stay between 5,000 and 10,000 words.

I hope you will be able to regard this task as a kind of professional duty. Some scholars in the future will write on educational trends and decisions in which you have been involved, and it will be your contribution to the profession to give testimony on your own role in these events and why you acted as you did.

A. *Family Background and Education*

1. *Your family background*—parents, grandparents, kin, siblings, cousins. What was your role in the family in which you grew up? What did the family members expect of you? What did you expect of yourself? With whom do you think you identified? Who do you think served as models for you?
2. *Your education*—formal and informal. When, where, what? Travel, reading, important persons.
   Your undergraduate and graduate education. Teachers and others who had a special influence on you.
   What proportion of the cost of your college education was paid by your family? Scholarship aid? Your own earnings?
3. *The bearing of your experience with religion on your career.*
4. *The kinds of communities in which you have lived* (rural, urban, ethnic composition, etc.) and how this may have influenced you in your early, middle, and later life.
5. *Friends and associates.* Who were influential in your development? How did they influence you?
6. *What books were important to you?*

B. *Career Choice and Preparation*

1. *Your career.* What have been the high points of decision or choice in your career? What turns or changes of direction have there been? When, where, and how were these decisions made? To what extent did certain persons influence your career choice? At what age did you become certain about your career?
   Important steps up the career ladder.
   Difficulties you overcame.
   Who helped you?
   What kinds of training and experience were especially important?
   What did you do over and above what was required on your job, that aided your career (e.g., learned a new foreign language; developed a hobby; made certain useful friends, or acquaintances)?
   Describe your extracurricular professional activities: memberships and offices in associations, etc.
   The balance between your work and other interests as time went on.
   Have you carried on any activities outside of your work which had major significance for you?

Personal qualities that have been most significant and useful in your career; and qualities that may have hindered you.

2. *Your personal motives and drives.* What is most characteristic of you as a person? What do you judge to be your strong and weak points? What kinds of activities or associations have given you most satisfaction? What disappointments have you had in your work when your ideas or products were misunderstood or ignored?
3. *Your social ideas.* How has your social and political ideology affected your career?

C. *Significant "Milestones" in Your Career*

1. *Your most significant achievements.* Can you rank or rate them?
2. *Major career activities.* Can you lay out your life since 1920 on a long vertical straight line by 5-year periods, and write down on the lifeline your major activities, preoccupations, achievements, etc.?
3. *Your work versus your citizenship.* Any conflict between your role as a worker and your role as a citizen? Any mutual support?
4. *Your own family and personal social life.* Did you marry? How do you evaluate the factor of marriage in your life? What about your children, if any? How have they influenced you? What are they currently doing?
5. *The past ten years.* Since reaching the modal retirement age, how do you feel about the most recent period? Did people push you out before you were ready? Did you desire to continue uninterrupted by retirement? Have you rearranged or reorganized your life in ways that enable you to make up for becoming disengaged in other areas?
6. *The meanings of time to you.* When did time move most rapidly?
When did you first realize that you did not have an indefinite and quasi-infinite amount of time ahead? How do time and money relate in your view of your life today?
7. *Money.* At what point did money cease to be an important factor in your career decisions?

D. *Appraisal of Career Contributions and Satisfactions*

1. *Major events or movements in education in which you were engaged.* How did you contribute to or influence these movements?
2. *Your judgment about yourself.* What have been your chief satisfactions? Regrets? What changes would you make if you had life to live over again? How much has your state of health influenced your career? What has been the relative importance of

social approval and of self-approval in the course of your life? How important has sheer pleasure in your work been?

Supplementary. If a biographer wishes to know how others have perceived you, would you give permission to solicit data from your close associates? Former students, or family members? What persons would you suggest for this?

Have you kept diaries or notebooks? At what ages? Have you used this material in your sketch?

Do you care to supply information on your financial condition at various stages in your life? At least, can you give a general rating of your financial status at ages 30, 60, and present?

May we have a bibliography or list of your writings as complete as possible?

Formal Agreement

The following "Memorandum of Agreement" was sent to each subject and biographer for signature and then was signed by Mr. Havighurst as the representative of the Board of Directors of the National Society. This seems to have worked out quite well.

MEMORANDUM OF AGREEMENT by All Participants in the Production of the 1971 Yearbook, NSSE, entitled:

LEADERS IN AMERICAN EDUCATION

This is the first of what may become a series of Yearbooks which treat the lives and achievements of contemporary leaders in American education. The general character of the Yearbook is as follows:

The Subjects will be ten people, aged 70 and over at the time the book is published. They will have come almost to the close of their careers, so that the Yearbook cannot influence their careers.

There will be two sections to the chapter which deals with a Leader. Each chapter will be limited to 13,000 words. One section will be an autobiography of not more than 10,000 words. The other section will be a biographical essay written by an appropriate person.

The Subject of the biography will not choose his Biographer—the choice will be made by the Yearbook Committee, with the concurrence of the Subject.

The Subject will write his autobiography, following an outline to be provided by the Yearbook Committee.

The Biographer may work as closely with his Subject as the two desire.

The Subject's formal responsibility will end when he supplies the Yearbook Committee with an autobiography which is accepted by the Committee.

In general, it appears that the Biographer may work with one of the following procedures:

1. Help the Subject amplify and improve his autobiography, and add only a minimum of supporting material. The Biographer would serve mainly as a catalyst and an editor. This would maximize the value of the autobiography and make it a better source of data for future historical work.

2. Accept the autobiography with whatever amplification seems clearly necessary. The Biographer to write a kind of "vignette" that supplies other kinds of information about the Subject.

3. Accept the autobiography with little or no amplification, and add to it about 50 percent as much wordage in the nature of a biographical essay and appraisal of the Subject's career and contribution.

Disposal of the autobiography and other material for the use of scholars.

After the Yearbook is completed, the Biographer will give the National Society for the Study of Education the file of correspondence and other material he has collected on the Subject, for placement in a set of archives, under conditions which protect the interests of the Subject and others concerned.

The Board of Directors of the Society will attempt to place these materials in a library or in some set of archives which may develop in the future.

The Subject and the Biographer accept these procedures and agree to abide by them.

Date____________________ Signed____________________

Date____________________ Signed____________________

Date____________________ Signed____________________

For the NSSE

Archives: Preservation and Use of Materials

The files that were collected on each subject vary in size. Several are quite voluminous, with letters, reprints, and first drafts of autobiographies that were reduced in length later, due to space limitations. These materials have all been deposited in the Archives of Education at the University of Washington in Seattle. Dr. Charles Burgess, a member of the yearbook committee, has made the arrangements and will be responsible for the rules governing the use of these materials by scholars. In most cases the files are open to scholars, but a few of the autobiographies contain material which is not published in this yearbook and which will be kept confidential for the next few years.

The Writers of the Biographical Essays

Charles Burgess (Ruth Strang) is associate professor of history of education at the University of Washington. The author of several articles and reviews in educational history, he has also written *What Doctrines to Embrace: Studies in the History of American Education* (1969) with Merle L. Borrowman, *Nettie Fowler McCormick: Profile of an American Philanthropist* (1962), and edited *Health, Growth, and Heredity: G. Stanley Hall on Natural Education* (1965) with Charles E. Strickland.

Raymond E. Callahan (George S. Counts) has been at Washington University since 1952, where he is professor of education. His special field of interest is the social foundations of education. His major publications include *An Introduction to Education in American Society* (1956; revised, 1960) and *Education and the Cult of Efficiency* (1962).

Geraldine Jonçich Clifford (Sidney L. Pressey) is associate professor of education at the University of California (Berkeley). She is the author of various journal and encyclopedia articles on topics in the history of American education. She has written a major biography of Edward L. Thorndike, *The Sane Positivist* (1968), and the forthcoming *Shape of American Education.*

Patricia Albjerg Graham (Carleton Washburne) has taught history and education at Indiana University and at Barnard College and Teachers College (Columbia University). She is the author of *Progressive Education: From Arcady to Academe* (1967).

Maxine Greene (John S. Brubacher) has taught at New York University, Montclair State College, and Brooklyn College before joining the faculty of Teachers College, Columbia University, in 1965. She is now professor of English and was for sometime the editor of the *Teachers College Record.* She has written *The Public School and the Private Vision* and *Existential Encounters for Teachers* and is now completing a book entitled *Philosophical Foundations of Education.*

J. Stephen Hazlett (William G. Carr) is assistant professor of the history of education at the University of Chicago. He has made a major study of the history of Chicago schools, entitled "Crisis in School Government: An Administrative History of the Chicago Public Schools, 1933-1947."

Vincent P. Lannie (George N. Shuster), formerly at New York University, is associate professor of education at the University of Notre Dame and faculty editor of the new *Notre Dame Journal of Education.* He is the author of the forthcoming volume, *Henry Barnard: American Educator* and is co-editor of "Studies in the History of American Education Series" published by John Wiley and Sons.

Jonathan Messerli (Robert Ulich) is dean of the School of Education at Hofstra University. A student of Robert Ulich while at Harvard, he has since taught at the University of Washington, Teachers College (Columbia University), Yale, and Sarah Lawrence. His scholarly interests are in the history of education in America, and he is presently completing a full-length biography of Horace Mann, to be published by Alfred Knopf. His writings have appeared in the *American Quarterly, Harvard Educational Review, British Journal of Educational Studies, History of Education Quarterly, New England Quarterly,* and the *Historian.*

Anne Roe (George D. Stoddard) took her B.A. at the University of Denver and her Ph.D. in psychology at Columbia. She has been active as a research psychologist in several problem areas. In 1947 she commenced a study of leaders in science which developed to be one of her principal professional interests since that time. Her other major professional interest has been in the psychology of occupations. She was professor of education and director of the Center for Research in Careers at Harvard from 1963-67. She and her husband (Professor George Gaylord Simpson) now live in Tucson, Arizona, where she continues with research and writing.

Robert E. Tostberg (Arthur I. Gates) is associate professor of education at the University of Washington. He is chairman of the Division of History, Philosophy, and Sociology of Education. He has published in the *History of Education Quarterly*.

Paul Woodring (James B. Conant) took his bachelor's degree at Bowling Green State University and his Ph.D. in psychology at Ohio State University. Since 1939 he has taught at Western Washington State College, Bellingham, where he is now a distinguished service professor. He is the author of several books about education, including the much discussed *Let's Talk Sense About Our Schools*. He served as education editor of *Saturday Review* from 1960-66 and is presently an editor-at-large of *Saturday Review*.

CHAPTER II

John S. Brubacher

Part I

An Autobiography

I

I have been introduced to many audiences but never more graciously than by Professor Frederick Eby when once I lectured at the University of Texas. From the Eby family lore he related how centuries ago in Switzerland the Ebys had Brubachers for neighbors. Then occurred one of those decimating plagues which racked Europe from time to time. A number of Ebys died and those who remained were in desperate straits. They only survived, Professor Eby said, because the Brubachers came over and nursed them back to health.

Of course, there is no telling whether the first John Brubacher to come to these shores had Ebys for neighbors. But we do know for sure that he did come from Berne, Switzerland, and that he came to this country at the opening of the eighteenth century at the behest of William Penn, who had made a missionary expedition up the Rhine about that time. Although recruited by the great Quaker, there is no evidence that he himself was or became a Quaker but rather that he probably was a Mennonite. When he arrived in this country, he, together with a Hershey (a forebear of the milk chocolate Hersheys), bought a tract of a thousand acres near Lancaster, Pennsylvania, where they and their progeny settled down and lived almost exactly as they had in the old world. They spoke German—hence were called Pennsylvania *Deutsch* (not Dutch)—and dressed like "plain" people, the women wearing white organdy bonnets and the men broad-brimmed black hats. As tillers of the soil they not only believed the Bible to be the word of God, but they lived it to the letter.

This manner of life had changed little if at all as late as the generation of my grandfather, Daniel. He, for instance, according to my father, never laid razor to his beard, thus keeping the Biblical injunction. My paternal grandmother was a Royer, whose family may have originated in Alsace-Lorraine. She arrived as a bride in my grandfather's house with a piano, which definitely profaned her husband's religious convictions. However, he never made an issue of it and in the end she came around to his point of view.

My father was the last of six children of this union. Growing up in this environment, he learned to speak German before English. Not only that—he was about twenty years old before he left the farm to concentrate on his formal education. As a result, he was considerably older than most of his class when he graduated with the rank of Phi Beta Kappa from Yale in 1897. After a year or so of teaching at Williston Seminary, my father returned to Yale where he took his Ph.D. in Greek philology. His ambition had been to become a professor of Greek. Ironically, however, he never fulfilled this aim. No sooner had he his Ph.D. in hand than his major professor took him aside and said, "Brubacher, how would you like to become a high school principal?" His decision to accept this offer was the first step in a lifelong career in educational administration. After being a principal in Gloversville, New York, he became principal of the high school in nearby Schenectady, then superintendent of schools, and finally president of the New York State College for Teachers in Albany, now become the State University of New York at Albany.

While the Brubachers had been rural folk and farmers, my mother's people were urban and merchants. Her father, a Haas, had married a Seiler and it is the latter name for which my middle initial *S* stands. My maternal grandmother was a most delightful person, indeed, a storybook grandma in her love for her grandchildren. My mother was the eldest of five daughters. Showing artistic talent, she was sent off to the New England Conservatory of Music. After graduating there, she joined the State Normal School at Hagerstown, Maryland, in charge of vocal and instrumental music. From there she went to Bloomsburg Normal in Pennsylvania, where she was at the time of her marriage to my father.

II

After their nuptials in 1897, my parents set up housekeeping in Easthampton, Massachusetts, where Williston Seminary was located. It was in this town that I was born October 18, 1898, the seventh generation of Brubachers in this country. We did not live long enough in Easthampton for me to have any recollections of the place. Indeed, I have only the barest recollections of New Haven where my parents next moved in quest of my father's Ph.D. Gloversville, New York, I remember much better, for there I began my schooling with attendance at kindergarten. It must have been a Froebelian one, for I remember the formal gifts and occupations to which we were exposed. However, so far as their awakening metaphysical notions was concerned, I have no recollection whatever. Nor is that surprising, since such expectations have long since gone into the pedagogical discard.

The following year I entered first grade where I had my first introduction to writing. No doubt, reading began at the same time but I have no memory of that. Writing I recollect, both because the teacher guided my hand with hers and because my tablet was ruled for upper and lower case, both practices now outmoded.

Following the next step in my father's career we moved to Schenectady, New York. There I attended the public schools till within a year of going to college. As I look back on my experiences in the lower grades, I can now distinguish two pedagogical theories by which I was taught. One was governed by the ancient axiom of proceeding from the simple to the complex. Thus, in reading I can remember clearly how our flash cards proceeded from the logically simplest element of language, the letter, to the next level of complexity, the syllable, from the syllable to the word, and so on. Similarly in music, we started with its simplest unit, the note, then proceeded to scales, then modified the scale with sharps and flats, and finally wound up with melodies. Unfortunately, I did not remain long enough to benefit from the revolution brought about by looking at this axiom from the psychological rather than the purely logical point of view. Of course, the key pedagogical question is, simple to whom?

The other method I am now aware of having sat under was the Herbartian. In the third and fourth grades the teachers had us keep notebooks of examples of the fundamental arithmetical processes. These still stand out in my memory as models of orderly progression in the steps of apperception. Yet, although through drill I became adept in these fundamental processes, I had difficulty when I came to problems. This perplexity, heightened by a poor fifth-grade teacher, pursued me right up into algebra in secondary school. No one showed me how to reason in mathematics; I did everything mechanically. Consequently I developed a mild dislike for mathematics which in retrospect seems to have been altogether unnecessary.

My elementary school had eight grades but by the time I reached the upper ones they were "departmentalized." In the sixth grade I had my introduction to a different teacher for each subject. My transition to this new organization was complicated by being in a group of students who were accelerated by spending the first half of the school year in the sixth grade and the second in the seventh. Doing two grades in one year went off fairly well except that English grammar in seventh grade baffled me completely and remained a bête noire till first-year Latin in high school.

III

As my acceleration indicated, I was taking home satisfactory report cards. In part, that was due to the fact that I conformed readily to the academic program. It never occurred to me to rebel against it or even to sabotage it. But for that matter I can recollect nothing in the school program which encouraged individuality on my part. At home I remember a balance between conformity and independence. Yet, even with encouragement I was slow to develop self-reliance because I had tremendous respect for my father's judgment, a respect my mother shared, too. Part of this respect he won by being an exceptionally self-disciplined man himself. He was not only strong of will, but physically strong as well. Years of farm work had seen to that. These characteristics added up to a man of some austerity at home and considerable dignity abroad. But such traits were not uncommon among men I learned to know in the Pennsylvania German community.

At this stage of my life I not only stood in the shadow of my father, but I was embarrassingly self-conscious. Perhaps part of this was due to being an only child. But that was not all of it. In addition, it was not easy to be the son of the superintendent of schools. On the one hand, I was anxious to be worthy of my father and hence was quite sensitive to falling short of his expectations. On the other hand, no matter how hard I tried to excel in school, any success I had was frequently ascribed to favoritism on the part of teachers seeking to ingratiate themselves with my father.

I must add that some of my sensitivity was also due to the fact that my parents set high standards for my conduct. My mother was more compassionate in holding me to them than was my father. Some spankings haunt my memory, but even more formidable than spankings was my father's putting me beyond the pale of his favor. Nor did he make it easy to get back in. In retrospect I have wondered whether he was treating me as Jehovah did his people Israel when He "turned his face from them."

Not all my early education, of course, occurred in the public school. My mother, being a musician, took charge of teaching me an instrument. Her own forte was the piano, so we started with that. Up in our attic one day I discovered her mandolin and begged to transfer to that. Subsequently, I came upon her violin and asked to learn that. I made my best progress with this instrument but still was handicapped, not by a disinclination to practice, but by a difficulty in learning to keep time. I learned time, unfortunately, not by tapping it out for myself, but by asking my mother to play the piece and then imitating it by ear. Naturally, one can't go very far this way and I didn't.

If I could not go far playing by ear, nevertheless the fact that I had an ear for music had its advantages. My mother had quite a repertoire of classical pieces which she played for her own enjoyment and that of company who always asked her to play when invited to our home. Though I paid little attention at the time, later, when I heard music away from home, I subconsciously used my mother's standard of taste as my own.

If my musical education occurred at home, my religious education was shared by home and Sunday school. From both I imbibed a traditional fundamentalism. Life was a moral tightrope by which, if you could keep your balance in the face of temptation, you might reach heaven. If you lost your balance, you tumbled into the discomforts of hell. As I was constantly being admonished by my parents, I had anxieties about being the kind of soul that was destined for heaven.

When I began to emerge from this theology is no longer altogether clear in my memory. One incident, however, I do recall. For a period our home was next door to a Unitarian church. At one time its pastor was a defrocked Catholic priest. On occasion our family attended this church because of its convenience. Once when there I heard this cleric say that he would never again wear the collar of any orthodoxy. That made a great impression on me and I resolved to go and do likewise. But it was some time before I had confidence in such independence. What if orthodoxy were the true faith? Then I would surely be punished for disloyalty to it. Fortunately, in due course it occurred to me that a just deity would not punish me or any one else for doing the best he could.

With respect to sex education, neither home, church, nor school was adequate. Evidently my father was aware of the problem because one day I accidentally found on his bookshelf a volume on the sex life of the child. For the most part it was beyond my ken but what I could understand I read avidly. The rest of my sex education I got from my peers. Indeed, in spite of being a superintendent of schools, my father seems to have shared the anxieties of his generation, for I recollect that twice he frowned on my having "girl friends" even in the elementary school.

Another out-of-school impact on my young life was summer vacations spent in Pennsylvania on the farms of my uncles and aunts. These vacations were notable parts of my education for several reasons. For one thing, they afforded me my earliest opportunity to travel. Of course we traveled by train, which gave me the chance to indulge my fancy for locomotives, the locomotive being my chief toy and the object I most often drew in pictures. But more important, travel to Pennsylvania left on me indelible impressions of farm life.

To some degree my emancipation from fundamentalist religion must have commenced on these trips. The folks down there were so much more fundamentalist in religion than were those where we lived that even I as a youngster noted it. Consulting my father, I learned that he had been regarded by his family as something of a black sheep because of his liberalism. Perhaps on this account I was frequently asked whether I was "saved," which meant whether I had experienced, as Jesus said to Nicodemus, "a rebirth of the spirit." Such regeneration was usually accompanied by considerable emotional stress. Since I could make no such witness to having cast the devil out of my life, my state of salvation was in doubt. In self-defense I argued with them about the meaning of salvation but finally gave up. Later, when asked whether I was "saved," I simply said I was, leaving each one of us to interpret the term as he saw fit.

IV

One summer when we came back from our usual vacation, I returned, not to the elementary school, but to the high school. Being overcrowded, Schenectady High was on double-session so I as a freshman had the afternoon shift. This left little time to play after school but more time to study before it. My high school years are chiefly memorable for my study of Latin and Greek. Of course I studied other subjects such as English and history, but it is the classics that stand out. Although on the decline at the time, they were still the backbone of my college preparation. I never complained about taking these subjects as did most of my classmates. My father had been a classicist and I just assumed that the classics were the main thoroughfare to intellectual respectability. Fortunately, these were the subjects in which I received my highest marks. In fact, in my last year I took both local and statewide prizes for excellence in Greek.

One reason I excelled in classics was the teachers I had, a Vassar graduate for Latin and a Mt. Holyoke one for Greek. The former was especially exacting in her demands. For learning our conjugations, 95 was the passing grade! Similarly with the rules of grammar. I believe I can still repeat all the prepositions which take the accusative. In translating Caesar and Virgil, she insisted on our understanding the syntax almost more thoroughly than the content. To insure against our using "ponies" or "trots," she made us translate each sentence literally no matter how awkward it might sound in English.

Successful as my Latin teacher may have thought she was in disciplining my mind, unwittingly she did me great harm. In my early professional career I was not the facile writer I wanted to be. By good chance our departmental secretary at Yale had previously some editorial experience with the *Atlantic Monthly*. I submitted some of my prose for her criticism. One thing she spotted right away was the persistence of some of those old awkward Latinisms.

If my teachers had been Jesuits, they would not have been guilty of such literary mayhem. The Jesuits taught classics to improve one's style in his native tongue. To this end they went over a passage several times, the first time for syntax, to be sure, but the second time for an idiomatic translation, and a third, to strive for grace and even elegance. My Greek teacher, happily, had a little more of this latter spirit. Thus, I recollect her calling attention to Homer's use of onomatopoeia to describe the pounding waves and the receding surf. And especially I remember how she called attention to the literary trick Homer used to convince long generations unborn that Helen was truly one of the most beautiful women who ever lived.

The chief residue I have from my concentration on Latin and Greek is my understanding and enjoyment of English word derivation. But what a price to pay for it! In all, I spent nine years on Latin and Greek—four years on Latin and three on Greek in high school and another year on each in college. If these years had been added to the total of four years spent on French and German—two years of German in high school and two of French in college—think what facility I might have had in these modern languages.

Meantime I was learning practically nothing from my high school courses in English to improve my prose style. Indeed, I recollect nothing more distasteful and frustrating there than writing compositions in my mother tongue. My father accounted for this by saying that I was too young and immature to have anything to say, but reassured me that later when I would, writing would come more easily. Well, it has come more easily but I still feel I have to content myself with a clear rather than a graceful style.

If writing was an unhappy experience in secondary school, reading was quite the contrary. Most of it I did outside of class as the pace there was discouragingly slow. Teachers thought they had to dissect novels chapter by chapter and dramas act by act, but I always read ahead to get the story as a whole. Perhaps nothing caught my imagination more than the Arthurian legend, which I read and reread in many versions. To this fascination I ascribe the fact that I later read nearly all of the Waverly novels. At another time I became absorbed in Cooper's Leather-stocking tales and even in many of his stories of the sea. On yet another occasion I had a passion for reading Robert Louis Stevenson. With such occupation I quickly learned how inferior the dime novels of the day were in plot, style, and character portrayal.

One reason I could read widely and concentrate on my studies was my home situation. There I had my own room where I could seclude myself for study. I don't know how children today study with a radio to distract them. My sons assured me they studied better to this accompaniment. I still doubt it. While I had parental encouragement to study, it was part of the atmosphere of the home rather than any direct exhortation. Both my wife and I have remarked how we were self-motivated, never needing "pep" talks by our parents on the importance of doing well in our studies.

Certainly fear of not being admitted to college was not the spur it is today, for I remember several occasions when recruiters from nearby colleges addressed our high school assembly urging us to attend. What a contrast to today when colleges must set barriers to reduce the mounting applications for admission.

Before leaving Schenectady High School I must mention one last product of my study of Latin and Greek. In both subjects we had social clubs to promote interest in the classics. The Latin club, for example, gave a Latin play in which I had a lead role. By belonging to these clubs I met my future wife, Winifred Wemple. She also was an excellent classicist so our mutual interests drew us together. I was proud of her indeed when she turned out to be valedictorian of our class.

But I did not graduate with the class. In sophomore year my physician thought my health required that I take only a half load of studies. Hence, although I identified with my class socially, I was half a year behind academically. This half year I was destined to make up in Albany where my father had become president of the State College for Teachers. He wanted me to go to a private school, the Albany Boys Academy, a fine old school, but I resisted, feeling it was more democratic to attend a public school. Why my father let me attend the Albany public high school against his better judgment, I don't know. But I do know that by Christmas I went to him and said I would never make college if I stayed there. I had some basis for knowing, for I had been taking my "college boards" one at a time as was customary then. I knew I would not continue to do that successfully from a school where I was on the honor role without doing a bit of homework.

So after Christmas I transferred to the Boys Academy. It proved the unhappiest half year of my whole academic career. I was so far behind my classmates that it was discouraging to try to catch up. In geometry, for instance, my grade depended on a weekly test, an "original" based on theorems studied during the week. At the end of the first six weeks my average was zero! The seventh week I got a two on the basis of ten and, although still failing, I was very proud of my progress. The next week I got a five and the following, a seven. In retrospect I am glad I had this experience, for I have some idea now of what it means to fail. I also know something of how private schools manage to have such good records of getting their clientele into college. Take that geometry class again. We finished all the required books of Euclid by early April. From then to the time for college boards we reviewed theorems and practiced on originals from previous college-board examinations.

Before leaving the academy, let me add that it was there I reached the pinnacle of my modest athletic career. I was enthusiastic about sports, playing on the tennis team and also on a champion hockey team as well. All the sports I ever played—and I played nearly all of them—I learned by watching others rather than taking instruction. This was a mistake, especially later when I took up golf. In a less strenuous mood I became very fond of chess during this period. It led to playing intercollegiate chess at college and many happy games with professional colleagues like George Axtelle, Jack Grinnell, and Paul Schilpp.

V

In spite of ultimately salvaging my academic prospects at the Albany Boys Academy, I was refused a diploma at graduation. The official statement was that the academy did not give diplomas for a half year's work. But I have always suspected that the faculty also had genuine misgivings that I was college caliber and might consequently besmirch the academy's reputation. Nevertheless, I had accumulated enough credits to be admitted to Yale and thither I went in the autumn of 1915. As a resident of Schenectady, I once thought I might go to Union College, which was located there, but my father assured me that Yale was the only place for a son of an Eli to go.

Freshman year was pretty much an added year of secondary school studies. Thus, I resumed my study of the classics but the pace was much faster. I was only getting B's in Greek, in which I won prizes in high school. The "prep school" boys in my class startled me with their superiority, especially Henry Luce, later of *Time* and *Life* magazines. I majored in history and minored in economics, but in spite of good teachers I cannot remember a single outstanding course. In particular I can't remember that they had any striking relevance to the period of the First World War, through which we were then passing. Looking back, for example, I don't remember the mention of Karl Marx once. The courses I do remember were outside my major and minor and were all in science. Freshman physics was a delight, as was also geology the next year. Both professors invited me to major with them.

But the most memorable course of my whole four years was introductory psychology in my sophomore year. It was the only course in which I read more than I was assigned and continually mulled over what I read. The point at which I caught fire was the glimpse the last part of the course gave me of the then budding field of Freudian psychology. Here I was ripe for what I read because, as it might be put today, I was suffering an "identity crisis." No doubt this resulted from the usual anxieties and inhibitions of an adolescent. At any rate, in Freud I found the key to understanding myself.

By a happy coincidence my roommate had much the same experience with this course that I did. We talked it over, even its moral implications, at great length after we had retired at night, and I am sure the course was my first step toward philosophy. Unfortunately, it was also my last one in college because I was so enamoured of science that I foolishly thought it would be a waste of time to study philosophy, which would surely be metaphysical. My roommate went on to take his Ph.D. in psychology and I have often thought how, with the guidance that is offered today, I might have become a psychiatrist.

To continue reference to my "identity crisis," another roommate also had a critical impact on me. In "bull sessions" with him he shook some of my basic convictions by arguments he purveyed from Bertram Russell's *Why Men Fight,* which he was reading coincident to the war. After a session I would retire to mend my fences only to have them torn down the next time we met. This was so unsettling that I nearly decided to dissociate myself from this roommate. But deep down I knew this was no solution. Instead of rebuilding old beliefs, I decided to build entirely new ones which could withstand any pressure. It was a fateful decision and one never regretted.

At the end of sophomore year my college education was interrupted by military service. I had been a member of the Yale R.O.T.C. during the preceding year, but in 1918 the Congress lowered the draft age to eighteen. That swept our whole unit into service. By some unique circumstance we were incorporated into the armed services as a unit. After spending the summer at Camp Jackson, South Carolina, about half our number were given commissions as second lieutenants in the field artillery. I was fortunate enough to be in the successful half but unfortunate enough to be the only one rejected at the medical examination for our commissions. According to the doctor, I had a serious heart murmur and about two more years to live. Startling as was this news, I took it quite calmly. Indeed, my chief concern was how my parents would take it. When I got home after being mustered out of the service, my father advised that I go at once to a local cardiologist, who happened to be the dean of the Albany Medical School. He too found the murmur but diagnosed it as unimportant. On the strength of his diagnosis, I was reexamined by the surgeon general at nearby Camp Devens, who confirmed the cardiologist's opinion. As a result I soon regained my commission, but before I could get overseas the war was over and I found myself in the reserve.

Under the circumstances, I rated as a veteran and was entitled to a sixty-dollar bonus from the state of New York. With this money

I made one of the best investments of my life, a portable typewriter. I started with the "hunt and peck" system but used all my fingers instead of just two. Soon they became so nimble that I glided almost imperceptibly into a "touch" system. The boon this has been to me professionally has been inestimable.

With my new typewriter in hand I returned to complete my college course. In my senior year I occupied by chance the same room on the "Old Campus" at Yale that my father had as a sophomore. The professor who made the most impression on me in this tag end of my college education was Johnny Berdan in his famous daily theme course. It was for him that I wrote my first essay affirming a philosophical way of life. Unfortunately, however, I did not take the even more famous courses taught by William Lyon Phelps and Chauncey Tinker. As a senior, though, I was permitted to attend lectures on American constitutional law by William Howard Taft, who had retired from the presidency to a chair in the Yale law school.

Although my brief military experience consumed the first semester of my junior year, Yale was generous in letting me graduate on schedule in June 1920. I took my A.B. with Phi Beta Kappa rank which gave me a measure of self-satisfaction. The farther my college education has receded into the past, however, the more dissatisfied I have become with it. My discontent centers in the fact that I was supposed to be getting a liberal education whereas I did not even know what it was. I am sure I could never have formulated the aim of a liberal education to guide and motivate my activities. I just assumed the faculty knew what it was offering me. What coordinating idea they may have had was never made clear.

VI

At the end of college I had no compelling notion of what sort of career to pursue. I had worked one summer on the farm, one in a bank, another in an insurance office, and yet another in a law office. None of these work experiences gave me decisive direction. Basically undecided, I finally determined on the law because, as my father pointed out, it was a kind of liberal education and could be turned to various careers such as business and politics. Consequently, the next autumn I entered Harvard Law School.

Almost from the outset I was not as successful in the study of the law as my undergraduate record had led me to hope. My undergraduate achievement had been largely built on an industrious memory. The study of law required more judgment. I tried to memorize precedents whereas what I needed was a critical ability to analyze them. I finally got my degree, but with a record short of what it should have been. I passed the Massachusetts bar examinations and started practice in an established firm, but my heart was not in it. I soon realized that I had had an academic rather than professional interest in the law. In retrospect, I think that with maturing judgment I might have made a teacher of the law.[1] But my record at the time was not good enough to suggest such a scholarly career.

Feeling that my basic aptitude was in education rather than law, I decided to change careers. It was a traumatic decision after such an investment in the law. But I made it and have had no regrets. Since administration is one of the general careers for which law is supposed to be good preparation, I decided to transfer from law to education via educational administration. Hence, I enrolled at Teachers College, Columbia University, for an M.A. under the famous team of Strayer and Englehardt. There I did well enough to earn a dean's scholarship in the middle of the year. By spring, two professional opportunities opened up. One was as an administrative intern in the Cleveland public schools and the other an opportunity to teach education at Dartmouth. Professor Reisner was responsible for making Dartmouth look more attractive as he offered to recall me from there to be his teaching assistant.

With that decision made, I got married and moved to Hanover, New Hampshire, in the heart of the Green Mountains and not far from the Presidential Range. This was New England at its best and the year spent there was like an extended honeymoon.

In retrospect I am amazed at what I with only an M.A. from Teachers College was assigned to teach Dartmouth undergraduates. My load included history of American education, philosophy of education, educational administration, and a section on higher education! No wonder academics came to complain about the incompetence of many educators and the superficiality of their curricu-

1. In my retirement I was to test this surmise by compiling a casebook on the law of higher education and then teaching a course based thereon.

lum. Yet, whatever my impact may have been on my students, it did me a great deal of good to familiarize myself with so many aspects of education. Like a Jesuit, I learned by teaching. I might add that the course in higher education consisted of readings compiled by the head of my department and was designed by the college to make better alumni of its undergraduates.

After a year of seasoning, I was back at Teachers College as Reisner's teaching assistant and in quest of my Ph.D. I took a wide variety of courses but, instead of continuing in educational administration, I now specialized in the history and philosophy of education. Looking back, I must confess that the intensive work required in these fields was considerably short of what it is now and should have been then. John Dewey was still teaching at the time, but a course of his on education and ethics proved nothing more than a rehash of his *Ethical Principles of Education.* Advance reports that he was not a scintillating lecturer proved only too true. The scholar who impressed me most was I. L. Kandel, with his sharp insights and high standards.

Meanwhile, I was teaching courses at both the graduate and undergraduate levels. To Reisner's credit, be it said that he sat in on my classes from time to time to advise me on my pedagogical progress. Only one of my students from these days stands out in my memory, Alice Keliher, whose academic star was already in the ascendant. For my dissertation topic I chose "The Judicial Power of the New York State Commissioner of Education." This topic enabled me to make a synthesis of my previous training in law with that in educational administration, all in a historical perspective.

VII

After receiving my degree I was retained at Teachers College as an assistant professor in educational history. But the appointment did not last long as I soon had an invitation to teach history and philosophy of education at Yale. I did not like to leave Teachers College, which was then the leader in the professional study of education, for Yale, where education was a much more marginal enterprise. On the other hand, at Yale I would teach not only educational history but also educational philosophy. Perhaps even more important, instead of being subordinate I would be in charge of these fields. There was a similar balance of attractions between New York City and New Haven. My wife and I were very fond of Broadway theatre, but we were also drawn to the size of New Haven, which was more like that of Schenectady, where we had been reared. The arguments for Yale and New Haven won out and there we spent the next thirty years of our lives.

When I reached Yale, I found myself teaching not only the history and philosophy of education, but occasionally courses in comparative education and educational sociology as well. I had studied these fields, to be sure, but, though they were closely related to my specialities, I had not prepared myself to teach them. Whatever the impact on my students was of spreading myself so thin, like Dartmouth again, the impact on me was to make me read widely and ultimately enrich my main interests. At first, the clientele I had in my various courses consisted on the one hand of graduate students and on the other, of extension ones. The latter were mostly experienced teachers who were trying to upgrade their two-year normal school diplomas to bachelor's degrees at a time when normals were rapidly being transformed into teacher colleges.

I had not been at Yale long before our departmental faculty embarked on a thorough reexamination of its role. This reexamination began with a realization that geographically Yale was flanked to the east and west by Boston and New York respectively, both of which areas had universities with conventional schools of education offering numerous courses to large clienteles at relatively low academic levels. With the small faculty we had—only five or six full-time members at the most—we decided at once that we could not compete with our neighbors in what they were doing. In contrast, we decided that the unique role of a faculty like ours at a university like Yale should be to put emphasis, not on quantity, but on quality. We decided, therefore, to limit our main activities to a small highly selected body of graduate students.

This body of students, in turn, we tried to serve with a superior program of graduate studies. If the reorganization of our department had any originality, it was in the "general seminar" which we designed for them. The chief character of this seminar was interdisciplinary. Indeed, it may have been the earliest attempt to introduce this approach into the graduate study of education. Whether it was an imitation at the graduate level of Columbia's highly successful "survey" courses for undergraduates, I cannot say. But I can say that a delegation of the faculty from Teachers College visited and complimented us before launching their well-known interdisciplinary "foundations" courses. In any event, our entire faculty was in constant attendance on the seminar. In it we took up current educational problems in all their concrete perplexity. Whatever aspect of one of these problems claimed the forestage of the seminar's attention, there was a faculty member present whose discipline was related to it, even some one from the Divinity School to represent religious education. The outcome of such a multifaceted approach was often confusing. Yet, if there was any single feature of our program which our graduates remembered and praised years afterwards, it was the clash of ideas in this seminar. Nothing, they said, taught them the necessity for independent thinking as did seeing the faculty disagreeing among themselves.

Originally, the "general seminar" was thought of as a basic grounding in the broad field of education preparatory to specialization in one of the fields represented by the faculty. As time went on, however, it was also viewed as an excellent means of integrating one's whole graduate course of instruction. In fact, the integrating paper which each student wrote at the end of the seminar came to be a substitute for the more conventional "prelims" for the doctor's degree.

The "general seminar" left a permanent deposit in my professional development, just as it did in that of the students. Particularly it left an imprint on the organization of my courses in educational history and philosophy. The conventional organization of these fields—the organization of history chronologically and the organization of philosophy by schools of thought—I found a handicap to my participation in the "general seminar." For instance, if some phase of curriculum or administration was up for consideration, about all I could recommend with conventional books was to read them passim and use the index extensively. But that was quite unsatisfactory as it afforded no continuity. Consequently I decided to organize my books *Modern Philosophies of Education* and *A History of the Problems of Education* topically. They are, I believe, the first to be so structured in the field.

The idea for my *Eclectic Philosophy of Education* preceded both of the volumes just mentioned, but I did not find a publisher till some time later. While at Teachers College I, like many others, was impressed with Professor Kilpatrick's course in educational philosophy. Two aspects stood out—his Socratic method and his book of readings. I found the discussion of the readings especially congenial because it was so similar to the pedagogy of the case method in the law school. Kilpatrick's *Source Book*, however, I felt was made up of too short selections and too frequently of material which, while educational inferences could be drawn from it, had not been written with education in mind. I resolved, therefore, to compile a book which met my personal requirements. When completed, I offered it to a publisher who disappointed me by rejecting it. His advice was to write something of my own first, and then my source materials would be more publishable. Hence, with the excellent preparation of wide and intensive reading, I sat down and wrote my *Modern Philosophies of Education*. Even then, it was more than a decade before I found a publisher for the book of readings. At one time I so despaired of finding a publisher that I proposed to Kilpatrick a joint revision of his own book wherein I would provide most of the new materials. I was quite encouraged when he lent his approval to the idea, but quite discouraged again when his publisher turned it down.

Let me add that in teaching educational philosophy, I have given original sources the first importance. While many of my colleagues use sources to supplement a text, I have always used a text to supplement the sources. I learned this order of importance in the law school. The faculty there was insistent that students learn to analyze and compare cases before they read treatises. So I have always preferred to have my students read and cogitate about philosophers firsthand before they resort to a textbook exposition. Students are challenged to think, not by learning abstract rules of logic, but by being confronted with unexpected discrepancies and incompatibilities between sources. And nothing encourages this kind of thinking as does the Socratic dialogue. If I have had any success as a teacher, it is because I have striven to develop a measure of artistry in this method.

VIII

Fortuitously, my teaching and writing received recognition both at Yale and beyond its campus. In due course I was promoted to associate and full professor and ultimately given the new chair of Reuben Post Halleck Professor of the History and Philosophy of Education. Since for long Yale had no summer session, I found myself free to teach on major summer campuses from coast to coast. Of the various professional societies I joined, I became president of the Philosophy of Education Society and of the National Society of College Teachers of Education. In addition, the National Society for the Study of Education invited me to chair two of its yearbooks, the forty-first and the fifty-fourth. As a graduate student I had already joined two professional fraternities, Phi Delta Kappa and Kappa Delta Pi. Just a few years ago I was elevated to the Laureate chapter of the latter.

With advance in rank and prestige came advance in salary as well. I started at Dartmouth at $2,200, which I increased by a multiple of about ten by the time I retired at Michigan. With careful budgeting, the purchasing power of my early salaries always seemed adequate. I even achieved a measure of comfort during the depression, of all times, because Yale did not reduce salaries when prices were falling. That margin of comfort became assured after the Second World War, when my books became established and I had a steady income from royalties.

But the recognition I have found most gratifying has been invitations to teach abroad. The first was to teach at one of the English red-brick universities, an invitation that was aborted by World War II. The second was to teach at the American University of Biarritz, a postwar university for soldiers awaiting transportation home. I did not accept, but when Habib Kurani offered me the chance to teach at the American University of Beirut in Lebanon, I accepted at once. It was a new experience to enter a different culture and then to view one's own from the new perspective. Both faculty and student body spoke either English or French (often both) in addition to Arabic. Certainly I never had a more earnest body of students; there wasn't a "deadbeat" in the lot. That is because higher education is a real privilege there and nearly every graduate is destined for a responsible post in his own country. The countries of the Near East served by A.U.B. are so many that in the early days of the United Nations more of its delegates were graduates of A.U.B. than of any other university. The high standards of A.U.B. stem from the little-known fact that it is incorporated under the regents of the state of New York. In addition to my teaching duties there, I chaired an all-university committee to review the aims and curriculum of the institution. When the incumbent dean of arts and sciences retired, I was invited to succeed him but declined the honor.

Our family found the Near East a fascinating place but not one where we wanted to settle down for an extended period. We traveled widely out of Beirut, going as far north as Istanbul and as far south as Cairo. To the east, we made several trips to Baalbek and Damascus. But the visit that most impressed us all was our trip to the Holy Land at Easter time. Indeed, Jerusalem overtopped visits to Rome and Athens, which we made on the trip from and back to the United States. The opportunity to visit these latter cities, whose ancient languages I had studied so diligently, had been one of my chief reasons for accepting the post in Beirut in the first place.

When I returned home, I was in demand to speak on the Near East to luncheon groups. Like most Americans who have lived in the Arab lands, I was quite sympathetic to the Arabs in their quarrel with Israel. Few Americans in 1952 knew how the state of Israel had been imposed on the Arabs. Fewer still knew how, by supporting Israel, the United States had thrown away an enormous budget of goodwill which the Arabs felt toward us because the American University of Beirut had been the center of the Arab nationalism which enabled them to throw off some four centuries of Turkish oppression.

Five years later I had another chance to teach at A.U.B. but this time for only the first half of a sabbatical, the second half of which I enjoyed on a Fulbright Fellowship at Kyushu University in Japan. My travel this time started as a member of a troupe from the Comparative Education Society, which spent the summer visiting schools and school authorities in several northern European countries. After this troupe returned home, my wife and I went on to Beirut, where we found things little changed from our earlier visit. When the autumn semester ended, I fortunately had a whole month before I had to begin teaching in Japan. This gave us an excellent opportunity to travel through Southeast Asia, stopping for several days in Teheran, Karachi, Rangoon, Bangkok, Manila, and Hong Kong, and a whole week in India, principally at Baroda and New Delhi. At each place a former student met us at the airport and arranged a program of visiting schools and sight-seeing. A month is scant time to cover such a vast area and yet the experience made a deep impression on us both. I read the news and watch the television now with ever so much more understanding.

The award of a Fulbright in Japan took its origin in a young Japanese woman, Masuko Otaki, who enrolled in my classes from the Divinity School at Yale. Coming out of an authoritarian culture and one which subordinates women, she could hardly believe that a professor would pay any attention to anything she had to say in the classroom dialogue. But soon she gained confidence in herself and became a most interesting contributor. Before Miss Otaki returned to her country, she made me promise that I would come to Japan and introduce Japanese students to the Socratic method. I protested there would be a language barrier but she insisted she would be my interpreter, indeed, that she would come and live with my wife and me and guide us about her country. Sure enough, within a year she had arranged a Fulbright. Unfortunately, on account of disturbed conditions at Yale (to be detailed later) I could not accept, nor could I accept when the invitation was postponed for a year. Tragically, when conditions did permit the year following, my protege had died. But I went, anyhow, out of respect to her memory. Her death was a great loss to Japan, for she had become the first woman professor in one of the old imperial universities.

Even with very good interpreters, I am sure my use of the Socratic method was not so successful as Miss Otaki had hoped. The interposition of an interpreter inevitably took the edge off the spontaneity of the class. Yet, many of the students were anxious to improve their English and so my wife, a former English teacher, was asked to conduct a class. Fortunately, she was not unprepared for the assignment for she had already been teaching such a class at the Beirut College for Women. The class at Kyushu started rather formally in one of the university buildings, but soon it was transferred to our home. Here, a social atmosphere soon replaced that of the school and we spent Thursday evening each week talking about Japan and America, even the late war. Needless to say, the students learned ever so much more English trying to enter the conversation than they ever would have in a formal classroom.

The success of this experience became the inspiration for another even more ambitious enterprise back in the United States. There, after we moved to the University of Michigan, my wife got permission from International Neighbors, a campus organization providing social contacts for wives of foreign students, to sponsor classes in English for these wives. Using her Japanese experience as a model, my wife began inviting these wives to our home. While the husbands were having ample opportunity to learn English and make friends incidental to the pursuit of their studies, the wives all too often were unhappy, shut up in the inadequate housing their meager stipends permitted. The first thing needed in many of these cases was to teach these girls English so they could become acquainted with American life. As in Japan, they learned this most readily in a social situation where they wanted to communicate with other wives. In no time at all, scores of American wives became interested in the project. Once communication had been facilitated, all sorts of activities were undertaken. Now, at the end of a dozen years, my wife has foreign "daughters" all over the world.

To return to Kyushu, the faculty there had weekly meetings. On alternate weeks they discussed educational policy and for my benefit discussed it in English. About a third participated fully, another third understood but did not trust themselves to speak, and the remaining third sat politely uncomprehending. But imagine an American faculty discussing educational policy in any language but English! Professor Hiratsuke, Miss Otaki's mentor and my closest friend, arranged for me to lecture at other universities besides Kyushu. In this manner I visited Sendai, Kyoto, and Tokyo among others. These lectures were finally gathered together and published by the Institute for Democratic Education. The proceeds at my suggestion were devoted to an award for the best student essay on an assigned topic in educational philosophy.

IX

By a happy coincidence, my first invitation to go to Beirut came when both our boys, John and Paul, were old enough to appreciate the advantages of foreign travel. By that time the older one had just graduated from college and the younger one was just entering high school. Both boys had had the good fortune to commence their education in Arnold Gesell's experimental nursery school at Yale. At the end of that experience each was a year short of the official entry age into the public kindergarten. I hoped the principal of our neighborhood elementary school would make an exception and admit our boys just to see whether their nursery school experience had readied them a year earlier for kindergarten. Unfortunately, the principal was more afraid of potential objections of other parents to her making an exception to the rule than she was eager to learn from pedagogical experimentation.

The remainder of their elementary and secondary education was fairly conventional, even traditional. At home, my wife and I tried to infuse their upbringing with some of the spirit of progressive education. We tried to encourage a balance of independence and responsibility, giving much time to talking through the problems which arose from practicing these traits. On the whole, we seemed to maintain our lines of communication very well till the latter years of college. These years coincided with the postwar years and the beginning of the "generation gap." When my wife and I were young, there was a "generation gap" too, but the situation was different from today in that we were anxious to close it as quickly as possible so we could be accepted as adults. The gap seems ominous today because the young see their culture as so markedly different from that of their elders. I know I almost despaired of closing the gap in our family. By the time, however, the boys had finished college, their military service, graduate study, and become married, the static in our communications disappeared.

While going through college, both boys swore they would follow any career other than their father's. As I had always thought my father had inclined me to the law more than he should have, I determined to let them freely choose their own. The fact that they took Ph.D.'s and chose educational careers, therefore, was strictly due to the attractiveness of a career in education. In any event, that now makes three successive generations of Brubachers in education.

During the war our family welcomed into our home one of the British children sent to the United States to escape the German bombing of English cities. She was of an age between our sons and the nearest approach to a sister either ever had. The experience, however, did not work out well. As nearly as we could determine, our guest thought both her American home and her school inferior to what she had left. We never heard from her after she returned home, nor from her family either.

In the period after the war I made other modest efforts at community service. One was political. Together with Sam Brownell of our faculty, later U.S. Commissioner of Education, I and an informal group of citizens tried to improve our local board of education by each member's trying to prevail on his political party to nominate superior candidates. Our efforts were only half successful. To our pleas the party leaders inquired what was wrong with the board members we had. We admitted they were good men but why not nominate the best? We learned that the public is little interested in the best, so few of them having the best of anything—homes, autos, clothes, jobs, and the like.

Another was religious. Just before leaving New Haven for Ann Arbor, I served as chairman of a committee of my local Congregational church, trying to establish closer relations with a black Congregational church, a number of whose parishioners were professional people. The plan was to exchange personnel at all levels and in all activities, not just for a Sunday, as is often done, but for several months at a time. Our committee, working slowly and piecemeal, won unanimous support from various organizations of the church. Finally, we thought we were ready to lay the matter before the whole congregation. In spite of our careful canvas, we lost by a single vote. Apparently the general laity feared we had a concealed design to prepare the way for blacks to buy homes in the neighborhood.

X

Attractive as Yale had been as a place to pursue my career, times began to change after returning from my first trip to Beirut. Then ensued the steps which ultimately led to the closing of the Department of Education at Yale. As this event attracted national concern without being fully ventilated, I shall recall it in a little more detail. The abandonment of such a major department by a major university would have been unthinkable under James Rowland Angell or Charles Seymour, who occupied the Yale presidency between the two world wars. With the celebration of Yale's two hundred and fiftieth anniversary in mid-century, however, A. Whitney Griswold succeeded to the presidency. He assumed the robes of office just as the cold war on the professional study of education was mounting in crescendo. That this attack was fully warranted, Griswold seemed to have no doubt.

His first step to improve the situation was to inaugurate a master of arts in teaching program similar to the one that had been so successful at Harvard. This program he wanted to put under the direction of our department, but our chairman thought it wiser not to accept. Our department had always respected competency in academic subject matter fully as much as competency in pedagogy, but apparently this was not enough for Griswold. Since he wanted a heavier emphasis, we thought he would more surely be satisfied if academicians directed it. Hence our chairman, Clyde M. Hill, proposed that rather than direct the new program, we should cooperate with it, providing the professional studies for state certification.

This cooperative arrangement seemed to work very well for the first few years. We had good relations with the director of the program, Tug Anderson, a member of the French department. In spite of this fact, Griswold was not pleased; he wanted professional interests reduced in importance and academic ones increased. Hence in 1954 he made an abrupt change of policy. As the principal feature of this change, he made the M.A.T. program the *sole* teacher training program at Yale. This entailed a number of changes. In the first place, he directed the graduate school to admit no more applicants for the department of education. The students already in the program—"in the pipe," as the president put it—could finish, but when the last one came out, that would be its end. Along with the remaining faculty in the department, I now took my leadership from a new director of the M.A.T. program, Ned Noyes, a member of the English department who had been director of admissions. Future students for the program Griswold planned to recruit from able college graduates attracted to Yale by handsome subsidies made possible through sizable grants from the Ford Foundation and the Carnegie Corporation.

This shift in policy was not only abrupt; it came as a complete surprise. Our chairman was just summarily called from a meeting across-town to the presidential office and told the news for the first time. Our faculty was the more astounded since some months previously we had addressed a letter to the president inviting him to meet with us on the future of the department because shortly it would be necessary to replace half our small staff. One had just retired, one was about to do so, and a third was about to become U.S. Commissioner of Education. Rather than replace this personnel one at a time, we thought it better to pick them all at once, each with reference to the other and the future development of the department. The only response we ever got to that letter was the change of policy just noted. Why didn't the president consult with us?

Well, he did consult with us, but ex post facto. He indicated to our chairman that future dealings with the department would be through me, although why, I never learned. At any rate an appointment for me to see the president was made shortly. At this meeting he told me that he was putting the department "on the back burner of the stove" for the time being. In the meantime he was proposing a committee to study what Yale's role in the professional study of education should be in the future. He wanted me to serve on this committee, together with two former high school principals now members of the Ford staff; three members of the academic faculty (Noyes and Anderson being two of them); Helen Randall, the dean of liberal arts at Smith; and William Sanders, the state commissioner of education and a former graduate of our department.

We met once a month for a year and a half, sending minutes of each meeting to the president. During this period Griswold's frustrations seemed to grow rather than abate. Principally, he still wanted to diminish the role of the professional study of education. Indeed, only state requirements prevented him from virtually eliminating it from the M.A.T. program. To enable students in that program to devote the whole academic year to the subject matter they were going to teach, he proposed they be allowed to pass off professional requirements after summer reading of a recommended bibliography. Of course, I could not admit that professional studies were that inconsequential. When I opposed the president on this point, he almost removed me from his study committee. In a final effort to discredit the professional study of education, he had the director of the M.A.T. conduct a student rating of all the instructors in the program, academic as well as professional. Evidently, he was confident that the students would see that the academicians were superior to the professionals. Probably to his chagrin, I am embarrassed to say that I received the top rating.

The longer the president's committee met, the more obvious it became that we were of one mind in favor of restoring the professional study of education as a proper part of the graduate program at Yale. This consensus too seems to have frustrated Griswold because at the end of a year and a half he let it be known that he thought we were getting nowhere. At the next meeting I recommended we invite the president to meet with us to discuss his disappointment. Then our meetings stopped altogether. Three months later we received word that the president would attend a resumption of our meetings. I still remember the occasion vividly. Griswold came and at once pulled out a summary of recommendations the committee had sent him and to our surprise approved of every one! Since the time and method of implementing the recommendations was an administrative matter, he suggested we could safely leave that in his hands.

The next year my delayed Fulbright to Japan became possible. I left New Haven with a light heart, assured the department would be in operation again before I returned. But even before I returned from Japan, I received news from home which could only be interpreted ominously. When I actually got back on campus, I found that the full report of our committee had been filed as a confidential document and that nothing was likely to come of it. I never learned exactly why this third abrupt change. However, the director of the M.A.T. initimated once that it was his impression that the Ford Foundation had decided not to back this new venture of Griswold's.

The end result of Griswold's policies enhanced neither his nor Yale's reputation. At mid-century there no doubt had been some shoddy teacher training programs around the country. But Yale's was not one of them. On the contrary, it was one of the best. In the quarter century of its existence graduates of the department had moved into significant positions of leadership.[2] The idea of a quality program, which was launched shortly after I came to Yale, had paid off handsomely. But the president either had not made the effort to inform himself of it, or, if he had, was unimpressed by it. Instead, he sold out a program leading to positions of administrative responsibility for one preparing only for high school teaching. Not only had he sold out this program, but he had alienated the whole alumni body of the department—to say nothing of leading educators of the country as well.

In partial explanation of Griswold's position, it should be added that his animus toward the Department of Education was not an isolated part of his policies. Each university, he thought, had a unique character and Yale's was to emphasize the basic intellectual disciplines—a view not unlike that of Robert Maynard Hutchins, although Griswold protested he was not a Hutchins man. Studies like nursing, industrial management, and engineering at Yale were all conglomerates of these disciplines and not autonomous disciplines themselves. For this reason they should be broken up and retracted into the small core of true disciplines. Hence all received the same unfriendly treatment as education. Even such nationally known bodies at Yale as the Institute of Human Relations and the Center for Alcoholic Studies got scant encouragement from the president.

The teaching of educational administration particularly drew the president's ire. Indeed, he emphatically promised me that that subject would only be taught at Yale again over his dead body. That there was no point to such a course he proved by pointing to his own career. He had passed from the professoriate to the presidency without formal instruction in administration; why, therefore, should anyone else have it. This lack of training could also prove

2. In 1960, among some 250 Ph.D.'s of the department there were: 9 college presidents, 34 deans, 24 superintendents of schools, 102 college teachers (of whom 63 were departmental chairmen), 13 school principals, 14 members of the U.S. Office of Education, 2 state commissioners of education, and 1 executive secretary of the A.A.S.A.

the narrowness of the president's policy, but of course I restrained myself from saying so. Ironically, since his death Yale is now offering a course in the problems of urban school administration by the very same man, Sam Brownell, who was the last to teach educational administration when Griswold was fulminating against it. But Griswold was not alone in his convictions on the Yale campus. George Pierson, for instance, author of a leading history of Yale, dismissed the half-century growth of the Department of Education with a mere brief footnote in his two-volume account.

Such slight consideration disappointed me personally. Earlier I had written a magazine article on the history of the department. At the suggestion of the secretary of the University, I sent a reprint of it to Pierson, who was then writing his Yale opus. Not a mention did he make of it. If it was poor scholarship, he could have criticized it in his footnote, but to neglect it altogether seemed to indicate the lack of importance he attached to the study of education at Yale. His attitude, however, was only part of a general academic snobbery toward professional histories of education. Thus, I was also irritated when the Ford Foundation subsidized a committee of academic historians to discuss ways and means for improving the writing of educational history. I did not doubt that better histories could be written, but I did doubt the implication that histories with a greater academic emphasis would be intrinsically superior to ones written from a professional view.

So far, the shortsighted policies of Griswold had not blighted my own prospects. But from here on my professional situation at Yale became increasingly untenable. In the autumn after my return from sabbatical I heard rumors that someone else was to be assigned the courses I had been teaching for the M.A.T. program. Of all persons it was to be Dwight Culler, a member of the English department whose chief claim to competence in the history and philosophy of education was the fact that he had written, as a young man, his dissertation on Cardinal Newman's education. By this time, the M.A.T. had its third director, Tom Mendenhall, subsequently president of Smith College. I went to him to inquire whether the rumor was true and, if so, where that left me. Apparently he was not unprepared for my visit, for he told me I had best consult the president, whom I now went to see for the last time.

After explaining my anxiety to him, he replied, "Brubacher, if only you were one of us." I protested that I was, having a Yale A.B. and with Phi Beta Kappa rank at that. In addition, I pointed out, I had the advantage of being a professional as well. To Griswold, however, this latter qualification was only a disqualification. Although it was to cost me my courses, Griswold assured me my tenure was not at stake. I could do research and write, but I was not to teach. In reflecting on this situation after leaving the presidential office, it occurred to me that a novel case of academic freedom might be in the making. Indeed, later a number of my colleagues from other universities started action to call my case to the attention of the American Association of University Professors.

XI

But it was not to go that far. It was at the peak of strained relations at Yale that Willis Rudy and I published our *Higher Education in Transition*. By an almost providential coincidence, Algo D. Henderson, who was then setting up the Center for the Study of Higher Education at the University of Michigan under Carnegie auspices, saw it and phoned me to join his staff. The invitation could not have been more opportune. It was hard to leave my alma mater after more than a quarter of a century in her service, but conditions there had obviously become intolerable. To be sure, I could have stayed on and been paid to be a scholar without teaching responsibilities, a situation some of my colleagues coveted. But, with our departmental faculty now rapidly dispersing, I would have neither colleagues nor students off whom to bounce ideas. Faced with such a bleak prospect I asked for leave to explore the opportunity at Michigan.

At the end of a most enjoyable year I was called back to Connecticut by the state commissioner of education to head a study to be financed by the Ford Foundation of the state's four teachers colleges. The seminal idea was to undertake the reform of teacher education on a statewide rather than single-institution basis. Connecticut was chosen because it had only four colleges, a number that was thought manageable. I met with faculty committees from each institution once a week. The planning was very time-consuming, no little part of our time having to be spent in overcoming faculty suspicions that Ford had some ulterior motive, possibly like that in Arkansas, in sponsoring this study. As it began to appear that a second year of planning would be necessary, these faculty committees asked Ford for a subsidy to release them part time from their regular academic duties. When the subsidy was refused, the Four College Study, as it was called, collapsed and I was glad to learn that I could return to Michigan. This time I remained there, though on an indefinite leave from Yale.

My wife and I made a roundabout return to Michigan by way of Brazil, where I was invited by the National Research Institute to give a series of lectures on educational philosophy, first in Sao Paulo and then in Rio de Janeiro. I gave rather abbreviated lectures to allow time for discussion, which I found very difficult to stimulate. This trip to South America was my last foreign travel but one. That last one came midway through my stay at Michigan when I joined a troupe of the Comparative Education Society again for a summer trip to six iron curtain countries. In each place we were the guests of the local trade union of teachers and so had ample opportunity to discuss educational issues with our opposite numbers. We pulled no intellectual punches and, so far as I could tell, they didn't either.

Looking back on my decade at the University of Michigan, I have no doubt whatever that it was a wise decision to leave Yale. In fact, this decade virtually opened up a second career for me. At Michigan I had a dual appointment—in the departments of higher education and social foundations, even becoming chairman of the latter. Yet, whereas formerly I had interested myself in the history and philosophy of education in general, I now gave the major portion of my efforts to the history and philosophy of higher education. The center's postdoctoral seminar for a half-dozen Carnegie fellows under the leadership of Algo Henderson I found especially exciting. Out of this seminar I drew many insights which I later incorporated into a revision of *Higher Education in Transition.* My *Bases for Policy in Higher Education* grew out of a course with the title "Critique of Ideas in Higher Education," which I inherited and came to enjoy as much as any course I ever taught. It was while teaching this course that retirement overtook me. Retirement from Yale occurred automatically while I was on leave so that, when I retired from Michigan, I became emeritus at two institutions at the same time, which must be some kind of record.

XII

In retrospect I must say I have found the professorial life very satisfying. The fields of history and philosophy of education have been most congenial. I like the scope they give for broad generalization. Yet I have often asked myself whether I should not have specialized in either history or philosophy to become thoroughly competent in one field rather than only modestly competent in two. As it is, I have been very ambivalent, preferring to write history but to teach philosophy. In either event I like the autonomy of the professorial life. Except for class appointments, one can regulate his hours of work to suit his mood. Even more important is the professor's autonomy to arrive at his own conclusions. Of course he must undergo the criticism of his peers, but this is usually meted out with academic decorum. In spite of some academic snobbery, I don't know any calling where one's associates are more likely to be gentlemen.

In pursuing a professorial career I do not see myself as having been an original thinker. Nor do I see myself as having been a crusader for political or scholarly causes. Rather do I see myself primarily as a teacher through the spoken and written word. But even as a teacher it has not been my chief purpose to win adherents to my own interpretations of history and philosophy. On the contrary, I have given first attention to developing students into independent and self-reliant thinkers. In using the Socratic dialogue I have always tried to conceal my own convictions. Yet, when asked by students, as has often been the case, what my personal views were, I did not hesitate to tell them.

My philosophical point of view happens to be pragmatic. Among pragmatists I find myself most closely drawn to John Dewey. Unlike some pragmatists, however, I am interested in ultimate questions in spite of an inability to reduce them to pragmatic terms. Since it is our nature to seek meanings, I can't escape wondering whether the cosmos has meanings which transcend our present ken. Indeed, it seems to me more than likely that there are such meanings. If evolution continues as many million years into the future as it extends back into the past, there seems every likelihood that *homo sapiens* will give way to *homo sapientior* or *homo sapientissimus* who will ferret out meanings far beyond our present capacities to do so. How I wish I might know the meanings they may know! So, as I approach the conclusion of this terrestrial tour, my principal regret is that I knew so little and my principal hope is that somehow the personal quest for meaning will not end or that at least this quest has been part of some overall increase in cosmic meaning.

A BIOGRAPHICAL SUMMARY

JOHN S. BRUBACHER. Born October 18, 1898, in Easthampton, Massachusetts.

Family. Married Elma Winifred Wemple, August 12, 1924. Children: John W., 1928; Paul W., 1937.

Education. Yale, A.B., 1920; Harvard, J.D., 1923; Columbia University, Ph.D., 1927.

Occupational history. Admitted to Massachusetts bar, 1923; instructor (education), Dartmouth University, 1924-25; associate in education, Teachers College, Columbia University, 1925-27, assistant professor, 1928; assistant professor of the history and philosophy of education, Yale University, 1928-34, associate professor, 1934-46, professor, 1946-59; Reuben Post Halleck professor of history and philosophy of education, 1948; director, Four College Study, Connecticut Department of Education, 1959-60; professor of education, University of Michigan, 1959-69; visiting professor, American University of Beirut, 1951-52 and 1956-57, and Kyushu University, Japan, 1957; Brazilian government, Center for Educational Research, 1959.

Memberships and affiliations. American Association of University Professors; National Society of College Teachers of Education (president, 1963); Philosophy of Education Society (president, 1942-46); History of Education Society; Association for Higher Education.

Part II

Selected Publications of John S. Brubacher

Books

1. *Judicial Power of the New York State Commissioner of Education.* New York: Bureau of Publications, Teachers College, Columbia University, 1927.
2. *Modern Philosophies of Education.* New York: McGraw-Hill Book Co., 1939 (rev. 1950, 1962, 1969).
3. *History of the Problems of Education.* New York: McGraw-Hill Book Co., 1947 (rev. 1966).
4. *Educational Frontiers.* Tokyo, Japan: Institute for Democratic Education, 1958.
5. *Higher Education in Transition* (with Willis Rudy). New York: Harper & Row, 1958 (rev. 1968).
6. *Importancia da Theoria em Educacão.* Centro Brasileiro de Pesquises Educationais, United States of Brazil, 1961.
7. *Bases for Policy in Higher Education.* New York: McGraw-Hill Book Co., 1965.
8. *The Courts and Higher Education.* San Francisco: Jossey-Bass, 1971.

Books Edited

9. *Henry Barnard on Education.* New York: McGraw-Hill Book Co., 1931.
10. *Philosophies of Education.* Forty-first Yearbook of the National Society for the Study of Education, Part I. Chicago: University of Chicago Press, 1942.
11. *The Public School and Spiritual Values.* New York: Harper & Bros., 1944.
12. *Eclectic Philosophy of Education.* New York: Prentice-Hall, 1952 (rev. 1961).
13. *Modern Philosophies.* Fifty-fourth Yearbook of the National Society for the Study of Education, Part I. Chicago: University of Chicago Press, 1955.
14. *Casebook in the Law of Higher Education.* Cranbury, N.J.: Associated University Presses, 1971.

Collections and Yearbooks

15. "Social Transition and School Administration." In *Educational Progress and School Administration*, edited by Clyde M. Hill, chap. 2. New Haven: Yale University Press, 1936.
16. "John Dewey." In *Les Grandes Pedagogues*, edited by Jean Chateau. Paris: Presses Universetaires de France, 1956.
17. "The Evolution of Professional Education." In *Education for the Professions*, chap. 3. Sixty-first Yearbook of the National Society for the Study of Education, Part II. Chicago: University of Chicago Press, 1962.
18. "How Responsible Has Our Discipline Become?" *Philosophy of Education Society Proceedings*, 1964, pp. 31-43.
19. "College or University—Dilemma of the Campus." In *Educational Imperatives in A Changing Culture*, edited by William W. Brickman, pp. 21-37. Philadelphia: University of Pennsylvania Press, 1967.

Brochures

20. *Philosophical Foundations of the Curriculum* (with Edward Ladd). New Haven: Yale University Press, 1956.
21. *Ten Misunderstandings of Dewey's Educational Philosophy*. School of Education, Indiana University, Bloomington, Ind., 1960.
22. *Higher Education and the Pursuit of Excellence*. A Scott lecture at Marshall University, Huntington, West Virginia, 1961.

Articles (Journals and Symposia)

History of Education

23. "Origin and Development of the Yale Department of Education," *Teacher Education Journal* 6 (1944): 116-22.
24. "A Century of the State University." *School and Society* 90 (1962): 227-31.

Philosophy of Education

25. "Democratic Education—The Vices of Its Virtues." *Educational Trends* 9 (May–June 1941): 10-16.
26. "Democracy, Education, and the Judeo-Christian Tradition." *Religious Education* 38 (1943): 352-58.
27. "Frontiers of Educational Philosophy." *Educational Forum* 12 (1947): 53-66.
28. "The Importance of Moral Option in Education." *Bulletin of the Research Institute of Comparative Education and Culture* (Kyushu University) 1 (March 1957): 16-28.

29. "Darwinian Evolution and Deweyan Education." *Rhode Island College Journal* I (December 1960): 67-75.
30. "The Anatomy of Power." *Teachers College Record* 70 (1969): 729-37.

Higher Education

31. "Should Liberal Education Bake Bread?" *Liberal Education* 45 (1959): 532-47.
32. "The Autonomy of the University." *Journal of Higher Education* 38 (1967): 237-49.
33. "The Theory of Higher Education." *Journal of Higher Education* 41 (1970): 98-115.
34. "Utopian Perspectives on the University." *Educational Record* 50 (1969): 213-19.

Miscellaneous

35. "State Education Departments as Administrative Judicial Tribunals." *School Board Journal* 77 (December 1928): 33-35, 78, 81.
36. "Constitutionality of a National System of Education in the United States." *School and Society* 46 (1937): 417-23.
37. "A Reargument of the Dartmouth College Case." *Educational Trends* 8 (May-June 1940): 6-11.
38. "Teaching as a Fine Art." *School of Education Bulletin* (University of Michigan) 16 (May 1945): 115-19.
39. "Conflicting Trends in Education in the Modern World." *Official Arabic Journal of the American University of Beirut*, Vol. III, September, 1952.
40. "Resolving the Conflict between Academic and Professional Training of Teachers." *School of Education Bulletin* (University of Michigan) 30 (1959): 81-88.

Part III

John S. Brubacher: A Biographical Essay

MAXINE GREENE

"My respectability is doubtful at best," John Brubacher told the 20th Annual Meeting of the Philosophy of Education Society in 1964.[1] His *Modern Philosophies of Education* was already in its third edition; the two NSSE Yearbooks he had edited on comparative philosophies of education had sold more copies than any other pair published by the NSSE;[2] he had been teaching philosophy of education for almost four decades. But he did not have a degree in the field; and "if anything has downgraded our discipline, it is having it taught by characters like myself." The modesty and irony are characteristic; so was the forcefulness with which he launched his argument. The man of "dubious respectability," who had been the society's second president, was prepared to present a number of imperatives to the young analysts and existentialists assembled before him. He charged them with attempting to become respectable "by playing variations on themes popular in academic journals of philosophy" in a reaction formation against James B. Conant's disdainful dismissal of educational philosophy in *The Education of American Teachers*.[3] Dr. Brubacher had lived through such rejection before. He had learned from bitter experience that, when academic philosophy's "cloak of respectability" was thrown over educational philosophy, education's distinctively complex problems were left to empirical study or a rule-of-thumb approach. As he

1. *Proceedings of the Twentieth Annual Meeting of the Philosophy of Education Society*, School of Education, University of Kansas, 1964.

2. *Philosophies of Education*, Forty-first Yearbook of the National Society for the Study of Education, Part I (Chicago: University of Chicago Press, 1942); *Modern Philosophies and Education*, Fifty-fourth Yearbook of the National Society for the Study of Education, Part I (Chicago: University of Chicago Press, 1955).

3. New York: McGraw-Hill Book Co., 1963.

had been doing for most of his professional life, however, he warned against the "academic cracker-barrel wisdom" which so often masqueraded as educational philosophy, against "quasi-philosophical" and "potpourri" courses which made serious inquiry impossible. He was demanding a scholarly approach to philosophy "relevant to the professional activities which are our main concern." In the language of contemporary students, he was linking "respectability" to "relevance"; but both were to be rigorously dealt with, with standards remaining high.

His conception of educational philosophy might differ from that of younger colleagues who objected to "drawing implications from general doctrines" and argued for "the extension of philosophical methods of analysis to educational contexts."[4] It might differ also from the view of those who laid their primary stress on "existence," "subjectivity," and choice.[5] It was, however, continuous with the efforts of twentieth-century pragmatists to overcome the fruitless dualisms of theory and practice, "liberal" and "professional" education, the "intellectual" and the "vocational." Moreover, it related directly to ongoing efforts to conceive of education, not as a discipline, but as "a professional field of study . . . organized by the societal problems that gave rise to the profession in the first place."[6] It is extremely unlikely that, without the work done by John Brubacher and a few of his contemporaries,[7] an autonomous "field of study" would have been defined.

A dominant theme in his autobiography has to do with the overcoming of dichotomies, the effecting of connections, the achievement of autonomy. One of the imperatives he offered to the Society in 1964 was to "deserve the autonomy characteristic of any profession by taking increasing responsibility for the thorough study of the philosophic bases of education and for the increasingly thorough preparation of our members. . . ." For him, autonomy

4. See, e.g., Israel Sheffler, ed., *Philosophy of Education*, 2d ed. (Boston: Allyn & Bacon, 1966); see also introduction to the first edition.

5. See, e.g., Van Cleve Morris, *Existentialism in Education* (New York: Harper & Row, 1966).

6. Harry S. Broudy et al., *Philosophy of Education: An Organization of Topics and Selected Sources* (Urbana: University of Illinois Press, 1967), p. 3.

7. For example: I. B. Berkson, Theodore Brameld, John Childs, I. L. Kandel, and Bruce Raup.

does not appear to be a "given"; it emerges dialectically. His father attained his by moving from the graduate study of Greek philology to educational administration; the son moved from "the shadow of my father" through a liberal arts experience to the study of law to (with "identity" at last secured) history and philosophy of education. Forming the materials of his life in retrospect, trying to account for what he is and who he is, John Brubacher has told a story of a man who created himself—or found himself—once he defined his professional goals. He did so with a rather remarkable sensitivity, it seems, to continuities and change. It is not accidental that his essay begins with an exploration of his family's past, which was also the American past, and that (because he is a historian) that past becomes usable in the present moment. The "persona" which comes to the fore is partly a consequence of the family history and the personal history and partly a response to acutely perceived change.

There are haunting resemblances between the experiences related in the autobiography and the lives of two educators who seem to have been of signal importance to John Brubacher: Henry Barnard and John Dewey. Barnard, about whom Brubacher wrote in 1931,[8] also went to Yale University, studied law, and discovered his heart was not in it. A chair in education at Yale was proposed for him in 1850, but nothing came of it; and he devoted most of his life to what he considered the "holy cause" of public education. Brubacher puts particular emphasis upon Barnard's interest in teacher education and tells how, when he was chancellor of the University of Wisconsin, he was more interested in his obligations to the state normal school than to the university. Like Brubacher, too, he was much interested in the history of education and had "a boundless capacity for human improvement." Almost as relevant as the content of *Henry Barnard on Education* is the organization of the materials chosen, since the pattern anticipates the great "problems" books Brubacher was later to prepare. Barnard, he wrote, was an "American Condorcet." Condorcet was, of course, one of the great *philosophes* of the eighteenth century, a pioneer of free universal education seldom mentioned in educational literature. It is

8. *Henry Barnard on Education* (New York: McGraw-Hill Book Co., 1931; Russell and Russell, 1965).

interesting that Brubacher's book of readings called *Eclectic Philosophy of Education*[9] contains a selection from Condorcet, introducing the chapter "Academic Freedom." In part, the selection reads: "any power which would forbid the teaching of an opinion contrary to that which has served as a basis for the established laws would attack directly the freedom of thought, would frustrate the aim of every social institution: the perfecting of the laws, which is the necessary consequence of the combat of opinions and the progress of knowledge."[10] The temperateness of the statement, like the regard for "combat of opinions," is somehow relevant to the tone and direction of Brubacher's career. There is a sense in which this country's twentieth-century pragmatists are heirs of the Enlightenment, and it is not difficult to envisage John Brubacher as a latter-day *philosophe*.

There were other, more indigenous influences. The memories of small towns, open fields, churches, talk of "salvation," and the actualities of work are not unlike the memories John Dewey must have had of Vermont. The period of Brubacher's childhood was significantly later; but he, too, had the experience of a home which provided an "educative environment" and a school whose formalism mattered relatively little to a boy encouraged to grow. As he was to realize before long, his was becoming a less and less "typical" educational experience. The era of his early youth was the tumultuous decade at the start of the century, when urbanization, immigration, and industrialization were transforming the American scene. The children of the new urban working class, coming out of chaotic slum environments, made an impact on the traditional common schools which exposed their insufficiency to all who chose to see. The classrooms, as John Dewey said,[11] were still dominated by a "medieval conception of learning." By that he meant an intellectualist conception, inherited from the days in which a "high priesthood" guarded "truth" as if it were a treasure and "doled it out to the masses under severe restrictions." In the larger society at that "progressive" moment in our history, intellectual revolution was taking

9. New York: Prentice-Hall, 1951.

10. *Eclectic Philosophy of Education* (New York: Prentice-Hall, 1951).

11. John Dewey, "The School and Society," in *Dewey on Education,* ed. Martin S. Dworkin (New York: Teachers College Press, 1959), p. 46.

place; "a distinctively learned class," said Dewey, had become an anachronism. "Knowledge is no longer an immobile solid; it has been liquefied. It is actively moving in all the currents of society itself."

The public school, however, had not changed radically in attitude or methodology in the face of the radical changes taking place. The shift to a more practical orientation was occurring very slowly; the school's role in the life of the child was expanding only haltingly. The prevailing confusion about techniques and aims created a situation in which the need for what Brubacher was to call "guideposts" [12] became shockingly clear. This was the moment when, as he wrote, philosophy "gave birth to yet a new form of herself, the philosophy of education." It was the moment when those "problems" he was to call perennial burst to the surface and became, at least for American educators, inescapable. "He used his deep scholarship in history," writes Lawrence G. Thomas,[13] "to illuminate his writings in philosophy of education. . . ." It is entirely likely that his later perception of the dislocations and discrepancies in the world outside his own child-world helped move him to the problem orientation which distinguished his philosophic writing and made his *History of the Problems of Education,* as Dr. Thomas puts it, "one of the few genuinely novel treatments of educational history."

Many of the public schools' deficiencies could be attributed to the inadequacies of teacher training at the time, and Brubacher's recognition of this was to affect his scholarly activity as well as his teaching career. Until about 1920, most elementary school teachers were trained in normal schools, while the majority of high school teachers were graduates of liberal arts colleges. The normal schools were not colleges and ordinarily provided only one or two years of instruction after high school, little of it at an advanced level. Their aim was, as Dewey wrote,[14] to provide nothing more than "immediate proficiency." The work Dewey had done at the Uni-

12. *A History of the Problems of Education* (New York: McGraw-Hill Book Co., 1947), p. 96.

13. Letter to the writer from Professor L. G. Thomas, School of Education, Stanford University, June 20, 1969.

14. John Dewey, "The Relation of Theory to Practice in Education" (1904), in *Teacher Education in America: A Documentary History,* ed. Merle E. Borrowman (New York: Teachers College Press, 1965), p. 150.

versity of Chicago, as well as the researches of Edward L. Thorndike in educational psychology and the contributions to child study made by G. Stanley Hall, constituted a groundwork for theoretical approaches to method; but the faculties and the student bodies of the normal schools were not equipped to utilize it. High school teachers, on the other hand, were generally opposed to the traditional liberal arts programs which excluded concern for anything as "practical" and "nonintellectual" as pedagogy. Yet, after the turn of the century, the high schools too were, as I. L. Kandel was to write,[15] "thrown open to pupils whose IQ ranges from that of a moron to the highest possible figure. The academically able students are less numerous than the less able who lack the intellectual ability needed to pursue a traditional academic course and who come from a less favorable background, social and cultural." The public high school teachers, almost entirely innocent of pedagogical expertise, were helpless when confronted with such students. Young Brubacher's experience was not exceptional; the gifted minority often had to move to private schools in order to pass the college boards.

His unfavorable response to his undergraduate experience at Yale was, according to everything we now know about the traditional college, warranted. There was no consistent philosophy governing the liberal arts curriculum; frequently, diverse assumptions underlay the teaching in different departments. In his *Bases for Policy in Higher Education,*[16] Brubacher himself points out that philosophical considerations were simply not extended to higher education early in the century, and few college presidents thought in terms of fundamental policy.

When, after a few brief years spent on the study and practice of law, he decided to go into education, he was certainly aware of the schism which existed between the "academic" and the "professional" educator. He went to Teachers College at the time when normal schools all over the country were on the verge of being upgraded and transformed into teachers colleges themselves. Paul Woodring says[17] that the county superintendents and experi-

15. *American Education in the Twentieth Century* (Cambridge: Harvard University Press, 1957), p. 210.

16. New York: McGraw-Hill Book Co., 1965.

17. Paul Woodring, *Let's Talk Sense about Our Schools* (McGraw-Hill Book Co., 1953), pp. 86-87.

enced elementary teachers who composed the faculties of most normal schools were forced to go to universities for additional graduate work in order to prepare to teach upper-division courses. "Those who did went most often to Columbia's Teachers College, for it was this institution which was most sympathetic with their problems." Master's degrees were offered there without oral examinations or a thesis being required.

> Moreover, Columbia's Teachers College had a way of convincing you that you really learned more about teaching within its halls than you could have learned in graduate school with the customary degree requirements. Here the student could sit at the feet of Dewey, Kilpatrick, and a host of lesser celebrities. Perhaps not quite at the back row where you could see little and hear less, but at least you could say you had had a course from the great men while others had only read their books.

Teachers College, nevertheless, was "conflict-ridden," as Merle Borrowman puts it,[18] "despite the fact that many of its critics erroneously described it as a temple dedicated to a single system of educational thought." James Earl Russell, who had been dean since 1897, hoped for a degree of mutual understanding between the "academic" and "professional" members of his faculty; he seldom thought in terms of unanimity. "The fundamental fact," he once said,[19] "is that teachers are either academically or professionally minded. Apparently we are born either pedagogical blonds or brunettes. . . ." It is difficult to know whether John Brubacher, as graduate student, was made aware of the schism at the college; but, whether he was or not, it was the existence of diversity in the field that prompted him repeatedly to present competing alternatives—and to ask his readers or students to examine each one critically and at length, and then to choose for themselves.

Because of his training in law, he gravitated at first to educational administration and studied with George Drayton Strayer, who was known to be a pioneer of new trends in educational ad-

18. Merle L. Borrowman, ed., *Teacher Education in America: A Documentary History* (New York: Teachers College Press, 1965), p. 209.

19. James Earl Russell, "A Summary of Some Difficulties Connected with the Making of a Teachers College" (1924), in Borrowman, *Teacher Education in America*, p. 210.

ministration.[20] Since 1910, he had been professor of educational administration and chairman of the department; and, since 1921, he had been head of the Institute of Educational Research in the Division of Field Studies. With the increasing complexity of American school systems and the need for new knowledge, men like Strayer (and the institutions they represented) were already beginning to be instrumental in effecting educational reform. One reason was the number of administrators they trained and dispatched to important superintendencies and commissionerships. Another was the growth of innovations like the school survey, for which Strayer —more than any other single individual—was responsible.

It was not really so surprising that Brubacher was asked to go to Dartmouth after one year of graduate work at Teachers College. The emerging teachers colleges were already competing with liberal arts colleges in the training of high school teachers, and "respectable" academics with even minimal acquaintance with pedagogy were few and far between. The Dartmouth experience, apparently, convinced Brubacher that history and philosophy of education represented his main interest. He was assistant to Edward H. Reisner, who headed the advanced school faculty at the time and clearly belonged to what Dean Russell would have called the "academic" side of the faculty. In Russell's sense, "academic" referred to the kind of work "which leads the student to a constantly expanding knowledge of the subject. It is scientific, logical, all-inclusive.[21] He proceeded to use, as example, "the subject called history of education," which had expanded to such a degree, he thought, that many questioned whether it was fulfilling professional needs. As Borrowman points out in a footnote,[22] Russell's conception of the subject turned out to be the contrary of views defined by modern critics like Bernard Bailyn. *They* consider history of education, as traditionally taught, to be overly "professional," inadequate, even nonhistorical.[23] Nevertheless, it may be assumed that

20. Lawrence A. Cremin et al., *A History of Teachers College* (New York: Columbia University Press, 1954), p. 57.

21. Russell, "Difficulties Connected with Making a Teachers College," p. 211.

22. Ibid.

23. See e.g., Bernard Bailyn, *Education in the Formation of American Society* (Chapel Hill: University of North Carolina Press, 1960).

John Brubacher was unashamedly "academic" in his teaching.

He himself mentions the skill he developed in Socratic teaching while he was at Yale, and numerous former students still comment upon his artistry. William J. Sanders, for example, commissioner of education for the state of Connecticut, writes:

> John Brubacher's work as a writer speaks for itself; his contribution to the history of education and to the philosophy of education is outstanding. I should like to remark upon his great gift for teaching. It has been his practice, in class, to use discussion and dialogue as a means of investigation. In his hands this method does not lead toward conclusions; rather it fosters growth in skill to use experimental logic. Concepts and principles tend to spin off from the dialogue. His seminars have always seemed most exciting and have been attractive not only to students but to visitors who enjoy participating in the "game"! In my opinion, his greatness as a teacher follows from his dramatic use of the dialectical method.[24]

James L. Miller, Jr., director of the Center for the Study of Higher Education at Michigan, writes:

> Brubacher is that rare and remarkable individual—the perfect Socratic teacher. No one attends Brubacher's classes unprepared because the class consists of genuine participation by all in attendance and the subject matter is the reading material assigned. The discussion is open and free, with Brubacher asking questions, challenging assertions, and pressing for the fuller development of ideas. Wonder of wonders, however, at the end of a two-hour block of teaching time, the discussion, as if of its own accord, has come full circle so that the questions raised in the beginning have indeed been dealt with and brought—not to resolution—but to a point of understanding sufficient to allay frustrations even as it encourages further thought and research on the part of the student.[25]

It seems obvious enough that the man of "dubious respectability" never taught a "cracker-barrel" or "quasi-philosophical" course when he was at Yale or anywhere else. Yet President Griswold of Yale, in his lordly certainty about the need to hold what he conceived to be "vocational education" at arm's length from liberal arts,[26] chose to consider what Brubacher was doing so "specialized"

24. Letter to the writer, June 27, 1969.

25. Letter to the writer, June 24, 1969.

26. John S. Brubacher, *Bases for Policy in Higher Education* (New York: McGraw-Hill Book Co., 1965).

and "instrumental" that it did not belong in a program focused on liberal arts.

Professor Brubacher has told the story of Yale in the 1950s more exhaustively than it has yet been told, and nothing need be added to what he has said. A selection from Griswold's own writing in that period, however, may well shed some light on Griswold's position and alliances in what I. L. Kandel once called the "academic civil war":

> My final suggestion is, therefore, that we give fresh thought to our teacher-training programs with a view to strengthening them in the subjects of the academic curriculum. I do not think there is any more crucial point at which the whole problem we have been discussing could be attacked than this. Generally speaking, these programs are replete with courses in methodology which I believe equip the prospective teacher less well than courses in the subject matter he is preparing to teach, combined with the actual experience of teaching, properly supervised, in practice and apprenticeship. Again, if students are to be sorted out according to the distinct aims of the vocational and academic curriculums, so, I think, should teachers be. . . .[27]

Considering this point of view, along with those of James B. Conant, Arthur Bestor, and Robert Maynard Hutchins, one can well understand what prompted Brubacher to keep asking for the examination of presuppositions, the clarification of the theoretical bases of policy. He writes at one point that Griswold "stoutly took the stand that we should take rational hold of events and try to redirect the current of history back into former channels."[28] The consequences of this attitude have become painfully evident on college campuses around the country. Surely it would have helped if more people had analysed such stands, had clarified the usages of "rational," had known enough to perceive the direction of history's current. Brubacher's effort throughout has been to equip individuals to see, to teach them to be clear.

Algo D. Henderson, who invited Brubacher to join the Center for the Study of Higher Education at Michigan and thus to begin a new career, now writes that Brubacher "is both an outstanding

27. A. Whitney Griswold, *Liberal Education and the Democratic Ideal* (New Haven: Yale University Press, 1959), pp. 57-58.

28. Brubacher, *Bases for Policy*.

scholar and also ranks exceptionally high as a stimulating teacher." [29]

Numerous colleagues have commented upon his ability to apply what he had learned in history and philosophy to the careful study of higher education and educational administration. Jerry Gardner, speaking at Brubacher's retirement in August 1968, said significantly:

> At a time when some college and university students are demonstrating their frustrations with faculty disinterest in teaching and lack of concern for students, you took the time and effort to ask some of your students how you might improve your course. . . . On another occasion you engaged Center students in an informal discussion of how you might organize a new course on "The College and the Law." These examples make clear your conception of the learning process in which both students and teachers are actively involved.[30]

James Miller has spoken, in his turn, about the influence Brubacher has had upon the center's students for the past ten years, similar to the influence he exerted during his twenty-five years at Yale. His Michigan students were people with teaching or administrative experience who had decided to move into college and university administration; and Brubacher's contribution to almost all of them has been "to provide them with a deep appreciation of the historical development of American higher education (and its antecedents in Europe) and to alert them to the fact that a 'philosophy of education' is more than a phrase; it is something each individual must have if he is to be effective in an educational setting." [31] Perhaps unfashionably, perhaps without "respectability," Brubacher has asked each student to develop his own philosophy of higher education; and he has done so Socratically, drawing out of each student "what the student himself thinks." Even after his mandatory retirement, writes Dr. Miller, he developed a new course, "Higher Education and the Law," complete with an 800-page casebook, to teach in the 1969 summer session.

29. Letter to writer from Algo D. Henderson, Center for Research and Development in Higher Education, University of California, Berkeley, June 27, 1969.

30. *Newsletter,* Center for the Study of Higher Education, University of Michigan, August 1968, p. 2.

31. Letter to the author from James L. Miller, Jr., Director of the Center, June 24, 1969.

"There is only one John Brubacher," says Dr. Miller, and he is joined by colleagues throughout the country. And perhaps that is the main point to be made. Father John E. Walsh, vice-president for academic affairs at the University of Notre Dame and a former student of Brubacher, said at Brubacher's retirement banquet:

> The philosopher has not always been highly regarded by the society in which he lives, probably because by his very devotion to the pursuit of wisdom he is often the conscience and the critic of his age. Wisdom is neither easy nor popular. Yet the philosopher is absolutely essential to any age and, if I may say so, I think particularly to our own. One who has tasted deeply of philosophy never tires of it or retires from it. For this reason I am certain we can look forward to Professor Brubacher's continuing to contribute to the solution of the two central problems of our day—problems he always considered well and often: The first is how to bring science and technology into closer contact with a higher, deeper, and more comprehensive wisdom; the second is how to develop a social philosophy in which human dignity (freedom and responsibility) and the system of values it implies are so clearly perceived that they are capable, as the students would say, of genuinely "turning us on."[32]

John Brubacher does not see himself as an "original thinker" or as a "crusader." He sees himself "primarily as a teacher through the spoken and written word." He has taught some of the best and most effective among us; his books continue goading and stimulating even those who do not totally agree. And so the man of "dubious respectability" has sought his meanings and made it possible for the quest to continue. There is no finer autonomy, no more significant specialization. There is only one John Brubacher, after all.

32. "Mnemosyne." Remarks by the Reverend John E. Walsh, C.S.C., at April 1968 banquet honoring John S. Brubacher.

CHAPTER III

William G. Carr

Part I

An Autobiography

In June 1924 I received my A.B. degree from Stanford University along with a document entitling me to teach mathematics, English, and French in a California junior high school. In August, Elizabeth Vaughan and I were married, and in September I began teaching at Roosevelt School in Glendale, California.

The end of my undergraduate education is an arbitrarily selected point at which to begin this essay. The editors have, however, asked me to comment on a few points about my earlier years.

I have been asked, for example, what role my family background played in the years of my youth. Had my parents been lazy or indifferent, hostile to education or to intellectual development, they might well have exerted an adverse effect. Fortunately, this was by no means the case. The best gift my parents offered for my development was the good example of an industrious, unselfish life. I can remember no parental pressure for good grades. They did not urge me to continue my formal education. Academic success, however, was not a major objective of our family life. If I had brought home school reports that were barely passing, I do not think I would have been scolded or urged to do better.

During my high school and college years our family struggled with serious economic difficulties, never experiencing actual want but always required to seek added income and to avoid nonessential expenses. From the age of about sixteen onward, I worked on Saturdays, before school, and after school. My work was unskilled and poorly paid. I picked apricots, cleaned chicken houses, dusted the high school auditorium from six to eight every morning, swept the school cafeteria every evening, worked in the Sunset Candy Factory in the longer vacations, ran errands, delivered newspapers, ushered at the race track and the opera house, and ran the elevator in a small hotel. This varied work experience was, of course, highly educational. I did not resent it. I felt, when I thought about the matter at all, that I was lucky to have the opportunity to work. In retrospect, I still think so.

I am also asked by the editors, "What did you expect of yourself?" The question implies sharpness of introspection as well as vividness of memory. I simply do not remember having given any thought to such questions in my childhood and youth. I did my best because life was more pleasant that way.

I am asked, "What is the bearing of religion on your career?" The answer is none, so far as I can tell or so far as any usual definition of religion is concerned.

I am asked whether the communities in which I spent my earlier years may have influenced my life. An English factory town, a homestead in the forests of Alberta, a small farm-market center, a rapidly growing western metropolis, a university town—none of these had any discernible relation to the events of my later life. Of course, had I lived in other places my life would probably have been different, but in what ways or for what reasons it is impossible for me to guess.

The editors have suggested that I write a few words about teachers who were important to me. There were many such. For instance, Miss Goudy in Red Deer (Alberta) High School taught me once and for all how an English sentence is constructed.

In college, Dr. Herbert Allen at U.C.L.A. and Dr. John Almack at Stanford taught me self-confidence. I had many teachers who were erudite, eloquent, amusing, or inspiring, but these two were interested in *me*. How they revealed that personal interest I cannot exactly say, but I was (and remain) certain that it existed. When Dr. Almack casually invited me to his home for a Sunday afternoon tea, the recognition meant more to me as an undergraduate than an honorary degree did thirty years later. Neither of these men were noted scholars or especially powerful teachers. They did care about their students and their intellectual growth. They made it clear that they had unlimited confidence in me to accomplish anything at all.

The influence of Dr. Cubberley at Stanford was somewhat less personal, but he did teach me and other Stanford men and women that public schools and democratic government are inseparable, that schools should anticipate the changing problems of our society, and that education can be a worthy career.

My teaching experience in Glendale was delightful but strenuous. Since I was the newest teacher on the staff, of course I drew the Z group for my homeroom and for most of my classes each day. I was also allowed, by common consent, the privilege of spending my lunch hour in playground supervision. The "dumb bunnies" —as my Z children cheerfully, unselfconsciously, and accurately called themselves—gave me no serious trouble. It was the clever youngsters who kept me on edge. The Z's were undemanding, polite, and appreciative. As for the playground, I enjoyed the California sunshine, which in those halcyon days came to us without the interposition of a blanket of smog, so I felt no resentment at all upon being "invited" to supervise the playground.

After my first year in teaching, it became necessary to decide whether to return to Stanford to seek a master's degree. I was by no means discontented in Glendale. Although we had saved as much as we could from my first year's salary, there was real doubt whether we could afford a year at Stanford. My wife, who might have been expected to favor Glendale, near her friends and family, was all for moving so that I might obtain further education. In September 1925 we moved to Palo Alto. By strict economy and by signing up for all of the extra paid work available, we managed to pay the bills and the tuition.

My dissertation for the M.A. degree was entitled "Desirable Qualities in a Textbook." My wife was typing page 89 of this remarkable document when she made an announcement which sent me hurrying according to plan to borrow a neighbor's car. A few minutes later we drove up to the ambulance entrance of Palo Alto Hospital. Our son was born there on April 11, 1926. I was so pleased with this event that I even finished typing the dissertation myself.

In 1926-27 I spent a busy and delightful interlude as *the* Department of Education at Pacific University, Forest Grove, Oregon. I taught the full range of courses offered by the department and was also in charge of freshman orientation. I also served as director of placement, supervisor of student teaching, and chairman of a faculty committee on each topic that I was careless enough to mention during faculty meetings.

In the fall of 1927, the award of the Cubberley Fellowship enabled me to return to Stanford where I completed the Ph.D. in education, with minors in Elizabethan literature and in French.

In those days the venerable chancellor emeritus of Stanford University, David Starr Jordan, used to give a public lecture every Sunday morning. I went to hear him as often as I could. One day after his lecture I was bold enough to tell him that I had written a small book on how schools could contribute to peace. Dr. Jordan immediately asked to see the manuscript. The next Sunday he returned it and recommended it for publication to the Stanford University Press.

Education for World Citizenship appeared in October 1928. In the foreword I said that I thought this was the first book on the subject and that it doubtless exhibited "many of the imperfections of a pioneer work in a rapidly growing and changing field of study." It was well that I put in some such disclaimer, for as I look at it today, I do not know whether most to admire the nerve of the author or to deplore the book's many inadequacies.

One copy of *Education for World Citizenship* landed on the desk of John K. Norton, then director of research for the National Education Association in Washington. In September 1928, a letter came from Dr. Norton inviting me to become assistant director of research for the National Education Association. This proposed dislocation required very careful evaluation. I could have certainly returned to Glendale or to Pacific University or secured other university teaching positions. I could have expanded my work with the California Teachers Association from part time to full time. But here was an invitation to go all the way to Washington, a tremendous distance, four nights and three days on the train.

On January 2, 1929, at six o'clock in the morning, the *Crescent Limited* pulled into Washington Union Station from California via New Orleans. My wife and I, with our two-year-old son, very tired after the long journey, climbed the stairs from the Southern Rail-

John S. Brubacher

William G. Carr

James Bryant Conant

George S. Counts

Arthur I. Gates

Sidney Leavitt Pressey

George N. Shuster

George D. Stoddard

Ruth M. Strang

Robert Ulich

Carleton Wolsey Washburne

way platform into the station and came thus to the capital of the United States. Those few who can remember will agree that the Washington Union Station was then an impressive piece of architecture—one great marble hall, vaulted, gracefully proportioned, uncluttered. No one had yet added the dirtly little shed for the station master, or defiled the elegance of the concourse with a garish corner for pinball machines, or hoisted neon signs to huckster whisky, tobacco, or detergents. In the great waiting room, high above the marble walls, pairs of heroic statues guarded what was then, I suppose, the railroad capitol of the United States. We went on through the station and emerged into the great square before it, a park with fountains where the bare trees of winter were just beginning to show through the morning mist. Our eyes were immediately drawn to the illuminated dome of the Capitol against the grey morning sky. The city and its splendour and challenge lay before us. I feel sorry now for people who come to Washington for the first time through a maze of superhighways which permits not one moment of contemplation, or through a cluttered, ever expanding airport which looks just like every other airport from Stockholm to Singapore.

The entire staff of the National Education Association was comfortably housed in a four-story remodeled residence known as the Guggenheim Mansion. Forty people could work there. Today, at the same address, the association staff of about twelve hundred occupies a modern office building.

Dr. John Norton, director of the Research Division, took a year's leave of absence in 1930-31 to study and teach at Columbia University. Early in 1931 he submitted his resignation. After a brief consideration, Mr. James W. Crabtree, the NEA executive secretary at that time, asked me to become director of research. I accepted and took up this office on my thirtieth birthday, June 1, 1931.

Most of the 1920s had been years of golden prosperity. Industrial activity expanded, incomes rose to new heights, and a wave of speculation hurried the prices of common stocks constantly upward. The end of an epoch came with the stock market crash of 1929. Not until 1933 was there a perceptible upward movement in the American economy. The interval was a period of severe hardships. The education system bore its full share and, as many thought, more than its full share of suffering.

School construction ceased. Children attended two-shift or three-shift schools. Many schools were closed. Staff salaries were cut, teaching loads were increased, and many teachers were unpaid for months at a time. Many school systems reduced the term by twenty days or more. Textbook purchases, health activities, music, art, home economics, physical education, kindergartens, evening schools, and classes for handicapped children were frequently eliminated. By 1933, confidence in public education was being rapidly eroded.

In February 1933 the National Education Association and its Department of Superintendence established the Joint Commission on the Emergency in Education.

I was assigned to serve as its executive officer and my former chief, John K. Norton, was named chairman. The commission aimed to help the schools to sustain morale and to meet the most catastrophic effects of the depression. We devised a number of procedures with these objectives in mind.

One of these procedures was to appoint a board of nine hundred consultants, announced with a public flourish in hometown newspapers. Consultants were invited to regional meetings as often as resources permitted. To save expense, the conferences were scheduled as closely together as possible. Here is a typical series of six in late 1934:

October 27, Chicago
October 29, Minneapolis
October 31, Cheyenne
November 1, Ogden
November 3, Portland
November 5, Oakland

I traveled by train and, as a rule, by night. Arriving at a regional conference city, I would proceed to the designated conference hotel, unpack and install the traveling exhibit, meet the press, hold the meeting, prepare a summary to be distributed as the conference ended, pay the bills, pack up the exhibit, and entrain for the next conference site.

The joint commission worked in close cooperation with the NEA Legislative Commission to secure emergency federal grants and loans to build schools, to pay teachers' salaries that were most seriously in arrears, and to reopen rural schools.

In its *Final Report*, July 1935, the joint commission made a recommendation which, when adopted, was destined to have great significance to American education, to the NEA, and to me personally. The joint commission proposed that the two agencies which had sponsored it create an educational policies commission "to bring a new type of thinking and higher statesmanship into the process of adapting educational institutions to the ever changing needs of our dynamic democracy." The joint commission, anticipating that its last recommendation would be accepted, had already opened discussions with Dr. Edmund Day, president of the General Education Board, looking toward a substantial grant to finance this proposed new unit in the NEA structure.

In the thirty months of its existence the joint commission spent $21,481.28. Commenting in its final report on the financing of its work, the joint commission noted that the salaries of the headquarters staff were not included. The joint commission added that "it frequently has been necessary for these employees to perform the work of the Commission as additional assignments to already overfilled programs." This added work, the joint commission said, had been accepted willingly and carried out with enthusiasm, devotion, and efficiency.

As it is now over a third of a century since these words were published, it may not be considered excessively boastful if, as the principal member of the joint commission's staff, I say that their report in this respect was absolutely correct. We worked our heads off.

In January 1936, the Educational Policies Commission met for the first time. Appointment to the commission was regarded as the highest honor that could come to any educator. No commissioner would have dreamed of proposing the excuse of a conflicting engagement for absence from a meeting. The absolute priority of the commission business was stressed. If some prospective member had declined to accept this priority, the invitation would have been immediately withdrawn. However, I never heard of such a contingency. When Dwight Eisenhower, then president of Columbia

University, attended his first commission meeting, he responded to greetings by saying with a smile, "If you had delayed my invitation much longer, I would have asked for the appointment." Even after he left Columbia to take command of NATO, General Eisenhower continued to be an active, highly concerned, and responsive member of the Commission. Other members were similarly devoted.

No one had any clear ideas as to how the Educational Policies Commission was to work. The large objective had been defined but the methods were yet to be devised. During its first meeting the commission went into executive session for the purpose of choosing its executive officer. I was genuinely surprised when a subcommittee came to ask me to assume that position.

In order that I might give the bulk of my time to the commission, Dr. Frank Hubbard became associate director of research and was in effect the executive officer of the Research Division. In 1941, he became director of the division while I was named secretary of the Educational Policies Commission and associate secretary of the NEA.

A word now about the working habits of the Educational Policies Commission. The commission met two or three times a year, each meeting lasting three or four days, normally three sessions a day. As long as most of the members of the commission came to the meeting by train, their attendance was much better than it was in subsequent years. Air travel has, in my opinion, impaired the quality of deliberative meetings, with ever increasing demands for shorter sessions, superficial debate, and hasty conclusions.

Younger readers may find it difficult to believe that only a few years ago it was by no means unusual for an important committee to meet for three hours at a stretch. The coffee break has put an end to such concentration and has, on many occasions, made productive debate all but impossible. However, the Educational Policies Commission in its early years never heard of such luxuries.

The continuity of discussion, the sense of history and of mission, the lack of pressure to try to catch a plane one hour earlier, and many other factors resulted in meetings of the Educational Policies Commission which were intellectually exciting and genuinely deliberative. After the commission voted to approve a prospectus or plan for a report, one of its members, or one of its staff, or an outside expert was assigned to prepare a first draft. It was not at all uncommon for these drafts to go through as many as ten revisions. The commission as a whole read the final text together and discussed it page by page, line by line. This was tiring, slogging work, both for the staff and the commission, but I believe it paid off.

Turning from procedures to substance, the commission began by dividing the whole area of education into manageable units and planning a series of publications on each. These plans were in an almost constant process of revision, but at any given moment it was possible to produce a chart which showed what the commission had done, what it was working on, and to what it would turn next.

Out of this procedure emerged a decision that the first major commission publication should deal with the historical and political roots of the American system of education. The commission made another decision, equally important; namely, that for any topic it would endeavour to secure as its author the most competent and distinguished person available. For the first project, entitled "The Unique Function of Education in American Democracy," we enlisted the services of Dr. Charles A. Beard, one of America's distinguished historians. Dr. Beard recognized the great prestige of the commission in educational circles and in a few months produced *The Unique Function of Education in American Democracy*. An immediate and immense success, the book is still quoted with respectful approval. It set a high standard for all future commission publications.

The second report of the commission, *The Structure and Administration of Education in American Democracy*, written by one of its members, Dr. George D. Strayer, easily upheld the high standards of the first.

The third volume in this series was titled *The Purposes of Education in American Democracy*. Here, the commission encountered its first serious difficulties in finding an acceptable author. Several well-known individuals, one after the other, accepted an invitation to prepare a prospectus for such a book. None of the drafts met with the commission's approval, the months passed, and the search for an author grew more anxious. At that point, I was handed the job of writing the book. Published in 1938, it was reprinted in whole or in part several million times and is still reprinted today. Other volumes in this series were then in various stages of preliminary discussion or drafting, but the volumes already produced established the commission for many years as the most respected voice of American education.

The longest and in many ways the most basic volume of this series was *Education and Economic Well-being in American Democracy*. After several false starts with other authors, it was completed in a remarkably short time by Dr. John K. Norton, a member of the commission. The series was completed by two final volumes: *The Education of Free Men in American Democracy* (1941) by commission member George Counts, and the culminating volume, *Moral and Spiritual Values in the Public Schools* (1951), which I wrote after a series of preliminary studies and drafts.

While the foregoing series of basic documents was being issued, other important commission enterprises were being prepared. One of the best known of the second group of documents presented a new approach to development of education for citizenship. We developed a list of ninety secondary schools which were judged to be unusually effective in training American citizens. Six men visited these schools for several weeks, took extensive notes, and then returned to the office to prepare the report. The results of our investigations were set forth in *Learning the Ways of Democracy*. This volume offered tested, practical ideas for teaching methods, curriculum, extracurricular activities, administration, and community relations in civic education.

A few days after Pearl Harbor the commission issued *A War Policy for American Schools*. I had been holding ready a first draft of this document for several months before the "Day of Infamy," hoping that it would never be used. A special meeting of the commission was called at once. With many revisions suggested by the members, the manuscript was approved for immediate distribution.

Immediately after the issuance of *A War Policy*, the commission began to plan for the postwar period in education. This forward look had at that time two major aspects: national and international. The latter will be considered more fully later. The commission's proposals for the reform and reconstruction of our own American school system took the form of two books: one for elementary schools and one for secondary schools. Each book described in detail the postwar schools of "Farmville" and "American City."

In his centennial history of the NEA, Dr. Edgar Wesley describes the Educational Policies Commission itself as "an instant success," its early publications as "timely and influential," and its continued achievements as the outcome of "sound analysis of educational issues and a strategic sense of timing and feasibility."

During the last years of World War II determination increasingly developed that education should be enlisted to help deal with international problems.

An Educational Policies Commission document, issued in 1943 and entitled *Education and the People's Peace*, immediately became a primary topic of conversation among teachers, school administrators, and members of the public. A substantial campaign, financed by the NEA War and Peace Fund, was launched to secure public consideration of the recommendations.

In April 1945 I went to San Francisco as a consultant in the U.S. delegation to the conference which drafted the United Nations Charter. Secretary of State Edward Stettinius told the consultants that he regarded their participation as "an experiment in taking the people through their unofficial representatives into the process of making foreign policy."

From the opening session to the concluding signing ceremonies, the San Francisco conference gave steadily increasing recognition to economic and social forces, including education.

There was, however, little original interest in education among the great powers. Thus, during the early days of the conference, only the small nations spoke of the possible educational functions of the new organization whose charter we were writing.

The difficulty in securing a charter reference to education centered around four points:

1. It was believed by many that references to education would make it more difficult to secure ratification by the United States Senate.
2. It was thought by some that the word "cultural" adequately covered what we had in mind and was less likely to raise objections.
3. The pressure of time made it difficult to consider any topic that was not in the early draft of the charter prepared at Dumbarton Oaks.

4. There was doubt as to whether the public really cared much about international cooperation in education.

At midnight of May 5, just under the deadline, the proposals of the United States for modification of the draft were filed. One of these proposals was to create a trusteeship council for the parts of the world then in colonial status. The draft, as submitted by the United States, contained no reference to education as a means of preparing the people of these areas for independence or self-government. I began immediately to get these points covered in the next revision.

Meanwhile, in Washington, Senators J. William Fulbright and Robert Taft sponsored a resolution in the Senate favoring the participation of the United States in an international office of education. A similar resolution was introduced in the House of Representatives by Congressman (later Senator) Karl Mundt.

In San Francisco the consultants met every day with key members of the United States delegation. On the question of educational cooperation we established an informal group of the consultants representing agriculture, business, labor, and education. This group was promptly called the ABLE group. (The representative of the National Council of Churches remarked to me later that if religion had been included, the ABLE group would have been ABLER!)

At 8:15 in the morning of May 16, the ABLE group met with the entire United States delegation. On the same day, the House Committee on Foreign Affairs voted favorably on Congressman Mundt's resolution. In fact, May 16 became the day of the break-through. The *San Francisco News* predicted a United Nations education conference within the next few months. The *New York Times* said that the discussion about education was one of the most significant developments of the conference.

On May 22, when the conference was exactly four weeks old, a definite reference to the promotion (not merely provision) of educational cooperation was unanimously approved in the drafting committee on a motion offered by the United States delegation. On the same day, the Mundt resolution passed the House of Representatives without a dissenting vote. On May 24 the Taft–Fulbright resolution passed the Senate unanimously. I began to make my plans to leave San Francisco a few days before the signing ceremonies.

The developments in San Francisco and in Washington were steps by which the profession of education not only registered a great achievement but also accepted a profound obligation.

Meanwhile, in London, there had been established the Council of Allied Ministers of Education, including the governments in exile.

Once the principle was established in San Francisco that the United Nations system would concern itself with educational co-operation, the London group sought an international conference on future intergovernmental activities in education.

The United Nations Conference for the Establishment of an Educational and Cultural Organization opened in London on November 1, 1945. I was sent to London by the United States State Department, at the request of the British government, to serve as deputy to Sir Alfred Zimmern, the secretary-general of the London conference. Hs assigned me the task of staffing the committee which drafted the preamble and the statement of purposes of the organization, under the chairmanship of Archibald MacLeish of the United States.

In delivering the address of welcome, Prime Minister Clement Atlee used a phrase which was later picked up in the Unesco Charter and which has often been attributed (incorrectly) to those who drafted the preamble to the charter. "Wars," said Mr. Atlee, "begin in the minds of men."

On November 15, 1945, the Unesco Charter was completed and adopted. That evening one of the colleagues of the British Minister of Education, Ellen Wilkinson, said to her, "Well, Ellen, it's a race now between your conference and the atom."

On November 12 the officers of the London conference had sent a telegram to the Soviet Union expressing the hope that a Soviet delegation might even yet join the work of the conference. Despite the provisions of the UN Charter, there had been no response to earlier invitations and there was no response to this telegram. In 1954, nine years later, without a word of explanation for its initial indifference, its subsequent hostility, or its final acceptance, Soviet delegates appeared to claim their places at Unesco conferences. The smaller countries of Eastern Europe, however, did participate in Unesco from the beginning. This arrangement permitted them to share fully in the advantages of Unesco programs for the rebuilding their shattered school systems even while they echoed Soviet policy by condemning Unesco as a tool of Western imperialism.

On June 30, 1946, I watched with a dozen other witnesses as President Harry S Truman signed the legislation confirming United States membership in Unesco. To coincide with this event, the NEA announced that it was inviting representatives of the national teachers' organizations of the world to a conference which would consider, among other items, how teachers could cooperate with the newly formed Unesco. Twenty-four of the world's teachers' organizations accepted the invitation.

I began the correspondence regarding the world teachers' conference in 1944. The teachers' associations in each of the United Nations were invited, plus those of Sweden, Switzerland, and Ireland. The conference met in August 1946 at "The Homestead" in Endicott, New York. In the closing ceremonies the delegates from each participating organization signed the constitution which they had drafted to establish the World Organization of the Teaching Profession.

A *Washington Post* editorial of September 1946 observed that "everyone talks about education as the key to peace; but it has remained for some of the teachers of the world to do something constructive about it." A similar editorial in the *New York Herald Tribune* said that careful preliminary work by the NEA and the congenial setting at Endicott had contributed to the success of the conference but that the decisive factor was the conviction of the delegates that education is an international fellowship.

Having recounted the establishing of Unesco and World Organization of the Teaching Profession (after 1952, the World Confederation of Organizations of the Teaching Profession—WCOTP), it will be best to bring my international activities down to date before returning to the national scene.

My own education occurred in three countries, and prior to the establishment of Unesco and WCOTP I had been involved in a number of international conferences either as organizer or delegate. Limitations of space, however, suggest that the story be picked up from 1945-46.

In 1946 I was appointed a member of the newly established

United States National Commission for Unesco. I served on its executive committee and engaged in other commission activities during the formative years of Unesco.

When the First General Conference of Unesco was held in Paris in 1946, I was invited to give one of the three Unesco lectures at the Sorbonne. My topic was "Conditions Necessary for the Success of Unesco."

The Second General Conference was held in 1947 in Mexico City. I was an adviser on the United States delegation and served as vice-chairman of the working party on education.

The 1945 General Conference on Unesco had been concerned mainly with the structure of Unesco; the 1946 conference, with its general goals; the 1947 conference, with its program. After the 1947 conference, I was never again invited to represent the United States at any general conference of Unesco. I have often wondered why. I have, however, maintained quite close connections with Unesco through other channels. For example, I lectured at the first Unesco Seminar on Education for International Understanding at Sevres in the summer of 1947. I have visited the Unesco headquarters in Paris for liaison and other purposes about once a year since then. In December 1951, on the invitation of Unesco, I attended as consultant a conference in Cairo on teacher exchange among the Arab states.

About 1962 Unesco became interested in a substantial recognition of the importance of the status of teachers. In my view, an international educational organization which found no time for teachers and their interests was cut off from one of its main sources of effectiveness and support. It took over ten years for this point to penetrate deep enough to produce a result.

I was named chairman of the first Unesco Expert Conference on the Status of Teachers, held in Paris in May 1964. At a further meeting on the same topic in January 1966 in Geneva, I was elected chairman of the Drafting Committee. The enterprise came to fruition in September 1966 with a Special Intergovernmental Conference at Unesco headquarters in Paris to adopt a recommendation on the status of the teaching profession. I was elected rapporteur for this conference. The conference produced a recommendation which, I believe, will bring greater recognition of the rights and responsibilities of the teaching profession throughout the world.

In 1967 I was appointed to the Unesco Liaison Committee on Literacy which meets annually in Paris under the chairmanship of Princess Ashraf Pahlavi of Iran.

Finally, to bring the account of my Unesco-related activities up to date, in May 1968 I attended the Unesco Conference on Higher Education in Arab States in Baghdad, and in October I went to Mexico to give the summary speech for the International Conference on Education and Sport. Leaving the Unesco-related activities, I now turn to more general types of international effort.

In September 1944 I edited one of the *Annals* of the American Academy of Political and Social Science under the title *International Frontiers in Education.* I wrote a substantial editorial foreword and organized eighteen papers from distinguished contributors.

In June 1945 I wrote for the Foreign Policy Association "Only by Understanding," a brief account of previous efforts to enlist education in the search for peace.

In February 1946, a few months after the adjournment of the San Francisco conference, I wrote for Ginn and Company *One World in the Making,* a guide to the then new United Nations Charter.

In July 1946, before the NEA Convention in Cincinnati, I delivered a paper outlining policies and programs to relate education to peace. By direction of the NEA Delegate Assembly, "On the Waging of Peace" was published for wide distribution.

From 1945 to 1966 I often appeared before congressional committees to testify on legislation affecting the international educational relations of the United States. My final, or at least my latest, appearance occurred in April 1966 before the Committee on Education and Labor of the House of Representatives, which was considering legislation eventuating in the International Education Act of 1966.

In January 1946 I took the initiative of inviting the cultural attaches in Washington to a meeting to promote useful contacts among these diplomats and a better understanding of United States private and governmental services of interest to them. With this start, the Round Table of Cultural and Educational Attaches has been meeting monthly now for twenty-two years.

In September 1946 I was active in starting the Anglo-American Teacher Exchange Program.

In August 1949 I visited the United States Occupation Forces in Germany as a consultant, meeting with members of the civilian staff, as well as with German educators. I made a second visit to Germany under the same auspices in September 1951 and have visited Germany on seven occasions since then.

In August 1953 we were in London, preparing for a long-sought week of vacation in Cornwall when the American-Korean Foundation in New York City telephoned to ask me to join a mission to Korea as the education adviser on postwar reconstruction and rehabilitation. The last thing I wanted at that moment was to go to Korea, but I reflected that many other Americans had been there recently under far less favourable conditions. Dr. Howard Rusk was in charge of medical and hospital aspects of the rehabilitation, General Van Fleet was our presiding officer, and Eugene Taylor, our administrator. As a side trip, we visited the prisoner exchange in Panmunjon and a number of villages.

In 1955 Dr. William F. Russell, former president of WOTP, became deputy director of the United States Foreign Aid Program. More than any of his predecessors or successors in that post, Dr. Russell recognized the role of elementary and secondary schools in nation-building. He organized a national advisory committee on elementary and secondary education. As a member of this advisory committee I was requested in 1956 to inspect the educational operations at United States Aid Missions in eight cities of the Caribbean and Central America and in eleven cities of Asia and to make recommendations to Dr. Russell.

In 1957 I helped to develop the Council on International Nontheatrical Events (CINE), which screens American films for international film festivals. I was elected president of the council in 1970.

In July 1962 I became a member of the board of directors of the People-to-People program with frequent meetings in Kansas City, Washington, New York, and Gettysburg. I was elected president in 1970.

The year 1965 was designated by the United Nations as International Cooperation Year. I served as chairman of the White House Conference Committee on Education and Training, organized four planning meetings of the committee, and presided over the appropriate sections of the White House Conference itself.

In early 1967 President Johnson suggested that a major international conference on education be held as an outgrowth of the International Education Act of 1966. At the President's request, an international planning committee met in Williamsburg in February. We selected the theme of the coming conference and completed other arrangements. The Conference on "The World Crisis in Education" was held in October 1967 at Williamsburg with President Johnson participating.

Curriculum experts of the United States, Canada, and the United Kingdom organized a conference on curriculum construction at Oxford, England, in September 1967. I served as chairman of the delegation from the United States and gave the closing address entitled "The Future of International Cooperation in Curriculum Construction." The United States will be host to a further conference in 1969. I became the 1969 conference coordinator and, as these words are written, am working on the plans for it.

As far as international events are concerned, it now remains only to trace the history of the World Organization of the Teaching Profession from the point where we left it at the adjournment of the 1946 meeting in Endicott.

Several serious difficulties arose between the 1946 Endicott meeting and the 1947 Glasgow meeting. First, we had for the Glasgow meeting no funds to pay the expenses of delegates. Second, many teachers' organizations in Europe were being assiduously taught to regard the United States with deep suspicion. Third, many European teachers' organizations were, and still are, organized with a sharp separation between the teachers of secondary schools and those of the primary schools. These two groups of European teachers, usually designated by the acronyms of IFTA and FIPESO, had been holding separate international meetings for many years. The advent of a comprehensive world organization which united teachers from every level of instruction was to many Europeans an unwelcome challenge to tradition. Fourth, the American Federation of Teachers (AFL-CIO), apparently appalled that the NEA might succeed in a major effort to help organize the teachers of the world, sent representatives and messages to other national teachers' organizations advising them to refrain from WOTP affiliation.

These were serious difficulties, but at this stage, and for a few months afterwards, the "iron curtain" did not affect WOTP. The Czechoslovak Teachers Union, in fact, was the first organization to join. The Polish Teachers Union was not far behind. The Union of Educational Workers of the Soviet Union did not respond to the invitation to participate at Endicott but, as far as I know, it made no effort to influence the meeting.

Two new forces entered at this stage to keep WOTP alive. One of these was the determination of the Scottish Education Institute that the new organization must survive. The other vivifying influence was the election of Dr. William F. Russell as president. He gave new energy and immense prestige to the struggling organization. At a special meeting of the executive committee in London in April 1948 we decided to hold the July 1948 meeting in London, although the English teachers at that time had not yet joined us.

From London I proceeded to Interlaken, Switzerland, where the two European organizations were simultaneously holding their separate meetings. So much hostility had been created by people who for various reasons wanted WOTP to fail that it was difficult for me to gain access to these meetings. However, I persisted, and steps taken at Interlaken ultimately led to a merger of the international bodies concerned.

The sixth (and last) Delegate Assembly of WOTP was held in Copenhagen in 1952, followed by a one-day organization meeting of the new World Confederation of Organizations of the Teaching Profession (WCOTP). In Copenhagen it became very clear how much was involved in the achievement of unity of teachers in the Western world. The teachers' organizations of the Communist countries hastily scheduled a meeting at the same time in Copenhagen. They tried to persuade European teachers not to join WCOTP, condemned the new organization, and predicted its early collapse. I had known for several years that the Communist teachers' organizations did not wish the teachers' organizations of the Western world to cooperate with one another, and events in Copenhagen revealed how deep was their hostility. Since Copenhagen, WCOTP has become the world's most powerful international professional organization, with branch offices around the world, regular and special publications in four or more languages, and a year-round program.

In summary, I have attended sixty-three international conferences on education since 1938 and have visited, in some cases quite frequently, most of the education ministries and teachers' organizations of the world.

And now, back to the United States and the National Education Association. Early in 1952 the NEA Board of Trustees voted to invite me to serve as executive secretary of the National Education Association for four years, the maximum term permitted under the NEA's charter from Congress. I accepted the appointment and was subsequently reelected by the trustees for four-year terms in 1956, 1960, and 1964.

As I stir my memory, I can see that here, more than elsewhere in this story, a comprehensive account is impossible, even if it were limited to matters of major importance. Accordingly, I propose to deal briefly with only four issues which arose in my work as executive secretary of the NEA: (a) the educational aspects of the civil rights movement; (b) the effort to maintain the independence of the teaching profession; (c) the role of the federal government; and (d) the search for quality in education.

Civil rights. The Supreme Court decision on school integration in 1954 inaugurated a series of events which changed the nation. In one aspect or another, civil rights profoundly concerned me for almost every moment of my term of office. During these fourteen years I clung to two major principles: first, that in the conduct of its own affairs the NEA itself should avoid and repudiate every evidence of racial discrimination; second, that the unity of the teaching profession should be preserved. To retain either one of these two principles would have been easy; to keep them both was often extremely difficult. I shall give a few examples.

When I assumed office in 1952 the association had already voted to hold its 1953 convention in Miami, Florida. When it became clear that only Miami Beach, Florida, could provide at that time integrated hotels and restaurants, we moved the convention to Miami Beach. Thus, the NEA became the first major national organization to hold an integrated convention in the South. There was much pressure on me to meet in Miami instead, but, between a segregated meeting and the ire of many southern members, I chose the latter.

This example illustrates the general policy which I tried to follow; namely, to go as far as I could and as fast as I could without splitting the association and rendering it ineffective.

In 1954 I changed the unwritten policy regarding employment opportunities for qualified Negro personnel in the NEA Washington staff. Soon thereafter the NEA was cited by the Urban League for pioneering in nondiscriminatory employment policy in the District of Columbia.

During my administration the association created, on my recommendation, a million-dollar "Human Rights Fund." Most of the expenditures from this fund were used to carry to the courts cases of unfair treatment of Negro teachers or children.

One other aspect of the civil rights controversies should be mentioned. In 1947, on the request of the leaders of the segregated Negro teachers' associations, the NEA had agreed to recognize a second affiliate in seventeen states where such segregation existed. By 1960 this number had been reduced to twelve.

In October 1960 I proposed to the principal NEA staff officers—a group which for convenience we called "the Cabinet"—an eight-year program to unify these organizations. We gave the matter no publicity but we decided to follow the following cautious schedule: (a) hold informal meetings of representatives of each pair of organizations; (b) hold at least one unified delegate meeting; (c) draft a new constitution for an inclusive organization; and (d) obtain action by the two organizations on the proposed constitution.

Each of these steps, I suggested, would require about two years or a total of eight years. When I left office in 1967 the dual affiliates in all but six of the original seventeen states had merged. The remaining six, I understand, are scheduled to complete their mergers this year (1969). Meanwhile, we unified the NEA and the American Teachers' Association in 1966.

There were members in the NEA, and others outside it, who urged a more rapid, radical, and direct involvement of the association in all the various phases of civil rights. They regarded the NEA policies as timid and ineffective. They yearned to make the white southern members "toe the line." I felt, however, that a united teaching profession would help, as few other groups could, to maintain the greatest possible unity, coherence, and strength of the nation.

This, it seems to me still, was not an unworthy or insignificant purpose. A major southern white secession from the NEA was possible on several occasions. Such a reaction in the 1950s or early 1960s would certainly have led to the emergence and prospering of another national teachers' organization, based in the South, but successfully seeking members everywhere, issuing its own publications, holding its own conferences, supporting its own state and national legislative programs, with a racially based, racially biased, states' rights, backlash policy. As it was, the NEA remained a powerful united force for securing equal opportunity in education. That, it seemed to me, was its primary responsibility. I used the considerable power of my office to promote the two principles to which I have already referred. One might say, I suppose, that I tried with some success to move the association "forward together" and with "deliberate speed."

Independence of the teaching profession. In 1960 it became clear that a major drive, generously financed by the Industrial Union Department (AFL-CIO), would be launched to make the teachers' union the sole voice of the employees on all matters affecting salaries, working conditions, and educational policy. The campaign began in New York City in 1961 where the NEA affiliate, a weak and temporary structure, lost the election to the United Federation of Teachers. The teachers' union thereupon took over control of New York schools with consequences that are now well known.

It appeared clear to me at that time that the leaders of organized labor had decided on an all-out campaign which would, if successful, profoundly modify the structure of American education. I perceived the affiliation of teachers' organization and organized labor as a serious threat to the integrity of the educational process. I believe that recent events provide ample evidence that I perceived correctly.

I never thought that the issue to which I reluctantly devoted a large part of my time between 1960 and 1967 was whether the initials of the major national teachers' organization would be NEA or AFT. I did not think of the conflict merely as a competition for members, or a struggle for power between rival organizations; or a question of whether teachers and school administrators should belong to the same organization; or even as a matter of relative emphases on teacher welfare versus improved teaching service. I thought, and still think, that the basic question was whether education should remain an independent, self-governing profession or become a subsidiary of one of the segments of American life and a weapon in its economic and political struggles.

The defeat of the NEA affiliate in New York City itself was not a surprise. Neither the union nor the NEA had ever mustered a substantial membership in this unique, self-centered, and self-sufficient metropolis. The leadership of the teachers of New York City, whether in the teachers' union or in the NEA affiliate, was with a few exceptions the worst I have ever encountered.

Thus the loss of the election in New York City was no great loss to the NEA, either in quantity or quality of members. Convinced, however, that New York was the first engagement in what would be a long war, I placed before the next meeting of the NEA Board of Directors, in February 1962, a detailed account of events in New York City and a series of recommendations to reorganize the association. The board of directors approved my proposal that each state affiliate should in 1962 set up enough regional forums so that substantially all members could attend a forum on a drive-in-and-back-the-same-day basis. These forums should clarify the basic reasons why an independent professional organization is better for teachers in the United States than a trade union and thoroughly review the programs of the state and national associations. If necessary, these forums should replace other scheduled meetings on less urgent topics. The board also voted that the local affiliates in every large city should hold similar but more extensive workshops attended by at least one person from every school building in the city. The state and local affiliates were urged to take immediate steps to convene these meetings.

In the next few years one of my principal problems was to prod the state and local education associations to act. In many cases I was unsuccessful. Many officers of the affiliated associations believed that what had happened in New York City would not affect them.

My proposal for a smaller representative assembly, followed or preceded by conventions devoted to general professional questions, was referred to various committees and, in effect, delayed until it lost the name of action. My proposal that the NEA Department of

Classroom Teachers concentrate solely on salaries and working conditions and be, in effect, the voice of the classroom teacher on these matters was also referred to a committee and "sunk without trace."

The association thus faced the teachers' union (largely, the American Federation of Teachers) in representation elections in city after city without any fundamental change in its structure and strategy. Only when this trend became clearly visible to anyone without a blindfold (and that was sometimes too late) could I secure serious attention to the challenge on the part of many of the local and state affiliates. My friends in positions of academic leadership, such as the college and university presidents and the deans and professors in schools of education, were, I found, generally unconcerned about this issue.

Federal support of education. Securing the assistance of the United States government to improve the public schools had been an important NEA objective long before I became its executive secretary and, indeed, long before I joined its staff. My first connections with this effort took the form of collecting data and writing memoranda for congressmen and congressional committees.

In 1950 an excellent bipartisan bill providing federal aid to public schools was sponsored by Democratic Senator Lister Hill and Republican Senator Robert Taft and passed by the Senate. The proposal then moved to the House where the Committee on Education voted thirteen to twelve against the proposal. We had hopes that somehow we could muster the one more vote needed, probably from among the younger members of the committee. On the Republican side we sought the support of Richard M. Nixon of California; on the Democratic side, of John F. Kennedy of Massachusetts. When the vote was taken both congressmen voted "nay." That decision was enough, as it turned out, to stop significant federal aid to education for fifteen crucial years.

Changing times and circumstances modify the judgments of men. During his term of office President Kennedy labored hard to secure legislation such as that he had helped to defeat some ten or twelve years earlier. And while this paragraph is being written, it appears probable that President Nixon will sponsor important school legislation.

In 1954 President Eisenhower sent to Congress a special message on the needs of education. The president said that the nation as a whole was not preparing teachers or building schools fast enough. He set aside the preparation of teachers as a state and local responsibility but asserted that the federal government could assist states which could not provide sufficient school buildings. To appraise the extent of the need, he announced that conferences on education would be held in each state, culminating in a national conference on education.

Pleased as we were that education was mentioned at all, we were also disappointed by the narrow range of this declaration and by the further delays inherent in another series of conferences. Nevertheless, as often happens in congressional relations, it was deemed advisable to welcome the message.

The National Conference on Education was held, as the president proposed, and it overwhelmingly approved the NEA position. In the end, however, even the school construction legislation failed to run the congressional gauntlet.

About one year later, after the conference had made its report and Congress had ignored it, the Soviet Union launched its first Sputnik. Swift and vindictive was the ensuing search in the United States for a scapegoat for our sin, if sin it was, of allowing our country to be embarrassed in this respect. There was no serious criticism of the Pentagon or of the White House, of the rocket manufacturers, or of the universities. The press leaped eagerly to the verdict, long before the evidence could be examined, that our primary and secondary schools were responsible for the brief period of a few months when a satellite bearing the Hammer and Sickle circled through space all alone.

The congressional reaction to the Russian performance was as hasty and ill-advised as its previous reaction to carefully documented recommendations had been lethargic or hostile. Less than a year after Sputnik inaugurated the space age, Congress enacted the National Defense Education Act of 1958. The act had the serious flaw of using federal funds to determine state and local educational policy. Congressmen and other public officials who had for years been expressing dismay at the possibility of "federal control" of education now spun their position full circle, like the artificial satellite to which their legislation was responding. In spite of serious defects, the legislation received NEA support and was claimed by us as an achievement. After all, it did provide some federal funds for some aspects of secondary education. We hoped too—and history has shown that the hope was reasonable—that the areas of education covered by NDEA could be expanded.

In September 1960, the nominee of the Republican party, Vice-President Nixon, issued a campaign statement entitled "A National Program in Support of Education." As is usually the case in political declarations by either party, Mr. Nixon's statement contained many exhortations regarding the great national importance of education. In practical terms, his position was less satisfactory. Although strongly in favor of better salaries for teachers, he would make no federal funds available for this purpose.

Senator Kennedy, on the contrary, during his campaign made it clear that he would support broad-scale federal aid for education limited to public schools. There can be little doubt that this assurance played a part in the narrow victory by which he achieved the White House.

President Kennedy kept this campaign promise but, after the administration bill had passed the Senate, it was sidetracked by a one-vote margin in the House Rules Committee. The President's proposals were vigorously attacked by most of the Catholic press, attacked (in my view) with unbecoming bias and a dismaying lack of fairness.

When President Johnson entered the White House, he continued to seek the goals of President Kennedy. Many people were seeking a way to resolve an apparent impasse. I remember, for example, one evening with Commissioner of Education Francis Keppel, discussing how some new approach could be discovered. It occurred to us that the key to the puzzle might be to relate federal aid to the "war on poverty." At Commissioner Keppel's request, I asked the NEA Research Division to compile some statistics showing the results of applying various formulas. Another new aspect of the proposals by President Johnson made it easier for students in parochial schools to be taught in the public schools with funds made available under the proposed law. Any child of any religious faith might enroll in a public school at any time. And if he might enroll full time, he should, subject to reasonable administrative convenience, be permitted to enroll part time. This slight change, plus the link to the war on poverty, plus President Johnson's deep concern and immense skill in negotiation and persuasion, was enough to bring about the enactment of the Elementary and Secondary Education Act of 1965, the most important breakthrough in federal school legislation in American history. The NEA gave full support to this legislation. The only important opposition came from the New York City Teachers Union.

In December 1968, about three weeks before President Johnson left the White House, I had the pleasure of organizing a group of leaders from the organizations in Washington which had worked for federal school legislation to call at the White House to express to President Johnson our gratitude for all he had done for American education. We gave the president at that time a volume recording the sixty major items of legislation affecting education passed during his administration. This impressive list ran all the way from Headstart programs for young children to aid to graduate schools. The volume included the names of the organizations participating in the ceremony and a brief tribute which I wrote under the title "The Teacher in the White House."

Quality in education. When I became executive secretary of the National Education Association, a varied and productive program for improving instruction was already in operation. The *NEA Journal*, for example, was publishing about one hundred pages every year on the improvement of teaching. The NEA departments and other units were publishing twenty-three specialized magazines and ten yearbooks mainly devoted to the improvement of teaching, with a combined annual distribution of about one and one-half million.

It seemed to me, however, that a serious gap existed between educational research and its practical application in the classroom. We therefore began at once to try to bridge that gap by publishing a series of small nontechnical pamphlets titled "What Research Says to the Classroom Teacher." The first three of these pamphlets dealt with reading, arithmetic, and spelling. Since then, the series has been expanded to include more than twenty areas of instruction.

Since many of the association's activities were isolated from each other, it also seemed to me desirable to develop some coordination of these efforts. Accordingly, we began the annual conference of officers of the NEA's largely autonomous departments. In addition, we began to hold every year at least one unified regional conference on instruction to which all NEA units with activities affecting instruction made their respective contributions.

An important turning point in this aspect of the NEA program was reached in 1957 when the association celebrated its centennial. I was asked to make the closing address before the centennial convention in Philadelphia with the title "The Past is Prologue." After considerable reflection I decided to propose that the emphasis of the teaching profession in the future should be on the quality of education. I said that America had hitherto been primarily concerned with quantity—with how many children we could get into school. Now, I suggested, we would in the decades ahead turn our primary attention to quality—to what each child could get out of school. Most of the editorial comments on the centennial convention referred to this declaration on quality and quantity as the most important theme of the meeting.

By vote of the centennial delegate assembly, the dues of members in the National Education Association were increased from five to ten dollars a year. This doubling the fees for individual memberships added substantial new revenue. I recommended, and the NEA officers approved, the allotment of a major part of the added revenue to "special projects" which dealt in the main, though not exclusively, with the quality of education. They covered such matters as automation, visual aids, juvenile delinquency, and education for the academically talented.

In the case of the special project on instruction I felt that the results were of such great potential value that I recommended it have a permanent place in the NEA structure, designated as the Center for the Study of Instruction.

Further illustrations of the association's attention to the quality of instruction could be added. However, perhaps enough have been supplied to make clear that in my view a professional organization should devote a substantial part of its time, energy, and resources to assist its members in doing a more effective job. I think the ability of the association to work simultaneously to elevate both the economic status and the professional competence of the profession was one of its major achievements during the years that I was its chief executive officer.

In the closing years of my service to the association, I became aware of a tendency among some of the elected leadership and the employed staff to give primary attention to power and the sources of power at the expense of attention to the purposes and achievements of the association. This tendency caused me some serious misgivings. In July 1967, therefore, in my last report to the board of directors, I made an emphatic statement that the time had come to put purposes and results at the forefront of official concern, that people who are deeply concerned about substance will become less concerned about status.

I shall conclude this account of my work with the National Education Association by describing the responsibilities of the executive secretary.

To begin with the obvious, the executive secretary must attend *meetings*. I found that the absolute minimum of time for this purpose, including preparation and immediate follow-up, was over 130 days per year.

Omitting activities in Washington itself and the meetings which have already been mentioned, I found that I was spending an average of 126 days per year in *field work*.

A third category of activity is *writing*—articles, speeches, testimony for congressional committees. This was rarely delegated.

In addition, *contacts with key individuals* need to be maintained. These include, for example, many members of Congress, White House officials, and cabinet officers concerned with education; members of the State Department concerned with educational exchange; members of the Defense Department concerned with training in the armed forces; leaders in business and industry; comparable officers in the professions, such as medicine and law; leaders of other national teachers' organizations; officials of the United Nations and Unesco insofar as their work involves education; university presidents and others in higher education; men and women involved in the preparation of teachers; scholars in various disciplines related to education; leaders in the news media and in the formation of public opinion; editors and columnists; civil rights leaders; and leaders of veterans' and civic organizations. Of course, the executive secretary had to delegate a great deal of this work to others.

The fifth area of activity may be described briefly as *the daily grind.* It required the executive secretary to relate himself swiftly to a kaleidoscope of personalities, events, issues, and problems. In the course of staff routine, most of the easy problems are sorted out and handled. Only the points of sharp controversy, the frustrations, and the emergencies get to the executive secretary.

What was done is perhaps less important than the spirit and method by which it was accomplished. In dealing with this kind of question one can scarcely hope to be highly objective, but I will venture a few observations.

I tried to discipline myself to remember that the association exists for the purposes stated in its charter. It is not, for example, an agency for the general promotion of civil rights or of international peace. Although I have strong personal views in favor of these ideals, as executive secretary of the NEA I believed my energies should be directed to agreed educational objectives. Many people, of course, try to *use* the association to advance various other purposes, but the executive secretary, like other officers, is committed not to acquiesce in such usage whether the goal be personal power or the highest altruism.

The executive secretary is not barred from endeavoring to influence the decisions of the association; indeed, in my opinion he is required to try to influence policy decisions by all legitimate means of evidence and persuasion. Almost everyone, I found, wants a chance to be consulted on every topic which even remotely touches his interests. Almost no one, however, wants the responsibility of decision or even of making a firm recommendation on difficult issues.

The habit of looking at specific issues in the light of future developments is, I think, highly important. The ability to do this, more than any other trait, is the prime component of what people usually call "good judgment." I doubt whether good judgment can be created by intelligence or by devotion, together or separately. I think experience is an essential added ingredient.

The pressure of time and sometimes of weariness suggested yielding to constant and dangerous temptations. To "make do," to "leave well enough alone," to delegate responsibility and then fail to check on performance, to attend a meeting without reading the background documents, to improvise a speech because the audience might be small or unlikely to be critical, to sign a letter without reading it because it was addressed to no one of great importance. to guess at the correct statistic without looking it up, to accept a clumsily worded sentence in a ghost-written article—these are the perils of complacency. No one, I suppose, is at his best on every occasion. No batter hits a home run on every trip to the plate. But a good player *intends* to get a solid hit, if he can, every single time.

In the instructions to contributors to this volume, the editors have asked us to respond to several general questions. Most of their questions have been answered in the course of the preceding pages. Responses to the few remaining questions will conclude these recollections.

I am asked whether I was retired before I was ready; my response is in the negative. I was under contract to serve as executive secretary of the NEA for a full year beyond the date of my actual retirement.

I am asked whether I wished to continue; I did not. I took the initiative in requesting the NEA trustees to amend my contract so that I might retire in 1967.

I am asked whether money (presumably money paid to me) was a factor in my career decisions. I think that it was never, except on one occasion, the sole factor. It was a substantial consideration in my earlier working years, declining in importance as the years passed.

Finally, I am asked whether I have rearranged my life to make up for "discontinued activity." This question is not answerable because I have not discontinued activity. I formerly gave my weekends and vacations to the work of WCOTP; now I give weekends, vacations, and the rest of my time to WCOTP. I find it an almost ideal arrangement. In addition, I am occasionally invited to speak at educational conferences and before university groups. I have particularly enjoyed this year the opportunity to teach a graduate course in the history of education.

A BIOGRAPHICAL SUMMARY

William G. Carr. Born June 1, 1901, Northampton, England. Came to United States, 1915.

Family. Married Elizabeth Vaughan, August 20, 1924. Son: Wilfred James (1926).

Education. Public schools of England, Canada, and United States; University of California, 1920-23; Stanford University, A.B., 1924, A.M., 1926, Ph.D., 1929.

Occupational history. Taught in Roosevelt Junior High School, Glendale, California, 1924-25; professor of education, Pacific University, 1926-27; director of research, California Teachers Association, 1928-29; assistant director of research, NEA, 1929-31; director of research, NEA, 1931-40; associate secretary, 1940-52; executive secretary, 1952-67; secretary, Educational Policies Commission, 1936-50; member, U.S. National Commission for Unesco, 1946-50; secretary, World Organization of Teaching Profession, 1946-70, President, 1970; visiting professor (summer), Stanford University, 1929, 31, 42; University of Michigan, 1930, 33, 34, 36, 37, 38; University of California at Los Angeles, 1935, at Berkeley, 1939; University of Oregon, 1940. University of Pennsylvania, 1941.

Memberships and Awards. Citation by Korean Federation of Educational Associations, 1956; honorary citizenship, Jaffna (Ceylon) Municipal Council, 1956; presidential medal in the Order of Cultural Merit, Seoul, Korea, 1966; member of the Chinese Academy, Taipei, 1966; fellow of the Educational Institute of Scotland, 1969; honorary member of the National Union of Teachers of England and Wales, 1970; president of Council on International Non-Theatrical Events (CINE), 1970; member, American Educational Research Association, etc.

Part II

Major Publications of William G. Carr

Books

1. *Education for World Citizenship.* Stanford University: Stanford University Press, 1928.
2. *The Lesson Assignment* (with John Waage). Stanford University: Stanford University Press, 1931.
3. *John Swett: Biography of an Educational Pioneer.* Santa Ana, Calif.: Fine Arts Press, 1933.
4. *School Finance.* Stanford University: Stanford University Press, 1933.
5. *The Purposes of Education in American Democracy* (for the Educational Policies Commission). Washington: National Education Association and the American Association of School Administrators, 1938.
6. *Education and the People Peace* (for the Educational Policies Commission). Washington: National Education Association and American Association of School Administrators, 1943.
7. *One World in the Making; the United Nations.* Boston: Ginn & Co., 1946.
8. *On Waging the Peace.* Washington: National Education Association, 1946.
9. *Moral and Spiritual Values in the Public Schools* (for the Educational Policies Commission). Washington: National Education Association and American Association of School Administration, 1943.

Edited Works

10. *International Frontiers in Education. Annals of the American Academy of Political and Social Science*, vol. 235, 1944.
11. *Values and the Curriculum.* Report of the Fourth International Curriculum Conference. Washington: N.E.A. Center for the Study of Instruction 1970.

Articles, Brochures, and Lectures

12. *Schools in the Story of Culture* (with Charles A. Beard). Washington: National Education Association, 1935.

13. *Educational Leadership in This Emergency.* School of Education, Stanford University, Cubberley lecture. Stanford University: Stanford University Press, 1942.
14. *Not in Our Stars But in Ourselves.* Sir John Adams lecture. Los Angeles: U.C.L.A. Press, 1958.
15. "Let us Keep Our Eyes Steadily on the Whole System. Address for the Inauguration of Andrew P. Holt as President of the University of Tennessee." *Tennessee Teacher* 28 (September 1960): 9-10.
16. *The Words of William G. Carr.* Washington: National Education Association, 1967.
17. "The Role of Teachers' Organizations in Assistance to Developing Countries," *Education Panorama* (World Confederation of Organizations of the Teaching Profession) 11 (No. 3, 1969): 1-17 (entire issue).
18. *The White Revolution in Iranian Education.* Washington: World Confederation of Organizations of the Teaching Profession, Occasional Papers, No. 11, 1970.
19. *Values in Teaching.* Pittcairn-Crabbe lecture. Pittsburgh: University of Pittsburgh Press, 1952.

Part III

A Commentary on the Career of William G. Carr

J. STEPHEN HAZLETT

Three educational principles, shared by many educators of his generation, importantly influenced the career of William G. Carr. The first states that education is indispensable to democracy, and the second is that democratic education is indispensable to international security. The third holds that the teaching profession must be united and independent.

Chosen in 1936 to be the first secretary to the Educational Policies Commission, Carr worked with leading figures in education who articulated for the profession a conception of education based on these principles. Because of the spirit of unanimity among the first members of the commission and the fact that he was its principal editor, the ideas set forth by the EPC appear to have been broadly representative of Carr's personal beliefs.

Several early EPC publications tried to explicate the relationship between education and democracy. As understood by the EPC and its secretary, democracy was far more than a political process; it was a method of living premised upon certain basal values.[1] The number of these fundamental values of democratic living was not precise—even for the authors of these documents—but, according to Carr, the general welfare, civil liberty, rule by reason and the consent of the governed, and the pursuit of happiness were "great elements" of democracy which "stand out in bold relief." [2]

1. Educational Policies Commission [William G. Carr], *The Process of Education* (Washington: National Education Association, 1938), p. 26; see also EPC [Charles A. Beard], *The Unique Function of Education in American Democracy* (Washington: National Education Association, 1937) and EPC [George S. Counts], *The Education of Free Men in American Democracy* (Washington: National Education Association, 1941).

2. Ibid., pp. 7-9.

From this conception of democracy the goals of education were derived. "Educational purposes," stated Carr, ". . . are a form of social policy, a program of social action based on some accepted scale of values."[3] Within this context educators should operate forthrightly, for "the responsibility of teachers is to the truth and to the promotion of the general welfare through the use of truth. . . ."[4]

That education was necessary for democracy meant that the members of the teaching profession should be united and independent. Whatever their rank or position, all educators should be united "in support of a few basic ideals" and should share "a common purpose and common leadership."[5] They should be independent because their mission would not permit them to serve exclusively any one segment of society or allow them to tolerate outside interference in the execution of their responsibilities. Even governments must recognize their limits in regulating school affairs. States may require the teaching of certain subjects, but if they attempt to legislate professional activities, such laws "may not only cripple the initiative of teachers but prevent the attainment of socially valuable objectives."[6] In fact, Carr asserted, "the immediate removal of all forms of political pressure and interference in the administration of schools would help greatly in the attainment of educational objectives."[7]

Carr accorded education an indispensable role in the attainment of world peace because he subscribed to the notion that wars begin in men's minds. He argued as early as 1928 that scientific evidence indicated that fighting was not an instinct but only a habit which could be suppressed by "the formation of habits of peaceful living."[8] The habits of peace were largely a function of understanding and cooperation. He claimed that students' understanding of other peoples could be stimulated by the study of foreign lands and

3. Ibid., p. 2.

4. Ibid., p. 129.

5. Ibid., p. 140.

6. Ibid., p. 138.

7. Ibid., p. 137.

8. William G. Carr, *Education for World Citizenship* (Stanford: Stanford University Press, 1928), p. 97.

customs and that learning the benefits of cooperation through practice in the classroom could lead to cooperation among nations.

International peace was then possible but it could not be attained, Carr believed, "unless each nation concerned is democratically controlled"[9] and unless teachers assumed responsibility for developing the appropriate attitudes and habits, for "if educational leadership does not undertake this task, it will not be done."[10] Therefore, in his *Education and the People's Peace*, published by the EPC in 1943, he proposed "nothing less than the systematic and deliberate use of education, on a worldwide basis and plan, to help safeguard the peace and to help extend the democracy for which this Second World War is being fought."[11] To this end, he recommended the creation of an international agency for education in the postwar period which would attempt, among other things, to proscribe teaching materials that were "aggressive, militaristic, or otherwise dangerous to the peace of the world."[12]

The publications of the Educational Policies Commission were widely disseminated, and hundreds and later thousands of EPC consultants had the duty of seeing that they were locally publicized and studied by educators and laymen. The implications of these documents for the conduct of public education are too numerous to be treated here. Basically, however, they stressed the view that the people and their elected officials were charged with major educational responsibilities, including the provision of ample resources, facilities, and moral support, but the actual organization and operation of schools were best left to professionals.

These publications also served another function. By their substance and tone, they sought to restore the morale and confidence of the teaching profession in a country badly shaken by economic depression and world war. The view of public education they affirmed aimed at instilling in all educators the sense of their import-

9. Ibid., p. 68.

10. William G. Carr, *Educational Leadership in This Emergency* (Stanford: Stanford University Press, 1942), p. 8. This was the Cubberley lecture delivered by Carr at the Stanford School of Education on July 20, 1941.

11. Educational Policies Commission, *Education and the People's Peace* (Washington: National Education Association, 1943), p. 9.

12. Ibid., p. 39.

ance for the preservation and advancement of American democracy and for the establishment of world peace on democratic values.

This conception was perhaps more useful as a source for watchwords than as a guide for educational practice, however. To assert that democracy is a way of life ordered by immutable values beyond those required for it to function as a decision-making process is a questionable description of the American experience. And the problems involved in the enumeration, explication, and ordering of these values confounded the best efforts of Carr and his colleagues to state their creed with precision. To view the teaching profession as an independent guarantor of democracy and peace seems to seriously exaggerate the capabilities of education. Further, to consider professional unity a direct consequence of shared ideals fails to recognize the very real differences of perception and interest among the constituent professional groupings and the difficulty, if not impossibility, of reconciling these differences by appeals to goodwill and reminders of the importance of the common enterprise.

But Carr stood by the articles drawn from this testament. They ordered his perceptions and inspired his activity. Yet, their extreme idealism predetermined their failure to be fully realized in the here and now and forced Carr into some untenable positions wherein he had to compromise certain principles to protect others. Examples of such compromise can be seen in his work with the World Confederation of Organizations of the Teaching Profession and the National Education Association.

At the end of World War II, Carr was involved in the efforts to achieve recognition for education in the emerging United Nations. He shared in the negotiations leading to the mention of education in the UN Charter, and he participated in the formation of Unesco, hoping that this agency would further the cause of peace through education in ways he had outlined earlier. That Unesco did not focus on elementary and secondary schooling at first was a disappointment to him, but he believes that it has recently shown more interest in projects designed to promote international goodwill by providing the schoolchildren of the world objective information about the values and aspirations of different cultures.[13]

13. Interview with William Carr, Washington, D.C., June, 1969.

The international enterprise with which his name has been most closely associated is the World Confederation of Organizations of the Teaching Profession and its precursor, the World Organization of the Teaching Profession. More than any other person, Carr was responsible for founding and developing this organization which was intended to unite national teachers associations in the service of democratic education and peace.[14]

To form this organization, however, Carr had to juggle his principles. In one instance, he minimized democracy for the sake of unity, and in another, unity for democracy.

In order to have any effective unity among the various national teacher groups—in order to gain the cooperation of Jews and Arabs, French and Germans, North and South Americans—it became evident that certain questions could not be considered by the organization, and the WCOTP constitution therefore contains a strict prohibition against discussion of political and religious matters.[15] Thus, to make WCOTP a viable structure, the intention to use it as a vehicle for the propagation of "democratic" education had to be abandoned. As secretary-general, Carr deals with education without the modifier and has had to approach situations socially and politically repugnant to him personally with tolerance and a sense of historical perspective. He claims that he acts pragmatically in such situations, basing his evaluations of need on relative, intuitive criteria aimed at the general improvement of the status of teachers and schools.[16]

The attitude shown toward cooperation with Communist teacher unions, however, has been an exception to this compromise. The creation of two postwar power blocs frustrated the hope of gathering all teachers throughout the world within a common professional association dedicated to common ends, and the cold war mentality did not leave Carr's organization unaffected. As WOTP (and later

14. See the comments of William F. Russell, dean of Columbia Teachers College and president of WOTP, in the National Education Association, *Proceedings of the Eighty-ninth Annual Meeting* (San Francisco, 1951), p. 77; also, interview with Forrest E. Conner, executive secretary of the American Association of School Administrators, Washington, D.C., June 1969.

15. Article II, Section I. The constitution appears in each of the WCOTP *Annual Reports*, 1953- .

16. Carr, interview.

WCOTP) sought recruits, it found itself in competition with a Communist-led rival, the Fédération Internationale Syndicale de l'Enseignement (FISE). Both claimed to desire fraternal relations and the unity of teachers, but the limited contact between them has been marked by mutual suspicion and hostility. As early as 1950, WOTP President William F. Russell told the NEA (which the previous year had passed a resolution banning Communists from its membership and declaring that "the responsibility of the schools is to teach the superiority of the American way of life,") [17] that "there is no use trying to deal with those people [in FISE]. They have no use for us and we have no use for them." [18] Carr expressed the same sentiment in 1953 when he informed the NEA representative assembly that WCOTP had rejected as "thinly disguised Soviet propaganda" an invitation to send delegates to a FISE meeting. He assured the NEA that its delegation to WCOTP would continue "to work for a strong, free, and democratic world organization of teachers." [19] When the matter of WCOTP relations with FISE was discussed at the 1956 confederation convention, he again stated his misgivings about contact with Communist teachers:

> A teachers organization that is merely a tool of the government of the country in which it exists is not likely to inspire confidence. Nor, in my opinion, does it deserve the ready confidence of free men and women. A teacher who is merely a pawn in a game of chess played by his government, who is restricted in his search for the truth, who is subservient to a single philosophy of life and society imposed on him by force or propaganda—such a teacher is not able to cooperate well with teachers who are free from such controls. We who do enjoy freedom have a duty to examine very carefully the overtures of cooperation from teachers who are not free.[20]

Carr maintains that he would welcome FISE affiliates in WCOTP—provided that they did not use their membership to spread Communism—but the history of mutual antagonism and

17. National Education Association, *Proceedings of the Eighty-seventh Annual Meeting* (Boston, 1949), p. 157.

18. National Education Association, *Proceedings of the Eighty-eighth Annual Meeting* (St. Louis, 1950), p. 131.

19. National Education Association, *Proceedings of the Ninety-first Annual Meeting* (Miami Beach, 1953), pp. 46-7.

20. WCOTP, *Annual Report*, 1956, p. 32.

Carr's own anti-Communist attitude leave little doubt that fruitful dialogue and cooperation between the two camps are not to be looked for in the near future. In sum, to foster the growth of WCOTP, Carr has shown flexibility in responding to political, social, and economic climates of the so-called Western and neutral nations, but in relation to countries clearly in the sphere of international Communism his policy has been more rigid and cautious.

WOTP-WCOTP has nevertheless survived and prospered and, to a large extent, it has overcome the hostility of some European and Latin American teacher groups that feared competition and American imperialism. The merger of WOTP with the International Federation of Teachers Associations (IFTA) and the International Federation of Secondary Teachers (FIPESO) to create WCOTP in 1952 reflected the diminution of these fears, and the recent increased cooperation between WCOTP and the Confederation of American Educators (CEA) indicates that similar progress is being made in Latin America. Further, the organization has grown. After a shaky start following the 1946 Endicott meeting, WOTP grew to represent national associations from 24 countries by 1951, and the 1952 merger further expanded the membership. In 1968 WCOTP claimed national members from 84 countries representing over four million teachers.[21]

The confederation has carried on many programs for the improvement of education internationally. In addition to the study of an annual theme, it maintains standing committees which treat particular aspects of education on a continuing basis. WCOTP participates in projects of Unesco through its consultative status with that body, and it serves as an international clearinghouse for the distribution of educational literature. In the late 1950s, the confederation increased its services to Africa, Asia, and Latin America, and it promoted regional committees and programs to relate specifically to the educational conditions of these areas. To finance program expansion, WCOTP has relied on membership dues, subsidies from Unesco and other groups, and support received from private foundations.

Amid WCOTP's conferences, seminars, meetings, studies, publications, and Unesco-related projects, the attempt to build and

21. See WCOTP, *Annual Report*, 1968, pp. 46-53.

stabilize strong teachers associations in every affiliated area has emerged as a major organizational purpose. At its third annual meeting, at Berne in 1949, WOTP began a detailed study of teacher organizations with this end in mind, and the confederation's activities in Africa, Asia, and Latin America have pursued the same goal. The WCOTP executive committee has referred to the "support [of] activities which foster strong, independent national teachers' organizations dedicated to the service of their members" as its "guiding principle" in program planning.[22] This policy well reflects on an international scale Carr's belief that the welfare of education is best promoted by an organized, independent teaching profession.

Carr is not pessimistic about the accomplishments of WCOTP. He thinks, for example, that some of the publications distributed by WCOTP have definitely contributed to international understanding. But he admits that in organizations as large as WCOTP one cannot always measure the efficacy of programs: sometimes the expenditure of time, energy, and money on a given project yields few perceivable results, whereas other times some small service may be hailed by its recipients as a breakthrough to the solution of a pressing problem. Nevertheless, it appears that the confederation has met with success in its efforts to elevate the dignity and self-esteem of teachers, especially in developing nations, to provide viable professional organizations for these teachers, and to make them feel that by way of WCOTP their colleagues in other countries stand ready to be of assistance to them. Moreover, as an international meeting-ground, WCOTP has given teachers the opportunity to share experiences which may throw new light on the complexities of the instructional process and temper unexamined educational prejudices.[23]

In the fifteen years that Carr was its executive secretary, the National Education Association grew. Membership steadily increased, surpassing the one million mark by his retirement in 1967; new facilities were added to house an expanding program which gave more attention to the problems of urban schools and the quality of instruction; and the NEA policy of greater federal

22. WCOTP, *Annual Report, 1966*, p. 19.

23. Conner, interview.

participation in financing public education was in large measure realized.

Carr's administrative style presented an interesting picture. On the one hand, he was a superb staff man. Diligence and conscientiousness characterized his work habits; his keen mind permitted him to define problems incisively; and he was able to cope with voluminous paperwork, whether as author, editor, or reader, with a facility that amazed his associates. On the other hand, he was more at ease with ideas and office matters than with people.[24] Although pleasant in conversation and given to occasional displays of wry humor, Carr was generally reserved, and it has been said that he lacked the temperament necessary to captivate those with whom he dealt and bend their wills to his.[25] The chief disadvantages of this efficient but taciturn administrative style were that Carr sometimes had difficulty implementing his plans and that, when major challenges to his leadership arose, he was unable to marshal his supporters fully in defense of his principles.

Within the NEA the first important test of his ideals came as a challenge to professional unity following the Supreme Court decision on school desegregation in 1954. Here, again, the protection of one principle caused him to give ground on another. Seeing in this decision grounds for dissension within the NEA itself, Carr enunciated a policy of working toward desegregation while maintaining the unity of the association. Carr was personally opposed to racial discrimination, and he pointed with pride to the NEA's efforts to remove racial barriers within the national organization. But the NEA *Proceedings* indicate that movement toward desegregation eventually came more from the representative assembly than from the executive secretary.

The NEA's resolutions on school desegregation between 1954 and 1960 failed either to condemn the principle of racial segregation in schools or even to urge compliance with the Supreme Court ruling.[26] Many delegates were displeased at the continued approval

24. Ibid.; also, from an interview with one of Carr's co-workers on the NEA staff who prefers not to be cited by name. This source will be referred to hereafter as, Informant, interview.

25. Conner, interview.

26. See National Education Association, *Proceedings of the Ninety-seventh Annual Meeting* (St. Louis, 1959), p. 186.

of a statement which, as one commented, merely asserted that "the problems engendered by integration can be solved if people are virtuous." [27]

By 1961, opposition to the association's official stand on the issue was powerful enough to strengthen the proposed desegregation resolution by amendments from the floor of the representative assembly. Thus, the NEA's support in 1961 for the Supreme Court decision and, in subsequent years, for fairhousing laws, techniques to minimize *de facto* segregation and promote interracial experiences, nonracial personnel policies in schools, and fair treatment of minorities in textbooks [28] came from members more concerned about speaking forthrightly on a major social question than guarding against possible disaffection from their ranks.

Likewise, the executive secretary's approach to merging the segregated state affiliates was cautious and depended for effect on the good intentions of those directly involved, the national association serving basically as honest broker. Carr designed in 1960 a timetable for the unification of these affiliates, and in 1963 the delegates amended the school desegregation resolution to make it apply to organizations affiliated with the NEA.[29] The following year, at the Seattle convention, Carr cautioned the assembly, however, against "any attempt by the NEA to coerce or threaten its affiliates," but it disregarded this advice and resolved that the merger of affiliates must take place by July 1, 1966.[30] The deadline was not met but, under pressure from the assembly, progress was made in the preparation and approval of merger plans. By the spring of 1969, only three states had yet to comply with the formal requirements for unification. Though Carr credits his policy with allowing him to hand over to his successor a united organization, this was still possible in spite of the actions of the delegate assembly.

27. Ibid., p. 188.

28. National Education Association, *Proceedings of the Ninety-ninth Annual Meeting* (Atlantic City, 1961), pp. 193-212; *Proceedings of the One hundred and fourth Annual Meeting* (Miami Beach, 1966), pp. 476-7; and *Proceedings of the One hundred and fifth Annual Meeting* (Minneapolis, 1967), pp. 496-500.

29. National Education Association, *Proceedings of the One hundred and first Annual Meeting* (Detroit, 1963), p. 463.

30. National Education Association, *Proceedings of the One hundred and second Annual Meeting* (Seattle, 1964), pp. 20, 444-45.

No administrator likes to see his organization dismembered by internal dissension. Carr's desire to preserve the unity of the NEA is therefore not in itself to be deprecated. However, his reluctance to encourage the nation's largest educational association to adopt a forceful position on an issue so critical to the well-being of the country is open to criticism and seems inconsistent with his ideology. His assertions that teachers are free to express their opinions as individuals and that race problems should be solved by political and judicial processes[31] seem antithetical to the proposition that education is the champion of democratic values.

Teacher militancy posed a second challenge to Carr's principles. This issue, which still threatens the existence of the NEA in its present form, indicated the extent to which growing numbers of teachers found Carr's conception of the profession inadequate for dealing with the realities they perceived.

Carr viewed the campaign of the American Federation of Labor to recruit more teachers as a serious assault on the independence of the teaching profession. He maintained his belief that teachers could not perform their vital services for all society without prejudice if they were organizationally allied with any one of its segments. Moreover, despite his statements to the contrary, Carr also opposed the American Federation of Teachers because the union was a potential threat to the NEA as an organization. Two of his associates have attested to this concern,[32] and Carr himself once spoke of the ominous forces plotting measures "which could destroy the Association."[33]

The executive secretary therefore tried to rally the NEA members around his view of professional organization and mobilize them against teacher unionism. In his annual address at the 1962 convention in Denver, he concentrated on this matter.[34] He reaffirmed what he called the four basic principles of the NEA—that it is professional, inclusive, democratic, and independent—and he prod-

31. National Education Association, *Proceedings of the Ninety-eighth Annual Meeting* (Los Angeles, 1960), p. 255.

32. Conner and informant, interviews.

33. National Education Association, *Proceedings of the One hundredth Annual Meeting* (Denver, 1962), p. 28.

34. Ibid., pp. 18-28.

ded the association to increase its services to the cities, where the AFT had enjoyed its greatest success. Further, he urged all local, state, and national NEA members to revitalize their organizations and to make a concerted effort to explain to their colleagues "why an independent profession is essential." Carr maintains that his warning of the dangers posed by unionism was timely and that his plans would have curtailed the union's growth even further had not some NEA leaders been so complacent.[35]

But whatever the effects of Carr's policy toward the AFT, the union's view of teacher organization acted as a stimulus to a more immediate problem for Carr—teacher militancy within the NEA. The issue here was not unionism but the degree to which the NEA should be a teacher-welfare association. The "new breed" of teachers, characterized by youth, better training, and a larger representation of men, wanted more occupational and material benefits and, with an eye on the AFT, was aware of the power of militancy in securing them. These teachers, too, championed democracy. They argued that, since classroom instructors constituted the majority of the NEA membership, teachers should have a controlling interest in the association and should rightfully expect more organizational recognition of their specific interests, even at the risk of alienating administrators.

The representative assembly exercised its formal legislative power to approve several measures motivated by these views. From the acceptance of sanctions in 1962 to the endorsement in 1968 of a resolution only a step away from condoning strikes, the NEA moved toward adopting coercion as a legitimate means for satisfying teachers' demands.[36] During the same period policies were mandated which called for collective bargaining between officials and employees of the NEA, majority status for teachers on all major NEA committees and commissions, and the election of the executive secretary by the more representative executive committee rather than by the board of trustees.[37]

35. Carr and informant, interviews.

36. National Education Association, *Proceedings of the One-hundredth Annual Meeting* (Denver, 1962), p. 398; *Proceedings of the One hundred and sixth Annual Meeting* (Dallas, 1968), pp. 526-27.

37. National Education Association, *Proceedings of the One hundred and third Annual Meeting* (New York, 1965), p. 417; *Proceedings of the One hundred and fourth Annual Meeting* (Miami Beach, 1966), p. 476.

For a time, after it was clear how wide the gap between him and the assembly had become, Carr stayed at his post, trying to remain a dutiful official, yet protect his principles. The task was impossible. He could accept sanctions as a means of last resort for correcting educational deficiencies, but he opposed their use for "trivial and transitory reasons." [38] However, under no circumstances would he countenance strikes, professional holidays, or whatever they were called. Once a teacher signed a contract, Carr argued, he was pledged to uninterrupted service for its duration. To approve bypassing the executive secretary in favor of direct negotiations between NEA employees and the elected officers of the association and arbitrarily to give teachers the dominant voice in all major bodies of the association, he considered unnecessary and unwise. And he defended the selection of the executive secretary by the board of trustees as a desirable means to balance the interests in the NEA and keep the association from becoming the captive of any one of them.[39]

To the end of his career with the NEA, Carr did not relinquish the ideal of a united, independent teaching profession in the service of democratic education. Of course the association should work for the welfare of teachers, but the welfare of education as a whole must remain its primary concern. Although educators will have their disagreements, he believed that their common devotion to the schooling of children should make possible the amicable resolution of such disputes and keep teachers and administrators bound together.

Hence, Carr's last few years in office were a holding action against the pendulum swing toward greater teacher militancy. Perhaps, had he been a more inspiring administrator, he could have resisted longer those trends he opposed, but, as he well knew, he could not unalterably reverse them. Ultimately, however, it was the failure of a new generation of teachers to accept his principles that led to the demise of his leadership in the association and contributed to his resignation one year prior to the expiration of his fourth four-year term.

38. National Education Association, *Proceedings of the One hundred and first Annual Meeting* (Detroit, 1963), p. 22.

39. Carr, interview.

It has been said that "a man's reach should exceed his grasp." Perhaps Carr's difficulty was that his reach extended too far into the realm of abstract ideals. But that does not mean that his grasp failed to close on anything substantial. As the sincere exponent of an ideology shared by countless other educators of his generation and before, he helped to formulate educational objectives and to restore professional morale at a time of grave national disquietude. He labored successfully to obtain formal recognition of education as one of the concerns of the United Nations, and he almost single-handedly created an international teachers organization which has been of benefit to education in many areas. Certainly not without accomplishment he bore the responsibilities of the NEA and perpetuated a specific ideal of its function. And though this ideal was challenged sufficiently to overturn his leadership, it would be a mistake to say that it is now but an ideological curiosity of the past. This ideal is still at large and, with enough accommodation for the realities of the profession, it may yet flourish.

Some might find it easy to conclude that Carr could have done better by being more practical, more realistic. Perhaps so. But in a sense that would be asking William Carr to be other than himself. From the standpoint of the possible, he and others of his time may have been the victims of their principles, and it is true that, on present rereading, their statements of belief often strike one as being nobly naive. Yet today, when it is hard to avoid the impressions that many educators, however well trained they may be, lack a sense of purpose beyond careerism, that much educational research hints of faddism and the desire to please rather than to know, and that the organization and administration of schools are often determined by considerations extraneous to education, then the profession may well profit from a new birth of ideals, more proximate than those of Carr, but ideals just the same.

CHAPTER IV

James Bryant Conant

Part I

AN AUTOBIOGRAPHICAL FRAGMENT

In a volume published by Harper and Row in 1970, I proclaimed that I had lived several lives *(My Several Lives: Memoirs of a Social Inventor)*. Two of these lives were concerned with problems of education. One of them comprised the twenty years of my presidency of Harvard University; the other was the period from 1957 to 1968 when I investigated the American high schools and the education of American teachers, and spent two years in Berlin, Germany, assisting the city authorities in establishing a pedagogical center.

During the war years I was engaged rather heavily in mobilizing science for the war effort; I was also one of a small group of college presidents who worried almost continuously about the impact of the war on the functioning of the colleges. Indeed, I might say that from 1940 to 1945 I led a double life: as an ex-chemist I was busy as a member and later chairman of the National Defense Research Committee and as deputy for Vannevar Bush insofar as nuclear research was concerned; as a university president I served on committees of educators and continued as well to carry the responsibilities of the administrative head of a large university.

After I retired from the presidency of Harvard in 1953, I served four years as President Eisenhower's representative in the Federal Republic of Germany (first as high commissioner and then as ambassador). It was only after my return to the United States in 1957 that I undertook the study of the American high school, which was generously supported by the Carnegie Corporation.

It will be evident from the capsulated autobiography I have just presented that my record as an educator in terms of chronology has been largely an in-and-out affair. In writing the following pages for the Seventieth Yearbook of the National Society for the Study of Education, I shall leave aside all accounts of my concern with scientific investigations, either as a chemist or as an administrator during the war years. I shall also not attempt to deal with my experiences as a diplomat.

I am a New Englander. My ancestors on both my father's and mother's sides inhabited the area around East Bridgewater, Plymouth County, Massachusetts. The village of Joppa, in which both my father (James Scott Conant) and my mother (Jennet Orr Bryant) were born, was a part of the town of East Bridgewater, which in the second quarter of the nineteenth century was a farming community with a bit of local industry. My Grandfather Bryant (born in 1800) owned and operated a shoe factory; my Grandfather Conant was a shoe cutter in the same factory.

In one respect, Joppa Village was not typical of Plymouth County communities. It was a stronghold of one protestant sect, the Swedenborgian. By the time my two grandfathers were raising families, the Swedenborgian or New Church appears to have been the center of their religious life. My mother and my father thus shared a rather special religious faith.

About the time I was entering kindergarten, my parents' adherence to Swedenborgian doctrine must have been slowly losing strength. There seem to have been differences of opinion among the faithful. My mother, I remember, used to speak rather forcefully against one group whose interpretation of Swedenborg's writings she did not like at all. I was thus aware at an early age of "schisms" among churchgoers. Far more important was my mother's complete condemnation of all Trinitarian doctrines. She never attempted to make me a Swedenborgian, perhaps because she had become less certain of the details as she grew older. Later she often attended a Unitarian church. In many ways she might have been classified as a Unitarian, as I have usually so characterized myself.

My father had volunteered as a boy when President Lincoln called for enlistments in the spring of 1860. He was too young to be enrolled, but went with a Massachusetts regiment of volunteers as a "captain's boy." After hospitalization for illness contracted in the Penninsula Campaign, he enlisted in the Federal Navy. At the conclusion of the war, he became a wood engraver. Because of his native ability as an artist, he became a competent draftsman with very little formal training. In the 1870s, he established with a senior partner a wood engraving firm in the city of Boston, married, and bought a house in the Dorchester section of the city, near the present Ashmont station on the subway which runs through the center of Boston, connecting the town of Milton with the city of Cambridge. It was in that house that I was born in March 1893 and in which I lived until 1910, when the house was sold and my father retired. Thus I grew up in a suburb of Boston which was relatively new and rapidly expanding.

When my father bought his house, the Ashmont section of Boston must have been composed largely of vacant fields. The process of cutting up an area into house lots and putting in paved streets and sewers was just starting. Suburban streets before the advent of the automobile were assumed to be playgrounds for youth and children. The "gang" of youngsters of which I must have become a member at about the age of four or five roved the streets and vacant lots without thought of danger from any vehicle. Except in winter, bicycles took the older ones all around the neighborhood. The geography of a suburb in process of expansion with many open spaces was certainly favorable to the kinds of activity which groups of boys favored before they were old enough to play baseball or football. War games with either Indians or Confederates as the enemy involved ambushes in unkempt bushes in fields dominated by large signs: "For Sale." About the time we started playing an organized sport on a vacant lot, the "gang" began to break up because of the different educational paths that some of us chose to follow. Up to this point in time, half a dozen of us of the same age had attended first the elementary schools and then the grammar school, which were part of the Boston school system. If we had continued along the normal route, we should all have entered the Dorchester High School in a year or two.

The high schools of the United States in the first decade of this century were generally regarded as providing what we now would call terminal education. The large majority of those who entered the Dorchester High School either went to work on graduation or dropped out before the course was finished. Those families who thought of college for their sons turned their eyes to the frankly college preparatory institutions. There were three which were available for me. They were: the Boston Latin School, a part of the Boston Public School System; the Milton Academy, a private secondary school chiefly for boarding pupils, but which admitted a few who lived at home in Milton or just over the city line in Ashmont; the Roxbury Latin School, founded in 1645 and still managed by a board of trustees. Attending any one of the three would involve a daily trip by trolley car of thirty minutes each way. My next-door neighbor decided to apply for admission to the Boston Latin School. My family chose the Roxbury Latin School largely because of my interest in mechanical and electrical toys and the reputation of the young science master. Therefore, one day in June 1903 I took a trolley car to the Roxbury Latin School then located near the Dudley Street elevated railway station. For three hours, I wrote my answers to a series of questions designed to test my spelling, my knowledge of arithmetic and geography, and my use of words. My friend next door went through the same entrance examination process in the building of the Boston Latin School in Boston. We were both successful, though my admission to the Roxbury Latin School was tempered by a condition in spelling.

In a section of my memoirs, entitled "Half a Lifetime as a Chemist," the curious reader will find an account of how a remarkable teacher in the Roxbury Latin School—Newton Henry Black—responded to my curiosity about chemical phenomena. When I entered Harvard College in the fall of 1910 I had not only anticipated freshman chemistry, but, under his tutelage, had advanced far enough to be allowed by the chemistry department to skip qualitative analysis and enroll as a freshman in quantitative analysis. Except for my last year in school, my "extracurricular" study of chemistry in no way interfered with the pursuing of the prescribed course of study. Thus I was exposed to the old-fashioned college preparatory course, six years in length. We started French and Latin in the first class and continued the study of both subjects until graduation. In the fourth year after entry, the student had a choice between Greek and German. I, of course, chose German since by that time I was convinced I was going to be a chemist. The mathematics sequence took the usual student only to trigonometry and logarithms. I was one of a few who studied these subjects as an "extra" in the last year of school and anticipated their study in college by passing an examination taken along with the other college entrance examinations. It is interesting to note that in those days the introduction to calculus was regarded as a course for college sophomores; today it is usual for the more talented high school students who are interested in mathematics to complete the first course in calculus before high school graduation.

My six-year record at the Roxbury Latin School was far from outstanding. Before I became consumed by a desire to master chemistry, my grades were about C+ or B—. Yet, as I look back at the hours of homework I spent on Latin and French, I cannot remember any feeling of resentment, though I am sure I had little sense of pleasure. In the first four years at the Roxbury Latin School, I regarded the prescribed studies as just one of the tasks which had to be performed if one wanted to go to college. I have no memory of ever having challenged the classical curriculum. If one wanted to enter Harvard College, one had to pass the college entrance examination in Latin. There were no two ways about it. The same was true as to French, though I could see that it might be convenient to be able to read French. Speaking the language or understanding the spoken word was not among the goals of either the French teacher or his pupils.

I entered Harvard College just when a new president was taking office. Charles William Eliot, who had been president of Harvard for forty years, was succeeded by Abbott Lawrence Lowell in 1909. My class—the class of 1914, which entered in the fall of 1910—was the first to be affected by the new regulations which drastically modified the free elective system. Yet the change for me was of little consequence, since my advanced standing had allowed me to register a number of credits towards an A.B. degree. My course of study had been planned by Mr. Black. The chemistry department, which was still dominated by the spirit of Mr. Eliot, had consented. Thus, in a sense, I was trained as a chemist in Mr. Eliot's university and educated in Mr. Lowell's, though the implied dichotomy in this sentence is too strong.

I received my A.B. degree after three years in college, which in Mr. Eliot's time was by no means unusual. I received my Ph.D. in 1916 for a double thesis in organic chemistry and physical chemistry. The summer of 1915 I spent in the laboratory of the Midvale Steel Company in Philadelphia and flirted with the idea of becoming a member of the small research group of that company when I had completed my Ph.D. program. The summer of 1916 I spent in Greater New York, together with two friends, in an endeavor to make chemicals then in short supply because of World War I. The effort ended in a tragic disaster in which one of my friends was killed. That autumn I was back in Cambridge, starting my career as a college teacher of organic chemistry. The entry of the United States into the war in the spring of 1917 led to my joining the Chemical Warfare Service. After the armistice in the fall of 1918, I came back once again to Cambridge and prepared to resume my teaching of organic chemistry with the status of an assistant professor. My lectures on organic chemistry were eventually turned into a textbook. I was tempted into the profitable field of textbook writing by my old and highly valued teacher, Newton Henry Black. He had made a great success with a high school physics text written in collaboration with a Harvard professor of physics. He now proposed that we produce a Black and Conant text in chemistry, which we did in 1921.

It is an unprofitable but nonetheless amusing exercise to rewrite history by introducing a few imaginary "if clauses." At least such a procedure highlights certain episodes or people. Applying this technique to my autobiography, I can say that if I had not been elected president of Harvard in 1933, the focus of my interest would have been chemistry for many years. If the Harvard Graduate School of Education had not been in budgetary trouble in 1933, I should not have made a study of the American high school in 1957. The demonstration of the correctness of this thesis runs as follows:

As a new president of Harvard, I conferred with the deans of the various faculties. Dean Henry Holmes of the faculty of education explained his worries about the future. As was true in all the faculties in those days of the deep depression, the basic problem was created by lack of money. Before considering ways and means of increasing the budget of the school, I suggested we should first explore a fundamental question, namely, why should Harvard have a school of education? Holmes knew quite well that my predecessor had not looked with favor on his school and that many members of the Harvard faculty of arts and sciences were indifferent if not hostile to what the graduate school of education had been trying to accomplish. Therefore, my question did not come as a particular shock. I appeared to be open-minded. Holmes set out to convert me to a belief in the mission of his school. To that end, he asked for a series of appointments in which we could discuss in a leisurely fashion the problem of how best to train school teachers in Harvard University. Before long, Dean Holmes brought with him to the conferences a younger colleague, Francis Trow Spaulding. He proved to be an able advocate. He opened my eyes to what the free public schools meant for the future of American society. If I have anyone to thank for starting me down the path which led in 1957 to my detailed study of American public schools, it is Francis Spaulding.

Before I had been convinced by the team of Holmes and Spaulding of the significance of their approach to teacher training, I developed my own idea of what should be done at Harvard. The source of my proposal was Dean Judd of the University of Chicago. At the suggestion of President Hutchins, I visited Judd one day in early 1934 and asked his views about schools of education. He emphatically recommended that the entire responsibility for instruction in subject matter fields be placed in the hands of subject matter departments. A faculty of education should be concerned with educational problems only. On my return to Cambridge, I evolved the idea of a new degree for future school teachers—the Master of Arts in Teaching. The responsibility for the new degree would be lodged in *two* faculties, at that time a novel idea. An administrative board would be composed of professors from the faculty of education and from various departments of the faculty of arts and sciences. This board would recommend those who were to receive the new degree.

A new president of the university was entitled to have his ideas tried. So thought many faculty members in 1934 and 1935. As a consequence, there was little or no objection to the establishment of the new degree. The administrative board of the graduate school of arts and sciences (a powerful body) recommended that the two governing boards authorize the degree and the appointment of the administrative board which I had proposed. The Harvard Corporation (a self-perpetuating body of seven) and the Board of Overseers (a board of thirty elected by the alumni) acted favorably upon the proposal in November 1935. I had made my first social invention.

Neither Holmes nor Spaulding was particularly enthusiastic about the new degree, and few members of either of the two faculties were ready to fight hard for its survival. As the inventor, I naturally did what I could to promote the idea in my capacity as chairman of the newly formed administrative board.

In a Charter Day address at the University of California at Berkeley in March 1940, I presented my social and educational philosophy as it had evolved up to that point. The title "A Free Classless Society: Ideal or Illusion?" clearly suggests what was on my mind. I combined what I had been saying in support of a drive for more funds for national scholarships (also one of my inventions) with my more recently acquired faith in the public schools. Spaulding's influence is to be seen in the broadening of my concept of "talent." Referring to the well-known phrase "careers open to the talented," I first spoke about finding and developing academic talent and then added the following: "This form of ability is only one aspect of the talents of mankind which can be useful to the nation. The skill of the artist and artisan are of equal significance for our national life. The possibility of careers open to the talented of all types must be provided." I ended the speech by asking the following question: What choice have those who teach our youth? I answered:

> "None, but to hope that the American ideal is not an illusion, that it is still valid; none, but to labor unremittingly for a type of education which will every day quietly loosen the social strata; none but to believe that through the functioning of our schools and colleges American society will remain, in essence, classless, and, by so doing, even in days of peril, preserve the heritage of the free."

Rereading this peroration in January 1970, I am led to remark that I still stand by it, equating the word "classless" with "casteless," a point which I did not make sufficiently explicit in my speeches and writings at that time.

Early in 1941, I was appointed to the Educational Policies Commission. I continued to be a member off and on until 1963, serving a total of five terms, an unusual distinction. My experiences with the commission had a profound influence on my subsequent career. The commission had been established in 1935 by joint action of the National Education Association and the American Association of School Administrators in response to the troubles which the Great Depression had created in the public schools. A series of excellent little books published by the commission in 1937, 1938, and 1939 had made the organization an important factor in public school affairs. The original plans had called for a review of the situation after five years. Such a review had been held and the commission was given a second lease on life beginning January 1, 1941. The composition was only slightly altered. One of the changes was my appointment.

When I attended my first meeting of the Educational Policies Commission in May 1941, I had just returned from a mission to England to establish a scientific liaison office with the British. I was a member of the National Defense Research Committee appointed by President Roosevelt in June 1940, with Vannevar Bush as chairman. I knew I would be carrying a heavy load of work in performing my duties in connection with the mobilizing of scientific talent for the defense of the free world. Indeed, in accepting membership to the commission I had stated that if my other commitments proved too time-consuming, I would resign. I had left myself an escape hatch. I have no recollection of ever having considered using it. I became fascinated with the task the commission had undertaken, namely, the preparation of *Education for All American Youth.*

The volume of four hundred pages published in 1944 was a product of the joint labors of all of the commission members under the skillful guidance of William G. Carr, the secretary. We struggled in small subcommittees and in the committee of the whole with drafts and redrafts. Just because I worked with others on the writing of the book, I became almost as attached to the volume as though I were the sole author. Therefore, my judgment must be heavily discounted when I state that *Education for All American Youth* was far and away the most important book published about public schools in my lifetime. Whether one agrees or feels as did many that it was a major disaster, of one thing I am sure: if I had not participated in the production of *Education for All American Youth*, my life would have been quite different. If the remaining pages do not demonstrate this fact, then I have completely failed as an autobiographer.

The first two or three meetings of the commission which I attended had been concerned with a pronouncement about the New Deal agencies which had been mixing into education. The first publication which carried my name was *Civilian Conservation Corps, the National Youth Administration, and the Public Schools.* It was dated October 1941. The manuscript had been essentially completed by the old commission but was placed before the new commission for approval before publication. In the discussion I learned for the first time of the alarm with which this group of teachers and administrators viewed what the Roosevelt administration had been doing.

The project of writing *Education for All American Youth* originated at the January 1942 meeting. The negative reactions which had been evoked by the publication of the pamphlet about the New Deal agencies required an answer. For example, my old friend Professor Spaulding in his critical review of the pamphlet had raised the question as to what the Educational Policies Commission had in mind when it spoke of "a sincere and comprehensive effort to meet the educational needs of youth." It was all very well, he wrote, for the commission to state that a new effort was needed which was to be implemented on a state-by-state basis through the public schools, but who was to formulate the details of such an effort?

The bold answer which the commission had decided to make was nothing less than: "We, the EPC, are to be the authors and here is a blueprint for American public secondary schools." Such a project would have been ambitious in times of peace. Pearl Harbor complicated the undertaking. Therefore, the steering committee, a month after Pearl Harbor, decided that the first priority had to be given to the formulation of policies designed to increase the contribution of education to the war effort. But second only to this should come the "preparation and promotion of policies concerning the education of all American youth, both during the war and in the postwar period."

One of the features of *Education for All American Youth*, when it finally appeared, was the separation of the recommendations into two parts. One applied to a rural area (a hypothetical Farmville) and the other to a city. Education in grades 13 and 14 was included in both plans; in Farmville a community school was to offer instruction in grades 7 through 13 to the youth in an area of two hundred square miles. In the "American City" a community institute was envisioned as a continuation of the high school. In both schemes, vocational courses occupied a central place. A new feature was a continuous course, "Common Learnings," which would take up a third of a student's time in grades 10, 11, and 12 and a sixth of his time in grades 13 and 14.

The common learnings course was planned "to help students grow in competence as citizens of the community and the nation; in understanding of economic processes and of their roles as producers and consumers; in cooperative living in family, school, and community; in appreciation of literature and the arts; and in the use of the English language." Guidance of individual students was to be a chief responsibility of the teachers in this course which had to be developed to answer two major questions asked by the community: (1) What are the learning experiences which all boys and girls should have in common? (2) How may these be organized so as to be most effective? The advocates of the new course rested their case on the ground that "people's daily work, their civic interests, their family life, their leisure-time activities, the things they think about, and their ways of thinking are all bound up together, each influencing the other." (With which hardly anyone could disagree.) The conclusion was that it was necessary to study problems as they were found in life outside the school, and to be aware of "interrelations which cut across conventional subject matter lines."

All such talk seemed extremely strange to me. Still, if the other members of the commission were convinced such an approach would work, I was not unwilling to have my name on a volume setting forth this particular educational novelty. I had already reached the position of admitting, on the basis of evidence presented, that the conventional pattern of disciplines (history, English, mathematics, chemistry or physics, and a foreign language) was not suitable for a majority of tenth- to twelfth-grade students. I had not the slightest idea of what would be a suitable substitute. So in an adventurous mood I raised few objections, though I was curious to see some examples of common learnings courses in action. Such curiosity was one of the factors (though a minor one) which was to lead me to visit American public high schools. Without knowing it in 1944, I had endorsed one form of a "core curriculum." Thirty years later I was to learn much more about such curricula and the difficulties of introducing them.

The famous Harvard report, *General Education in a Free Society*, was written during the war by a joint committee of the faculties of education and arts and sciences. I appointed the committee but played no part in the preparation of the report. The emphasis on the relation of secondary education to college work pleased me greatly and, in general, I concurred with the findings and recommendations.

As the war came to an end, I was invited by Teachers College, Columbia University, to give the Julius and Rosa Sachs lectures. I decided that I would use the opportunity to express my views about the education of American youth. *Education for All American Youth* had appeared a year before. The report of the Harvard committee had just been published and was receiving excellent reviews. *Education for All American Youth*, however, had been either ignored or condemned in private conversations by all my academic friends. I was annoyed by what I felt was a misunderstanding of the book by professors of the university faculties (except the faculties of education). I was equally annoyed by the reaction of some of the public school people to the Harvard report. They failed to see any significance in the fact that I had appointed a committee on which members of both the faculties of arts and sciences and of education served. Spaulding was critical. Too much about our old friend Plato, he remarked. Those who looked to schools of education for guidance tended to consider the Harvard report as one more defense of the old liberal arts with only a change in name. They hailed the *Education for All American Youth* as the true gospel. I was convinced the diverse appraisals were a reflection of two sets of prejudices. I endeavored in the Sachs lectures, therefore, to reconcile the two books with whose preparation I had been connected in one way or another. This is, in part, what I said:

> One cannot help having the feeling that different descriptions of general education at the high school stage are the result of focusing attention on different types of public schools, or, what amounts to the same thing, focusing attention on different types of students. For example, the phrases used by my colleagues in Cambridge in describing a general education in high school seem to me excellent, if one has in mind a school where a large proportion of every graduating class is headed for college. On the other hand, the Educational Policies Commission in their document *Education for All American Youth* are obviously concerned primarily with the vast majority of high school students who are going to terminate their formal education either at the end of school or in a junior college. Compare the two descriptions of general education: the Harvard Report reads as follows: "At the center of it would be three inevitable areas of man's life and knowledge: the physical world, man's corporate life, his inner visions and standards. . . . In school . . . general education in these three areas should form a continuing core for all, taking up at least half a student's time." The authors of *Education for All American Youth,* also talking about a common core of general education, describe a course entitled "Common Learnings." This course, they declare, should be "continuous for all, planned to help students to grow in competence as citizens of the community and the nation; in understanding of economic processes and of their roles as producers and consumers; in cooperative living in family, school and community; in appreciation of literature and the arts; and in use of the English language."
>
> At first sight these two descriptions seem to be very different; I say seem to be very different, for I believe in reality they are not far apart. And having participated to a slight degree in the preparation of one volume (*Education for All American Youth*) and looked over the fence at the writing of the other, I am, perhaps, in a position to judge. If I am correct in my hypothesis that, unconsciously at least, the authors of the two volumes had in mind two different types of students, then the two descriptions may almost be merged in one. For, if one examines the actual content of the two prescriptions as far as they are specified in terms of classroom work, there is a surprising agreement as to conventional subjects studied. But the subjects are put together in a different way, one according to a pattern which corresponds to the rational method of handling areas of knowledge traditional in our universities, the other in terms of stimulating the interests of those students who have no natural bent for scholarly work. As a consequence, the two books give somewhat different reasons for the need for a common core of

general education, and they argue differently as to why certain subjects must be included in a course of common learnings. Yet, even this difference is largely one of emphasis.

I concluded this section of my second Sachs lecture as follows:

Many a disagreement about education arises because we fail to differentiate in our thinking about the needs of different groups.

Let it be agreed by the professors in our colleges and universities that the high schools of the country today have a job to do which is not to be measured primarily in terms of their success or failure in the formal education of specially gifted youth. But on the other hand, let those concerned primarily with high school education agree: (a) to provide a greater motivation among many groups to evolve a higher degree of intellectual curiosity; (b) to explore more sympathetically the ways and means of discovering special talent at an early age; and (c) to provide better formal instruction for those of high scholastic aptitude—all this to be accomplished without a segregation which might turn the boys and girls in question into either prigs or academic snobs.

Along some such lines, it seems to me, we may look forward to a united front in education. Along some such lines we can hope for the development of various patterns of general education which are tied together by their basic aims. As a contribution toward such unity I venture to close by subscribing to the doctrines as set forth in both volumes to which I have referred at length. Armed with *General Education for a Free Society* in one hand and *Education for All American Youth* in the other, I should hope to answer all critics of the future of our American schools!

The Educational Policies Commission was reconstituted in 1948. Carr's assistant, Wilbur F. Murra, traveled around the country looking for ideas. He remembers interviewing me in my office at Harvard and my pushing for the publication of a statement about the education of the gifted. The suggestion was placed on the agenda for the September meeting in the form of a question: "How can we reconcile the concept of education for all with the need to provide maximum education for the especially talented?" When we came to this item, I spoke up and said:

I may have had something to do with that going on the agenda. I have heard a number of people criticize the volume entitled *Education for All American Youth* on the grounds that it was like all public school documents, concerned only with mass education and that it does not do a proper job for the gifted children. I do not think it is a fair criticism. But it is one I have heard more than once. It would seem to me that if this group, representing the NEA as it does, as well as the superintendents, could make some statement to show that the representative body was concerned not only with education for all American youth, but also concerned with giving especially suitable education for gifted children, this would have a good public relations effect, even if it did not do anything else.

My suggestion was not immediately greeted with enthusiasm. Quite the contrary, it required a considerable amount of gentle prodding before the steering committee in April 1949 asked for a memorandum to be presented to the October meeting. Carr himself drafted a document which was laid before the whole commission and discussed at length. The final outcome was the appointment of a subcommittee, of which I was chairman, to write the first draft of what would be an eighty-page pamphlet.

I turned to Murra to do the writing. In early 1950 (two years after I had raised the issue in a meeting of the reorganized commission) a document entitled *Education of the Gifted* was circulated to the members prior to the final discussion and revision at the March meeting. I wrote to Carr on February 27 saying that, in general, I liked the document very much indeed; I hoped it would not be too greatly mutilated when it was subjected to the scrutiny of the commission.

The second paragraph of the foreword to *Education of the Gifted* contained the essence of what I had been trying to get the commission to say for over two years. I, therefore, quote it in full.

> Acquaintance with present educational practices has convinced the Commission that the gifted members of the total school population constitute a minority which is too largely neglected. Part of the neglect stems from attitudes widely held among the American people, attitudes which tend to obscure the great social need for able and educated leaders and to withhold needed funds for making adequate educational opportunities available to all gifted youth. Part of the neglect results from the circumstance that inadequate buildings and equipment and an insufficient supply of teachers prevent schools and colleges from doing as much as they would like to do in differentiating instruction. But the education of gifted children and youth also suffers from a too frequent failure on the part of teachers and administrators to give enough attention to the problems of identifying the gifted, counselling them, and making special provisions for their education. Although many excellent programs designed to meet the special needs of the gifted are in operation, such

programs could doubtless benefit from further improvement and from a broader base of lay and professional understanding as to their purpose and importance.

A year later, at the thirty-seventh meeting of the commission in March 1951, Carr reported that the little pamphlet which had cost me and the others so much effort had been selling at the rate of about six hundred a month. Everybody seemed to like it. People were pleased that the commission had a kind word for the gifted. Surprisingly enough, nobody had had anything to say of a critical nature. Nobody (to Carr's surprise, I gathered) had written a review saying that the commission was undemocratic or reactionary.

In 1948 I published *Education in a Divided World.* In this volume I set forth my ideas about the relation of American schools and colleges to the structure of our society. I praised our system of tax-supported schools; I wrote of the need for a greater degree of social mobility and a lesser degree of social distinction between occupational groups; I stressed the importance to the nation of the doctrine of equality of educational opportunity. Yet nowhere in the 220 pages is there even a hint of my understanding the difference between a *selective* secondary school and a comprehensive school. What was to become a central point of my concern is totally lacking. In contrast stands *Education and Liberty*, published in 1953.

One has no difficulty in finding in it an explanation of the American concept of "the comprehensive high school." Indeed, one of the ten suggestions for the future was that "we adhere to the principle of a comprehensive high school with a common core of studies and differentiated special programs, but in so doing we make far more effort to identify the gifted youth and give him or her more rigorous academic training in languages and mathematics."

Between 1948 and 1953 I had found a new focus for my writing about public secondary schools. How had this happened? As far as I can reconstruct the evolution of my ideas, the shift was largely a consequence of my study of schools and universities in Australia and New Zealand in the summer of 1951. What I saw and heard in those countries made me ready to speak out boldly on two educational issues of which I had been aware right along but about which I thought it well to be silent. The first was the pros and cons of selective academic public secondary schools (exemplified by the Boston Latin School). The second was the place of private schools (particularly parochial schools) in the American picture.

The reason for my trip to the Antipodes was my hope that by studying the Australian and New Zealand schools I would be doing a little study in comparative education. I had been told that the educational systems in the Australian states reflected a philosophy of education somewhere between the American and the British views. I found that what my informant had said was in fact the case.

What impressed me most in my inquiry into Australian and New Zealand schools was the influence of the historical facts of the development of secondary education in these two countries as contrasted to the United States. Because of my many arguments with EPC members, I knew something of the reforms in public secondary education in the United States at the time of World War I. I now began to appreciate the true significance of a document which was a sort of Bible for public school people. I refer to the *Principles of Secondary Education* published in 1918 by a commission of the National Education Association. In this document, the thesis was put forward that secondary education was essential for all youth. One of the recommendations was to the effect that "education should be so reorganized that every normal boy and girl will be encouraged to remain in school to the age of 18 on full time if possible, otherwise on part time." The comprehensive or composite high school was set forth as the ideal school. Vocational instruction was to be provided in such a school and not in separate vocational schools. The existence of private secondary schools was simply ignored by the NEA. It was assumed that the vast majority of American youth would attend free tax-supported secondary schools.

No such assumption could have been made in Australia at any time in its history. The system which had grown up was a dual system. As a consequence, those concerned with tax-supported schools did not have to be concerned with the wide diversity of educational conditions as did those who were responsible for American high schools. The idea that the schools could be instruments of democracy had found few if any supporters in Australia. The basic assumptions of the Educational Policies Commission in writing *Education for All American Youth* did not apply to a nation with a dual system. Examining secondary education in several of the Australian states and New Zealand thus forced me to think more deeply about public secondary education in the United States. I began to appreciate what might be called the social arguments in favor of the comprehensive high school.

When I returned from my summer in Australia and New Zealand, I was invited to give three lectures at the University of Virginia (published as *Education and Liberty*). I used the opportunity to contrast the educational systems of the United States, England, Scotland, Australia and New Zealand. I placed considerable emphasis on the distribution of the youth of every nation among the various educational institutions. For example, I took some pains to obtain reliable information about the percentage of each age group which was in school full time. The unique position of the United States stood out clearly. The fact that, of the five countries, only the United States was involved in providing full-time education for a large proportion of youth made it appropriate for me to consider the nature of the American comprehensive high school. I spelled out my own interpretation of what I had absorbed during the sessions of the Educational Policies Commission.

In the last of the three lectures, I dealt with the use of public money for the support of church-connected schools. I repeated the lecture at a regional meeting of the AASA in April 1952 in Boston. What I said did not endear me either to proponents of church-connected schools or to those who favored private secondary schools in general. The argument I presented was based on the assumption that it was essential for the future of our type of society that children and young people with a great variety of beliefs come to know each other. The public high school should be the place where *all* American youth learned to understand each other. I quote one paragraph from the speech as it appears in *Education and Liberty:*

> During the past seventy-five years all but a few per cent of the children in the United States have attended public schools. More than one foreign observer has remarked that without these schools we never could have assimilated so rapidly the different cultures which came to North America in the nineteenth century. Our schools have served all creeds

and all economic groups within a given geographic area. I believe it to be of the utmost importance that this pattern be continued. To this end the comprehensive high school deserves the enthusiastic support of the American taxpayer. The greater the proportion of our youth who fail to attend our public schools and who receive their education elsewhere, the greater the threat to our democratic unity. To use taxpayers' money to assist private schools is to suggest that American society use its own hands to destroy itself. This is the answer I must give to those who would advocate the transformation of the American pattern into that of England.

The case against using tax money for parochial schools was thus presented in unusual form. I did not raise the issue of separation of church and state. My objection to the use of federal or state money for a private school was irrespective of whether the school was or was not church connected. What I was arguing for was the comprehensive high school. What I was arguing against was the taxpayer's supporting competing schools, though I underlined my belief in the right of such schools to exist.

My arguments were violently attacked, not only by Catholic educators, but also by advocates of private secular schools. Because I did not rest my case on the constitutional separation of church and state, I was looked at a little askance by those who had spent their lives fighting against the state support of church schools. Particularly my separation of the school issue from the college issue placed me in a different camp from many. Yet I found people who readily conceded the distinction I was making, once I had a chance of presenting my views in logical fashion. Thus, I was glad that in 1968 a New York state committee of five, of which I was a member, separated clearly the question of state aid to church-connected colleges from state aid to parochial schools.

I became the United States high commissioner for Germany in February 1953. A few of my experiences in that post are recorded in six chapters of my memoirs. A fuller account of my four years in postwar Germany remains to be written. As an educator, I was no longer active. The important decisions about German education, including the creation of the Free University of Berlin, had been made by my predecessors.

The four years away from the United States were not totally barren of connections with current developments in American education. I was able to arrange my trips to the United States to accommodate an invitation to be the main speaker at a dinner in New York of the National Citizens Commission for the Public Schools. The commission had come into being in 1959 largely as a result of a suggestion of mine at a meeting of the Educational Policies Commission. I was glad, therefore, to be able to salute the commission in general and Roy E. Larsen, the chairman, in particular for accomplishments of the past five years.

From time to time I kept in touch with William Carr and the new president of the Carnegie Corporation, John Gardner. As a consequence of my conversation with these two gentlemen and Francis Keppel, the relatively new dean of the Harvard School of Education, I formulated a rather ambitious project to study American public high schools. In part, my experiences in trying to explain American schools to German audiences were responsible for the project. My knowledge was all secondhand. I spoke about the high school for *all* youth, but I had never even been inside such a school. I wanted to make at least a few visits to American high schools if for no other reason than to satisfy my curiosity as to the accuracy of what I had been telling German audiences.

During the Christmas vacation period 1956, I returned to the United States for a week or so. By prearrangement, John Gardner and I talked specifically about the idea which had been taking concrete form in my mind for a year or more. I dictated to his secretary a long memorandum which began with the following paragraph:

> What is proposed is a study of the education of the talented youth of a community in an American comprehensive high school (senior and junior high schools). The study would be conducted by me personally with the assistance of three or four collaborators. I would propose to be responsible for the findings and the conclusions. Any recommendations would be put forward under my own name and on my own responsibility. To be useful the project must be completed, including publication, in two years. The proposed date for starting the work would be October 1, 1957.

Starting from this memorandum, John Gardner developed plans for a meeting in March 1957 in New York of a small group of educators as advisers. The group was unanimous that the study had to have a much wider geographic coverage than I had suggested in my memorandum. The possibility of creating a study committee of educators and laymen which would visit the schools in question was discussed and discarded. The verdict was clear. I must visit many schools myself; a few trips to sample a few schools would not suffice. I could not complain. The whole idea of a study had originated in my mind because of my desire to obtain some first-hand information. Now it would appear that I was going to become directly involved in obtaining a great deal of information.

In March 1957, I resigned from my post in Germany and Mrs. Conant and I took up temporary quarters in New York City. I devoted a month to assembling a staff for the work which would start in September 1957. I was most fortunate in securing the services of Eugene Youngert, the principal and superintendent of Oak Park and River Forest High School outside of Chicago; Nathaniel Ober, a teacher from a small high school in Maine; Bernard S. Miller, assistant principal of a school outside of New York City; and Professor Reuben H. Gross, representing the field of higher education.

By the time Mrs. Conant and I were ready to start on a trip to Switzerland in April (to be followed by a summer in New Hampshire), the plans for the study were complete. A well balanced staff of four men had been chosen; plans for getting underway after Labor Day were completed; an office on the sixth floor of 588 Fifth Avenue had been rented; and most important of all, the Carnegie Corporation had made a grant to the Educational Testing Service of Princeton, New Jersey, which would provide the "logistic support" of the enterprise. Henry Chauncey, the president of the ETS, had been one of the small group of consultants from the start. I was, at that time, one of his trustees. Therefore, it seemed natural to turn to his organization for assistance. The arrangement proved to be highly satisfactory in every way.

The search for a model comprehensive high school started after Labor Day. We all realized that there was no such thing as a typical high school; that no sampling procedure would be adequate to give us grounds for generalizing about even one class of schools such as comprehensive schools. What we set out to find was one or more schools which met our three requirements for a satisfactory comprehensive high school. These were: (a) the forwarding of a democratic spirit among students from widely different family backgrounds; (b) a satisfactory elective program for the intellectually able; (c) a satisfactory offering of vocational courses. Starting with a list of schools which had been recommended by knowledgeable persons, we sent out questionnaires. From the returns, we spotted schools which appeared to meet our standards. These, Ober and I visited together. On the basis of what we learned and the staff work of the other members of the team, I rapidly evolved some recommendations addressed to school board members and administrators. These I tried out in addresses to educational gatherings. Dr. Youngert was extremely helpful by introducing me to principals and superintendents at various meetings of educators. My discussions with them of our tentative conclusions and recommendations were invaluable.

The report in manuscript form was complete in July 1958 when the group dispersed. It appeared in print as *The American High School Today* in February 1959. During the first half of the academic year 1958-59 I traveled extensively in the United States addressing educational meetings. I presented in capsule form my forthcoming recommendations as well as my findings. The latter were the result of my having spent at least a day in each of fifty-five schools. I reported that I believed no radical alteration in the basic pattern of American education was necessary. "If all the high schools were functioning as well as some I have visited, the education of all American youth would be satisfactory except for the study of foreign languages and the guidance of the more able girls." To this declaration I added the following criticism: "The academically talented student, as a rule, is not being sufficiently challenged, does not work hard enough, and his program of academic subjects is not of sufficient range."

I found only eight of the fifty-five schools I personally examined satisfactorily fulfilling the three main objectives of a comprehensive high school. Using letters to designate the schools, I published a summary of our rating of twenty-two schools on such points as "Adequate General Education for All," and "Adequacy of Nonacademic Elective Program." I also included for each of these schools what I called an academic inventory for boys and girls.

These inventories were prepared from the data supplied by the principals of the twenty-two schools. We asked for the courses taken by each of the upper 15 percent of the graduating class as measured by an I.Q. test or its equivalent. The results showed the wide diversity even among schools all of which were comprehensive. For example, in one school a majority of the boys in the top 15 percent had studied seventeen academic subjects, including three years of a foreign language. In another school, none of the boys or girls in the 15 percent group had studied seventeen academic subjects, and only 25 percent had studied a foreign language for more than two years.

The phrase "academically talented" had been used in the title of a conference called by the NEA in Washington in early 1958. It proved useful, though there were difficulties as to the criteria to be used in defining the top 15 percent of a class. I was quite ready later to make it 15 to 20 percent. The distinction I wished to emphasize was between those who could carry without undue difficulty a heavy load of academic work and those who could not. The critics of this concept concentrated on the difficulties of definition and also on the obvious fact that there was no necessary connection between the years of study of a foreign language and how much was learned.

The audiences to which I had spoken, particularly those in which school board members predominated, were enthusiastic. The timing was right; the recommendations were clear-cut and briefly argued. The Russian success with Sputnik in the fall of 1957 had triggered off a continuing series of blasts against the American public schools. Much of it was unfair. Administrators and school boards were looking for a reply to the critics. I offered one which seemed to fit the need. I was really simply describing and endorsing the best practices we had found in our journeying around the country.

When the book was ready for distribution, no one could say it had not been well advertised by my speeches. The publishers had been worried lest my talks and the publication of a twelve-page summary by the National Citizens Council for Better Schools would destroy the potential market. Such worries proved false. The little book of 140 pages had a tremendous sale for several years.

A number of recommendations were soon accepted by many administrators who were quick to point out to school boards that additional money was needed for their implementation. Critics were not lacking, however. Some professors of education wrote reviews in a hostile tone. I was not surprised. After all, I was an intruder barging into a province which was theirs by right of professional ownership. They were joined by a group of laymen who had been distressed by the failure of many high school principals and school superintendents to be concerned with providing adequate academic fare. They liked my criticisms of the schools, but did not agree with my advocacy of vocational courses or my belief in the value of the widely comprehensive school. In general, I was considered by this group to be too much of a defender of the status quo. The NEA leaders had praised the book, which fact condemned it in the eyes of many.

In presenting my recommendations about the high school curricula, I left aside the question of what should be the admission requirements of a four-year college. I was well aware that, just at that time, many institutions were becoming highly selective. I neither endorsed nor attacked this trend. I thought my position about college education had been made plain in earlier books. I had long been a proponent of the two-year community college. Therefore, I was clearly on the side of those who believed that everyone should have at least a start in collegiate education, irrespective of his or her academic talent. Nevertheless, my advocacy of a stiff academic program for the academically talented in a comprehensive high school could be misunderstood. To some, I appeared to be endorsing the growing tendency to limit admission to college to those who had a high degree of academic talent. Such was not my idea at all. I felt then and still feel that the admission requirements of each college must be settled within the college itself. I believe that a student may obtain a highly satisfactory education by attending a two-year college and then transferring to a four-year institution for the final two years if he shows a real interest in obtaining the kind of academic education suitable as a base for the learned professions. I recognize that the situation the nation over is such that the ideal of a first-rate, local two-year college is far from being as yet reached. But I hope that the increasing number of community colleges will, throughout the nation, provide adequate intellectual nourishment for a whole range of talent. Under such conditions, there would be many among those entering the freshman class of the local community college whose potentialities would not place them in the class of the academically talented. Nevertheless, on the basis of the kind of comprehensive high school I envisaged, such students, at the completion of the two-year course, would be in a position to take up a worthwhile task. For those who were academically talented, I would hope the two-year college would be as rewarding as two years in a four-year college. In other words, the importance of determining the degree of academic talent of a high school student would be to guide the pupil's choice in the elective system of the high school and later at the college level.

At the end of the academic year 1958-59, I was ready to expand my investigation of American high schools. I had not only been spreading my prejudices by my many addresses, but I had been learning about many high school problems not covered in my book. During the year 1959-1960 I continued writing articles and speaking about the comprehensive high school. I also undertook to have a quick look at junior high schools. In both undertakings, I was greatly assisted by E. Alden Dunham. The results of our junior high school investigations were published by the Educational Testing Service under the title *Memorandum to School Boards.* The chief conclusion was that there was no general answer to the question of whether a school system with junior high schools was better than one without. The fourteen recommendations were on the whole well received as a supplement to *The American High School Today* but, taken by themselves, attracted little attention.

In arranging my travels to see junior high schools in operation, I made a point of visiting several large cities and their suburbs. Out of these visits came the volume *Slums and Suburbs.* In it I contrasted the affluent suburban schools which had become essentially college-preparatory schools with the under-supported schools in the large cities. At a time when it was considered un-American to refer to the color of the skins of the pupils in a public school, I reported frankly on what I had found in the 100 percent Negro schools in Chicago, St. Louis, and Detroit. I was disturbed and shocked. My associate, E. Alden Dunham, suggested I use the phrase "social dynamite" to describe the conditions which I found. The words, alas, have proved to be prophetic. The attention I directed to the dangers of allowing so many out-of-school Negro youth to be unemployed in our large cities had been too little heeded. I expressed a negative view of attempts to improve Negro education by token integration across attendance lines. I said that, given money enough, education could be made satisfactory in a 100 percent black school. I pointed out the vast expense which would be involved in any attempt through bussing to make all large city schools integrated schools. These statements left me open to attack by many leaders who were then integrationists. Now, another group appears to be agreeing with my conclusion of 1961. I might note my point 16, which read: "Big cities need decentralized administration in order to bring the schools closer to the needs of the people in each neighborhood and to make each school fit the local situation." It was years before any steps were undertaken along these lines. Whether the delay has been fatal to the idea remains uncertain as I write.

The negative reaction of the Negro leaders to *Slums and Suburbs* made it evident that I was not in a position to be helpful in solving the problems which I raised. Therefore, I turned my attention to the education of American teachers. Thanks to a grant from the Carnegie Corporation, I made a two-year study of this field. Two small teams of educators—one each year—made the undertaking possible. We traveled widely and visited many institutions and not a few state departments of education.

The report was a voluminous document, *The Education of American Teachers*. It is impossible to summarize either the findings or recommendations. Suffice it to say it was welcomed by those who had been bitter critics of schools of education, but not by most of my old friends with whom I had served on the Educational Policies Commission. I was thought by many to have turned from being a friend of public school teachers and administrators to being a hostile critic. In a little book published in 1964, *Shaping Educational Policy*, I analyzed the activities of certain teachers' associations without mincing words. I also spoke harshly of the inadequacies of most state departments of education. A suggestion about the creation of an interstate educational agency by a compact between the states was made a reality by the former governor of North Carolina, Terry Sanford, who brought into being the Education Commission of the States.

I had gone to Berlin, Germany, on the publication of my report on the education of teachers. In that city, I was educational adviser to the city government in connection with the creation of a pedagogical center to serve all of Europe. On my return, I settled again in New York City with the intention of writing my memoirs. But before starting the enterprise, I accepted a generous invitation of the officers of the National Association of Secondary School Principals to undertake a second study of the comprehensive high school, largely at their expense. The study, carried out by means of a questionnaire, was published in early 1967 under the title *The Comprehensive High School: A Second Report to Interested Citizens.* It was in the nature of an inventory of the educational offerings of medium-sized, widely comprehensive high schools. It showed that in some schools almost all the changes advocated in *The American High School Today* had taken place. The reader was left in no doubt as to my strong belief in the widely comprehensive high school. Noting the wide differences between the financial resources of school districts within a state, I raised the issue of local financing of public schools. At the second annual meeting of the Education Commission of the States in 1968, I made the radical proposal that we should reexamine our belief that local financing was essential to local control. I pointed to the fact that in many states two neighboring districts might differ in their financial resources by a factor of two or three. I concluded that: To say that we have equality of educational opportunity in our system is, frankly, to misstate the case.

In the last two years almost all my working time and energies have been directed to the writing of an autobiography of which this document is a fragmentary summary.

A BIOGRAPHICAL SUMMARY

James Bryant Conant. Born March 26, 1893, in Boston, Massachusetts.

Family. Married Grace Thayer Richards, 1921. Children: James Richards, 1923; Theodore Richards, 1926.

Education. Public schools in Dorchester section of the city of Boston, Roxbury Latin School, Harvard College, A.B., 1913 (as of the class of 1914), Ph.D. (chemistry), Harvard University, 1916.

Occupational history. Captain, Sanitary Corps, U.S. Army, 1917; major, Chemical Warfare Service, U.S. Army, 1918; assistant professor of chemistry, Harvard University, 1919-1925; associate professor of chemistry, 1925-1929; professor of chemistry, 1929-1933; president, 1933-1953; president emeritus, 1953—; U.S. high commissioner for Germany, 1953-1955; U.S. ambassador, 1955-1957; director, A Study of the American High School, 1957-1959; studies of American education for Carnegie Corporation of New York, 1960-1963, 1965-1969; educational adviser to the Ford Foundation in Berlin, Germany, 1963-1965; author and educational consultant in U.S., 1965—.

Membership. Committee Scientific Aids to Learning, National Research Council, 1937-1942; National Defense Research Committee, 1941-1946 (chairman, 1942-1946); Educational Policies Commission, 1941-1946, 1947-1950, 1957-1963; National Science Foundation, 1950-1953; General Advisory Committee to the U.S. Atomic Energy Commission, 1947-1952.

Affiliations. American Chemical Society; American Association for the Advancement of Science; National Academy of Sciences; American Philosophical Society; American Academy of Arts and Sciences; Royal Society of London; Royal Society of Edinburgh; honorary member, Chemical Society (Great Britain).

Awards. Chandler Medal, Columbia, 1932; Priestley Medal, American Chemical Society, 1944; Freedom House Award, 1952; Commander Legion of Honor; Honorary Commander of Most Excellent Order of British Empire; Medal of Merit, oak leaf cluster, 1948; Medal of Freedom, 1963; Great Living American Award, 1965; Sylvanus Thayer Award, West Point, 1965; Arches of Science Award, 1967.

Part II

Major Educational Publications of

James Bryant Conant

Books

Sciences

1. *Practical Chemistry: Fundamental Facts and Applications to Modern Life* (with N. H. Black). New York: Macmillan Co., 1920.
2. *Organic Chemistry: A Brief Introductory Course.* New York: Macmillan Co., 1928.
3. *The Chemistry of Organic Compounds.* New York: Macmillan Co., 1933 rev. 1939; later revisions, with A. H. Blatt).
4. *On Understanding Science: An Historical Approach.* Dwight Harrington Terry Foundation Lectures on Religion in the Light of Science and Philosophy. New Haven: Yale University Press, 1947.
5. *Fundamentals of Organic Chemistry: A Brief Course for Students Concerned with Biology, Medicine, Agriculture, and Industry* (with A. H. Blatt). New York: Macmillan Co., 1950.
6. *Science and Common Sense.* New Haven: Yale University Press, 1951.
7. *Modern Science and Modern Man.* Columbia University, Bampton Lectures. New York: Columbia University Press, 1952.

Education

8. *Our Fighting Faith: Five Addresses to College Youth.* Cambridge: Harvard University Press, 1942. (Same, *Six Addresses to College Youth.* 2d rev. ed., 1944).
9. *Education in a Divided World: The Function of the Public School in Our Unique Society.* Cambridge: Harvard University Press, 1948.
10. *Education and Liberty: The Role of the Schools in a Modern Democracy.* Cambridge: Harvard University Press, 1953.
11. *The Citadel of Learning.* New Haven: Yale University Press, 1956.
12. *Germany and Freedom: A Personal Appraisal.* Harvard University Lectures on the Essentials of Free Government and the Duties of Citizens. Cambridge: Harvard University Press, 1958.

13. *The Child, the Parent, and the State.* Cambridge: Harvard University Press, 1959.
14. *The American High School Today.* New York: McGraw-Hill Book Co., 1959.
15. *Education in the Junior High School Years.* Princeton, N.J.: Educational Testing Service, 1960.
16. *Slums and Suburbs: A Commentary on Schools in Metropolitan Areas.* New York: McGraw-Hill Book Co., 1961.
17. *Thomas Jefferson and the Development of American Public Education.* Jefferson Memorial Lectures. Berkeley: University of California Press, 1962.
18. *The Education of American Teachers.* New York: McGraw-Hill Book Co., 1963.
19. *Two Modes of Thought: My Encounters with Science and Education.* New York: Trident Press, 1964.
20. *Shaping Educational Policy.* New York: McGraw-Hill Book Co., 1964.
21. *The Comprehensive High School: A Second Report to Interested Citizens.* New York: McGraw-Hill Book Co., 1967.
22. *Scientific Principles and Moral Conduct.* The Twentieth Arthur Stanley Eddington Memorial Lecture delivered at Princeton University, 15 November 1966. Cambridge, England: University Press, 1967.
23. *My Several Lives: Memoirs of a Social Inventor.* New York: Harper & Row, 1970.

Part III

James Bryant Conant: A Biographical Commentary

Paul Woodring

Most of the men and women whose autobiographies appear in this volume have devoted their entire lives to education as school or college administrators, professors of education, or psychologists working in areas closely related to education. James B. Conant, a man of many parts who had a variety of careers and has lived many lives, is an exception. Had he not accepted the presidency of Harvard, he might well have become one of the most noted scientists of his generation. Had it not been for World War II, he probably would have lived out his days as one of the outstanding presidents of Harvard. But, responding to new challenges resulting from changes in the world about him, Conant became an advisor to the president of the United States and then a diplomat. Throughout all these careers he retained his interest in education and, when his other assignments were completed, he again made education his primary concern. His career is an excellent example of the fact that the men who make the most notable contributions to mankind often are those who rise above their specialties and play a variety of roles on an ever expanding stage.

Though he calls his career in education an "in-and-out affair," from the time he became president of Harvard in 1933, Conant was never very far out of education. As a university president he saved and rebuilt the Harvard Graduate School of Education at a time when the president of Yale was rejecting teacher education as a university responsibility and was liquidating his own school of education. Between 1941 and 1963 he served a total of five terms as a member of the Educational Policies Commission and played a notable part in the activities of that organization. He was instrumental in the establishment of the National Citizens Committee for the Public Schools—Roy Larsen, who became the head of that organization, gives Conant credit for arousing his own concern for the problems facing the schools. In 1951 he made a study of the schools and universities of New Zealand and Australia. While he was United States high commissioner and later ambassador to West Germany, he took an active interest in German education. Since returning to the United States in 1957, he has devoted most of his time to investigations of various aspects of public education and teacher education in the United States. Although he has no professional degrees in education, his impressive bibliography on education would entitle him to a distinguished professorship of education in any university. Very few men who have made full-time careers of education have made comparable contributions.

At the time of his return from Germany in 1957, Conant might quite legitimately have retired to enjoy the fruits of his labors, for he was already sixty-four and had contributed as much to his nation and to the world as can reasonably be expected of any man. Or he could have selected from any of a number of fields. He might have elected to work in graduate education, on the problems facing the undergraduate colleges, in his own discipline of organic chemistry, or he might have continued service to the federal government. Instead, he chose to devote his efforts to the improvement of public education at the secondary level.

Other scientists and scholars expressed surprise at this choice and doubted that a study of the American high school offered the best outlet for the talents of a man of Conant's stature. But these doubters revealed an ignorance of history and a failure to recognize what is most important in determining the course of the nation's future. Conant's choice would not have seemed strange or irrelevant to men such as Jefferson and Franklin, for they also accepted it as a responsibility of statesmen and men of affairs to think long and deeply about the problems of educating free men and to make vigorous recommendations for improving the people's schools. When the history of twentieth-century America is written, Conant's contribution to secondary education will no doubt be given space equal to that of his contributions to science, diplomacy, and higher education.

Conant's first report on the American high school came at a time when the American people had grown weary of the endless debate over the schools, the reckless attacks on professional educators and the replies that the critics were unfair or did not know what they were talking about. The people were convinced that something was wrong and they wanted to be told what to do about it, but they did not trust either the educators or their critics to tell them. They did trust Conant, whom they saw as a man of unquestioned integrity who had taken a close look at a great many schools and who had no axes to grind.

At the time he undertook his study, Conant had never been inside a comprehensive high school but he had become convinced that selective preparatory schools, such as he himself had attended as a boy, are inappropriate in a nation that undertakes to provide secondary education for all and that European models for secondary education are inappropriate for this side of the Atlantic. He had expressed the opinion that nonpublic schools are a divisive influence because they separate students on the basis of social class, or religious background, during a period of life when all young Americans ought to be learning to live together.

After he had visited a number of public high schools which enrolled students from a wide range of social backgrounds and of varied academic talents, Conant became convinced that the best of these schools provided a model which others might appropriately emulate. Consequently, his recommendations were not revolutionary. He proposed only an upgrading and improvement of what already existed, for he was convinced that if all high schools could be made as good as the best already were, most of the problems of secondary education would be solved.

Some of his critics have expressed surprise that a man who emphasizes, as Conant does, the importance of a vigorous academic program with high standards for those who plan to enter college should also be the leading exponent of the comprehensive high schools, which enroll many students who do not plan to enter college. But there is no true inconsistency here. Conant was well aware that a high school is a social as well as an academic institution—a place in which adolescents learn to associate in a wide variety of nonacademic activities and hopefully to understand and respect each other. If, during the adolescent years, students are segregated on the basis of race, religion, social class, or academic talent, they will not be properly prepared for living in a democracy.

But Conant was also aware of the wide range of individual differences in learning capacity and motivation for academic work. Regardless of whether these differences are in part genetic or entirely the result of early childhood experiences, they are so well established by the time a boy or girl reaches high school that the school program appropriate for one group of students may be totally inappropriate for others. Consequently, he recommends a kind of secondary school in which students of varied backgrounds can associate for a part of the day as social equals and can then be reassembled for other parts of the day for different programs of study. Since a variety of programs, vocational and academic, are necessary to meet the varied needs of students from a wide range of backgrounds, possessing a wide range of talents, and with a wide range of vocational prospects, Conant came to the conclusion that no high school could be truly comprehensive unless it had an enrollment of sufficient size to assure a graduating class of one hundred.

Public high schools which enrolled all the adolescents in the community, regardless of academic talent, social class, or vocational plans, and which offered a choice of academic or vocational programs, had existed in one form or another for many decades before Conant discovered them—indeed, the majority of Americans living west of the Alleghenies had never known specialized secondary schools such as are common along the Atlantic Seaboard and particularly in New England. In spite of this fact, it may well be that the comprehensive high school will stand as Conant's monument. It was he who gave nationwide publicity to such schools and proposed definite standards for measuring their excellence. And although educators had previously emphasized the need for a wide range of programs to satisfy the needs of all American youth, Conant was more successful than the others in making school board members and other laymen aware of the need.

In *The American High School Today* Conant recommended a rigorous academic program (four years of mathematics, four years of one foreign language, three years of science, four years of English, and three years of social studies) for only the academically talented, a group which he defined as consisting of those scoring in approximately the upper 15 percent (on a national basis) on scholastic aptitude tests. Even at the time he wrote, the percentage of high school graduates going on to college was much larger than this and now is closer to 60 percent. As this proportion increases it seems obvious that the number for whom vocational training in high school is appropriate will fall sharply, and if the time comes when nearly all students attend community colleges or trade schools after high school graduation, Conant's emphasis on vocational training in high school will become outmoded—vocational courses could be moved up into the thirteenth and fourteenth years, thus providing more time for courses of a general and liberal nature during the high school years.

Although rigorous courses in mathematics and foreign language do not seem appropriate for students of low academic ability, a different kind of liberal education could well be provided for those who must proceed at a slower pace. Students from a deprived cultural background—the ones most likely to be guided into vocational courses at the high school level—are the ones most in need of cultural enrichment, and, if it is not provided in high school, those who do not go on to college will never get it.

Conant was not unaware of this problem but he was also aware of the wide range of individual differences in academic talent, and he doubted that more than 15 percent could handle the rigorous program which he proposed for the talented. It is not entirely clear what kind of college preparation he intended for the students—now 40 or 45 percent—who enter college even though their abilities do not place them within the "academically talented group."

Some of Conant's critics, notably the disciples of Robert Maynard Hutchins and some of those identified with the Council for Basic Education, protested that he was recommending only a watered-down academic program for the great majority and insisted that the program he proposed for the talented should be required for all high school students. On the other hand, many professional educators protested that Conant placed too much emphasis on academic subject matter and pointed to the Eight-Year Study and other evidence that the traditional academic program does not necessarily provide the best preparation for college. This controversy remains unsolved but the great majority of high schools have, in recent years, raised their academic requirements for the college-bound students including a percentage much larger than the 15 recommended by Conant.

Even for students taking vocational courses, Conant recommended a substantial program of academic work including four years of English, three or four years of social studies including two years of history, a year of general mathematics, at least one year of science, and a senior course in American problems or American government. If such courses were well planned and well taught, they would provide a considerable amount of general education even for the students enrolled in vocational courses.

In his most prophetic book, *Slums and Suburbs,* Conant saw more clearly than most of his contemporaries the "social dynamite" that was building up in the central cities as a result of the migration of white families to the suburbs and their replacement by Negroes from the rural South who were unprepared to meet the educational requirements of city schools and unable to find suitable employment after graduating from or dropping out of school. It is tragic that the cities dawdled for many years before undertaking the reforms that Conant recommended, including decentralization of school systems; equally tragic that Negro leaders rejected the assistance that Conant might have given them in bringing about necessary changes. Even though his perception of the problem differed somewhat from theirs, he could have assisted them in their search for solutions and his support would have been invaluable.

In his own evaluation of his contributions to education, Conant is neither modest nor immodest—he simply tells it as it is. In an interview with Terry Ferrer which provided the basis for a profile in *Saturday Review,* Conant said, "I have to confess that there was a lot of luck in the timing of *The American High School Today*—the Russians really put Sputnik up right on schedule in 1957 for my purposes. That book was addressed to 20,000 local school boards all under tremendous pressure from Sputnik." But, he added, "I'm not sure that *The Education of American Teachers* has been successful. Maybe the timing was wrong. Maybe I was not wise to delve into teacher-education reform." [1]

It is true that the effects of Conant's proposal for the reform of teacher education have been less influential than his recommendations for changes in the high schools. The school board members to

1. Terry Ferrer, "Conant Revisited," *Saturday Review,* March 18, 1967, p. 57.

whom the recommendation for changes in secondary education were addressed were willing to accept Conant's judgment as to what was needed, but the professional educators who made policy for teacher education were much less willing to accept his advice. As a result of the steady barrage of lay criticism that had been directed at them during the fifties, many professional educators had become defensive. They were prone to look upon Conant as an outsider, almost an interloper, and, with some exceptions, were reluctant to accept his counsel and leadership. Moreover, Conant was seen as a threat. He recommended a reduction in the number of professional courses in education. This would reduce the demand for professors of education in the universities and colleges and no professional group can be expected to accept a demand for a reduction in its services with equanimity.

In his writing, Conant rarely comments either positively or negatively on the work of other educational writers and does not rely on quotations from others to support his own position. Though his conclusions always seem to be based upon evidence, he does not always cite the evidence, assuming, perhaps, that professional educators are familiar with it and that others are more interested in his conclusions than in his way of reaching them. When criticized he rarely defends himself or offers a reply. He simply stands firm—a response that can be infuriating to critics who know that since Conant's prestige is greater than theirs, at least outside the educational fraternity, he will probably win out.

Conant avoids becoming involved in philosophical disputes, especially those involving the definition of education. Instead of reasoning from first principles concerning the nature of man, he prefers to take a close look at the schools as they are and then ask how they can be improved within the limits of available resources and within the democratic process. He is an educational statesman rather than an educational philosopher but probably would not object to being called a pragmatist. William James undoubtedly would place him in his "tough-minded" category—he faces reality and works within its limits. He is definitely not a romantic and wastes no time tilting with windmills.

There is no invective in Conant's writing, no sarcasm, and only occasionally a touch of irony. Though winning friends does not appear to be high on his list of personal goals—he would rather be right and influential than popular—he does not make enemies unnecessarily. Though he avoids controversy, he never avoids controversial issues when he thinks it necessary to take a position.

Conant the man does not emerge clearly from his autobiography—he wants to be judged by his work rather than by his personality. But it is obvious that he has a high sense of duty and a deep commitment to the betterment of the lot of mankind. Though he probably does not believe in the perfectibility of mankind, he clearly believes in the possibility of its improvement and looks upon education as one of the major roads to improvement.

The younger educators who worked closely with Conant on his various studies of education have great affection for him, as well as respect and admiration. Merle Borrowman says, "I had been told by one who knew him long ago that Conant was cold, aloof, and tough and when I first encountered him several years past these adjectives seemed appropriate. I was surprised, therefore, in our first conference to see how relaxed and free to joke and argue with him were the relatively young and not yet fully established men who had worked with him the year before. Several of the younger collaborators have since reported feelings of great tenderness—even protectiveness—toward him, though at the same time they describe such feelings as ridiculous 'since obviously Dr. Conant can take care of himself.' In conferences with students or classroom teachers, many of whom enter his presence in awe, I am constantly struck with how quickly they can speak in ease and humor, with thoughtfulness and candor. These typical responses are, I would guess, the result of his tendency to treat people as respected colleagues." [2]

2. Merle Borrowman, "Conant the Man," *Saturday Review,* September 21, 1963, p. 60.

CHAPTER V

George S. Counts

Part I

A Humble Autobiography

To give an accurate description of what has never occurred is not merely the proper occupation of the historian, but the inalienable privilege of any man of parts and culture.

Oscar Wilde

I

This observation by the great British wit and writer should apply with particular force to any person engaged in writing an autobiography. And it is certainly applicable in the present case. Consequently, I would like to warn my readers, as in my later years I have warned my students, to beware of everything that I tell them. To give strength to the warning, I repeat an old English proverb: "Old men and far travelers may lie by authority." Then I tell them that I am both. An "old man" can say that he remembers this or that very well. It happened when he was in the eighth grade or in high school or in college. To illustrate, I tell my students that the only time I ever saw Abraham Lincoln on the television screen was when he read the Emancipation Proclamation. A "far traveler" can, of course, say that he visited this or that country, and that he knows what he is talking about. If any question is raised about what is happening in the Soviet Union, I just tell them that in 1929 I drove my own Ford automobile six thousand miles over that country, a large part of the time entirely alone. And this happens to be true.

According to the family record, I was born on December 9, 1889. But this is an important event in my life that I cannot clearly recall. I was told later that I was somewhat underweight and that my grandmother wondered "whether it would pay" to raise me. As a boy I was known as a "redhead." The period of my life embraces seventy-nine years at this time (January 1969). And it has been a period of unprecedented changes in my country and the world. According to Henry Steele Commager, a distinguished historian, "the decade of the nineties is the watershed of American history"—a watershed between an "America predominantly agricultural" and an "America predominantly urban and industrial." And another distinguished historian, Carl Bridenbaugh, tells us that "the greatest turning point in all human history, of which we have any record, has occurred within the twentieth century." If anybody had told me at the beginning of this century that I would live to witness the phenomenal changes in the condition of man that have occurred, I would not have believed him. And my parents or grandparents would not have believed him either. So many things have happened that just could not happen. In what follows I shall depend almost entirely on my memory. When I retired from Teachers College, Columbia University, I destroyed practically all of my correspondence. And I never kept a diary, except during my automobile trip through the Soviet Union.

II

I was born on a farm three miles from the town of Baldwin in northeastern Kansas. The land was beautiful, quite unlike the prevailing view of the state as a vast and unbroken prairie. It was a land of hills and forests and streams. With very few exceptions the years of my childhood and youth were lived on this farm and a second farm which my father bought closer to the town so that his children could attend a town school. Consequently, those years were lived before I passed over that great "watershed" in American history. For power we depended on human muscle, the horse, and the windmill; for food we depended largely on the cow, the pig, the chicken, the garden, the orchard, and wild fruits, and rabbits and squirrels and ducks. I saw my first automobile when I was thirteen years old. I was driving a riding cultivator drawn by a team of horses from one of our farms to the other. As I drove over the brow of a hill I saw that first automobile coming toward me. And the horses saw it too and dashed off the road into a field.

In terms of labor, life on the farm was hard, not only for father and mother, but also for the children. From the time we were five years old, both boys and girls had chores to perform. I began by carrying in wood and corncobs for fire in the stoves. And then I climbed the ladder toward maturity: milking the cows, feeding the animals, removing manure from the stable, cutting down trees, sawing logs, tending the garden, gathering fruit, pitching hay, pulling weeds and morning glories in the corn field, and finally plowing the land, planting grain, cultivating the fields, and harvesting crops of many kinds. In the spring, summer, and autumn the working day was long, from before dawn to hours after sunset. It was in this way that I acquired most of the practical skills and knowledges necessary for life on the farm in those days. I well recall when, at thirteen years of age, I was permitted and able to plow a large field with a "single plow" drawn by a team of horses. And the point should be emphasized that the youngster acquired not only knowledges and skills, but also moral character and discipline. From the earliest years he or she, boy or girl, contributed to the welfare of the family and the rural neighborhood and without being paid in dollars and cents. And by watching the animals they received a good sex education. After passing over the "watershed" into the urban and industrial society, we have given little thought to the question: Where are our children and youth going to be, what are they going to do? As yet we have not found a substitute for even the milk cow, one of the most important educational institutions of preindustrial America. The traditional school does not and perhaps cannot provide the answer to this question.

In spite of the heavy burden of labor on the farm, I did find time for many kinds of recreation during both day and night. Among these were swimming and skating, "playing Indian," "snipe-hunting," camping in the woods, visiting haunted houses, hunting "bee trees," participating in "spelling bees," breaking and riding horses, fighting wasps and bumblebees, snapping off the heads of snakes, going on school and Sunday school picnics, sleigh-riding and making snowmen, and reading stories of adventure. I longed to climb the Rocky Mountains and go down the Mississippi on a house-boat. A major interest was collecting birds' eggs, arrowheads, and postage stamps. I even learned the elements of taxidermy. Among my heroes were John James Audubon and Daniel Boone. And I did a tremendous amount of reading in the fields of botany, zoology, and natural history. My father had a good library, including a set of encyclopedias.

My major interest during my years of childhood and youth, however, was hunting and fishing and, particularly, trapping the game and fur-bearing animals of the region. In fact, until I was halfway through college my great ambition was to spend my life as a trapper. During autumn, winter, and spring (in all months containing the letter *r*) I would rise before dawn, visit my line of traps by lantern-light, do my chores, and then walk a mile and a half to school. The animals which I trapped were, for the most part, opossums, skunks, civet cats, and minks. I even developed a conditioned reflex which caused me to like the smell of the skunk. The only time I was ever dismissed from school was when I was in the fifth grade—the reason being that I had found a few skunks in my traps that morning. The pupils revealed my condition to the teacher with their noses. However, from the sale of my furs I made practically all the money that I could call my own. During my youth I planned from year to year, usually with one of my brothers, to go to Canada and float down the Churchill River toward Hudson Bay, find a good region for hunting and trapping, build a log cabin, and live there the rest of my life. Every year we would open the catalogue of Montgomery Ward and Company and calculate the cost of such an expedition in terms of traps, firearms, axes, shoes, clothes, blankets, etc. From my life in the woods, on the streams, and in the hills I acquired many of the interests of the naturalist and a deep love of nature which persists to this day. The beauty of the flowers in the spring and of the foliage in the autumn still enthrall me. I have often said that in a certain sense I am a Shintoist—a worshipper of nature.

This suggests a major recreational interest which I developed after going to Teachers College. In 1931, at my wife's insistence, we bought a small farm of fifty acres near New Hope, Bucks County, Pennsylvania, about seventy-five miles from our apartment in New York City. Very soon I became interested in flowering trees and shrubs from all over the world. Whenever I visited another country I would collect seeds, bring them home, and plant them.

The result was the most beautiful place in the world! As the time for my retirement approached I planned to go into the nursery business. I built a greenhouse and began to grow thousands of azaleas and other shrubs from cuttings. Unfortunately, invitations to lecture or teach here and there from the Atlantic to the Pacific began to pour in. I usually accepted these invitations and thus changed the course of my life. This reminds me of a remark by my old friend Harold Rugg: "You are lucky, George, that you were not born a girl, because you can't say 'no'."

III

My people came, according to the available records, altogether from colonial and pioneer stock. I know of no ancestor who came to America after the War for Independence. But this is a question which in the days of my childhood out on the Kansas frontier received little attention. In fact, it was regarded as undemocratic to boast about one's forebears. There was a saying, directed primarily toward persons coming from the East wearing a silk hat or any other sign of aristocracy, that "one man is just as good as another, if not a little better." (This was long before George Orwell wrote *Animal Farm.*) The important question was: "What can he do?" Under the conditions prevailing at the time, it was generally agreed that the Harvard graduate or the man with a silk hat could not do very well anything of real importance. We called them "city slickers." When, as a boy, I asked my father about our ancestry, he warned me as follows: "George, I would advise you not to inquire into that too far, because you would probably find that one of your ancestors was hung as a horsethief."

However, in the course of time I have obtained some data about my ancestors. My mother, whose maiden name was Mertie Gamble and who was born in Kansas, visited relatives in Pennsylvania when she was close to eighty years of age. They gave her a genealogical chart which showed that she was descended from William Bradford, a leader of the Pilgrims, a signer of the Mayflower Compact, and governor of the Plymouth Colony for thirty years. Long after his death I learned that my father, born on a farm in Ohio, was descended from John Counts (Kuntz), who probably came from Germany to Virginia about 1714. But the fact should be emphasized that, since my first ancestors came to America, there has been much mixing with other ethnic elements. The available evidence seems to show that this mixing embraces English, Scotch, Irish, Welsh, German, and French sources. While many of my ancestors remained in the East, many migrated westward from Massachusetts, Connecticut, New York, Pennsylvania, and Virginia with the advancing frontier.

Neither of my parents went to college, though both of them attended high school for a period. As I remember them, however, they were well educated. My father did a great deal of reading, had an excellent command of the language, and was something of an artist. The same could be said of my mother. She was a talented musician. She played the organ and sang beautifully. I can still see her standing at the washtub and singing songs as she scrubbed the clothes of the family. But perhaps the most important thing about my parents was their system of values and their code of ethics. My father would often employ a "hired hand" to work on the farm or a "hired woman" to help mother in the house. Generally these people were from neighboring families. And some of them were Negroes. In every case the "hired hand," whether white or black, was treated as if he or she were a member of the family. My parents always endeavored to live according to the principles of the Judeo-Christian ethic. They took seriously the second of the two great commandments and believed in the brotherhood of man. As I look back over my life, clear back to my early childhood, I can see how they influenced me. When I was seven years old, a Negro boy, Johnny Hawkets, a close friend of mine, was attacked by four white boys. Even today I can see blood streaming from his nose. I took his part. But my one regret regarding my parents is that I never fully appreciated them until they went down into the grave.

I was the third of six children, three brothers and two sisters, with whom I played and worked and quarreled during childhood and adolescence. Although our parents loved us most sincerely, they knew that if you spare the rod, you spoil the child. My own research into the causes of juvenile delinquency supports the idea that such delinquency is "the result of parents trying to train children without starting at the bottom." My parents believed this, but whenever they resorted to corporal punishment they assured me that it hurt them more than it hurt me. And they also warned us that, if the teacher in the school applied the "hickory stick" to us, they would have to repeat the process at home. Nevertheless, we were a closely knit family and we loved each other, even though I sometimes thought of running away from home and going west, in the tradition of my family. But we derived some satisfaction from a version of Parkinson's law: "One boy is a whole boy, two boys are half a boy, and three boys are no boy at all." Whenever we three older sons were asked to work together, we could always think of other things we wanted to do. All six children are still living.

I was reared in the strict discipline of the Methodist church. The first dollar I earned was given to me at the age of six by my grandfather for learning in order the names of the books of the Bible. According to the family tradition, Sunday was the "Lord's Day" and a "Day of Rest," except for attending religious services and doing the necessary chores on the farm. Playing games was practically forbidden. The same may be said of cards, tobacco, alcohol, and swearing in even its mildest form. However, I enjoyed learning the hymns of my faith, and I still love to sing them whenever opportunity presents itself. And I didn't always obey the rules. After all, everybody in those days knew that "boys will be boys."

IV

My formal education began in a one-room rural school which was about one mile from home. I started at five years of age, but became a "dropout" during the first month. When the teacher asked me to do something, I would always respond by saying, "I can't." But I returned to the same school the next year and completed four grades in two years. This experience has convinced me that the ungraded school is superior. My father then bought a second farm nearer Baldwin. Thereafter, except for one year when I was thirteen and remained at home to help with the work on the farm, I attended the public school in the town until I graduated from high school in 1907. This involved walking a mile and one-half to and from school every day in all kinds of weather. The idea of remaining at home because of snow or ice on the roads never occurred to me. In fact, we liked both snow and ice—the deeper and slicker, the better.

I received my undergraduate education in Baker University, located in Baldwin, a Methodist institution, and the oldest and finest college in Kansas, founded in 1858. My field of specialization was the classics—Latin and Greek—seven years of the one and four years of the other in high school and college. I also took courses in history, philosophy, and the natural sciences, graduating at the head of my class and receiving the degree of bachelor of arts in 1911. During the four years my grades were all A's, except one, which was a B+.

In both secondary school and college I was active in student affairs. I was elected president of my class, my social fraternity, the athletic association, and other organizations. I was both fond of and successful in sports. I was a member of the varsity football and basketball teams and captain of the latter one year. As I look back to those days I sense something quite prophetic. I played left end on the football team and left guard on the basketball team. And, according to many of my critics, I have been on the "left" all the rest of my life. With reluctance I must add that in my junior year I aroused the displeasure of the college authorities by participating in an unauthorized and unchaperoned excursion of the college basketball team to St. Louis, Chicago, and other distant places during the Christmas vacation.

In the summer of 1913 I went to the University of Chicago for graduate study with a scholarship in sociology. My reason for going to this institution, according to my recollection, was that it was regarded at that time as a champion of radical ideas in the fields of biology, social science, philosophy, and theology. During that summer quarter I was persuaded by my future brother-in-law, William Bailey, to discuss with Dr. Charles Hubbard Judd, dean of the School of Education, the question of seeking my graduate degree in education. He persuaded me to do this and thus changed profoundly the course of my life. However, I did not abandon my interest in sociology and thus became the first of Judd's students to take a minor in that field. Previously, all of his students had chosen psychology. This may have been due to the fact that he himself was a distinguished psychologist and presumably did not see how sociology could contribute significantly to the training of a professional educator. During my three years at the University of

Chicago I took more courses in my minor than in my major. I took all of the courses offered in sociology and anthropology and some in economics and political science, including the principles of law. I supported my wife and myself by working at various jobs and winning scholarships and fellowships. I was awarded the degree of doctor of philosophy, *magna cum laude,* in the summer of 1916.

V

I began my teaching career on graduation from college in 1911. I did this in spite of the fact that I had never planned to become a teacher and, while in college, had not taken a single course in pedagogy. The reason for this will be explained later. My first job was teaching science and mathematics in the Sumner County High School in Wellington, Kansas, for a monthly salary of eighty-five dollars. In view of the fact that my father had employed "hired hands" for seventeen dollars a month, this seemed pretty good to me. The next year, 1912-13, I served as principal of the public high school in Peabody, Kansas, for one hundred dollars a month. Again I taught biology and introduced my students to the theory of organic evolution. Although I was the only member of the teaching staff, including the school superintendent, who accepted this theory of the origin of man, I was subjected to no criticism. This may have been the result of my faithful attendance at the Methodist church and active membership in a Sunday school class for men. In both schools, besides teaching various subjects, I coached athletics. Perhaps I should add that the only job in the teaching profession I ever sought was my first one, the one in Wellington. All of the others throughout my long career sought me.

After completing my graduate program at the University of Chicago in 1916, I became a college or university professor for the rest of my professional life. In that first year, I joined the staff of Delaware College (now the University of Delaware) in Newark, Delaware, as head of the Department of Education and director of the summer school. In addition to offering all the courses in education, I taught courses in psychology and sociology. While there I planned to write a comprehensive volume entitled *The Story of Human Progress* to be used in the secondary school. Unfortunately, I never completed the manuscript because H. G. Wells did the job and published his great work *The Outline of History* in 1920. In 1918 I went to Harris Teachers College in St. Louis; in 1919 to the University of Washington in Seattle; in 1920 to Yale University; in 1926 to my alma mater, the University of Chicago; and in 1927 to Teachers College, Columbia University, where I remained until I retired in 1955 at the age of sixty-five. Thus, I seem to have lived in my early years as a gypsy, moving from one place to another, even though I liked every college or university where I taught and always assumed that I would remain there the rest of my life. After moving to New Haven in 1920, my wife received a letter from her mother warning us that a rolling stone gathers no moss. I suggested that she reply at once and say that we didn't want to gather any moss at all. Since retirement I have taught at the University of Pittsburgh, the University of Colorado, Michigan State University, Northwestern University, and now Southern Illinois University. An important point to emphasize is that, wherever I have taught and regardless of the titles of my courses, I have always worked in the realm of the social and cultural foundations of education.

VI

Early in my professional career I became interested in the cultures and societies of other countries. This interest undoubtedly derived in part from my study of anthropology, sociology, and other social sciences at the University of Chicago. But my first personal experience beyond the borders of my native land occurred in 1925. In that year, at the invitation of Dr. Paul Monroe, a distinguished historian and student of comparative education, I became a member of the Philippine Educational Survey Commission, which made a study of the educational system of the Philippine Islands. After traveling by yacht to practically all the islands, we went up to Baguio in the mountains of Luzon, one of the most beautiful spots in the world, and wrote our report. On this trip I also visited China and Japan. Because of the role I played in this survey, I was invited, at the suggestion of Dr. Monroe, to come to Teachers College as associate director of the International Institute, of which he was director, an agency established with funds from the foundations to foster the interchange of ideas among educators, teachers, and students of the world. My acceptance of the invitation certainly marked a turning point in my life.

Each member of the staff of the institute was expected to study the language, the schools, and the basic social institutions of some country or region of the earth. Since no one had chosen the Soviet Union and since I had been interested in the Russian revolution through the years, I decided to fill the gap. In the summer of 1927 I made my first trip to the Soviet Union, traveling from Leningrad to Moscow to Tblisi to Nizhni Novgorod and other places. In the following years the study of the Soviet Union and communism became a major interest in my life. Moreover, as a boy in the public schools of Kansas I had been taught to regard the tsarist government as a peculiarly unenlightened and tyrannical despotism and to expect a revolution. Consequently, when the regime of Nicholas II collapsed in March, 1917, I hailed the event as a great victory for the cause of democracy and human freedom. After the seizure of power by Lenin and his Bolsheviks in November I was challenged by the proclaimed goals of the Soviet government to extend educational opportunities to all, to eradicate racial and national prejudices and hatreds, to prevent depressions, and to bring the economy, science, and technology into the service of all the people. At the same time, from the first I had grave doubts and misgivings about the dictatorship which shaped the course of the revolution. I hoped that these evils would weaken and disappear with the passing of the years. But the exact contrary happened. The dictatorship became ever more ruthless and assumed the totalitarian pattern of rule. It also became clear that, in spite of its professions, the Communist movement throughout the world is profoundly hostile to democracy and human freedom.

My interest in the Soviet Union, however, has continued down to the present. In 1929 I had a Ford car, Model A, sent from the factory in Michigan to Leningrad. During the months of June, July, August, September, and October I drove that car approximately six thousand miles through the Soviet Union west of the Urals, a large part of the time entirely alone—from Leningrad to Moscow to Kharkov and across the Caucasus Mountains and over the Black Sea to Odessa to Kiev and back to Moscow and on to Nizhni Novgorod. This experience was overwhelming in many respects and I was told in Moscow that no other person had attempted such a trip. I saw the backwardness of the Soviet Union during the first year of the First Five-Year Plan, which launched the program of industrialization that has transformed backward Russia into the second great power of the world. Most of the roads over which I drove my Ford were ungraded and I lived in the villages with peasants who in many cases had never seen an automobile. Consequently, when I returned to Moscow late in October about one o'clock in the morning, the tires for the rear wheels were tied on with ropes and the light bulbs were dead. At the same time, there was one aspect of that experience which I recall with pleasure. I found the Russian people everywhere extremely friendly and hospitable. A single illustration of this must suffice. On one occasion I spent the night in a rooming house belonging to two elderly ladies. When I went to my automobile in the morning to continue my trip, both of them came out to say good-bye. One of them gave me a bottle of milk, the other handed me a bouquet of flowers, and said: "I thank God that my eyes have at last rested on a foreigner."

On returning to New York in early January, 1930, I wrote my first full-length book on Soviet Russia. It was published in 1931 under the title *The Soviet Challenge to America* and with an opening chapter, "To Surpass America." Naturally this aroused quite a bit of criticism because every "sound thinker" knew that it was utterly impossible for a backward country ruled by a dictatorship to challenge America. One of the Hearst papers carried an editorial with the heading, "George Soviet Counts." The Soviet leadership also turned against me after my third long visit in 1936. In fact, my closest Soviet friend, Dr. Pinkevich, a leading educator who bid me good-bye at the railroad station at the end of December, was sent to a forced-labor camp in January and died there two years later. However, I am still hoping that we can live in peace and friendship with the Russian people.

I should add that my experience abroad has not been confined to the Soviet Union. In the twenties and the thirties I visited Britain, France, Belgium, Holland, Denmark, Switzerland, Austria, Germany, Poland, and Czechoslovakia. In 1946 I served on the Educational Mission to Japan to advise General MacArthur on the reconstruction of Japanese education to support democratic purposes. Although we probably didn't know what we were doing, it was a most interesting and educative experience. In the fifties and sixties

I lectured in Brazil, Venezuela, and Puerto Rico. Altogether I have given lectures in eleven countries. A basic conclusion which I draw from my experience around the world and with a great many students from other lands is that the age of narrow nationalism in education is closing and that, if the human race is to survive, what we need throughout the world is some form of *international* education—an education designed to promote peace, understanding, and friendship among all the races and nations of homo sapiens.

VII

During the course of my life I have been active in professional organizations and commissions at home. From 1929 to 1934 I was a member and from 1931 to 1934 research director of the Commission of the American Historical Association on the Teaching of the Social Studies in the Schools, which undertook a comprehensive study of the problem of civic education in the present fateful age. This also was a most interesting and challenging experience. The members of the commission, for the most part, were distinguished scholars, and among them was the great historian, Charles A. Beard, with whom I became very closely associated down to the time of his death in 1948. From 1936 to 1942 I was a member of the Educational Policies Commission of the National Education Association. This commission endeavored to formulate broad educational policies for the nation. During the Second World War I served as a member of the nationwide Committee on Education and National Defense. I have also served on many other commissions and am an emeritus member of the National Academy of Education. Perhaps I should add that I have held membership for years in the American Historical Association, the American Sociological Society, the American Academy of Political and Social Science, the American Association of University Professors, the National Society of College Teachers of Education, the John Dewey Society, the P.E.N. Club, and other learned societies. Perhaps I should add that in the early forties a friend and I launched the American Society of Former Coon-Hunters.

I have also been active in social and political affairs. Reared in the tradition of the American frontier, I have always regarded myself as a product and champion of our American democracy as outlined in the Bill of Rights and the Declaration of Independence. Sensing from early manhood the great dangers threatening that democracy due to the rise of our urbanized and industrialized society, I have ever sought to make organized education serve the purposes of democracy—democracy conceived both as social ends and as social means. In pursuing this course I have been bitterly opposed at times by totalitarians of all brands—left and right, foreign and domestic. The Fascist-minded have sometimes called me a "Communist," even as the Communist-minded have called me a "Fascist." In fact, like my people, I regard myself as a cross between a Jeffersonian Democrat and a Lincolnian Republican, struggling with the old problem of human freedom and equality in the age of science and technology. I enjoy surprising my students by telling them that I am a conservative, that I have striven throughout my life to "conserve our radical tradition." I have been a member of the American Civil Liberties Union for almost half a century and a member of its National Committee for approximately thirty years.

My "conservatism" is expressed in my decision to become a member of the American Federation of Teachers, an association of classroom teachers affiliated with the American Federation of Labor and carrying on the masthead of its publications the great slogan Education for Democracy and Democracy in Education. Doubtless I was influenced to some extent by studies which I had made in the twenties of the impact of social class on high school attendance and on the social composition of boards of education. These studies revealed clearly that our "common school" was controlled by the middle and upper classes and that the public high school, in spite of its phenomenal growth after 1890, remained down to 1920 largely a school for the sons and daughters of the more fortunate. It seemed to me, therefore, that the American Federation of Teachers would contribute to the democratization of our schools. In August 1939, at the convention of the federation in Buffalo, New York, I was elected president. And I was reelected in 1940 and 1941. The big issue in these elections was the elimination of organized Communist influence from the federation. This was accomplished in what came to be called the "First and Second Battles of Buffalo," the city where both conventions were held. After the conclusion of the "Second Battle," I calculated that I had had six hours of sleep out of ninety-six. As president I traveled from the Atlantic to the Pacific and from the Gulf of Mexico to the Canadian border, speaking at meetings of the locals of the federation. One thing impressed me greatly. I found elementary school teachers standing up and expressing their ideas and convictions at meetings of school boards and even Chambers of Commerce. I concluded that the federation was converting the school teacher into a human being and a citizen of our democracy.

All of this was in accord with my own social philosophy. For years I have told my students that our society has demanded that the teacher be an "idiot" in the original meaning of the term among the ancient Greeks, that is, a person who takes no part in community affairs. Yet we expect the teacher to teach citizenship to the members of the younger generation. These considerations led me to accept the chairmanship of the American Labor party in 1942, and I served for two years. Then in 1944 the more independent members of the party launched the Liberal party of New York State, which continues down to this day. In its mode of operation it is unlike any other party that I have ever known. As a general rule it does not nominate its own members to run for office. It waits for the two major parties to make their nominations and then selects the better one. However, occasionally it cannot accept either and nominates one of its own members. This happened in 1952 in the election for the United States Senate and I was chosen to run for that office. I accepted and went all over New York State speaking to audiences of great diversity. At the same time, I met my classes in Teachers College. One of my themes was criticism of the policies and activities of Senator Joseph McCarthy. In the election I received approximately five hundred thousand votes. Perhaps I should close this account of my political activity by stating that I have generally followed an independent course. In the presidential campaigns since I came of age I voted as follows: in 1912, for Theodore Roosevelt; in 1916, for Woodrow Wilson; in 1920, for James M. Cox; in 1924, for Robert M. LaFollette; in 1928, for Alfred E. Smith; in 1932, for Norman Thomas; in 1936, 1940, and 1944, for Franklin D. Roosevelt; in 1948, for Harry S. Truman; in 1952 and 1956, for Adlai E. Stevenson; in 1960, for John F. Kennedy; in 1964, for Lyndon B. Johnson; and in 1968, for Hubert H.

Humphrey. So, it would seem that I have been something of a maverick in politics, as well as in other spheres of activity, but always on the "left."

VIII

As I look back over my long, but to me brief, life I can see that the course of that life would have been profoundly different if certain events had not occurred. Of course, my life has been shaped by the obvious factors which included our American culture and my parents with their family heritage. Particularly important in my case were the geographical frontier, the rural household and neighborhood, the Judeo-Christian ethic, the democratic tradition, the warfare between science and theology, and, with the passing of the years, the transformation of our society and the annihilation of distance. But I would like to direct attention to a few particular events.

In the month of June 1907, when I was seventeen years of age, with my older brother and seven or eight other students at Baker University, I "shipped" out to a lumber camp in the Big Horn Mountains of Wyoming as a common laborer. My experience that summer was thrilling. I acquired some of the skills of the lumberjack, such as riding logs and breaking jams on the river. The morning I first attempted to ride the logs I fell into the ice-cold water of the mountain stream six times. Shortly after my arrival at the camp I became acquainted with three or four French-Canadian trappers who were there just for the summer. We became very good friends and I discussed with them the possibility of accompanying them back to Canada when the trapping season began in the autumn. They liked the idea, and so it seemed that my ambition from early childhood to spend my life as a trapper of fur-bearing animals was about to be fulfilled. But, unfortunately, I was fired in August and ordered by my boss to leave the camp. I had learned to ride logs down the flume and loved to do it. And I continued to do this after being ordered to stop it. This was the only time I was ever fired from a job and the event affected profoundly the course of my life. Instead of going to Canada with my friends, I went back home to Kansas to continue my formal education in Baker University.

The year of 1907 proved to be a fateful year for me as a result of a second event. During the Spanish-American War I became very much interested in our navy. Admiral Dewey's victory in Manila Bay had a tremendous impact on me. From the time of that event through the rest of my childhood and into my adolescence I watched the newspapers for reports on the launching of new warships. I became a specialist in this field, learning the name, the tonnage, and the armament of every ship in our navy. As a consequence, my commitment to trapping as a life career had a rival. I wanted to join the navy and see the world. In the autumn of 1907 I persuaded my father to write to the congressman representing our district in Kansas and ask him to give me an appointment to the Naval Academy in Annapolis. In response my father soon received a letter from him stating that the appointment had already been made but that he could give me an appointment to West Point. This, of course, did not interest me in the slightest degree. I had no desire to become a soldier and remain on the land. I wanted to sail the "seven seas" and experience the adventures of Columbus. And so again I turned back to Baker.

In my junior year my father urged and persuaded me to take the examination for the Rhodes Scholarship. The examination was rather severe, embracing Greek, Latin, mathematics, history, and some other subjects, but I soon received a card from Oxford University stating that I had passed the "Responsions" and would be admitted, if. . . . But here I encountered difficulties. Four colleges in the state of Kansas had qualified to participate in the competition, and the selections committee, to avoid charges of bias, had adopted the policy of rotating the scholarships. And it happened that the candidate from Baker had received the last one. But in 1913 the chairman of the committee wrote me a letter asking me if I would accept the scholarship. I imagine that I would have accepted it if I could have, but I had just married Lois Hazel Bailey in September. At that time a Rhodes scholar could not be a married man. Since this rule was changed recently, I have often wondered how different my life would have been if I had gone to Oxford. And back in 1913 I came to realize that marriage is a very important institution, even though Albion W. Small, head of the Department of Sociology at the University of Chicago, told me that I could not learn anything at Oxford that I could not learn at Chicago.

The very important event that probably changed the course of my career had its beginnings during my junior year in college. I was standing at a street corner in Baldwin when I saw a very attractive girl or young woman walking across the street. I soon discovered that she was a sister of a very good friend of mine, Herbert Bailey, who played quarterback on the varsity football team. I soon became acquainted with her and was greatly impressed with her beauty, talents, and character. Although I had always had girl friends, beginning with my first grade in the one-room country school, I had never seriously contemplated courtship and marriage. But now the situation was changed. I lost interest in all other girls, dated Lois Hazel Bailey practically every week, took her to many parties, and invited her to visit my parents out on the farm. Finally, in June 1911, when we were on a picnic on the banks of a stream about twelve miles from town, I proposed marriage to her and she accepted with a smile. This event put an end to my desire to become a trapper in Canada. Also it was responsible for my becoming a teacher. With the assistance of the chairman of the Rhodes Scholarship committee, I was invited to join the staff of the Sumner County High School in Wellington, Kansas. The following year (1912-13), as already reported, I became principal of the Peabody High School. Thus, for two years, being away from my parents, I had to make all decisions by myself. This was more than I could bear. Consequently, we were married on September 24, 1913, and life became much easier. Whenever I had to make a decision, I would go to my wife and she would always tell me what to do. On our golden wedding anniversary in 1963 I presented her with a dark blue banner with the following words in white letters: The Banner of Heroic Matrimony. I still have difficulty in understanding how she endured me for so many years! But I would like to add that we had two wonderful children, Esther and Martha; and I have always contended that the years when one's children are growing up are the "happiest years of life."

IX

Persons, as well as events, are always powerful influences shaping the life, the character, and the interests of every individual. Permit me, therefore, to mention briefly the roles of a few such persons in my life, in addition to my parents and other members of my family. The latter, of course, as already emphasized, constituted the most basic of these influences.

I shall begin with my teachers from the first grade in the country school to my last year in the graduate division of the University of Chicago. My experience may be unique, because I can only say that I liked every teacher with whom I studied. I cannot remember ever quarreling with any one of my scores of teachers in nineteen years of formal education. I recall today with affection my first teacher in the country school, Miss Stewart, under whom I made four grades in two years. At the end of the day she would often ask me to help her clean the room and then she would drive me to my home in her one-horse buggy. I really loved her, perhaps because she seemed to love me. And so it was in the town school, from the fifth grade through high school. In Baker University I had wonderful teachers who were both scholars and human beings. Limitations of space permit me to mention only a few of my major professors: Homer K. Ebright in Greek, O. G. Markham in Latin, Charles S. Parmenter in biology, Alice D. Porter in English literature, and Joseph K. Hart in philosophy. At the University of Chicago I was extremely fortunate. In the field of education there was Charles Hubbard Judd, head of the department and a truly distinguished psychologist, who was born in India of missionary parents and received his doctor's degree from the University of Leipzig in Germany. I should also mention Franklin Bobbitt in the field of the curriculum and Frank N. Freeman in psychology. In the social sciences I took courses with some of the foremost scholars of the land. Outstanding among them were Albion W. Small, head of the Department of Sociology; William I. Thomas, whose course in "Social Origins" was famous throughout the country; Carl Richmond Henderson, in the field of penology; Frederick Starr, an extraordinary character and teacher in anthropology; Charles E. Merriam, who came to be rated the dean of American political scientists; and Harold G. Moulton in economics, who, after some years, was chosen to head the famous Brookings Institution in Washington. After my first course with Dr. Moulton he called me into his office and offered me a fellowship in economics. I often wonder whether members of the younger generation today can be as fortunate as I was in the quality of their teachers, from the first grade through the university.

I owe a great deal to other persons, living and dead, who might also be called my teachers. I think, first of all, of John Dewey and Charles A. Beard. While I never enrolled formally in a course with either of them, they taught me a great deal. Before going to Columbia University in 1927 I had read their books, sometimes as textbooks. Shortly after arriving in New York, I became personally acquainted with John Dewey. We had many interests in common and worked together on committees and in the Liberal Party. I often quote the citation by the dean of the Faculty of Letters of the University of Paris when Dewey was awarded an honorary degree. With true insight the dean characterized him as "the most profound, most complete expression of American genius." And he was one of the most modest men I have ever known. Charles A. Beard was also a truly great man and scholar. As I have already stated, I came to know him personally when we served together on the Commission of the American Historical Association, beginning in 1929. With A. C. Krey, we were responsible for the writing of the *Conclusions and Recommendations.* From the very first we found that we shared many common concerns and interests. And he contributed greatly to my understanding of the history of our American democracy. We visited back and forth (he lived in New Milford, Connecticut) down to the time of his death in 1948. In fact, I was the last of his friends to see him before he started on his final journey. In several of his letters to me he referred to me as his "son." I was also influenced greatly by my many colleagues at Teachers College and Columbia University. I can only mention Jesse Newlon, John L. Childs, William H. Kilpatrick, William F. Russell, Harold Rugg, and F. Ernest Johnson. Then there were my friends in the Liberal party: David Dubinsky, chairman of the International Ladies Garment Workers Union; Alex Rose, chairman of the Cap, Hat and Millinery Workers Union; Harry Uviller, impartial chairman of the garment industry; and Matthew Levy, a distinguished lawyer and judge. Among noncontemporaries also there were many who influenced me through their writings. I would have to include, of course, the great prophets of Israel and the philosophers of ancient Greece and Rome. Among those of a more recent age I would include Charles Darwin, Karl Marx, Peter Kropotkin, William Graham Sumner, Herbert Spencer, Charles Horton Cooley, Edward Alexander Westermarck, Alexis de Tocqueville, and many others. And I should not omit my many brilliant students from all over the world from whom I learned a great deal. And I always liked them, even when they disagreed with me.

Another person whose name should be included in this list is the woman who was my personal secretary and research assistant throughout my career at Teachers College. I refer to Mrs. Nucia P. Lodge, who was born Nucia Perlamutter in St. Petersburg, Russia, in 1900. Her father was a distinguished lawyer who died just before the First World War. Her mother then brought her to America with two sisters. Shortly after arriving here, she took a master's degree at Clark University and served as a secretary for G. Stanley Hall. Then she went to Chicago and was employed by Charles Hubbard Judd as his personal secretary. It was there that I first met her. And, when she learned that I planned to make the study of Soviet education my major interest, she came to New York and assisted me for almost thirty years. She was very talented and had excellent command of several languages. This, of course, included the Russian language of which she had complete mastery. But it also included French which, as customary in privileged families in Russia at the time, she learned from a French nurse. She also had a fairly good command of German and several Slavic languages other than Russian. In my opinion few scholars ever had a more talented and industrious secretary and research assistant.

X

In spite of my activities in politics and social affairs, I have found time and energy to do a good deal of writing. I have written in whole or in major part twenty-nine or thirty books and monographs and several hundred articles for professional and popular magazines. Unfortunately, I have in my possession only about one-half of the books and perhaps ten or fifteen of the articles. I never thought that I would need them.

My first publication, according to my recollections, was a report in 1915 on the policies and programs of the North Central Association. The next was my doctoral dissertation, entitled "Arithmetic

Tests and Studies in the Psychology of Arithmetic." I took this subject at the suggestion of Dr. Judd, although I wanted to do research in the domain of educational sociology. After getting my degree, my studies and writings, with practically no exceptions, involved the relation of education to society and culture. I have already mentioned my monographs, published in the early twenties, which reported the results of my research into the impact of social class on educational opportunity and the control of the school. Also during this early period, while at the University of Chicago in the academic year 1926-27, I offered a course dealing with the subject of education and social forces. The result was a volume entitled *School and Society in Chicago*. In 1924, my colleague at Yale, James Crosby Chapman, and I published *Principles of Education* which was used widely as a textbook. My partner, who was a psychologist, was responsible for the psychological foundations and I for the social and cultural foundations of education. During the past year I found a copy of this book, which I had given to my mother in 1924, and was surprised to discover that I had used the expression, the "Great Society," ten times. Most of my later books directed attention to the transformation of our American society which was the result of the advance of science and technology. I would mention *Secondary Education and Industrialism*, the Inglis lecture at Harvard in 1929, *The Social Foundations of Education* in 1934, *Education and American Civilization* in 1952, and others.

In the 1930s I gave particular attention to the thesis that the school should assume responsibility for the improvement of our society, for the fulfillment of the age-long "promise of America," for bringing our actions into harmony with our professions. This philosophy was expressed most vigorously and even militantly in *Dare the School Build a New Social Order?*—published in 1932. Many persons who never read the book have criticized it on the grounds that the school not only should not but could not do this. On page 24 I wrote that "the school is but one formative agency among many, and certainly not the strongest at that." And on page 37 I defined the goal of the school in these words: "This does not mean that we should endeavor to promote particular reforms through the educational system. We should, however, give to our children a vision of the possibilities which lie ahead and endeavor to enlist their loyalties and enthusiasms in the realization of the vision. Also our social institutions and practices, all of them, should be critically examined in the light of such a vision." Other books dealing with the same theme are *The Schools Can Teach Democracy*, 1939; *The Education of Free Men in American Democracy*, 1941; *Education and the Promise of America*, 1945; and *Education and the Foundation of Human Freedom*, 1963. I should also mention in this connection *The Prospects of American Democracy*, 1938, which John Dewey appraised as follows: "Since the publication of this book, any one assessing the prospects for democracy in this country must reckon this book as a great asset on the favorable side, if only it is widely read and studied." I was also editor of *The Social Frontier*, a journal launched in 1934, which had a similar orientation. The title was derived from a realization that the "geographic frontier" was closed. Beginning in 1931, I outlined in detail a plan for launching at Teachers College a program entitled "Institute of Social Research." Dean Russell was very much interested in the projects as were several of the leading social scientists and philosophers at Columbia University. But we never succeeded in getting financial support from the board of trustees.

Perhaps I should close with a brief reference to my books dealing with the Soviet Union and communism. The total number was nine, including two which, for the most part, were translations. One of these books, *New Russian's Primer*, a translation, was a Book-of-the-Month Club selection in 1931. Another, *The Challenge of Soviet Education*, received the American Library Association Liberty and Justice Award. The jury "adjudged (it) the most distinguished book of 1957 in contemporary problems and affairs." And there was a prize of five thousand dollars. Naturally, my interest in the Soviet Union aroused substantial criticism in certain circles in the U.S.A. Also, some of my publications, notably *The Country of the Blind*, which attempted to tell the story of the purge of the intelligentsia following "The Great Patriotic War," was *not praised* in the Soviet Union.

XI

A concluding word. After fifty-five years of experience as a teacher in secondary and higher schools, I am convinced that teaching is the greatest of the professions in terms of service to our people and to all mankind. Also, I think that it is the most interesting and challenging of all occupations and ways of life—with the possible exception of trapping and hunting, unless one views the latter from the point of view of the animals. It is so interesting and challenging that I just could not retire when I was informed officially in June 1955 that I had finally served my term in Teachers College, Columbia University. And when I do retire completely and finally, I do not know what I shall do. However, since I believe in metempsychosis, I look forward to continuing my professional career on some other planet in the universe!

A BIOGRAPHICAL SUMMARY

George S. Counts. Born on December 9, 1889, near Baldwin City, Kansas.

Family. Married Lois Hazel Bailey, September 24, 1913. Children: Esther Mae, Martha Lou.

Education. Baker University, A.B., 1911; University of Chicago, Ph.D., 1916.

Occupational history. Head, Department of Education, Delaware College, Newark, 1916-18; professor of educational sociology, Harris Teachers College, St. Louis, 1918-19; professor of secondary education, University of Washington, 1919-20; associate professor of educational sociology, Yale University, 1920-24; professor, 1924-26; professor of education, University of Chicago, 1926-27; professor of education, Teachers College, Columbia University, 1927-56. Visiting professor: University of Pittsburgh, 1959; Michigan State University, 1960; Southern Illinois University, 1962—. Editor, *Social Frontier*, 1934-37.

Memberships and affiliations. Commission of the American Historical Association on the Teaching of the Social Studies in Schools, 1929-34 (research director, 1931-34); American Sociological Association; American Association of University Professors, John Dewey Society; Educational Policies Commission, 1936-42; American Federation of Teachers (president, 1939-42); National Commission, Civil Liberties Union, 1940—; American Labor party (New York State Chairman), 1942-44; Liberal party, 1955-59; National Academy of Education.

Awards. Teachers College medal for distinguished service, 1954.

Part II

Major Publications of George S. Counts

1. *Principles of Education* (with J. Crosby Chapman). Boston: Houghton Mifflin Co., 1924.
2. *The Selective Character of American Secondary Education.* Chicago: University of Chicago Press, 1924.
3. *The Social Composition of Boards of Education.* Chicago: University of Chicago Press, 1927.
4. *School and Society In Chicago.* New York: Harcourt, Brace & Co., 1928.
5. *The American Road to Culture.* New York: John Day Co., 1930.
6. *The Soviet Challenge to America.* New York: John Day Co., 1931.
7. *Dare the Schools Build a New Social Order?* New York: John Day Co., 1932.
8. *The Social Foundations of Education.* New York: Charles Scribner's Sons, 1934.
9. *The Prospects of American Democracy.* New York: John Day Co., 1938.
10. *The Schools Can Teach Democracy.* New York: John Day Co., 1939.
11. *The Education of Free Men in American Democracy.* Washington: National Education Association, 1941.
12. *America, Russia and the Communist Party in the Postwar World* (with John Childs). New York: John Day Co., 1943.
13. *Education and the Promise of America.* New York: Macmillan Co., 1946.
14. *I Want to Be Like Stalin* (with Nucia Lodge). New York: John Day Co., 1947. A translation of a Russian text on pedagogy with a long introduction by George S. Counts.
15. *The Country of the Blind* (with Nucia Lodge). Boston: Houghton Mifflin Co., 1949.
16. *Education and American Civilization.* New York: Teachers College, Columbia University, 1952.
17. *The Challenge of Soviet Education.* New York: McGraw-Hill Book Co., 1957.

18. *Khrushchev and the Central Committee Speak on Education.* Pittsburgh: University of Pittsburgh Press, 1959.
19. *Education and the Foundations of Human Freedom.* Pittsburgh: University of Pittsburgh Press, 1962.

Part III

George S. Counts: Educational Statesman

RAYMOND E. CALLAHAN

In this brief biographical sketch I want to try to do three things: First, I want to try to assess the role that George Counts played in American education; second, I want to discuss his ideas about education—his educational philosophy, if you will; and, third, I want to write about George Counts the man, as I have known him, first as his student and then as a fellow educator for the last twenty years.

My experience has been that labels or slogans, while useful, tend to be inadequate, especially when they are used to try to describe complex phenomena or intelligent, complex human beings. Still, I think that the label "Educational Statesman" comes close to capturing the essence of George Counts as a professional person. For more than forty years, from 1927 to the present, he has thrown his great ability and energy into the effort to improve American education and, through it, American civilization. In some ways, as I reread his works and as I think about them in the context of the history of American education in the twentieth century, I am tempted to say that he is the Walter Lippmann of education. He has Lippmann's penetrating insight and his ability to get to the heart of a matter and he has, like Lippmann, a gifted pen. But, perhaps because he is a professional educator, he is more of an advocate of policies. In his career he has been analyst, critic, and advocate of policies—necessary ingredients for statesmanship in any field.

But it would also be accurate to describe him as a teacher-scholar. Eminent psychologist Hadley Cantril has testified (in a letter to the NSSE editor) to Counts's great ability as a teacher and, especially, as a lecturer, and I am sure thousands of graduate students from Teachers College would concur in this testimony, as would the thousands of educators who heard him in the hundreds of speeches he gave at professional meetings all over the country. He is also a great teacher through his writings, and I personally think I have learned more from his books and articles than from his lectures or from our many conferences. It is true that the lectures and speeches and, especially, the conferences had a direct, personal, emotional quality that the written page cannot match. For example, there is no doubt that his great speech before the Progressive Education Association in April of 1932 left his audience stunned. But a lecture or a speech is a momentary thing even if one takes notes; a book has the potential, through reading and rereading and sober reflection and absorption, of having a more lasting impact. But, whether writing or speaking, he is a great teacher.

He is also a tremendous scholar. I suppose that from a technical standpoint his *The Challenge of Soviet Education* (1957) has to be ranked as his most scholarly work, representing as it did thirty years of study and research. (Talk about scholarship! Here was a man who in his middle thirties began the study, and attained mastery, of the Russian language and then continuously devoured the literature from the USSR.) As scholar and teacher he would consider himself (and I would consider him) a student of society, especially of American society and Russian society. He is not a researcher in the narrow sense of working intensely on highly specialized problems, e.g., in educational sociology. He has recognized and respected the necessity of such research. But his interest has been in the broad social and educational issues of his time. The closest he came to specialized empirical research was in his studies of the selective character of the American secondary school and of the social composition of school boards, both done in the early and middle twenties. Even in these studies, however, he was at least as much interested in considering what the data meant for educational policy as he was in reporting the findings. And this has been his style throughout his career. Research, reading, study, travel—he has engaged in and obviously enjoyed them all, but he has always been concerned, especially after 1932, with the implications of his knowledge for American education and American society.

As I consider his role in education from another angle, I think it would be appropriate to see George Counts as serving as a kind of conscience for American educators. A large part, if not the major part, of his work has been devoted to analyzing American society and American education and in pointing out where the real fell short of the ideal. His writing, especially in the thirties, has an impassioned quality, which, together with his dogged singleness of purpose, makes him appear not only an educator and teacher-scholar but also almost a missionary. His mission or the central purpose in his career has been to humanize human society, to make the world a place where men could live decently and with dignity. And for him America has a unique contribution to make. He frequently cites historian James Truslow Adams's contention that America's chief contribution to the heritage of the human race rests not in the field of science, or technology, or politics, or religion, or art, but in the creation of the "American Dream," which Counts describes as "a vision of a society in which the lot of the common man will be made easier and his life enriched and ennobled." In his writing and teaching he has continuously tried to spell out what needs to be done to help bring that "dream" closer to reality. And he has continuously urged educators at all levels to make their central task the creation of an America "more just and noble and beautiful than the society of today." In this endeavor he has not sought to develop a sense of guilt in American educators as he has criticized them (and his criticisms have never been personal). Rather, he seeks to inspire and encourage. He has continuously stressed that, while educators in the twentieth century have problems to face that are unprecedented in human history, they also have unprecedented means at their disposal to create a great and noble educational system and, through this, a great and noble society. In fact, an appropriate general title for all of his work could well be the one he gave to his Kappa Delta Pi lecture in 1945. The title was *Education and the Promise of America.*

Educational statesman, teacher-scholar, missionary—he has been all three at one time or another. But I think the weight has to go to the statesman role because he is more of an activist than the men we ordinarily think of as teacher-scholars, and he is more open-minded than the persons we ordinarily think of as missionaries. He has a faith, but he has not tried to jam it down anyone's throat. He asks his students and his readers to think with him and to contribute to the solution of America's problems. He has his own ideas, his own solutions, but his system is open and flexible, not closed and rigid. He insists, of course, that whatever programs Americans come up with, whether in education or in politics, they cannot ignore the reality of the interdependent industrial society in which they live, and he hopes they will accept and use the basic democratic values as their frame of reference.

In placing my emphasis upon George Counts as an educational statesman, I am assuming that a statesman would be engaged in the world of policy-making and of attempting to translate these policies into action. He has described in his "Autobiography" his work in prominent educational and political organizations and his connection with important commissions, such as the Commission of the Social Studies of the American Historical Association. I think his most impressive actions were, first, his successful fight, as president of the American Federation of Teachers from 1939 to 1942, to keep the Communists from gaining control of that organization; and second, his campaign for the U.S. Senate as the candidate of the Liberal party in New York State. In these efforts, of course, he stepped outside the classroom into the rough and tumble world of politics. But he was an activist, too, in the educational world, both in his teaching and writing, and this was especially so in the thirties.

It seems to me that there are three rather distinct periods in his career in which his behavior in his role as educational statesman has been markedly different. During the first period, in the twenties, his work is scholarly and analytical and, compared to what was to come later, only mildly critical. For example, the tone of his work *The American Road to Culture* (which I think is one of the most penetrating studies of American education ever written) is more one of disappointment and impatience than of criticism. But that mildness disappears in the second phase, in the thirties. Beginning with his powerful speech to the Progressive Education Association in 1932, he criticizes repeatedly the ineffectiveness of the American school and the weakness of the teaching profession. He charges educators (even the able ones) with a failure to develop a social philosophy, and he urges them to throw aside their timidity and engage in the task of building a great civilization. After World War II, in what I see as the third phase, his writing is forceful, but the militant tone is gone. In *Education and American Civilization* (1952), he is still analyst, critic, and advocate. The analysis is just as insightful in these volumes as in his earlier work, and the educational program he proposes is just as revolutionary, but it is presented in a moderate tone.

Why the dramatic changes in his actions from the twenties to the thirties, and then the apparent mellowing after 1945? There were, I think, two reasons for his shift to a militant stance in the thirties. The first and most obvious was the development of the Great Depression. George Counts was too intelligent, too well-educated, too sensitive to human beings to accept that catastrophe with tranquility. He knew there was nothing inevitable about it. He knew there was no reason why millions should be hungry in a country that could produce all the food the people could eat. He knew there was no reason why fifteen million men should be unemployed. The whole thing was stupid. He worried about the needless human suffering he saw around him, and he also feared his beloved democracy might fall if the country continued to drift without direction. The great question in a modern industrial society, he said, was whether man could control the machine. His answer was that of course he could but it would take courage, intelligence, and imagination, and he did not see much of these qualities in either politics or education. I think the other reason for his aggressive, militant action in the early thirties was that he had seen at firsthand what the Russians were doing. He had visited the USSR in 1927 and again in 1929. He was impressed by the effort the Russians were making to control the machine and to make it serve all the people. He was impressed with their attempt to use human intelligence to plan the economy. And he was impressed by the enthusiasm and the dedication he had seen, especially in the leaders. It was clear that many of the Russian leaders had a dream, and they were working to make it come true. The American scene he saw when he returned late in 1929 was just the opposite on every point. The machine was benefiting the privileged few. There was no plan, no leadership. The country seemed paralyzed. And Progressive educators were discussing the child-centered school! No wonder he boiled over.

I think that his change to a more moderate style (not program) after 1945 is understandable. Free men, and especially the British and the Americans, had shown that they cherished freedom and would fight for it. They had beaten the Fascists. And by 1952 (when

Education and American Civilization appeared) it looked as though the United States was learning to cope with its economic problems, providing some assurance that the terrible days of 1930 would not occur again. It is true that by 1952, although the domestic scene looked better, the world situation looked bleak, and he was certainly deeply concerned about it. Perhaps the mellowing was simply a result of his growing older.

In conclusion, then, it is my considered judgment that any historian who will take the trouble to read George Counts's work and who will study his professional activities from 1918 to 1968 will agree that he deserves the label "Educational Statesman." This will be especially true of the historian has even a mildly liberal point of view. From a conservative point of view, of course, the judgment will be different. He will be described (and he has been described) as a Communist sympathizer, a Socialist, a dangerous radical, a fanatic, and, by those inclined to be more friendly, as an unrealistic utopian. But, looking back from 1970, I think the statesman verdict will predominate. This would not have been quite as true in 1932 or 1935 or 1940. In the thirties, in the midst of battle, educators were usually either enthusiastically with him or vigorously against him. It was hard to be neutral about George Counts. Of course, the hostility and the fear he engendered in those years were partly a result of his praise of and hope for the Russian experiment at a time when the Communists and communism were hated and feared. It was also due to his forthright criticism of American society and American education. Nobody likes to be criticized, even impersonally, and certainly not in public, and I can imagine that there were very many members of the Progressive Education Association (even some who agreed with him) who resented his remarks. Then, too, his programs were pretty far out (radical if you were unfriendly, visionary if you were friendly) and certainly controversial. Despite all this, he was appointed to the Educational Policies Commission of the NEA in 1936, and he wrote some of that group's major policy statements. And, in 1939, he was elected president of the American Federation of Teachers. So even at the peak of the hostility against him he was honored by his profession. Certainly those who so honored him recognized his statesmanlike qualities.

II

Some of the major elements in the educational philosophy of George Counts have already been alluded to, and John Childs, who knows him well, has written an excellent statement of his educational philosophy.[1] Counts is a pragmatist in the Deweyan tradition and he shares Dewey's great faith: faith in human beings, and especially in educated human beings. Writing in 1962, he said, "the truly critical mind is one of the most precious resources of a free society. At the same time such a mind must be highly disciplined. It must be armed with knowledge and understanding, and perhaps with a modicum of humility and wisdom."[2] And although he recognizes the limitations of the school, he also views it as an institution with great potential. But to realize this potential the school has to have a special quality. Throughout his career, but especially after 1932, he has repeatedly issued the following warning—a warning which also spells out a major theme (if not the major theme) in his philosophy:

> We must abandon completely the naive faith that the school automatically liberates the mind and serves the cause of human progress. In fact, we know that it may serve any cause, that it may serve tyranny as well as freedom, ignorance as well as enlightenment, falsehood as well as truth, war as well as peace, death as well as life. It may lead men and women to think they are free even as it rivets upon them the chains of bondage. Education is indeed a force of great power, particularly when the word is made to embrace all of the agencies and organized processes for molding the mind, but whether it is good or evil depends, not on the laws of learning, but on the conception of life and civilization which gives it substance and direction. In the course of history education has served every purpose and doctrine contrived by man. If it is to serve the cause of human freedom, it must be explicitly designed for that purpose.[3]

And the conception of civilization which he advocates is a civilization based on and devoted to the democratic values.

1. *American Pragmatism and Education* (New York: Henry Holt & Co., 1956).

2. *Education and the Foundations of Freedom* (Pittsburgh: University of Pittsburgh Press, 1962), p. 83.

3. Ibid., p. 54.

He has labored throughout his career to educate Americans concerning the nature of the democratic creed which he believes provides the basis for a great and noble society. In his great work *Education and American Civilization* (1952) his purpose is "an effort to develop a conception of American education which will support the values of free society in the present troubled age as effectively and vigorously as the educational conceptions of the totalitarian states support the purposes of despotism." He seeks to achieve this end through "an analysis in historical perspective of the broad features of our American civilization, an exploration of the dynamics of industrial society, an examination of the major realities of the contemporary epoch, and an affirmation of the values which should guide us in the rearing of the young in the coming years." Then he repeats his basic theme. The book, he says, is "based upon the assumption that an education always expresses a conception of some living civilization and that a great education must express a great conception of civilization." Then he adds a sentence which contains the essence of his philosophy. The book, he says, is "based . . . on the conviction that our American civilization contains the elements out of which such a conception of civilization can be fashioned."

To the cynic these words probably sound like the words of a naive idealist. George Counts was an idealist, but he was not naive. He was (and is) a gentle man without a trace of bitterness or hostility in him, but he was a realist. He had lived through and had seen the stupidity and tragedy of World War I, of the Harding and Coolidge administrations, and of the Great Depression. Furthermore, he was a keen student of history, and almost every page of his writing provides evidence of his awareness of man's brutality and ignorance and insensitivity. He saw, and pointed out in 1924, the essentially undemocratic character of the American secondary school, which is all too evident today. He saw the need in 1927 for broader representation on school boards, which is one of the burning issues of our time. He pointed out repeatedly, beginning in the twenties, the immoral, undemocratic, indefensible discrimination against and neglect of our minority groups, and especially of the Negro. As early as 1938 he pointed out the violent aspects of the American tradition and warned that we would be in trouble if we ignored them in the education of our children. No, he was not naive. He saw the problems in America. But he also saw the potential for greatness. For my part, I do not think there is a better historical analysis of the American heritage and of American values than that contained in part two and part four of *Education and American Civilization.* And in part five of this volume George Counts spells out the dimensions of his educational program. I think the chapter titles will convey the essence of the program. They are as follows: "The Resources for a Great Education," "Education for Individual Excellence," "Education for a Society of Equals," "Education for a Government of Free Men," "Education for an Economy for Security and Plenty," "Education for a Civilization of Beauty and Grandeur," "Education for an Enduring Civilization," and "Education for a World Community."

But George Counts did more than provide a great vision for American educators. He understood that men and women, and especially young men and women, needed something to live and work for—something to give meaning to life. Throughout his career he urged teachers to enlist the energy and talents of students in the task of building a great civilization. And perhaps he had some influence. The students who went to New Hampshire and Wisconsin in the spring of 1968 to work for Eugene McCarthy and many of those who led the moratorium in October of 1969 appeared to me as though they had the idea in mind of using their energy and talents in the great social tasks.

What kind of a man is George S. Counts? Physically, he is about six feet tall and of a trim and muscular build. When I met him for the first time in 1949, he was sixty and had a full head of red-gray hair and wore a mustache. He wore metal rimmed glasses, and smoked a pipe, which must have been constantly going out for he seemed to be continuously engaged in relighting it. He must have been powerfully built as a youth, for at sixty and even at seventy-five he gave the impression of great physical strength. He has enjoyed excellent health, in general, throughout his life, and has great energy and a zest for life that is remarkable. He is still strong and active and eager to discuss his favorite subjects—education and world affairs. And in these discussions, as in his classes, the mood is never entirely a deadly serious one. For George Counts has a great sense of humor; he loves to tell stories and he has quite a repertoire.

He is a tremendously hard worker (as his literary production alone would indicate) and I think he loves his work. In the course of preparing this essay, I have given a good deal of thought to the question of the forces that have motivated him. How does one account for the prodigious amount of work the man has done? He didn't even slow down when he retired from Columbia University at the age of sixty-five, and he is still working hard at the age of eighty! My hunch is that there were two major factors. The first and most obvious is that he is a product of the midwestern version of the Protestant ethic. If he didn't use the McGuffey Readers in school, he used books like them. Besides, the same values (especially the importance of work) were being stressed and put into operation by his family. He states it in his "Autobiography"—a man was judged by what he did. George Counts grew up expecting to work hard, and everyone important around him expected him to work hard. How else could one get ahead? I think the other major factor is that his work in education has given him a purpose in life which has transcended his own personal ambition and welfare. I think George Counts, with his great ability and energy, would have been successful at any career, e.g., farming, law, politics, or business. But he found in his work in education a significance capable of fully engaging all his great gifts because he has believed it could make a difference in preserving and even improving the country which he loves.

George Counts is a hardworking professional but he is not a slave to his work. He loves his family and has spent a lot of time with them. He also loves and enjoys the good life. He appreciates good food and good bourbon. He also loves good company, and he has always had very many good friends. As I think about it, I realize that he is one of the most gregarious men I have ever known. He even seemed to enjoy professional meetings! But he has the knack, apparently, of balancing concentration and hard work on the one side with recreation and relaxation on the other. Let me give an example. After I graduated from Columbia, where George Counts was my adviser, I was invited and stayed several times with Dr. and Mrs. Counts at their New York apartment. During the week the routine was always the same. He would rouse me out of bed no later than seven o'clock and he would be in his office by eight, ready to work. In the evening dinner was served late, but not too late, and always after a couple of drinks. (Mrs. Counts is a marvelous cook and a very gracious hostess.) The meal would be leisurely and long with lots of conversation—a pattern of behavior he might have developed as a result of his experience in Russia. There would always be an after-dinner drink to go with what to me were stimulating and enjoyable conversations. But somehow, as I remember, we were all in bed by 10:30 or 11:00 P.M. to be ready for the next day's work. I am sure that he was forced to vary this schedule frequently, but my guess is that he maintained it most of the time he was at home. So he has really enjoyed the good life, but he has not let it interfere with his work. On the contrary, his ability to relax and enjoy life has probably enabled him to return to his work refreshed. I think this quality plus his great ability and energy helps to explain his long and brilliant career as an educator.

I wish that space permitted me to tell what it was like to study under George S. Counts. I can only allude to his endless patience with his students, the sense he gave of always having time to spare for us, and the encouragement he gave us to do some worthwhile work. I think he has wanted to train all his students in such a way that they would clearly see everything that was wrong with the world but, far from being discouraged, would go forth with determined and permanent optimism regarding their ability to change things. To just the extent that he has succeeded, his students will resemble him, for a clear grasp of all the wrongs of our society and an incurable optimism about the future are the very essence of his personality.

CHAPTER VI

Arthur I. Gates

Part I

An Autobiography

The majority of my ancestors back through several generations were similar in their characteristics and movements. They had migrated to New England mainly from England and Scotland and moved slowly westward to Pennsylvania, on to the Illinois region, and then to the northern plain states. They were predominately middle-class Protestants—farmers, storekeepers, traders, real estate dealers, with a scattering of preachers, teachers, musicians, minor politicians, and brewers. The most frequent surnames were Gates, Gaylord, Truman, and the like. My father's education was interrupted and his parent's occupational progress was upset by the Civil War. My father joined the Union Army at a little less than the minimum age for enlistment. After the end of the war he moved about the Middle West for a time, sampling several occupations. During this period he met my mother who, with a young son, had lost her husband. Soon thereafter my father decided to enter the lumber industry then flourishing in the northern plain states, a decision soon followed by marrying my mother and moving to Minnesota. Soon after my birth on September 22, 1890, in this state, my parents decided to join a large lumbering company's venture in northwestern California.

In 1892 my family, then, including two older brothers, settled down near a small town, Fortuna, in the heart of the northwestern California redwood belt. My father built a house on a six-acre plot about a mile and a quarter from the town, on the edge of a seemingly boundless redwood forest. He pursued a variety of assignments with a nearby large lumber company until he retired.

My mother told me that I learned to read with a bit of help from her soon after my third birthday. I entered school nearly a year late since my birthday came about two weeks after the fall term opened. Suffering from lack of occupation during school hours, I began early to engage in minor mischief, until one discerning teacher allowed me to spend some time daily in the "library," a dark attic room, really a storeroom, rarely open to anyone except teachers. Shortly after entering the third grade, I organized and became the captain of a sandlot baseball team, which became a joyful enterprise through the seventh grade. We played similar teams in all the nearby towns.

During these early years I helped take care of the home garden, the berry patch and fruit trees, chickens, cow, and "buggy horse." The activities were all very pleasant except two—the task of catching the horse when she felt frisky with three acres of meadow in which to dash about, and a chore which made me resolve never to be a farmer—cleaning the big chicken coop. Even with these duties, I usually took a half-time job during the summer—picking berries or fruit, splitting redwood stovewood, weeding fodder beets or corn on nearby farms.

The year before I entered the small high school which had only recently become a public institution, I was hired by the elementary school principal to do all sorts of work after school and on Saturdays in the insurance and real estate business which he conducted on the side. Shortly after I entered high school, which didn't keep me very fully occupied, I was offered another job by the owners of a "general merchandise" store during all the time I could spare from school and full time during the summer. The owners of this large store, the Friedenbachs, pioneer California emigrants from Germany, were a marvelously warm and helpful family. The work, which I kept up until I entered college, was one of the most satisfying and rewarding experiences of my lifetime. While in high school, I largely administered the grocery, men's furnishing, and hardware departments, made the window displays, wrote the advertisements and sales booklets, as well as serving as clerk.

During my third high school year, encouraged by the editor and the very intelligent typesetter of the local weekly newspaper, I began to write news items and feature reports for their paper and for a daily paper published in the county seat twenty miles away. My daily contacts with a wide range of people and events in the store made it easy for me to pick up items to report. I found the editors of both papers more exacting than any school teacher I ever had. They gave me, along with frequent headaches, an apprenticeship that helped me to support myself in college.

Teachers in the local schools were exacting, and, although I was a mischief-maker in both elementary and high school, they were all generously helpful to me. The principal of the then small high school, "Professor" P. S. Inskip, who came to this small isolated school from England after the death of his wife, was, I came later to realize, one of the most highly cultured, well-informed, and supportive human beings I have ever met. I shall never forget his talk with me after I had messed up my first debate in my freshman year while trying to give it verbatim from memory. The tact and understanding he showed resulted in my determination to become a good debater. Nor will I forget the obvious joy he revealed when, in my senior year, I won the individual debating championship of the county schools.

Before I graduated from high school I was faced with the necessity of making a vocational decision. Three opportunities, all unexpected, opened up. In that day the king of the sports and of summer entertainment in my part of the world was baseball. The players on intertown and intersectional professional teams were the popular heroes. Just before my graduation I was offered a surprising salary to play professional ball. Almost on the same day I received notice that I had been awarded a small scholarship to attend the University of California at Berkeley. A tempting offer was the third, a proposal to continue with Friedenbach's general store with the prospect of soon becoming a partner. Mr. Inskip and my high school teachers overcame any reluctance I might have had to give up this opportunity. Actually, attending the university was the course I really wanted to take.

I entered the university in vocational uncertainty. My friends and former teachers had suggested the law, journalism, education, medicine, and business administration. All appealed to me. I took two of the excellent "vaudeville" courses offered to help a student make a choice. In one of these, a series of units on both the physical and the social sciences, I listened with great curiosity to George M. Stratton's polished lectures concerning what psychology was all about. I was fascinated. I asked to take my half-dozen "laboratory sessions" in this field. Here I was taken in hand by Warner Brown who encouraged me to pursue further work, which I did. This was for me a very important action. At the end of my sophomore year I was offered the job of student assistant in the department. I promptly became a major in psychology and served as assistant from my junior year until I left after two years of graduate study to complete my work elsewhere.

During my first two years at Berkeley I seized upon opportunities to continue some of my former interests. I became a freshman reporter and editorial worker for the *Daily Californian*, the college newspaper, a post I gave up early in the second year when I tried more lucrative work as a free-lance writer for a miscellany of publications. I also tried out for the freshman debating team for which about forty contestants appeared. I "made" the team, but we lost our final major contest, a debate with the sophomore team which contained an extraordinarily adroit performer. I started "fall" practice with the freshman baseball squad, but found it demanded more time than I could spare. I spent a day now and then as clerk or advertising writer for stores within commuting distance. Early in my first year I had joined one of the campus house clubs, which a couple of years later became a chapter of a national fraternity. During my junior year I became the manager of the chapter house and directed all its business affairs, a post I held until the end of my first graduate year.

I took a year off after completing my sophomore year to try to build up a better financial status and to think about my future plans. I spent this period working during the day in the Fortuna store and during the evenings until midnight or later writing for a nearby daily paper and various other publications. The psychology department and the fraternity kept the jobs available to me until I returned.

When I returned to college, I took a course with Professor Alexis Lange, a former professor of English, who had been made director of the School of Education. What he lacked in familiarity with the professional side of education was compensated for by frequent appearances of other more practical members of his staff and by his own extraordinary wit, charm, and warm concern about the welfare of his students. In my senior year I took more work in education, unwittingly thereby accumulating enough credits to meet the minimum needed to qualify as a charter member of Lambda Chapter of Phi Delta Kappa. Later, joint meetings of this chapter with the Stanford group led to my making the acquaintance with the Stanford staff, among them Ellsworth Cubberley and Lewis M. Terman. Each of these men offered me a post at Stanford within a few years after I had taken my doctorate, but I decided to stay at Columbia, perhaps mainly because of the greater novelty and challenge it then offered.

When I began my work as assistant, the psychology department had a relatively small offering of formal courses at the advanced level. Warner Brown and shortly an additional young instructor conducted a number of courses in the well-equipped experimental laboratory, and George M. Stratton took care of most of the large lecture courses in his admirably polished and charming manner. As his assistant, I set up the apparatus for his demonstrations, took rolls, kept class records, and read the examination papers. I worked more intimately with Warner Brown, a superbly thorough and exacting laboratory experimentalist. One of the most thrilling intellectual experiences of my lifetime was that of conducting subjects through a series of nearly thirty tests of "suggestibility" which Brown had developed. The subjects were volunteer students examined singly. Each was told, for example, that he or she would be given a series of tests to determine how slight a sensory stimulus he could detect. Among them was a test to determine the lightest touch on the concealed palm, the faintest odor, or the weakest taste of sweet, sour, or bitter. I was astonished and fascinated by the range and variety of the students' responses and especially by the very high degree of error—the alleged effects of suggestion. A student might swear that he had been shocked by an electric current when, after the "now" signal, the apparatus clicked as in all trials but the current was not turned on. Or he might describe the color and shape of an image on the darkroom screen when none was projected. Before the experiments were over, Brown approved of my adding a few informal tests which I had arranged to reveal the exceptional undependability of the subjects' reports about their bodily and organic sensations. One test I gave up in hurry and fright when a student who declared he felt a suggested burning in his stomach after swallowing a spoonful of distilled water shortly reported great distress to the college physician. For a few hours until reassured, I feared that my career as a psychologist had come to an end.

I was advised to study largely on my own from the middle of my junior year. I surveyed carefully the major works of the world's leading psychologists available in English or German—such as those of the German leaders Wilhelm Wundt, H. von Helmholtz, and Ernst Meumann; the translated French reports of Alfred Binet and H. Bernheim; and the publications of Englishmen such as E. B. Titchener (later at Cornell) and of many Americans, especially William James, James McKeen Cattell, R. S. Woodworth, Charles H. Judd, L. M. Terman, and E. L. Thorndike.

Brown advised me to follow what was then a rather unusual program for an undergraduate student. He suggested that I read more and attend lectures less, mainly because I could cover so much more ground. He urged me to avoid becoming too tied down to books, however, and to engage in a variety of more practical explorations such as giving Binet intelligence tests to different kinds of children and adults, talking with psychiatric cases, and investigating by laboratory and clinical techniques other exceptional individuals. Among those I studied was an overconfident trumpet medium (in which Brown joined), the world's champion rifle shooter, and youngsters being investigated by the San Francisco Juvenile Court.

But Brown's most important innovation resulted from his belief that study and experience in research should come very early and not, as was then and even today is the usual practice, very late in one's program. He told me to begin at once to study the major methods of research then employed in psychology and to learn how to use them, including what I could master of the statistical method being introduced in America mainly by Cattell and Thorndike at Columbia. I was advised definitely that I should be ready to launch, at the beginning of my senior year, one or more pieces of research. His view was that a major question about pursuing a career as a college teacher of psychology was whether one had a real interest in and aptitude for research and the sooner one found out the better. Accordingly, early in my senior year I presented to Brown a proposal for several investigations. He gave me free choice, but I followed his tip not to undertake a couple of my early choices because he realized that they were too large or too subtle for me to handle at that time.

I undertook two lines of research, one a typical laboratory study of the physical and physiological symptoms of students as they went through several typically exasperating sessions in learning to trace figures shown only in a mirror. The other larger enterprise embodied a research pattern that I used frequently in later years—a combination of group tests or experiences yielding data which could be analyzed by statistical methods followed by relatively extended laboratory, observational, or "clinical" study of some or all of the cases individually.

I finished these studies late in the spring of my senior year and wrote four reports which were submitted to Brown at the end of the term. Three of them were later published.[1] The report of the "mirror-drawing" study was quite properly never published.

During the following two years of graduate study I continued a similar program of work. I served as manager of the fraternity house for one more year, but greatly reduced my free-lance writing. My work as departmental assistant was widened. I arranged my own program of study and undertook several pieces of research. I became gradually more and more attracted to the work of Cattell, Woodworth, and Thorndike at Columbia, which was then widely regarded as the leader of American universities in psychology. Almost at the same time in the spring of my second year I was offered a fellowship at Stanford by Terman and a choice of a fellowship or teaching assistantship at Columbia. I chose the assistantship at Columbia. There I became responsible primarily to Cattell, but served several departmental needs and taught the graduate course in experimental psychology. One of my most difficult jobs was getting ready various complex pieces of apparatus for Cattell to demonstrate before his graduate seminar class. Many of these were unfamiliar, unique inventions of Cattell (including de-

1. In the *University of California Publications in Psychology*, Vol. I, No. 5, 1916, pp. 323-44; No. 6, pp. 345-50; and Vol. 2, No. 1, 1916, pp. 1-156.

vices for observing and recording visual perception) which, because of long use, were inclined to be balky. Woe descended like a cloudburst on any assistant who failed to make Cattell's apparatus work properly during a demonstration. Professor A. T. Poffenberger, youngest of the psychology staff at that time, and one of the warmest, friendliest, and most helpful persons I have ever known, saved my professional life on numerous occasions.

I did not enroll in but was permitted to visit freely in several courses outside the department. One was with anthropologist Franz Boas, another with John Dewey. Since Dewey's course came at an inconvenient time for me, I heard him less often than I liked. I saw more of him informally a few years later. I had hopes of taking considerable work with Thorndike at Teachers College. When I called at his office I was surprised when, instead of suggesting that I take his "advanced" educational psychology or his course in mental measurement, or both, he advised me to take his course that was open to all Teachers College students, the "Psychology of the School Subjects." He stated that his work in this field would be more novel to me because he had published very little of it. He was right. It was new, ingenious, exceedingly interesting, and often puzzling to me. I remember that when he began to talk about teaching reading, he mentioned the term "phonics," which I didn't understand. There are many persons who, years later, have insisted that this is still the case.

Early in the year I discussed the choice of a dissertation problem with my advisers. I showed them some of the data I had gathered in California during the preceding year. They all seemed chiefly interested in some hunches I had developed about the strikingly different mental activities which appeared among children when they were engaged in trying to learn, in one case, by reading and rereading material in comparison with those which appeared when after the first reading they recalled as much as they could, and reread only when their memory failed. I reported that my data seemed to conflict with the learning by "repetition" idea and to suggest the tremendous importance of restructuring the complex learning procedure at every step. They suggested too the importance of emphasizing the techniques of learning, of mastering the "tricks of the trade" as one went along in contrast to mere review, mere "stamping in the bonds." I had no intention of trying to offer this collection of data as the basis of my dissertation. Cattell, however, asked me what I would like to do next to round out this study. I said I would like to conduct extensive laboratory tests and observations of and conferences with more expert and sophisticated subjects, such as graduate students in psychology already experienced in self-analysis and "introspection." To my surprise, I was told after the staff completed their private review that they all approved of my adding these studies to my present data and of my trying to complete my work for the doctorate in the following June, instead of a year later, as I had expected. This I managed to do.

My dissertation, given what I now regard as a very poor title, "Recitation as a Factor in Memorizing," was approved by the committee consisting of Cattell (chairman), Woodworth, Thorndike, and Poffenberger. During the spring term Cattell offered me a summer job doing editorial work on his book *American Men of Science* and his several professional journals, including the recently launched *School and Society*. Soon thereafter Thorndike rendered me utterly speechless by offering me a place on his staff at Teachers College. When I stuttered that I had never taught school a day in my life, he arose with a broad grin, saying, "Neither did I."

And then the country became deeply involved in World War I. Thorndike, Terman, Guy M. Whipple of Cornell, and others shortly persuaded the national administration to launch for the first time a wide program of psychological services. This is the group that developed the famous Army Alpha and Army Beta Intelligence Tests, the Army Personality Inventory (mainly the work of Woodworth), and other classification devices. Thorndike was asked to become chairman of the Committee on Classification of Personnel, which he agreed to do providing he served as a civilian. Appointments as commissioned lieutenants were available to persons who had received a Ph.D. in psychology. When I reported to Thorndike in the late spring that I felt I should apply for a commission, he suggested that I first talk it over with Cattell and Woodworth. When I met them, Cattell told me bluntly that Thorndike would accept the assignment as chairman of the committee only if someone would take much of the teaching load off his shoulders, and that, unless I felt that I could as a lieutenant be of greater service to the country than Thorndike would, I should not apply for the commission. Needless to say, I hurried to tell Thorndike I would remain at Teachers College.

My summer at Cattell's mountaintop residence and business offices in the Hudson Valley was richly rewarded. He had long fathered the American Association for the Advancement of Science. He supported all movements in psychology with the exception of Freudianism and psychoanalysis in other forms. A brilliant laboratory investigator, as his early work on visual, especially word, perception in Wundt's laboratory attested, he was also the first to promote in America the statistical method to which Galton had introduced him in England. Although he admired the "system builder" type of psychologist, especially William James, whose student Woodworth he appointed to the Columbia department, and Thorndike, whom he induced James E. Russell to employ at Teachers College, he was somewhat skeptical of the value of most systems and never developed one! He defined psychology behavioristically —"Psychology is what psychologists do." He greatly admired top-notch philosophers, especially the converted psychologists James and Dewey. I think he regarded Thorndike as I did—as the most inventive and versatile psychologist of his generation. He was a very strict perfectionist possessed of a piercing, caustic wit which made life miserable for many, notably President Nicholas Murray Butler, whom he regarded as a bit pompous. I thought of Cattell as a very loving father, but a quite naughty child. I developed a great affection for him.

When I took up quarters at Teachers College, having taken there only one of Thorndike's courses, I was given a first-level course in educational psychology and shared with Thorndike his "Advanced Educational Psychology" and his "Psychology of the School Subjects." He asked me to take a desk immediately behind him in his office and I assisted him, as best I could, in many of his arduous duties as chairman of the very important committee on personnel. I worked on copy for tests, analyzed all sorts of data, wrote up tentative reports, and supervised considerable experimental work and testing in the New York area, especially the trial runs of tests on factory workers, automobile drivers and repairmen, machine operators, etc. I suffered in teaching the Teachers College students who were almost all experienced teachers, administrators, and specialists, and older than I. I remember one large school principal of about forty years of age who, during a lecture I was giving on child development, stated in a loud and confident voice, "Young man, when you get a little older and have a few children of your own, you won't make such foolish statements as those!"

During the war I started little research or writing on my own, but I did try to achieve some understanding of professional education and the role I might play in Teachers College. I got well acquainted with a number of the college leaders—Dean James E. Russell, Paul Monroe, George Strayer, William Kilpatrick, Henry Johnson, and many others. Thorndike was always encouraging and helpful but anxious that I follow my own inclinations. I do not recall that he ever suggested I explore any particular field especially, except a rather casual comment that he felt that the study of learning in the case of the school subjects would be as rewarding as he found it difficult and complex.

In the fall of 1919 I noted in the sizable course in advanced psychology which I shared with Thorndike a girl who was obviously younger, more vivacious, and more beautiful than anyone else in the room. I sighed inwardly as I thought that she would probably turn out to be one of the youngsters who occasionally enrolled in the course because of convenience or curiosity and that, after the first written examination, I would have to carry out Thorndike's request to ease her out. When the results of the first objective tests were ready, I was astonished to discover that she had the top score. I found out soon that she was Georgina Stickland, a Phi Beta Kappa student at Barnard, who had just been asked to serve as assistant to Professor H. L. Hollingworth, head of the Department of Psychology. I soon encountered her often at psychology affairs and found out she was shortly to get her Ph.D. from the tough Columbia department at the then unheard of age of twenty-two. Having fallen in love with her completely, I found as I pursued her that her social charm, grace, and warmth at least equalled her intellect. After she agreed to marry me, I remarked to my two roommates that not only did I adore her but I realized that if I didn't make a go of it professionally, she certainly would!

After receiving her doctorate, she was appointed instructor in psychology at Barnard. She continued at Barnard after we were married in 1920 and was soon made assistant professor, a post she kept on a full-time basis until our first child, a boy, was born. She went on half time until soon after our daughter was born, when she resigned. Needless to say, she has been of inestimable help to me professionally as well as a perfect partner in every other way.

Our son, Robert Gaylord, born October 7, 1929, went through the college's Horace Mann Elementary and Lincoln High schools, then to Columbia College, and finally to the Columbia School of Engineering, where he took a doctor of science degree in a combination of mechanical engineering and metallurgy. He is now engaged in research in the research center of a large industrial corporation. Our daughter, Katherine Blair, born January 15, 1934, went to the same elementary and high schools until the latter closed, after which she went to other private high schools, then through Vassar College, and, after a year spent in Oxford on a Fulbright Fellowship, returned to take a Ph.D. degree in the Harvard-Radcliffe program in English literature. She has since been teaching English in a liberal arts college. Both of our children are married.

As the pressure of the war demands began to ebb, I realized it was high time for me to consider thoroughly what I should undertake to do in the future. Probably the most pressing problem was the choice between cultivating what Dean James E. Russell called the "academic and the professional" mind. He made it clear that he felt that Teachers College should chiefly reward the persons who sought primarily to solve the professional problems of education. The person devoted primarily to "pure" psychology, to academic schools or theories of psychology, should be supported by the older, more numerous, more affluent academic departments. The issue as he saw it was not quite the same as that based on the popular distinction between pure or theoretical psychology on the one hand and applied or practical on the other. He was clearly aware that Thorndike, Dewey, and many others developed general theories which had clear and immensely useful professional implication whereas others had evolved theories which, however valuable they might be for "academic" psychology, were not very intelligible or useful in practical fields. Since I had devoted my student days to theoretical psychology with about as great enjoyment as with the experimental discipline, I felt I must decide soon whether to try to do something in it. I elected to try my hand at developing the general theoretical concepts, at conducting experiments aimed primarily to reveal general principles, and to study and consult with a few highly competent persons who seemed to have somewhat different convictions.

Among the early experiments I conducted was one designed to test whether the development of particular practical skill involved any general constitutional change or an increase in capacity, or merely the acquisition of techniques or tangible abilities or "tricks of the trade" as my dissertation suggested.[2] Another was an experiment designed to reveal whether putting a person through an undeveloped skill by artificial means, such as moving a child's hand through the movements of tracing the letters, would impress the skill into the child's system, or whether such a skill would result only from the child himself giving birth to the proper movements.[3] Another was an effort to see whether two related aspects or components of a skill could be combined by a mathematical formulae as in the physical sciences. I found that it was possible to combine the rate of speed and the level of quality in a specimen of handwriting by such a formula,[4] but I was unable to do this with anything else I tried.

I soon began to feel that the more I examined this ancient distinction, the more indistinct it became. For example, when I reflected on Thorndike's many investigations, I concluded that his greatest contribution to psychological theories—to pure science—was the series of learning "laws" or theories he conceived to explain the activities of cats and other animals endeavoring to solve the crude puzzle boxes in which food was placed. This was his famous doctoral dissertation. What could be more practical or pro-

2. "The Nature and Limit of Improvement Due to Training," *Nature and Nurture*, pp. 44-60. Twenty-seventh Yearbook of the National Society for the Study of Education, Part I (Bloomington, Ill.: Public School Publishing Co., 1928).

3. "The Acquisition of Motor Control in Writing by Pre-School Children," *Teachers College Record* 24 (1923), 459-69.

4. "The Relation of Quality and Speed of Performance: A Formula for Combining the Two in Case of Handwriting," *Journal of Educational Psychology* (1924), 129-45.

fessional or more typical of daily activities than a cat's efforts to find its way to food in a clutter of box-like slats, or a thicket of shrubs, or a pile of garbage and rubble!

From the day these studies by Thorndike were reported they have been regarded by the profession as singularly brilliant and important examples of "academic" or general or "pure" psychology, but they seem to me to be equally significant examples of practical or professional psychology. When it is stated that "applied" psychology is a different activity, a case of viewing a practical situation by applying to it the investigator's stock of "principles," it should be noted that Thorndike clearly stated that he vigorously "applied" to the animal behavior such explanatory principles and theories as he knew and that he was forced to evolve new ones when he was convinced that the old ones were unsatisfactory. The feature that made his studies an admirable case of scientific or general or pure psychology was not the form of the activity under observation, but the way the investigator brought to bear upon it all the technical and intellectual skills, the insights, controls, facts, theories, and principles he had at hand—the way he sought for a deeper, fuller, more revealing explanation of the phenomenon. The more characteristic of typical daily activities the experimental operations are, the more likely the explanatory principles are to be sound and useful. Perhaps the artificial experimental situations should be resorted to only when the variables cannot be satisfactorily controlled in more typical activities.

My study of psychological theory led me gradually to certain other convictions. One was that the psychological laws or principles are unlike most of those evolved in the physical sciences, like which most psychologists hoped they would become. They are not "laws" in the same mathematically exact sense. They are more like succinct summaries of the major revelations of investigations. They are close kin to practical maxims; they resemble brief practical guides.

I soon became convinced that psychological principles were not so widely applicable as the typical laws of the physical sciences. Thus, when the Gestalt psychologists insisted that Thorndike's "trial and error" formula did not provide a satisfactory explanation of the monkey's deliberate use of sticks and other objects or "tools" in certain puzzle situations (and even if they were correct in assuming that their principles rationalized these "more intelligent" forms of learning better), they seemed to me to be wrong in assuming that they had better explanatory principles for all forms of learning, particularly for the kinds of problems which were presented to Thorndike's cats.

In any event I gradually reached the conviction that I could do more for education by applying my kit of scientific concepts and techniques to some of the multitude of complex and puzzling problems one must face in the daily tasks of teaching than to confine them to work in the typically narrow and artificial situations then so characteristic of the pure, theoretical psychology and the more artificial experimental laboratory tasks I had been trained to do. If no general principles appeared in a study of typical operations in teaching reading or grammar or solving a problem in algebra, or in controlling one's emotions when one fails to solve a problem, thorough, analytical study of the phenomenon is at least more likely to lead to some observations useful to a teacher.

I decided, however, to divide my time for a few years between work on general or theoretical psychological issues and the practical problems in education. Thorndike approved heartily and said, to my surprise, that I would find the latter more difficult, partly because one must avoid being blinded or led astray by the confusion of uncontrolled variables in which they are typically enmeshed.

An excellent opportunity for tackling problems professionally soon opened up through the overtures of one of the students who was in the first class I taught (with Thorndike) at Teachers College, Wilford M. Aikin, who had become principal of the private experimental Scarborough School and later became the director of the famous Eight-Year Study. He suggested to the founder of the school, Mr. Frank A. Vanderlip, that I be asked to direct studies of some of the problems in which the latter was interested. Arrangements were soon made. With my student Miss Jessie Lasalle as my assistant, I carried out during the following year an array of group and case studies which were published in a small book, *The Psychology of Reading and Spelling with Special Reference to Disability*.[5] Needless to say, I carried into these analyses many devices

5. New York: Teachers College Bureau of Publications, Teachers College, Columbia University, 1922.

and techniques I had used in the psychological laboratory and I tried to invent additional ones to meet the new problems.

During this period I maintained a full program at the college and started work on two texts in general psychology, one primarily for students of education and the other for students in all fields. I also tried to maintain some experimentation in general psychology. The college provided some quite expensive apparatus which I used in an effort to analyze certain physiological and emotional reactions to pleasant and unpleasant emotions and to states of relaxation and fatigue. One of my hunches was that the percentage of sugar in the blood and the contraction of the stomach muscles would prove to be a delicate index of these conditions. After spending many long and trying hours, I gave up this enterprise partly because I failed to develop a stomach balloon that subjects could swallow without distress and partly because I learned that a college medical officer felt that a doctor should supervise my analysis of blood sugar. A few years later, one of my students, a brilliant young Japanese girl, Tomi Wada, soon referred to as "Tummy Waddle," designed a tiny balloon which, swallowed and inflated, served without distress to yield valuable data reported in her doctor's thesis.[6] My plans to do further work along this general line were never carried out.

The writing of the texts proceeded with fewer headaches. *Psychology for Students of Education* was finished in the summer of 1922 and published in early 1923. *Elementary Psychology*, largely written during the following two years, came off the press in 1925.

Certain features of these two texts aroused quite a stir of interest and resentment, especially from older educators and psychologists. I think the former was the first text to include a full treatment of "mental adjustment." It introduced some Freudian and other psychoanalytic ideas. Although these were reformulated into psychological mechanisms and given such innocuous names as "sour grapes mechanism," "substitute activities," "compensation adjustment," etc., the publisher and author received many indignant protests of this and certain other rather novel sections of the book which later became the most popular ones, especially among the students and younger instructors.

6. Tomi Wada, "Experimental Study of Hunger in its Relation to Activity," *Archives of Psychology*, No. 57, New York, 1922.

The basal theoretical principles adopted in these books, after careful deliberation, were largely modifications of the Thorndike-Woodworth formulations. For Thorndike's "formation of bonds" formulas I substituted a "reaction hypothesis" structure, somewhat similar to Woodworth's scheme. I found this more helpful than anything else I could locate or contrive for formulating general psychological concepts and enlightening professional problems. That I still feel the same is probably in large measure the result of habit and inflexibility. But I still retain the conviction that the choice of a theoretical system in our field is largely a personal matter. Some can function better with one, others with another. None is as yet all right or all wrong. Each has been, and properly can be, modified greatly to take into account new data and ideas. One is justified in selecting the system that helps him most, somewhat in the way he chooses a "life-style," to use Gordon Allport's phrase, or even a religion.

I found that the work in the experimental study of professional school problems and the work in the general theoretical field were about equally fascinating. I realized indeed that all that I learned about one enriched my understanding of the other. The combination of the two, call it what you will—pure, professional, applied—is the ideal, at least for most purposes.

In December 1927 Thorndike provided me with an opportunity to explore a wide range of school activities. He asked me if I would like to join him in revising his *Education: A First Book*, which he published in 1912. I was of course flattered, but I asked him to consider the difficulty I might make for him if I employed the variations from his terminology and systematic theories I was then accustomed to use. As was always so characteristic of him, he said he would enjoy seeing what would come forth and discussing any differences which might lead to serious consequences. It was agreed that I would rewrite the whole book, as I saw fit, before showing him any of it. I took the summer off, retreated with my wife to Maine, and presented him with my complete revision when the college opened in September. Modifications acceptable to both of us were worked out during the next three months and the book was published in 1929, but we never found time to revise it.[7]

7. *Elementary Principles of Education* (with E. L. Thorndike). New York: Macmillan Co., 1929).

Before I reached the end of my first year of work at Scarborough, Dean James E. Russell asked me to use the college's Horace Mann Elementary School for my experimentation. There I undertook to subject some broad educational patterns to reliable tests. The most successful of these studies was published: "A Modern Systematic Versus an Opportunistic Method of Teaching,"[8] methods which had been debated for years but never investigated objectively. I also conducted or supervised studies of the initial stages of learning such skills as reading and handwriting and I made a kind of laboratory-test, clinical analysis of disabilities and difficulties in the school subjects. These lines of attack were shortly expanded and extended for use with other classes in the public schools, youngsters in institutions such as the Lexington School for the Deaf, and community clinics and hospitals. In such enterprises as these I spent as much time as I could spare from my teaching and administrative work at the college during the remainder of the 1920-1930 decade.

I was most productive in research on practical educational problems between 1920 and 1935. A major purpose was to see what improvements I might suggest in everyday teaching of the common branches by application of psychological theories, devices, and techniques. I became convinced that the most crucial and revealing way to test an educational material or method was to try it out on children who had an extreme aptitude or limitation or disability for a particular type of learning. For example, the most crucial test of the value of "phonics" or word-sound approach to learning to read would be to see how children deaf from birth could learn to read by other methods. Coming to grips with individual abilities and limitations was obviously important for wholly practical, as well as theoretical, values. Accordingly I sought methods of diagnosing and prescribing for individual cases in the hope that sooner or later schools would provide teachers and specialists who could rival in their field the expertness of a well-trained physician in his. I carried out and published many studies by myself and supervised many others reported mainly in doctoral dissertations by my students. In 1927, I published a program of diagnostic and remedial

8. *Teachers College Record* 27 (1926), 679-701. (With Mildred I. Batchelder and Jean Betzner)

study of difficulties in reading, spelling, and a battery of tests and diagnostic materials.[9]

Early in the decade, I supervised the preparation of a series of what would now be regarded as programmed materials both for reading and spelling courses.[10] One of the former consisted of over twelve hundred pages of classroom material for teaching beginning reading for less than a school year. Other similar outfits variously supplemented by the teacher were tried in numerous other public and private schools and with deaf-mutes and many other exceptional children. The results were reported over the years in various articles, monographs, and several books.

During the two decades following 1930 I found myself so increasingly occupied with duties as teacher, administrator, committee member, worker in professional and scientific organizations, and with family and social activities that time for research and scholarly enterprises became harder to find. I tried, however, to devote more attention to advanced students and to writing or revising comprehensive texts. I did as much research as I could. I kept alive several of my major textbooks by a series of revisions. *Elementary Psychology* went through two revisions before I gave it up to concentrate on my work in the field of education. *Psychology for Students of Education,* which was translated into several other languages, was repeatedly revised. With the cooperation of Arthur T. Jersild, T. R. McConnell, and Robert C. Challman, a more comprehensive work, *Educational Psychology,* was brought out in 1942 and revised later. *The Improvement of Reading,* with its diagnostic and remedial program, was repeatedly revised until I retired, after which with the cooperation of Anne McKillop the diagnostic materials were reconstructed.

I published during this period a number of other books, mainly smaller volumes, such as *Reading for Public School Administrators* (1931), *The Acceptable Uses of Achievement Tests* (with Paul R. Mort, 1932), *Generalization and Transfer in Spelling* (1935); wrote chapters or sections for many other books and yearbooks; and edited a few, such as the Forty-eighth Yearbook of this Society,

9. *The Improvement of Reading* (New York: Macmillan Co., 1927).

10. Assisted by such remarkable students as Ruth Strang, Margaret Mead, and Dorothy Van Alstyne.

Part II, entitled *Reading in the Elementary School* (1949). A large array of books, workbooks, practice exercises, and other classroom materials, together with more than three thousand pages of teachers' manuals, were brought out and revised from time to time.

During the decade following 1930 I engaged in several large-scale enterprises made possible and desirable by the Great Depression. Soon after 1930, unemployment among New York City teachers, especially of the younger ones, reached alarming proportions. In 1933 George Chatfield, then assistant (later associate) superintendent of schools, and I drew up plans for a city-wide remedial reading project, a plan to deal individually or in small groups with the worst cases of reading difficulty to be found in the city's elementary schools. When the Federal Civil Works Administration support was provided, I selected twenty-three supervisors, mainly from students I had trained in diagnostic and remedial work, to join me in giving two weeks of intensive training to about two hundred previously unemployed teachers, and then sent them out to tackle the city's toughest educational problems. Their phenomenal achievements during the following four months provided me with one of the most thrilling experiences of my professional life. These (mainly) young, but previously deeply worried, teachers became remarkably devoted, determined, and successful apostles; they gave a genuine educational resurrection to more than 90 percent of the city's "hopeless" cases. During the second and third years, this continually growing project was directed by my lieutenant, Dr. Annette Bennett, after whose untimely death it was taken over by the city's staff and continued for several more years under the general administration of Dr. May Lazar of the Bureau of Educational Research. At times it gave a rich apprenticeship and modest salary to as many as seven hundred teachers who probably would otherwise have been unemployed.

A second enterprise, called "The Writers' Project," I sketched out with Mr. Chatfield, who succeeded in getting federal funds to support it. For the sizable group of "writers," mainly unemployed feature writers for many kinds of publications, but including also teachers who wished to try their hand, and several previously successful authors of children's literature, I sketched a plan of developing small books of relatively easy reading material but of more advanced interest levels. Once the project was well under way, it was supervised by one or more city school officials. Unemployed artists were added. I have now in my files over three hundred published small books, sixteen to forty-eight pages, of fully illustrated materials of all sorts, prose and poetry, adventurous, humorous, fanciful, historical, factual. The New York City school children loved them. It is true there was once a battle—a near riot in one school—after an author, having read one of his own manuscripts to a group of overage, mainly "nonreading" boys, showed several of his others on which he wanted the boys' advice before committing them to the printer. The fight occurred during recess when the lads found there were not enough "books" to go around! They were found guilty—of never before having stayed in a classroom during recess on their own accord.

The third WPA project was worked out jointly by my Teachers College colleagues, William Featherstone (administration), Leta S. Hollingworth (psychology), and myself, with Benjamin B. Greenberg, later an associate superintendent of the city schools. Known as the Speyer School Experiment, it was based on five classes of bright children (I.Q. 120 and above) and seven classes of "low-normal" pupils (I.Q. 75-95). Professor Hollingworth carried out her curriculum with the bright, and I worked with the low-normal pupils. The principal, supervisor, and all the teachers were selected from the New York City schools. My chief lieutenants were Guy L. Bond, joined later by David H. Russell and Andrew Halpin. The school carried on for five years. More than a dozen reports of the experiment and various experiences were published.

When Teachers College began to open its doors around 1920 to part-time and in-service teachers, our teaching loads increased. My "service" course in educational psychology, like many other offerings in other fields, often attracted more students than could be accommodated in our largest classrooms. The number of full-time, advanced students also increased rapidly, and during the several years preceding 1927 when I relieved Thorndike at his and Dean Russell's request as chairman of two large departments—psychology and research methods—I had been carrying much of the administrative detail. These ever increasing demands slowed down my research and writing considerably during the following two decades.

The rapidly increasing enrollment of part-time students seeking practical advice and training resulted in a gradual change in the character of the college. Those engaged extensively in research and scholarly work tended to devote more time and attention to dealing with the professional problems which these faced. To provide for the increasing number of students, the college employed more and more instructors predominantly expert in the practical school tasks. Many members of the staff feared that the scholarly component of the college's activities would dwindle.

In 1933, Paul R. Mort, with Dean William F. Russell's approval, launched a plan for a relatively independent Advanced School within the college which would primarily promote advanced research and study. It was to include two divisions, one emphasizing professional preparation and leading to the new doctor of education degree, the other emphasizing the more theoretical type of research and scholarly work leading to the doctor of philosophy degree. Nicholas Engelhardt was invited to serve as chairman of the former and I as head of the latter. Paul Mort was the overall director.

During the following several years only promising advanced students were accepted and only a portion of the staff was assigned to the Advanced School. Plans for certain separate quarters and research facilities were worked out. Opposition to the venture became increasingly apparent. Many members of the staff and student body felt that it represented an undemocratic division of both groups into the sheep and the goats. Finally, Dean Russell called for a secret ballot which showed the opponents of the Advanced School to be in the majority, and it was abolished in 1937. Many believed that the college thereby started a march toward the trade school pattern. I felt that special provision for encouraging advanced study in both lines was desirable and needed. I have always thought, however, that the best arrangement for the college was to provide approximately equal emphasis and power for the two concerns, as seemed to me to prevail when I first joined it. At that time, for example, George Strayer was as respected and influential as Thorndike, and each admired and supported the other. If the emphasis swung too far one way following the abolition of the Advanced

School, I feel that in Teachers College and other schools of education it has in recent years been moving back toward a happy medium. I feel that the two should represent merely a degree of specialization growing out of a larger area of common knowledge and concern.

During these decades, keeping informed about developments in many other rapidly growing fields such as philosophy, sociology, anthropology, as well as new, more practical fields such as curriculum and guidance, became increasingly difficult. Although I had few personal contacts with John Dewey, I tried to maintain a reasonable degree of familiarity with the stream of challenging ideas which flowed from him throughout his long life, especially those related to educational policies and practices. Fortunately, Dewey was a prolific writer and a number of my colleagues at the college kept well informed about his views. I have always believed that many of his ideas, properly interpreted, including his conceptions of educational methods in the narrower sense, were enormously important. Interestingly enough, I was often criticized during my first professional quarter century for being unresponsive or hostile to Dewey's ideas and during the second for being a naive victim of his "permissive" or "progressive" notions. I have long felt that his views of certain crucial features of good method such as those described under such terms as interest, effort, purpose, drive, motivation, goal-seeking, self-diagnosis, self-direction, and self-determined insight were highly insightful and valid. I think he sensed the essence of many modern notions of "understanding" psychology, on the one hand, and of such behavioristic concepts as B. F. Skinner's reinforcement theories on the other, although I expect many followers of both disciplines will be scandalized by this statement. I have treasured many of his succinct, classic expressions of method, such as the following.

> The question of method . . . is no longer a question of how the teacher is to instruct and how the pupil is to study. The problem is to find what conditions must be fulfilled in order that study and learning will naturally and necessarily take place, what conditions must be present so that pupils will make the responses which cannot help having learning as their consequences.[11]

11. I quoted this in my *Interest and Ability in Reading.* (New York: Macmillan Co., 1930).

In my earliest work at Teachers College I felt I was striving to develop a program which embodied something of this sort. Soon thereafter I adopted the phrase "intrinsic method" (of teaching reading or indeed anything), which I feel is validly suggestive, even if it has been widely misinterpreted. I was trying to achieve similar objectives when I was developing, for example, the previously mentioned, very detailed, carefully controlled twelve-hundred-page programmed materials for teaching beginning reading. My associates and I sought to embody certain principles of learning in this program—the choice of realistic, everyday material, interesting and challenging activities and projects organized in ways that "could not help having learning as their consequence"—and to realize the then Thorndikian and the current Skinnerian ideas of guiding learning by revealing detailed successes and errors and omissions at small steps in its course. Finally, we were attentive to the importance of "concomitant" or "simultaneous" learnings (Dewey-Kilpatrick terms), especially of satisfaction in the process and the acquisition of techniques of learning, "tricks of the trade," ways of maneuvering and of achieving insight into one's own ways of learning. Among the "techniques of learning," etc., should be included, in my view at least, all those operations, maneuvers, and subtle activities involved in what are referred to as comprehending, perceiving, understanding, thinking, reasoning, imagining, problem-solving, concept-forming, and the like.

If the sketch of the desirable components of the learning process I have drawn seems pretentious and unattainable, I must insist that James, Thorndike, Judd, and especially Dewey long ago quite clearly recognized them as ideals of education, as objectives to strive for, not occasionally or in separate formal exercises but during every hour in every school subject and activity. This, I think, is really a psychologically sound substitute for the old, faulty faculty theory—a promising possibility for realizing, by tangible even if obviously more complex and difficult means, objectives similar to those mistakenly sought by the methods of formal discipline.

I recall from my early years similar expressions, both by Dewey and Thorndike, of the difficulty and danger of giving an opinion about a practice when it must be based not on a thorough study of the program in operation, but on a limited observation or an incomplete description. The greatest difficulty, each said, was to see the whole program in sufficient clarity and detail to tell whether it embodied the principle of learning which he thought was desirable and was free of too many omissions or conflicting features. During the remainder of my professional life I felt the point of their comments with increasing frequency and sharpness. This explains why "applying" principles to practical situations is so frightfully difficult and risky, why all manner of practices and theoretical formulations have been advocated as examples of Dewey's or Thorndike's convictions. I can illustrate this point by a striking example which I encountered in working on a yearbook of this Society.

In 1940 T. R. McConnell and his committee set out to prepare a much needed yearbook on the then, as ever, numerous and apparent divergent theories of learning. I approved of inviting a former student of Thorndike, then an outstanding Canadian psychologist, Peter Sandiford, to write the chapter devoted to Thorndike's views. When I reviewed the manuscript for McConnell, I had to report that Sandiford's account represented a theoretical and practical emphasis, indeed, a whole verbal structure that was very different from my own. At McConnell's invitation I wrote another chapter, embodying my own conceptions. Both were published in the yearbook.[12]

Retirement at Teachers College is mandatory at the end of the academic year which includes one's sixty-fifth birthday, a time I reached on June 30, 1956. During my last year I received the approval of President Hollis Caswell and the college trustees to set up an institute for research which I had agreed to finance. The title "Institute of Language Arts" and my designation as "supervisor" (since a retired person could not be given any official title then in use in the college) had no particular significance. It was understood that I could do whatever I wanted—within socially acceptable limits!

I began by trying to do some reading and to observe certain research enterprises I had long wanted to investigate. I provided a

12. *The Psychology of Learning*, chaps. iii and iv, Forty-first Yearbook of the National Society for the Study of Education, Part II (Bloomington, Ill.: Public School Publishing Co., 1942).

few internships in research for carefully selected advanced students, who were either put on my payroll or given the Gates or Macmillan fellowships. Among these have been a number of very brilliant young persons who now hold important posts in colleges and other institutions. Gradually I followed my inclination to reduce the amount of time and money put into particular investigations in order to devote myself more fully to exploring a few general theoretical ideas and especially to encouraging research and scholarly work relating to problems in every field of education. During the last eight years prior to the present date (November 1968) my writing and speaking and my activities in societies and committees have been primarily directed to this end. I have found especially rewarding the study of two professional fields, agriculture and medicine, in which scientific and scholarly work has been almost incredibly fruitful. I have repeatedly urged that we in education learn more of their ways and those of many other disciplines and practical fields.

I think it appropriate for me to conclude this fragmentary account with some recent suggestions for increasing our ability to advance the welfare of the human race by means of education. The first of these is taken from an address I made following a banquet in celebration of the fiftieth anniversary of the establishment of the Lambda Chapter of Phi Delta Kappa fraternity in Berkeley.[13]

> Science can be described only as a variety of attacks made by a number of quite different men. Science was the early theoretical work of William James, whom many regard as the greatest psychologist of all time, despite the fact that he made but one experimental study, the design of which was quite faulty. James was a theorist whose pen was guided by the angels. The scientific movement at Columbia included John Dewey, trained for and inventive in a career in psychology, who began early to attack the most complex social problems with the slow, deep persistence of the oxen which plowed the soil of his native Vermont. There was James McKeen Cattell, head of Columbia's Psychology Department, whose savage brilliance illuminated the educational significance of both the experimental and statistical approach. And there was Charles Judd, the crusty [but vastly talented] Chicago advocate of laboratory experimentation, and Edward L. Thorndike, the scientific movement's most prolific worker, possessed of a most brilliant and

13. "Science or Sanity?" *Phi Delta Kappan* 45 (1964), 297-302.

versatile mind, one which threw shafts of lightning into the most unpredictable places.

There were others, but these illustrate the range of differences in personality, in methods, in fields of work. These men, especially James and Dewey, were both scientists and philosophers, sometimes one, sometimes the other, or both in some degree all the time. . . . The essence of science is a kind of thinking. Science comprises the kinds of thinking these men did.

The second, based on several convictions arrived at in recent years, points to the need for a greater amount of experimentation than I had previously thought necessary. This belief, which I arrived at after reviewing the results of similar experiments conducted at intervals over my professional life, I recently expressed as follows:

The values of most reading materials and methods [for example] depend more upon what children do at the time in school and out, upon attitudes and abilities they possess, and upon the skills and habits of their teacher than upon any inherent, absolute virtue of the material or method itself, or on any basal psychological principle. Experimental results obtained before 1930 are often very different from those secured today, and practical recommendations made then were and should have been different. We should expect that most of them will not be valid now. Note also, if you try to reach conclusions about desirable practices today by summing up the results of studies done over a span of many years, you merely get ambiguity. Any study done in the past is meaningless when taken out of context, that is, when interpreted without taking fully into account the vital characteristics of the time. "Sufficient unto the day the [educational practices] thereof." [14]

This, of course, means that we must reinvestigate the values of school materials and practices at frequent, perhaps increasingly frequent, intervals in the future.

The following quotation is the last paragraph from the last address I have made to this day (November 6, 1968). It was a talk to a world congress, composed of societies from more than twenty-five different nations concerned especially with problems in communication and the language arts, held in Copenhagen, Denmark, during the first three days in August of 1968.

Lest my comments today and those of many other critics, both qualified and unqualified, during recent years cause you to doubt that

14. From address, "The Tides of Time," delivered at the Annual Convention of the International Reading Association in Boston in 1968.

scientific and scholarly study can contribute richly [to the improvement of education], let me urge you to reflect for a moment on the fact that we have had a trifling amount of it in comparison with many other fields, such as medicine, agriculture, and mechanical engineering. Educational research has lived on the crumbs during my days, but I believe that it is soon to join other groups at the table. Indeed, it has already had at least a few substantial handouts. For example, in several recent instances the amount of money made available for *each* of a few short-time (two- to five-year) investigations has been greater than I received for all the research work I have carried out during my entire lifetime. If some of those in our field now show signs of getting indigestion from the unaccustomed feast at the main table, we need not worry. They will soon get adjusted to a rich diet. In a long run a bountiful table for scholarly and scientific study will provide much that we need to give full vigor to our profession. I hope especially that the members of the organizations which have honored me today will be assigned reserved seats at the main table and as a consequence will enjoy long, happy, and fruitful lives.[15]

A BIOGRAPHICAL SUMMARY

ARTHUR I. GATES. Born on September 22, 1890, at Red Wing, Minnesota; moved to Fortuna, California, in 1891.

Family. Married Georgina Stickland, 1920. Children: Robert Gaylord, 1929; Katherine Blair, 1934.

Education. Elementary and high school, Fortuna, California; University of California (Berkeley), B.L., 1914; M.A., 1915; Columbia University, Ph.D. (Psychology), 1917.

Occupational history. Teaching fellow in psychology, Columbia University, 1916-17; instructor to full professor, 1917-56; head, Department of Psychology and Research Methods, 1933-36; director, Institute of Educational Research, Section D, 1921-30; head, Department of Education Research in Advanced School, 1933-42; director, Division of Foundations of Education, 1948-56; professor emeritus, 1956—; supervisor, Institute of Language Arts, 1956.

Memberships and affiliations. American Psychological Association (president of Section on Educational Psychology, 1948-49); American Educational Research Association (president, 1942); American Association for Applied Psychology (chairman, Education Section, 1940); American Association for the Advancement of Science (chairman, Edu-

15. Published slightly revised as "Reflection and Return," in *Reading: A Human Right and a Human Problem*, Second World Congress in Reading, Copenhagen, 1968 (Newark, Del.: International Reading Association, 1969), pp. 9-14.

cational Division, 1932); National Academy of Education; Century Club.

Awards. Medals and citations for distinguished service from International Reading Association, 1961; American Educational Research Association and Phi Delta Kappa, 1964; American Psychological Association, 1967; Teachers College, Columbia University, 1968; and World Congress on Language Arts, 1968.

Part II

Selected Publications of Arthur I. Gates

Books

Psychology, Education, and Educational Psychology

1. "Recitation as a Factor in Memorizing." *Archives of Psychology* (ed. R. S. Woodworth) 26, No. 1 (1917): 1-104. (Ph.D. dissertation.)
2. *The Psychology of Reading and Spelling with Special Reference to Disability*. New York: Columbia University Contributions to Education No. 129. New York: Teachers College, Columbia University, 1922.
3. *Psychology for Students of Education.* New York: Macmillan Co., 1923 (rev. 1930).
4. *Elementary Psychology*. New York: Macmillan Co., 1925 (rev. 1928).
5. *Elementary Principles of Education* (with E. L. Thorndike). New York: Macmillan Co., 1929.
6. *Educational Psychology* (with Arthur T. Jersild, T. R. McConnell, and Robert C. Challman). New York: Macmillan Co., 1942 (rev. 1948).
7. *The Effect of Mothers' Diets on the Intelligence of Offspring* (with Ruth F. Harrell and Ella Woodward). New York: Bureau of Publications, Teachers College, Columbia University, 1955.

Reading and Spelling

8. *Spelling Difficulties of 3876 Words.* New York: Bureau of Publications, Teachers College, Columbia University, 1937.
9. *The Improvement of Reading: A Program of Diagnostic and Remedial Methods.* New York: Macmillan Co., 1927 (rev. 1935, 1947).
10. *New Methods in Primary Reading.* New York: Bureau of Publications, Teachers College, Columbia University, 1928.
11. *Interest and Ability in Reading: A Report of Investigations.* New York: Macmillan Co., 1930.
12. *Reading for Public School Administrators.* New York: Bureau of Publications, Teachers College, Columbia University, 1931.

13. *Generalization and Transfer in Spelling.* Bureau of Publications, Teachers College, Columbia University, 1935.

Diagnostic and Instructional Materials

14. *The Gates-Strang Health Knowledge Test.* (Complete Series). *Manual of Directions* (with Ruth Strang). New York: Bureau of Publications, Teachers College, Columbia University, 1925.
15. *A Reading Vocabulary for the Primary Grades.* New York: Bureau of Publications, Teachers College, Columbia University, 1926 (rev. 1935).
16. "The Gates Primary Reading Tests." *Teachers College Record* 28 (1926): 146-78. The first is cited; most recent (with Walter H. MacGinitie) was published in 1969.
17. *Gates-Russell Spelling Diagnosis Tests* (with David H. Russell). New York: Bureau of Publications, Teachers College, Columbia University, 1937.
18. *The Story Book of Nick and Dick* (with F. T. Baker and C. C. Peardon). New York: Macmillan Co., 1937.
19. *Methods of Determining Reading Readiness* (with G. L. Bond and D. H. Russell, assisted by Andrew Halpin and Kathryn Horan). New York: Bureau of Publications, Teachers College, Columbia University, 1939.
20. *The Ranch Book* (with M. B. Huber and Frank S. Salisbury). New York: Macmillan Co., 1943.
21. *Teaching Reading* (First in a series, "What Research Says to the Teacher"). Washington: Department of Classroom Teachers and American Education Research Association, 1953 (rev. 1962, 1967).

Articles

Psychology and Educational Psychology

22. "The Relative Predictive Values of Certain Intelligence and Educational Tests Together with a Study of the Effect of Educational Achievement Upon Intelligence Test Scores." *Journal of Education Psychology* 14 (1923): 517-40.
23. "A Critique of Methods of Estimating and Measuring the Transfer of Training." *Journal of Educational Psychology* 15 (1924): 545-59.
24. "The Nature and Educational Significance of Physical Status and of Mental, Physiological, Social and Emotional Maturity." *Journal of Educational Psychology* 15 (1924): 329-58.
25. "A Study of the Role of Visual Perception, Intelligence and Certain Associative Processes in Reading and Spelling." *Journal of Educational Psychology* 17 (1926): 443-45.
26. "The Nature and Limit of Improvement Due to Training." In

Nature and Nurture: Their Influence Upon Intelligence, pp. 441-61. Twenty-seventh Yearbook of the National Society for the Study of Education, Part I. Bloomington, Ill.: Public School Publishing Co., 1929.

27. "Observed Facts and Theoretical Concepts." *Journal of Educational Psychology* 19 (1928): 381-91.
28. "Contributions of Research to General Methods of Instruction." In *Scientific Movement in Education*, pp. 79-91. Thirty-seventh Yearbook of the National Society for the Study of Education, Part II. Bloomington, Ill.: Public School Publishing Co., 1935.
29. "Connectionism: Present Concepts and Interpretations." In *The Psychology of Learning*, pp. 141-63. Forty-first Yearbook of the National Society for the Study of Education, Part II. Bloomington, Ill.: Public School Publishing Co., 1942.
30. "The General Nature of Learning" (with G. Lester Anderson). In *Learning and Instruction*, pp. 12-36. Forty-ninth Yearbook of the National Society for the Study of Education, Part I. Chicago: University of Chicago Press, 1950.
31. "Educational Psychology, Twenty-five years of Educational Research" (with Arthur T. Jersild, Anne S. McKillop, Harry N. Rivlin, Edward J. Shoben Jr. and Goodwin Watson). *Review of Educational Research* 26 (1956): 241-67.

Reading

32. "An Experimental and Statistical Study of Reading and Reading Tests." *Journal of Educational Psychology* 12 (1921): 303-14, 378-91, 445-64.
33. "The General and Specific Effects of Training in Reading with Observations of the Experimental Technique (with Dorothy Van Alstyne). *Teachers College Record* 25 (1924): 98-123.
34. "Problems in Beginning Reading." *Teachers College Record* 26 (1925): 572-91.
35. "A Modern Systematic Versus an Opportunistic Method of Teaching" (with Mildred T. Batchelder and Jean Betzner). *Teachers College Record* 27 (1926): 679-701.
36. "Recent Developments in Diagnostic and Remedial Teaching in Reading." *American Educational Association Annual Report*, February 1935, pp. 83-91.
37. "Viewpoints Underlying the Study of Reading Disabilities." *Elementary English Review* 12 (1935): 85-90, 105.
38. "An Experimental Evaluation of Reading-Readiness Tests." *Elementary School Journal* 39 (1939): 497-508.
39. [Needed Research] "In Reading." *Journal of Educational Research* 40 (1947): 381-88.

40. "The Role of Personality Adjustment in Reading Disability." *Journal of Genetic Psychology* 49 (1941): 77-83.
41. "Character and Purposes of the Yearbook." In *Reading in the Elementary School* (Arthur I. Gates, Chairman), pp. 1-9. Forty-eighth Yearbook of the National Society for the Study of Education, Part II. Chicago: University of Chicago Press, 1949.

Part III

Biographical Essay on Arthur I. Gates

ROBERT E. TOSTBERG

Arthur Gates's autobiographical statement is an informative and instructive document. It sets forth, in straightforward fashion, those incidents and motives that have shaped his distinguished career and draws together certain conclusions distilled from his experience. It is, however, a modest recounting of his accomplishments. In this companion essay, I will introduce material that shows his stature among professional colleagues, present an examination of bases for his reputation, and put forward some tentative comments about leadership in American education.

The place of an individual in the history of American education is secured largely by his peers' assessments. A look at the public record provides ample evidence of Gates's professional reputation and the work upon which it is based. "I am probably the only man you know whose career was founded upon a yawn," said Gates in a recent address.[1] He was referring to his first published study, "Variations in Efficiency During the Day." [2] In the case of both the subject of that study and Gates's career, the yawn was followed by a period of increased activity, efficiency, and visibility. Studies that Gates and his collaborators conducted during the next half century have added substantially and significantly to the literature on reading research and instruction. In the judgment of those who have reviewed it, the work has been consistently sound. Note the appraisals of these careful observers of the field of reading. William McAndrew, reviewing *Psychology for Students of Education,* wrote, "Among the helpers this age is giving us in remarkable

1. Arthur I. Gates, "Science or Sanity?" *Phi Delta Kappan* 45 (1964): 297.

2. "Variations in Efficiency During the Day, Together with Practice Effects, Sex Differences and Correlations," *University of California Publications in Psychology,* Vol. II, No. 1, pp. 1-156.

numbers I think you will put Arthur Gates in the front rank. He has a genius for selecting facts that are pertinent and for putting them into form adapted for the schoolman's immediate use."[3] Of *Interest and Ability in Reading*, Miles A. Tinker said, "The development of a program of research dealing with materials and methods of the teaching of reading by Dr. A. I. Gates and his associates in the Institute of Educational Research of Teachers College has resulted in contributions that may be classified as among the most important appearing during the past decade. . . . Dr. Gates gives an outline of what promises to become one of our most effective method[s] of teaching reading."[4] Donald D. Durrell's judgment regarding *The Improvement of Reading* was that "this book is without question the best treatment of diagnosis and correction of defects in reading that has yet appeared."[5] Not only were Gates's books well received but—and this is perhaps a more telling indicator of his status—his individual studies have been regularly prominent and favorably discussed in the major longitudinal reviews of research on reading and reading instruction.[6]

Certain features of his work have been consistently noteworthy: his concern to supply a "factual" basis for reading instruction and his ability to make his findings applicable to classroom situations. These are the stuff of which his career has been made and on which his reputation has been founded. David H. Russell, in a biographical sketch written at about the time of Gates's retirement from Teach-

3. "Psychology That Beats the Morning Paper," *School and Society* 32 (1930): 779.

4. *Journal of Educational Psychology* 23 (1932): 73-74.

5. *Education* 56 (1935): 58.

6. See, *Ten Years of Research in Reading: Summary and Bibliography*, ed. Arthur E. Traxler and Margaret Seden (New York: Educational Records Bureau, 1941); *Another Five Years of Research in Reading: Summary and Bibliography*, ed. Arthur E. Traxler and Agatha Townsend (New York: Educational Records Bureau, 1946); *Eight More Years of Research in Reading: Summary and Bibliography*, ed. Arthur E. Traxler and Agatha Townsend (New York: Educational Records Bureau, 1955). See also articles under "Reading" in *Encyclopedia of Educational Research* 2d ed., Walter S. Monroe, ed. (New York: Macmillan Co., 1950); *Encyclopedia of Educational Research*, 3d ed., Chester W. Harris, ed. (New York: Macmillan Co., 1960); David H. Russell and Henry R. Fea, "Research on Teaching Reading," *Handbook of Research on Teaching*, ed. N. L. Gage (Chicago: Rand McNally & Co., 1963), 865-928 passim.

ers College, offered this assessment: "The desire to get at the facts has characterized most of Arthur Gates's professional work, a career marked by wide-ranging interests and tremendous productivity in general psychology and educational psychology as well as in the study of reading problems. . . . In the field of reading instruction Gates's original researches and wide-ranging writings have made him one of the most influential figures in the United States and throughout the world. . . . His [intrinsic] method, with some later variations, has become standard practice in most American schools. . . . It is no exaggeration to say that [Gates's] books largely changed reading from an isolated and mechanical exercise to a series of consecutive, meaningful, and zestful activities for American children." [7] That others who know his work well have come to similar conclusions regarding the value of his contributions to reading is indicated by two honors bestowed upon him during the past few years. One was the Citation of Merit Award presented in 1961 by the International Reading Association.[8] Also under the auspices of that association, he was chosen to receive, in 1968, the first World Congress in Reading Award for "his distinguished service and many contributions to a better understanding of the reading process and to reading instruction throughout the world." [9]

Further recognition has come from outside the ranks of reading specialists. In a 1957 issue of *Phi Delta Kappan*, Robert Beck counted Arthur Gates among those persons he saw fit to name as leaders in education during the period 1906-1956. Of Gates he said, "His research in learning, his studies in diagnostic and remedial reading, and his contributions to the field of testing place Dr. Gates among the education leaders of recent decades." [10] If one is to be judged by the company he keeps, it is worth noting that Gates appears

7. "Pioneers in Reading: Arthur Irving Gates," *Elementary English* 34 (1957): 397-98.

8. Arthur I. Gates et al., *Invitational Addresses*, 1965 (Newark, Del.: International Reading Association, 1965), p. 2.

9. *Reading: A Human Right and a Human Problem*, ed. Ralph C. Staiger and Oliver Andresen (Newark, Del.: International Reading Association, 1969), p. iii.

10. Robert H. Beck, "Educational Leadership, 1906-1956," *Phi Delta Kappan* 37 (1956): 159-65.

(between Frank N. Freeman and Arnold L. Gesell) with Cubberley, Dewey, Hall, Rugg, Strayer, Thorndike, and others of similar stature.

Perhaps the most significant evidence of the reputation he now enjoys across a relatively broad spectrum of American educators is the honor accorded him in 1964 as the first recipient of the Award for Distinguished Contributions to Educational Research, now given annually by the American Educational Research Association and Phi Delta Kappa. The plaque presented to him on that occasion reads:

> Distinguished contributor to educational research, author of the seminal study of recitation as a factor in memorizing, and of many basic investigations in reading, influential leader in improving practices, his scholarly career has had profound influence on education.[11]

The judgment is clear and conclusive. Arthur Gates is, by consensus of his professional colleagues, a leader in American education.

Dankwart A. Rustow, in an issue of *Daedalus* given over to studies in leadership, has noted, following Erik Erikson, that the role of a leader "must be explained concurrently on two distinct levels: the personal or psychological and the social or historical."[12] It is tempting to undertake an examination of Gates's leadership in these two dimensions. Even more intriguing is the prospect that the connectionist psychology espoused by Gates might prove to be a useful conceptual tool for explaining the behavior of this leader. A more modest, more manageable, and for the purposes of this volume a more pertinent inquiry, however, is to ask about the basis for Gates's recognition as a leader. Though his autobiography provides an abundance of descriptive material about his professional life, and judgments proffered about his work contain references to his accomplishments, a closer examination of certain features of his career may help to understand better how it is that Arthur Gates has come to be seen as a leader in American education.

Consider first the timing of that career. When Gates began his

11. American Educational Research Association, *Newsletter* 15, No. 2 (1964): 6.

12. "Introduction" of the issue "Philosophers and Kings: Studies in Leadership," *Daedalus* 97 (1968): 688.

studies of reading, he was entering a field that was, at best, embryonic. His investigations took him into an area that was, as a focus for scholarly endeavor, not yet clearly differentiated from its progenitors, psychological research and general pedagogical method. He has described his decision to pursue a career in research as a choice between science and sanity. His recollection that "to choose to become a psychologist, then regarded by many as some kind of vagrant mind-reader, was to family and friends sheer insanity"[13] dramatizes the novelty of taking seriously even psychological research as one's lifework. When it is further recognized that the first doctoral dissertations in American universities to deal explicitly with reading appeared in 1917[14] (the year of both Gates's and William S. Gray's studies), Gates's place as a pioneer in the scientific study of reading is patent.

As important as the circumstances of his entry into the field is the duration of his concern. For over half a century now, Gates has been intensively involved in and widely identified with psychological and pedagogical studies that pertain to reading. Three of his major books illustrate the focus of scholarly interests that he has sustained. *Psychology for Students of Education, The Improvement of Reading,* and *New Methods in Primary Reading,* all published initially before 1930, represent areas of inquiry that he has developed and elaborated upon. Not only has he contributed substantially to answering questions about reading, but he has been instrumental in forming the fundamental questions to which students of reading have addressed themselves for over half a century.

Another important facet of Gates's career is the extraordinary visibility that he and his ideas have gained through his publications, his institutional location, and his professional affiliations. The sheer quantity of his published works (currently about three hundred books, articles, and addresses) would be enough to establish him as a paramount figure in the field of reading research and instruction. Since 1921, six yearbooks of this Society have dealt explicitly with reading. Taken together, they provide both a history of the study of reading and a register of the persons who made that history; the

13. Gates, "Science or Sanity?" p. 297.

14. This date is assigned by Nila Banton Smith in Gates, et al., *Invitational Addresses, 1965,* p. 38.

four most recent of those volumes include contributions by Gates.[15]

If he had intentionally sought a place in which to be highly conspicuous, what better location could he have chosen than Teachers College during the era of its greatest renown? There, for forty years, in the company of Cattell, Thorndike, Woodworth, and others of equal eminence, he occupied a platform from which he could be seen and heard by a vast audience of American educators. It takes nothing away from Gates to suggest that his association with such colleagues contributed, initially at least, to his gaining prominence in a number of important professional organizations. Just to list some of those organizations and the offices he has held in them is to be reminded of his peers' view of him: American Association for the Advancement of Science, chairman and vice president of Section Q (Education), 1925; American Association of Applied Psychologists, chairman of Education Section, 1940-42; American Educational Research Association, president, 1942-43; American Psychological Association, president of Educational Psychology Section, 1948-49. A highly visible figure, indeed.

These features of Gates's professional life must be seen against the background of certain broader developments in American education with which his career has been contemporaneous and closely interwoven. Particularly important is his relationship to the movement called "the scientific study of education." The theme of scientific investigation is a primary one in his career choice, his publications, and his professional affiliations and, most significantly, it serves to set his work firmly in the context of a movement that reflects the dominant persuasion of American educators during the twentieth century. Whatever the subject of inquiry and whatever the technique of investigation, proponents of the scientific study of education have generally agreed that, as a coherent movement, it has been

15. *The Teaching of Reading: A Second Report,* Thirty-sixth Yearbook of the National Society for the Study of Education, Part I (Bloomington, Ill.: Public School Publishing Co., 1937); *Reading in the High School and College,* Forty-seventh Yearbook of the National Society for the Study of Education, Part II (Chicago: University of Chicago Press, 1938); *Reading in the Elementary School,* Forty-eighth Yearbook of the National Society for the Study of Education, Part II (Chicago: University of Chicago Press, 1949); *Development in and Through Reading,* Sixtieth Yearbook of the National Society for the Study of Education, Part I (Chicago: University of Chicago Press, 1961).

"an effort to secure as exact information as possible to serve as the basis for practice."[16] This is a succinct statement of the informing concept underlying Gates's scholarly studies and pedagogical prescriptions and, as noted in his autobiography, it is the answer he developed to Dean Russell's question about the relative merits of the "academic" and "professional" mind. The suggestion made earlier in this essay that Gates has been a force in marking out certain domains of inquiry with regard to reading does not imply that he has provided definitive answers to the questions raised, nor that he has claimed to have done so. On the contrary, he has regularly maintained that there are many ways to teach reading, perhaps as many as there are pupils to be taught. What he has advocated, however, is that rigorous, systematic methods of investigation should be utilized, that research must provide the basis for every program of reading instruction, and that further scientific study is prerequisite to progress in all educational practices. Though constant in his praise of method, Gates's own approaches to educational research have varied over time. In a retrospective address to the International Reading Association in 1968, he said, "my first love was the analytical, experimental, and theoretical psychology. . . . [During the] years I still regard as my best, I used these approaches as my primary ones. . . . [Later, for reasons of efficiency] I shifted more and more to the mass-statistical approach. . . . [But now] I would happily return [to the] analytical-experimental . . . approaches."[17] If a dispassionate investigator is permitted one passion, "method" has been Gates's. Given this identification with the scientific study of education and the honorific status accorded science by American educators, Gates's visibility within that movement takes on the aura of esteem.

These points regarding Gates's prominence and importance might be emphasized by contrast. If the first five decades of the twentieth century are taken as the era of Progressive education and the scientific study of education is viewed as part of that complex movement, then one might expect that a person of Gates's stature would enjoy

16. Frank N. Freeman, "Introduction," *The Scientific Movement in Education,* Thirty-seventh Yearbook of the National Society for the Study of Education, Part II (Bloomington, Ill.: Public School Publishing Co., 1938), p. 2.

17. *Reading,* ed. Staiger and Andresen, p. 13.

similar repute across a wide range of Progressive educators. This seems an especially plausible assumption when it is recalled that Gates, in his autobiography, acknowledges his general agreement with the pedagogical point of view expressed by Dewey and Kilpatrick and when it is noted that the persons and ideas that make up the several strands of progressivism have overlapped and intertwined throughout Gates's professional life. But such, apparently, is not the case. Neither the writings most often taken as representative of Progressive education nor subsequent historical accounts of that much studied movement give significant notice to Gates. This is not to suggest that he has not been, in some sense, a "progressive" educator, but only—and most importantly— that he has stood in a different relationship to other groups of educational reformers than to his own primary reference group.

Other persons concerned to improve the condition of American education (principal among them some of Gates's Teachers College colleagues) set out to remake American society and its intellectual foundations or to secure for the child a new and central role in the scheme of things educational. While Gates was collecting evidence on which to base new methods for teachers of reading, George Counts was daring the school to build a new social order, John Dewey was reconstructing philosophy, and Harold Rugg was promoting the child-centered school. During a period of widespread reexamination of matters both internal and external to schooling, Gates put his professional energies into trying to provide a better knowledge base for the teaching of reading, a set of abilities that he has considered foundational to all formal education and, thus, fundamental to enhancing the quality of living, in both its individual and social dimensions.

Those reformers who focused their attention on factors external to the psychological laboratory and the classroom were heavily involved with political questions and ideological conflicts. Gates was not; it would seem fair to characterize his interests and his activities as apolitical and nonideological. Perhaps partly because he did not engage in the rhetoric of radical reform, he has not been a controversial figure. He has, with regard to major issues, taken the position of moderate—sometimes moderator—or, to use his own term, "nonsectarian." His "on-the-one-hand-but-on-the-other" assessment of the "activity movement" at a time when it was the center of vigorous debate illustrates this stance.[18]

Considered comparatively, then, Gates's reputation turns out to be a function of the setting in which his career is viewed. In the community of scientific investigators of education, he is paramount and highly regarded. In the community of social reformers of education he is, in a word, undistinguished.

The notion I am advancing is that leadership is contextual and contingent and that, in order to account for Gates's stature as a leader, the primary contexts in which he has spent his public, professional life and the relationships upon which reputation depends must be given first consideration. In Gates's case—using evidence from his own record of his career, his published works, and public reports of his reputation—the relevant background is the scientific orientation of that group of educators with which he has been most closely identified. That is the setting, both substantive and normative, for his professional activities. There his contributions have been recognized as appropriate and judged according to criteria generally agreed upon. It is the conjunction of visibility and value within his primary reference group that constitutes grounds for Gates's acclaim as a leader in American education.

Gates himself has suggested my concluding point. He notes, in his autobiography, that the value of particular research studies, curricular materials, or teaching methods is dependent upon their time and circumstances. That observation seems pertinent to the matters considered in this essay. To paraphrase both Gates and the authority he cites: "Sufficient unto the day the [educational leadership] thereof."

18. "Statements by Various Members of the Committee," In *The Activity Movement*, Thirty-third Yearbook of the National Society for the Study of Education, Part II (Bloomington, Ill.: Public School Publishing Co., 1934), 189-90.

CHAPTER VII

Sidney Leavitt Pressey

Part I

An Autobiography

Now at the age of eighty, I am still battling long-continuing gross faults in our schools which first irked me as a boy in the grades. Trained as a laboratory psychologist, I was soon declaring the laboratory too piddling artificial and psychology either too biological or too theoretical to come helpfully to grips with major human problems. That, I tried to do first by relating to psychiatry; but fortunate circumstance soon moved me into very practical educational research from which base I forayed wide—as, with increasing age, into gerontology. An earlier autobiographical sketch [1] followed those meanderings. This one focuses on issues educational, hoping yet more adequately to elucidate them.

Stimulating Home, Stuffy Schools

My parents both came from a charming little old southern New Hampshire village near which both families had long lived—and where in my childhood we often vacationed. My mother taught school, attended the New England Conservatory of Music, played the pipe organ in the Congregational church where Grandfather Pressey long served as deacon. My father graduated from Williams College and Union Theological Seminary, thereafter serving Congregational churches mostly in the Midwest—though his first parish was in Brooklyn, New York, where I was born December 28, 1888.

1. "Sidney Leavitt Pressey," *A History of Psychology in Autobiography*, vol. 5, ed. Edwin G. Boring and Gardner Lindzey (New York: Appleton-Century-Crofts, Educ. Div., Meredith Corporation, 1968), pp. 311-39. The permission of editor and publisher is here gratefully acknowledged, that I might again tell my story, but now with different emphases.

For his denomination and his time, he was a liberal; and he tried to relate to the entire community—besides the usual services there were lectures, entertainments, and organizations of various sorts with opportunities for all to participate. My mother was devoted to her little family (I had a sister six years younger) and her husband's work, though often herself not well. Since during my childhood and youth my father's church was in a suburb of the Twin Cities not far from the University of Minnesota, community contacts and resources for enriching the total program of the church were many and various. In much of this I was involved. Thus I printed tickets for lectures on my little press and ran the stereopticon if there were slides, played in the Sunday school orchestra, helped plan and then delivered the parish newsletter. Some contacts in the role of minister's son and some tasks might be irksome—but they were all educative. Though I came to question beliefs my father preached, I admired my parents' selfless devotion to his work.

With my mother's help, I began to read before entering school. The family subscribed to excellent magazines, my father's library was sizable and included such compendia as the *Encyclopaedia Britannica;* I became an omnivorous reader. I also had a workbench and early developed an interest in handicraft and gadgets which has remained with me. But the local elementary school took no account of such factors: every child started in the first grade and stayed eight years, and all did the same work in the same way—mostly drill in oral reading, arithmetic, grammar, spelling, and handwriting, largely rote learning in the geography and history of places and events. Eight years of such drudgery, being taught what I already knew, or could learn in a third the time! Long before this "thorough grounding in the fundamentals" was over, I was wishing it was.

In high school my most valuable courses were in typing and shorthand, which resulted in a secretarial job the next summer (in a college of agriculture office concerned with livestock) and which have aided me ever since right up to and including the writing of this paper, and also improved my composition more than any course so labeled. A "literary society" gave experience in debate. Four years of Latin was drudgery with negligible profit. Mostly, high school was dreary and the last year redundant. The most broadly educative experience of these years was a summer job in a department store;

there I wrapped bundles, made special deliveries all over town including the red-light district, and chummed with fellow workers very different from people I had known before.

My first college year was at nearby University of Minnesota. There I delighted in a literature course dealing with current magazines and recent American books—my only escape, in all my schooling, from authors mostly English and all dead. There in the physical education program I learned to swim, play handball and tennis—my physical recreations so far as I had time, for years thereafter. Then the family moved to a parish in Massachusetts and my father urged me to transfer to his alma mater, Williams, where his classmate Harry Garfield had just become president. I found Williamstown a lovely little place in the Berkshire Hills but student life dominated by athletic interests and fraternities and a curriculum indeed conservative: required were a fifth year of Latin and mathematics, and composition and literature largely repetitive of work had before, much of it in high school. I majored in American history, studied and restudied wars and political maneuverings long past, only in the last half of my senior year getting within twenty years of the then present. But a course in social psychology, using as major reading McDougall's book with that title and taught by a young assistant professor formerly a student of William James, suggested that there might be a science of human behavior yielding some understanding of those historical personages, of my former teachers (many so stodgy), of the people I had known in the department store, of the folks in my father's congregations, of my overworking ever anxious parents, and, mostly, of unhappy me. Here, I decided, was what I had been wanting, and I obtained a scholarship to begin graduate work at Harvard in 1912.

There, psychology was then in the department of philosophy, and my first adviser was a philosopher who urged more background of epistemology and metaphysics; he found unprecedented my desire to take some courses in the newly forming graduate school of education—where I sought ways schools might be made less bumbling than I had found them. And he was aghast at my wish to take Walter B. Cannon's medical school course in physiology as a foundation for psychology—though Cannon was already internationally known for his brilliant research on the physiology of the emotions. But finally my requests were granted, and I found the mix of psychology with education and physiology richly stimulating, not only in content but also in diversity of associates and indeed of basic points of view in graduate school, medical school, and school of education. There I remember Dean Holmes mentioning promising new materials called tests, as in arithmetic, which might make possible educational measurement.

For further study I needed money; and if, as I now thought, I desired to teach in college, I should try it. Here, my father had not only a suggestion—why not broaden my experience by teaching a year in a missionary college—but had found a place, a little home-missionary institution in Alabama. So there I went, never having known a Negro except for one classmate nor been in the South. Not only did the race prejudice there shock me, but also the gross irrelevance of the educational program to student needs. For those students, attending at great sacrifice and presumably seeking understanding of their problems and preparation for such opportunities as conceivably might open to them, there was a conventional arts program; in the little theological seminary Hebrew was taught, but nothing about problems likely to be met in a struggling Negro crossroads church. The students sensed these inadequacies; a protest meeting turned into a mild riot so blunderingly dealt with by the president that the faculty chose a committee (of which I was a leader) to ask the home office in New York to review the whole situation. That review was made with such arrogant disregard of basic problems that all the younger faculty left at the end of the year. I again had a Harvard scholarship and returned there almost exhausted.

The next year was a dreary struggle with ill health, language requirements, and a Titchenerian psychology barren of significance for me. For a thesis project I was given an investigation of effects of hue and brightness of surroundings on productivity in work—this being one of Munsterberg's efforts in applied psychology. After much tedious experimenting, I obtained some data suggesting greater productivity with bright lighting as compared to average or dim—all this with tasks not involving use of the eyes and so a general dynamogenic effect. Hue made no difference. A general alerting or stimulating effect of brightness seemed in accord with general observation and, if verified, of possible profit to electric light companies and importance for those planning lighting in shops, offices, or schoolrooms (51).[2] But twelve minutes with a given brightness in a laboratory darkroom at odd inconsequential tasks (and a total for three years of only twenty-six subjects) told little about possible effects of similar brightness continued throughout the day while working at tasks more substantial. I became impatient of the artificialities and limitations of the laboratory. And meantime I had begun work with the man most influential on my career—R. M. Yerkes.

Yerkes was the most active in research of the Harvard psychologists, probably greatest of all comparative psychologists and certainly most wide-ranging—at this time he was also directing psychological work at the Boston Psychopathic Hospital. Venturing into this work, I found it fascinating, and Yerkes appointed me a psychological intern there, where I was in residence for over a year while completing my thesis and disposing of the doctoral examinations. The hospital was a relatively new institution handling about 2,000 cases a year, keeping each long enough for first diagnosis and reference to a state hospital, social agency, or other provision for treatment. To it the police brought chronic alcoholics, criminals (possibly psychotic), girls off the streets; to it physicians, employers, and social agencies referred persons exhibiting symptoms of mental illness or disability; into the outpatient department came problem children from schools, courts, and agencies for child care. The staff included outstanding psychiatrists, another psychologist, and social caseworkers. As intern I made acquaintance with all these various groups, had access to the wards, case records, and excellent library, and attended morning staff rounds and staff meetings.

My work was chiefly testing children in the outpatient department, using the Yerkes Point Scale (having essentially Binet-type material but with like items together rather than scattered through age levels) plus Healy form boards and a variety of other material. However, on occasion I was also asked to test psychotic adults to seek evidence of intellectual deterioration. Such tests were then still new and their value in measuring the growth of "general intelli-

2. In this chapter, the numbers in parentheses refer to the numbered items in "Selected Publications of Sidney Leavitt Pressey."

gence" in children much questioned. The use of such materials to measure possible decline of abilities in adults and especially their use with those mentally ill to appraise possible effects of this or that type of illness on abilities—such were indeed pioneering ventures needing appraisal. That, Yerkes suggested I attempt. And in a little series of studies I compared in detail the responses on each test question (and each move on each form board) of normal and feebleminded children with the responses of dementia praecox and chronic alcoholic patients, all testing as of the same "mental age," but the psychotics having histories indicating that they had attained adult intelligence. Records of adult feebleminded were also examined. Certain items were found especially differential of the psychotics; these I combined into a "differential unit" with tables from which I could read off the rough probability that (for example) a patient was feebleminded with a few odd symptoms rather than a deteriorated alcoholic. Yerkes was much interested, arranged that I present the first of these studies at a state meeting, and helped me prepare it for publication (45). And he obtained for me, for the coming year, an outstanding appointment (at a better salary and with far more research opportunity than any other contemporary Harvard Ph.D.) at Indiana University to investigate problems of mental deficiency and disease in that state.

So, at long last, in 1917 at the age of twenty-eight I had my Ph.D. and a job, having essentially completed two doctoral projects and other research besides—really two doctoral programs—and utilized Harvard's rich resources for advanced training more widely than any of my associates. In the process I had taken four graduate years instead of the then usual three, and had become almost physically exhausted from overwork (plagued with insomnia, episodes of dizziness, and indigestion). As I now look back at my total education, I can see that three main thrusts in my total career, into which I threw myself with the evangelical devotion of my parents to their work, had already formed: (a) From the insistence in the first grade that I learn to read although I already knew how; through all that Latin to the language requirements and all the cramming about theories and psychologists already then out of date to get the doctorate, the schools had wasted my time. *I would seek more realistic determination of educational goals, of young people's abilities, and of their progress toward those goals.* (b) Whenever I escaped from school into the work world, as in the department store or the hospital residency, I felt freed from stale-air passivity into exhilarating participant worth. *I would try to make students active and participant in their education—and release them earlier into the challenges of a career.* (c) Not until Yerkes did anyone in college or university help in planning or furthering my career. Not only did he get me my internship and my first paper-giving and first publication and first job; until shortly before his death he helped me get research grants and advised me in sundry matters. *I would try to make myself continuingly helpful to my students.*

The hospital residency enlarged my life in a further very important way. Williams was a men's college, and both staff and students in the Harvard laboratory were male. But in the hospital, some resident there and thus so easy to chum with, were many able, friendly career girls—nurses, secretaries, social caseworkers. One of these last was a Vassar graduate, with some work in psychology there, who showed interest in my research. Though a childhood victim of polio, corrective operations and exercises had carried her through to unusual physical vigor, but with some emotional residuals as morbid fear of operations, cancer (from which her mother had died), childbirth, storms, closed places—on a European trip she slept on a deck chair, finding a cabin intolerable. We talked over our problems and our work, became very well acquainted, planned marriage. Postponement of both job and marriage seemed imminent when I was drafted shortly after this country entered the First World War, and again when Yerkes offered me a commission for participation in the army psychological work which he headed. But both times I was rejected as physically unfit for any form of military service. So out we went to Indiana where my wife, desiring a career, began graduate work and obtained the doctorate with my guidance, using part of the total program there for her thesis project.

Toward a Technology and a Science of Education

The initial task at Indiana University was to determine the number of subnormal children in the schools of the county in which the university was located—the county comprised Bloomington, then a city of about 12,000 population, and the surrounding countryside, then with some one-room schools in hollows as primitive as in isolated areas of Kentucky. But the university was also much interested in locating gifted children; a class for them in Louisville was then attracting much attention—and was disturbing conservative schoolmen since the youngsters were zestfully doing two years' work in one. To cover territory so diverse and such a range of childhood abilities, a first sorting with group tests was clearly needed. Nothing satisfactory being then available, my wife and I developed a 200-item, ten-test examination for grades 3 to 12 in which we tried to keep the easy rapport of a Binet in an apparently informal group procedure (actually well standardized) yielding objective scores. This examination we ourselves gave to those grades in the city, also in the country schools with the help of a graduate student. Pupils scoring especially high or low (and children in the first two grades so judged by the teacher) were then given the Stanford Binet. These last testings indicated that the group examination was making a good first sorting; but for further evidence to that effect we went to Louisville and found that those "whiz kids" did test very high on our examination, then visited the state (Indiana) school for the feebleminded and found that those there who could take the test at all scored very low.

Clearly, certain schools of this largely rural southern Indiana county were burdened with many subnormal children; there were also goodly numbers of bright youngsters, mostly held to a slow-average, lockstep pace, though a few who had accelerated illustrated how successful such expediting could be—and we persuaded the schools to accelerate a few more. All this was reported in local and state meetings, and the need for more special classes or other special treatment for the very dull and very bright was discussed. Mostly, the schoolmen considered such efforts not then feasible; but they were much interested in certain school and city comparisons of "pupil material." The children in one of Bloomington's three elementary schools averaged a year in "mental age" below the other two; the principal felt his teachers thus largely cleared of blame for the poorer work their children were doing. A second school showed an exceptional range of abilities, and this seemed explanatory of difficulties its teachers had had in keeping their classes together. And the analysis of the group intelligence examination that had been given in another small city with a school system supposedly inferior presented the anomalous finding that the pupils in its upper grades averaged a year in mental age above those in corresponding grades in Bloomington and provided an explanation of great importance for school policy. The inferior school system failed so many pupils (a dull child might be kept in the first grade three years) that the less able dropped out of school before reaching the upper grades, and the pupils there were on the average four months older than in the school with a more lenient promotion policy. Age for age, the children in the two little cities averaged the same. In short, by an outrageously heavy retardation and negligible acceleration, an inferior school system might show a spurious superiority in grade comparisons as to its pupils' ability and presumably also in achievement in the school subjects (46). Schoolmen were much interested and asked for tests facilitating such comparisons.

We therefore constructed two very inexpensive and easy-to-give-take-and-score test folders markedly different from the elaborate "batteries" then appearing and prevalent since. For grades 3 to 12 the first cross-out test, (on the front page of a little six-by-nine-inch four-page folder) consisted of twenty-five items such as "see a I man on," the task being to cross out the word not belonging in the sentence. On the next page the second test consisted of twenty-five items such as "dog cow horse oak cat," the task being to cross out the item not belonging with the others. A number series and an abstract meanings test were similarly simple (47). The blanks cost only a penny apiece, a class could be tested in twenty-five minutes, blanks scored one per minute. In contrast, another survey "battery" then widely used cost seven times as much, was nine times as bulky, took five times as long to score—and showed no better correlations with independent indications of ability. Another inexpensive easy-to-use folder made up what is believed to be the first group objective examination for appraising general ability in the first three grades. On the first page were twenty-five patterns of dots with one extra and this to be marked off; the second page had twenty-five groups of pictures, as of two dogs and a cat, and the incongruent item was to be crossed, a paper form board and a picture absurdities test followed, having surplus or wrong elements to be checked. Very practical validating research showed that this little four-test folder, given in the first month of the first grade, sectioned pupils better than a teacher could then do, in terms of the sectioning she had arrived at by the end of the school year.

The two cross-out tests thus seemed very convenient, inexpensive devices, making it feasible for any school to make a first appraisal of the general abilities of its pupils, from grades one through twelve. They thus seemed a contribution to a practical educational technology. But they also facilitated educational research as exampled by a little series of papers most often published in collaboration with students, thus giving them recognition. Children from poor hill farms tested in ability below those from good farming country—but both tested below city children. In the city, both cross-out tests (one for grades 4 to 12 and one for grades 1 to 3, the latter involving no reading) agreed in showing the ability of children of professional parents to be much above that of the children of unskilled laborers, but showed a few of the latter to be very bright and deserving of encouragement in their schooling. Comparison of school youngsters with inmates of a girls reform school and with attendants in a state hospital showed these last two groups and especially the attendants exhibiting such irregularity on the different tests as to raise doubts regarding the significance of their relatively low scores.

My cross-out technique facilitated testing in the school subjects also. Thus, a reading vocabulary test consisting of seventy-five lines such as "is do ki at in," the directions being to cross out in each line the one item that wasn't a real word, proved an easily understood and enjoyed game, differentiating the first four grades more clearly than any other reading test then available. A child's understanding of a sentence was well evidenced if he crossed the changed word in "The chill wind blew the snow and made the house warm." An occasional child was found who at entrance to first grade could read—and more fifth-graders who could not. We issued simple inexpensive easy-to-use tests in all the major elementary school subjects—and results were sometimes startling. On one occasion a big-city superintendent asked us to measure how much less children learned in a primary school so crowded as to have only half-day sessions than did the children of a neighboring school which kept them the full school day. We found no significant differences—and our tests were thrown out as discredited. They were inadequate for the purpose. But when I considered how weary both pupils and teachers in this last school were by mid-afternoon (and how weary I had been in those grades), I thought maybe our tests told some truth. At least, shouldn't tests be used as one means of determining how long a school day should be?

So we had exceptionally usable tests of ability and of attainment in the school subjects and had evidenced their usefulness. But I felt the need also for an easy-to-use personality inventory applicable down into the grades. After much exploring, I issued a little folder which on three six-by-nine-inch pages had a total of 450 items, all covered by the average student in about twenty-five minutes—a record as regards compactness and yield of score per unit of time spent which apparently still stands after almost fifty years. On the first page, the directions were to cross out everything considered wrong in twenty-five lines listing a variety of borderland social and moral taboos such as "begging smoking flirting spitting giggling," then go back and circle the one item in each line thought worst—in effect, each word was a question and each line one more. The second and third pages similarly sampled worries and interests. These were called "X-O Tests" because of the crossing and circling. The total number of words a person crossed out was considered his total affect, and the number of lines in which he circled a word other than the one which had been found modal was his total idiosyncrasy. The form was found usable as low as the fifth grade, was tried out in several clinics and a psychopathic hospital, and systematically used in ways to be described shortly.

The four years at Indiana University resulted in fifty-three papers by myself, my wife, local teachers, and students—whenever possible I brought others into the program and gave them recognition. I had some clerical and secretarial help; usually taught one class, sometimes in extension; presented papers at local, state, and national meetings; and worked in schools and state institutions. It was an almost ideal way to begin a professional career (in contrast to a fellowship for postdoctoral study, which for me would have been a stifling continuance of mere going to school) and resulted in an invitation to Ohio State University as assistant professor in 1921, where I insisted on an appointment for my wife also.

There the feverish pace continued. It was an exciting time: psychology was becoming applied and education becoming scientific—and we were in the middle of it all! In the next dozen years were produced three books, two laboratory manuals and a monograph, some seventy-five professional papers—and four teaching machines. I also had a full teaching load, increasing numbers of graduate students, and committee assignments. And I attended regional and national meetings in both psychology and education, usually participating in some way. It was a marvelously stimulating, challenging life. In 1926 I was given the rank of full professor.

The first book (1) brought together in very practical nontechnical form the then current work in testing of both ability and attainment in the school subjects. It was widely used, reissued in England, and brought out in a French translation. The second text (2) was based on the experience at the Boston Psychopathic Hospital and in the Indiana surveys; it attempted a nontechnical overview of the full range of mental diseases and deficiencies, with avoidance of both psychiatric and psychoanalytic technicalities. The purpose was especially to give school people more understanding of such diseases and deficiencies and of the ways they might be dealt with and, more generally, to give an orientation regarding problems of mental health which we thought every educated person should have.

Most original was a volume (4) in which I summarized eighteen investigations regarding problems of higher education, with which two-thirds of all doctoral projects under my direction have been concerned, on the double ground of need therefor and appropriateness for students looking toward college positions. The first chapter differentiated most effective methods of study by contrasting those used by superior and by failing students; a laboratory course based on those findings was shown to be a great help to students in academic difficulty; case studies made vivid their problems. In the volume it was also shown that some students beginning a required course in educational psychology were already able to pass the final examination; some matter was found better learned in independent study than in class; some important professional topics were shown not to be included anywhere in a curriculum of teacher preparation

—research regarding programs and methods in the preparation of teachers seemed much needed. When the already mentioned X-O Tests were given to 1734 subjects from the sixth grade through college, it was clear that the college years were the period of greatest change in moral and social attitudes and in interests. An informal inquiry form given to a sample of college undergraduates showed all of them reporting adjustmental problems of one sort or another but not one in ten receiving any help on these problems from the university, in either classes or conferences. Data on student use of time made clear that classes and study were often only a minor part of student existence—and the university seemed mostly indifferent to those parts most important for them. Most difficulty-causing deficiencies in preparation for college were found not in those secondary school subjects stressed in entrance requirements, but rather in elementary school tool subjects, such as arithmetic needed for science and grammatical terminology for foreign language: a so-informed educational diagnostician in a remedial laboratory with appropriate self-instructional materials, it was then noted, should usually be able to soon dispose of such difficulties. Indeed, the value of much conventional secondary school work was questioned: in this connection a simple little test of sensitivity to blank verse showed a majority of college freshmen to have none—really, is all that Shakespeare appropriate for high school kids! Contrast of data about classes (judged by students as good or poor) differentiated instructional features of merit. Analyses of college textbooks showed them overburdened with petty detail. It was demonstrated possible to teach a large college class by a social project method with evidenced good results. A majority of psychologists and educators thought those planning to teach in college should have some training therefor. I concluded this 1927 volume (believed first of its kind) with the naively optimistic prophecy that, through educational research, higher education would be "remarkably improved" within ten years!

Toward this end, I introduced a graduate course on problems of higher education and gave it for many years. And throughout my first twenty-five years at Ohio State (until my many other obligations forced me to give up the responsibility) I was in charge of the required freshman first course in educational psychology and tried to make it outstanding in content and method. It was taught under my direction, in sections of about thirty, mostly by doctoral candidates who often had thesis projects involving this course. Usually, some research was going on and this the students found stimulating, never objectionable, since the projects were always practical and where relevant their findings were promptly applied. But research and its prompt application ranged over all my university work. Thus I persuaded a graduate student to take four oral examinations for the master's degree under four different faculty committees with concealed stenographers keeping record. Two committees passed the candidate and two failed her; the questions in one examination were largely irrelevant (38). This is believed the first attempt at empirical appraisal of graduate oral examining. Split-half determinations of the reliability of a doctoral comprehensive written examination showed it to be low. As a result, the department made certain improvements in its examining procedures—but they didn't last!

Research regarding public school work was continued, but with applications to adult life. Thus, having noted a remark by Leonard Ayres that certain features of handwriting harmed legibility though not appearance, I collected samples of handwriting from elementary school through college and also from adults, had these read by students in a class in educational psychology, checking where they had trouble making out what was written, and found that a few malformings (as *d* and *cl* written so as to be easily confused, also *a* and *u*, *g* and *y*) accounted for most difficulties in reading (34). A simple chart facilitated identifying such errors and tabulating their frequency for each pupil. Remedial work concentrating on each pupil's specific difficulties was found very effective: thus a fourth-grade class so aided gained over a control group not only in speed and quality of writing but also markedly in the rate at which its writing could be read. A similar analysis of the writing of arabic numerals, found not only in school and college work, but also on business sales slips and on checks, again located a few common confusions (as 7 and *1*, *6* and incomplete *8* or *0*); and another little folder made easy the analysis and count of likely errors in reading each person's figurings—obviously such errors might be serious. It also seemed obvious that such very simple little charts might not only facilitate and improve the initial teaching of handwriting, but later, as very simple helps in keeping writing and figuring legible in college and business, might be very helpful. But publishers of handwriting systems weren't interested in anything so much simpler and less profitable to sell than those systems already established in the schools—after a few years these two little charts were discontinued as not used!

"Efficiency engineering" in improving correctness in English composition was analogously attempted. Thus, use of capital letters in newspapers, magazines, and business letters was tabulated; also, capitalization errors in samples of writing from school and college and from adult correspondence were compiled. Both usage and error data were then brought together in one simple table in terms of frequencies per ten thousand words. The few needed usages not mastered were then evident (32). Individual conferences with pupils about their capitalization errors gave insight as to causes (35). Rules for capitalization were then formulated taking account of all this, and a little six-by-nine-inch test sheet was made up systematically covering these rules. Essentials in punctuation, grammar, and sentence structure were similarly determined; similar simple diagnostic tests were published. Also published was a little pamphlet, *Guide to Correctness in Written Work*, giving rules which, if followed, would eliminate nine-tenths of all errors in written work. These materials were very widely used—but in supplementation to conventional composition books with all their formal grammar and syntax rather than as replacement therefor, as intended.

A simple thousand-word sample method of appraising the vocabulary burden of various types of reading matter showed marked differences (31). All school subjects had technical vocabularies; a college science text had over four-thousand words (almost all technical) outside the Thorndike list of the most common ten-thousand. But a series of studies taking account of frequency of use in various texts, judgments as to importance by experienced teachers, and adult needs showed essential technical terms to be perhaps a quarter of those used in a given textbook—most were barnacled with excess terminology. Classified lists of essential terms in the important school subjects and simple tests covering them were prepared as aids to teachers and pupils—and in hope of exercising some restraint on over technical textbook writers. All this was part of the great interest around 1925 in what was then often called "the psychology of the school subjects." But the "teaching machine" I exhibited at the meetings of the American Psychological Association that year proved ahead of the times.

In a window of the little apparatus there was shown a four-choice question to which the student responded by pressing the key corresponding to the answer he thought right. If it was, the next question turned up, but if not, he had to try again until he did find the right answer—meanwhile a counter kept a cumulative record of his tries. Moreover, the apparatus had two features no device since seems to have had: if a little lever were raised, the device was changed into a self-scoring *and* rewarding testing machine—whatever key was pressed, the next question turned up, but the counter counted only rights; also, when the set on a reward dial was reached, a candy lozenge was automatically presented (52). A paper the next year reported a device which, when a student went through an objective lesson sheet a second or yet more times, presented him only those questions on which he had made a mistake in finding the right answer the previous time through—that is, the device automatically provided selective review. And a third device automatically marked each error on a student's test-answer strip, printed on it the total number of his errors, and kept a cumulative count of number of errors on each question so that the instructor could at once see which questions had been most missed and center his discussion on them (54). Carefully controlled experiments evidenced that class use of this last little machine as an instructional aid significantly increased learning in a college course (educational psychology); and the first type of device aided even more, with its immediate feedback correction of errors and attesting of all right answers. My former student Hans Peterson and his brother devised and similarly attested the value of a very simple paper feedback "teaching machine": if a wrong answer on a test-answer slip was moistened, it at once turned red, but a moistened slip with a right answer turned green. If such feedback devices came into general use as aids in both instruction and study, an "industrial revolution" greatly facilitating both teaching and study seemed possible.[3]

However, by this time the Great Depression was making it ironic to accelerate the progress of young people into careers when there were none to be found or to save labor in teaching when there were many more teachers than jobs. The manufacturer of the one crude teaching machine I had been able to get on the market withdrew it from sale. The publisher of my tests went out of business. And—my wife asked for a divorce, having plans for a second marriage. The fault may have been mostly mine: we were too much together, I too often insisted on changing what I considered hasty in her work while she thought me fussy; undoubtedly my compulsive absorption in my work was hard to live with. So not only my marriage, but a professional partnership, broke up. After thirty-seven years, the hurt is still with me. But two good colleagues, who had been more aware than I of my wife's disaffection, willingly served as witnesses in my obtaining a divorce on grounds of desertion. The departmental chairman and dean assured me that my university status would not be affected. And when I talked with the woman (also on the university faculty as director of teacher education in home economics) who had long been my wife's best friend, her sensible, kindly understanding was in healing contrast to the tense irritability to which I had been accustomed. The association ripened into a marriage which now for thirty-five years has been vital to my well-being and the most precious experience of my life. Thus at the age of forty-five both my personal and my professional life were largely reconstituted. So far as possible I dropped work, especially at the public school level, with which my first wife had been associated and which she wished somewhat to continue; and I sought something of a second career. For that, a major undertaking was already underway.

3. These early papers are reprinted, with slight condensations, in pp. 32-93 of *Teaching Machines and Programmed Learning: A Source Book* edited by A. A. Lumsdaine and R. Glaser and published by the National Education Association in 1960. My brief comment, in that year, on then current work in this field is also included on pp. 497-505. The generous recognition by Lumsdaine and Glaser of this early work is very much appreciated.

Toward Making Teacher Training "Progressive"

In 1929 the College of Education began, under the general chairmanship of W. W. Charters, a sweeping attempt to remake its entire program; I was on the central committee, the committee on required courses—some seventeen committees in all. As chairman of a committee on honors I pushed through a program the central feature of which was a project involving actual work in the schools or with young people—and possible release from boresome required courses (39). Able students liked the challenge, school superintendents looking for teachers liked such students, and a little follow-up twenty years later indicated that an exceptional number of them later went on for the doctorate (37). But it was hard work for the faculty involved and was soon dropped. Inquiry having shown some students socially isolate and some too run-about, some vocationally naive and some too much on jobs even while in school, a card was prepared on which each quarter each student had to list not only the courses he wanted to take the next quarter but also any activities and any employment he then anticipated. And the adviser had to consider and approve the total plan (41). Advising was thus made much more adequate—but more bother. So the plan was dropped although it served a purpose, as will be seen shortly.

In the committee on required courses I agreed to criticisms that textbooks in educational psychology then current derived too much from experiments and theories distant from the everyday realities of public school classrooms. I insisted that certain required courses in education were also not close to those realities, also notorious as poorly taught and inconsistent—two hundred students given an uninterrupted formal lecture on the importance of small classes with full pupil participation! And I accepted the challenge to so remake the required course in educational psychology that in content and method it would be accepted as basic to a sound program for the preparation of teachers. In this effort I brought out a text (7), radically different from those then available, with a congruent sourcebook and laboratory manual. And instructional methods were made yet more venturesome.

The first half of the text was titled "Development during the School Years." It included chapters on physical growth and health, stressing interrelationships with personality; on interests as manifested in play and in reading, radio, and movie choices; on the social psychology of these years with emphasis on the often conflicting social worlds of home, school, peers, and adults; on emotional stress, with causes seen especially in those conflicts; on intellectual efficiency, with recognition of the importance of constitutional differences in abilities but with stress on influences hampering or fostering their development; on the individual child, with brief case studies emphasizing the importance of understanding each as a person. Material came from pediatrics and sociology as well as education and psychology. The book's second half, "Learning in School", began with graphs showing progress in reading, composition, arithmetic, and foreign language, with evidence that curricular and instructional research could make such learning much more effective. The chapter, "The Results of Schooling," began with distressing evidence as to how little was recalled of a school or college course a few months after it had been taken. Research on transfer showed study of Latin mostly a gross waste of time. But meaningful learning was found to be more retained and generalized; a cognitive rather than a stimulus-response learning theory was advocated. A chapter was devoted to general training, as in methods of work, and to development of character traits and aesthetic appreciations. And an enthusiastic final chapter foresaw notable advances soon, as a product of educational research. The text was very widely used and the revised edition yet more, with translations even into Japanese and Turkish.

Also distinctive was the *Casebook of Research* (10): seventy-six reports, edited to be very readable, showed that, for instance, a fine nursery school program seemed to increase somewhat the "general ability" of preschool orphans, that a brief test near the end of a college class hour substantially increased what could be recalled of that lecture two months later, that a motion picture may have long-continuing effects on the attitudes of high school students, that a school safety program did substantially decrease accidents. The twenty-five projects in the little *Laboratory Workbook in Applied Educational Psychology* (9) began with a data sheet to be filled out and turned in by each student regarding his background and interests, thus acquainting his instructor with him and illustrating information a teacher should have about his pupils. A condensed version of the handwriting chart already mentioned enabled the students to locate each other's illegibilities. Simple practice exercises dealt with methods of tabulating, finding percentiles, and making and interpreting graphs. All the exercises were thus practical. Two other forms helped each student select and appraise three professional journals and three tests of interest to him, using files of such materials available in the laboratory.

This freshman course was now taught by very informal social laboratory methods, in sections of about thirty students each, in a large room reserved for this course and having round tables seating five (discards from a dormitory dining room), also cabinets holding the sample tests and other materials, and cases displaying frequently changed exhibits, many brought in by students and explained to classes by them. Such furniture was made as class projects by industrial arts students in this course. On the walls were relevant pictures and charts and above them a frieze depicting children at play and in school, crayon-drawn on wrapping paper by fine arts students in the course. Perhaps half of the five fifty-minute class hours per week went into very informal class discussion, but during the remainder of the time the students worked together at the tables, going to the cases for materials as needed, talking freely with each other and the instructor. But despite all this stir, standards as shown by examinations were maintained. The staff (mostly doctoral candidates in educational psychology) met weekly; it was agreed that anyone might visit any class (including the one I usually taught) anytime (61, 64). Near the end of each quarter we picked the dozen or so students in the course we thought most outstanding and offered them laboratory-assisting jobs the coming quarter to look after all the "lab" material and help in any way possible; so even freshmen got a professional start—and a good proportion went on to fine careers, several mentioning to me since the value of this early experience.

Helped by the student data sheet, each instructor was expected to get acquainted with his students. At each table the students usually were soon chummy, and they often circulated about, sometimes moved by the instructor, to extend acquaintance. Sociometric appraisals evidenced that students became much more widely and more closely acquainted than in the average class (65). Socially sensitive instructors could note students not adjusting well; often, like a tactful host, they could foster easier acquaintanceship—also sometimes venture broad guidance as hoped for in the earlier mentioned adviser card.

As a result of the effort at curriculum revision mentioned a few paragraphs back, all other departments in the College of Education were done away with, and all other required courses merged in a series labeled Education number so and so. But the course in educational psychology had gotten itself a new and distinctively practical text, sourcebook, and laboratory manual, and had become the most colorful, unique, and lively classroom in the college, often shown to visiting educators. It was handling some eight hundred students a year in classes of about thirty by methods advocated (but not used) by the Progressive educators on the faculty., with tight supervision obtaining excellent instruction from graduate students while both training them in teaching and fostering relevant research. Appraisals by seniors and recent graduates rated the course outstanding. The college agreed that educational psychology should remain independent and the required course be under my direction. But outcomes were not merely local. The very wide use of the text and other materials, the reports I gave at meetings and published (as 61, 64), and the influence of my participating students, many of whom soon moved into positions of some influence, all spread the gospel that educational psychology should be based on realistic research in the schools and taught in accord with its own teachings—and, if these criteria were met, it was fundamental in any adequate program of preparation for teaching.

Life-span Psychology; and Acceleration

Meanwhile, I was working on what I consider my best book, *Life: A Psychological Survey* (11). I was now fifty and my friends mostly that or older; all those books on developmental psychology, which ended around eighteen with the completion of gross physical growth for certain left out most of life! And their orientation was biological; but this time of the Great Depression and of international turmoil made clear that the socioeconomic and cultural environment was major (62, 67). Increasingly, my work was so oriented. We regularly entertained our graduate students in our pleasant home and learned their problems and uncertainties of career. To assure their careers, I took them to meetings and got them on programs and placed most of them well. Sundry NYA and WPA people were now working for me and with them I had lunch and got acquainted; and I was involved in a statewide adult education project (40). So I set out to write a book which would cover human development and change throughout the life-span and would place emphasis on the socioeconomic and cultural environment.

For the wide ranging library work involved, I assembled a little staff of able, needy students, paying them myself; the two who stayed with the project throughout I made coauthors. And we used "quarters off" to get out and see things ourselves—to visit settlement houses and housing developments and courts in New York and Washington; to go to congressional hearings and government bureaus, to CCC camps and WPA projects, to Mexico for a glimpse of a more primitive economy and culture. After a summer's teaching at the University of Hawaii in 1937, we stayed on for four months for contacts with the many racial groups in the Islands and for use of the excellent resources there for study of relevant problems in the Orient. Fishing and golf were major means of contact in preparation of the book.[4]

The volume was divided into three parts. The first, titled "Conditions and Circumstances of Life," noted the "population explosion" (not much noted then) and the lengthening life-span, provided data on marriage, divorce, and the family, on occupations and employment, etc., and described differences in different places with respect to these variables. The following chapter brought together again in simple tables and graphs very extensive data on wealth, income,

4. Having taken up fishing and golf as chatty middle-aged recreations, I so chummed with a miscellany of folk in Ohio, Michigan, Canada, Mississippi, Colorado, California, Hawaii. And irked by the game's frustrations, I invented "softball golf": a bright-colored sponge rubber ball ¾ inch bigger than the standard required no tee, raised no divots on the fairway, was never lost, hurt no one if it hit him, and floated in water. Since it went only about a third as far as the standard ball, about three times as many foursomes could be on the fairway at the same time. All relaxed jocular fun, especially for the more elderly. So I finally wrote it up—"Why Not Softball Golf?" *Recreation* 44 (1951): 485, but to no effect. I have had no luck with any of my inventions.

education, and living conditions. Another chapter "The Invisible Environment—Culture" stressed this topic of major importance for psychology, then strangely neglected, and dramatically illustrated changes, as in the status of women, codes of conduct, science, and technology. Part II, "Development through the Life Span," dealt first with physical growth and change (not only through adolescence but specially thereafter and into old age) in physique, strength, skill, morbidity; then with the growth and decline of mental abilities—not only how abilities grow through the growth years but do they (as some tests suggest) cease growing or even soon decline: When is there most creativity, most aptitude for leadership, and such decline as to warrant retirement? How should education coordinate with growth, when make way for career? Indeed, what is and what should be the course of the work life? How do interests change not only from five to fifteen, but to thirty, sixty, eighty? Obviously, the social life changes and then changes again through all these years; how are those changes best made? What changes occur in attitudes, character traits, and personality; and are these primarily constitutional and presumably inevitable or more a product of the circumstances associated with each age? How do very brief biographies of morons, criminals, psychotics, average citizens, and famous men and women illustrate these phenomena? A final applicational section, "Problems of Life," focused on the practical question of how might a reader best try to increase his efficiency, better his adjustments, and plan his life?

The book was well received as a pioneering venture, tried in a few colleges as a beginning text, found increasing use in courses in developmental psychology extended to cover the life-span and in adult education for courses on "the psychology of adult life." I increasingly turned my efforts in these directions, gave such courses, and in 1948 initiated the Division on Adulthood and Age of the American Psychological Association (22). In 1957 I published, with Kuhlen, *Psychological Development through the Life Span* (14).

Certain issues were probed with research. Thus, the already mentioned X-O Test survey of 1923 was followed systematically by others in 1933, 1943, and 1953, showing over these thirty years increasing liberalism in attitudes and increasing rate of change from child-home to college-senior attitudes and interests. And the 1953 survey, which included adults up into the sixties, found their attitudes were sufficiently similar to college-senior attitudes in 1923 to suggest a retention of attitudes established early rather than an increasing conservatism with age (43, 44). The X-O Tests are odd scatter-gun devices and such findings are little more than agreements with what everybody knows; but the possible values of regular gatherings of data over long periods of time seem too little recognized. With change now increasingly rapid, such planning for its measurement would seem especially needed.

The famous Binet scale for measuring the general ability of children rightly has childish content and tasks. The Wechsler so-called adult scale does not differ greatly therefrom. Most group tests of "intelligence" are largely clerical in nature. So it really is not surprising that both types of tests show little gain or even a loss in the middle and older ages. But tests built with content and problems systematically chosen as adult in nature showed substantial increases in ability through those years (26). Again the material is insufficient. But it seems generally recognized that adult abilities may continue somewhat to "grow" (as in knowledgeableness, shrewdness, wisdom) even into the older years. If so, tests recognizing and appraising such growth should be of great value in personnel work, in adult education—and in portraying the nature and worth of maturity.

The outbreak of the Second World War brought great interest in possibilities of educational acceleration. I urged on Dean Klein of the College of Education the need for broad investigation of that topic—and the relevancy of much of my work. And he arranged that for several years I was largely freed for that investigation, with the help of a small staff and good campus cooperation. The total project was reported in twenty-four papers and a monograph (12), with important supportive papers since.

A sweeping historical review (12: 5-27) turned up much research indicating that able children might well begin school at the age of five instead of the conventional six; seven-year elementary schools had presented evidence they could do as much as those lasting eight. Terman reported that those boys in his famous gifted group who graduated from high school at a mean age of 14.9 more often went on to fine vocational success than those in that group who graduated at 17.3, though their childhood Binet ratings were substantially the same. Many attempts have been made to shorten the college four years to three or even two; Clark for twenty years had a three-year program and President Eliot long advocated a three-year program for Harvard—as was established practice in English universities. Students in a number of colleges who entered young were found more likely to graduate, and those who entered and graduated young were more likely to have good academic records than those who entered and graduated at the conventional ages. In short, there was no research justification for the rigid age-grade situation almost universal in this country thirty years ago—and now.

We piled up more data showing that students who entered college young not only did well academically but participated more in student activities, were more likely to go on to advanced training, and more often were successful in their careers. Students who during the war years completed a four-year undergraduate program in three years (a few in two calendar years) did better academically than students attending four years paired with them in ability and age at entrance, and were about as active in student affairs; and a follow-up ten years later showed the accelerates still doing better. There were intimations that functioning ability might be increased by some liveliness of educational pace. Indeed, precocious geniuses may be the product in no small part of opportunities to progress rapidly (18). As a result of the historical circumstance that when a hundred years ago the Ph.D. program was imported from Germany where it followed the gymnasium (largely a secondary school), it was made in this country to follow the American four-year college, Americans ever since have been getting the doctorate four or more years later than do German students—and thus losing years from their careers in the potentially most productive years of the prime. Congruent with this last inference is the finding that in several professional fields leaders obtained their doctorates several years earlier than average for that field (19, 20), also the psychiatric observation that those getting the doctorate late tend to be neurotic. Thus a variety of evidence supports Lehman's findings that age of maximal potential for achievement is in the early adult years and more broadly that those are the years of greatest total vigor (14).

As increasing numbers of students go on for advanced training and such training tends to lengthen, means of expediting educational progress become more important, from preschool head starts, through nongraded schools, and grade-skipping even in high school (21) to credit by examination and advanced placement, lengthened school year, "heavy" loads, and independent study perhaps with feedback aids (56). With such means wisely used, there seems reason to believe that programs of advanced training could be completed several years earlier than now, those years being added to productive career in the prime—and the educational system relieved that much in enrollments with all their cost. Perhaps student unrest would then be very substantially reduced.

Automation; Aging

Early in the Second World War, I wrote the Navy Office of Research and Invention, telling of my teaching machines, and offering to bring them to Washington and demonstrate them. There was no reply. But shortly after the war, several psychologist friends joined that office; at their suggestion I applied for a grant which was awarded and renewed and which supported extensive further work designed to accelerate learning. My most satisfactory "teaching machine" was simple—a little three-by-five-inch card with thirty four-choice answer spaces and an invisible ink in the "right" boxes so that when a right mark was made, a change of color followed. Using such very simple feedback materials, I again evidenced that, used with simple tests on each assignment, either informal instruction or independent study was much aided, as was shown chiefly by experiments with the subject matter in that required course in educational psychology which had long been my pride and joy and in which as always the students seemed much to like trying new devices which might help them now as students, perhaps later as teachers. The most dramatic success was with a "learning laboratory"—a little study room with all the course materials (including teach-tests with answer cards on all assignments), open every afternoon with an assistant to help as needed. Each student could come in as he wished, work alone or with others, and consult with the assistant if he felt the need. All the students (to be sure a good group) finished the course in half the usual time or less, all with high grades. But the navy office changed staff again, the new people were not interested—in disgust I vowed never to touch that ill-fated topic again.

However, my former student Leslie Briggs continued such work. Lumsdaine wrote me as did Skinner, with whom I had several delightful conferences. Being now near retirement, I planned no further work in this field. Then I was startled, at an Air Force conference on automated learning in 1958, by the learning theorists' ignorance of all the research regarding learning in school and their assurance in applying concepts there, derived from rat maze-running or paired-associates memorizing. And I was shocked by the commercialization soon following: hundreds of teaching machines put on the market, some sold door to door with extravagant claims; programs sold with as many as sixteen thousand "frames." Reluctantly I attacked both programming methods and basic theory, centering on the Holland-Skinner programmed college text *The Analysis of Behavior* as an authoritative pioneer of its type involving, as had my research, an undergraduate course in psychology—and processes of reading and study which I had much investigated. Such investigations had stressed the importance of reading for larger meanings and of noting paragraphs, headings, and summaries to find and structure those meanings and also to guide preview and review of main points. But the programming eliminated such cues to structure and aids to overviewing; instead, there was interminable bit-learning of specific responses to interminable "frames," with interminable writing-in of "constructed" completions to each, and interminable page-turning. I evidenced with simple little class experiments that (a) such time-taking busywork brought no more learning than simply reading silently, (b) objective questions with immediate feedback did not, with meaningful matter, mislead the learner with their wrong alternatives (as Skinner had assumed on a priori grounds) but did clarify meanings, and (c) such objective questions with feedback used to check on and clarify the understanding of organized subject matter could bring about better understanding than Skinner-type programs at a fraction of the cost in student time (55, 57, 58, 59, 60). Such simple use of feedback devices to help in the understanding of but not displace organized matter as in texts, I called adjunct autoinstruction.

In the background are issues of learning theory: does stimulus-response or cognitive theory most helpfully explain meaningful learning? But right up front now are strategies in educational technology including use of computers in aid of instruction, into which the big money is going but which might nevertheless often be going wrong. I have consistently argued that, in meaningful learning, structure should be kept and enhanced, and where possible the larger setting and significance also; and that, mostly, learning should be social. But computer-assisted instruction (CAI) more often isolates each learner in a carrel with itsy-bitsy tasks in sequence and no chance to see things whole or move about except as it is cut-and-dried in the programming, or to innovate with a friend. Surely computers may help, perhaps not so much take over, the teaching process. But I am foolhardy, being now so distant from research, to venture such comments.

At the Boston Psychopathic Hospital I had seen many senile cases, usually with complicating disease and of poor socioeconomic status. But sundry elderly faculty friends, seen at the faculty club, certainly remained sprightly. Then in 1944 my eighty-eight-year-old father came to live with us. He was still relatively active and alert and read widely; there even seemed certain gains with age—a relaxed mellowing of mood, more humor, good humor, and more tolerant judgment. Though slowing down physically, in intellect and personality he remained essentially intact until his death at the age of ninety-three. Here was an issue relatively neglected but both appropriate for investigation and of personal concern to a developmental psychologist now sixty: What are the potentials in contrast to the liabilities of age, and how might those potentials be increased?

To make practical contacts and see problems at first hand, I became active in local, state, and national organizations concerned with the old, and in adult education programs, offered a seminar and an evening course on problems and potentials of age—for which I had a variety of materials since we were now, in connection with summer school appointments and meetings, visiting recreation centers and institutions for the old all across the country. As a visiting professor, I gave such a course at the age of seventy-five. Local business firms, concerned with retirement policies, supported fellowships for study of them. We found one company insisting on retirement at sixty-five but a big department store keeping on a few good salespeople half time till eighty—still maintaining their fine sales records. A survey of psychologists past seventy found three still active at eighty in a big western state permitting a carefully selected few to continue half time to that age; one was teaching a course on the history of psychology rich in personal reminiscences, another was editing a journal, yet another was doing student counseling for which his relaxed grandfatherly good humor admirably suited him. Elsewhere a woman of eighty-one was continuing some work on child welfare. A zoologist at ninety-six served as a director on a state biological board. A man of eighty-five and a woman of eighty-two served on VISTA. And such notable men as Michelangelo, Voltaire, Franklin, Jefferson, Churchill did notable work after eighty. Policies seem needed, perhaps especially in education, permitting a tapering-off rather than arbitrary retirement at a set age—the policies to be selective according to health, capability, and desire for continuance (23, 24, 25, 29).

How long might capability continue, and what influences operate? Two centenarians were studied, both still prominent in their small communities. Constitution is of course the major factor but others are important. A widow of 102 though of course not still earning (or needing to) seemed as alert as the average person thirty years younger, the revered oldest member of her church and graduate of the little local college—such affiliations, roles, and status surely were important in maintaining that alertness. A three-year study, supported by the National Institutes of Health, of two hundred superior aged people in a city of some 400,000, emphasized the importance of such factors and ways in which they might operate more fully (13). But even these superior aged could less and less maintain such supports; and in every area we studied were many largely invisible aged, burdensome on relatives or stranded in cheap rooms—in the South and Southwest they were legion. To us it seemed wise, in advance of such debility, for old people to affiliate with a carefully chosen institution for the old and in advance of necessity go reside there. The task of clearing out one's old home can still then be manageable, and energies remain for making friends and finding some roles in this new last environment. So, that we have done, and we have studied the process and something of the nature of life in a fine retirement community (28). We are continuing such study.

Retrospect—and Prospect?

So now at the age of eighty I attempt assessment and understanding of my life. From my home came the earnest altruistic purposefulness of a liberal clergyman's family, also its cultural richness and awareness of community. From my education, excellent for its time, came nevertheless impatience with its rigid time-wasting inefficiency, its apartness from the full richness and complexities of living, and its indifference to the individual. With the first dozen years of my career, and first marriage, came an explosion of professional activity reaching wide, trying much to improve the practicality of tests and of their use, but endeavoring especially to exemplify, in the college courses with which we were associated, the best thinking and research bearing on their content and method —with a special fruition of all this in the invention and first appraisal of teaching machines. With my second marriage came an enriched personal life and an endeavor to make the curricular reorganization of the College of Education really exemplify the "progressive" gospel it preached; in especial, by innovating with a new textbook, sourcebook, laboratory exercise book, and a room as gay as a primary room before Thanksgiving, I tried to make the required course in educational psychology a lively social laboratory which would be both educative and fun. In mid-life, and under the stresses of the Great Depression, I reached wide to write a book which would see life at full length and in its socioeconomic and cultural environment. Then the educational urgencies of the Second World War exhausted me by intensive research evidencing need for flexibility in pupil progress, with earlier release of the most able from prolonged college-going into the full opportunities and responsibilities of life's young prime. In my seventies my great interest in educational automation was pleasantly rewarded by the generous recognition of my early work thereon, but I was deeply troubled by the turn in its development; hence, my reluctant efforts to rescue that movement from animal laboratory rigidities of thinking. Meanwhile, my age led me to study age.

And now—any prospects, when one has reached the age of eighty? Hopefully, this paper may show that there is some value in being able to look back a long way and see things in a long perspective. And here I am at eighty, a gerontologist now myself in a home for the aged. Mostly, gerontologists are, comparatively, young; and the prospectus for the upcoming international congress of gerontology urges more young gerontologists. But younger people know age only at a distance, in those shuffling oldsters often viewed with impatience. Now I am inside old age—and getting further and further into that condition. And I am in a domiciliary for the old. I hope that study of myself and my companions here, and of this little community as a residence for us, may contribute more intimate understanding of the aged and the modes of living most conducive to their welfare.

A BIOGRAPHICAL SUMMARY

SIDNEY LEAVITT PRESSEY. Born December 28, 1888 in Brooklyn, New York.

Family. Married Louella Cole, 1918, divorced 1933; married Alice Donnelly, 1934.

Education. Williams College, A.B., 1912; Harvard University, A.M., 1915, Ph.D. (Psychology), 1917.

Occupational history. Intern and assistant psychologist, Boston Psychopathtic Hospital, 1916-17; research associate and assistant professor, Indiana University, 1917-21; assistant professor of Psychology, Ohio State University, 1921-26; professor, 1926-59; professor emeritus, 1959—; professor, University of California at Los Angeles, 1959-60; University of Arizona, 1962-64. Summer Sessions: Teachers College, Columbia University, 1930; University of Utah, 1932; University of Hawaii, 1937; Colorado State College, 1939; University of Southern California, 1948; University of British Columbia, 1949.

Memberships and affiliations. American Educational Research Association; Society for Research in Child Development; Society of College Teachers of Education; American Association of Applied Psychology; (chairman of its section on educational psychology, 1941-42); fellow, American Psychological Association, member of its council, 1943-45, initiator and first president of its Division on Maturity and Age, 1947, president of its Division on Teaching of Psychology, 1948; president, Midwestern Psychological Association, 1942-45; fellow, American Association for the Advancement of Science, vice-president and chairman of its psychological section, 1946.

Awards. First E. L. Thorndike Award for Contributions to Educational Psychology, 1964; elected to emeritus membership in newly formed National Academy of Education, 1965. Gold Medal, American Psychological Foundation, 1970.

Part II

Selected Publications of Sidney Leavitt Pressey

Books and Manuals

1. *Introduction to the Use of Standard Tests* (with L. C. Pressey). Yonkers-on-Hudson, N.Y.: World Book Co., 1922, rev. ed., 1930.
2. *Mental Abnormality and Deficiency* (with L. C. Pressey). New York: Macmillan Co., 1926.
3. *Methods of Handling Test Scores* (with L. C. Pressey). Yonkers-on-Hudson, N.Y.: World Book Co., 1926.
4. *Research Adventures in University Teaching* (with L. C. Pressey and others). Bloomington, Ill.: Public School Publishing Co., 1927.
5. *Student's Guide to Correctness in Written Work: For Grades 7-12, with Teacher's Manual* (with F. R. Conkling). Bloomington, Ill.: Public School Publishing Co., 1926.
6. *Essential Preparations for College* (with L. C. Pressey). New York: Ray Long & Richard R. Smith Co., 1932.
7. *Psychology and the New Education.* New York: Harper & Bros., 1933; rev. ed. (with F. P. Robinson), 1944.
8. *Student's Handbook of Essentials in Methods of Work and Study, Written English, and Mathematics* (with J. F. Fullington). Columbus: Ohio State Department of Education, 1935.
9. *Laboratory Workshop in Applied Educational Psychology.* New York: Harper & Bros., 1936; rev. ed. (with M. E. Troyer), 1945.
10. *Casebook of Research in Educational Psychology* (with J. Elliott Janney). New York: Harper & Bros., 1937.
11. *Life: A Psychological Survey* (with J. Elliott Janney and Raymond G. Kuhlen). New York: Harper & Bros., 1939.
12. *Educational Acceleration: Appraisals and Basic Problems.* Columbus: Ohio State University, Bureau of Educational Research, 1949.
13. "Potentials of Age: An Exploratory Field Study." *Genetic Psychology Monographs* 56 (1957): 159-205.
14. *Psychological Development through the Life Span* (with R. G. Kuhlen). New York: Harper & Bros., 1957.
15. *Psychology in Education* (with F. P. Robinson and J. E. Horrocks). New York: Harper & Bros., 1959.

Articles

Acceleration

16. "Age of College Graduation and Success in Adult Life." *Journal of Applied Psychology* 30 (1946): 226-33.
17. "Time-saving in Professional Training." *American Psychologist* 1 (1946): 324-29.
18. "Concerning the Nature and Nurture of Genius." *Scientific Monthly* 81 (1955): 123-29.
19. "Age and the Doctorate, Then and Now." *Journal of Higher Education* 33 (1962): 153-60.
20. "Two Basic Neglected Psychoeducational Problems." *American Psychologist* 20 (1965): 391-96.
21. "Fordling Accelerates Ten Years After." *Journal of Counseling Psychology* 14 (1967): 73-80.

Aging

22. "The New Division on Maturity and Old Age: Its History and Potential Service." *American Psychologist* 3 (1948): 107-9.
23. "Case Study Comparisons of Successful and Problem Old People" (with Elizabeth Simcoe). *Journal of Gerontology* 5 (1950): 168-75.
24. "The Older Psychologist: His Potentials and Problems." *American Psychologist* 10 (1955): 163-65.
25. "Certain Findings and Proposals Regarding Professional Retirement." *Bulletin of the American Association of University Professors* 41 (1955): 503-9.
26. "Tests 'Indigeneous' to the Adult and Older Years" (with J .A. Demming). *Journal of Counseling Psychology* 4 (1957): 144-48.
27. "Most Important and Most Neglected Topic: Potentials." *Gerontologist* 3 (1963): 69-70.
28. "Two Insiders" Searchings for Best Life in Old Age." *Gerontologist* 6 (1966): 14-17.
29. "Genius at 80; and Other Oldsters." *Gerontologist* 7 (1967): 184-87.

Autobiography

30. "Sidney Leavitt Pressey." In *A History of Psychology in Autobiography*, vol. 5. Edited by Edwin G. Boring and Gardner Lindzey, pp. 311-39. New York: Appleton-Century-Crofts, 1967.

Educational Concerns

31. "A Method for Measuring the 'Vocabulary Burden' of Textbooks" (with Bertha Lively). *Educational Administration and Supervision* 9 (1923): 389-98.

32. "A Statistical Study of Usage and of Children's Errors in Capitalization." *English Journal* 13 (1924): 727-32.
33. "Fundamental Misconceptions Involved in Current Marking Systems." *School and Society* 21 (1925): 736-38.
34. "Analysis of 3,000 Illegibilities in the Handwriting of Children and Adults" (with L. C. Pressey). *Educational Research Bulletin* 6 (1927): 270-73, 285.
35. "The Causes of Children's Errors in Capitalization" (with Pera Campbell). *English Journal (College Edition)* 22 (1933): 197-201.
36. "A University Activity Program." *Journal of Higher Education* 8 (1937): 211-14.
37. "Outcomes of a Special 'Honors' Program, 20 Years Later." *School and Society* 82 (1955): 58-59.

Higher Education

38. "The Final Ordeal" (with L. C. Pressey and E. J. Barnes). *Journal of Higher Education* 3 (1932): 261-64.
39. "The New Program for the Degree with Distinction in Education at the Ohio State University." *School and Society* 36 (1932): 280-82.
40. "Outstanding Problems of 'Emergency Junior College' Students." *School and Society* 43 (1936): 1-4.
41. "A New Type of Record-Advisory System." *School and Society* 60 (1944): 110-12.
42. "Some Data on the Doctorate: With Special Reference to Postwar Education." *Journal of Higher Education* 4 (1944): 191-97.
43. "Changes from 1923 to 1943 in the Attitudes of Public School and University Students." *Journal of Psychology* 21 (1946): 173-88.
44. "1923-1953 and 20-60 Age Changes in Moral Codes, Anxieties, and Interests, As Shown by the 'X-O Tests'" (with A. W. Jones). *Journal of Psychology* 39 (1955): 485-502.

Psychological and Educational Testing

45. "Distinctive Features in Psychological Test Measurements Made upon Dementia Praecox and Chronic Alcoholic Patients." *Journal of Abnormal Psychology* 12 (1917): 130-39.
46. "A Comparison of Two Cities and Their School Systems by Means of a Group Scale of Intelligence." *Educational Administration and Supervision* 5 (1919): 53-62.
47. "A Brief Group Scale of Intelligence for Use in School Surveys." *Journal of Educational Psychology* 11 (1920): 89-100.
48. "Two Important Points with Regard to Age-Grade Tables." *Journal of Educational Psychology* 11 (1920): 355-60.
49. "An Attempt to Measure the Comparative Importance of General Intelligence and Certain Character Traits in Contributing to Success in School." *Elementary School Journal* 21 (1920): 220-29.

50. "A Group Scale for Investigating the Emotions." *Journal of Abnormal Psychology* 16 (1921): 55-64.
51. "The Influence of Color upon Mental and Motor Efficiency." *American Journal of Psychology* 32 (1921): 326-56.

Teaching Machines and Programming

52. "A Simple Apparatus Which Gives Tests and Scores—and Teaches." *School and Society* 23 (1926): 373-76.
53. "A Machine for Automatic Teaching of Drill Material." *School and Society* 25 (1927): 549-52.
54. "A Third and Fourth Contribution Toward the Coming 'Industrial Revolution' in Education." *School and Society* 36 (1932): 668-72.
55. "Teaching Machine (and Learning Theory) Crisis. *Journal of Applied Psychology* 47 (1963): 1-6.
56. "Psycho-technology in Higher Education versus Psychologizing." *Journal of Psychology* 55 (1963): 101-8.
57. "A Puncture of the Huge Programming Boom?" *Teachers College Record* 64 (1963): 413-18.
58. "Auto-instruction: Perspectives, Problems, Potentials." In *Programed Instruction*, pp. 355-70. Sixty-third Yearbook of the National Society for the Study of Education. Chicago: University of Chicago Press, 1964.
59. "Auto-elucidation without Programming!" (with J. E. Kinzer). *Psychology in the Schools* 1 (1964): 359-65.
60. "Re-program programming?" *Psychology in the Schools* 4 (1967): 234-39.

The Teaching of Psychology

61. "The Laboratory Concept and Its Functioning" (with others). *Educational Research Bulletin* 19 (1940): 187-216.
62. "Fundamentalism, Isolationism, and Biological Pedantry versus Socio-cultural Orientation, in Psychology." *Journal of General Psychology* 23 (1940): 393-99.
63. "Report of the Committee on Contributions of Psychology to Problems of Preparation for Teaching." *Journal of Consulting Psychology* 6 (1942): 165-67.
64. "Social and Useful College Classes." *School and Society* 55 (1942): 117-20.
65. "The Class As a Psycho-sociological Unit" (with David C. Hanna). *Journal of Psychology* 16 (1943): 13-19.
66. "Place and Functions of Psychology in Undergraduate Programs." *American Psychologist* 4 (1949): 148-50.
67. "Teaching in the Ivory Tower, with Rarely a Step Outside." *Psychological Bulletin* 52 (1955): 343-44.

Part III

The Autobiography of Sidney Leavitt Pressey: A Commentary

GERALDINE JONÇICH CLIFFORD[1]

Invitations to contribute autobiographical writings are essentially pannings for historical gold, undertaken in hopes of acquiring "as much as possible of the inner life and private action relevant to our understanding of large events." [2] Twice Sidney L. Pressey was asked to open his life to public account; twice he accepted.[3] What motives impel a man or woman to consent to write autobiography? Whether or not one knows the craft and has the tools of the historian, acceptance of so clearly a historical mission implies at least a *disposition* to act the historian. Age, wrote Pressey, enables one to see certain issues "in a long perspective" (30:313).[4] Moreover, a certain measure of psychohistorical interests led him to teach courses on "Psychology in Biography" from time to time (30:328).

The autobiographer may play *other* roles than that of historian, however; some may complement and others distort historical vision. This paper intends to analyze the autobiographical writings of Sidney L. Pressey as they illustrate various alternative functions—for the larger purpose of demonstrating the utility and the limitations

1. The author is indebted to Robert J. Havighurst for help in conceptualizing this paper, to Lana Brown Muraskin for help in researching it, and, especially, to Sidney L. Pressey for unfailing patience in responding to questions, for supplying additional biographical data, and for reprints of and comments upon some of his other writings.

2. Roger Brown, "The Secret Drawer": Review of *A History of Psychology in Autobiography*, vol. 5, *Contemporary Psychology*, 14 (1969): 51-53.

3. First, by a committee of the American Psychological Association, for the aforementioned volume 5 and, second, by the committee responsible for this yearbook.

4. Numbers run into the text, e.g., (30:328) refer to "Selected Publications of Sidney Leavitt Pressey," Part II of this chapter.

of the genre of autobiography for historical and psychological usage.

1. *To create a work of art, to act the man-of-letters,* to continue a venerable tradition of distinguished memoirs and famous "confessions" motivates some autobiography—for virtually all who write their life story must hope that it will be judged literate, if not "literary." Thus, autobiography resembles historical writing in the Western world in its earlier, unspecialized, and unprofessional days—when histories were typically "composed" by the literate and when historians, as a class, did not yet exist.

An introduction, however brief, exists to interest the reader and establish a mood. In this regard Pressey's second autobiographical effort is artistically superior to the first; from the historian's viewpoint it is also somewhat better in placing his life and work in relation to larger developments. There is throughout, however, a marked unevenness: The writing is, at points (*e.g.*, on test constructions), highly detailed and, on others (on machine inventions), generalized and even vague. Since, in the case of autobiography, the *facts* are all *equally known* (if not equally well-remembered), other preferences more powerful than literary consistency must be working.

The language of Pressey's autobiographies is simple and straightforward, although the construction is frequently complex. It is not poetic language, and rarely is an emotional response evoked by mood. With the sensible discussion of a sensible adjustment to old age, a response of grateful admiration arises in the reader. Another feeling follows Pressey's treatment of the ending of his first marriage, where one's impression is of labored effort, not artlessness, and the effect comes primarily from the interstices—i.e., less from the hurt admitted than from the bitterness and sense of betrayal imperfectly concealed.

2. *The desire to tell a story, to reminisce,* seems humanly universal; who has not told a story "on one's self!" His autobiographical writing, especially such passages as that on the teaching of a freshman class in psychology, brings Pressey's work alive as a dedicated and generous teacher—as he is perhaps best remembered by those who know his person. He offers, too, some recounting of

those personal "preferences, antipathies, and small ironies that are the background of great events" [5]—viz., his remarks on laboratory application and pithy explanation of public loss of interest in teaching machines. The value of frankness he recognizes, writing that, at 76, "I can comment more freely than a younger man about certain issues . . ." (30:313).

Yet, Pressey's is an incomplete story because autobiography is first and quintessentially the story of man qua man. Pressey leaves us unsatisfied here. Beliefs and convictions appear, but not his *reflections* upon them and upon himself. In a few words he tells us far more of his *opinions* of his first wife's inner feelings than of his own makeup. We are not told the substance of his part of "our problems." Is Pressey simply of an extremely reserved and nonintrospective temperament—such as was E. L. Thorndike, whose own autobiography was made, thereby, of scant usefulness? [6] Pressey's autobiographies do not otherwise suggest this quality about him.

Ordinary facts are absent: the names of his parents and of that New Hampshire village, the name and fate of his sister, identification of his first [7] and second wives (later supplied at the request of the editor), the title of his Harvard thesis, the identity of that southern college in whose rebellion he participated. From an oblique remark one may infer childlessness, but Pressey does not say.

Pressey handles well the telling of his reaction against what he perceived as the commercialization and "misguided" psychology behind the teaching-machine boom. This tale is, however, incomplete for neglecting what motivated the original work, what ideas inspired it, the thought processes by which the devices were conceived. The same problem inheres in discussions of the early testing work, expanded and elaborated upon over his first telling. The great detail and attention provided suggests that Pressey took special

5. Brown, "The Secret Drawer," p. 51.

6. Thorndike autobiography in *A History of Psychology in Autobiography*, vol. 3, ed. Carl Murchison (Worcester, Mass.: Clark University Press), pp. 263-70. Compare Thorndike's with the self-story of John B. Watson in the same volume, for an instructive exercise in character-reading through autobiography.

7. The late Luella Cole (who subsequently married anthropologist Robert H. Lowie). Generally speaking, fewer names appear in this than in the earlier Pressey autobiography. Pressey has since told the author that he considered it unnecessary, in an article of this kind, to name his birthplace and sister.

pleasure in it, experienced success at it, and came to regard the period of this work as the most rewarding years of his life; we can, however, only infer this.

3. *The role of record-keeper, the wish to "set the record straight,"* is more goal-directed and purposeful activity than is the spontaneous and nearly irrepressible tendency to tell a tale. At two points in his autobiographical writings Pressey *seems* to play this role: on the professional matter of the teaching-machine phenomenon, and on the personal topic of his first marriage. While the first gets more words, and second has, perhaps, more impact.

"The most extraordinary commercialization of a new idea in American educational history" (30: 332) is Pressey's description of the latter-day response to autoinstructional devices. Despite his "shock," he formally acknowledges the "generous recognition" of his early inventions as the pioneering work that it was and the pleasure that such notice affords him. Yet, he also goes on record to indicate that the teaching machine figured no *larger* in his career than did any other of his researches.[8] It is as if Pressey fears the losing sight of his other work in the lamentable, distorting glare arising from educational, psychological, and commercial interest in machines.

After B. F. Skinner presented his experimental work on teaching devices in his paper "The Science of Learning and the Art of Teaching" in 1954 (published in the *Harvard Review* and elsewhere), Pressey sent Skinner a most cordial letter and reprints of his own related work—acquainting Skinner with accomplishments previously unknown to him.[9] Pressey's disagreements with Skinner's theoretical system and with the programmed approach appeared first in 1959 [10] and prominently after 1963—in several Pressey articles (55, 57, 58, 60) and in those of some of his supporters, and in his first auto-

8. The teaching machine is not mentioned among Pressey's interests in the entry submitted by him for publication in Jacques Cattell and E. E. Ross, eds., *Leaders in Education: A Biographical Directory*, 4th ed. (Lancaster, Pa.: Science Press, 1948). It is included in the much later sketch in *American Men of Science: The Social and Behavioral Sciences*, vol. 8 (New York: R. R. Bowker & Co., 1968).

9. Letter of Skinner to the author, January 27, 1969.

10. In Eugene Galanter, ed., *Automatic Teaching: The State of The Art* (New York: John Wiley & Sons, 1959).

biography (30: 332f). Pressey also sharpened somewhat his theoretical criticisms of Skinnerian psychology for this present work.

While Pressey's concern with the placement of automated devices in a *total* educational context seems greater than does Skinner's, the two employ the same arguments in support of their use: immediate knowledge of results with each response, the reinforcing effect of manipulation itself, an active student working at his own pace, the release of teachers from supervision of drill work. Apparently there exist certain broad pedagogical and psychological principles so well accepted as to bridge the research generations.

4. *The psychological need to convert or convince, to act the preacher or the polemicist,* sometimes motivates human behavior, including some autobiographical writings; the *Confessions* of Saint Augustine is a most ambitious example. Pressey himself mentions the "evangelical devotion" which his career assumed and the marvelous stimulation and challenge which it gave to life.

The messianic drive could issue from grievances deeply felt; of such, as much has been already commented upon as can be inferred from this autobiography. Or it could stem from *ideological commitments.* One such commitment (and the one that so passionately moved his peer, E. L. Thorndike, that it acquired an ideological character) is the application of psychological science to man's affairs. "Throughout, I have worked with the conviction that psychology has major contributions to make to human welfare," Pressey wrote in the 1967 autobiography.

Yet the message of Pressey's autobiographical accounts is that he was a profoundly *nonideological* man—for our and for his times, a refreshing quality! If, indeed, he had an ideology, where was it acquired? What, if anything, did he read which made a lasting impression? He mentions an English course at Minnesota which finally allowed him to study contemporary magazines and recent American literature, but does not even say that it gave shape to his later reading tastes. McDougall's book is cited as leading him to psychology, but with even more restraint than Thorndike he writes of the experience of reading William James. That Pressey was moved to study with McDougall or can be considered a McDougall disciple cannot be said— even though Pressey exemplified, in his teaching, an educational psychology of far more social content than the average. The effect of his experience, then, seems uncertain but far removed from a religious conversion.

To say that Pressey is nonideological or nonphilosophic is to say merely that he does not *appear* to be a man moved by abstract ideas. It is not to maintain that he is without theoretical preferences. Neither did he avoid personalizing his work. On the contrary, his activities in educational psychology were intimately informed by his own schooling and teaching, and he appropriately took such progressivist colleagues as Gordon Hullfish and Boyd Bode to task for being ideologues who did not animate their own beliefs by their teaching practices. Similarly, Pressey's gerontological work was evoked by interactions with the aging and his own progress toward old age. Still, his discussion of what he considers his best book, *Life: A Psychological Survey*, represents his nonphilosophical approach—suggesting why Pressey's does not (unlike George Counts's furnish an example of messianic autobiography. Although his autobiography primarily offers a list of headings from his book, it suggests preoccupation first with questions of fact (e.g., do abilities decline with age), and second with technique (e.g., how to better coordinate growth and education). Normative questions—the "should" and "why should"—are not apparent.

In autobiographical form Pressey's educational preferences and antipathies are amply and consistently demonstrated. Does he not, then, demonstrate possession of a philosophy of education? He has, for example, written elsewhere that ". . . the purpose of education is to further the total development of children and young people and aid them to achieve the best possible adjustment to their total world. . . ." (63: 30). His department store work was, he judges, the most "broadly educative" experience he had in youth. This and other references to training for occupation mark Pressey as in the tradition of the early Progressive education movement.[11] But he was a nonideological progressive (broadly defined) revealing, autobiographically, no preoccupation with large-scale educational reform or with national organs of progressivism. At some points his activities contravened Progressive ideology: his work on accelera-

11. "I was sympathetic with the general point of view of the progressive educators . . . but disgusted with their smug assurance of having enlightenment. . . ." Letter of Pressey to the author, February 15, 1969.

tion for able students seems unlike progressivist emphasis upon the *equal* needs of all children and its overriding concern for the social outcomes of schooling.*

John Dewey wrote of education as growth, without end. The humanists judge education by its creation of lifelong appreciations and sensitivity, sharply distinguishing education from training. In *Pressey's autobiography* education is something to get done with, to leave behind, best when it enables one to "get on with" a career. Hence he describes his Indiana position as superior to postdoctoral study—"a stifling continuance of mere going to school"—because it provided a better initiation to a professional career. It is not that Pressey had little faith in institutionalized education; a lifelong devotion to improving educational practice in specific ways denies that. But his life sketches do suggest that Pressey's concern manifests less a philosophy *of education* than a "lived-in" philosophy *of teaching.*

5. Finally, autobiography may have *a professional purpose: the application of one's expertise to the understanding of his own life, the use of one's experiences to test his own field.* Most undergraduate students of psychology, wrote Pressey, "expect our subject to be of help to them in their own problems of living" (66). We must, he once argued, give prospective teachers a psychological knowledge that will not remain "abstract and depersonalized" (63). "So now," writes Pressey, "I attempt assessment and understanding of my life" (see closing paragraphs).

Because Pressey's is obviously and admittedly an *applied* psychology, his failure to employ psychological language or to reveal psychological insight into the analysis of his own behavior is especially surprising. Pressey's is autobiography bereft of psychodynamics. It may be that he tried and found his science inadequate to the task; if so, the effort is not herein revealed.[12] In this failure Pressey's autobiography is not remarkable. As Roger Brown has noted, "The genre—psychologist's autobiography—is uniquely suited to the treatment of private lifelong experience as psychological data;" but, with rare exceptions, the language and "the *concepts*

12. Near the conclusion of the earlier sketch Pressey wrote, "So at seventy-six I look back at my life, trying to decide whether my psychology helps me understand it. It doesn't much!" (30: 337).

*Editorial note: Dr. Pressey does give careful and detailed attention to the problem of acceleration from a social and broad intellectual view.

are ones that might be used by any successful man writing his memoirs."[13]

Leaving aside psychological terminology (like "extinction") and forgetting the use of theoretical constructs (like "reinforcement"), it would be instructive to the general purpose of assessing autobiographical adequacy to note the treatment given by Pressey's life story to certain major *topics* of psychological interest. One of these, prominent in educational and social psychology, is *motivation.* Pressey does not treat motivation as a psychologist would be expected to regard it; indeed, motivational questions far exceed answers. For example, among the men whose work influenced him only Robert Yerkes is mentioned.[14] But the engaging personality sketch of the first autobiography is omitted here, making the dynamics of Yerkes's impact quite obscure. *How* did a devoted worker in animal, laboratory experimentation, like Yerkes, influence a psychologist like Pressey—who was doubtful of laboratory work while still at Harvard, cool to its applications to education, and rejecting of the comparative studies which underlay Skinnerian work on programmed instruction? Surely the people who "inspired" Pressey did so beyond helping him win fellowships (as did J. B. Pratt) or find jobs (as did Yerkes).

When asked whether his work on aging owed any debt to G. Stanley Hall—Whose *Senescence* (1922) was as unique in its day as was his *Adolescence* (1904)—Pressey reported that, on the contrary, Hall "seemed superficial" to him.[15] No negative influence is suggested here, but as Pressey makes abundantly clear, his strong *negative* reaction to poor schooling became a *positive* influence of surpassing degree. What is missing are indications of *why* and *how* this stimulus worked: in what fashion did the boredom, tedium, and antipathy which school created arouse him to an academic career?

13. Brown, "The Secret Drawer," p. 52. Italics added.

14. "You ask about psychologists in addition to Yerkes who influenced me. Thorndike would come next; I saw him often at meetings, had him as conference speaker at Indiana and here, followed his work closely." Letter of Pressey to the author, February 15, 1969. But Thorndike is not mentioned in the autobiography by name, nor is Pressey's receipt of the first E. L. Thorndike Award from the section on educational psychology of the American Psychological Association in 1964. Since Pressey rejects S-R psychology, the substance or character of Thorndike's influence is unclear.

15. *Ibid.*

In his theoretical orientation Pressey identifies with cognitive psychology. Yet, that motivation which he does mention could be explained more easily by stimulus-response theory. This S-R characterization is an admittedly superficial analysis, but one which the autobiographies support more fully than any other explanation. For example, of his research Pressey writes, ". . . fortunate circumstances soon moved me into very practical educational research." And, ". . . my research in gerontology was stimulated by concern over my father's problems of aging and my own" (30: 313) without indication that a "higher-order" analysis led him to *choose* this field. Because his first testing experiences were with abnormal subjects he accepted, for his first job, similar testing responsibilities. Pressey's first avocational interests were the things he learned to do at school. Such "connections" are understandable, clearer than why —if he found his experiences at the Boston Psychopathic Hospital "fascinating" and the participation there "exhilarating"—he never developed a substantive interest in abnormal psychology. Also murky is why, laboratory-trained, he soon declared the laboratory "too piddling artificial and psychology too biological or too theoretical . . ."—even though the scientific temperament reportedly rejoices in experimentalism's artificialities, abstractions, and primitivisms. The lesson here may be simply that S-R explanations are easier (more natural?) to slip into, even though one's conscious preference is for an explanatory system of a "higher-order" rationality.

"The prevailing psychiatry," writes Pressey, "saw causation as organic rather than psychogenic, but . . . I saw cultural conflicts and socioeconomic stresses as often major but neglected causative factors" (30: 317). Nevertheless, Pressey continues this neglect in his own autobiographies; in no way do they support his reported *environmentalist* concerns.[16] He offers little information or speculation about parental impress; a section, "Stimulating Home, Stuffy Schools," lacks illustrative detail. The first sketch offered the generalized interpretation that "I am a product of the Puritan ethic of work and hope for a larger usefulness. . . . (30: 337). Elsewhere his

16. Pressey titled one article (62) "Fundamentalism, Isolationism, and Biological Pedantry versus Sociocultural Orientation in Psychology."

liking for handiwork Pressey connects to Yankee gadgetry[17] inviting one to relate the teaching-machine boom to America's historic use of capital-intensive approaches in production and of labor-saving devices at home. But little is included concerning social forces, except reference to the depression's effect upon his teaching machine. In describing his early productivity, a brief environmental note appears: "Psychology was becoming applied, and education becoming scientific—and we were in the middle of it all!" But of the theoretical and organizational battles within and around psychology, education, and science there is barely a hint.

Despite Pressey's participation in national meetings, his even greater national involvement in work on aging, and his frequent visiting teaching posts at various campuses, the impression persists that his environment was essentially an immediate one: that of his institution, department, his courses, his students, recognized duties. In the academic vernacular, he appears to have been a "local," not a "cosmopolitan." Sidney Pressey probably would be an idol of today's students—clamorously seeking from their professors involvement, dedication to teaching, meaningful guidance, and personal concern—as he indeed was to many among earlier generations of students.

Conclusion

The conviction with which this commentary was begun was that autobiography provides a potentially rich source, especially for writing the *intellectual* history of education, psychology, and science. The purpose of this commentary was to test this conviction by attempting an analysis of an autobiography—taking in this analysis a methodological, and primarily an historiographic, slant. Are any conclusions yet warranted?

For biography writers one conclusion is that autobiography can generate and sharpen necessary research questions—those concerning both internal, personal, and private factors and the social and cultural contexts within which personality operates. For historians using the autobiographical genre to supplement or in lieu of other data, the familiar question of motive reappears. The writers of these

17. Letter of Pressey to the author, February 15, 1969.

personal sketches were all men of good will and good intentions; not all autobiography is written by such. But, then, neither do documents, newspapers, and other sources represent impartiality and dispassionate record-keeping. All of this volume's contributors received an outline to guide their writing; the great diversity in substance, style, and mood that nevertheless resulted is instructive. Other historical (*and experimental*) data also reproduce human variability in interests, temperament, talent, veracity, sensitivity—only doing so in more subtle, impersonal forms.

Finally, the utility of an approach must, as the pragmatists observed, be measured by its consequences, in this case specifically by reader involvement; impeccable scholarship aridly framed has few takers. Autobiography's advantage is that, after all, the most fascinating and compelling subject to man is man himself—and especially as bright and warm a man as Sidney Pressey.

CHAPTER VIII

George N. Shuster

Part I

AN AUTOBIOGRAPHY

I was born in what still is one of the most charming small towns in Wisconsin, even though progress as understood during the early twentieth century destroyed some gracious structures and replaced them with hideous ones. Lancaster, when I appeared on the scene, was a county seat and therefore assured of a permanent complement of judges, lawyers, sheriffs, and similar dignitaries. The jail was, to be sure, usually occupied only by a couple of old soaks, who as they recovered from their hangovers stared gloomily through the grilled windows. Our asylum and "poor farm" just outside the city limits were more lugubrious institutions, and as youngsters our blood curdled at the news that somebody we knew had been sent off to one or the other. But above all, we were dominated by memories of the Civil War. Lancaster erected the first monument in memory of the boys in blue in the whole of the United States, and surprisingly this was and remains in its simple way very beautiful. Of course we likewise had our surviving heroes, intact or minus an arm or a leg. Because of what the area economy had been, namely a blend of lead mining and farming, our best families had come from the East or the South. We therefore had, though the temperature tumbled to twenty degrees below zero in winter, charming southern style houses with great french windows, as well as New England colonials. Our own house was New York colonial, to which my father had added a long annex in no style whatever.[1]

1. The pertinent dates follow. I was born on August 27, 1894, was admitted to Notre Dame in 1912 and awarded an A.B. three years later. After military service (1917-1919) I returned to Notre Dame as professor of English and, later, chairman of the Department of English, earning an M.A. degree in 1920. During 1924 I joined the staff of the *Commonweal*, later becoming managing editor. Having left the *Commonweal*, I was a fellow of the Social Science Research Council from 1937 to 1939. Then I became acting president and, a year later, president of Hunter College (1939-1960). In 1961 I returned to Notre Dame as professor of English and assistant to the president.

Both of my grandfathers lived on farms, though this was more or less accidental. The one on my paternal side had come over because his father, a notary public, had been forced to leave Germany in a hurry by reason of what happened in 1848. It was a staunchly Catholic group, though by no means puritanical. My father was born as one of a sizable family in a stone house built in a picturesque little valley, and apparently there was plenty of singing and storytelling. My mother's parents had been lured from Pennsylvania by an adroit real estate man, who had given them a most alluring description of the farm on which they made a down payment. It turned out to be mostly woodland, with a relatively large log house and an orchard from peddling the products of which my grandfather paid his bills for quite some time. He was a Lutheran, but gave little or no attention to what this implied. His wife, however, was deeply religious. I still have her book of daily devotions; and if she lived up to what this advised she must have lived austerely indeed. But she appears to have been rather genial and to have sung innumerable German folk songs with considerable ability.

I was reared a Catholic and sent to the parochial school. My mother did not, however, transfer her allegiance from Lutheranism until years after she married. But until quite a bit later we saw little or nothing of our Lutheran relatives, who then proved to be very likable. I have described the religious aspects of my youth in an essay which anyone can consult should he so desire.[2]

My most vivid boyhood memories have to do with a retired U.S. Navy captain, presumably Congregationalist, who built the replica of a battleship on his front lawn in which his two orphaned grandchildren and I played day in and out, sinking pirate vessels or enemy cruisers with little wooden replicas of cannons and doing similar deeds of valor. The captain had also rigged up a telescope in the attic of his house, with the help of which we could see the Mississippi twelve miles away, though there was only a small gap in its magnificent range of bluffs. I am afraid that these experiences, plus all the Civil War heroics, filled me with romantic dreams of martial valor, which virtue, if it be one, was markedly absent from my family tree. As a matter of fact, I came later on within half a

2. *American Spiritual Autobiographies*, ed. Louis Finkelstein (New York: Harper & Bros., 1948).

foot of embarking on a military career, but desisted for reasons which are of no special interest. The captain's estimable lady, settled by a strange quirk of fate in our town, was one of the earliest graduates of Smith College. When I was ten or so, she began giving me copies of *Harper's* which introduced me to a world of which I had never dreamed. I believe she rather enjoyed talking with me, because her husband was a dour man who never approved of entertaining anybody. In retrospect this seems a great pity for there were some people in the town who might have interested and entertained her.

There was a good deal of interreligious bickering in Lancaster, though the small Catholic minority normally ran for cover only when some itinerant ex-monk came to town and relit the fires of the Inquisition. It never bothered me very much, except that in school we were asked to pray for the poor Protestants who as a consequence of not having the true faith would all doubtless end up in hell. I was distressed about this, particularly because a very pretty little Methodist girl with long blond hair lived just down our street. Otherwise our prejudices were purely political. My mother was invariably greatly impressed by her favorite candidate for the presidency, but if after eight months in office he had not espoused her recipes for the improvement of the nation she referred to him at best with veiled contempt. My father and I became partisans of Robert La Follette, Sr., by reason of hearing him speak for two hours from the rear of a little whistle-stop train.

A few of the leading merchants in our town were later on revealed as German Jews. My father talked with them in their native language and held them in high esteem. It never occurred to us at the time to think of them as being Jewish, and if it had it would not have mattered in the least. Of course, I should have thought, yes, the Jews did crucify Christ, but Mr. Schneider and Mr. Blumenthal weren't there at the time. As for Negroes, my grandfather's farm was surrounded by a semicircle of farms which a Southern planter had bought for the slaves he freed. As a result, my mother was for some time the only white child in the one-room school she attended. She was treated like a princess; and all during my boyhood a former classmate or other used to drop in for a chat. And then there was Tom Greene, one of the freed slaves, in whose wagon I rode for days during summers, listening to yarns which I have long since wished I could remember.

Then for some reason or other I belatedly took an interest in my studies and was held to be a bright boy. My mother having been taken seriously ill, it was decided that I should go to a boarding preparatory school. No Catholic boy in our area had ever done that before, excepting one who had left to enter a seminary. The parish priest was therefore consulted and it was decided that I should go to St. Lawrence College, which was as like a seminary as could be managed. It turned out to be a Swiss preparatory school transplanted to the United States. The course of study would induce in a modern American lad feelings akin to despair. Bed and board were spartan, indeed, but the atmosphere was warm and human. There I met Father Corbinian, beyond any question the greatest teacher I have known. He taught German and Greek, and as a result I devoted myself to the tasks he assigned and the vistas he opened with all the enthusiasm I could muster. I read immense quantities of German literature, from Goethe at one end of the spectrum to Karl May on the other. But the farthest point I reached in Greek was a couple of Plato's *Dialogues* and one or two of the orations of Demosthenes.

The next stage in my development was Notre Dame, then called a university because by so doing it was easier to get a charter. Frankly, I chose to go there because it had a football team and therefore sounded less formidably academic than St. Lawrence College. One afternoon of practice convinced me that football was not for me. I was strong and wiry at the time, but no match for the replicas of Hercules who had been recruited. Soon, however, I found myself in great demand for totally other reasons. Because of the intensive work done in preparatory school, I was adjudged to have amassed credits well in excess of those demanded by Notre Dame for matriculation and therewith triumphantly became a sophomore. This fact must have been very impressive because I was besought by a professor of English to correct his freshman themes. A more dreadful assortment of scrawling attempts at prose cannot be imagined, but there was one boy who wrote so well that I sought him out. We remained friends until he died, though he never lived up to his promise. Not long thereafter the librarian looked me up and suggested that during certain hours I sit at the front desk of his establishment and dole out books. This proved to be the most desirable employment I have ever had. In those days of teaching by textbook, virtually no one disturbed my leisure. Owing largely to the efforts of two or three extraordinary men, the library was for its time far better than anyone could have expected.

I read widely and thus began my first personal intellectual adventure. The course offerings in psychology were perfunctory but on the library shelves were the books of James, Ladd, and other Americans, as well as those of the Germans on whom they had leaned. If I had thought at the time of an academic career, psychology would no doubt have been my chosen field. But—and this will probably show how isolated we were from the mainstream of university life—all the devotees of the liberal arts at Notre Dame at that time thought that the rainbow's end was a great career in journalism or creative writing. Some of us succeeded in a measure, though none won Pulitzer prizes. At any rate, James remained a strong influence on my intellectual life. Let me add that the two chores, neither of which I had asked for, netted enough to enable me to pay my way at Notre Dame. My parents were thereby enabled to send my sisters to college.

I majored in the classics, which were avoided by virtually all students except those belonging to the captive audience assembled by the seminary which trained priests for the Congregation of the Holy Cross, which governed the university. It was fortunate that I did, because Scheier, educated at Leyden in Holland, was an excellent if eccentric scholar. We ranged far, at a rapid rate, doing the whole of the *Odyssey* in one semester and nearly all of *Appolonius Rhodius* in another, ending later with the corpus of Greek drama, from Aeschylus to Aristophanes. The courses in Latin literature were more perfunctory, though we did some rather unusual readings. Then I discovered one day that I could read Plato in Greek with no more than cursory help from the dictionary. To me that seemed a feat as unusual as finding the North Pole.

The rest of my course of study was routine, excepting for the university's debating team, which demanded wide reading about some selected theme of current interest as well as writing and speaking skills. There were distinguished scientists on the campus, for example, Julius Nieuwland, who found out how to make artificial rubber, but to my great regret in later life I learned nothing of what they had to offer excepting for some work in general biology. There was a good course in early Greek philosophy, but all the others in this field were taught against the background of a series of textbooks thought to be neo-Scholastic in character. The references to Aquinas or Augustine were perfunctory. But my hours in the library brought me close to Newman, who with Plato no doubt steered my thinking in the way in which it was to go. I suppose, in essence, this meant that I came to believe that, although tradition and the conclusions at which it had arrived are important and even in some sense conclusive, emphasis must be placed on the discovery of new ideas and their development.

The Notre Dame of those days was provincial, rather lazy (only the engineering students seemed to work hard), not too inquisitive, and permeated by religious feeling. The old Latin Liturgy was rendered well, the Sunday sermons were usually good, and receiving the Sacraments was taken for granted. Nobody pushed compendia of dogma down our throats. Not a few students were disturbed by evolution, but this had no terrors for me because of Zahm's *Evolution and Dogma,* way ahead of its time. But I was uneasy about some trends in modernist theology and brooded over Winston Churchill's *Inside of the Cup,* which was both novel and tract. But for the most part these were passing moods. The university campus was beautiful, the atmosphere friendly, the rules normally circumventible. Nobody went home on weekends. The student body ate in common and the president was seated at the head table with some other campus dignitaries. No one had a car or even dreamed of owning one. There was a street car which clattered to and from South Bend, but most of our locomotion was done on foot, sometimes on walks many miles long. Good theater was brought to South Bend by companies on tour, an amiable practice to which TV called a halt, so that we could see Maude Adams, Julia Marlowe, and many another person of ability and fame. No doubt we boys, glued to our chairs in an era before that of picture magazines, could be completely bowled over by the beauty of an actress. There were also flourishing athletic programs, notably in football and baseball, though there was then only a small attendance on the part of the general public. In short,

Notre Dame was what the people of the United States have forgotten there could be, namely, an academic community in which everybody knew everybody and in which friendships were fostered and communication made an art.

Leaving, I had some chance to learn the hardships of becoming a writer. I supplemented my earnings in various ways, some of them fairly lucrative and others not. Trying my hand at being a reporter, I found myself in various situations often boring and sometimes dangerous. Rejection slips in number went into the waste basket, there were some acceptances, and I wrote a novel, the only copy of which was lost by a publisher's reader. At the time I could have shot him, which treatment was being accorded by most of my novel's heroes to their human environment, but I have long since been grateful. Then I was mustered into military service.

Having been a captain in the Notre Dame cadet corps, remote from the realities of Verdun though that was, I could have had a commission virtually for the asking. But I could not bring myself to accept one. The war seemed to me unnecessary and the decision to enter it fallacious. On the other hand, it appeared to me completely obvious that I could not reconcile with my conscience not sharing the burden with others of my age. Why should I imagine that because of my superior education and presumably superior outlook I should burn up my draft card and let others do the grimy job? And so I entered military service as a private, was transferred to an intelligence unit because of my knowledge of the German language, and then found myself at the front as a member of a Franco-American group assigned to pick up enemy telephone and telegraph conversation. I was very lucky to emerge from the fighting a very much alive, though in many ways worn to a frazzle, sergeant first-class. From this vantage point in time I should like to salute my French comrades, now surely all passed on to the land of shadows and benediction. Whatever people have said latterly about the country of de Gaulle does not apply to them. They were soldiers, sometimes scoundrels after their fashion, but gentlemen. I would have walked confidently with any of them through a night of fire.

Then, because of my knowledge of German, there followed several months of service as an interpreter for an Intelligence colonel in Occupied Germany. This was my first visit to the country the literature of which I had read so diligently. Since most of my days in the performance of this kind of duty were spent in the beautiful Moselle Valley (I was sent farther east upon occasion), I drank my fill of the landscape and what it meant. To some extent I fell in love with a girl, but she viewed me with indifference verging on contempt. I must add that none of this experience led me to change my mind in the least about the war.

I should now say something about my war experience because of its impact on my outlook on life. First of all, there was the discovery of France. We landed at Nantes after eleven stormy and most disagreeable days on the sea, our ship being escorted by a ring of destroyers bobbing up and down like corks in the agitated waters. Then because of the privileged character of our unit we went eastward in a third-class coach on a regular train. For a young man who then knew only the Middle West from Indianapolis to the Minnesota Iron Range, the historical character of the landscape through which we passed was breathtaking. We finally got off the train—how little needed is sleep when one is young—and were driven in a kind of bus to Langres, in the moonlight, over the drawbridge and through the great gate. This I knew was Caesar's city; and later on Christendom had built the huge hulk of the cathedral which now loomed up out of the dark in the golden shimmer of the night. Then we went up to the shattered front, first to Baccarat, where I slept on the front step of a half-ruined building, listening to the booming of guns still far away. Then further on to a louse- and rat-filled dugout north of Pexonne.

Our troops were very green, blunders were frequent and unavoidable. The Germans staged fairly extensive raids, lasting for hours. The roar of exploding shells, the heavy thuds of belching mortars, the smell of gas—all of this left the four of us on duty in the dugout in a state of superanxiety during a fifty-two hour attack. We were wearing masks, bayonets were on our rifles, and grenades were in our hands. But the storm passed us by, my first real wartime storm; and when we went up next morning to repair the lines on which our work depended, I came upon my first dead soldier, that is, one not in a casket or on a stretcher. He was a young French lad, not more than eighteen, with a love letter to his girl in the Loire country still in his pocket. My companion and I carried him back, cursing so vehemently that if the Lord God was listening He must have been shocked. Later on came Chateau Thierry and St. Mihiel, each with its rivers of blood. I was a veteran now, and like all veterans I do not talk about such things.

Finally, I was sitting in a room in Toul, to which some of us had come to serve as instructors, listening to the news on Morse code. And so I overheard the German request for an armistice. The first person I ran into outside, jubilant as I was over the news, happened to be a French machine gunner whom I had met on some segment of the front. "What shall I do now?" he asked gloomily. "I have been a machine gunner since before the day the war started, and there is nothing I know about except fighting." Years later I met him by accident, an old drunk, with the ribbons which are France's greatest tribute to valor faded on his shirt. I have concluded that this is the way in which I could sum up the war. But I must add that when it was all over, I found myself for the first time genuinely religious. Before that, I had lived up to all the rules and tried to believe what I was supposed to as a Catholic. Now I was personally religious, deeply so, but no longer a subservient soul. It seemed to me that I had found God across all the suffering I had seen. Many men I knew had lost every vestige of belief, and one could not blame them. Just what happened to me I cannot easily explain.

Since demobilization had to take a long time, the army decided that it ought to shunt its critical, restless, college-educated soldiers somewhere. And so one morning I found myself in Poitiers, enrolled in the old university of that city. What I knew of the French language I had picked up on the Vosges front. Our bereted companions in blue became good friends; and face to face with the problem of conversing I acquired a truly terrifying kind of French. I taught myself to read a little, while sitting in dugouts, by putting New Testaments in English and French side by side. And so I was not completely speechless when I came to Poitiers, a marvelous place in which to begin acquaintance with a France not torn by shot and shell. It was and still is a city the structures of which proceed from Roman to Romanesque, from Gothic to Renaissance. Every day I walked up the street along which Jeanne d'Arc had once ridden and passed the palace of Eleanor of Aquitaine. I grew very fond of the university and some of its professors, emerging finally with a *Certificat d'Aptitude,* which somewhat rashly announced to the world that I was prepared to teach French culture.

After I was mustered out, I could find no job to my liking and therefore responded affirmatively to an invitation to come to Notre Dame and teach English. This was attributable to some things I had written. I had no intention of staying, but at the end of my first year I made an important decision. A lucrative job offer had come in just the kind of journalism I liked, but I allowed the president of the university to talk me into staying. The Rev. James Burns, C.S.C., was by far the most creative and imaginative Catholic educator of his time, though he was then known primarily as a pioneer in the history of Catholic schools. He saw that if Notre Dame was to build a worthy institution of higher learning round the nuclei of quality it already possessed, notably in some of the natural sciences, it would be necessary to assemble a lay teaching staff having some semblance of academic stature. This in turn would require an endowment; and he took the first steps in the university's history to create one. It was a busy life I led at Notre Dame, teaching, helping to edit a local magazine, the *Ave Maria,* spending endless hours with students, and writing my first book. When Father Burns's tenure in office came to an end, I made, in 1924, two decisions which would affect the rest of my life. First, I married one of my summer school students, the beautiful and pert Doris Cunningham. Second, I decided to go to New York, find a job (I had saved some money, so that it was not of immediate importance), and study for the doctorate at Columbia. Fortunately, Ashley Thorndike, then chairman of the Department of English, had recommended my book to its publisher, and I could enter through the front door.

Then I made another fateful decision. The *Commonweal* had just been founded and I cast my lot with it. At first this seemed reconcilable with the quest for a doctorate and fortunately I did make considerable headway. It was hard, often grueling work, but it was fascinating. The *Commonweal* was a distinguished if perilous venture. Michael Williams and his friends who founded it were bent on proving that not all Catholics were priest-ridden or devotees of Tammany Hall. Therefore, it was to be edited and published by laymen and given as much of an ecumenical flavor as the circumstances permitted. This flavor was limited, to be sure. An Episcopalian served on our advisory board, and another was on the staff. The magazine was to be as like the *New Republic* as possible, though serving Catholic interests primarily. From the beginning it had an interested group of non-Catholic readers. But though its "snob appeal" was obvious enough to be resented by not a few, the magazine was quite liberal in tone and temper. Two fellowships were sandwiched in by me for study in Germany, and as a result I wrote three books, the second of which was the first eyewitness account of what was going on there after Hitler's seizure of power. This and its predecessor were favorably received and I acquired a reputation as a commentator on German affairs. I had rather thought that all this was forgotten, but to my surprise young delvers have now ferreted much of it out. I left the *Commonweal* in 1937, primarily because of the unpopularity resulting from my advocacy of neutrality toward Franco, exiting with a magnificent two-year fellowship for study abroad, generously sponsored by Carlton Hayes and Lindsay Rogers of Columbia.

Summarizing very briefly the impact of European experiences on my intellectual formation, I would say that the first important change in my outlook was caused by the discovery of French literature and thought, which had played only a small part in my earlier education. Now I came to know, in addition to poets and novelists (my master's degree thesis was a study of Huysmans), Montaigne, Fénélon, and Pascal, with the last of whom I still sense great affinity of spirit, though he was far more Jansenistic than I ever cared to be and hostile to the Jesuits, whose history I greatly admire. France likewise made something of a medievalist of me by reason of Chartres, Bourges, and Paris's Notre Dame, to mention only a few of the cathedrals.

Still, it was always Germany which interested me most. In addition to the associations growing out of variegated studies of the political and social situation, I saw a good deal of German university life and came to know writers and artists. The heart of any university of my acquaintance was of course the *institut*, presided over by one or more professors. Here, research was carried on with unflagging zeal with the help of assistants who often toiled like slaves chained to Roman galleys. From among these the explorers

(*Forscher*) of the future would be selected. It seemed to me a rigorous system which we Americans could imitate but seldom manage to duplicate. Meanwhile the German university's student body as a whole moved along rather haphazardly through a series of lectures, seminars, and examinations, often quite impersonal and mechanical. The liveliest institution in Berlin during pre-Nazi times was the *Hochschule fuer Politik*, in which political and social problems were discussed from a variety of points of view, liberal, radical, and conservative. I could not spend more than a month there, but that provided a most rewarding experience. German theology was then noted for meticulous exegesis and tireless historical delving. But there were among Catholic scholars some original thinkers and impressive lecturers, Guardini, Adam, and Lippert among them, who came to occupy places in my scheme of things beside Friedrich von Huegel, who had meant so much to me during my *Commonweal* days.

Fortunately, all this did not entirely wean me away from pursuing the doctorate later on to be awarded by Columbia University, my gratitude to and affection for which have never waned. It taught me what a great university is like and what scholarship truly is. During the fellowship periods abroad I had managed a number of weeks at the British Museum and the Bodleian filling in gaps in the research done for *A History of the English Ode from Milton to Keats*, which promises to be the most enduring of my books. Through this I acquired a key to the academic door, at a time when reopening the journalistic one did not seem alluring. Indeed, the field of comparative literature then being relatively untilled, the road ahead seemed promising. Then to my complete amazement I found myself being talked to by members of New York City's Board of Higher Education and members of the faculty of Hunter College. Then came an offer of appointment to the presidency of the college with which I was to be identified for more than twenty years. I hesitated a long while, first, because of the obvious fact that I knew nothing about being a president, and then because of the intergroup conflict in which members of the faculty were embroiled. It was John Burke, son of old Eli, president of Altman's and one of New York's most prominent Catholic laymen, who more than anyone else induced me to risk trying it out. To be sure, the position also provided a platform as a commentator on totalitarianism, and as things worked out I put that visibility to good use. I have dealt with that part of my story in a book of memoirs, *The Ground I Walked On*, and will not discuss it further here.[3]

When I took office in 1939, Hunter was a college for women, waiting for the completion of its new multistoried building on Park Avenue and meanwhile cramming seven thousand fully matriculated students into buildings on its Bronx campus and into various structures downtown. New York was still wallowing in the Great Depression, which I have called the Great Disaster. Many of the girls came from very poor families and would indeed in many instances not have thought of higher education if they could have found jobs. Indeed, quite a sizable number could not find them even after graduation. As for the faculty, it was struggling to come to grips with the democratic reorganization which had been decreed by the board of higher education. Virtually everything was to be entrusted to committees of the faculty; and it certainly looked for a time as if such feathers as had been left on the presidential skin were to be plucked to the best of everyone's ability. We also had a rather small but potentially noisy group of left-wing students organized as the American Student Union, the counterpart of which was the then Communist-dominated teachers' union. This last bears no relationship whatever to the teachers' union currently active in New York. The municipal colleges were supposed to be populated by Communists, which surmisal of course added not a whit to their reputations. As a matter of fact, the Catholic portion of the Hunter student body made it "the largest Catholic college for women," as we sometimes pointed out half facetiously and half in earnest. If there could have been anything these young ladies did not possess, it was sympathetic sentiment about communism.

But in a relatively short time much that was good and experimentally useful in the democratic procedures had been retained and the rest discarded. The true structure of the college emerged. What had been a teacher training institution some forty years earlier became a college of liberal arts, which of course continued to prepare teachers for their careers of service but did not permit them

3. New York: Farrar, Straus & Cudahy, 1956.

to major in education. There were two demonstration schools under its auspices, one housing children of nursery and elementary school age, the other a high school the pupils in which were selected in accordance with their ability.

The faculty was, to be sure, in part masculine, and this portion was by no means lacking in distinction. Nevertheless, the high academic quality of Hunter was largely attributable to its "learned lady" professors, whom at that time only institutions which were professedly colleges for women would employ. There were eminent, sometimes even internationally respected, scholars in English, in other languages and literatures, history, the social sciences and, indeed, one or another of the natural sciences. In due time we built up a very distinguished art department, too, and strengthened our work in music. In some areas of inquiry, notably the humanities, the Hunter faculty ranked very high among the academic institutions of the United States in the number and quality of its scholarly publications. We had an amiable custom of honoring the author of a scholarly volume with a luncheon to which he or she could invite friends from other colleges and universities. One by-product of this was unsought advertising of Hunter's virtues.

Not a few of these women had done their undergraduate work at Hunter and, never having married, dedicated themselves to the college with greater enthusiasm than is shown by many mothers to their children. We all lived in a deep or moderating depression during the ten years after 1939. Budgets were pared down, promotions were hard to come by, teaching loads were inordinately heavy. And yet some of our faculty developed innovative instructional programs or dedicated themselves to student leadership. It was also a source of satisfaction to me personally that we were dealing for the most part with poor youngsters, some of them almost desperately poor. A coat stolen from a student locker room could cause a family tragedy. Often enough a girl would faint because of not having enough to eat. To be sure, we had wealthy girls too, who refused to go to the exclusive private colleges their mothers had attended. In many respects our students were insulated and often tightly homebound. I knew young women from Brooklyn who had never seen the Hudson River, let alone what lay beyond it. We therefore arranged for no end of field trips, notably those organized by our geographers, and so got to places far remote from New York City. On the whole, exceptions having been duly noted, the moral climate was one of surprising innocence. You can therefore imagine the furor in the offices of the deans of students when some girls reported that they had been queried by a stranger about their sex lives. If the interviewer believed everything he was told, he was definitely a misguided social scientist. All this occurred during the research phase of the Kinsey report.

Some of our students came from families enamored of the radical Left, while the backgrounds of others were decidedly conservative. The Left often made a good deal of noise, while the Right retreated into its bastions of indignation. The faculty was overwhelmingly conservative but would allow no deviation from its predominatingly liberal views. It resented the fact that the American Student Union was active on the premises, but any attempt to curb or suppress it would have created a wall of opposition that would have been defended by the majority. I have sometimes been accused of having been "soft on the Communists." But, quite apart from the fact that I grew up in Wisconsin with a Farmer-Labor—La Follette climate about me, I very soon concluded that administration opposition to student extremism is futile and that the only way of redressing the balance is to create a strong liberal-conservative student movement. This we succeeded in doing, with magnificent assistance from Eleanor Roosevelt.

Insofar as the academic program was concerned, I was persuaded during my first years in office that education in the strict liberal arts sense was not adequate. Girls had to bring to the labor market after graduation some skill which would enable them to find employment, at least until such time as the demand for teachers grew larger. I had to use all my persuasive powers to introduce courses in typewriting and stenography, offered at first without credit. These courses I called a "vocational inlay." Of course I nevertheless subscribed to the ideals of Phi Beta Kappa, to which nearly all the distinguished members of the Hunter faculty belonged. During all my years at Hunter I taught a course at the request of my colleagues, first in comparative literature and then in modern German government and politics. We also had a sheaf of honor societies, each cherished by its initiates. I have tried in vain to recall how many of these invited me to honorary membership, as of course they would have any other president. Let me add that I came to the college deeply prejudiced against sororities. But I must candidly say that without these, life on the Hunter campus at that time would have been far less satisfactory than it was. Members of the Hunter faculty established the first truly interracial sorority, having a charter of its own. It collapsed when what we then called Negro students no longer wished to belong to it.

Everybody will understand that not a few of our students entered with chips on their shoulders. They would have preferred to go to some private alma mater having a campus and a more savory social reputation. But after a while, in spite of subways and the social atmospheres of their homes, they helped to create a climate of quite singular friendliness. If I passed a student without being greeted with a smile, I knew that she was a freshman. When anyone asks me whether a "day college" can have a sense of cordial solidarity, I look at him with astonishment. To be sure, it soon became apparent that anyone who tried to run that kind of show was bound not to lead a leisurely life. There were dances, games, teas, and whatever else a feminine constituency could dream up. But a still far greater occupational hazard was attending innumerable meetings of the Board of Higher Education and its various committees. Not that the board was a disagreeable body—quite the contrary. Not a few of its members became my close friends. But they sometimes seemed to suffer from a really puritanical sense of their responsibilities and to want to take a picture of every leaf on the educational bush.

The war years brought great changes. To begin with, our enrollment dropped for the first time, due to a congeries of circumstances. There was a trough in the birth rate. Many young women could find lucrative employment. Others married soldier boys before they left for the wars. And so we were not too gravely affected when the Navy commandeered the whole of the Bronx campus in order to make provision for the training of WAVES. Downtown there was a great flurry of patriotic activities, particularly in the form of dances and receptions to which service men were invited without it being at all clear which kind of hero would show up. Some affairs were urbane and successful, even leading to correspondence and in subsequent years to matrimony. But there were comical situations, too. One evening I looked in on one of the many dances to which I was invited only to find that in the center of the room there was a solid phalanx of sailors who just wouldn't be pried apart. I spent a busy hour shaking hands with individual seamen and introducing them to girls. Even so, they were in sum total the unhappiest group of terpsichoreans on record. They had been rounded up and ordered to attend.

I do not wish to give the impression that everything at Hunter was charming and played to soft music. It certainly was not. During the early depression-ridden years some members of the faculty loathed the unwashed and often quite foreign young women they taught. And some of these in turn were so unhappy at home that the bitterness never rubbed off. Not a few had been thrust out of a foreign language environment and had little if any idea of how they could overcome their handicaps. Others had sordid, unhappy love affairs which left scars on their personalities. At the time, we could afford practically no professional counseling other than that provided for strictly academic affairs. The assistance we offered was made possible by able volunteers, some of whom far overstepped the boundaries of what could legitimately be expected of persons from whom all this was a labor of love.

After the war was over, affluence began to heat up the frigid atmosphere of depression-time New York. When the UN Security Council finally ended its ill-starred and bizarre occupancy of the Bronx campus, that part of Hunter became coeducational. This created new problems. Many of the first young men to enter had not been admitted to other municipal colleges and were genuinely averse to invading what had been a feminine precinct. Gradually this hurdle was surmounted, too. One reason was a first-rate athletic program for men, supervised by a professor the college was very fortunate to acquire. Another reason was that the service fraternities, organized in New York high schools from among former Scouts of both sexes, exercised leadership of a kind I had not imagined could exist. As a result, uptown and downtown we breathed in fresh air.

We boldly changed the climate of what had been known as the Evening Session and which soon took on the luster of the title, School of General Studies. This had been frequented for the most part by young people who did not qualify for matriculation. It was a sort of institution akin to that which would later on be established as a community college, though the teachers had no pension or tenure rights and were for a long time scandalously underpaid. Even for their sakes we could not close down this part of our activity because most of them would have had no employment whatsoever. The other municipal college presidents and I tried in every possible way to improve the situation and at long last were in some measure successful. But the tragedies which occurred when an instructor reached retirement age and had subsequently to try to exist on welfare doles were dire indeed. When one remembers the resistance of a great part of our people to social security, which at long last mitigated some of this distress, one is sorry to remember how callous a republic like ours could have been.

As I have said, the climate changed and nothing was affected more than that which was known as the School of General Studies. Hunter being where it was, on Park Avenue, we threw the doors wide open to educational activities of many kinds. Groups could ask for the use of rooms or even of halls where these were free. There were all sorts of goings-on—classes taught under the auspices of labor unions, Negro choral groups, instruction for amateur silversmiths (astonishingly successful, this). Hunter began its now quite famous concert series and organized an opera workshop. As I have already indicated, the warm spirit of Eleanor Roosevelt hovered over the campus during all the years I was there. She came again and again and again, asking no emolument whatever, always attracting everybody who could get into the hall. With the help of friends we had purchased the old Sara Delano Roosevelt house for use by student social and religious groups. I am sure Mrs. Roosevelt was much happier being with our students than she had ever been in that house.

We also professionalized our offerings to some extent, first by establishing a collegiate nursing program at the request of the city, which badly needed it, and second by creating the privately financed Graduate School of Social Work. Both, I may gratefully say, have flourished ever since. Meanwhile, in view of the very great need for teachers in the schools of New York City and its environs, the State provided funds for the development of a training program extending over the first year of graduate study. On the basis of this, there was rather hastily erected the Graduate School of the City University of New York, which has since survived any number of growing pains. This belongs, however, to an era after my time.

Meanwhile, my family lived in a pleasant old house on Shippan Point, which juts into the Connecticut Sound just east of Stamford. We were fated to have only one child of our own, our son Robert, who, in addition to other enterprises, now manages one of New York's numerous art galleries. But we filled the house with other people's children—Felicity, Jennifer, Inge, Bruce, and Ali. Other young people stayed there, too; and sometimes we bedded down more than a dozen, for it was a roomy house. I commuted regularly from New York, which often meant that on rainy or starry nights the Sound splashed on my ears at an hour near midnight. Of course I had sometimes to stay in the city; and when the periods of government service began in earnest I was obliged to be away for lengths of time. Inevitably the house grew emptier and emptier, as the young people got married or embarked on careers. There were also almost always grown guests, ranging all the way from Heinrich Bruening to Van Wyck Brooks. My wife managed none the less to become deeply involved in the affairs of Stamford as well as those of New York. We lived for twenty-three years in that house; and when we finally turned the keys over to another owner, so many memories were left behind that it almost seemed as if they would suffice for eternity. But we left sorrows behind us, too, some of them great ones, for which I learned to be thankful, because I think it is only through suffering that one can gain insight into the true meaning of the human pilgrimage. As a good though now forgotten poet wrote,

> Sweet sorrow, play a grateful part,
> Break me the marble of my heart.

I come now to an aspect of higher educational administration which has always astonished Europeans, who know nothing of our identification of the academic presidency with relative permanence. This is involvement in government service and in civic as well as scholarly organizations. Once I tried to justify this by saying that if a president could not be seen off the campus, he could not be seen on it either. But, though there is truth in this statement, the fact is that during the war and its aftermath it would have been impossible not to do what one was asked if it was at all within the area of one's competence. Refuse I did, of course, upon occasion; and, though I accepted more than a dozen assignments they did not add up in terms of time or importance to those taken on by men like James Conant or Henry Wriston. It should be added, perhaps, that being a municipal college president was irreconcilable with political activity. We simply had to make every effort to get along with any city or state administration.

My first two assignments were not overly time-consuming. The Committee Advisory to the Department of State on Cultural Affairs was established in 1942 as part of the good-neighbor policy toward Latin America. This was already "cold war" in a sense, since both the United States and Great Britain deemed it expedient to offset Nazi propaganda in the countries to the south of us. Cultural affairs in any but a random sense were then novel and so the committee was able to establish guidelines which to a greater or lesser degree have been followed ever since. Many of its members, James Conant and James T. Shotwell among them, I had known previously, but others, in particular Vice-President Henry Wallace and G. Howland Shaw, then assistant secretary of state, were new acquaintances. Mr. Shaw was not only one of our best experts in the field of Islam but also a man with a deep, broad concern for underprivileged youth. The committee was disbanded when the Office of War Information was established because it was unwilling to consider itself a propaganda organization. The other assignment was to membership on a commission assembled by the Council on Foreign Relations shortly after the entry of the United States into the Second World War to consider the form which the peace in Europe might take once the fighting was over. The commission met regularly, its guests being representatives of governments in exile, or in such cases as those of Germany and Austria, distinguished men who had been compelled to leave their countries. It was an excellent commission, though unfortunately nothing came of its work because of the astonishing concessions made to the Soviet Union as the war came to a close.

My next involvements became increasingly time-consuming. Sitting on an Enemy Alien Board to consider whether detained Germans, Italians, and Japanese should be released, paroled, or confined may not seem particularly impressive in retrospect, but it meant many nights and days either in New York or Santa Fe, New Mexico. Fortunately, I was young enough then to take this pretty well in stride and show up at Hunter not too dazed by all the late hours. My family, to be sure, often saw very little of me. The value of my personal experience, however, seemed to me great. For the first time I met Japanese, some of them simple folk, cooks especially, while others were merchants or students. Then I spent the summer of 1945 in Europe as chairman of a group formed by Secretary Robert Patterson to interview captured erstwhile foes, from Hermann Goering and Franz von Papen to the generals who had fought on the eastern front. I believe we did manage to collect information which would not have been available otherwise, and this was duly deposited for the benefit of whomever cared to look at it. At any rate, I picked up my study of Germany again, at least to some extent, for after 1934 I had been unable to get a German visa. All of us on the commission likewise saw the havoc wrought by the war, which had taken so great a toll that one hardly dared dream that restoration would be possible. Who could have imagined then that twenty-three years after the defeat the currency of the West German Federal Republic would have become the strongest in the world?

Then came the founding of Unesco. I served on the U.S. delegations to the London and Paris conferences which established the organization, later on took the chairmanship of the U.S. National Commission at the request of John Foster Dulles, and finally became the representative of the government of the United States on the Unesco Executive Board. The London conference drafted the constitution, opening with the since famous preamble urging that the "defenses of the peace" must be erected in the minds of men. We were then, in 1945, strongly under the influence of the dread war which had just ended and which was attributable to the evil genius of Adolf Hitler. Could not education, if dedicated to the cause of understanding, greatly help to insure that the peoples of the world would henceforth take recourse to peaceful means of settling disputes? This hope was also dominant throughout the Paris Conference (1946), which perhaps assembled the most brilliant body of scholars, writers, journalists, and representatives of the educational systems of many countries ever to come together up to that time. But when the moment came to develop leadership for the organization, the post of director general went by default to Julian Huxley. There was an informal but at the time binding agreement that if Unesco headquarters were established in Paris, the director general should not be French; and of course the Germans, Austrians, Spanish, and Japanese nations were not represented. Although cordially invited to do so, the Russians sent no delegation. As for the United States, it put forward no candidate seriously and publicly, though had it done so, he could easily have been elected.

The British really had two candidates but the Labour government's Ministry of Education strongly supported Mr. Huxley, and he was chosen in spite of grave doubts as to his ability to manage the enterprise. Then he began to circulate a pamphlet bound in green which set out to prove that his version of an ultra neo-Darwinian and humanistic faith ought to be adopted as official Unesco doctrine. This aroused violent opposition on the part of church groups of all kinds, especially in the United States. The State Department, to which this part of our cultural foreign policy was assigned, went to great pains to tell the citizenry that it had not the slightest interest in supporting Mr. Huxley's theological proposals.

Unesco thus came into being under two great handicaps. It had been created on the assumption that the Soviet Union would subscribe to the constitution and take its place among the nations. Stalin had not the slightest intention of doing so and meanwhile proceeded to fasten his grip on the European satellite countries which had so thoughtlessly been turned over to Communist domination. Years later the Soviet Union did join the organization but for some time used the position it thus acquired to keep up a continuing and sometimes raucous political drumfire. The second handicap was that after Mr. Huxley's fiasco it was impossible to establish any generally acceptable Unesco philosophy of education. And so, after many good and bad starts, the organization gradually became what it now is—a genuinely necessary and effective international educational service agency. I believe that it has in many ways proved that if it did not exist it would have to be created. To be sure, it has suffered by reason of the declining prestige of the UN itself and from budgetary stringencies. But, like some of the other subsidiary organizations, it has given a good account of its stewardship. The amount of time required for service as U.S. Representative became so large that I was compelled to resign from the post in 1962.

My major departure from college routine grew directly out of my German interests and I shall confess that I accepted appointment in 1950 as land commissioner for Bavaria (or, more realistically, as John J. McCloy's deputy for that country) with reluctance. But there was no way out of doing so, especially since the Board of Higher Education was greatly impressed by the glory which this assignment would presumably bring to the municipal colleges. And so, excepting for some decisions which had to be made via long distance, I was away from Hunter for the better part of two years. But of all such assignments I have accepted this was by all odds the most interesting and rewarding. I am probably the only American who can say that he has visited almost every city and town in Bavaria. This was because the High Commission had field offices all over the beautiful country and it was part of my assignment to visit as many of them as possible. Here I shall make only a very brief comment on education. I had several times been requested by General Clay to accept the post of director of education in his military government. But, despite my sincere admiration for him, I repeated that I would do so only if that post were separated from military government. In 1950, when the State Department took over, we looked back on the history of a dogged attempt to remodel German education according to the American pattern. Only so, it was thought, could the virus of nazism be exterminated. Textbooks were to be rewritten, coeducational high schools were to take the place of the *gymnasia*, and teaching about the evils of nazism was prescribed. Much of this the Germans stoutly resisted, though some beneficial changes did occur, especially in the teaching of history and political science. Of course, the effort was greatly lamed by the fact that the British and the French did not do in their zones what we were trying to do in ours. Now the time had come to propose cooperation with the Germans, and this led eventually to a broad program of exchange of students and professors, as well as to the establishment of institutes of American studies. We assisted worthy innovative efforts whenever we were invited to do so. But the old order of educational reform by fiat had to be abandoned.

I have been often asked to express an opinion about which persons during my long career have seemed to me especially impressive. All attempts to do something like this are probably rather meaningless enterprises because one does not manage to take advantage of all the opportunities provided to know important people. Thus, I could no doubt have become very well acquainted with General deGaulle if a number of things had not intervened. Let me nevertheless present my catalog of the distinguished personages I have known. As heads of states, I would nominate Harry Truman and Konrad Adenauer. There was little in the earlier record of either to indicate that he would master the problems which confronted him with such consummate skill. It was not my good fortune to meet Winston Churchill more than casually. If I say that John Foster Dulles was perhaps the most eminent diplomat of my time, please do not misunderstand what I mean. He and to a greater degree General MacArthur pursued a policy to which I did not subscribe. But at least the policy had an objective and was not a vague nebulous something without substance. I have also greatly admired Dean Rusk. Among authors I have known, I probably would choose Thornton Wilder and Thomas Mann. In the field of education it would seem to me necessary to choose Nicholas Murray Butler and Robert Hutchins, if only because they challenged existing ideas of what education was all about. And if you ask me about senators, I would give the accolade to John Sherman Cooper, liberal Republican from Kentucky, and to Hubert Humphrey. This is all I shall say except that I believe that Henry Luce and Iphigene Sulzberger, for a long while the guiding spirit of the *New York Times*, were the most illustrious publishers I have known, with Alfred Knopf leading the procession in a different category.

The last years of my presidency were troubled because the Fineberg Law, enacted by the state of New York and approved by all the courts, compelled the Board of Higher Education to take disciplinary action against members of the faculty who belonged to the Communist party. There was certainly little reason why I should have entertained deep affection for many such members, nor did I have any responsibility other than to furnish such evidence, pro or contra, as the college records contained. Some of our faculty had long since overtly cut off relations with the party with which they had been affiliated for a short period of time during the turbulent thirties. A very few, however, had permitted a Communist noose to be knotted round their throats. There was a good deal of faculty and student sympathy with these colleagues and teachers, largely because it looked as if our proud record in defense of academic freedom was being tarnished. Few knew as I did how stupidly some of the accused had behaved. Meanwhile I was subjected to a great deal of abuse off the campus for having said that instead of being investigated by him, the universities should investigate Joe McCarthy. Still I received a great many compliments, especially from faculty men and women in the Middle West, so that the balance was more than even.

I retired from the presidency of Hunter in 1960, after more than twenty years in office, before I would have been obliged to simply because I was very tired and because the ever increasing involvements in the total municipal college administration appeared to be turning my life into something I no longer found rewarding. Many of my associates were kind enough to regret my decision; such regrets might not have endured a longer tenure. The convocation marking my departure was quite a glorious affair. Henry Heald delivered the obituary address, and the erstwhile enemies, Cardinal Spellman and Eleanor Roosevelt, were seated on the stage, he in the resplendent robes of his office and she in her Oxford cap and gown. Thus the twenty-one years at Hunter came to a close.

It had not seemed to me that anyone would be likely to request my services and I looked forward to little more than some writing and lecturing while continuing my service on Unesco's Executive Board. But almost in the twinkling of an eye there was a spate of interesting job opportunities. I decided to cast my lot with Father Hesburgh at Notre Dame and see if a distinguished Catholic university could be created there. The gamble, in view of his leadership, was worth taking. Many of my friends doubted that anything significant would come of it, and indeed some of my former colleagues at Hunter were quite distressed by reason of their assumption that I had preferred going to Notre Dame instead of lasting out my years with them. It seems to me that the decision I made was very much the right one. It is true that whether Father Hesburgh, despite his truly remarkable gifts, can manage to achieve excellence is still open to question. The sportswriters of the nation have long since had their idea of Notre Dame; and whether any president, however able, can weave his way to academic distinction between football and basketball is still an open question.

But I have been on the campus long enough to know that a new idea of how a Catholic university can emerge into fellowship with the other great universities of the United States is being formulated. Notre Dame was a small institution when I first knew it and extremely fortunate to have a kernel from which distinction could be evolved. This was satisfactorily enough a natural science kernel. John Zahm, friend of Theodore Roosevelt and his companion in explorations of the Amazon River, was a very great geographer as well as a brilliant student of evolution. Julius Nieuwland discovered among other things how to make artificial rubber. There were others. Around this somewhat mysteriously organized nucleus, would it be possible to build a university eminent also in the social sciences and the humanities? This was the question to which at Notre Dame I have devoted such energies as have been given to me, and I think the answer is affirmative. That is, it will be if the university can enlist the enduring enthusiastic dedication of its best young faculty members. This is going to be difficult because of the strong and indeed sometimes bitter competition for scholars of quality, at any age. If Father Hesburgh and his associates can hold their own in this arena, the future seems most promising. Of course Notre Dame is already strongly committed to freedom and the ecumenical spirit. This commitment it will have to strengthen and I have no doubt that it will. At any rate, I am grateful for the opportunity I have had to participate in what is both a hope and an achievement.

A BIOGRAPHICAL SUMMARY

George N. Shuster. Born August 27, 1894, in Lancaster, Wisconsin.

Family. Married Doris Cunningham, 1924. Children: Robert, 1925; Inge, adopted.

Education. Parochial school; St. Lawrence College (preparatory); Notre Dame, A.B., 1915, M.A., 1919; Columbia University, Ph.D., 1940.

Occupational history. Chairman, Department of English, Notre Dame, 1925; managing editor, *The Commonweal,* 1925-37; president, Hunter College of the City of New York, 1939-60; assistant to the president, Notre Dame, 1961—.

Memberships and affiliations. American Academy of Arts and Sciences; trustee, Carnegie Endowment for International Peace; trustee, Notre Dame University; director, Fund for the Republic; U.S. representative on the Executive Committee of Unesco; chairman, U.S. National Commission for Unesco.

Awards. Chevalier, Legion of Honor; Great Gold Medal of Honor (Austrian Republic); Knight Commander's Cross of Order of Merit (Germany); Butler Medal, Columbia University; Laetare Medal, University of Notre Dame; Insignis Medal, Fordham University; Pestalozzi-Foundation Medal; Campion Award; Pax Christi Award, St. John's University.

Part II

Selected Publications of George N. Shuster

Books

1. *Catholic Literature: A Reading List* (with Charles L. O'Donnell). Notre Dame: University of Notre Dame Press, 1914.
2. *The Chief Things About Writing: A Syllabus of Freshman English*. Notre Dame: University of Notre Dame Press, 1917 (2d ed., 1920).
3. *English Literature*. New York: Allyn & Bacon, 1926.
4. *The Hill of Happiness*. New York: D. Appleton & Co., 1926.
5. *Catholic Spirit in America*. New York: Dial Press, 1927.
6. *The Catholic Church and Current Literature*. New York: Macmillan Co., 1930.
7. *The Germans: An Inquiry and An Estimate*. New York: Dial Press, 1932.
8. *Strong Man Rules: An Interpretation of Germany Today*. New York: D. Appleton Century Co., 1934.
9. *Like A Mighty Army: Hitler versus Established Religion*. New York: D. Appleton Century Co., 1935.
10. *Brother Flo*. New York: Macmillan Co., 1938.
11. *Look Away!* New York: Macmillan Co., 1969.
12. *The English Ode from Milton to Keats*. New York: Columbia University Press, 1940.
13. *Germany: A Short History* (with Arnold Bergstraesser). New York: W. W. Norton & Co., 1944.
14. *Cultural Cooperation and the Peace*. Milwaukee: Bruce Publishing Co., 1953.
15. *Religion Behind the Iron Curtain*. New York: Macmillan Co., 1954.
16. *In Silence I Speak*. New York: Farrar, Straus & Cudahy, 1956.
17. *Education and Moral Wisdom*. New York: Harper & Bros., 1960.
18. *The Ground I Walked On*. New York: Farrar, Straus & Cudahy, 1961.
19. *Unesco: Assessment and Promise*. New York: Harper & Row, 1963.
20. *Albert Gregory Cardinal Meyer*. Notre Dame: University of Notre Dame Press, 1964.
21. *Catholic Education in a Changing World*. New York: Rinehart & Winston, 1967.

Editions

22. Newman: *Prose and Poetry*. New York: Allyn & Bacon, 1925.
23. Thomas Walsh, *The Catholic Anthology*. rev. ed. New York: Macmillan Co., 1932.
24. *Pope Pius XI and American Public Opinion* (with Robert J. Cuddihy). New York: Funk & Wagnalls Co., 1939.
25. *The World's Great Catholic Literature*. New York: Macmillan Co., 1942.
26. *Freedom and Authority in the West*. Notre Dame: University of Notre Dame Press, 1967.

Translations

27. Siegfried Behn. *The Eternal Magnet*. New York: Devin-Adair Co., 1929.
28. Enrica Ludovica Maria Handel-Mazzetti. *Jesse and Maria*. New York: Henry Holt & Co., 1931.
29. Peter Lippert. *Job the Man Speaks with God*. New York: Benziger Bros., 1936.
30. Paul Schulte. *The Flying Missionary*. New York: Benziger Bros., 1936.

Introductions

31. Introduction to *The Wall*, by John Hersey. New York: Marchbanks Press, 1957.
32. Introduction to *Sieg Heil!* by Morris D. Waldman. New York: Oceana Publications, 1962.
33. Introduction to *The Problem of Population*. Vol. 3. *Educational Considerations*, edited by George N. Shuster. Notre Dame: University of Notre Dame Press, 1965.

Articles in Books

34. "Spiritual Autobiography." In *American Spiritual Autobiographies*, edited by Louis Finkelstein. New York: Harper & Bros., 1948.
35. "Christian Culture and Education." In *The Church in the World*, edited by Charles O'Donnell. Milwaukee: Bruce Publishing Co., 1967.
36. "Dr. Bruning's Sojourn in the United States (1935-1945)." In *Staat, Wirtschaft und Politik in der Weimarer Republik: Festschrift fuer Heinrich Bruning*, edited by Ferdinand A. Hermens and Theodor Schieder. Berlin: Duncker & Humbolt, 1967.
37. "The Nature and Development of United States Cultural Relations." In *Cultural Affairs and Foreign Relations*, edited by Paul J. Braisted. Washington: Columbia Books, 1968.

Part III

George N. Shuster: A Reflective Evaluation

VINCENT P. LANNIE

High on the eleventh floor of the University of Notre Dame's Memorial Library, George Shuster maintains a large but unpretentious office. From this citadel overlooking the campus, "the old man," as many of his university colleagues refer to him, directs the Center for the Study of Man in Contemporary Society. With a vision that transcends the confines of any one nation, he has geared the center to study the many-faceted dimensions of man's role and destiny in an ever changing world and expanding universe. Still vigorous and alert at seventy-six, he spends most of his days in his office unless he is giving a speech or attending a conference in this country or abroad. Although his steps are somewhat slower than in the past, he maintains a lifetime habit of rising early and spending several hours at his desk before breakfast. His cherished belief that graciousness and courtesy are human virtues of the highest order has not left him—even when he bemoans their absence in today's world or is harassed by an interviewer seeking information about his fascinating life.

In a home filled with the mementoes of an active life, Shuster lives with his wife of forty-six years, Doris. A charming conversationalist with strong views of her own, she believes that she is married to a great man who nevertheless is human enough to be imperfect. She regards Shuster as a brilliant intellectual as well as a man of action who has always exhibited a remarkable degree of courtesy, gentleness, and strength—qualities which attracted her to him when she first met him as her teacher nearly half a century ago. As admirable a man as she thinks Shuster is, Mrs. Shuster had her share of arguments with him. This is not too unusual since she believes that occasional quarrels are an important ingredient for a successful marriage. Yet she would not trade a day in her many years with her husband and would treasure at least another forty-six years with him. Shuster is much too reserved to express his deep feelings for his wife. But on one occasion he did pay tribute to "the light in my own house." He had just retired from Hunter College and had finished writing his recollections as president of that institution. In the last paragraph of *The Ground I Walked On*, Shuster, reminiscing about the bitter and the sweet he and his wife experienced together, ends the book with these sentiments: "It is often said a wife is the shadow of her husband, or that a husband is the shadow of his wife. That is not true of us. We made one shadow, and for it I am in this place saying thanks." Shuster wrote these words in 1961 and has lived them all his married life.

Shuster wrote his memoirs in the same year that he retired from the presidency of Hunter. Many offers came to him but he accepted President Theodore Hesburgh's invitation to come to Notre Dame and serve as the first lay assistant to the president. For Notre Dame was a second home to him even if he had not lived there for a long while. He spent his undergraduate days there before World War I and returned as an English instructor after military service "over there." Several years later, he departed for New York for a journalistic position with the liberal Catholic magazine *Commonweal*. In time he resigned this position rather than compromise his views concerning Franco during the Spanish Civil War. While in New York he completed his doctorate in literature at Columbia University, and a fellowship enabled him to visit Germany (though not for the first time) where he got a firsthand view of the rise of nazism in the home of his ancestors.

In 1939 Hitler was about to engulf Europe in a second world war and Shuster was back in New York. One day he received a call from Carlton J. Hayes, noted Columbia historian and Shuster's friend from *Commonweal* days, to attend a tea at his home. Not knowing the purpose of this invitation Shuster arrived at Hayes' house to find the chairman of the Board of Higher Education of New York City seated with his friend. He was surprised—perhaps even stunned—when he was offered the presidency of Hunter College. In a city where religious affiliations are integrally related to the political realities of life, it had been a tradition for the president of

Hunter to be a Catholic. A prominent Catholic New Yorker and a good friend, John Burke, urged Shuster to accept the position since he was a leading Catholic liberal who could effectively work with the contending groups within the Board of Higher Education as well as within the college. Because of the political influence of the "Power House" on Madison Avenue, the residence of the Archbishop of New York, Burke advised Shuster to seek an interview with the then Archbishop Francis Spellman "for the purpose of sniffing out what the climate might be." The meeting with Spellman went well and the churchman promised not to interfere with any of Shuster's policy decisions at Hunter. Spellman did suggest that Shuster refrain from voicing opinions on controversial noneducational issues (he had done so regularly through his editorials in *Commonweal*)—advice which quickly "went through both ears without delay." When he told his wife about the offer, she was delighted because it would give him a platform from which to express his views on education as well as on world events. Overcoming initial doubts about his qualifications for an administrative post and with the encouragement of his wife, Shuster accepted the position, and Hunter had a new president.

For twenty-one years Shuster presided over the destiny of Hunter College—years that witnessed the depression merge into the nightmare of World War II and the beginnings of the "cold war" and the anti-Communist purges of the McCarthy era. His love of Hunter became an integral part of his life and he affectionately referred to it as "the greatest college community center to be found anywhere in the world." Although abortive Communist attempts to penetrate both faculty and students caused him many a harried day during his administration, they never diminished his belief in academic freedom and the right of faculty members to pursue the truth as they saw it. In his role as college administrator of a municipal college, Shuster came into contact with the leading politicians of New York City. He came to know quite well three of the city's mayors—Fiorello LaGuardia, "The Little Flower," who had "a concern for humanity no social worker has ever equalled"; William O'Dwyer, whose "Celtic charm, presence, and a measure of the rarest kind of social tact" did not preclude benefacting old cronies who did not merit such help; and Robert Wagner, whose "remarkable urbanity" proved that a "gentleman's government can in some measure survive in New York." On the academic side, Shuster had a profound respect for Nicholas Murray Butler of Columbia University and a fondness for Alvin Johnson, founder and first president of the New School of Social Research. Butler was the dean of college presidents at that time in the United States and detractors often referred to him as "Nicholas Miraculous" as he became more dogmatic with each passing year at Morningside Heights. Butler's "great mistake had been," declares Shuster, "that he knew not when the time had come to go." Shuster would not make this "mistake" and would take his leave of Hunter before his retirement age would come to pass.

During Shuster's presidential tenure, Hunter inaugurated its concert series and opera workshop, which enjoyed increasing success in the years that followed. In addition to expanding the fine arts, Shuster opened the doors of the college to the many talented refugees who had fortunately escaped the Nazi terror which was brutalizing most of Europe in the late 1930s and early 1940s. In a macabre way, Europe's loss was America's gain since an assortment of intellectuals, both Jewish and Gentile, found their way to the safe shores of this country. On many an evening during those dark years of totalitarianism, the Hunter College auditorium was packed to capacity to hear these learned victims talk about contemporary tyranny as well as about their scholarly and professional interests. Partisan political activities were forbidden on campus, though various groups were free to express their views about a host of civic matters. Occasionally, this open-forum policy drew criticism from groups sponsoring different viewpoints and solutions. At such times Shuster, reared in the midwestern La Follette liberal tradition, would call attention to the motto inscribed on the south wall of Hunter's building: "We are of different opinions at different hours, but we may always be said to be at heart on the side of truth." Shuster had come across this passage in Emerson's *Conduct of Life* and abided its message faithfully during his years at the College and throughout his life. It was during these somewhat turbulent Hunter years that Shuster was awarded Columbia University's Butler Medal for Service to Education. He considered this a major compliment.

Traditionally, American college presidents have engaged in public service in behalf of their country. In this connection, Shuster gave more than full measure in expending his talents for the common good. During and after World War II, he served on numerous national commissions at home and abroad. With the outbreak of war in 1941, he sat as a member of New York's Enemy Alien Boards which screened Germans, Italians, and Japanese who had been brought into detention by the Federal Bureau of Investigation. Later, the Department of Justice established appeal boards at various internment camps throughout the country. And, although Shuster was a specialist in German affairs with a native's command of the language, bureaucratic inefficiency assigned him to "Santa Fe, New Mexico, at a camp for Japanese." After the War, he was commissioned as deputy to John J. McCloy, then United States High Commissioner for Germany, "for the beautiful but presumably cantankerous state of Bavaria." As a leading American educator and Catholic who spoke fluent German and who had previously visited the area, Shuster was asked to aid in the restoration of this wartorn region and especially to offer his professional recommendations for the reformation of its educational system. In an attempt to democratize Germany according to American models, newspapers, communication media, and schools were reformed; and organizations such as PTAs and civil liberties groups came into existence as examples of a vibrant democratic life. No doubt these efforts introduced a kind of leaven. But Shuster felt that "in the end the Bavarians would remain what they had always been, just as Virginians will perennially be Virginians. The Bavarian dearly loves freedom, but it is not our kind. He is tolerant of others because fundamentally he is tolerant of his own foibles." And, unless technological changes directly affect his country and his life, "he will go right on being a person who on the one hand piously makes a pilgrimage to some shrine like Andechs and on the other has a love affair at Fasching time."

In another postwar assignment, Shuster interviewed captured German generals and Nazi officials to secure information that would be useful in a future evaluation of wartime policies. He thought that the generals were a superior lot to the other prisoners and felt that they should not have been put on trial for directing Hitler's war effort. "What can a soldier do but try to win the battles which the civilians make it necessary for him to fight?" asks Shuster in regard to the perplexing dilemma of public duty and private conscience. But for Nazi officialdom Shuster had no such reservations. These were the vermin who supported and encouraged Hitler's inhuman cruelties throughout Europe but he meditated not so much on these men who were really prisoners of a warped genius and a diabolical idea as upon the countless Germans who understood Hitler's intentions and gave up their lives in opposition to them. Shuster can never forget the Nazi evil and the "human wolves" who screamed their fanatical glee as millions were fed to the ovens as sacrificial victims upon the altar of a twisted ideal.

During the early 1940s, Shuster participated in a Department of State committee to advise the government's newly organized cultural relations program. The long and arduous hours spent with such men as James B. Conant and Archibald MacLeish discussing a variety of conceptions of cultural relations were not in vain since Shuster felt that the work of this committee was to find its expression in the creation of Unesco. For he was to serve as a member of the American delegation to the conference which gave birth to this branch of the United Nations. Not a few associates believed that Shuster was wasting his time with an organization that would never be of much value toward the improvement of world conditions. Certainly he experienced discouragement when the organization was used as a pawn in the cold war struggle between East and West. But he remained committed to Unesco as an effective educational instrument in improving the lot of the underdeveloped nations of the world. "I cannot imagine that any agency could plot for itself a larger task," concludes Shuster who is obviously proud of his association with Unesco, "or one more likely to prove worthwhile if it were accomplished."

Shuster experienced pangs of guilt because his national and international responsibilities caused him to be absent from Hunter for long periods of time. Yet he remains convinced that these excursions into world affairs brought to him a deeper awareness of human society which he could never have acquired by remaining in his presidential chair. But in 1961 he was tired, and he had been Hunter's president for over twenty years. Remembering the painful consequences of Nicholas Murray Butler's overstay at Columbia many years before, he had earlier informed the Board of Higher Education of his intention to resign from his position. With his wife's support, he remained adamant in his decision to leave Hunter and even resisted a tempting offer to become chancellor of all the municipal colleges of New York City. Even though he left Hunter, the College would never lose his interest or esteem, for "I remain deeply grateful for every year I was privileged to spend at Hunter."

Though he had sometimes been critical of Notre Dame, Shuster's affection for his alma mater had never waned. But it was in quite a dispassionate mood that he accepted Father Hesburgh's invitation to attempt to develop the idea which the university and the Ford Foundation had spelled out as the Center for the Study of Man in Contemporary Society. It was to provide the core round which research in the humanities and the social sciences was hopefully to develop. Since Shuster also wished to encourage studies in religion, he conceived of what is now the Institute for Advanced Religious Studies. Finally, as a member of Notre Dame's board of trustees he could also share in the discussion of administrative and policy matters.

II

A man of national and international affairs, Shuster has remained primarily an educator and is most at home within a university setting. He has always loved the classroom but has spent most of his years administering one college and serving as an advisor for another. It is not surprising, therefore, that he should have strong views about the nature and functions of a college president.

In 1968, Shuster was asked to deliver the "Founder's Day Address" at the installation of Robert D. Cross as president of Hunter College. In this speech of reminiscence about the old Hunter and of encouragement to the new president, Shuster presented his view of an effective academic administrator. He thought that there was no better description than that penned by St. Benedict for his monastic community fifteen hundred years ago:

> Let one of the community be chosen; . . . who is wise, mature in character, temperate, not a great eater, not arrogant nor quarrelsome, not insolent, and not a dawdler, nor wasteful, but one who fears God and is a father to the community. Let him have charge of everything . . .

and not make the brethren sad. If any of them shall perchance ask something unreasonable, he must not vex him by contemptuously rejecting his argument, but humbly and reasonably refuse what he wrongly asks. . . . Above all, let him . . . give a gentle answer to those to whom he can give nothing else, for it is written that a good word is above the best gift. . . . [I]f the community be large, let him be given helpers, by whose aid he may without worry perform the office committed to him. What is given let it be given, and what is asked for let it be asked at suitable times, so that no one is troubled or distressed.

Although some of these Benedictine admonitions must be refined and seen within a contemporary context, Shuster believes that they summarize the functions of a top administrator and enable him to be "courageous and forward-looking, resourceful and wise." Even before he addressed Benedict's maxims to the young Robert Cross, Shuster had categorized the qualities necessary for an effective college president. Such a person must be able to speak with large groups persuasively, meet countless and diverse people with equanimity, possess an iron stomach for public dinners, be a good public relations man and an excellent fund raiser, and "be in tune with the traditions of a given campus . . . without being hidebound about his allegiance to them." He must be accessible to students, genuinely fond of them, and aware of their problems and hopes. He must learn to delegate authority but be prepared to shoulder responsibility for decisions which are his alone. In the last analysis, Shuster, looking back over his many years as an administrator, contends that a college president must have "a stout heart, a tough skin, a sense of humor, and . . . a core of unflinching and indestructible honor."

Shuster has never been interested primarily in administrative theory and practice. Rather, he has given priority to goals and ideals in any discussion of his educational scale of values. In attempting to understand the nature of education, he has not been oblivious to the fact that any educational ideal ultimately depends upon its underlying concept of human nature. Such a task becomes even more difficult in a philosophically and religiously pluralistic country as the United States. But this has not deterred Shuster and he has set forth his understanding of education and its implications for society.

Shuster has always related religious thought to human behavior and he has made the same application with his educational philosophy. A deeply religious person with an abiding conviction in man's moral integrity, he has affirmed, as another commentator has declared on one occasion, "the spiritual roots and moral overtones of all American education with its historic democratic convictions and purposes." His creed that learning and wisdom without moral purpose are of little significance emerges clearly in a group of essays published in 1960 under the title *Education and Moral Wisdom.* Knowledge is important but moral wisdom is indispensable to man's most noble and ultimate values. As a result, human virtue always takes precedence over the acquisition of human knowledge. Above all, the seeking after truth is more important than its discovery because the search itself is a "heartening, cleansing, [and] ennobling experience." Nor does a particular environment affect this quest for truth and beauty; its significance is not lost simply because "the world in which one happens to be living is false and tawdry." Shuster happened upon this insight one evening while lying in a "louse-infected" trench in Lorraine during the First World War. Next to him lay an old French soldier who nightly read a battered volume of Aeschylus before he slumbered into a few hours of restless sleep. It was as if this Frenchman were telling him that Greek poetry is as impervious to war "as the sunset is to a man's desire for day." Shuster had studied Greek literature for many years in school, but it was on the Lorraine battlefield that he discovered its rich dimensions. In the final analysis, declares Shuster in language reminiscent of Platonic thought, "the sole thing that matters is that a boy or girl go away from college with an unfettered mind, knowing that the only treasure which will not trickle away is the small change of beauty and truth he keeps in his soul." This is why he can define education as "human nature trying to become more human, in the best sense of the term." With regularity he has stressed the view that moral decision is indispensable to man's intellectual life. "One cannot honestly or successfully live the life of the mind," he once reminded incoming students as they were about to begin their college career at Hunter, "unless one is committed wholeheartedly to what is true and what is free."

Such views about the general nature of education are consistent with Shuster's understanding of the liberal arts, which he places at the core of the college experience. And yet he is quite candid about certain "myths" which he believes are associated with the meaning of a liberal education. The first myth is that merely "taking a program in the liberal arts will prepare people to earn a livelihood." For a knowledge of all the great ideas of the world and a familiarity with the leading figures of history will not equip students to cope with the world in which they find themselves. Thus, at Hunter Shuster urged students to take such courses as typewriting and stenography and advised his girls to understand the psychology of the male and the problems encountered in raising a family. It has always seemed incredible to him that a college should "help young people fail in everything else than their classes." The second myth is that colleges can offer a complete education for the professions or specific vocations. Certainly they can offer preparatory instruction and some training. But no more. The other ingredients are obtained on the job and depend in good measure upon the moral integrity and determination of the practitioner. The good physician, for instance, has knowledge, character, insight, and magnanimity, while the bad doctor is an imposter "who sells patients his wholly worthless degree." Shuster reflects that students are harmed when a college conveys the impression that competency in a prescribed course will prepare them for a lifetime work; for example, that piecemeal courses in educational psychology will adequately ready a teacher for competent classroom instruction.

In this connection, Shuster has recorded his observations about the educational views of John Dewey and Robert Hutchins—both of whom he came to know personally. A reformer of education whose prose style unfortunately clouded his thought, Dewey persuaded the American public that youthful participation was an important dimension in the business of education. But Shuster contends that Dewey's followers overestimated "the prowess of the junior members of the firm" and that the master was somewhat romantically naive in thinking that "making democracy interesting in school would also make it work outside of school." More important, however, Dewey's philosophy of pragmatic relativism has always been alien to Shuster's religious absolutism. He has never been able to understand Dewey's proposal "to bridge the gap between the 'liberal' classroom and his new way of looking at the world, in which Relativism had become the only Absolute and so made the past obsolete." Although many of Dewey's strictures of traditional pedagogical methods were valid, and some of his ideas on the teaching process are still relevant, Shuster believes that the Columbia professor's grand mistake was to see the enemy "in caricature rather than in the round." At the same time, Shuster argues that Hutchins's thought is really understood only within the context of Dewey's *Democracy and Education,* which stresses "the fostering of community, and the formation of character." For Hutchins, learning means the mastering of a "common language" of the mind, that is, familiarity with the basic literature of mankind (hence his emphasis on great books) and the ability to use this language in reasonable dialectic. The true end of education is the formation of a community of persons competent in these abilities which would then establish a democratic society—one, it might be added, envisioned both by Hutchins and Dewey. Thus, all other educational goals (especially many of those promulgated by the Progressives) are peripheral or meaningless to the main task of education.

Within his own intellectual perspective, Shuster thinks that it is almost impossible to define a liberal education; rather, it seems to be "an experience to be lived through, a banquet that is served, a journey entered upon and only in a certain sense completed." But at another time and in a less poetic mood, he did characterize the liberal arts as "a course of study designed to encourage tentatively integrated learning about man's most fruitful insights into himself and the reality about him, so that a student may feel the texture of the known in order to be able to realize, sooner or later, that this is only the garment of the unknown." When he talks about the pursuit of truth, therefore, he is referring to a person who comes to grasp at least a part of reality regardless of where he finds it. As a result, he feels that the real value of Hutchins's program of the great books lies not so much in the books themselves as in the methods proposed to discuss them, namely, the *disputatio* and the *colloquium.* Thus, influenced by "Dewey's idea of the community, Hutchins's practice of dialectic, and Martin Buber's philosophy of the dialogue," Shuster maintains that the "great conversation" is indispensable in the college experience of all students. But this emphasis on dialogue leaves room in the college curriculum for vocational subjects or, as Shuster labels them, "vocational inlays" which he describes as "modest essays in the art of preparing for life." Although knowledge can be systematized and constantly organized, Shuster concludes that it can never finally be synthesized even if all the encyclopedias of the world were added to the hundred or thousand great books. For at this point each human being is on his own. In its ultimate and final sense, integration is something quite different. "It is silence." Or to put it in the thought of St. Paul, to whom Shuster pays deep devotion, one sees in part now and in full only later. And so in a utopian stance, Shuster offers a "dream of a new world":

> . . . [a world] in which anyone who desists after his fiftieth year from gainful employment, in order to devote time and energy to the task of thinking through his experience for the benefit of himself and his fellows, will be exempt from all taxes. Such men will not write a great deal. But from time to time, I trust, they may say something in which humor, caution, and learning are blended with a deep concern for everlasting values. Perhaps in that blessed era one or two of them will receive honorary degrees, even though they cannot endow the university with a chair for the study of Belgian marbles and Egyptian miniatures. It may even be that someone will be honored for having suggested that prayer is an intellectual exercise.

Interest in higher education kept Shuster at Hunter for over two decades; concern for Catholic education returned him to Notre Dame as a teacher thirty years after he had left his alma mater. Just as he has voiced his beliefs about higher education in general, he has presented rather strong views about its Catholic dimension. A Catholic college must be primarily a good college which happens to be at the same time Catholic in its religious orientation. He has little sympathy with the numerous Catholic colleges which confuse their intellectual responsibilities with their religious commitment. In this respect, he quotes the brilliant and ascetical John Henry Newman: "Knowledge is one thing, virtue another; good sense is not conscience, refinement is not humility, nor is largeness and justice of view faith." The personal holiness of a cleric, nun, or lay person can never be a substitute for effective teaching and sound scholarship. Shuster first recorded these thoughts in an essay "On Catholic Education" written in 1958. Nine years later, with the educational repercussions of the Second Vatican Council clearly before him, he wrote

Catholic Education in a Changing World, which offers fresh insights into the present state and future progress of Catholic higher education. In this volume, Shuster argues that the Catholic college, like any first-rate institution of higher learning, must alert students to new problems and solutions facing contemporary man, must be staffed by competent teachers who will stimulate students and be given freedom to pursue their scholarship, must be concerned with the aesthetic as well as the intellectual life of man and, as a specifically Catholic institution, must foster man's social responsibilities within the spirit of Vatican Council II. No longer can a Catholic college justify its existence on the nineteenth-century immigrant rationale of preserving its students' religious faith in a hostile and increasingly secularistic society. The only viable alternative for Shuster (other Catholic educators have reached a similar conclusion) is that these colleges demonstrate their capability of providing a "first-rate education within the context of a Catholic community." Otherwise, they will simply dry up and fade into a happy but justified oblivion. This means that such colleges emphasize not only the past but the present, not only the heavenly city but the earthly one as well. These are the guidelines that were proposed at the Vatican Council and to these Shuster subscribes.

In some ways, Shuster's ideas about a Catholic university have remained intact, but in other ways his thinking has been somewhat altered by the intellectual currents prevalent in post–Vatican II days. Whereas formerly he subscribed to Newman's contention that the primary justification for a Catholic university was an unfettered school of theology, in *Catholic Education in a Changing World* Shuster concedes that such a rationale can no longer account for its contemporary existence. For theology offers some ways to study the family of man and the life of God. But only some ways. The social sciences have their own methods, the physical sciences offer other alternatives, and the arts still other avenues. As far as he can observe the present and glimpse the future, Shuster would place the following sentiments upon the lips of faculty members and students:

> We are men and women who have resolved to lead the life of the mind in a way which only a genuine university, combining rigor with courtesy, can provide in every dimension of scholarly venture and

worth. At the same time, we have accepted with all our hearts Pascal's wager that God is and has spoken. We have done this for a variety of reasons, so that in our diversity we offer, as does life itself, testimony which is one through many.

Nevertheless, this change of focus has not altered Shuster's other basic contentions about a Catholic university. All points of view must be present and yet be justified before the exacting demands of their respective disciplines. Such a condition is by no means a watering down of a Catholic university (at least not in its new conception). On the contrary, such diversity alone can "provide the breadth of association with the whole human family which is the proper mode of the life of the Church. Indeed, it is not too much to say that a Catholic university without such a leaven would be stale bread." In this environment, the freedom to explore and challenge is indisputable and the new function of the Catholic university is to "replace censorship with criticism." A competent scholar must proceed where his evidence seems to lead him regardless of his conclusions and despite their real or apparent antagonism to official Catholic belief. Within such an intellectual milieu, administrators must come to accept this freedom of inquiry the more they realize that "only the unfettered mind can be unimpeachable."

Shuster is convinced that diversity of viewpoint is essential if Catholics are to comprehend the diversity of experiences, disciplines, and aspirations in the life of man. Once again picking up Pascal's reference to the human–divine wager, Shuster judges that "it makes all the difference which side of the wager a man is on, but, above everything, all are members of the human family, guided by conscience and the laws of evidence." Thus, the university must always be open to those who are qualified to enter and must give ear to all who have something to say. In addition, the university must never prostitute its intellectual or moral position for financial gain, though it "must do many things which are in the public interest" even when the "work may be distracting and sometimes disappointing." With such a thought Shuster seems to be reflecting Dewey's concern that an educational institution become a part of the total community in which it finds itself.

Shuster has consistently asserted that Catholics have traditionally lived in social and intellectual isolationism and have had little inclination to enter into the nation's total life. But the university environment has now changed, just as church and country are in the agonizing process of change. American Catholics must now take their place on the national intellectual scene—not with any chauvinistic pride that they alone possess *the* truth, but rather as partners engaged with their fellows in the human pursuit of truth and light. Hopefully, the new Catholic university will help them "sense more acutely the blessing which lies on all Being, all truth about Being, because it is of God."

Does such a Catholic university exist anywhere in this country today? In 1958, Shuster evidenced pessimism in response to this question. "We have as yet no such university, and unless there is a change in the way things are going we never will have one." But that was before the Second Vatican Council opened wide the gates and allowed fresh air to come into the many doors of its Church. Shuster arrived at Notre Dame before the sessions of the Council had begun. Since then he has tasted of its substance and has feasted upon its possibilities. He came to Notre Dame to contribute toward the transformation of the college into a great Catholic university. And although the academic millennium has not as yet arrived, Notre Dame is at least going in the right direction. For this, Shuster is pleased and has youthful confidence in the work yet ahead.

CHAPTER IX

George D. Stoddard

Part I

An Autobiography

Family Background

The one grandfather I knew, a retired farmer, was born in 1815. Living to be ninety-six, he almost spanned the long period from Napoleon to World War I. He farmed from boyhood to the age of eighty. He was a tough, forthright perfectionist, hard on himself but gentle with others. My father owned a modest insurance business. He was sincere, upright, and highly respected. He was always encouraging and obviously proud of his children. My mother was the recessive member of the family, sweet and obliging—the old-fashioned "helpmeet" to her husband. My father expected me to be a lawyer, but the ones I had contact with in my small town were uninspiring. My older brother had married into a manufacturing family, my younger was off early to California with his hometown buddies. My sister, Etna, ten years older than I, from the first supplied the strong feminine influence in my life. She was forever *for* me; she blatantly kept her ambitions in my behalf up to or well beyond anything I felt able to accomplish.

Thus, for rectitude, my father and his father who lived with us during my teens; for ambition honeyed over with love, my sister.

Education

The only elementary school teacher I vividly recall was Alice Rashleigh, a full-blooded, exuberant person who, I thought at the time, kept riding me to do better. Everything on my report card had to fall between 96 and 100. This brought gladness to my father's heart and a I-knew-you-could-do-it response from my sister. Although I kept this up through high school, I finished only in second place there—a matter of a few decimal points. Actually, I did not "find myself" at all in high school, fluctuating between literary subjects and science. The only bright spot was a remarkable teacher and, years later, friend and counselor, William D. Bryden, who taught German and admired young people and art. Fifty years ahead of his time, he joined the "in" group in communicating with youth. For me, he set my eyes on college—at the time a rather uncommon goal in the little anthracite town of Carbondale, Pennsylvania.

After high school, I worked in the town's principal bank for a year. I disappointed its president by clinging to my ambition to go to college. He remarked that I probably would not make much money, for chemical engineering (my first collegiate love) was certainly not as lucrative as banking. Since this particular bank failed during the Depression, the goal of making money, then as now a faint lure for me, would have proved a blind alley.

Still, in college I did not care much for engineering, either. Mathematics? Delightful. Physics? Yes. Pure chemistry? An intriguing game. But shop work, machine design, industrial chemistry? These soon bored me, especially in an academic matrix practically stripped of the arts and humanities. So, I switched to education as a major and found incidentally the world of psychology. It was a close call between education and sociology, for among Penn State's truly inspiring scholars and teachers was O. Fred Boucke. When I was only a junior in college, Professor Boucke gave me an inscribed copy of a book he had just published. What a treasure for a student threading his way through the academic maze! But even back there I had an intuitive feeling that education was my true love—a choice aided and abetted by another wise counselor of youth, David Allen Anderson, dean of the School of Education. So it turned out to be. In the next two years as a student I "flourished," graduating with almost six years of "credits" and hungry for the intellectual life that chemical engineering had denied me.

Before the shift I spent seven months in the army, starting in the Medical Corps and finishing (after the war) in the Field Artillery. It was only in an officers' training camp far removed from Penn State that I screwed up my courage to write the redoubtable "Swampy" Pond of my intention to drop industrial chemistry—a decision that brought forth from him such a denunciation as to arouse awe among my barracks mates.

After Penn State, I applied for a fellowship in order to study a year at the Sorbonne. My request was denied for a reason that seemed fair enough even to me: I had no French at all. Nevertheless, after teaching English a year in the local high school, I went to the University of Paris on my own, with my father's help, that is. Thus my three significant career decisions, in this order: (a) to go to college; (b) to transfer to education; and (c) to move into psychology, a la Simon, Dumas, Piéron and company at the Sorbonne.

In Paris everything was seen "through a glass darkly." The first skull-penetration for me was not really through lectures and laboratory work, but through the arts—literature, the theaters, the museums, the concert halls. Dead broke most of the time, students used to haunt the American agencies for "hand-outs," not for food or wine—they were cheap—but for free tickets. This was the Paris of the early 1920s, but for me, above all, it was an intimate contact with Simon and the work of his brilliant collaborator, the late Alfred Binet.

From Penn State to Paris to the University of Iowa in the then small town of Iowa City was an unlikely journey. However, Dean Anderson's mentor over the years was Carl E. Seashore, head of the Department of Psychology and dean of the Graduate College at the University of Iowa. As presidents came and went, Seashore guided the University along lines that still today sound daring to many a university executive. He believed in art and music and literature; he was at the same time a distinguished scientist, a member of the National Academy. At Iowa he immediately placed the gangling graduate student "fresh out" of Paris under the tutelage of G. M. Ruch, a hard-driving perfectionist in tests and measurements, the significance of whose work to this day is undervalued. Himself a student of L. M. Terman's, Ruch was not enthralled by the web-spinning that accompanied the successful attempts of the Stanford group to translate and adapt the Binet-Simon Scales for the measurement of intelligence. Ruch taught me all I ever learned about the art of testing, while Professor Henry Rietz, head of the Department of Mathematics, rounded out my scanty knowledge of statistics.

The Bearing of My Experience with Religion on My Career

Having dutifully attended a Methodist Sunday school and, under the watchful eye of my father, gone to church occasionally and eschewed Sunday games and the colored comics, I suddenly pulled away from all that. At age twelve I found intolerable the wooden answers to burning questions (of the kind Piaget found to be rampant among European nine-year-olds). For a dozen of us, action followed insight: we literally stalked out of the little church school never to return. Years later in college there appeared professors in the flesh and in books (who remembers Roy Wood Sellars?) who shed new light on the age-old question of man's relation to the universe and to his fellowmen. Thus it was an easy step to Unitarianism. Marginal as my religious practices were, and are, I have accepted a limited amount of religious involvement by becoming a moderator of the church, a contributor to its publications, and a life member of its Laymen's League. This degree of commitment, if not more, I still regard as a valuable counterpoise to the pressures of organized superstition. There is indeed something in life that reaches beyond work and play and art and ethics; for me it is found in a liberalizing religion devoid of cant.

The Kinds of Communities in Which I Have Lived

As indicated, I was born and brought up in a small coal town which was entering a decline. It had schools with gravelly playgrounds—or none at all in the case of the high school. In earlier more prosperous times it had built a few handsome churches and business blocks. Its public library was puny and repulsive. Its tiny municipal park was fenced in like a cemetery and just as lifeless. Its art consisted of two competing "concert bands" which in turn competed with two glamorous fire companies. What saved it for the children of my day was the accessibility of wooded hills and streams and lakes. There a boy and a dog could walk a lot and dream a little. Our neighbors were kind and responsive; together with parents, like mine, they made this otherwise drab small-town life bearable and often enjoyable. Still, ever since, I have turned to college towns that create their own culture pattern or to large cities

(Paris and New York) that have something to offer for every taste. I cannot "go home again."

Friends and Associates

I have already mentioned the Brydens, Bouckes, Andersons, Ruchs, and Seashores, who gave me friendly advice and encouragement at various choice-points. These were indeed my guides and counselors through high school, college, and university. And there were many others. But among my fellow students at any academic level, none stands out. Friends and associates—yes, but not of the lasting till-death-do-us-part variety. Looking back, I believe that my early intellectual interests shut me in somewhat. Besides, I was frail, not given to athletics, and no hail-fellow-well-met. Until I was twenty-five, girls interested me not in the least. In the army at age twenty, the best I could do was to carry on a desultory correspondence with this or that hometown girl (every soldier was supposed to get a scented pink letter now and then). In short, for me the "influence" came from my elders almost exclusively.

What Books Were Important to Me?

Through high school and college I read everything I could get my eyes on, but for the long years before college the fare was neither rich nor extensive. I had a bent toward the scientific and a strong interest in the shape of things to come. The battle scenes that dominated the teaching of history from first grade up interested me less than what the leaders said; I was by nature no archivist, no reciter of dates, names, and places, no tracer of military campaigns. But the ideas and plans of the French, English, German, American, and Russian revolutionaries in politics, like their radical counterparts in sociology and religion, invariably caught my attention.

But the question is, *What books, what writers?* A few do stand out, although at the time I was too enamored of almost any author to be discriminating. These I remember for the good reason that I read them, or turned to them, over and over: Frazer's *The Golden Bough;* Karl Pearson's *Grammar of Science;* Lewis Mumford's *The Golden Day;* the writings of Rousseau, Darwin, Huxley, Freud, Janet, Poincaré, Binet, Bertrand Russell, Sherrington, Piaget, and the early Gestalt psychologists; of Americans (U.S.), the work of the geneticists, Morgan and Castle, and of Horace Mann, William James, Thorndike, Dewey, and the behaviorists. Threaded in were the usual potpourri of literary offerings: Shakespeare, Tennyson *(The Vision of Sir Launfal)*, Victor Hugo; the science fiction of H. G. Wells; the writings of Emerson and Thoreau, and later of Frost and Sandburg. Before these stalwarts came a series of readings common at the time, Eliot's Five-Foot Book Shelf, the one constantly sampled set of books, cheaply bound but rich in content, that graced my private "study" in a corner of my bedroom. No handsome set of *The Great Books* on today's shelf is comparable in its impact! I should confess, too, that the various Bibles that dogged my steps at home and away from home (Gideons be praised) were opened only at the New Testament, and there at the well-thumbed marker for the Sermon on the Mount. Only Plato on the last days and death of Socrates has ever so enthralled me.

My Career

Several critical choice-points in my career are clearly discernible, as has already been noted. The first important step was the firm decision to go to college. To the college-oriented youth of today that must seem strange; nobody who wants to be "somebody" ignores the collegiate route. Not so in 1915. Perhaps 10 percent of the college-age population was in college; from my hometown the percentage was smaller. There were many local opportunities for work. Mine was a job in a bank—in the biggest bank in town, headed by a leading figure in the community. My father knew him as did almost everybody. Actually, this banker offered me a job while I was cutting his lawn one summer day; perhaps he had checked on my high school record. I worked a year in his bank, plotting meanwhile to escape to college. At the time, he expressed disappointment but he got over it. I went back to the bank each summer, pinch-hitting for vacationers up to the rank of teller in the "cage." That was my first and last experience with a stack of yellowbacks and greenbacks; they soon became as common to the touch as old newspapers. However, it was only the beginning of my contact with the petty intrigues of grown men who are called upon to use only 20 percent of their mental capacity to keep up with a job.

So, in 1916, I went off to college. The choice of a college was easy: Penn State was tuition-free and word had penetrated to Carbondale that its science and engineering rated high.

The second choice-point I have already alluded to: the slowly thought-out intention to abandon chemistry and engineering for education and psychology. This was a significant change of direction and it sprang from inner conviction. I have never been thing-minded. As a half-engineer my ineptitude with anything mechanical is to this day a source of hilarity. Doubtless I have cultivated this reputation in order to avoid doing things I could do but would rather not.

The third decision-point came right after graduation from Penn State. My erstwhile roommate and I cooked up a scheme to spend a year in graduate study in Germany. Since we were both hard up—and I in debt to my indulgent father—each of us decided to work a year while living at home. With the savings, we might eke out the cost of study abroad. We went our separate ways, with a difference. I did what I had planned to do. At age twenty-four, still sponging off the family (my parents were pleased to have me at home), I had saved enough money to set off for France. Germany, after all, was not in good odor so soon after World War I. Her lustrous universities that had sired my professors were tarnished. Besides, psychology was taking over my mental life and the brilliant, intuitive forays of the French school appealed to me more than the solid but less glamorous work of the Germans. In retrospect, this was a wise decision, for the French stayed in France and could only be reached there, while the whole complement of German gestalt psychologists, threatened by Hitler, came to the United States. Thus, as a graduate student at the University of Iowa, with my year at the Sorbonne's Institut de Psychologie neatly in reserve, I could turn hungrily to the writings of German and American scholars who were shaping the course of psychology—to Wertheimer, Koffka, Koehler, Lewin; to Thorndike, Watson, Thurstone, and Ruch. For a time I also turned to Ruch's preceptor, Terman; but, as we shall see, I reluctantly turned away and finally wound up in a camp hostile to him and his followers. (What happened to my ex-roommate? Well, he too "saved up," but soon married and settled down.)

The next important decision as a student was to accept the half-time research assistantship in psychology offered to me by Dean Seashore of the University of Iowa. As indicated, the connecting link was Dean Anderson in whose School of Education I had majored at Penn State. Anderson flatly told me I had "promise," swayed no doubt by the temerity of a student tackling a graduate program at the University of Paris without benefit of an hour of formal study of the French language. The rest was clear sailing, for with these two men Scandinavian (Norwegian) was speaking to Scandinavian (Swedish).

Of course, Seashore soon discovered that his principal scholarly interests (experimental psychology and musicology) were not mine. I kept up the love of art and music so magically fostered in Paris, but not of their *psychology*—nor the psychology of anything else, except childhood education. In Ruch, a tireless innovator who creatively applied statistics to tests and measurements, I found a true comrade and, as I thought then, a parallel career.

To sum up at this precareer point:

From one high school teacher, Mr. Bryden, I learned enough German, but beyond that, I learned what it meant to be a teacher, a scholar, a gentleman, and a friend of youth. Of course, this insight was an after-burner phenomenon; over the years the fire would be rekindled.

From only three or four professors in the course of four years at college, I learned the same lessons in more depth. Through reading I was brought intimately into contact with the works of great thinkers. I learned to place a high value on intellectual accomplishment—for its concentration of energy and, indeed, its downright scarcity in any historical period, past or present.

If I had a hobby, it was not in sports, games, mechanics, stamps, or anything of the sort. It was the search for the inner life of persons as expressed in their speech, writings, and behavior. My interest veered toward mathematics for awhile and then toward philosophy but, through inner forces hardly noticed at the time and not easily brought to light now, I would not settle for science or logic anymore than I would for mechanics or any craft or skill. In this respect I drew away from my mentor, Ruch, and moved toward the more wide-ranging Seashore. Ruch was a master of the art of applied social science; his tests and examinations were far ahead of their time. Nevertheless, like Terman and T. L. Kelley before him, he did not develop new theories or establish basic principles. In fact, Binet's brilliant hypotheses as to the nature of intelligence were lost on Terman. For decades the Stanford group was highly successful in translation, test improvement, normative tabulation, and promotion without so much as a nod to Binet's fundamental theories of intelligence.

I did not sense at the time that the significant academic experiences I had at the Sorbonne were only two in number: first, a direct contact, through Simon, with the original work of Binet; and second, an introduction to the remarkable contributions of scholars like Charcot, Freud, Janet, Dumas, Delacroix, and Piéron. American students in educational psychology, fascinated as they had a right to be by the burgeoning field of tests and measurements that culminated in World War I Army Alpha and Army Beta, rarely had any grasp of the underlying hypotheses. Entranced by the seeming exactitude of the Pearson product-moment coefficient of correlation and a false transfer to human abilities of exciting discoveries in genetic determinism—it made no difference whether the subjects were rats, fish, or fruit flies—students became the easy victims of wishful thinking. It would be so much better scientifically if something could be forever fixed and determined in the genes! Of course some things were, but hardly the precise range of one's vocabulary or general information.

I can think of no personal qualities that led me to question everything; at the time I supposed this was a natural consequence of being young. Today there is nothing strange about such an attitude. Everything is being examined, with or without the tools of thought needed for the task. At any rate, as graduate students and young instructors, we did not stop with critical analysis—we were not allowed to by our superiors. We were expected to move on to a better test, a new idea, a new application, a new frontier. At the University of Iowa, creativity was in the air, not only in psychology and measurement, but also in speech, poetry, music, theater, and the graphic arts. Much of this ferment is still to be found there, but to indulge the sin of nostalgia, I find it hard to name the counterparts of Seashore, Horn, Ruch, Mabie, Clapp, Bush, Schramm, Engle, and

Grant Wood. We come close to it in contemplating the remarkable achievements of Lindquist, VanAllen, and the late Wendell Johnson.

Personal Motives and Drives

I suppose one of my characteristics is a willingness, but no relentless drive, to accept responsibility, to undertake diverse tasks and see them through—somehow to bridge the gap pinpointed by T. S. Eliot:

> Between the idea
> And the reality
> Between the motion
> And the act
> Falls the Shadow.

Such a drive may border on the ruthless, but as a rule only in artists or scientists with a touch of genius. An artist sees and hears and understands and he goes further—he strives to produce something to which others must attend and respond, if only negatively. Those of us whose drives lead to scholarly productions or administrative acts move men, if we move them at all, by the force of ideas or the circumstance of change. The true artistic achievement is a boon that needs no discernible practical effect. Not so the administrative act: in itself it is neutral. It may mark a small step forward or a great reform. It may, on the other hand, be regressive, obnoxious, or brutal. We may indulge in wonderful thoughts and still be regarded as a dilettante, an escapist, if nothing is communicated. So, I regard myself as no poet, no artist, but as no empty-minded administrator either—a blend, if you will, of a scholar more than skin-deep but not profound and an educational administrator plagued by ideas. My inner and outer lives intersect but not equally. In the midst of committees and telephones, chameleon-like, I usually stay alert though the mix eventually palls. Absorbed in putting thoughts on paper or mapping out an innovation, I resent interruption. My constant inner life makes me seem deafer than I am, though hard-of-hearing at the best of times; it imparts an air of remoteness or indifference to the speech of others. It can become a source of unintentional rudeness but, I think, not of malice.

My inner satisfactions relate to this ambivalence. I cannot pretend to be a hail-fellow-well-met, a hearty, grinning slapper of backs. I am guilty of the cold eye and the dour look. If persons bore me, I probably show it, although a bore by definition is the last one to take notice. On the other hand, I am apt to "take fire" and display an emotionally tinged response. At such times I become compulsively articulate. The hardest stance for me is to remain cool to what I regard as original and exciting, or, on the other hand, to what strikes me as stupid, corrupt, or malicious. My most intense pleasure is to be in touch with a warm creative person who represents what human nature is or could be. To me, the self-righteous person is distasteful at best and repulsive if insincere. I find it hard to admire saints, and I could never worship them. Perhaps one further characteristic of my personality (as seen from within) is an intuitive rejection of hypocrisy and pretense. I literally cannot endure the "phony," whether his defect is displayed in a series of small acts or in a complex structure of self-deception. Even when, as a psychologist, I sense the need revealed by a person in conflict, a paranoid for example, I prefer to reform him or avoid him rather than give in and let him take out his meanness on me. That is why I probably did well to skirt the field of clinical psychology and stay out of psychiatry altogether. In like manner, social welfare as a worthy endeavor to salvage persons and lead them to a better life became meaningful to me chiefly through the influence of education from infancy upward. There are other significant factors, of course, such as health protection, good housing, job opportunities, and human rights, some of which I have paid attention to in a collateral way. Penetrating every attribute of Socrates' "examined life" is education, broadly conceived. Were I to use the Biblical concept of "evil," I would reserve it for crimes against the rights, safety, and freedom of *persons*. Deviations that turn inward to debilitate or destroy the self I view with curiosity and a desire to be helpful. Thus, for decades I was rated by poll-minded sociologists as a "liberal"—with a footnote which recorded, but did not explain, the fact that I believed in capital punishment. Nor have I ever explained, until now. Actually I did not believe in capital *punishment*, but only in deterrence through the killing by society of murderers. To me, one murder by itself alone marked a man not for life but for death, provided that by such means society had found a genuine hedge against this particular crime. There, of course, lies the heart of the matter. Is capital punishment a reliable deterrent? I still believe it would be if judges and juries could be persuaded of its justice and efficacy. Unhappily, apprehension of the murderer is difficult, and a conviction, even when the evidence of guilt is overwhelming, is a rarity. It may be that life imprisonment will offer more protection. In either case punishment remains as an ingredient. While some may view life in prison as a basis for personal reform, I am dubious about that in the case of the murderer. At best, it provides a time for remorse. Generally it evokes a widespread mawkishness in the public press that gives aid to the criminal while ignoring the victim and his living circle of family and friends. So, not unfairly, I hope, I tend to save all tears for the actual or potential victims. It must be emphasized that when I use the term "murderer," I mean just that—a person convicted of the crime under the very best legal procedures that our social structure can provide. Any form of perjury, of racial or other prejudice, any departure from a strict application of legal and ethical principles of justice, I regard with repugnance.

In any event, capital punishment in the United States is now scarcely an issue. What counts is the effectiveness with which we lead children and youth into lives of usefulness, decency, and good cheer. The failure of a delinquent or criminal is in us, too, as an element in the social structure, and this can be said of a failure to prevent hookworm, malnutrition, malaria, typhoid, polio, or tuberculosis. When we find such a condition, we treat it and try to prevent its spread, but the injustice sets in long before that and it may spring from a defect in the total social structure. Again, a sovereign ingredient of reform is to be found in child, parent, and community education.

As to my ideas being understood or misunderstood, the truth is that trouble more often has followed understanding than the reverse. In Illinois, for example, it was well known that I was hostile to fraud, to medical quackery, to malicious deception. I questioned dubious procedures; I probed and exposed. Any corrupt person can tolerate sanctimonious rhetoric—the familiar expounding and viewing-with-alarm of editors, preachers, and educators. Perhaps he welcomes it as a diversionary exercise; it makes his conniving not only profitable but attention-getting. A real antagonist, such as the uncorrupted policeman, he fears and hates and seeks to destroy.

In education no one expects ideas to be accepted or even noticed simply because they are proclaimed. Understanding, modification, and acceptance are slow to come and may not come at all in one's lifetime. In that respect I have been fortunate, for I have lived long enough to see some improvements toward which I have contributed to a slight degree. The best example in my career was the fierce hostility a group of us experienced in reporting research findings on the nonfixity of the IQ: a hornet's nest then, a textbook commonplace now. Ever since, I, for one, have sensed what young people mean when they lash out against the "establishment." The whole affair finally was more of a venture than a frustration.

My Social Ideas

As indicated, my social ideas are for the most part on the liberal side. In religion it was not so much a matter of liberalism versus conservatism as it was a matter of uncommon sense, uncommon, that is, among middle-class, church-going families. All we children had to do was to apply a touch of reason and the scientific approach to witness a quick deflation of dogma. It became clear that to behave properly through fear of semieternal or eternal punishment, and for no other reason, was in itself a shameful human condition. The moral was that evil would dominate persons deprived of such surefire horrors. There was a prodigious disparity between crime and its punishment. My young mind was asked to believe that the more vague and subjective the "sin," the more certain and horrible the retribution. Children who could read learned that for centuries organized religion had found easy ways, through money or repentance, of absolving a person of guilt and its dreadful consequence. Through an intense interest all through college in the mechanism of heredity, I applied the same thought processes to the question of life-after-death, a personal God, the revealed Truth, and all that. As with the soul itself, no entity, condition, structure, or necessity was revealed. The whole structure was so obviously humanoid as to make the inquiry itself irrational and fruitless. Beyond adolescence and throughout adulthood I retained a sense of wonder toward unanswerable questions about the universe, the galaxies, the physical forces at work, and the emergence of life itself. Long before I ran into the term *teleology* I rejected its implications. There was perforce a *Beginning* sensed as a dramatic event and there would be an *End* of equal proportions, but the one was preceded by infinite beginnings and the other would be followed by unending cataclysms. Through it all the tinyness of man in relation to the cosmos was clearly depicted; he could mean nothing to it, and it to him would forever be an unresolved mystery.

I pick up this train of thought again only because it still tempers my social and political ideology. Up to a point the approach is, I trust, scientific and technical, but beyond that we may as well be reconciled to our fate through thought, art, and love. Thrown among practical human beings, we need not relinquish our wonder at Nature's ways, but rather apply it to the vast complexity of human affairs. There is elegance in fitting man's theories, laws, and discoveries to the so-called laws of nature; it is a handsome way to reach out, not to some all-seeing, all-controlling divinity but rather to the hope of man's control of his own destiny as man. We can think, work, and help others; we can share in the human experience of art and love here and now. To fail to do so at this time and in this place is to fail in all the ways given to man.

As to the immediate effects of such ideas and their social counterparts, there is little to add. I have yet to find a board of trustees which is not, as a composite board, fearful of thinking. There was, and still is, administrative safety in the orthodox, the innocuous, the sterile. Acts can be condoned or vetoed but thoughts, if expressed, are ever so much harder to subdue. I can think of no college executive who lost his job by advocating McCarthyism (Joseph) but some were harassed for supporting McCarthyism (Eugene). On the whole, the respect of a faculty or a student body is won in exactly the reverse fashion. Similarly, agnosticism, ethical culture, or Unitarianism are not tickets to preferment in the ranks of academic administrators, although tolerance is on the upswing. The commonest religion of all, namely, "no religious preference," is in fashion and sustains an aura of open-mindedness. Actually I have found it to be rather an attitude of indifference to matters that are significant in human affairs. There is a profound need to find some meaningful ritual when one is faced with such ceremonies as those of marriage or death. The lesser sacraments carry little weight with the people I have known. What academic authorities fear to this day is any critical pronouncement on such matters or any action that smacks of nonconformity. The decline in religious faith has had the effect of turning the attention of the paranoid to deviations seen as unpatriotic, socialistic, communistic, or treasonable. It is still all too easy to be tagged with one of these names on the basis of simple disagreement or the exercise of free speech.

Having long felt free to speak and write on such matters, although not belligerently or cynically, I did indeed fan a few flames. Eventually they subsided.

My Most Significant Achievements

Any such valid ranking must come from an external source. One grows in personality and character along a scale not to be measured by "success" or "failure"; in fact, at times there is a negative correlation in this respect. So, in a not very reliable rank order:

1. The presidency of the University of Illinois during the seven years following World War II
2. The directorship of the Child Welfare Research Station of the University of Iowa, 1928-1942
3. The commissionership of the state of New York during World War II
4. The editorship of the NSSE yearbook, *Intelligence: Its Nature and Nurture* (1940)
5. The authorship of *The Meaning of Intelligence* (1943)
6. The deanship of the Graduate College of the University of Iowa, 1936-1942
7. The principal authorship of New York University Self-Study (1956)
8. The executive vice-presidency and chancellorship of New York University, 1960-1964
9. Activities in Unesco, 1945-1951
10. The authorship of *Krebiozen, The Great Cancer Mystery* (1955)
11. The authorship of *The Dual Progress Plan* (1961)
12. Activities in *National Educational Television*
13. Membership on the board of *Lincoln Center for the Performing Arts*, New York
14. Membership on the board of trustees of the *American Shakespeare Festival Theatre and Academy*, Stratford, Connecticut
15. Membership on the board of directors of the RAND Corporation, Santa Monica

16. Chairmanship of the U.S. Educational Mission to Japan, 1946
17. A series of assignments in international education: Korea, Iran, Cambridge University, University of East Africa
18. Again, administration in higher education—at Long Island University, beginning in 1967

Major Career Activities

On a vertical straight line by five-year periods:

1920-1924

1921	Graduated from Pennsylvania State College
1921-22	Teacher of English, Carbondale (Pa.) High School
1922-23	Graduate student, University of Paris (Diplôme, 1923)
1923-25	Graduate student and research assistant, University of Iowa

1925-1929

1925	Ph.D. in psychology; associate in psychology and education, University of Iowa
1926-28	Assistant professor of psychology and education, University of Iowa
1928-29	Associate professor and director, Iowa Child Welfare Research Station, University of Iowa
	Professor, University of Iowa, 1929

1930-1934

	Professor of psychology and education, University of Iowa
	Director, Iowa Child Welfare Research Station

1935-1939

	Professor of psychology and education
	Director, Iowa Child Welfare Research Station
	Dean of the Graduate College (1936), University of Iowa

1940-1944

1940-42	Professor of psychology and education
	Director, Iowa Child Welfare Research Station
	Dean of the Graduate College, University of Iowa
1942-	Commissioner of education and president of the University of the State of New York
1943	*The Meaning of Intelligence* published

1945-1949

1945-46	Commissioner of education and president of the University of the State of New York
1946	President of the University of Illinois

1950-1954

1953	President, University of Illinois—to September 1953
1954	Chairman, the Directing Committee, Self-Study, New York University

1955-1959

1955-56	Director, Self-Study, New York University
1955	Fulbright lecturer, Cambridge University
1956	Dean, School of Education, New York University

1960-1964

1960-64	Chancellor and executive vice-president, New York University
1964 Summer	Salzburg Seminar on American Studies
1964 Fall	Distinguished professor of education, New York University

1965-1969

1965-67	Distinguished professor of education, New York University
1967	Vice-chancellor for academic affairs, Long Island University
1968 Fall	Acting chancellor, Long Island University

Work versus Citizenship

Along cultural lines my extracurricular activities have been local, national, and international. As a citizen with a capital "C" in political or welfare matters, I have been inert—a contributor to "worthy causes," yes, but a participant, no. The fact is I have regarded the profession of education itself as a uniquely powerful force in the advancement of citizenship. I have not run for public office or served on a school board. (As commissioner of education of the state of New York I served *ex officio* on the board of trustees of Cornell University.) To seek a competitive office in a psychological or educational hierarchy was devoid of appeal. In fact, I do not recall ever having applied for a job or a promotion. Opportunism of a sort was the result, but I have not taken a job I disliked or lived in a place deemed undesirable. True, in Iowa City I was a Kiwanian briefly in order to serve as chairman of its local committee on child welfare. It was a good cause but the mechanics of the service outweighed the results, and the little rituals of the club left me cold. Very likely I was its least promising and most short-lived member.

Family and Personal Social Life

In 1925, a few months after receiving my doctoral degree at the University of Iowa, I married a bright and beautiful girl from my hometown. She was twenty-one and I twenty-eight. Unlike me, she was a scion of the socioeconomic elite of the community, granddaughter of the founder of almost everything in town and daughter of a leading engineer and industrialist. (Since my elder brother was already married to her elder sister, the ice was easily broken.) Thus our marriage spans forty-five years. It is by all odds the greatest event of my life. Margaret from the beginning "tuned in" with the early struggling life of the college teacher, and effortlessly advanced with him to the so-called higher rungs of the educational ladder. To this day she has been my chief editorial assistant and adviser.

We have three boys and two girls, the four oldest married, with families of their own. We have thirteen grandchildren spread over the land from New York, Washington, D.C., and Ohio to Southern California. They have always meant much to us and they always will. After all, my wife is strongly but intelligently maternal in her ways, while I, less openly affectionate, buttressed a strong attachment to the young by a fourteen-year term as director of a university division of child development and parent education. With help from others whose approach was more intuitive, I wrote forty articles on the child for a popular magazine. This was about my only gesture toward a mass audience, for I never wrote a textbook or anything else of wide sale. My few efforts in radio and television confirmed an incompatibility toward performance although, as mentioned earlier, I was active for many years in promoting educational television.

Now that my religious and social sentiments have been discussed in this essay, I may add that my deep sense of the "hereafter" is enriched in contemplation of my five handsome children and thirteen equally attractive grandchildren. Does not the sole hope of immortality lie in the unbroken line of parent-offspring down through countless generations? That it will stay unbroken for the human race I believe but, like everybody else, I sometimes doubt it. We can count on fertility and the control of disease—on mastering every natural or man-made force except one. The human race is still a murderously warlike society, with no real safeguard against genocide. Under massive nuclear radiation, all sources of food, water, and air could be poisoned, and the living genes be turned into carriers of monstrosities. While thus far we have kept a step ahead of such corruption, we live in a time of dangerous alienation of technology from human values. The same slow business of evolution, on which is superimposed a long period of infancy for the individual, can hardly cope with the instant success of new means of self-destruction. Still, from long prebomb conditioning, I remain basically optimistic.

In sum, the liveliness and the loveliness of children, especially in my own family line, take all such gloomy prospects out of the realm of abstract indifference into the orbit of the here and now. Henceforth, these young people have ten times as much influence on me as I have on them.

The Past Ten Years

On retiring from university administration five years ago, I accepted a full-time teaching assignment for a three-year term at New York University. All of us know administrators whose lament is that they had to relinquish teaching or research; some of them are sincere, others, I feel, are only deceiving themselves. Given a free choice, I turned from teaching to administration but managed to write numerous papers and a few books on the side. Those not based on administrative experience suffered in consequence of my dual professional life. While writing I felt that I should be doing something else; while "administering" I had to guard against the intrusion of nonadministrative thoughts. I abandoned neither but kept up a not unhappy shuttling and switching. On returning to full-time teaching at the age of sixty-six, I found the experience richly rewarding. In fact, it was a kind of "pay-off" for my continued, if spotty, attention to the scholarly demands of my twin fields of psychology and education. Appropriately, I taught educational psychology after an intensive summer drive to get abreast of the field. I need not have worried. The newer younger researchers were still beholden to the group I knew; their breakthroughs were neither esoteric nor, it seemed to me, fundamental. There was a strong stabilizing factor in the resistance to change in psychology and education. Patterns of growth and behavior were familiar and the methods employed to study them not radically different from what had gone before. Essentially, the change in my field of interest was away from massive findings and wide generalization toward a series of retail operations. The main exception to this trend was found in a deepening sense of the significance of early childhood as a period of growth and experience. The "whole child," once only a slogan, had become the true center of new studies and insights. Also at N.Y.U. I conducted a seminar on higher education which the students seemed to enjoy. Beyond most ex-university deans, presidents, and chancellors, I was able to expound firsthand the seamy side of the business!

After these three years given to teaching graduate students (over four hundred altogether), I had planned to retire from such steady demands. My extracurricular activities would continue. In the aggregate they could be expected to take up perhaps one-fourth of my time and energy. (The reference is to board and committee memberships in National Educational Television, WNDT, Channel 13; Lincoln Center for the Performing Arts and its subsidiary, the Vivian Beaumont Repertory Theater; the American Shakespeare Festival Theatre and Academy; the Institute of International Education; Encyclopaedia Britannica Films; to the editorship of *Living History of the World*, and to various writing assignments.) To these pleasant chores would be added part-time consulting in a well-known New York firm of advisers on higher education. However, this was not to be. Right after my last class meeting I became a part-time consultant to the chancellor of Long Island University, a burgeoning institution of twenty thousand students with four locations on the Island. Soon thereafter, due to an unexpected resignation, I was appointed to the number-two administrative post at the university, vice-chancellor for academic affairs. With this last assignment I cheerfully gave up some of my extracurricular activities. Henceforth, beyond some short-term pinch-hitting engagements, as in East Africa, I planned really to retire to my study at home. There would be a chance to put the thoughts of my declining years in order and to have more time to attend to the flourishing Stoddard family tree.

It follows that during long stretches of intensive involvement in affairs, I was a healthy animal losing scarcely a day through illness or any other cause. No Christian Scientist, my attitude toward illness is not to deny it, but rather mildly to resent it—a nuisance to be guarded against.

The Meaning of Time

In the lives of the Stoddards, old and young alike, time was generally well filled and always in short supply. Neither my wife nor I have ever really loafed, although she is a harder worker than I. Raising a large family of activists, meeting the manifold social demands of the wife of a professor-executive officer, assisting with every major writing project—these duties were taken in stride. She says of me, "You accomplish a great deal with your sixty-hour week," and I of her, "You accomplish still more in your eighty-hour week." That is the truth even now when our family is grown up and we do not need the extra income. Avoiding budgets of any description, I do not systematically lay out my time. It is enough for me to establish priorities—to meet deadlines, that is—and plow through. In the press of things to be done in a given time-bind, I follow the Chinese laundry system: start with the item on top and work through the batch one after another. In any case, since a rigid stopwatch allocation would not square with my administrative work, I set up instead a place-bind: if in my study, only important interruptions were in order. The thing to do, as one child after another discovered, was to get me out of that forbidden spot to a play space, a pond, or, on rainy days, into a card game or a round of chess.

Money

At no time was money an important factor in my career decisions. The University of Iowa, where I taught for seventeen years, was not outstanding in its salary ratings; in fact, it had made no financial provision whatever for transfer benefits or retirement. From the thirties on, I declined offers to go elsewhere—Columbia, Chicago, California—on one occasion with a 50 percent increase in salary. Except during a few years of the depression we did not need the money. What counted was the opportunity to work creatively. Looking back, I feel that in certain areas, educational psychology in particular, no university in the United States offered a better opportunity than Iowa for growth and achievement. Thus, the Iowa Child Welfare Research Station, which I directed immediately after my predecessor Birt T. Baldwin died, had at its disposal a research grant of over $1 million. In those days that was a munificent sum. Perhaps it was too much to leave behind. A more compelling reason for staying was the quality of such persons as Beth Wellman and Kurt Lewin in the station, alongside the Iowa "greats" I have already mentioned.

Of course, I did leave in 1942 at a time university life came almost to a standstill and the student body was melting away. The war years in Albany improved our financial position through everyone's inability to get help or to purchase much of anything. There, too, we had a beautiful Mt. Vernon-type house surrounded by thirty-two acres of lawn, garden, and woods. It was essentially a self-contained unit in a handsome suburban village. It helped to knit us together in work and play during the dark days of World War II. The subsequent move to Urbana, Illinois, was expensive but there we lived in the large President's House, rent free, with an expense account for its upkeep. The four children soon to be in college were becoming expensive. At the end of my Illinois term we had little capital and for the first and last time felt a financial pinch. (The Wall Street crash had depleted our assets. My knowledge of financial matters was slim and a Chicago brokerage firm had given us bad advice.)

At no time since has money entered into our decision-making. We have gone where the work was to be done. Henceforth, however, New York City or its suburbs will be our home.

Appraisal of Lesser Contributions and Satisfactions

MAJOR EVENTS OR MOVEMENTS IN EDUCATION IN WHICH I WAS ENGAGED

The principal event which formed the spearhead of a movement was the editorship of the Thirty-ninth Yearbook of the National Society for the Study of Education, a two-volume work entitled, *Intelligence: Its Nature and Nurture.* I was chairman of a committee of eight that included Leonard Carmichael, Frank N. Freeman, Harold E. Jones, and Lewis M. Terman. Among the fifty associated contributors were John E. Anderson, Edgar A. Doll, Arnold Gesell, Kurt Lewin, Willard C. Olson, Harold M. Skeels, Robert L. Thorndike, and Paul A. Witty. Much of the resultant controversy centered in such issues as the fixity or changeability of the I.Q.; the effect of environmental experience on mental growth; gene-related factors; the racial distribution of intelligence; the validity of intelligence tests; the soundness of various hypotheses. It is not too much to say that the movement, like the persons at the center of it, has not been quite the same since 1940. My individual follow-up came through the publication of the book, *The Meaning of Intelligence;* it went through ten printings.

A second principal event was the development of the Dual Progress Plan culminating in my book by that title in 1961 and in Glen Heathers's book *Organizing Schools through the Dual Progress Plan* (1967). The Ford Foundation under the presidency of Henry T. Heald contributed liberally to this project. It contemplates a reform movement in elementary education in which the *cultural imperatives* (English, arithmetic computation, and the social studies) are sharply distinguished from the *cultural electives* (mathematics, science, art, music, and foreign languages). The former constitute the grade location and the basis for grade promotion of the pupils; the latter are ungraded. Both types of subject matter are taught by experts in the subject fields who meet all the state requirements for teachers. Embedded in the plan are various forms of team teaching. The plan was put into operation in two school systems (Long Beach, New York, and Ossining, New York) on a five-year demonstration basis and retained thereafter. However, as a "movement" the scheme has made little headway. One stumbling block is the expectation that students very low on the curve of intelligence or relevant aptitude will be allowed to drop a course, say, in mathematics, in order to strengthen the cultural imperatives. To many teachers and supervisors such a plan is downright sinful; *everybody* must endure a full measure of mathematics even though the subject as taught in elementary school is often sterile and self-defeating. Orthodoxy in teaching, but not in psychology, holds that the dull will approach the bright in any subject if given enough time. The fact that few American adults, apart from scientists and engineers, know anything about mathematics and have little need of it beyond simple arithmetic is ignored. Up to the time a pupil reaches a ceiling in abstract "electives," after expert teaching and counseling in the Dual Progress Plan, he gets more mathematics and science than he would in standard programs. Again, critics ignore this factor. In brief, it strikes me that the theory underlying the Plan is sound, even though some administrative "bugs" must be overcome.

Writing had to be done on the side, since most of the time I was engaged in promoting the plans of professors, department heads, and deans. Some of these activities were untried in a particular locus. Thus were found in a series of wave movements: Progressive education; the junior high school; the 4-4-4 plan; preschool education; parent education; the year-round school; the platoon system; ungraded schools; language laboratories; team teaching; teacher aides; programmed instruction; instructional television; advanced placement; general education; honors courses; survey courses; cluster colleges; student power. Each plan or fashion was accorded some kind of a run, and a few gained the impetus of a genuine movement. Wide acceptance may run well ahead of validation. As a teacher I have touched on every one of these subjects, usually in a superficial way. As a part-time researcher I gave only the few subjects previously mentioned more than a nod.

THE KREBIOZEN AFFAIR

And now a flashback to the most upsetting event in my professional life: the vote of "no confidence" in my administration carried by a majority vote of the board of trustees of the University of Illinois at a midnight session, on "Black Friday," June 24, 1953. There is not space here to chronicle the events leading to this climax nor to portray the characters involved. Rather than try my hand at a new version, I shall simply quote from past writings, thus sparing the reader the I-told-you-so and now-it-can-be-told syndrome.

As a prelude there was a series of charges, some of them serious but most of them trivial or diversionary. The big gun was "Krebiozen."

To quote from my book *Krebiozen: The Great Cancer Mystery* (1955):

> Why did the controversy [at the University of Illinois] arise?
>
> 1. Because "Krebiozen" was announced and publicized in a manner foreign to medical research.
> 2. Because it had received little laboratory and animal experimentation before it was tried on human beings, and because it had had no controlled clinical investigation—that is, it was not given to some patients and withheld from others in order to compare results under statistical controls.
> 3. Because distinguished medical commissions that later examined the evidence could find no value in "Krebiozen" for the treatment of cancer, although a few individuals—some of them doctors—continued to claim that it had valuable effects.
> 4. Because an air of mystery surrounded the life and career of the promoter of the drug.
> 5. Because a high official and leading physiologist at one of the nation's top-ranking universities became the guardian of the drug.
> 6. Because "Krebiozen" itself could not be obtained for an analysis of its nature by any of the investigating groups.
> 7. Because the false hopes raised by a simple "agent for treatment" lessens attention to, and faith in, the truly notable success achieved by surgery and radiation in the treatment of cancer.
> 8. Because "Krebiozen" became the focal point of political and social groups that found in the issue an outlet for opposing points of view.
> 9. Because, as long as cancer is a mystery, men will fight hard to solve it. Those who are dying—or in whose family someone is dying—will seek hope even where there is no hope, and will deny the truth when the truth means death.

The notorious semipublic meeting to announce and promote the cancer "cure" was held in the Drake Hotel on March 26, 1951. From that time on, in spite of the utter lack of cooperation on the part of its promoters, scientists at the University of Illinois, aided by experts from other universities, tried hard to ascertain the nature of the concoction and its effects, if any, on patients. Samples of the drug, presumably prepared in Argentina, were denied the committee on drug analysis. A long authoritative report on the effect on cancerous patients emphasized the worthlessness of the drug and the necessity of stopping its clinical usage until it had been analyzed. "Krebiozen" was not harmful as such. It was deadly in the sense that it encouraged patients to turn away from irradiation or surgery; in the long run several thousand persons in the advanced stages of cancer did so. They died sooner than was necessary.

Six members of the board of trustees had not been happy with a university president who was so foolhardy (in Illinois) as to: fight financial fraud, endorse the UN and help to found Unesco, espouse Unitarianism, defend academic freedom for alleged "pinks" —that is, critics of Illinois politicians; question loyalty oaths; support Governor Adlai Stevenson; push for a University-owned-and-operated TV station (clearly a trend toward socialism)—and now, crowning misdemeanor, to interfere with "research" on a secret drug, especially when millions of dollars were pouring in to its owners. After all, it *might* benefit mankind.

This was the background of the midnight action, following which I immediately resigned. By law, the president served "at the pleasure of the board of trustees," an item I had paid no attention to until that moment. The same brutal action was applied also to Provost Coleman R. Griffith. Naturally, neither of us could stomach that kind of trusteeship. In the days and months that followed, the official faculty bodies attacked the board's procedure and its "cooked up" decision, as did the American Civil Liberties Union in a formal citation. Many friends and colleagues in the academic world expressed outrage, but there was nothing to be done. As a member of the board of trustees remarked, it was "yesterday's mashed potatoes."

A word by way of epilogue. The "Krebiozen" of those days was later analyzed by two chemical experts, one at the University of California and the other at Stanford University; the official verdict was the same: "Krebiozen is nothing more than mineral oil." A few years later, following new laws passed after the thalidomide scandal, samples of "Krebiozen" were forcibly obtained from a Chicago "laboratory." Analysis showed it to be mineral oil to which had been added a small quantity of creatinine—a cheap chemical of no potency. (At the time, the cash price of "Krebiozen" was moving up from $7.00 per ampule to $9.00.) There is general agreement in the medical world that "Krebiozen" was the meanest and most expensive fraud in the annals of modern medicine. My book precipitated a libel suit against me for $300,000. It dragged on in U.S. courts for eleven years. I paid nothing except my lawyer's fees.

My book on "Krebiozen" closed with these paragraphs; fifteen years later I can think of nothing to add:

> Finally, what of the true villain of this story—the disease men call cancer? Cancer, in its numerous forms, has continued to reap a harvest of death. Many patients who would have had no hope a generation ago are now alive because of recent advances in early diagnosis, in surgery, and in radiology. Still, the world waits for the discovery of a true preventive or curative drug that will do for cancer what has already been done for typhoid, smallpox, and diphtheria—what may soon be done for poliomelitis. We have a right to hope that cancer, too, will fall within the range of the understandable and the curable. It will take time. It will take the kind of research that is being carried on patiently and undramatically in hundreds of laboratories over the world.
>
> And when an effective treatment or cure for cancer is found, there will be no secrets—no holding back. When the scientists know, they will spread the good news. This greatest of all medical achievements will be shared.
>
> There are many who regard the story of "Krebiozen" as a tragedy. For some it was. But, like most human experience, it should bring new insight and, in the end, new hope. There would be no mystery and no drama if men, loving life, did not try to understand it and to prolong it.

BEFORE AND AFTER KREBIOZEN

Doubtless, for dramatic effect, I should let the Illinois affair end at this point, but to do so would overemphasize what was really a late-appearing phenomenon. In my 1946 installation address at the University of Illinois I stated:

> The aim of education is to develop a structure of thought and to improve human relations. A university is not a dictionary, a dispensary, or a department store; it is more than a storehouse of knowledge and more than a community of scholars. University life is essentially an exercise in thinking, preparing and living.

In a four-year report (1950) at the peak of my "salad days" at the University of Illinois, I wrote:

> The mental maturity that is gained on a campus is a permanent acquisition of the student. Habits of adjustment and reasoning that have been learned will continue to serve our graduates in their lives.
>
> The public often thinks of service from the state university in other terms. Some know of the work of the extension division in agriculture, family living, education, business, government, labor relations, music, or library and think that the help they receive is all that is meant by service. Others know of extra-mural classes, of short courses, both on and off campus, of correspondence courses. Still others know the bulletins and publications of the university, the films and recordings made available, the paintings exhibited throughout the state or the tests that are rented to high schools. All these activities are desirable; we intend to continue them, although they cannot be expanded to meet all the needs of all of the people. If the people of the state are to receive valuable help, they must come to know the latest discoveries in many fields. It is not enough to acquaint them with something that will work well enough, when another procedure will work twice or three times as well. Whatever the University communicates through its service to the people of Illinois should be of the best. What is best is discovered through scholarly work and fundamental research.

In March 1968, when the University of Illinois awarded me an LL.D.—an event that produced standing ovations for Mrs. Stoddard and myself—a citation was presented that reads in part as follows:

> During seven critical years he guided the University of Illinois through a period of growth unparalleled in its previous history. New campuses for returning war veterans, the Institute of Labor and Industrial Relations, the Institute of Communications Research; the Institute of Government and Public Affairs, the Institute of Aviation, and the College of Veterinary Medicine were all established during his presidency. One of his most notable achievements was the inauguration of the Festival of Contemporary Arts—a recurring occasion that continues to enrich the cultural life of the campus.

For the whole Stoddard family that was indeed the "week that was!"

My Judgment of Myself

My chief satisfactions have already been revealed and sketchily documented. It was pleasant, at times exhilarating, to accomplish something personally. In this matrix, a few pieces of "creative writing" are intermingled with a few "good decisions," in both instances confirmed by subsequent commentaries or events. Generally, in advance of such confirmation, there is a sense of euphoria. One test I have long applied to department heads, directors, and deans is the evidence that they deeply want their staff members and associates to succeed. An administrator given to vagrant ideas—perhaps plagued with them—should do more than just be reconciled when someone "steals" them. He should actively encourage such deviationists. Otherwise, let him stay in his study, laboratory, or classroom; let him keep clear of any supervisory relation to others. I don't remember when I learned this lesson, nor can I recall having departed from it. My chief fault along this line is the difficulty I have had in listening to the views of other people; my own self-centered mental life gets in the way. Perhaps weeks or months later, I sense the true worth of ideas that at first seemed trivial or irrational. I can only report that on these occasions I feel remorseful and try to make amends.

On the main events of my life, I have no regrets. Thus, in a self-review twenty years later, I wrote of *The Meaning of Intelligence* (*Phi Delta Kappan,* October 1963):

> My book punctured certain cherished but sham ideas that encouraged various forms of escapism. Not that genetic and other prenatal factors were unimportant; they were indeed important and sometimes crucial and my book is explicit on this point. Rather, it was necessary to break through with the idea and the evidence that environmental factors were important too, and, further, that up to that time the work on human abilities had been sterile in its attempts to separate heredity from environment.
>
> Were I to write *The Meaning of Intelligence* in the 1960s I would scarcely refer to long-dead controversies, but would concentrate—and thus be more fruitful—on closely knit theory, on scientific experiments and demonstrations, and particularly on the ways in which our tested theories of intelligence throw light on pervasive problems in education and the social structure. For this reason, I am still rather taken with Part V of my book, entitled "Intelligence and Society." There, for example, are some timely intimations with respect to such troubles as poverty, racial prejudice, and superstition.
>
> Now, as then, established forces would take offense at my statements about the final reliance of man on his own brain and heart, joined at all times by a social structure that plays up and makes effective the best that any man has thought or said or done in this world. My ad-

vocacy of the concept of *this* world as the final world spreads an alarm. Now in 1963 I see no point in a retreat from reason.

Writing this piece for the Seventieth Yearbook of the NSSE, I am still impressed by man's remarkable gift for self-deception.

On such choice-points as going to college, switching from engineering, entering the University of Paris, joining the University of Iowa (and staying there nineteen years as student and staff member), going to Albany—there are no regrets whatever. The question that counts is, What about the decision to accept the Presidency of the University of Illinois? Nobody could have foretold the sad outcome, now a matter of record. Still, my answer is, *no regrets.* My wife and family, like myself, had seven fruitful years there, and no harassment lasting a few months or the bitter climax of a few days could erase those wonderful years. Nor do I regret refusing to condone a scheme which, I am proud to say, struck me as a fraudulent and nasty business years before readers of *Life* or *The Saturday Evening Post* must have come to the same conclusion. At Illinois I placed self-esteem ahead of board approval. My self-esteem was not lost. It would have been had I kept quiet; that was really all the majority of the trustees were asking of me. Massive approval of my stand on the part of faculty, student body, alumni, and former trustees offered a powerful antidote to the smears of a "little group of willful men."

The reader who is not only unfamiliar with such events but also vague about the very names of us septuagenarians will find the revelations in this volume unenticing. Are we not writing these pieces for our "friends and relations"—and for historians who are trained to distill the truth from this welter of introspection and boast? The final act of communication, if there is to be one, will be assumed neither by the biographer nor the historian; it will be that of the dramatist. In the dusty business of educational administration, of late so frustrating to its practitioners, there is character, there is plot, there is action. Once more in the cycle of human affairs, "the play's the thing."

A BIOGRAPHICAL SUMMARY

GEORGE DINSMORE STODDARD. Born October 8, 1897, Carbondale, Pennsylvania.

Family. Married Margaret Trautwein, December 26, 1925. Children:

Philip Hendrick, 1929; Arthur Dinsmore, 1931; Eleanor, 1933; Caroline, 1936; Alfred Eugene, 1942.

Education. Carbondale High School, 1911-15; Pennsylvania State University, A.B. (Education), 1921; University of Paris, Diplôme (Psychology), 1923; University of Iowa, Ph.D. (Psychology), 1925.

Occupational history. Professor of psychology and education, University of Iowa, 1929-42; director, Iowa Child Welfare Research Station, 1928-42; head, Department of Psychology, 1938; dean of the Graduate College, 1936-42; president, University of the State of New York and commissioner of education, 1942-46; president, University of Illinois, 1946-53; chairman, New York University Self-Study, 1954-56; dean, School of Education, New York University, 1956-60; chancellor and executive vice president, 1960-64; distinguished professor of education, 1964-67; vice-chancellor for academic affairs, Long Island University, 1967-68; chancellor, 1968-69. Summer sessions: Columbia University, 1935; University of California (Berkeley), 1939; University of Chicago, 1940; Fulbright lecturer, Cambridge University, 1955; Salzburg Seminar, 1964.

Memberships and affiliations. American Council on Education (chairman, 1946-47), University Club (New York), New York University Club, Century Association, Unitarian.

Part II

Selected Publications of George D. Stoddard

Books and Reports (Author or Editor)

1. "Research in Child Development." In *Educational Research: Its Nature, Essential Conditions, and Controlling Concepts* (Henry W. Holmes, Chm.). American Council on Education Studies, Series I, vol. 3, no. 10. Washington: The Council, 1939.
2. *Intelligence: Its Nature and Nurture.* Part I, *Comparative and Critical Exposition;* Part II, *Original Studies and Experiments,* edited by George D. Stoddard (Chairman of the Society's Committee on the Yearbook) et al. Thirty-ninth Yearbook of the National Society for the Study of Education. Bloomington, Ill.: Public School Publishing Co., 1940.
3. *The Meaning of Intelligence.* New York: Macmillan Co., 1943.
4. *Report of the U.S. Mission to Japan.* George D. Stoddard, Chairman. Department of State, publication no. 2579, Far Eastern Series, no. 11, 1946.
5. *On the Education of Women.* New York: Macmillan Co., 1950.
6. *The New York University Self-Study, Final Report.* 2 parts. New York: New York University Press, 1956.
7. *The Dual Progress Plan.* New York: Harper & Row, 1961.
8. *New Departures for the Brooklyn Institute of Arts and Sciences.* Brooklyn, N.Y.: The Institute, 1967.
9. *Living History of the World.* George D. Stoddard, Editor-in-Chief. New York: Parents Magazine Press, 1967 (also for 1968).

Articles in Journals and Symposiums (Including Addresses)

10. "The Problem of Individual Differences in Learning." *Psychological Review* 32 (1925): 479-85.
11. "Ferson and Stoddard Law Aptitude Examinations." *American Law School Review* 6 (1927): 78-81.
12. "Extending the School Downward." *Educational Administration and Supervision* 15 (1929): 581-92.
13. "The Arts College and Contemporary Life." *Bulletin of the Association of American Colleges* 25 (1929): 204-12.
14. "Guiding the Emotional Health of School Children." *Educational Method* 14 (1935): 163-66.

15. "What of the Nursery School?" *Progressive Education* 14 (1937): 441-51.
16. "The Teacher as a Person." In *The Teacher and Society*, edited by W. H. Kilpatrick, pp. 68-91. New York: D. Appleton Century, 1937.
17. "Intellectual Development of the Child: An Answer to the Critics of the Iowa Studies." *School and Society* 51 (1940): 529-36.
18. "On the Meaning of Intelligence." *Psychological Review* 48 (1941): 250-60.
19. "Teach Them the Ways of Democracy." *International Frontiers in Education*, pp. 25-32. *The Annals of the American Academy of Political and Social Science*, vol. 244, Philadelphia, 1944.
20. *Tertiary Education.* Cambridge: Harvard University Press, 1944.
21. "Statewide Planning for Postwar Educational Needs." *Higher Education and the War*, edited by T. R. McConnell. *Annals of the American Academy of Political and Social Science*, Philadelphia, 1944.
22. *Frontiers in Education.* Stanford: Stanford University Press, 1945.
23. "Education and Public Policy." *Educational Record* 28 (1947): 362-74.
24. "Ferment in Education." In *Ferment in Education*, edited by George Stoddard et al., pp. 3-14. Urbana: University of Illinois Press, 1948.
25. "The Role of Education in International Affairs." In *Inauguration of Joseph Hillis Miller as President of the University of Florida*, pp. 12-18. Gainesville: University of Florida Press, 1948.
26. "Public Relations Aspects of Academic Freedom." *College Public Relations Quarterly* 7 (July 1956): 3-10.
27. "Creativity in Education." In *Creativity and Its Cultivation*, edited by Harold M. Anderson, pp. 181-202. New York: Harper & Bros., 1959.
28. "The Merging Patterns of Outdoor Recreation and Education." In *Trends in American Living and Outdoor Recreation*, pp. 115-32. *Reports to the Outdoor Recreation Resources Review Commission* (L. S. Rockefeller, Chm.) ORRC Study Report no. 22, 1962, Washington, D.C., 1962.
29. "An Exciting Time to Be in Education." In *Frontiers of Education*, edited by Arthur E. Traxler, pp. 13-22. Washington: American Council on Education, 1963.
30. "America's Tomorrow: The Long View." *Official Report of the American Association of School Administrators*, pp. 76-86. Washington: The Association, 1964.
31. "Art As the Measure of Man. In *Art, Art, Art*, pp. 7-28. New York: Museum of Modern Art, 1964.
32. "On the Meaning of Intelligence." In *Invitational Conference on*

Testing Problems, pp. 3-11. Princeton, N.J.: Educational Testing Service, 1965.

33. "The Evaluation of Arts and Sciences in Land-Grant Institutions." *Proceedings of the American Association of Land-Grant Colleges and State Universities*, edited by Charles P. McCurly, Jr., pp. 63-67. 75th Annual Convention. Washington: The Association, 1962.

34. "Fifty Years of Research, 1917-1967." In *The Institute of Child Behavior and Development*. Iowa City: University of Iowa, 1967. (Includes sixteen references to Stoddard's publications on intelligence and other subjects.)

Part III

George D. Stoddard: A Biographical Essay

ANNE ROE

One approach to biography is to read, sequentially, what the biographee has said, looking for such things as attitudes, recurring or changing themes, intensity of involvement in different causes, and breadth of interests. It was possible for me to start with such an approach, although the selection of material available was somewhat random—chiefly reprints and copies of books which Dr. Stoddard could spare. These reached me in New Zealand, and were a main interest for me on the long voyage home. It was clear that there were a number of missing elements, but several very interesting themes appeared which further reading confirmed.

The first and most pervasive one had to do with what has apparently been an almost lifelong battle with one "establishment" or another. He has clearly never hesitated to take on any outfit which he felt was restricting anyone in any way. Any psychologist would immediately pose two obvious questions: What were his relations with his father? What was his earliest battle against entrenched forces? (It would be assumed that he had won it.) His story answers these questions in part.

With or without a battle, he has clearly never been satisfied with things as they are, never been unwilling to query the old ways of doing things and to search for others. He has always been looking for some better way to accomplish his continually broadening goals. He has always relied along the way and in the end on his own judgment (sometimes, perhaps, more openly than prudent tact would suggest) and has been willing to accept responsibility for his actions. Time has usually shown him to have been on the right side.

Another theme, particularly in all the early papers, and of course not unconnected with the first, is seen in his passionate concern with freedom of thought.

Throughout all of his papers, there are many references to the basic dignity of man, and more recently such statements as that in the long run man has only his own brain and heart to rely on.

In his papers of the last decade or so there has also been a good deal that showed an understanding of the forces now so clearly in action in education and the culture in general, although they do not convey a sense of urgency. But who among us even five years ago would have predicted the current college situation—or coped with it so effectively?

In what follows, I will try to comment on various aspects of his life and work in approximately chronological order. I do not need to rely only upon my own appreciation of what he has written, but I can also call upon comments and descriptions by persons who were associated with him at various times.

His earliest "battle with the establishment" was hardly a battle. He and a group of like-minded friends simply left the church school for good. Asked for further details he reported: "My 'leaving the church' was in no sense traumatic. Had I ever been in it? Surrounded by like-minded children (think of it, in a small coal-mining town in the early 1900s) I had found it easy to be a leader if only through articulateness. At home the subject was not brought up, perhaps because I continued politely to go to the Methodist church with my parents." But the matter was not really simple, and it is an early illustration of several continuing characteristics: the questioning of the usually unquestioned; the habit of making up his own mind and acting on his own judgment; the ability to gather like-minded persons into action with him. In this instance his consideration for his parents does not foreshadow some later episodes when more tact might have been helpful to him.

His report of his nonathletic, somewhat nonsocial, early years is rather more characteristic of natural than of behavioral scientists. Reading everything one could get his hands on has been so important for so many who have become contributors to society that it almost has come to be a sine qua non. He was fortunate, in a small town with only a "puny and repulsive" library, that he had at home the Five-Foot Book Shelf. Although neither parent had more than a high school education, his father read widely and enjoyed conversation. That his father suggested law for him was apparently just because it was one of the professions of high standing.

Asked for further comment on his starting college in engineering and shifting to education, he replied.

The truth is, since chemistry, physics, and mathematics fascinated me in high school, it made sense to point toward a career that would draw upon them—hence chemical engineering. Unhappily for me, the college curriculum soon moved away from these "pure" attributes and hence away from my central interests. It became clear that my solid interests lay in the social studies, with overtones in English and literature. Psychology was on the march and that for me became the "drumbeat." Its professional application in education was a later and somewhat accidental outcome. Had I stayed exclusively in psychology, it would surely have been clinical, educational, social psychology. Animal psychology appealed to me only as a game and the whole Wundt-Titchenerian School not at all.

His decision to go abroad for a year at the Sorbonne can be seen as an indication of his reaching out for experiences beyond the usual run. Very few U.S. college students were doing this at the time, and few of those going to France to study psychology. He greatly admired Binet and he studied under Simon, and it is possible that his strong feeling for them was a factor in the intensity of his disagreement with Terman over the nature of intelligence and its measurement. He felt strongly that the Stanford Binet contained the mechanics but not the substance of Binet's major contributions. In fact, the first few chapters of Terman's *The Measurement of Intelligence*[1] tend rather to refute Stoddard's statement that "Binet's brilliant hypotheses as to the nature of intelligence were lost on Terman . . . the Stanford group [did not give] so much as a nod to Binet's fundamental theories of intelligence." The constancy of the I.Q. and the relative roles of nature and nurture are other issues on which disagreement was profound. Few professional organizations can have had as extreme a conflict as that which took place at the 1940 meeting of the National Society for the Study of Education. The disagreements were not discussed as such in the Thirty-ninth Yearbook which Stoddard edited, but it is only necessary to

1. Lewis M. Terman, *The Measurement of Intelligence* (Boston: Houghton Mifflin Co., 1916).

read the papers to see how sharp the cleavage was. It was Stoddard's sense of outrage over some of those events and his feeling of frustration that the full extent of his own position had not been appreciated that led him to write *The Meaning of Intelligence.*[2] This was a very thorough and intensively critical review of intelligence testing, and he was not, as he acknowledges not at all ruefully, noticeably tactful. Twenty years later, reviewing his own book for the *Phi Delta Kappan,* he said, "it still looks good to me," and added that after that experience he "resolved to eschew all further yearbook services." Fortunately for us he has reconsidered. He felt then that the nature-nurture controversy was a thing of the past. Certainly it seems well accepted that the two variables interact intricately, but the issue is still far from settled[3] and has become inextricably involved in the racial issues of today. In considering some of the implications of his position on intelligence, he sensed many problems which now, a quarter of a century later, have become increasingly acute:

> Placed in a dreary cocoon of life, without much guidance at home, a life that, for millions of children from two to five years of age, is characterized by negation and restriction, the child fails to grow satisfactorily; from the standpoint of mental and social experience, he endures a season of undernourishment. . . . It can be predicted with some confidence that when homes and schools give the child what he truly needs, at all ages from the first year upward, there will be a radical revision in the norms and standards for mental tests. But this is a minor consideration. More important to the welfare of children, and of the nation as a whole, is the idea that we must develop the unused reservoirs of mental power. The process will take courage. An abler and better informed youth population will demand changes in home, school, and community practice that transcend our traditional concepts of the young in society. Eventually such a program, if developed into a movement with social, economic, and political implementation, will lead to a way of life so truly democratic and American in its ideology as to frighten all but the firm believers.[4]

In the light of researches in child development and experience with in-school and out-of-school youth, *voting for all persons at age eighteen*

2. George D. Stoddard, *The Meaning of Intelligence* (New York: Macmillan Co., 1943).

3. See, for example, Arthur Jensen, "How Can We Boost I.Q. and Scholastic Achievement," *Harvard Educational Review* 39 (1969): 1-123. See also pp. 273-356 for responses by seven authors and pp. 449-483 for Jensen's reply.

4. Stoddard, *Meaning of Intelligence,* p. 392.

is clearly indicated. . . . Moreover, by voting they might learn what voting means.[5]

Although this book was written after he had left Iowa, it of course stems from his experience as Director of the Child Welfare Station there. He left Iowa to accept the position of Commissioner of Education and President of the University of the State of New York and remained in that position until 1946. The two offices covered the whole school and college system of the State of New York, public and private. Subsequently the two offices were separated. He has said relatively little about that period, although he rates it as his third most significant experience. J. Cayce Morrison, who knew him well, has provided much significant detail for us.

The history of public education in New York State has many distinctive features, which resulted in a number of functions being assigned to the office of the commissioner of education which are not the responsibility of that office in other states. For example, his jurisdiction includes the State Library, the State Museum, Archives and History, and the licensing of all professional groups for which this is required—incidentally, something of a shock to psychologists when they were attempting to obtain a licensing law in New York. He also has administrative supervision over all state institutions of college rank, including teachers colleges, agricultural schools, and state colleges, and considerable judicial powers.

Among other particular accomplishments, Stoddard, continuing his concern with early childhood education, established a program for special training, adding a specialist in kindergarten education to his staff. He encouraged advances in the development of compresensive scholarship examinations (the New York Regents' Examination) and in the use of testing for guidance purposes. He put through a provision for residence facilities for students on a self-liquidating basis at the state colleges for teachers. He promoted centralization of rural schools. He developed a state science service in connection with the New York State Museum. He instituted research in a wide variety of areas. A study of projected needs and resources for higher education made it possible for the state's institutions to handle their share of veterans returning to school under the

5. Ibid., p. 475.

GI bill. Another study resulted in the recommendation for the creation of a state university system, although this was not implemented until 1948, after he had left. Under his direction, new curricula were developed for technical schools in terms of job clusters, and the curricula for the state agricultural schools were revised.

A particularly good example of his research-mindedness and the promptitude with which he could take action was provided when the budget for the Bureau of Adult Education came up for a hearing. The bureau made quite a modest request for continuing the established program. Stoddard is reported to have said, "I would be willing to request $100,000 to find out what New York should be doing in adult education, but I will not ask for a dollar to increase what we are now doing." In an extraordinarily short time he had informed himself about many problems and needs in the field and had secured the funds. His goal: "The provision of adequate opportunities throughout the State for all adult individuals to continue to learn and develop in all phases of their lives: work life, family life, public life, cultural life."

In exercising the judicial power allocated to the office of commissioner of education, Stoddard heard many appeals. One, during the 1943-44 school year, had to do with a charge against the board of education in one school district of discrimination in drawing district lines to maintain an all-Negro school. This was the first appeal made under a New York State law of 1938, and Stoddard ruled for the plaintiffs, agreeing that there was "discrimination," not only in the way zones were set up, but, more importantly, in that the direct consequence was the maintenance of an inferior school. That school was ordered closed.

These were fantastically busy and productive years. Throughout them, the insistence on looking for better ways of doing things, the willingness to tackle problems on a large scale, and a demand for and reliance upon inquiry into the facts are characteristic behaviors.

He left this position to become president of the University of Illinois, where he remained for seven effective years, until forced out by the board of trustees in what is surely one of the most remarkable episodes in the history of higher education in the United States—an episode which did no credit to the politicians of Illinois and the trustees of the University. To his own remarks on this, I should like to add only one comment.

When Ivy's almost incredibly irresponsible behavior became a serious embarrassment to his colleagues, the board of trustees asked Stoddard to take action. Instead of any more direct action, which was well warranted, he arranged a leave of absence for Ivy to facilitate his further studies and insisted upon a thorough rereview of reported cases, in keeping with Stoddard's continual turning to research. But as always he insisted that research be open as well as competent. The Ivy story also exemplifies his characteristic willingness to uphold individual freedom of action at least until it becomes a threat to others.

Even with his lifelong insistence upon freedom to think, he does have one qualification: "We are free in all respects but one; we are not free to tolerate the destruction of our freedom. If we ignore this age-old principle, we shall soon be at one another's throats." [6] On this basis, he notes in a number of places that we are not free to accept communism.

He went to New York University in 1954 where he remained in a variety of positions (except for periods abroad) until 1967. One of his more notable contributions to education during this period was the development of the "Dual Progress Plan" for elementary education, which he has described. It should be added that this plan would also require modifications in teacher training and that he has also spelled them out. As always, with Stoddard, he was concerned not only with a technique but with its implications. It was his belief that such a plan would make it possible for every child to develop his own particular capacities much more fully than in the standard system and through this become more fully a "thinker up to the top level of his talents."

As we sense the need for freedom that impinges on every one of us, we should be able to accept the full consequences of a scientific approach. The blocking, as we know from the bitter struggle against cosmology and biology, is not in the inherent nature of the subject matter but in the fear of consequences. When men are free to think

6. "Teach Them the Ways of Democracy," *International Frontiers in Education*, pp. 25-32. *Annals of the Academy of Political and Social Science*, vol. 244, Philadelphia, 1944.

in *all* areas, they will think differently from the constituted authorities. The young free student will question the pronouncement of his elders, whether they be parents, professors, priests, or politicians.[7]

(I, for one, am not completely assured that the questioning student of today is one who can also think constructively.)

Stoddard's innovations in education have not, of course, been limited to the elementary schools but have extended throughout the college years and to special situations, as was noted in reviewing his work as commissioner of education. He has suggested new kinds of curricula for liberal arts colleges, for women, for land-grant colleges, for example. And he has been much concerned with general social problems as well as educational ones, both nationally and internationally. A few quotations will give the flavor of this thinking.

There is no sharp dividing line between the specialized core (in college) and related subjects. The student should feel equally at home in both. In fact, this feeling of "at homeness" is crucial. An engineer studying English has not left the field of engineering. Poetry is not written for other poets; it is written for everyone.[8]

To some persons the liberal arts signify fuzziness, futility, and escape, a pecking around the edges of subjects without biting into their tough core, a prolonged romp in the green pastures. In relation to this concept of the liberal arts, the revolt that leads to a concentration upon great masters is understandable and salutary. But professors need not be driven to this extreme of reform if they will insist upon learning, even sweated learning, as a prerequisite to enjoyment and orientation.[9]

The time has come to give as much attention to homemakers seeking a good education in college as to physicists, chemists, or engineers. The latter, almost exclusively men, have done well within their restricted technical spheres. They have discovered how to destroy that part of the world on which life depends. The women have not done well. They have been confused by the red herring of an education identical to education for men.[10]

Nobody wants delinquency, but almost everybody contributes to it. The failure lies in our ignorance of the deep-seated drives of children and youth. We fail properly to feed, house, guide and educate children

7. George D. Stoddard, *The Dual Progress Plan* (New York: Harper & Row, 1961).

8. "Ferment in Education," in *Ferment in Education*, ed. George D. Stoddard et al., pp. 3-14 (Urbana: University of Illinois Press, 1948).

9. *Tertiary Education* (Cambridge: Harvard University Press, 1944).

10. *On the Education of Women* (New York: Macmillan Co., 1950).

and then worry about the defective outcome. For millions of parents over the country, such concepts as self-reliance, mental hygiene, recreation, social development, and emotional outlet are just big words used by persons who have nothing better to do with their time. . . . The child is not naturally rebellious or delinquent, but he is naturally a bundle of energy and a personality. . . . It is amazing how scarce these articles become, even in a democracy.[11]

It can never be said too plainly that a decent preparation for university life should begin in the nursery school. The speech and habit patterns gained in these formative years under good conditions are a firm rock for all subsequent growth (Unesco Universities Conference, Utrecht, Holland, August 4, 1948).

Through his activities in Unesco, as chairman of the U.S. Education Mission to Japan, as consultant for the International Cooperation Administration with special reference to Korea, and in other activities listed by him, his influence has spread far beyond the United States in education, and beyond education into other cultural activities. A few quotations from men with whom he worked in these fields are of interest.

Sir Julian Huxley writes of Stoddard's work with Unesco: "I always found him helpful, in that his views on education were both sane and progressive and that he had great courage in facing any opposition, while always remaining good-tempered and reasonable."

William Schuman states:

I first came to know George Stoddard in the late fifties when, as president of the Juilliard School, I wanted to see that institution become a constituent member of Lincoln Center. I found him to be most sympathetic and understanding as to the need and desirability of having top-flight professional education in the arts as an adjunct of Lincoln Center's professional performing organizations. . . . His leadership role as a director (of the Lincoln Center Fund for Education and Creative Artistic Advancement) was always strong and supportive and his criticisms ever constructive. Since every man has his weaknesses, I am sure that George Stoddard has his, for he is indeed a man, but from the point of view of this observer I never had the opportunity of discovering them. In his dealings with education at Lincoln Center he was all strength.

Stoddard's autobiography does not take him beyond his position

11. "Educating American Citizens", in *The United States After War*, pp. 161-80. Cornell University Summer Session Lectures (Ithaca, N.Y.: Cornell University Press), pp. 169-70.

as vice-chancellor for academic affairs at Long Island University. Since he wrote that, he was made chancellor the end of October, 1968. The preface to an interview with him in *Seawanhaka* (the student newspaper) of April 18, 1969 notes that his appointment roused great resentment, both because he had upheld the previous chancellor in some bitterly contested actions and because the trustees appointed him out of hand, without consultation with anyone. But the interviewer states further:

> With the progressive outlook of a man half his age, the elderly Stoddard has revamped the Chancellor's cabinet, played a leading role in reorganizing the statutes, and, in general, sought to obliterate the image of dictator replacing dictator that most student and faculty leaders at the Brooklyn Center have of him.
>
> One of the first things Stoddard did, after assuming the Chancellorship, was to enroll student and faculty leaders in ex officio membership in the Cabinet . . . But even more startling was that Stoddard coupled this reform with an even broader one pressing for student-faculty voting membership privileges both in the Cabinet and in the University Council . . . This provision has now been incorporated into the new statutes and, unless the Board of Trustees repudiates both Stoddard and all the University constituents who worked on these far-reaching by-law revisions, students and faculty will, starting in July when the new statutes take effect, be exercising as much power as the administrators who previously ran these bodies autonomously.

Need one add anything to this?

CHAPTER X

Ruth M. Strang

Part I

An Autobiographical Sketch

Family Background and Education

One of my cousins, who amuses us by being interested in the family genealogy, has traced my father's ancestry back to a Daniel L'Estrange who left France during the reign of Louis XIV to escape the Huguenot persecution. Later, he settled in New York and taught French and philosophy in King's College, the predecessor of Columbia University. I somewhat facetiously attribute whatever originality I have and my delight in a good theory to my French ancestry.

My mother's ancestors came over from Holland, having migrated originally, I think, from Sweden. Perhaps it is the Viking strain that has encouraged my exploration in the realm of thought. My mother's ancestors settled in the New York area and were related to several of the old Dutch families.

MY IMMEDIATE FAMILY

My father, Charles Garret Strang (1854-1926), an only child, grew up in Greater New York City. I regret now that I did not ask him to tell me more about the earlier days of life in New York City, but I was always too busy to listen. He went to college for two years and wanted to become a lawyer. At that time, however, his father bought a large farm in South Jamaica and needed his only son to help him run it. I imagine my father felt frustrated over the enforced change in his vocational plans. During the years following he worked very hard on the farm to make both ends meet. At the present time the chief impression that remains of my childhood years is one of an atmosphere of anxiety.

My mother, Anna Bergen Strang (1854-1927), was gentle, "always a lady," as one of the relatives said. My father was the disciplinarian; my mother would be more likely to cry when we were bad. Her remark very shortly before she died was typical. I had said to her, "You've got three bad children. We all have worried you in different ways. I worry you by working all the time. Ben worries you by speculating in the stock market. Arthur worried you by enlisting in the war." And she replied in her reassuring way, "No, I've got three good children."

My brother, Arthur Cornelius Strang (1880-1945), was fifteen years older than I; he was always good to his little sister. He was the most thoroughly kind person I have ever known. As a member of the 23d Regiment he went "Over There" in the 165th Infantry, Rainbow Division, at the beginning of World War I and was severely wounded at Chateau Thierry. One of my saddest recollections and regrets is that my birthday present for his last birthday did not reach him in time. He died that day from a heart attack without having that little last indication of my affection for him.

As a child I resented the preference most people seemed to have for boys. It was taken for granted that my second brother, Benjamin Bergen Strang (1889-1963), would go to college. Since scholarships were rare in those days, my parents paid his tuition from their meager income. He majored in mathematics, graduated from Columbia College, and immediately obtained a position at Georgia Tech teaching calculus, theory of functions, and other courses. After teaching three years there, he returned to New York, obtained his master's degree at Teachers College, and took a position teaching mathematics in high school. His main interest was finance, however, not education.

He was opposed to my giving up my teaching position in the New York City schools to study further at Teachers College. When I retired from Teachers College in 1960, he urged me to give up my professional work. Instead, I accepted the position of professor of education at the University of Arizona. During his last illness I visited him at the hospital twice daily. At the end of the summer I again made the decision to put my work first and returned to the

University of Arizona for the fall semester. He died about two weeks after I left. This is another instance of the frequent conflict between the demands of human relations and of the work that I felt destined to do.

There were three cousins who may have had some influence on me. One had been a much respected high school teacher and "had a way with children." Another was my only first cousin, who was a baby when I was about seven years old. My most pleasant association with her was during weekends at Wellesley College in her senior year. The third cousin, an only child, gave me my happiest social experiences. Visits in her home introduced me to an entirely different world of friends and freedom from financial anxiety.

My role in the family. As the only girl, my role as viewed by my parents was a domestic one. I was not expected to go to college, and my school marks were accepted without special comment.

So far as I can remember, I had no clearly defined self-image during childhood or adolescence. I did "what my hands found to do" but always wanted to do something new or different. This tendency toward originality, which was very strong, was not encouraged.

There was no one with whom I identified. I had a strong sense of individuality; I wanted to be different. Even characters in fiction were not models, although they had certain qualities I wanted to emulate.

In summarizing my family background, it appears that I was fortunate, inheriting to a certain degree what Piaget has described as an "organizing, relating quality of mind" and a tendency toward originality. The atmosphere of anxiety in which I grew up during my early elementary school years may have reenforced a strong, persistent tendency to worry and to anticipate the worst, "to see a calamity in every opportunity."

EDUCATION, FORMAL AND INFORMAL

My first educational experience was in the first grade of a one-room rural school. I have no recollection of being taught phonics or any other special reading method, but seem to have learned by "being confronted with printed words" from which I was expected and wanted to derive meaning.

As soon as I had acquired reading ability I began to read any books available, mostly my older brothers' books. My reaction to these books was similar to that described by Somerset Maugham in *Of Human Bondage;* I was completely absorbed in the stories.

When we moved from New Jersey back to the farm in Greater New York I walked a mile four times a day—morning, noon, afternoon, and after school—to the elementary school. My dominant recollection of these years was fear of the principal, who terrorized all the children. The only subject I had trouble with (and still have) was spelling. To help me, my mother used to "hear me" on the list of spelling words.

I changed schools a third time when we moved to Phoenix, Arizona, for two winters because of my father's bronchitis. The fourth elementary school I attended was in Brooklyn after my father had sold the farm. This was a fairly good public school in a residential neighborhood.

When I graduated from elementary school, I went to a private high school, Adelphi Academy. One teacher, a Mr. Johnson, interested me in English history to the extent that I assembled a collection of poems about various events in English history. He was also sponsor of the Walking Club, which was one of the most enjoyable of my high school experiences. The other extraclass activity I enjoyed was basketball.

During the middle of the senior year I discovered that I needed a year of physics to meet admission requirements for Pratt Institute, which I expected to attend. The physics teacher, Mr. Jewett, set up certain experiments and gave me special instruction after school so that I passed the regents examination in June. I remember his kindness and the vistas of the physical world he opened up to the class.

I had no educational guidance during these years, but association with other students made me eager to go to college. I begged to go to Wellesley. Perhaps my father did not have the money at this time, or perhaps he did not think girls needed to attend college. Consequently, I went to Pratt Institute, which was two blocks away from home. I took the two-year normal program in household science. The courses, except the one in sewing, involved no difficulty. Most enjoyable were the courses in art and interior decorating, taught by Mary Jane Quinn, who encouraged me to continue in that field and recommended me for a job with an interior decorator. This work proved disappointing. After staying home to care for my mother, who was ill at the time, I began teaching home economics in a slum area of New York City.

After three years of teaching, I decided to continue my education. Despite the strong opposition of the principal and of my brother Ben, I persisted in my determination and completed my bachelor's degree at Teachers College in two years with a major interest in nutrition. The dominant person in my education during these years was Professor Mary Swartz Rose, who asked me to assist in the elementary course in nutrition and in a rat experiment. She adjusted her schedule to make it possible for me to take an advanced course in chemistry and the sixteen-point course in physiology at the Columbia Medical School. She also often sent me to the New York Academy of Medicine library to summarize articles on nutrition. Thus she deepened tremendously my academic background, for which I have always been grateful.

On Dr. Rose's recommendation, I took a part-time position in the Department of Health Education at Columbia. In addition to teaching a graduate course, I supervised health education in the Horace Mann School. Out of these two years' experience I wrote a course of study in health for the elementary school; this was published jointly with Dr. Thomas D. Wood.

During these years I was meeting the requirements for the doctor's degree while commuting back and forth to Brooklyn where my family still lived. By means of the part-time work I was able to finance my education.

At the end of the second year with Dr. Wood, Dr. Arthur Gates interested me in preparing exercises for his primary reading test and in an experiment in teaching reading to deaf and mute children. Realizing my lack of background in the field of reading, I went to the University of Chicago for a double summer session. I took the course in teaching reading in high school by Dr. Gray, and also courses with Dr. Buswell, Dr. Judd, and Dr. Barr. Dr. Judd's course, "Psychology of Elementary School Subjects," stimulated me to explore several fascinating theories. He asked me to stay on at Chicago for the coming year, but I had already signed up for the experiment with the deaf and mute children.

In this experiment I worked with Dr. Helen Thompson. I prepared twenty-six practice books of reading material and she did the teaching. At the end of this experiment in 1926, I completed all the requirements for my Ph.D. degree. I had not told my family I was working for a Ph.D.; they found it out by reading the announcement in the paper! So ended my formal education.

The only traveling I did during these years was a month's trip to France and Holland with a cousin who wanted to visit the town in Holland from which her ancestors came. One memorable experience of this trip was seeing the Rembrandt exhibit brought to the Ryks Museum from all over Europe.

The persons who influenced me most during this period were Dr. Rose and Dr. Judd, whom I have already mentioned; there were also Dr. E. L. Thorndike and Dr. Leta S. Hollingworth. I was especially impressed by their kindness and their integrity. While still a student I was a member of a panel teaching a class of about five hundred graduate students in psychological foundations. In that capacity I was associated with Dr. Kilpatrick, the chairman; Dr. Leta S. Hollingworth; and Dr. Kandel.

To summarize: My most important education was acquired through jobs that were offered me for which I had practically no preparation. This necessitated an intensive search for knowledge and the preparation of original material. I also elected courses in other fields which I was able to relate to education by putting ideas together in a new and meaningful way.

At the same time, I was in close touch with children in the Horace Mann School and the New York School for the Deaf. Added to this experience were my previous three years of teaching in a slum area of New York City, the teaching of a settlement class of undisciplined little Italian boys in another deprived area, and teaching of a Sunday school class of girls in a residential area which I taught for about seven years. It was this intimate association with children and young people on weekend trips as well as in Sunday school that gave me the background for my work in child study and guidance. From these children I learned much more than they learned from me. With so many anchors to the reality of teaching children and adolescents, I could not rest serenely on a comfortable cloud of untested theory.

RELIGIOUS INFLUENCES

Agnes Repplier described the Puritan as one who "understood that life is neither a pleasure nor a calamity. It is a grave affair with which we are charged, and which we must conduct and terminate with honor." [1] This statement best expresses my philosophy of life. Judged by usual standards, I have had few pleasures. I have fulfilled every obligation that I have accepted.

Early in adolescence I gravitated toward pessimistic poetry. Whenever a poem appealed to me strongly, it slipped into my memory without effort. Consequently I still know by heart many poems and passages of this kind, such as Mathew Arnold's "Dover Beach," Keats's "When I have fears that I may cease to be," and Sophocles's "Who craves excess of years beyond life's common span . . ." from *Oedipus at Colonus.* As an antidote, I also remember selections from Wordsworth, Browning, and Sydney Lanier. In my thirties I read a passage in *Young Henry of Navarre* which suddenly gave me a sense of destiny, a feeling that I, too, had a mission to accomplish.

Formal religion also played an exceptionally dominant role in my life, and probably in my career. All during childhood, every morning and evening my father read from the Bible. Many authors have testified to the influence of the King James Version on their literary style. Certainly I had daily opportunity to acquire the sound of language. The compliment to my writing that I most prize was in Dr. Laurence Shaffer's review of one of my books in which he said that it "had a deceptive simplicity."

I have no definite impressions of the influence of the years when I attended Sunday school. My religious education really began when I taught settlement and Sunday school classes of my own. I still keep in touch with some of the women whom I taught as children so many years ago.

In my own attendance at church I was fortunate in having two outstanding ministers. Dr. Cleland B. McAfee associated religion in

1. Agnes Repplier, *Eight Decades: Essays and Episodes* (Boston: Houghton Mifflin Co., 1937), p. 88.

my mind with kindness to and understanding of children. Dr. Charles C. Albertson appealed to me during my adolescence through his love of poetry. He frequently quoted poetry in his sermons, and in one Lenten season devoted a series of Wednesday night meetings to the reading of Sydney Lanier's poetry: "The Marshes of Glynn," "Sunrise," "The Crystal," and other poems. This perhaps was my deepest religious experience.

It seems strange that with this constant church attendance during childhood and adolescence I have not attended church during my professional years. My withdrawal from church attendance was not, however, a withdrawal from the influence of religion. I still listen to recordings of religious music and seek guidance in prayer. Intellectually I accept the idea of a God like Jeremiah's, who is not all-powerful but needs the help of Man to create a better world.

Although not specifically religious, my activities with the Camp Fire Girls reenforced my deep love of nature and included many memorable experiences such as overnight camping trips and a story hour by Ernest Thompson Seton around a campfire at his Greenwich, Connecticut, home.

In summary, my experiences with religion not only contributed to my style of writing, appreciation of literature, and understanding of children and adolescents, but also to a sense of destiny and a feeling of being a co-worker with Something bigger than and beyond myself. Religion has also offered "a very present help in time of trouble."

KINDS OF COMMUNITIES IN WHICH I HAVE LIVED

One of Joseph Conrad's unfinished novels had as its theme the influence of vast, open spaces on a child even in infancy. I think that my early childhood experiences with nature have permeated my lifelong thinking and feeling. I tune in readily with many of the thoughts about nature expressed by Wordsworth.

My most vivid recollections of nature are of the period on the farm when I was between six and ten years old: the wonder of spring coming to the woods, first a gray-green mist, then the fresh green leaves; the progression from blossom to blossom—marsh marigold, hepatica, spring beauties, dogtooth violets, and through summer into ironwood, goldenrod, purple asters, and the last red shining berries. The bay and the ocean were also part of my early childhood: the little fish and other sea animals flashing through seaweed; the "movement and change and beauty" of the edge of the sea; the "in-rolling wall of the fog"; and the storms when the breakers were high and strong.

It is the continuation of these childhood experiences that has furnished much of my happiness in later life. They have made possible a deeper appreciation of literature and a continuing interest in rural life, eventuating in my work with Dr. O. Latham Hatcher in Breathitt County and Harlan County, Kentucky, and my active participation for seven or eight years in the Columbia University Seminar on Rural Life.

The influence of preadolescent and adolescent years in a residential section of Brooklyn was not due primarily to the location but to friends in the church and schools I attended. In the summer we went to our home on Long Island where I again had contact with the land and the sea. After my mother and father died, I continued to commute and keep house (after a fashion) for my two brothers.

When the strain of commuting became too great I rented a small room near Columbia University and lived there during the remaining years I was employed at the university. Living thus in the university community made it possible for me to become completely absorbed in my teaching and writing. I was too busy during the academic year to enjoy a home of my own or to entertain.

The summer of 1960, immediately following my retirement from Teachers College, I spent in Berkeley, California, teaching two courses at the university. I lived in the residence for women faculty on campus. That was the most delightful living arrangement I have ever had—a quiet, beautiful setting, ideal summer climate, swimming in the outdoor pool, pleasant walks, and very good friends.

The contrast between Berkeley and Tucson, Arizona, was most distressing. The heat was intense when I arrived in Tucson early in September. The noise of airplanes from the mammoth air force base kept me awake at night and disturbed me by day. In time, either the noise of the planes declined or I learned to ignore it. Again my work at the university absorbed practically all my time and energy, leaving very little for social or community activities.

In summary, the kinds of communities in which I have lived have influenced me a great deal. My early childhood experiences in meadows and woods and near the sea have made a lasting impression. City life has become increasingly distasteful to me, though I appreciate its stimulating effect. Ideally, both experiences would be desirable, "the solace that comes from nature and the stimulus that comes from man," as Horace put it. I did have this combination to some extent after I built a little house in the woods of Montrose, New York, where I "reclused" during June and August vacations and where I spent a long spring during one of my sabbaticals.

My living arrangements during most of my life have been subordinate to my work. I ignored discomforts and unattractive surroundings during my years in New York City. Thus far I have not fully enjoyed the more pleasant Tucson environment because of illness and pressure of work.

FRIENDS AND ASSOCIATES

During my years on the farm there were few children to play with outside of school. The most influential friend during preadolescence was two years younger than I. With her I played handball and went roller-skating. This was a completely satisfying relationship. During high school years I was quite intimate with two girls in my class at Adelphi Academy. We went to each other's homes and shared many experiences. I enjoyed being with classmates, many of whom were wealthier and more socially adept than I but friendly and outgoing. At Pratt Institute I made no close friends among my fellow students, but spent the little free time I had with my church associates.

During the forty years at Columbia University practically all my friends were my students, both while they were in college and after they had graduated and moved into responsible positions. I was interested in each one's progression of experience and did much to further it.

Five of these students became lifetime friends who contributed largely to whatever happiness I have had and to the reinforcement of my ideals. With Esther Dayman, who was dean of students at Mills College, I had stimulating talks about philosophy of life and education, with emphasis on the idea of living most fully in the present.

Virginia Ballard, one of my doctoral students, became director of guidance and psychological services in the Long Beach city schools. She was my opposite in personality—optimistic, outgoing, dependent upon friends, of which she had many. In her life she exemplified the philosophy of "accentuating the positive."

Frances Wilson, who became director of educational and vocational guidance in New York City, was my closest associate for almost twenty years. She taught half of one of my evening guidance course at Teachers College. Our visits were mostly about our work, but sometimes we discussed poetry and literature. Her illness and indomitable spirit were similar to those of Virginia Ballard. Her impact on many persons in the field of guidance was very great.

Marian Brown, another of my doctoral students and a loyal friend, became director of vocational guidance and information in Oakland, California. She, too, was extrovert in nature. I visited her the summer I taught at Berkeley, and several years ago she collaborated with me on a paperback book on guidance for adolescents.

For the person with whom I have been most closely associated during the past fifteen years I have provided a progression of professional experiences, from assistance in obtaining her doctor's degree to obtaining for her the position of assistant professor at the University of Arizona in 1960, when she completed her dissertation. In Arizona we lived together and worked on the development of the reading program for eight years.

Another person, Dr. Thomas Briggs, now ninty-two years old, has become influential in my life through his letters and an occasional visit to Tucson. His undiminished intellectual interests and ability and his fortitude in facing physical accidents and illness have been an inspiration reminding me of the refrain in Chaucer, "What he endured, that also can I."

My brief association with Barbara Burks was an experience with a truly gifted, generous person. A casual association with Dr. Philip E. Vernon has been most pleasant and stimulating. We have corresponded intermittently and he has shared some of his research studies with me and sent me copies of his books.

In summary, my friends and associates have had an important professional influence on me. Being chosen almost exclusively from among those interested in guidance and reading, they have reinforced rather than interfered with my work. It was natural and mutually satisfying to "talk shop" with them. These associations have not been coldly professional; I have felt warmly toward these friends and found much satisfaction in their success.

INFLUENCE OF BOOKS

I have read few books other than those related specifically to my work. What I lacked in breadth of reading I may have made up for in intensity—not an analytical intensity, but a complete involvement in the content and style. Other books I "spot check," pausing to consider and elaborate an idea that catches my attention because of its significance or the felicity of its expression. I read magazines in the same way.

My professional reading, however, has not been confined to one narrow field. I enjoy reading in a field unfamiliar to me; it is like traveling in an unknown country. Even if I do not understand it, I catch glimpses of significant ideas. I do not regret these excursions into other fields, for it is important to know something about them all if we want to understand the many-sided aspects of child and adolescent development. Any new theory in physiology or medicine, any new psychological insight, any glimpses of anthropology have possible applications to guidance and reading.

Career Choice and Preparation

MY CAREER

I have had no formal vocational guidance and have done practically no vocational planning. My career has grown in response to needs in the situation and to opportunities that were offered me. Preparation for a position has often followed its acceptance. At other times I acquired the competencies needed while on the job. Thus, my vocational history has zigzagged from one apparently unrelated field to another. Yet each of the diverse kinds of work has contributed in some way to my competency in subsequent positions.

The main turning points in my career were many. My first full-time work grew out of two art courses in which I attracted the attention of the teacher by unusual color schemes and original designs. I went into interior decorating without exploring any other possibilities. The next job grew out of my previous preparation in home economics and the need for a home economics teacher in a slum area. Again, the job came to me, unsolicited and unsought. The next move involved a determined decision, made in spite of opposition from the school principal, my family, and the teacher with whom I was working. This was the decision to resign a teaching position and study full time at Teachers College, Columbia.

During my graduate study, already described, several part-time jobs were offered me. The first was assistant in nutrition, which geared in with my study and contributed greatly to my understanding of the field. The move from nutrition to health education involved a more difficult decision which was influenced by Professor Rose's desire to have someone with a nutrition background in the Department of Health Education and by the appeal which the unknown has always held for me.

The position in health education offered many opportunities for learning. It was stimulating to teach a large class of graduate students and to have contact with the gifted teachers and children in the Horace Mann School.

The next move, which involved teaching beginning reading to deaf and mute children, is more difficult to explain. It seemed to throw aside most of my previous professional preparation; I was totally unprepared for it. I can only account for this decision by the appeal of a new experience and by Dr. Gates's effective presentation of the need of these children to acquire reading skills.

After the two-year experiment with these deaf and mute children was completed, another opportunity entirely different was offered. This was in the new field of student personnel administration. The elder Dean James Russell offered me a scholarship in this newly developed field. He foresaw its possibilities and suggested that my contribution would be to build up the professional body of subject matter in the field. I assisted in the teaching of Sarah Sturtevant's major course, and immediately began to follow Dean Russell's directive about building up the literature in the field. I commenced by a review of theory and research on major aspects of student personnel work. This, Dean William Russell later facetiously compared with Bacon's compendium of all knowledge. The series eventually took the form of three volumes: *Behavior and Back-*

ground of Students in College and Secondary Schools, *Counseling Technics*, and *Group Activities*. I had originally planned a fourth volume on vocational guidance, but other books in that area were in print before I got around to it.

During the next few years I was given more teaching responsibility in the major course and, in cooperation with Frances Wilson, developed courses in counseling techniques and in group activities. The course in which I was most interested and for which I was solely responsible over a period of almost thirty years was "The Role of the Teacher in Personnel Work." For this I wrote a book of the same title, which has been revised four times. It was a "first," written at a time when the prevalent point of view was that guidance was the responsibility of specialists, not teachers.

Around 1930, realizing that many guidance problems involve reading inability, I became interested in the improvement of reading. As there were already well-established courses in the teaching of reading at the elementary level, I developed a reading program for high school and college. In this program I had several part-time assistants who had been my doctoral candidates: Beulah Ephron Wray, with clinical psychology and psychiatric background; Nancy Young, supervisor of reading in the junior high schools of New York City; Dorothy Withrow and Helen Carey, psychologists in charge of the Philadelphia Reading Diagnostic Clinic. During the summer sessions I invited outstanding people to teach a two-week unit of my basic reading course: John McInnes, Paul Witty, Dorothy Bracken, and Constance McCullough. All these were my good friends as well as my professional associates.

A stimulating and valuable part of my work during the first part of this period was participation in a counseling practicum with members of the Teachers College psychology department, a psychiatrist, and a Rorschach expert. Another stimulating and valuable experience during Teachers College years was my participation in the Strayer surveys.

In addition to my teaching, writing, and participation in surveys, I sponsored many doctoral dissertations and served as a member of many dissertation committees.

To my college duties were added responsibilities in various organizations: attendance at conferences, editorship of the *Journal of the National Association of Deans of Women* for about thirty years, and the writing of articles and chapters in yearbooks. A most pleasant and rewarding association was as a member of the Board of Directors of the National Society for the Study of Education over three three-year periods.

In my early days at Teachers College I accepted a number of summer teaching positions elsewhere. The first was as instructor in child study and child psychology at the Women's College of the University of North Carolina. It was during three summers there that I became interested and built up my background of knowledge in the field of child growth and development. At the end of that time I had written the manuscript for my first book, *An Introduction to Child Study*. As a totally unknown author I submitted the book to the Macmillan Company with only a brief note of explanation. Within an astonishingly short time I received a letter of acceptance. Other summer positions at the University of Colorado, the University of Maine, University of Chicago, and the University of California were stimulating and pleasant.

I persisted in my career in spite of difficulties. These included not only lack of encouragement and support of my efforts to achieve, but also active opposition from family and certain friends who tried to discourage me from working so hard. A second difficulty was the frustration of working in the guidance department during the years after Professor Sarah M. Sturtevant retired. A third difficulty was physical. Even after I stopped commuting from Brooklyn I was always tired. In addition, I was susceptible to respiratory diseases and suffered from severe headaches. I spent most of one sabbatical undergoing and recovering from an operation.

Apart from the secretarial and student assistance to which a professor with such a heavy load is entitled, but which was actually most inadequate, I had very little help. I never consulted anyone about the books I was writing. During my years at Teachers College, the only financial assistance to carry on my work was a small grant made by the Time-Life Magazine Research Committee.

As time went on, my work continued to dominate my life. In fact, work was my life. Physically I could not engage in both social and professional activities. Fortunately, I obtained much pleasure from professional associations. Work, when not carried to the point of fatigue and not frustrating, was not distinct from recreation.

PERSONAL MOTIVES AND DRIVES

Among the personal qualities that have been most significant and useful in my career I should put first originality, the desire to do something new and different, to choose "the road not taken." This quality, I think, has been shown in my books and other writing. So far as I know, each of them was in a sense a "first" and has had many imitators.

Next to originality, I think my most important quality was a strong sense of "closure," a need or desire to complete whatever I had undertaken and to make it as good as possible. This often led to a dogged persistence in the face of fatigue and opposition.

A third quality is a strong sense of commitment. It is accurate to say I was motivated to persist in the laborious process of writing not by financial reward or even by desire for prestige, but by a sense of people's need for the information in the books or articles I was producing. In addition to this conviction of the importance of my work, there was the more mundane motivation of finishing a job—a specific deadline to meet, marks that had to be handed in, a report that was due.

Motivation arising from the self-concept or self-ideal—in fact, the whole personality with its predispositions, habits, experiences of previous successes or failures, values, standards, and commitments—comprises a complex network and defies analysis here. One other kind of motivation is more mystical than psychological. It is a sense of destiny, a search for "the unknowable," a desire and an obligation to develop one's potentialities and at the end of life to avoid having to say in Tagore's words, "The song I came to sing remains unsung."

Among the personal qualities that have hindered me is too complete absorption in my work to the neglect of sociability. In social situations where proficiency in "chit-chat" is a requisite I have usually felt inadequate. I am much too brusque or even impolite when interrupted while my attention is focused on an idea or a task to be completed. Yet in other instances I am sensitive to the way people are thinking and feeling. This quality led my brother to say that I was rude to people's faces but kind behind their backs. A related quality that has already become evident to the reader is my egotism. Perhaps "egotism" or "egocentrism" is not the right word, for I am work-centered more than self-centered.

Another characteristic is anxiety combined with pessimism and imagination. Granted that a minimum of anxiety or tension is essential for achievement, a high degree of either disrupts thinking. Periodically I have been completely distracted by situations which seemed to threaten the things I cared for most. At such times, emotional equilibrium was most often restored by getting down to work again. Successful writing and teaching have been the most important therapeutic influences in my life.

The activities and associations that have given me the most satisfaction have been (1) the success of my students in completing their doctoral requirements and, later, in their profession; (2) favorable reviews of my books; (3) letters or comments of appreciation from students and other people with whom I have worked; (4) evidence of my contribution to the field; (5) stimulating theoretical discussion, as with colleagues in a good oral doctoral examination or in a class or faculty group; (6) reading or hearing a lecture or TV program that opens a new vista of thought; and (7) suddenly getting a new bright idea. A class period in which students are interested and responsive is most satisfying; conversely, a dull, drab class period is most depressing.

METHODS OF WORKING

Problems for investigation have arisen out of my work with children, from discussions in classes of graduate students, or from recognized need for the study. Reading also may have suggested a topic, elaborated it, and suggested methods of study. In recent years most of my writing has been in response to requests for articles or chapters on a particular topic, or to revise and bring up to date a book I had previously written. Four of my books are in their third or fourth editions.

In thinking out a research topic I often sketch my own ideas for it first and then read to verify, modify, or change them. In addition to the systematic review of the literature, I have often obtained important ideas from unexpected sources, serendipity-wise. Instead of submitting an outline or a first draft to someone for criticism, it seems more satisfactory for me to complete the article, chapter, or report of research to the best of my ability before letting others see it.

I have usually not tried to convince others of the value of my ideas or theories. After presenting them in writing or in lectures, I have often found there was a time lag in their acceptance. Some of my books have sold better in their third or fourth years than in the beginning. Some ideas I advocated ten years ago are only now being widely accepted. Sometime I should like to trace the history of some of these ideas, e.g., (a) the role of the teacher in guidance, (b) the use of introspection as a research technique, (c) the case study approach to evaluation, (d) the inconclusiveness of control-group experiments and the greater value of detailed descriptions of the subjects, the methods, and the results, (e) the importance of describing in detail the method by which research results were obtained, (f) the reporting of individual deviations as well as central tendencies, (g) the importance of studying the reading process, and (h) the incongruity of insisting that research should result in generalizations when the uniqueness of every individual has been clearly established.

Significant Milestones in My Career

SIGNIFICANT ACHIEVEMENTS

Achievements which in my more optimistic moments seem to be of significance may be ranked as follows:

1. Whatever influence for good I have had on the lives and contributions of my students. I think there is no substitute for "the impact of life upon life and personality upon personality."

2. The books I have written. Several of these have been translated into other languages.

3. The ideas I have developed. The ideas mentioned in the previous section, if fundamentally sound, may have influenced research and practice to a slight degree.

MAJOR CAREER ACTIVITIES

1920–1925

Obtained M.S. from Teachers College
Summer session at the University of Chicago
Assistant in nutrition, two years
Supervisor of health education, Horace Mann School, two years
Instructor in health education, Teachers College

1926–1930

Obtained Ph.D. from Columbia University
Research assistant in psychology, Teachers College
Assistant professor of education, Teachers College
Took courses in psychology
Prepared reading material for experiment with deaf and mute children, two years
Worked on Gates's Primary Reading Tests
Taught child study and child psychology at Women's College, University of North Carolina, summer sessions
Wrote *An Introduction to Child Study;* began work on *Health and Growth* series
Obtained fellowship in student personnel work

1931–1935

Assistant professor of education in the field of student personnel administration, Teachers College
Introduced and taught first course in the improvement of reading in high school offered at Teachers College
Taught guidance, summer session, University of Colorado
Published first editions of *The Role of the Teacher in Personnel Work*, and *Personal Development and Guidance in College and Secondary Schools*
Moved to a small room a few blocks from the University
Went on Strayer surveys
Became editor of *Journal of the National Association of Deans of Women;* continued as editor until 1960
Became member of Sigma Xi, Kappa Delta Pi, Pi Lambda Theta

1936-1940

Promoted to associate professor of education in the field of student personnel administration, 1936; to full professor, 1940

Developed further the high school and college reading center

Active in N.A.W.D.C. and the reading association

Published *Behavior and Background of Students in College and Secondary Schools*, and *Problems in the Improvement of Reading in College and Secondary Schools*

1941-1945

Taught heavy program of courses in guidance and reading during both academic year and summer sessions

Participated in conferences and surveys and wrote many articles

Published *Pupil Personnel and Guidance; Child Development and Guidance in Rural Schools,* with Latham Hatcher; *Explorations in Reading Patterns; The Role of the Teacher in Health Education,* with Dr. Smiley

1946-1950

Professor of education, Teachers College; continued to teach a heavy program of courses in guidance and reading, plus more work with doctoral candidates

Invited to teach summer session at Harvard but was obligated to remain at Teachers College

Participated in conferences, wrote articles and chapters for yearbooks

Board of Directors, N.S.S.E., 1948-1954

Published *Counseling Techniques in College and Secondary Schools,* and *Educational Guidance—Its Principles and Practice*

1951-1955

Same program at Teachers College, with expanding reading center

Similar participation in conferences, surveys, and writing of articles

Published *Gateways to Readable Books*

Spent summers in cousin's guest house, Candlewood Isle, Connecticut

Active in American Association for Gifted Children

1956-1960

Same program at Teachers College, increasing in intensity in spring semester of 1960, with several doctoral students trying to complete requirements before I left in June

Published *Making Better Readers*, with Dorothy Bracken; *The Adolescent Views Himself; Helping Your Gifted Child*

Summer session 1960, taught graduate course in reading and mental health at University of California, Berkeley; visited with old friends there

Taught two-week workshop at Flagstaff, Arizona, on my way to new position in Tucson

Began work at University of Arizona in September 1960 as professor of education

Board of Directors, N.S.S.E., 1958-61

1961-1965

Served as full-time professor of education at the University of Arizona and built up a program in reading for undergraduates and graduates. Both the president of the University and Dean Moore of the College of Education, as well as public school administrators, were pleased with my work

A third member, George Becker, added to the staff of the reading center

Spoke at many meetings

Published *Helping Your Child Improve His Reading*, *Helping Your Child Develop His Potentialities*, *Diagnostic Teaching of Reading*, and *Understanding and Helping the Retarded Reader*

Bought a house within walking distance of University

During 1965 the work became heavier than ever while I was trying to complete revision of the fourth edition of *The Improvement of Reading*. There was little time for social activities except for occasional dinners with Mr. and Mrs. McCurdy, former friends who had come to Arizona for the winter

1966-1968

Continued as full-time professor of education

Published fourth revision of *The Improvement of Reading*, and several chapters in books of readings

Obtained grant for and conducted five-week N.D.E.A. Institute in summer of 1966

Sabbatical leave due but deferred to Dr. Melnik so that she might take trip abroad and visit reading centers in the U.S. during fall semester 1966. As substitutes were not provided for persons on sabbatical leave, I carried the extra teaching load plus all administrative duties in the reading center during this semester.

Obtained state approval of the University of Arizona reading program

Achieved state certification of reading

Obtained U.S. Office of Education grant for Experienced Teacher Fellowship program, which I conducted during academic year 1967-68

Elected to membership on the Board of Directors, N.S.S.E., spring 1968 for three-year period

Full retirement requested by Dean Paulsen as of June 1968

Spoke at general session of the 1968 Copenhagen Second World Congress on Reading in August 1968 and at the Fifth Annual Study Congress in Edinburgh

Accepted the Peter Sandiford Professorship for 1968-69 at the Ontario Institute for Studies in Education, University of Toronto, as soon as I knew I would no longer have connection with the University of Arizona. The program proposed at the Institute seemed ideal in every way.

MY WORK VERSUS MY CITIZENSHIP

Perhaps I am rationalizing here, but it seems to me that nothing is more important for the nation and for a better world than reducing illiteracy and helping every child develop his potentialities. Through my health books, preschool "Guide" in the *PTA Magazine* during the past ten years, books and articles for parents and children, and teacher education in guidance, child study, and reading, I hope I have made some small contribution to the world of today and tomorrow. At least, the work I have done has been in the area of my greatest competency, and the time devoted to it should have been more productive than time devoted to political action, for which I am poorly qualified.

Perhaps my professional correspondence, an average of two hours a day, should be mentioned here since much of it consisted of replies to letters asking for advice or information.

FAMILY AND PERSONAL SOCIAL LIFE

My family and personal social life has been briefly described in other sections of this autobiography and needs only be summarized and supplemented in a few respects. Not having married and had children of my own, I perhaps had more affection to give other people's children, such as those in my Sunday school classes and in public school, to the reading cases with whom I have worked, and even to my college students. I have been financially helpful to children of my relatives and friends.

As already stated, my social life has been almost entirely connected with my work. Other social activities that interfered with my work have brought little pleasure or relaxation. The most enjoyable recreation has been the noon swimming sessions during my summers at Montrose, New York, and all the year around in Arizona; and walks and talks with friends and students.

THE PAST TEN YEARS

As the policy at Columbia University of retiring at the age of sixty-five is rigidly enforced, I had no feeling of being "pushed out." Still, I did not feel ready to retire. I was offered positions at a number of universities, but the one at the University of Arizona appealed to me because of its location and because of the opportunity to build up the reading program almost from scratch.

Actually, I did not retire but moved into an equally exacting position. I did this against the very strong opposition of my brother. His arguments were: "You have made your reputation and have the respect of people in your field. Why continue the strain and stress of professional life any longer? There is the danger that past achievement may be dimmed or blotted out by future failure. If you retired on Long Island you would have a pleasant, inexpensive home; you could write; you could keep in touch with your friends in the New York area who also want you to stay here." Perhaps he was right. Much of my present satisfaction stems from associations and achievements of the pre-Tucson days.

During the first five years at the University of Arizona, the president of the University and Dean Hollis Moore of the College of Education were appreciative and supportive of the unified sequential reading program we developed leading to master's and doctor's degrees. This program met the need for reading consultants in elementary and secondary schools, and it provided more adequate preparation for beginning teachers in self-contained classes and in subject areas. After Dean Moore left, the next dean, determined to promote his own form of organization, became increasingly antagonistic to the reading program until in the spring of 1968 he decreed that the reading courses and staff be allocated to other departments, thus fragmenting and destroying the integrative program that had been built up during the previous seven years. He was prevented from carrying out his plan by a spontaneous, dignified protest from students and members of the community.

Two major satisfactions during the past two years have been the N.D.E.A. Institute and the Experienced Teacher Fellowship program, for which I received federal grants. The latter is perhaps best described by one of the participants in an anonymous evaluation made at the end of the year:

> I think that if any aspect of the program had been left out I would not feel I could do as effective a job of teaching and consulting as I now feel capable of doing. Each part seemed to complement the other and broaden our understanding of some facet—the lectures gave us ideas and suggestions; the field work permitted us to try them out, and the seminars encouraged an exchange of ideas and how to best implement these ideas and the background obtained through the field work. I was exposed to theory and practical approaches to reading, one complementing the other. The theory in the classroom was put to practical use in our field work. The program was exceedingly well coordinated. The courses dovetailed into one another so that you came out with a clear picture of how to find out where a pupil was on the growth continuum and what and how you should teach him.

Some decisions are irreversible; they start you on "the road of no return." Once you've made the decision, other doors are closed to you. So it was with my decision to go to the University of Arizona. My anticipation of better health and less stress and strain was not fulfilled. Nor was my hope, expressed in Sara Teasdale's words, "It may be with the coming on of evening I shall be granted unassailed repose."

THE MEANING OF TIME TO ME

There has never been enough time. Time has always moved too rapidly. It still does. I haven't had time to think much about the "time that is still mine." If I can meet immediate demands, that is my only concern at present.

Money plays little or no part in my view of life today other than an impatience at the amout of *time* it takes to write checks, pay bills, and fill out income tax returns. I have always contributed a large proportion of my income to schools, churches, colleges, and welfare organizations. In addition I give quite a bit more, which is not deductible for income tax purposes, to students and other needy persons whom I know personally. Until recently my living expenses have been small; I've been too busy to spend money shopping, traveling for pleasure, and the like.

Appraisal of Career Contributions and Satisfactions

MAJOR EVENTS OR MOVEMENTS IN EDUCATION IN WHICH I WAS ENGAGED

1. The movement in health education from primary concern with physiology and physical exercise to much more concern with practical nutritional problems, mental and physical health. My contribution here was through the Horace Mann course of study, and the *Health and Growth* series published by Macmillan.

2. The guidance movement, from a narrow vocational guidance emphasis and reliance on specialists to a broad developmental view with emphasis on the fulfillment of each individual and the responsibility of the teacher assisted by the guidance specialist. My contribution here was through publication of *The Role of the Teacher in Personnel Work* and through the literally thousands of students who have taken my courses, "Guidance for the Classroom Teacher" and "Counseling Techniques." During peak years often more than three hundred students were enrolled each semester.

3. The movement toward improvement of reading in the secondary schools, from practically no recognition of the reading problem in junior and senior high school to the present increasing interest as evidenced by several magazines devoted to reading in

high school and college, many articles in other magazines, large attendance at sections on high school reading at conferences, and books and pamphlets on the subject. My contribution was through (a) *Problems in the Improvement of Reading in Secondary Schools and College*, first published in 1938 and subsequently revised and expanded four times; and (b) the high school and college programs begun at Teachers College in 1932 and at the University of Arizona in 1960.

4. The movement toward a broader, less statistical, more individually oriented type of research instead of control-group studies as the dominant pattern of educational research. I don't think I have influenced this rather recent tendency, but have been advocating it for years.

MY JUDGMENT ABOUT MYSELF

My chief satisfactions, as suggested, have been in the evidence of (a) growth in the children, adolescents, or adults with whom I have worked, (b) the value and usefulness of my writings, (c) successful completion by my students of their dissertations, (d) responsiveness of classes and other audiences, and (e) the soundness of ideas that have occurred to me. There has also been satisfaction in the moment of discovering a new idea or relationship. Non-professional satisfactions have been the enjoyment of poetry and literature, flowers and other "things of beauty," and physical activities, especially hiking and swimming.

My regrets in the professional area are few. I feel I have done what I could, as well as I could. I did regret that I was not free to stay on at Berkeley after the summer of 1960. A personal regret is that I did not or was not able to contribute more to the happiness of my two brothers in their last years. Both of them led lonely lives. But this regret is mitigated by the probability of my not having been temperamentally able to have done so.

If I had my life to live over, I really do not know what changes I would make. It seems to have been an organic whole, each stage growing almost inevitably out of the previous stage as opportunities were offered. However, I should try to keep one day a week, Sunday preferably, entirely free from regular professional work and devote it to rest, reading, music, religious services, and enjoyable physical activity. I should also like to be free from professional responsibilities after a seven o'clock dinner hour and be able to retire by ten o'clock. Perhaps if I had lived a less hectic life, illness would not have been necessary as a reminder or a reprimand. Illness seems to be part of a gestalt involving regrets for the past and fear of the future as well as pain in the present.

My state of health has had a great influence on my career, surely contributing to my pessimistic outlook and my habitual fatigue. I was seriously ill as a baby, having malaria and typhoid fever in addition to the usual children's diseases. I've always been susceptible to headaches and respiratory diseases, have had three or four severe colds each winter, and flu whenever it came around. Then there was the serious, more recent operation for cancer. The trouble with surgery is that it disrupts many good habits and creates new problems. To produce desirable changes after surgery, the conditions that gave rise to the problem initially must be changed. One's way of life and ways of thought must be given a more favorable direction.

How did these illnesses influence my career? Perhaps in two ways: by making me more introvert than I might have been, and by making it impossible for me physically to engage in the "normal" amount of social activities, thus giving me more time for reading and study. On the other hand, illness has prevented me from working as long and as hard as I might have otherwise and has caused a constant undercurrent of anxiety.

Social approval has influenced me more than I like to admit. I should like to resemble the French mathematician who said people's opinion did not affect him, only his own judgment of his work. Perhaps I've depended more on people's expression of appreciation and appraisal of my work because my own opinion of it is usually quite low. Only once in a while do I feel, when I have written an article or book or taught a class, "This is good."

Work has been an important, therapeutic, integrating factor in my life. If I can only get to work when I'm emotionally disturbed about something else, I become calmer and more content. Moreover, there is the pleasure in finding the apt word, in seeing a new relationship, or in getting a glimpse of a new theory.

The future is unknown and unknowable. Like Cezanne at Aix,

I hope to keep on working to the end. I should like to use whatever wisdom and competencies I have acquired over more than seventy years to make some further contribution to child development and guidance and to the more thoughtful and critical reading of adolescents. These seem to me two effective ways of making a better world.

A BIOGRAPHICAL SUMMARY

RUTH M. STRANG. Born on April 3, 1895, in Chatham, New Jersey.*

Education. Public schools in the Greater New York area, Adelphi Academy (secondary school), Pratt Institute (two-year course), Teachers College, Columbia University, B.S., 1922, Ph.D., 1926.

Occupational history. New York City public schools, 1917-20; assistant in nutrition, Teachers College, Columbia University, 1923-24; instructor in health education, 1924-25; research assistant in psychology, 1925-26; assistant professor to professor of education, 1926-40; professor of education, 1940-60; professor of education, University of Arizona, 1960-68; Peter Sandiford professor of education, Ontario Institute for Studies in Education, 1968-69. Editor, *Journal of the National Association of Deans of Women*, 1935-60.

Memberships. International Reading Association, National Society for the Study of Education (Board of Directors, 1948-54, 1958-61, 1968-69); American Association for Gifted Children; National Association of Deans of Women.

*Editorial note: Word of Miss Strang's death was received just before this book went to press.

Part II

Selected Publications of Ruth M. Strang

A most comprehensive and easily accessible bibliography of Ruth Strang's writings (up to the time of her retirement from Teachers College in 1960) may be found in Amelia Melnik's "The Writings of Ruth Strang," *Teachers College Record* 61 (May 1960): 464-76. The following bibliographical selections therefore make no pretense of comprehensiveness; they rather serve to suggest the sweep of Ruth Strang's professional activities by calling attention to the books she wrote over an exhaustively productive career and to articles written since 1960.

Books

Guidance, Student Personnel, and the Gifted

1. *A Personnel Study of Deans of Women in Teachers Colleges and Normal Schools* (with Sarah M. Sturtevant). New York: Bureau of Publications, Teachers College, Columbia University, 1928.
2. *A Personnel Study of Deans of Girls in High Schools* (with Sarah M. Sturtevant). New York: Bureau of Publications, Teachers College, Columbia University, 1929.
3. *Personnel Development and Guidance in College and Secondary School*. New York: Harper & Bros., 1934.
4. *Behavior and Background of Students in Secondary School and College*. New York: Harper & Bros., 1937.
5. *Child Development and Guidance in Rural Schools* (with Latham Hatcher). New York: Harper & Bros., 1943.
6. *Pupil Personnel and Guidance*. 2d ed., rev. New York: Macmillan Co., 1946.
7. *Educational Guidance: Its Principles and Practice*. New York: Macmillan Co., 1947.
8. *Counseling Technics in Secondary School and College*. 2d ed., rev. New York: Harper & Bros., 1949.
9. *The Role of the Teacher in Personnel Work*. 4th ed., rev. New York: Bureau of Publications, Teachers College, Columbia University, 1953.

10. *Helping Your Gifted Child.* New York: E. P. Dutton Co., 1960.
11. *Guidance in the Classroom* (with Glyn Morris). New York: McGraw-Hill Book Co., 1964.
12. *Parent-Teacher Conference* (with Virginia Ballard). New York: McGraw-Hill Book Co., 1964.
13. *Target: Tomorrow.* New York: Dell Publishing Co., 1964.

Reading and Communication

14. *Problems in the Improvement of Reading in High School and College.* 2d ed., rev. Lancaster, Pa.: Science Press, 1940.
15. *Explorations in Reading Patterns.* Chicago: University of Chicago Press, 1942.
16. *Teen-Age Tales.* Books 1, 2, 3, 6 (with others). Boston: D. C. Heath & Co., 1954, 1955, 1958.
17. *Problems in the Improvement of Reading* (with Constance M. McCullough and Arthur E. Traxler). 2d ed., rev. New York: McGraw-Hill Book Co., 1955.
18. *Making Better Readers* (with Dorothy Bracken). Boston: D. C. Heath & Co., 1957.
19. *The Administration and Improvement of Reading* (with Donald Lindquist). New York: Appleton-Century-Crofts, 1960.
20. *Diagnostic Teaching of Reading.* New York: McGraw-Hill Book Co., 1964.
21. *Gateways to Readable Books* (with Ethlyne Phelps and Dorothy Withrow). 4th ed., rev. New York: H. W. Wilson Co., 1966.
22. *Improvement of Reading* (with Constance M. McCullough and Arthur E. Traxler). 4th ed., rev. New York: McGraw-Hill Book Co., 1967.

Health Education

23. *A Tentative Course of Study in Health Education* (with Thomas Wood). New York: Bureau of Publications, Teachers College, Columbia University, 1925.
24. *The Role of the Teacher in Health Education* (with Dean Smiley). New York: Macmillan Co., 1951.
25. *The Health and Growth Series,* Grades 1-8 (with others). 4th ed., rev. New York: Macmillan Co., 1955.

Psychology and Mental Health

26. *The Adolescent Views Himself: A Psychology of Adolescence.* New York: McGraw-Hill Book Co., 1957.
27. *An Introduction to Child Study.* 4th ed., rev. New York: Macmillan Co., 1959.

28. *Helping Your Child Develop His Potentialities.* New York: E. P. Dutton & Co., 1965.

Group Work

29. *Group Activities in College and Secondary Schools.* 2d ed., rev. New York: Harper & Bros., 1946.
30. *Group Work in Education.* New York: Harper & Bros., 1958.

Journal Articles

31. "The Able Reader." *Instructor* 74 (March 1965): 83-108.
32. "Beginning Reading for Slow Learners." *Education Digest* 31 (December 1965): 51-54.
33. "Clinical Study of High School Students' Reading." *Perspectives in Reading*, pp. 103-15. Newark, Delaware: International Reading Association, 1964.
34. "Communication and the Counseling Process." *Journal of the National Association of Women Deans and Counselors* 26 (October 1962): 11-15.
35. "Controversial Programs and Procedures in Reading." *School Review* 69 (1961): 413-28.
36. "Counseling Adolescents." *Adolescence* (1966-67): 297-303.
37. "Counseling Service in Schools of the United States." *Unesco* September 1962.
38. "Creativity in the Elementary Classroom." *N.E.A. Journal* 50 (March 1961): 20-22.
39. "The Current Status and Enduring Value of 'On Their Own in Reading' by W. S. Gray." *School Review* 75 (1967): 114-21.
40. "Developing Oral Expression." *National Elementary Principal* 45 (1965): 36-41.
41. "Developing Reading Skills in the Content Area." *High School Journal* 49 (1966): 301-6.
42. "Diagnostic Teaching of Reading in High School." *Journal of Reading* (1965): 147-54.
43. "Discipline Isn't Dated." *PTA Magazine* (November 1966): 26-28.
44. "A Dynamic Theory of the Reading Process." *Merrill-Palmer Quarterly of Behavior and Development* 7 (1961): 239-45.
45. "Effective Materials for Teaching Reading." *Instructor* (Textbook Supplement) 74 (March 1965): 53, 76-80.
46. "Exploration of the Reading Process." *Reading Research Quarterly* 2 (Spring 1967): 33-45.
47. "Getting Off Self-Center." *National Parent-Teacher* 55 (November 1960): 24-26.
48. "Group Guidance as Students View It." *School Counselor* 8 (1961): 142-45.

49. "Guidance and the Teacher." *Professional Growth for Teachers,* vol 8, no. 9. New London, Conn.: Croft Educational Services, 1963.
50. "Helping Your Child with His Homework." *National Parent-Teacher* 56 (November 1961): 24-27.
51. "How the Child's Identity Grows." *PTA Magazine* (October 1965): 28-30.
52. "Jealousy When A New Baby Arrives." *Growing* 13 (April-June 1961): 6-11.
53. "The Linguistically Handicapped: Learning English as a Second Language—A Theoretical Model." *Exceptional Children* (September 1963): 14-16.
54. "Motivation: As Adolescents See It." *Education* 86 (1966): 473-78.
55. "NAWDC, Perspective and Prospectus: A Symposium." *Journal of the National Association of Woman Deans and Counselors* 29 (Spring 1966): 99-105.
56. "Needed Emphases in High School Reading." *Reading in High School* I (Winter 1964): 35-38.
57. "Normal Adolescence." *Christian Home* 21 (June 1962): 5-7.
58. "Preparation for Teachers of Reading." *Journal of Developmental Reading* (Autumn 1960): 53-57.
59. "Progress in Reading Through Continuous Appraisal and Practice." *Educational Horizons* 46 (Fall 1967): 38-42.
60. "Progress in the Teaching of Reading in High School and College." *Reading Teacher* 16 (1962): 170-77.
61. "Reactions to Research on Reading." *Educational Forum* 26 (1962): 187-92.
62. "Readily to School." *PTA Magazine* 59 (May 1965): 10-13.
63. "The Reading Ability of Disadvantaged Adolescence." *Adolescence* 18 (October-December 1966).
64. "Reading Instruction in Secondary Schools: 'Need' and 'Know-How'." *Arizona Teacher* 53 (May 1965): 12-13.
65. "The Relation of Guidance to the Teaching of Reading." *Personnel and Guidance Journal* 44 (1966): 831-36.
66. "The Role of Guidance in Developing Adolescents' Potentialities." *Naya Shikshak: The Quarterly Journal of the Department of Education* (Rejasthan, Bakiner, India) 9 (July 1966): 63-70.
67. "The Role of the Junior High School in the Teaching of Reading." *High School Journal* 50 (1966): 132-36.
68. "Secondary School Reading As Thinking." *Reading Teacher* 15 (1961): 155-61.
69. "Self-Concepts of Gifted Adolescents." *High School Journal* 48 (1964): 102-6.
70. "Scope of Adolescent Interests." *Education* 83 (1963): 463-67.
71. "Should Parents Teach Reading?" *National Parent-Teacher* 57 (March 1963): 7-9.

72. "Some Principles of Learning Applied to Reading." *Arizona Teacher* 56 (November 1967): 11-12, 25.
73. "Step-by-Step Instruction in Beginning Reading for Slow Learners." *Exceptional Children* 23 (September 1965): 31-6.
74. "A Synthetic Approach to the Teaching of Reading." *Elementary English* 39 (1962): 558-61.
75. "Teaching Reading to the Culturally Disadvantaged in Secondary Schools." *Journal of Reading* 10 (1967): 527-35.
76. "Teaching Reading to the Culturally Disadvantaged in Secondary Schools." *Developing High School Reading Programs*, edited by Mildred Dawson, pp. 146-54 (Newark, Del.: International Reading Association, 1967).
77. "Teaching Slow-Learning Children in Elementary School." *Education* 81 (1961): 338-40.
78. "Teen-Age Readers: How They Got That Way." *National Parent-Teacher* 55 (June 1961): 24-26.
79. "They Have to be Taught to Play." *PTA Magazine* 32 (November 1963): 32-34.
80. "A Unique Workshop." *Arizona Teacher* 52 (March 1964): 20-21.
81. "War Talk and War Games." *PTA Magazine* 62 (January 1968): 18-23.
82. "What is Maturity?" *Church School Worker* 15 (January 1965): 55-57.
83. "What the Pastor Should Know about Special Education." *Pastoral Psychology* No. 142 (March 1964): 19-23.

Part III

Ruth Strang: A Biographical Sketch

CHARLES BURGESS

Ruth Strang, the only woman appearing in this volume of *Leaders in American Education*, began her professional career at a time when women seemed at last to be rising from the world of the economically and politically disenfranchised minorities. In 1926, when she received her assistant professorship at Teachers College, she gained entrance to one of the least forbidding of the few professional fields open to her sex. As a college teacher she became part of a female group that had increased 510 percent since 1910. Even so, women then constituted only 18 percent of the faculties of institutions approved by the American Association of Universities. The overwhelming majority of women employed in professional or semiprofessional fields found niches in nursing, where they comprised 98 percent of the field, and in school teaching, where nearly eight of ten were female. The small cadre of women at the collegiate level gravitated toward such fields as domestic science, health, and education. There they found general if grumpy agreement that their sex could make special claims of promise. There they further happily discovered less open hostility to the idea of having female colleagues.[1]

Thus Ruth Strang helped form a new minority of American women—the female professor. For it was one thing to get through the door of academe and quite another thing for a woman to pass beyond the level of instructor or assistant professor. Approximately

1. S. P. Breckinridge, "The Activities of Women Outside the Home," in *Recent Social Trends in the United States*, one volume ed. (New York: McGraw-Hill Book Co., 1933), pp. 722ff. Forty years later, the percentage of women professors still resembles the 1929 figures.

three of every four women then worked at these two levels.[2] The one woman included among the leaders appearing in this volume is in many ways a prototype of those few females who entered the academic world and succeeeded according to the reward system created almost exclusively by males in higher education. Regularly limiting her contact with colleagues to pleasantly formal professional conversations, she built a usefully protective reputation as a "loner," as one who did her work with quiet dispatch (and boundless energy) and left departmental affairs to the men—and to more socially aggressive women—on the faculty. Single all her life and devoted to her students, she carefully called forth from them their finest potential for ego integrity and professional competence and won from them a reputation as one who would stand by her charges in even the most discouraging trials of graduate experience. A prolific writer and excellent teacher left to her own devices, she thus enhanced the reputation of her parent institution by carving positions of leadership in several educational fields.

Reminiscences of Ruth Strang as colleague, teacher, collaborator, or acquaintance often transcend fondness. Such phrases as "plain eloquence" may have described her professional pronouncements. But it was in face-to-face meetings—especially with her students—that Miss Strang undoubtedly made her deepest impression. She had an elusive "special quality of caring" and showed an unusual concern "for the maximum development of others, whether they be students or colleagues." Students credited her for their own best traits.

> Her faith in you engenders faith in yourself. She sees the best in each individual and knows the worth of a human soul. She gives moral support. She is gentle, patient, and understanding. . . .
>
> What I remember most vividly is her use of public school students in panels before her classes. She had an uncanny ability to draw out these students—even "dead-end kid" types. Her decision to teach through the voices of children and adolescents, as well as the effectiveness of her relaxed, obviously empathic, and low-keyed style in opening people up seem important to me. One sensed that the kids felt totally unthreatened by her, and also that they considered themselves as her colleagues in helping us (her class) to see things as they were. . . . She was never

2. Ibid., p. 726.

eager, as most of us are, to lock up a judgment about what people are really trying to say. Here in the Jamesian sense not only is the universe open-ended, but a particular person is also.

Add to all this a thorough commitment to professional objectives, modesty, and a sense of humor and one recognizes not only why so many beheld her as a teacher of towering prominence—but why she, even willy-nilly, would have made many devotees. "Whenever I am discouraged or disheartened by the frustrations in my work, I can turn to her for encouragement—she is 'the shadow of a rock in a weary land.'"[3]

She would spend long weeks in nightly sessions helping a colleague's young son overcome his reading disabilities, donate her lecture fees to scholarship funds, become so involved in her work that her students would take her out to buy clothes and meet hairdresser appointments they had previously made for her. Slender of frame, with warm eyes framed in grey hair, and a soft, thin voice that made an intimate circle out of an otherwise undistinguished group, Ruth Strang worked for a lifetime to live up to the ideals she taught and to develop the combination of concern and competence she tried to foster in her students.

Those who were directly associated with Ruth Strang remember her principally as a "presence." As she once described good teaching, her own ideas were caught, rather than taught. One must turn to her publications to sketch her intellectual biography. What might one learn from or about her from her writings alone? She addressed her professional attention to a wide range of educational matters—from nutrition to reading improvement—but in all of her writings one theme survived in virtually unaltered form: Guidance. One former student spoke for many: "Dr. Strang was essentially a one-idea person. As she once said, toward the end of one course, 'If you remember nothing else from our work together, remember that it is the guidance point of view that must permeate your entire school and build its esprit.'" Strang recalled that her popular course on the role of the teacher in personnel work sustained her greatest classroom interests throughout most of her long

3. This and the items in the preceding paragraph were selected from reminiscences from several associates. Copies of all reminiscences in my possession. I am particularly indebted to Merle L. Borrowman for his critical comments here and throughout the essay.

tenure at Teachers College. It is not surprising that her writings are chiefly—either directly or indirectly—concerned with guidance under both exceptional and general teaching conditions.[4]

Reviewers of her books regularly and correctly noted that she relied heavily upon anecdotes and "concrete examples," and explained that she viewed her readers as generalists rather than specialists. Admittedly not inclined toward analysis, Ruth Strang often managed to satisfy her more critical reviewers with elaborate bibliographies and sketchy references to research (much of which often yielded conflicting hypotheses for teaching effectiveness). However, not all reviewers appreciated this, even if intended as a conciliatory gesture. After reading her 1938 revision of *Introduction to Child Study*, Richard T. LaPierre accepted the work as an appropriately unsentimental "nontechnical, practical treatment." But, he concluded, Strang's "analytic materials are lost in a wealth of homely advice. . . ." And David Snedden, on noting that her guidance point of view would put one-third of the American population under "guidance," sputtered, "is she not clasping hands with Utopians?"[5]

Utopian? Ruth Strang's ideals rested comfortably with some of the most familiar values in the American experience. Two of those ideals are illustrative: the Protestant ethic and the tribal values of small-town and rural America. She accepted wholeheartedly those elements of the Protestant ethic that advanced work, duty, self-improvement, and the doctrine of stewardship as worthy guidons for man. Fond of quoting the parable of the talents, she taught that

4. As Harold H. Punke, in a review of her book *Educational Guidance* typically remarked, there was a clear "similarity in viewpoint between the present book and some of the author's earlier writings." *Educational Guidance: Its Principles and Practices*, reviewed by Punke in *School Review* 56 (1948): 58. See also Verne Faust, *History of Elementary School Counseling* (Boston: Houghton Mifflin Co., 1968), p. 88.

5. See, e.g., the G. T. Buswell review of Strang's *Introduction to Child Study* in *Elementary School Journal*, 30 (1930): 795f. He described the book as "a commendable contribution to the popular literature on child study," but also noted that her "treatment is frequently brief and at points somewhat more positive than the evidence available would warrant." Her bibliography was found to be "excellent." Also see Ruth Strang, *An Introduction to Child Study* (rev. ed.) reviewed by Richard T. LaPierre, *American Sociological Review* 3 (December 1938): 904; and Strang, *Pupil Personnel and Guidance*, reviewed by David Snedden in *School and Society* 54 (1941): 93.

all humans are expected to give returns for their gifts in the forms of self-development and social usefulness. The former had the latter as its crowning achievement. No narrowly intellectual notion of those gifts suited her. Intellectual precocity in fact often worked against social usefulness. It too easily bred arrogance, a contemptuousness of incompetence, and self-centeredness. Rather, she stressed the need for recognizing as necessary the union between "excellence" and an equality of concern for all in a system based upon diversity of talents and begging for the sustained cultivation of individual differences. "No occupation," Ruth Strang declared, "should be considered high or low; the only question is whether it is suited to the individual and of service to society." [6]

Spiritual and social values twined inseparably through Strang's writings on education. Tenderness, indignation in the face of injustice, awe and wonder of nature, being loved and loving in return—these themes undergirded her work; and even her volume on the gifted child served as reminder of the "true nature" of giftedness. "The truly great are humble in spirit; they have the quality of loving-kindness, of sympathy with all mankind, of pity for the weak." Conscious religious allusions summed up the central task of the teacher—"to secure the best development of his pupils, to help each one of them grow in wisdom and stature and in favor with God and man." [7]

Ruth Strang described herself as a puritan, but she advocated more generous notions of man and God than are commonly conjured by the term. Attributes of goodness, truth, beauty, and brotherhood described her God better than did those of vengeance, wrath, anger, and remoteness. Where the puritan might have found evil to be man's natural attribute, she discovered the Emersonian God dwelling in each person. She borrowed even more from Emerson than such ideas as that of "the God that is within us. . . ." She further drew from Carl Rogers's "client-centered approach," as well as from Kahlil Gibran's mystic sense of human divinity, to support her contention that "each student has within himself the

6. Ruth Strang, *Helping Your Gifted Child* (New York: E. P. Dutton & Co., 1960), pp. 6, 218f.

7. Ibid., p. 6; and Ruth Strang, *Every Teachers Record* (New York: Bureau of Publications, Teachers College, Columbia University 1936), p. 2.

capacity to guide himself." With the divine spark found in each child, Ruth Strang took encouragement from Emerson's insistence that ultimately "help must come from the bosom alone. . . .The world is nothing, the man is all; in yourself is the law of all nature. . . . [Have] confidence in the unsearched might of man." [8]

Sustained guidance, often indirect and subtle, conducted in an atmosphere of friendliness and shared planning, however, first taught the child to "know himself." Self-reliance and social responsibility came with intelligently and warmly arranged experiences in childhood and youth. The child then should grow into an awareness of himself as an emanation of divinity with worthy gifts to develop and a social purpose to serve. If he early exhibited traits that were inferior or causes of embarrassment, the teacher helped him gain a more satisfying sense of self. If he displayed a self-conscious feeling of superiority, the teacher worked to turn the child toward a more becoming humility in the face of greater social expectations. Strang's message here combined the talents parable with overtones of Walt Whitman's "divine average" man. And again, with Emerson, she implicitly agreed that "everything must have its flower or effort at the beautiful, coarser or finer according to its stuff." [9] And she too cut through the anomalies and contradictions of life by accepting the imperfection as well as the divinity shared in common by all mankind.

One must, she argued, "accentuate the positive" and dwell on the divinity—the talents—of man. As man was *homo faber*, so work was Ruth Strang's life. Few beneficiaries of the Protestant ethic gave themselves more fully to this directive. But no ideological gulf separated work and play. Elements of play—joy, spontaneity—gave work its leaven. Echoing Froebel, Strang noted that human activity ideally unified the best elements of both work and play. "Child's play" was the purposeful work of childhood; and work,

8. She cited Dewey's *Common Faith* with approval on this subject. See, e.g., Ruth Strang, *Group Activities in College and Secondary School*, rev. ed. (New York: Harper & Bros., 1946), p. 139; Ruth Strang, *The Role of the Teacher in Personnel Work* (New York: Bureau of Publications, Teachers College, Columbia University 1932), p. 299; quotation from Emerson's *American Scholar* in Ruth Strang, *Educational Guidance: Its Principles and Practice* (New York: Macmillan Co., 1947), p. 114; see also Strang, *Gifted Child*, p. 5.

9. Ralph Waldo Emerson, "Nominalist and Realist," in *Emerson's Essays, Complete* (Chicago: Henneberry Co., n.d.), p. 267.

to be purposefully rewarding for an older person, should be well-grounded in the spirit of play. In Strang's writings as in her life, however, necessity was the mother of invention and virtue. No Aristotelian appreciation for the creative potential of leisure found its way into her views. "No great achievement," she insisted, "grows out of an easy, comfortable existence." [10]

While the Protestant ethic shaped Strang's sense of ideal self-development, it made similarly impressive contributions to her sense of community. She rarely developed sustained commentaries about community. Hints of her tribal values, however, appeared regularly in her works. Based implicitly upon the ideals of small-town life, her communal views elevated neighborliness, the cooperative spirit, and above all else a sense of esprit. No communal existence could be termed satisfactory, no communal innovation could hope to succeed, without love and goodwill. One who would "improve upon" the quality of life in his community should ever make haste slowly. Repeatedly, Strang cautioned teachers and administrators to seek first goodwill, then educate for and introduce their superior innovations. Each progressive step taken should have its own firm foundation already laid, carefully and painstakingly.

In the ideal community no devil lurked to snatch the hindmost. Each individual played an approved and worthy role; and the community needed no special instruction on the manifold nature of excellence. In the community as in the classroom the sense of personal unworthiness and failure weakened the effectiveness of the group. Early in her career, Strang had held that a little failure now and then should come to each child. In reasonably tolerable doses and offset with successes, failure developed fortitude. Children who "occasionally meet failure, and face it squarely. . . ," may be aided by the teacher to gain strength from the experience. Over the years, however, as Strang developed a clearer sense of community and fashioned a firm faith in the power of guidance, failure lost its pedagogical value. Indeed, "educational guidance should eventually lead to the prevention of failure." She noted approvingly that Pestalozzi had demonstrated the enlightened attitude toward failure in school by diverting attention "away from the child's failure to

10. Strang, *Gifted Child*, p. 14.

learn and. . . [emphasizing] the teacher's failure to interest the child and hold his attention."[11]

The notion of the "late bloomer" and the "late flowering" of youth bolstered her arguments against the value of failure. Increasingly, her stress fell on the need to develop a sense of success, to build self-confidence. Her mood change was subtle but impressive in light of her expanding view of community and deepening suspicion of competitive activities.[12] Whereas earlier she noted that a taste of failure could be turned to constructive purposes, she later preferred to advise that success—in endeavors carefully tailored to each individual's talents—better served those same constructive purposes. "Accentuate the positive" had now become a universal.

Thus the "good community" adopted an experience-based, generous view of success; it harmonized its component talents and educated for good will, self-fulfillment, and service to the community. Strang's message seemed to be essentially the same for the ideal community as for the ideal school. The school served as the community writ small. As Ruth Strang advised one young principal, new to his community, he should first gain a solid sense of "the existing situation." Then he should develop a well thought-out program for bringing about desirable changes. . . . work for the support of the staff and then *gradually* with their active cooperation make whatever changes seem feasible." Repeatedly she warned: "Don't attempt too much the first year."[13] She never abandoned her faith in the irresistible power of gradualism based upon goodwill.

Community institutions seemed to have been accepted as essentially sound, with the exception of the mass media which came to be viewed narrowly as the purveyor of, at worst, malevolent ideas and, at best, dubious values. Widespread social reform hinged upon changing individuals, their values and sense of purpose. Hav-

11. See, e.g., Ruth Strang, *An Introduction to Child Study* (New York: Macmillan Co., 1930), p. 339; Ruth Strang, *Guided Study and Homework*, pamphlet (Washington, D.C.: Department of Classroom Teachers, AERA, NEA, 1955), p. 11f; and Strang, *Educational Guidance*, p. 103.

12. Strang, *Gifted Child*, p. 23, e.g.; and Ruth Strang, *An Introduction to Child Study*, 4th ed. (New York: Macmillan Co., 1959), pp. 185, 306f.

13. Handwritten note by Ruth Strang on a student term paper. Copy in my possession.

ing joined the faculty at Teachers College at a time when "social reconstruction" made pedagogical headlines, Ruth Strang quietly but firmly expressed her preference for reform of the individual as superior to massive social engineering. She acknowledged the "increased emphasis on recognizing social forces which impinge on the individual," but insisted that "there should be no diminution of the effort to adapt and modify educational offerings to individual needs." From the outset of her professional career she advanced her version of the child-centered approach to education and, as she expressed the importance of child study, of "learning children as well as teaching them." [14]

Teachers should indeed try "to help students develop a better way of living in modern industrial society with its economic and social problems." But she argued for individual commitment to enduring values as the key to social reconstruction. "Teachers have a responsibility for showing students that they have a part in the reconstruction of society and in working out ways and means of satisfying the novel religious needs of today." The critical problem, then, grew out of divisiveness and militancy. Spiritual drift had loosed these forces. "If 'religion is life,' then religious behavior includes all social activity." [15]

Those deeply committed to the Enlightenment faith argued that the study of human nature had proved men to be alike in all most important respects. It followed that the most powerful efforts for Good might be wrought through refashioning the communal environment into alignment with man's general nature. But Ruth Strang explored the recesses of human nature and returned to advance vastly different truths. Each man bore the stamp of unique-

14. Strang, *Role of the Teacher,* 1st ed., p. 11. Even with the mass media, however, she did continue to accentuate the positive, stressing the potential power of the media for good. She remained throughout her career innocent of systematic concern for the complex, disturbing issues of the school in American society. In the ideological confusion of today's world, indeed one might suspect that racist motives led her to recommend using *Birth of a Nation* as a film which would "improve children's attitudes toward the Negro." Given her uniformly sympathetic but simplistic posture in her other writings, one might more reasonably guess that she neither saw the classic film which debased the black man and sang a paean to the Klan nor studied with a critical eye the research on the values taught by the film. See Strang, *Introduction to Child Study,* 4th ed., p. 403.

15. Strang, *Role of the Teacher,* 1st ed., p. 296.

ness as his most important attribute. Human differences rather than human similarities emerged most clearly from her observations of human nature. The perfunctoriness of her attention to rigorously controlled experiments with human subjects grew logically out of this view of man's nature. Each such experiment served as a potential guide to possible behavior; but it could never serve as a rule for behavior. For Ruth Strang it remained incongruous to insist that "research should result in generalizations when the uniqueness of every individual has been clearly established." [16] Over the years her aversion to social reconstruction continued unabated. In 1961, when James B. Conant was preparing his major study of teacher education, she asked him to pay particular attention to "the extent to which courses in history, philosophy, and sociology actually contributed to the effectiveness of the teacher. . . ." [17] The teacher needed firsthand experience in the classroom, commitment to youth, confidence in self, and wide knowledge of the guidance point of view; but studies of education in societies past and present or systematic analyses of modes of inquiry had only questionable value.

Social reformation eluded massive efforts to rearrange the conditions of life. Slower yet more certain social melioration came from adopting the view that the reform of the individual had the cumulative effect of reforming the society. No heroics or political liberalism here, but a cautious confidence in progress under Providence. The social aim of treating each person as teachable and unique, after all, "is to help every individual *change himelf* so that he can make the world better." Once again, "love, not force, is the path toward human betterment." [18]

If Ruth Strang was often evangelically vague in describing the direction of desirable individual change, it may well have stemmed as much from her sense of priorities as from what she believed to be her own difficulties with analysis. Throughout her career she argued in effect that one who simply worked quietly to instill values from the Protestant ethic could unleash vast power upon society.

16. See the Strang autobiography, supra.

17. Letter from James B. Conant to Ruth Strang, May 23, 1961. Copy in my possession.

18. Ruth Strang, *The Adolescent Views Himself: A Psychology of Adolescence* (New York: McGraw-Hill Book Co., 1957), p. 556 (emphasis mine); and Strang, *Child Study*, 4th ed., p. 400.

Religion was life indeed. It was more a Deweyan sense of a "common faith" than a celebration of orthodox credal sacraments; but it was generally Christian in senses spiritual and ethical.

If she seemed to bank more heavily upon "anecdotal research" than upon controlled "experimental research," it may have had as much to do with her overriding concern for developing a teacher's style and attitudes as with her consistent stress on individual differences. She preferred longitudinal case studies and the "clinical approach" consistently. Vocational guidance had its place, minimal subject matter mastery could not be ignored, and a certain amount of regimentation could not be avoided in American schools. But what a child (with his unique "bundle of possibilities") "may become" had more to do with attitudes and values than with those accomplishments which yielded readily to the calipers. Much of Strang's work amounted to an elaboration of William James's confidence in the power of "good habits." One who carefully guided the conduct of the young "in the plastic state," James declared, gave them the best education. Let the child work faithfully at his immediate tasks (as Strang put it: help the child grow in wisdom and stature and favor with God and man) and "he may safely leave the final result to itself. He can with perfect certainty count on waking up some fine morning, to find himself one of the competent ones of his generation. . . ."[19]

But did competence owe more to gumption—or to genes? As a student of human development Strang might have been expected to face publicly the torment of discussing the place of heredity in setting the ground rules for competence. In her earlier writings she prodded at the heredity-environment problem and pondered the meaning of the Kallikak family studies. "The importance of social heredity on the personality of a child should not be ignored," she advised in the first edition of her *Introduction to Child Study*. But by the time she prepared the fourth edition of that popular volume, her own voluntarism and years of stressing "success" and "cooperation" and "accentuating the positive" led her to view the heredity-environment controversy as a problem of values rather than of research design. "We should not take a fatalistic attitude toward

19. William James, *Talks to Teachers on Psychology* . . . , (New York: Henry Holt & Co., 1925), p. 78.

heredity," she added to that last edition of *Child Study*. "We should have a dim, discouraging view of man if we thought he was helplessly driven by his innate predispositions or unresistingly molded by his culture." The question thus became whether to perpetuate doubt with a recital of evidence on either side of the issue (as in the earlier editions of *Child Study*) or to cut free of ambiguity on the strength of will alone. Will prevailed. "Man has more nobility when he feels responsible for what he is and what he becomes." The child must be taught to accept responsibility for his behavior in order to become a social being.[20]

A truly social being is a loving being. The finest expression of love, in Strang's estimation, appeared in a letter from St. Paul (I Cor. 13). St. Paul's abstract views, however, drove deep lines between physical and spiritual love. What of sex? In the course of developing her concept of love, Strang made certain important revisions in her own attitude toward sex and its relationship to the ideal of love. Masturbation is a case in point. In 1930, Strang listed masturbation as "a noticeably bad habit." She advised against punishment for the offense "because it increases the emotion connected with the habit and drives the child to secrecy." Rather the child's behavior should be discouraged in the "same matter-of-fact tone of voice in which he is told not to put dirty fingers in his mouth."[21]

A generation later Strang's treatment of the subject had become more casual and sympathetic. The child should never be allowed to think of the habit as "bad" (as the analogy of "dirty fingers" had earlier done). Strang searched for a more suitable solution to the "problem." The child "can learn not to shock the excessive respectability of neighbors. 'People are funny; they don't like it,' is sufficient reason for him to conform to social conventions."[22]

In 1930 she approached the question of sexual activity in adolescence with similar caution. She weighed the merits of sexual segregation but still preferred coeducational schools, accepted sex

20. Strang, *Child Study*, 1st ed., p. 22; Strang, *Child Study*, 4th ed., pp. 19f, 401.

21. See Strang, *Adolescent Views Himself*, p. 327; and Strang, *Child Study*, 1st ed., pp. 199, 339, 359.

22. Strang, *Child Study*, 4th ed., p. 213. In both periods of time her views on this subject shaded toward a side of greater conservatism than did those held by many professional contemporaries.

interest as "normal," and asked parents and teachers to be frank and fair in dealing with sex. But she also argued that "sex impulses must be suppressed." As with masturbation, however, her attitude toward heterosexual behavior—even light petting—shifted. Instead of flatly insisting that the sex impulse be suppressed, she later tended to express her caution more circumspectively: "There is some convincing evidence that premarital sex repression does not necessarily cause frustration or emotional conflict." [23]

Her discussions of "crushes" took particularly interesting turns over the course of her professional life. She consistently defined a "crush" as an intimate attachment between two adolescent girls. Her definition may have been quaint; but its implications, at least during the 1930s, were most serious. It was a dangerous relationship. "This type of prolonged intimacy of one girl with another may result in inability to make a normal heterosexual adjustment during an entire lifetime." In her later years Strang continued to describe the phenomenon of "crushes," but began to see them as normally more nettlesome to the adult who worked with adolescent girls than permanently injurious to the girls involved.[24]

Her aversion to Freud remained constant. Although her own notion of love came close to the Neo-Freudian libations to Eros, she continued to associate Freud and the Freudians with physical sex. (One should also note that Strang consistently turned from system builders of all kinds. Instead of selecting any given system from the psychoanalytic schools, she borrowed sparingly and judiciously, especially from Carl Rogers. Assembly-line rules or pat generalizations won little enthusiasm from Strang.) And the bohemianism of the 1920s, with its "down repression, up libido," erected a permanent barrier between her and Freud. Freud's own generalizations, moreover, were regularly uncomplimentary to females. Strang could argue that "falling in love is a sign of emotional maturity; it indicates the ability to feel for and give to another person." But Freud, whose ability to accentuate the negative was undisputed, raised questions about one who either never fell in love or achieved sexual fulfillment. Freud reasoned that one who

23. Strang, *Child Study*, 1st ed., pp. 501, 513; and Strang, *Adolescent Views Himself*, p. 327.

24. Strang, *Child Study*, 4th ed., p. 506.

does not satisfy one's "strong sexual instinct will also assume a conciliatory and resigned attitude in other paths of life, rather than a powerfully active one. . . . [The] undoubted fact of the intellectual inferiority of so many women can be traced to that inhibition of thought necessitated by suppression." [25]

Such an observation would have been found wanting in truth as well as in kindness by Strang. It would also have served as an index of what she believed to be the exaggerated role given to sex by Freud. Certainly children and youth should learn about sex, she agreed. But such learning should ever be under the aegis of parents and teachers who taught approved values and treated sex as an attitude more than as an activity. Thus there should be no special instruction in sex in the schools. "Social hygiene," rather than sex education, should be taught in various courses whenever the subject might be timed for logical inclusion as part of the course. The teacher should above all remember that sex education "is not mainly a matter of facts; it involves feeling more than thinking." As with the development of character and personality, feelings about sex are "caught, not taught." [26]

"Caught, not taught." One might confidently assume that she would have said as much for the leading ideas which threaded throughout her writings. Those who knew her may often have remembered the gestalt of her presence above all else, but her goal was as much to teach others her familiar ideas as to gain an undisputed reputation as a gifted stylist.

25. Quoted by David Riesman, *Individualism Reconsidered And Other Essays* (Glencoe: The Free Press, 1954), p. 373. Strang, *Child Study*, 4th ed., p. 505.

26. Strang, *Child Study*, 4th ed., pp. 447, 508. Strang's stress on "feelings," "client-centeredness," and what could legitimately be identified as "permissiveness" might profitably be considered from the perspective provided by Fred N. Kerlinger. See, e.g., Kerlinger's "Implications of the Permissiveness Doctrine in American Education," in *Educational Theory* 10 (April 1960): 120-27.

CHAPTER XI

Robert Ulich

Part I

An Autobiography

The editorial committee of this yearbook has suggested that the contributors tell something about their family background. Although a historian of a sort, I have left the search for ancestors to several of my relatives, who were men of affairs. From them and the genealogies they composed and to a degree from my father I learned that, even before the Thirty Years' War, the Ulichs had been Protestant pastors or scholars and had generally intermarried with families of similar background.

I directly became acquainted with my ancestors when at the State Library of Dresden I looked for the name Ulich and found it mentioned in various theological yearbooks of earlier centuries. There I discovered that one of my forebears must have been a great linguist. About 1700 he wrote, in Latin of course, an enormous volume on the question of what kind of language the Lord spoke to Adam and Eve in paradise. After all, if the scholastics of the Middle Ages discussed the problem of how many angels could dance on the point of a needle, whether Adam had a navel, or what the future of the human race would have been if Adam and Eve had remained innocent inhabitants of Eden, then why not discuss what language the Lord used when he made the most momentous decision about the human race?

My grandfather and my father went into business. Except for a career officer who retired as a general and with whom we had no contact, they were the only ones without university training. Certainly, my father would have been happier in an academic profession; he would have made an excellent lawyer, and it was his ardent wish that I study law. But he never tried to influence me when he discovered that I had developed other interests.

Except for the usual disturbances by wars, my father's forebears lived the quiet and probably conventional life of Protestant pastors and scholars. From my mother's side, however, there came a strand of religious dissenters. Members of her family, originally Spanish, had become suspect as possessors and readers of books by Erasmus of Rotterdam, condemned as heretical by the Church. This cannot be a mere family legend. An old aunt of mine, totally unversed in ecclesiastical history, asked me before her death in 1910 what the word "Erasmians" meant, which she had heard from her grandfather. I did not know it myself, until later I discovered its meaning. Whether my Spanish ancestors were declared-Protestants or merely doubters of the Catholic dogma, I do not know, but they did prefer exile to the stakes of the Inquisition and went to Nantes, the asylum of the French Huguenots until 1685, when Louis XIV revoked the treaty named after that city. Thus from Nantes they went to Belgium and from Belgium to Germany, where the father of the family was welcomed as a "mechanic," or "engineer," as we would say today. He was an expert in setting up complicated weaver's looms then unknown in Germany and may thus have contributed to the impoverishment of the German weavers in the middle of the nineteenth century. My mother looked exactly like one of the French beauties so lovingly painted by the French impressionists.

Since I myself was expelled from my home country, I sometimes ask myself whether there is some kind of hidden destiny in certain families.

My early youth was spent near the small village of Lam in the *Bayrische Wald* (Bavaria), where my father was co-owner of an industrial enterprise that still exists. I cannot say for certain whether the silent grandeur of the *Bayrische Wald* has made a deep and lasting impression on my mind, but I am inclined to believe that my philosophical pantheism has its roots in my early youth.

The question of the editors of this volume of whether I "identified" with anyone else, I can answer only in the negative. Nor can I remember that I had a "model" or a "hero." This may be due to the fact that my father, an outspoken liberal, was critical of so-called great men, and my mother possessed the wonderful gift of humor.

There was no cynicism in my family. On the contrary, there was much reverence for the depth and beauty of life, but it was never lodged in any fallible mortal. I also believe that even the most skill-ful psychoanalyst could not have discovered an Oedipus complex in the dark corners of my soul, unless he had succeeded in talking me into it.

At the customary age of six, I had to be broken in to go to school. The teacher whom I still think of with a sense of undivided reverence was an old and simple elementary school teacher in the little Saxon town of Bischofswerda, where my parents had moved after leaving Bavaria. When I was nine, he prepared me for the entrance examination of the classical gymnasium of the neighboring city of Bautzen. Its old walls, towers, and baroque streets can well compare with those of the most famous of the old German towns. flooded every year by thousands of visitors. Fortunately, it was off the typical tourist route. It greatly impressed me that the nave of the Cathedral of St. Peter, built in the sixteenth century, was divided by a magnificent fence, with the Catholics—mostly Wendish —preaching and praying on the one side and the Protestants on the other. There has never been any disturbance. Bautzen now belongs to the Russian-dominated East Zone of Germany, and the street signs are in both German and Wendish, a slavic dialect closely related to Czech.

Again, I do not know to what extent the wealth of perceptions I received in the old capital of Eastern Saxony has influenced my mind. Youth inhale impressions without being aware of them; only later one begins to reflect upon them, and then one's memory may blend facts and illusions. But one thing I know is that none of the teachers of the gymnasium, in history, geography, or Latin (there were Latin inscriptions all around) ever made use of the rich chances which Bautzen offered to connect verbal instruction with historical concreteness.

This leads me to some highly contradictory observations about my experiences as a pupil in the three gymnasia which I attended because my parents moved from Bischofswerda to Leipzig and then to Dresden. On the one hand, I am deeply indebted to the linguistic training I received, not only because later in my historical studies I could read the originals instead of being dependent on secondary sources, but also because the introduction into our intellectual tradition prevented me from being lost in the present. It gave me perspective and provided me with some insight into the depth, the beauty, and the failures of the human situation. The language I liked most was Greek.

But I sometimes feel that the inner enrichment I derived from the nine years of the gymnasium came to me despite more than through my teachers. Only a very few taught me more than just plain surface knowledge. One of them was the rector (headmaster) of the Dresden Royal Gymnasium, a cousin of my father, with whom twice a week in the last grade we read some of the plays of Sophocles. From any pedagogical point of view, his method of teaching was inexcusable. Of the twelve pupils in my class, all of them already selected for advanced classical studies, ten were to the rector, a great scholar and contributor to a well-known world history, nonexistent entities. Why lose time with them? Instead, he concentrated on my friend Hans Schauer and me, and under his guidance we entered deeper into the language and spirit of Sophocles than we could have hoped to do under any famous university professor. He also was the man who during my university years introduced me to Hegel. I have never become an "Hegelian" or a "Kantian" or a sectary of any system of thought, but I still believe that the sweep of Hegel's ideas, combined with a gigantic dialectical power, represents one of the greatest attempts of the human mind to comprehend its place in the evolution of history.

Despite all gratitude for my classical education, I have become increasingly convinced that it was a pedagogical scandal. Most of the teachers despised or ridiculed any attempt on the part of educational reformers to improve the teaching methods and the teacher-pupil relationship in the secondary schools. The outcome of their instruction was extremely low. After nine years of Latin (seven to eight hours a week), six years of French and Greek, and three years of English or Hebrew, only a very few of us could read a foreign text with joy and facility, though most of us certainly had a good I.Q., came from relatively cultured families, and were from Monday to Saturday overstrained with class attendance and homework.

I have often asked myself one question, already raised in 1861 by the Englishman Herbert Spencer in his famous essays, *Education: Intellectual, Moral and Physical.* He expressed the opinion that men growing up in the oppressive school environment of the old English public schools would, when entering positions of power, be tempted to let out their pent-up resentments on their inferiors. I, too, believe that aggressiveness (which is the reverse of anxiety) and chauvinism (which often is the overcompensation of inferiority complexes), as well as the tyrannical father role in many European—by no means exclusively German—families, have their origins partly in the atmosphere of mutual siege and hostility between teachers and pupils.

During the later years of adolescence, I intended to study theology and instead of English chose Hebrew as my fourth language. But even before I left the gymnasium I decided otherwise. Lessing's great drama of tolerance, *Nathan the Wise*, which we read in the eighth grade of the gymnasium, taught me that there may be infinitely more greatness of mind in a Jew or in a follower of Islam than in a Christian. About the same time, I read the book on Buddhism by the Englishman, Rhys Davids. And when I bought some books on the history of Christianity, I discovered its missionary complex as a consequence of its claim to superiority, its alliance with insidious political powers, its hatred against free minds, and its persecution mania even within its own ranks. Evidently, every organization that claims to be absolute and tries to control the passage of man to the holy invites the devil of totalitarianism.

Nevertheless, despite my disillusion, I have never forgotten what Christianity gave to millions of mankind and could have given to even more if its teachings had been heeded by the powerful of the world, especially by the churches themselves. The "Grand Inquisitor" and "Father Zossima's Conversations" (both in Dostoevski's *The Brothers Karamazov*) are still for me the greatest symbolizations of Christianity: on the one hand, trust perverted into power-seeking institutionalism; on the other, the gospel of love and mutual responsibility. It is idle to muse whether both the bad and the good would also have occurred if Christianity, partly by its inner persuasiveness and partly by sheer power, had not defeated its religious rivals. However, we have to accept history as it has come down to us, even if we would like to change it.

Philosophically untrained, as I still was as a boy of seventeen, I believed for a while in the crudely materialistic philosophy of the Darwinist Ernst Häckel, whose *Welträtsel* (*Riddles of the Universe*) was then a bestseller all over the world. But only in the juvenile state of rebellion against everything that smacked of tradition did I lose the conviction that man's way of transcendence from self to world eventually leads into metaphysical and ontological grounds, which, at least for me, have a religious relevance.

When, at the age of nineteen, I entered the university, I naturally tried to find clarity in the study of philosophy. I had already read some Schopenhauer as a gymnasiast, now I occupied myself intensely with Kant's *Critique of Pure Reason.* I still believe that no one has a right to teach philosophy (whatever his convictions) who has not vicariously participated in the gigantic struggle of this little man of Königsberg to clarify the boundaries between human intelligence (*Verstand*), human reason (*Vernunft*), and the ultimate essence of life (Das Ding an sich).

I also read Hegel, who, before World War I, was much more popular in Russia, and even in Holland and England, than in Germany. Only Professor Georg Lasson of the University of Berlin, editor of Hegel's works, was a stalwart Hegelian. Among the students, perhaps even among his colleagues, he was considered somewhat queer. Since then, there has been a kind of Hegel renaissance in every country.

In spite of my prevailing interest in philosophy, I saw so many avenues toward knowledge in the fields of higher learning that it took considerable time before I knew whither to go. Germany offered the great opportunity to study at different universities. So, in order to listen personally to a professor whose books had attracted my interest, I studied, after Freiburg, at the universities of Neuchatel, Munich, Berlin, and Leipzig where finally I wrote my doctoral thesis, a monograph on the rather obscure German poet Chr. F. Scherenberg, and also passed the examination required for teachers of secondary schools. My fields were philosophy, German language and literature, history, and Latin. I never attended a course in "*Pädagogik*", which is probably the reason that I later became interested in education. Just as in this country, the typical courses in the history and methods of that field enjoyed no great reputation. In addition, I did not intend to become a teacher.

At the end of my academic studies, World War I broke out. I never shared the war enthusiasm of my contemporaries, for I saw no reason why the assassination of the Austrian archduke Ferdinand in the Bosnian city of Sarajevo, where he had no business in the first place, should throw the civilized world into the holocaust of officially legitimized, but nevertheless inhuman, mass murder. Perhaps, so I often thought later, that which we call "civilization" is only a thin veneer laid over an intellectually and technically highly organized barbarism. Only in certain individuals there burns the light of humanity. When mass instincts are unleashed (and all great institutions, states as well as churches, have used them for their purposes), these individuals are pushed aside, if they are not shot or burned.

When, in 1918, the war was over, I was a young man of twenty-eight and had to decide about my professional career. Do we, so I ask myself sometimes, really "decide" our future, or are we not more the driven than the drivers in our vocational as well as in our personal life, in our actions as much as in our idleness, in our alienations as much as in our love? There are, of course, persons who from their early youth know exactly what they want to become—physicians, scientists, lawyers, or teachers. I never belonged to that group, simply because I had too many interests.

Soon after I had passed my doctoral examination, I was invited to become a fellow in the *Institut für Kultur und Universalgeschichte*, founded by the historian Karl Lamprecht, one of the main participants in the awakening interest in comparative historical, religious, and anthropological studies. Karl Lamprecht and Wilhelm Wundt at Leipzig, Max and Alfred Weber, Ernst Troeltsch and Gerhart von Schulze-Gaevernitz, at other universities, were those to whom the intellectually more ambitious German students listened in their desire to jump the fences of narrow specialization. When I entered the institute, Lamprecht had already died. The war brought to nil his plans of international historical cooperation. I myself had planned to devote my time to two projects, not being certain which one to choose: either a study of the impact of the revolutions of 1840 and 1848 on German belles lettres or a study of medieval Latin poetry. As it developed, I found time only to prepare the translation of the *Carmina Burana, Vagantenlieder aus der lateinischen Dichtung des zwoelften und dreizehnten Jahrhunderts,* published in 1927 by the famous German publisher Eugen Diederichs.

When the shortage of teachers became more and more urgent during the war, I resigned from the institute and accepted an appointment at the Thomas Schule of Leipzig. The school was famous, not only for its high scholastic standards, but also for its boys' choir, a reputation stemming from the days when Johann Sebastian Bach had been the organist of the Peterskirche, where the concerts of the choir took place. I probably did well as a teacher of German literature in the upper grades of the gymnasium, then the equivalent of the first two years of an American college, but my Latin instruction in the first grade with boys at the age of ten was an unforgivable sin. Unable to arouse in myself any enthusiasm for the first rules of syntax and the daily vocabulary drill, I taught just as I had been taught myself, which means I taught miserably. But, at least, I had a bad conscience about it.

I believe there is a deep problem involved in teaching young children. The creative type of man might well engage in research in teaching methods or, as did the great Erasmus of Rotterdam, offer models for it. But he would despair of being forced to teach the rudiments of knowledge to young people year after year. Only the love for children, the interest in their development, the participation in their efforts and sorrows, and the contact with their parents can change the routine of teaching into an ever self-renewing event. Therefore, women with a motherly spirit should be the teachers of the very young, though not exclusively as in the United States. Even here difficulties arise. Once, when lecturing before a Canadian audience, I expressed my admiration for women who devote their life to the instruction of little children and thus deprive themselves of many natural and intellectual experiences given to other women. At the end of my lecture a prioress approached me. She had that spiritualized and somewhat ascetic, yet friendly, face we sometimes meet in truly priestly persons: "Professor, you should not admire nor pity them too much. For thirty years I have observed hundreds of these females. After some years most of them have little left to sacrifice. They have become themselves like children, many, alas, even childish."

Added to my professional difficulties was my fear of spending life at an institution such as the Thomas Schule, with teachers who enjoyed the glory of a long tradition without adding anything to it. Also, I had become deeply critical about the value of mere erudition in human culture. Too many of the learned in academia had dipped into a lot of scholarly books, but had not read in the book of life. When compared with my parents, who had not studied, their immaturity was patent. After a year at the Thomas Schule, I gladly accepted an opportunity to work at one of the middle-sized metal plants in the industrial center of Berlin. Though as a child at Bischofswerda I often had accompanied my father through the glass factory of which he was a co-owner, I now observed for the first time as a mature man the life of the industrial worker at the beginning of this century. During the war, these highly skilled workmen were in demand and were reasonably well paid. But in 1917 food had already become scarce and the wives, who themselves had been working before they married, were incapable of preparing something palatable out of little. The men were tired; for three years they had had no vacation or weekends. Furthermore, they had become aware of the serious shortage of raw material caused by blockades of the Allies. Understandably, they listened to leftist Socialists and Communists who called for a revolution, although such agitators were not even necessary. The workers had but to listen to returning wounded soldiers in order to understand the military and moral gravity faced by the nation. Government spies were identifying the more outspoken workers, who suddenly were dispatched to the most perilous places at the war front. There, unexpectedly, some of them still lived long enough to spread the gospel of revolution.

In Berlin I began to change my whole conception of education. What society needed—so I now began to understand—was a form of total reeducation or re-formation of the social body in its entirety. There was some truth in the claim of Karl Marx that the worker has no fatherland. Indeed, a large part of the population lived under humiliating conditions and could well believe that they were exploited by the unholy trinity of state, church, and money. But just as I never became a Kantian or a Hegelian, likewise I never became a Marxist. The typical Socialist meetings disappointed me. The orators used Marxian slogans, especially that of the "class struggle," without penetrating deeper into the thought of Marx. It never dawned on them that he, as all mortals, was influenced by his time and environment. I was especially disturbed by the fatalistic character of his materialistic determinism, which was in striking contrast to the evangelism of his *Communist Manifesto* and his utopian image of the classless society. Nevertheless, just as my historical thinking was partly influenced by Hegel, so it came to be also partly influenced by Marx, who, as modern research has proved, was philosophically closer to Hegel than was originally understood. But whatever one may think about the relation of Marx to Hegel, I can no longer believe in the older personalistic forms of humanism or in the omnipotence of the individual in shaping the course of human events. Have we not all felt that insane powers sweep over us like breakers and that in spite of our best intentions we are unable to help the millions who are thrown against the rocks? Under the influence of Marx I have also become increasingly critical of all those high-sounding slogans that work like narcotics on the instincts and minds of men until, like drunks, they no longer see that their path leads to a precipice. Nothing is more dangerous to mankind than the divine gift of faith uncontrolled by the equally divine gift of reason.

Observing the tragic forces which century after century have foiled the human desire for progress and happiness, I sometimes have difficulty in avoiding the traps of disillusionment. But to all the sources which so far have sustained me—a happy youth, poetry, philosophy, and the contemplations of the great religious prophets —I must also add the conviction that nothing rusts the springs of action and leads to corrosion of the heart more quickly than continual criticism and emphasis of the negative. Schopenhauer's pessimism and the Buddhist negation of life can be easily defended on empirical grounds, for the will to live can create more suffering than joy and more errors than truths. Conversely, all love, hope, work, and joy involve a risk, but only through them can we fulfill our lives. Withdrawal is cowardice.

After these personal confessions, let me now go back to the influence of my Berlin experiences on my thinking regarding the role of education in the life of man. What forces do really educate us? I would answer, the family and schools to a degree, but in addition there are also the traditions which form our judgments and prejudices; the communal and national environments; the people with whom, under whom, and above whom we have to work; our loves, hopes, and disappointments, and infinitely more. In comparison with the magnitude of these surrounding powers, how narrow our typical concepts of education seemed to me then, a narrowness which still prevails today in our teacher training institutions. Of course, our teachers have to be trained for the specific methodological and psychological tasks in the classroom, but unless they see their pupils as growing participants in the struggle of man for a decent society and help them to understand what constitutes human greatness or human baseness and what causes the rise or fall of civilizations, teachers are not the trustees of the intellectual and moral capital of society but merely part of its bureaucracy.

Such were the thoughts that began to germinate in me when I walked from the factory in the midst of Berlin's *Arbeiterviertel* (workers quarter) in the eastern part of the city to my apartment in one of the western suburbs. How welcome, then, was a letter from Walter Hofmann, director of the Leipzig public libraries, who invited me to assist him in a new adventure in adult education. Hofmann, originally an engraver (if I remember correctly), had been invited by a major industrial company to organize a library for its workers, only to discover that they, their wives, and their older children came, often with baskets, to borrow books that could lead only to confusion and bewilderment. He also refused to use the library's money for buying and lending cheap entertainment literature. Only books of artistic, literary, scientific, and general educational value were distributed, and for each reader a card was kept in the library from which one could observe his interests. Soon it was discovered that the majority of the users were totally without the experience needed to know which books they wanted to read or should and could read. Young men and women, eager to improve their education and perhaps their vocational opportunities, borrowed books that were too difficult and could only cause a sense of frustration. Others who had sought books for their leisure had never heard that the German literature, as any other great literature, contained hundreds of highly valuable books which could enrich a person's life, widen his horizon, and yet entertain him and even make him laugh. Trash is not necessary. In other words, that which was indispensable in our nonprofessional public libraries was not only books but advisers who could tell people how to use them.

When the city of Leipzig, then Germany's greatest center of publishing and printing, decided to establish a public library with branches in the different parts of the community, it invited Walter Hofmann to be its guiding spirit. After some years he asked me to join him. That was the beginning of my work in adult education, which I still consider one of the happiest parts of my professional work. With Walter Hofmann I edited the journal *Die Bücherhalle*. My work at the Leipzig *Bücherhallen* was also the beginning of my personal contact with the trade unions of such highly trained artisans as printers, compositors, and binders. Of course, many of my former academic acquaintances disapproved of my venturing into such a plebeian enterprise as popular education. Moreover, they were convinced, and rightly, that my contact with Socialists would spoil my hopes for a university career.

The situation changed when the outbreak of the revolution, November 3, 1918, made them afraid that Germany might follow the way of Russia. Then several of my so-called friends who recently had avoided my company visited me in my library, situated in one of the poorer sections of the city. They diligently assured me of their sympathy with the new cause and asked me for referrals, erroneously believing that I had influential connections.

Such turncoats, found in all ranks of society, I later encountered in the Ministry of Education, especially after the murder of Walter Rathenau when for a short while it looked as if the leaders in the republic had gained enough courage to clean out the reactionary officials from its higher bureaucratic echelons.

After several years of my activity in the field of adult education, the Saxon Ministry of Education followed the example of the Prussian government and established a special office for adult education in 1921. Since I was the only person with the necessary academic credentials who had worked in this field, I was appointed to organize the new department. Only a very few members of the bureaucracy had any understanding of my work. They were convinced that nothing but the desire for a quick career had caused me to join the Socialist party, which in their opinion had been responsible for "the stab in the back" of the otherwise "victorious" German army, for the inflation, and, of course, for the decay of German patriotic self-consciousness.

Permit me a little ancedote about officialdom which, I am afraid, applies to many countries. On my first round of official visits in the Ministry of Education I met a relatively young man who was a member of the Democratic party and thus as far left as a self-respecting person could go. With a serious expression he said to me: "May I give you some advice? If you want to stay here, never assume any responsibility. Always shift it to your superior." Not long after, I discovered that he had said so in a mood of bitter irony. When the Nazis came to power, he committed suicide.

In spite of all the obstacles at the beginning, I succeeded in changing Saxon adult education from a rather conventional and somewhat charitable enterprise into a truly educational movement that attracted not only the middle classes, but also workers whom we particularly wished to reach. A large part of my time was spent on the education of the educators. Having taught mostly in secondary schools, largely gymnasiums, and having studied at universities, these teachers were totally unprepared for the new task. Not realizing that true popularization is by no means a cheapening and dilution of knowledge, but rather an illumination of its essence by elimination of its technical accretions, they struck the foreign words from their old university notebooks and other academic paraphernalia. In other words, they "taught down to the people" instead of lifting their own learning to the level of true humanity. But how to change the attitudes and behavior of an instructor so that he may go beyond being a pedantic purveyor of mere subject matter to be a teacher of meaning? The same problem that hung over the schooling of the young appeared now with special intensity in the courses for adults.

Attempting to get out of the predicament, I organized special weeks for adult educators during which outstanding scholars and teachers from various fields, mostly well-known university professors and artists, explained how they had gradually found their way from the stuff of knowledge into its essence. Naturally, we also provided ample room for discussion and for the friendly meeting of minds. To help disseminate our ideas, with my Thuringian colleague, Reinhold Buchwald, I edited a journal on adult education. In such ways we gradually succeeded in forming groups of men and women who understood how to attract striving individuals from all social classes. They in turn formed the core of culturally active groups in intellectually dormant small towns. In contrast to organizations for political or religious indoctrination, we laid value upon the free discussion of controversial topics. Everybody was invited to express his opinion. Needless to say, the rise of the Nazis was the death of free adult education. The evenings I spent for several years with a group of young workers belong to the fondest memories of my life as a teacher. These workers formed the nucleus of the first underground movement of Dresden against the Nazis and often met at my home. Unfortunately, they were inexperienced in the techniques of resistance, were soon detected and cruelly murdered in the cellar of a Dresden police station—unsung heroes who sacrificed their lives long before the resistance of others who names are now praised as symbols of the German love of liberty.

In 1923, the counselor in charge of higher education, Geheimrat Apelt, tiring of administrative duties under inefficient ministers, resumed his professorship at the University of Leipzig and recommended me as his successor. Thus, at the relatively young age of thirty-three, I became the official in charge of university affairs and professional appointments for all the institutions of higher education in Saxony. My main responsibility extended to the University of Leipzig (after Berlin and Munich, the largest German university) and the Institute of Technology (*Technische Hochschule*) of Dresden. In addition, I was in charge of the many cultural and scholarly responsibilities which connected Saxony with the other German states and the federal government. Somewhat distrustful as I had become of professorial politicking and intrigue, I considered it my right and even my duty not merely to accept the proposals of the faculties for new appointments, but to ask for the opinions of well-known experts at other scholarly institutions. Soon I discovered that Jewish scholars, though highly recommended by impartial experts abroad, were not even mentioned in the faculty nominations. Frequently, friendly negotiations helped to correct the injustice, but I was bold enough to persuade the Social Democratic or Democratic ministers to appoint Jewish or leftist scholars rejected by the faculty out of mere prejudice. Needless to say, the universities complained about the "violation of academic freedom" by the new Social Democratic administrator (though I was the one who had defended it). A special parliamentary committee was appointed, but in no case did the complaint of the universities go before the plenum. Later, in the United States, I discovered to my satisfaction that the scholars whom I had appointed under the protest of the faculty were men of international reputation. From my point of view, permanent university appointments should never be made without far-reaching inquiries. The danger of ingrowth or of the tyranny of special groups is great in every institution and especially immanent in scholarly circles.

The most time-consuming controversy in which I was engaged was the reform of the education of elementary teachers. Previously they had been educated at the so-called *Lehrerseminare* (normal schools), many of them founded at the beginning of the nineteenth century. No doubt, the old *Lehrerseminare* had their merits. They kept the profession of the elementary teachers close to the life of the common people because they were inexpensive and thus enabled parents in low-income groups to give their sons a better education than they themselves had received. The money which the state shrewdly spent for the education and housing of the seminarian it got back later by paying miserable salaries. During a large part of the nineteenth century the seminaries were almost the only centers of pedagogical interest. Through them the educational ideas of Pestalozzi, Froebel, and Herbart were transformed into practical media for the schooling of the young. Some of the leaders of the new movement became courageous defenders of the rights of the people against reactionary governments, with the result that between 1815 and 1860 the seminaries were looked at with some suspicion by state and church. But with the prolongation of school age, the advancement of knowledge, and the social requirements of a more urban democratic society, the old seminaries became obsolete and almost all teachers with an independent mind scorned their professional education as "pedagogy" of the narrowest kind, combined with religious and patriotic indoctrination. The teachers also resented the fact that in spite of their cultural responsibilities their profession was regarded as inferior by businessmen and the academic professions.

Sensing the need to raise the intellectual and social level of the school teacher, I believed these were two possible approaches. One, to establish special *Paedagogische Academieen,* the other, to combine the education of the elementary teacher with the programs of the universities. Heinrich Becker, the Prussian minister of education, an admired friend of mine and the last educational statesman Germany could boast of, contended that since the universities would always consider the education of the school teacher an unwelcome addition to their humanistic and scientific departments, he would choose the first alternative. Saxony and Thuringia, the two most leftist states in Germany, maintained that prospective teachers needed the broad cultural perspective of a university, not just an improved normal school. They should have the benefit of sitting at the feet of some great teachers, who, of course, would not even think of accepting a position in a segregated teacher training institution. In addition, my friends in Saxony and Thuringia believed they would never have a unified body of teachers if the education of the elementary school teacher remained separate from that of the teacher in secondary schools.

The resistance I met against the plan of a full academization of the elementary teacher was almost insuperable. Financial difficulties were advanced, though the unavoidable repair of the old seminaries would have been more expensive, and though at the same time millions were already being spent for secret rearmament. Furthermore, it was contended that the influx of inferior students (for who else would choose the career of an elementary school teacher) would dilute the academic standards of the university. This position was emphatically held by the organizations of the secondary school teachers who were afraid of losing their social status with unification of the teaching profession.

Unfortunately, whenever I had to battle for a new cause, I received only timid support from the Social Democratic ministers. Insufficiently educated, they stood in awe or with a feeling of lower-class resentment before the old officials, especially when they came from titled families. Paradoxically, when in about 1928 the political constellation changed and a lawyer from the rightist *Deutsche Volkspartei,* a certain Dr. Kaiser, became the minister of education, I met for the first time a superior with whom I could talk freely about political and educational problems. All the parties of the Right—so he told me—had given him orders to remove "that Social Democrat Ulich who apparently governs the Ministry of Education." He was also the man who, on the request of the philosophy department of the Technical University, signed my appointment as honorary professor in that department, an action that required considerable courage. I lectured first mainly on the problems of adult education. Then I changed over to the interpretation of the concepts of man as espoused by our great classical writers, especially Kant, Goethe, and Schiller. I also devoted considerable time to Nietzsche.

Increasingly, I became interested in comparative education. Through the good offices of Isaac Kandel and Abraham Flexner, I was given the welcome chance to lecture and travel in the United States for half of the year of 1930. It was a great pleasure for me that thirty-eight years later, on the invitation of my friend and former pupil, Professor George Bereday, I wrote the introduction to the new edition of Abraham Flexner's book, *Universities: American, English, German*, some parts of which I had discussed with him in New York. I then warned him that he thought too highly of the German universities, which, from my point of view, had declined after World War I. I wish he had been right and I had been wrong.

When, in the fall of 1930, I returned to Germany, the National Socialist party, which we believed to have been defeated some years before, had won a major victory in the elections. My freedom of action became increasingly limited, and I felt that I could be more useful if I devoted myself full time to my professorship and to writing. The new minister of education, who had been a highly placed judge and one of the leading men in the reactionary *Deutschnationale Volkspartei*, was afraid of doing anything that could offend the Nazis, then a still relatively small group of young, noisy, and uneducated men who gleefully joined the Communists in the mutual endeavor to destroy the republic. *Les extrêmes se touchent.* Although I never had any illusions about the reactionary attitude of the majority of the German judges, I had difficulty in believing my ears when one day the new minister told me that he could not approve my plan to name a new foundation for the support of young writers in honor of Lessing (who was born in 1729 in the

Saxon town of Kamenz and whose two hundredth birthday had been celebrated throughout Germany). "Yes," he said, "I first supported your idea. But I don't want to have difficulties with my friends in the party and especially with the National Socialists. After all, Lessing wrote *Nathan the Wise*, in which the Jew Nathan is portrayed as a figure of supreme virtue. This is impossible."

I followed the old Buddhist advice to breathe three times deeply when one fears to be overcome by blind rage. But even this wise counsel would not have helped me if I had not just been prepared for the shock during a recent vacation in my Bavarian home village where I learned that children in school and church were told that the Jews were "Christ-killers" and would have to pay for this sin at the day of judgment. Ignored was the fact that apparently God himself had selected the Jews to bring about the "salvation of mankind." Could this be, I asked myself, the Germany that boasted of a Kant, Goethe, and Schiller?

About 1930 trouble began also in the universities. A growing number of students disturbed the class when a professor explained the development of the idea of freedom and tolerance in the eighteenth century, or spoke objectively of democracy and efforts for international conciliation.

The genesis of the Nazi regime has been so often described—though still not yet in all its various political and ideological ramifications—that I need not carry coal to Newcastle. I should only mention one experience which might be of interest to the political historian. After the dismissal of Chancellor Brüning by the decrepit *Reichspräsident* von Hindenburg, there came first the cabinet of von Papen. Its slogan was the same we now hear in the United States: "to restore law and order in an immoral society." Unfortunately, von Papen was not a person to serve as an example to the bewildered German citizen. He was soon succeeded by a General von Schleicher, the last hope to break the rapidly swelling wave of Hitlerism. During Schleicher's chancellorship I suddenly received a direct call from the Reich government to attend immediately a conference of the highest political importance. This invitation contradicted all the rules of protocol, according to which an official of a state could be invited by the Reich only via his own chancellery. When I came to the meeting, I met a most unusual gathering of about twenty people: a group of trade union leaders and, surprisingly enough, a relatively large group of army officers, mostly young. However, I was not too much surprised because I knew that, facing the imminent danger of nazism, contacts had been established by otherwise alien groups, the trade unions and the army. They apparently hoped that their combined opposition might prevent the seizure of power by Hitler. So far, the officers had welcomed the rearmament, but they did not want an Austrian corporal as their highest commander. The meeting began hopefully. But before long, a retired general known as an outright reactionary and leader of the movement of the "*Ertüchtigung*" (reinvigoration) of the "corrupt German people" began a long tirade in which he said almost everything that should not have been said. Heaven knows how he had heard of and could intrude upon this meeting. Certainly spies were everywhere.

But it was now too late anyhow. Too many conservatives had hoped to use the Nazis as a gadfly on the body of democracy. Many officers, retired after the defeat of 1918, now found a new occupation in training Nazi brownshirts and storm troopers. I once asked a close relative of one of these officers whether they were not afraid of saddling a horse that would throw them off when led out into the open. He only smiled: "Don't bother. We have learned how to ride a horse."

I am now sorry for the man. After the invasion of Dresden by the Russians he was, together with some of his relatives, carried in an overloaded truck to one of the so-called *Adelslager* (nobility camps) on the island of Ruegen. I heard later that he died from exhaustion.

Also, a goodly number of capitalists were duped by the National Socialist party and helped finance it in 1931 when it suffered severe setbacks and ran out of money. Hoping to get rid of the trade unions and socialism (which they stubbornly identified with communism), of atheism (although they themselves did not believe in anything), of the ever swelling number of bureaucrats (although they had themselves had an unduly great influence in the ministries), and even of taxes (which they had carefully evaded), they believed whatever they wanted to believe in the wild array of Hitler's promises for the "Thousand Year Reich." Surely, one can apply to them what Dostoevski, in *The Brothers Karamazov,* says about dogmatic scientists: "But they have only analyzed the parts and overlooked the whole, and indeed their blindness is marvelous." To certain industrial captains, even this would be a compliment. They did not even "analyze the parts."

When the Nazi flag was hoisted on the government buildings, I went to the Nazi minister, who had just arrived. Without waiting for what I wanted to say, he told me that he had already signed the dismissal of racially and politically undesirable professors. "Well," I said, "I just wanted to make sure that I am among them." During the following days, most of my political friends were imprisoned. I myself would certainly have been among them, if I had not been married to Elsa Brandstrom, daughter of the Swedish general and ambassador to Russia, Edward Brandstrom. She had been living for years with the war prisoners in Siberia and saved thousands of the inmates of the Russian war camps from starvation, freezing to death, and mortal diseases, mostly typhus. (Many German towns have now a street or girls' school named after her.) I am now certain that the Foreign Office, knowing of my Swedish connections, had intervened on my behalf. Nevertheless, the situation was highly unsafe. My house was watched, and I had to tell my students who wanted to continue our seminar at my home that they were followed by the Nazi police. Some of them, first seduced by the Nazi promises of German restoration, were totally perplexed and literally wept on my shoulders.

Under these circumstances, my wife and I were extremely happy when in the fall of 1933 I received an invitation from Dean Henry Wyman Holmes to lecture in the Harvard Graduate School of Education for one year. Initially, my appointment was supported by the Karl Schurz Foundation and then by the Carnegie Corporation, whose president, Frederick Keppel, had met me at the Conference on Examinations at Eastbourne, England, in 1931. President Keppel was the father of Francis Keppel, who served as dean of the Graduate School of Education from 1948-1962. In 1935, I was appointed to a professorship.

The first years were difficult. Having had Hebrew at the gymnasium, I had acquired my English through a correspondence course. I still admire the patience of my first American students. In addition, despite my interest in comparative problems, my knowledge of the American educational scene was inadequate, philosophically as well as historically. I began with a thorough study of the works of John Dewey, who was then the guiding spirit in a large majority of philosophy departments and especially departments of education. Much though I admired him as a thinker, and still more as a person, I was unable to join the overwhelming number of "Deweyites" who from their center at Teachers College, Columbia University, at that time placed their disciples in most of our institutions for the training of teachers.

Although fully agreeing with John Dewey that we have to replace older dogmatic views, be they philosophical or religious in nature, by a more dynamic and empirical outlook toward the problems of life and man, I refused to make a new dogma out of "empiricism," "instrumentalism," or whatever the "isms" were. I simply asked the question: How *can* man be empirical, how *can* he invent and use instruments, physical as well as intellectual, and how *can* he experiment within a systematic sequence of ideas and with some hope for success? My own answer was only by transcending his subjective self towards a greater self; only because he lives, physically as well as mentally, within a self-directing whole which he can intuit only by dint of such images as the Indian Atman, the Greek *Hen kai Pan* (the One and the All), cosmos (which means order, just as with Confucius), or Logos (the spiritual principle), or God. Man does not invent his own logic, just as he does not invent himself. Rather through learning, in the widest sense of the term, can he grow into, or become a participant in, man's common search for meaning and for a permanent reality within the ever changing flux of appearances. Otherwise we could not explain the transmission of ideas from generation to generation, which is the requisite of all culture and civilization. If each of us thought and experimented just for and out of himself, at his particular place and his particular time, how could we still read Plato, or how could an Indian scholar check on the solution of a mathematical problem attempted by a Frenchman? Thus, in my first book on educational philosophy, *Fundamentals of Democratic Education* (1940), I coined the awkward phrase of "self-transcendent empiricism," not satisfactory, but the best I could find. Some parts of this book were republished in my *Philosophy of Education* (1961).

In spite of my metaphysics or "mysticism" at it was sometimes pejoratively called, I have never abandoned the Kantian assertion that our human reason can move only within the world as it *appears* to us. There is no guarantee that it may enter into the innermost secret of being. Nevertheless, what we call "truth" is not merely a theoretical fiction of the human mind. It is a never ceasing attempt to live, mentally as well as physically, according to the inner order we try to discover in the universe of being. Therefore, truth is not only of intellectual and moral nature; it is also eminently practical. The more we live according to truth, the greater is our chance for individual and collective survival. And the more certain sinister powers within and without us try to distort, to deflect and abuse man's natural desire for spiritual, rational, and moral truth, the more they contribute even to his physical decline. The mass murder of modern wars is cruel proof of it.

It is a truism which does not need to be constantly repeated that men, dependent as they are on time and environment, have different concepts of the *bonum, verum,* and *pulchrum.* And we have all met a so-called human being who apparently has no room nor the slightest desire for such values in his sick soul. This, however, does not take a gram away from the weighty fact that only man's aspiration for what I have sometimes called "the Ever Greater" changes humanity from a mere mass of struggling creatures into a moral community.

I have developed these ideas more systematically in my *The Human Career* (1955). This book, as several others, has been translated into various languages. But, against the high hopes of the publisher, in spite of most favorable reviews by outstanding philosophers, and in spite of the almost embarrassing praise of a number of individual readers, it had little success either in the United States or in Germany. In the former, the book was an embarrassment to the still dominating schools of Deweyism, positivism, and relativism; in the latter, it was silenced by the churches which then dominated the educational press. For nothing irritates the ecclesiastical powers more than writers who are religiously open to the *tremendum et numinosum* in all life, but refuse to have it chained by dogmatic assertions. Nevertheless, it is in Germany that *The Human Career,* (published under the title *Weg und Weisung* in an excellent translation by Count Stanislaus von Kalckreuth, the best friend of my eldest son who was killed in the war) has been welcomed by a steadily growing free religious movement, *Die Religionsgemeinschaft Deutscher Unitarier.* The best and rather extended analysis of *The Human Career,* as of my whole philosophy, has been made by the Italian scholar Giustini Broccolini under the title *L'emprismo transcendentale di Robert Ulich* (*I Problemi della Pedogogia, Anno XI, Maggio-Guigno,* 1965).

Soon I discovered that the one-sided admiration for John Dewey was partly due to the lack of historical knowledge on the part of educators. It seemed to many of them that his *Democracy and Education* (1916) was the only treatise on education worthy of reading. Moreover, before and after World War I, the courses on the history of education leaned heavily on Ellwood Cubberley's several histories of education and the accompanying source books. When in Europe I was grateful for them (as a first source of orientation about the United States). But used by teachers without some knowledge of the broad cultural developments of which education is but a part, they must have been deadly. Indeed, they enjoyed the reputation of organized boredom all over the country. "You are teaching education?" College graduates would tell me with a benign smile, "Oh yes, we still remember Cubberley"!

So I wrote my *History of Educational Thought* (1945) in which I tried to prove that those men who determined the course of Western education were not concerned merely with schools and with didactic methods, but were great thinkers and often courageous reformers. Most of them harbored a profoundly mystical trend—even Dewey, despite all his struggles against it. Education was for them a continual process of the examination, transmission, and re-formation of human values and, most of all, a process of inspiration.

Not satisfied with merely writing *about* these men and their ideas, I later published my *Three Thousand Years of Educational Wisdom* (1947), an anthology with large introductions to every major chapter. Here I could do—at least in some groping beginnings—what I would have liked to do in my *History of Educational Thought* and still would like to do if it were not for my inadequacy for the task, namely, to give Western readers some insight into the thought of the great educators of the East: the authors of the *Upanishads*, Buddha, Lao-Tse, Confucius, the teachers of Yogi, and many others. The task still remains to be done. Unfortunately, I was unable to convince any of the major American foundations to support my plan to create a comprehensive international thesaurus of educational philosophy. On one side of each page the original would have been printed, on the other side the English translation, both carefully edited by scholars of the particular country. In this way, we would have created the opportunity for a worldwide perspective of the educational ideals of great cultures and perhaps also for a better understanding of their differences. I still feel a mixture of fury and frustration when I remember the empty gaze in the eyes of the more or less prominent foundation clerks. Incredible though it sounds, they just did not understand what I was talking about. Was not everything "OK" in American democracy, especially in the schools? Why look around? This was at the end of and shortly after World War II. Today, in 1968, we think differently. Perhaps we may learn, and some younger scholars may take up my idea.

In the course of my historical studies I became increasingly aware of one deplorable lack in our historical knowledge. Except for two inadequate and obsolete books, I could discover no account of the history of religious education. This lack was probably a result of the growing secularization of American education and American thought in general. Even in church-affiliated circles I found an amazing degree of ignorance. Yet, it is a fact that before the nineteenth, perhaps to the middle of that century, the schools in most Western countries worked under the control of the churches and considered religious instruction an essential part of indoctrination. In several nations this is still the case. I therefore accepted an invitation of the Harvard Divinity School to join its ranks and give a course in this area. The outcome was *A History of Religious Education: Documents and Interpretations from the Judaeo-Christian Tradition* (published by the New York University Press, 1968).

But I will leave this earth with one plan unfinished—a history of universities. For more than twenty years I gave a course on this subject in the Harvard Department of the History of Science and

Learning to which the great historian of science, Professor George Sarton, had invited me. A tentative outline of the book has been published in the *Goals for American Education* (Conference on Science, Philosophy, and Religion, 1948). It was a real satisfaction to me that the commentators on this essay expressed the hope that it might be extended into a book. Here again, I must leave the younger generation to finish what I left uncompleted.

Another area of my scholarly interest was, naturally, comparative education. A considerable amount of literature already existed when I came to this country. But most of it—as is still the case today in comparative literature and similar fields—was not comparative at all, but consisted merely of a juxtaposition of the educational events in different countries. The only real exception was I. L. Kandel's *Comparative Education* (1933). This was a momentous undertaking which contained excellent chapters of general comparative character but drowned inexperienced teachers and their pupils in a mass of details in which they could not distinguish the important and permanent trends in a nation from the unimportant minutiae. In addition, the book suffered from the fact that the large chapter on Germany was already obsolete when the book became known. The Nazis had taken over. In my own attempt, as in the *History of Educational Thought*, I tried to incorporate the educational developments of the different countries into the broad stream of general culture. In the initial chapters I described the universal basis of Western education in ancient and mediaeval thought and culture; only after that introduction did I think I could count on the reader's understanding of the specific developments of education in the major nations of Europe. The success of the book, entitled *The Education of Nations* (1961), indicated the merits of this approach.

But who for long can compare the educational attempts of various nations without feeling an urgent concern for humanity as a whole, especially in a historical situation such as ours. Certainly, the nation encompasses and largely directs modern man's existence. But however much chauvinistic and totalitarian minds may regard the state as the final and absolute achievement in human history, it should be but one step in the development of the person from the cave dweller to the world citizen.

Therefore, I welcomed the invitation to join a group of Chicago professors who had formed a committee for the systematic discussion of our obligations (and also of our failures) in a period of tremendous global transitions. The result of my cooperation with these scholars was the book *Education and the Idea of Mankind* (1964), now published in paperback by the University of Chicago Press.

Among my literary efforts I will mention only one more, *Crisis and Hope in American Education* (1951; published in paperback in 1955). Here I attempted to develop the scheme of a secondary school that would combine unity and diversity: unity in fields where young people could be united, as in basic social obligations and the enjoyment of sport, dance, theatre, and certain kinds of manual work; differentiation where their interests and aptitudes varied, as in the pursuit of science, the humanities, administration, artisanship, and so on. I also tried to show that the execution of such a plan would require a completely new school architecture, not only a new type of classroom, but large workshops for all pupils—fields, gardens, and opportunities for farming. When I worked on the book, I thought I was writing of another utopia, for the financial expenses involved would be exorbitant. Last year we spent many billions on the Vietnam War and lived through a crisis which along with the lunacy of the Vietnam adventure is to a large part reducible to the meaninglessness of what goes on in our schools under the name of education. Though here and especially in England my book has induced some communities and their architects to reorganize their ideas about school grounds and buildings, I doubt whether it will have any great effect. One still prefers the futility of patchwork to the courage of reconstruction. Nothing sticks so tenaciously to the past, however obsolete, as habits of thinking. Some reviewers called the book "undemocratic." I thought I had written a truly democratic book.

So much about some of my literary productions. I now ask myself whether they influenced American education and the education of other countries. I am probably the last who could give an objective answer. But if I trust the opinions of my pupils and friends in many countries, my books rendered at least some service to American educators critical of the one-sided advocates of narrow empiricism, relativism, and environmentalism. I may also have productively irritated the kind of American progressive educators who mistook the absence of inner direction as evidence of progress. I remember that in my classes some students laughed when I mentioned such concepts as "discipline," "reverence," and "authority." They had never thought that bringing up a young person without the help of guiding concepts is just as much a crime against him and society as subjecting him to the dominion of fixed and externally imposed ideas which cripple or distort his inherent chance for individual maturity. "Culture" is not "nature" but nature productively transformed without being violated.

In the field of philosophy I am still a "controversial figure." To many of our young educators my work is of little significance in our age of computers, teaching machines, school strikes, and street riots; they are deeply involved with the immediate and have little time for the contemplative. On the other hand, if the continuous sales of my books and the several translations indicate the degree of influence of my labors devoted to the history of education and to comparative education, then I have apparently helped in changing the ahistorical or even antihistorical attitude of many teachers. The awareness seems to grow that in spite of all changes and revolutions there exists not only something like a *philosophia perennis*, but also an *educatio perennis*. How can one wisely change without knowing the roots of that which one wants to change?

With regard to my attempts at reforming American institutions of learning—well, I don't know. Some of my ideas came too early, though being early is better than being late. Certainly the growing integration of education within the whole structure of the universities as I recommended it in several of my writings proves to me that I was on the right path.

One last and probably surprising confession. When looking back on my life I do not know where its main emphasis lay, whether I was more of a scholar, a politically active administrator (as in Germany), or a poet. My first two larger publications were poetry, and now, while I am writing these lines, my German friends have prepared editions of two volumes of poetry, one with the title *Mensch und Kosmos*, the other with the title *Das Grosse Geheimnis* (both published 1968). Whatever their value, I know that poetic productivity gave me the opportunity to express the deep joys I could experience, as well as the deep sorrows I had to go through. Without this form of self-expression, I might not have survived the cruel calamities of my life—the rise of the Nazis, the forced emigration, and the destruction of some of my most cherished plans for the future of German higher education, the loss of my wife, Elsa Brandstrom, and the death of one of my two sons from my first marriage, who was fatally wounded at the battle of El Alamein.

However, I should not be ungrateful. I have continued to travel in many parts of the world. The months in 1966 which I was allowed to spend in Japan and Korea under the care of former students have enriched my life beyond all expectation. The continued loyalty of many of my best students and the blessing of long and enduring friendships have also been to me a source of profound encouragement. And despite my advanced age, I have still maintained some characteristics generally ascribed to healthy youth: physical elasticity, eagerness to learn and to enrich myself through the treasures of art and thought, the hope to grow with my plans and my work, the enjoyment of the company of young people, the love of nature, and the admiration of cultured men and women. I cannot imagine what my life would have been without them.

A BIOGRAPHICAL SUMMARY

ROBERT ULICH. Born April 21, 1890, in Lam, Bavaria, Germany.

Family. Married (1) Else Beil, 1918-27; (2) Elsa Brandstrom, 1928-46; (3) Mary Ewen Palmer, 1947-63. Children: Eckart, 1921; Konrad, 1923; Brita Brandstrom, 1931.

Education. Humanistisches Gymnasium, Riedermühl, Bavaria, 1900-09; Universities of Freiburg, Neufchatel, Munich, Berlin, Leipzig; Ph.D., University of Leipzig, 1915.

Occupational history. Research fellow, Institute of Comparative History, Leipzig, 1915-16; teacher and tutor in Thomas Gymnasium, Leipzig, 1916; librarian, public libraries of Leipzig, 1917-20; director, Department of Adult Education, Ministry of Education, Saxony, 1921-23, director of higher education, 1923-33; honorarprofessor, Dresden Institute of Technology, 1928-33; lecturer, Harvard University School of Education, 1934-36, professor of philosophy and history of education and comparative education, 1936-61.

Memberships and affiliations. American Academy of Arts and Sciences; Medieval Academy of America; National Academy of Education; Commission on Humanities of the American Council of Learned Societies.

Part II

Selected Publications of Robert Ulich

Books and Pamphlets

1. *Christian Friedrich Scherenberg: Ein Beitrag zur Literaturgeschichte des neunzehnten Jahrhunderts.* Leipzig: R. Voigtlander, 1915.
2. *Europa und seine Revolutionen.* Leipzig: T. Weicher, 1919.
3. *Carmina Burana. Vagantenlieder aus der lateinischen Dichtung des zwoelften und dreizehnten Jahrhunderts,* (Latin text, Max Manitius). Jena: E. Diederichs, 1927.
4. *A Sequence of Educational Sequences. Traced through Unpublished Writings of Pestalozzi, Froebel, Diesterweg, Horace Mann, and Henry Barnard.* Cambridge: Harvard University Press, 1935.
5. *On the Reform of Educational Research.* Occasional Pamphlets of the Graduate School of Education, Harvard University, no. 2. Cambridge: Graduate School of Education, Harvard University, 1937.
6. *Fundamentals of Democratic Education.* New York: American Book Co., 1940.
7. *History of Educational Thought.* New York: American Book Co., 1945 (rev. 1968).
8. *Conditions of Civilized Living.* New York: E. P. Dutton & Co., 1946.
9. *Three Thousand Years of Educational Wisdom: Selections from Great Documents.* Cambridge: Harvard University Press, 1947 (2d ed. enl., 1963).
10. *Man and Reality; Three Dimensions of Human Experience.* Hazen Pamphlets no. 21. Edward H. Hazen Foundation, Haddam, Conn., 1945.
11. *Religious Perspectives of College Teaching in the Preparation of Teachers.* Edward H. Hazen Foundation, Haddam, Conn., 1950.
12. *Crisis and Hope in American Education.* Boston: Beacon Press, 1951 (paperback, 1966).
13. *On the Conflict between the Liberal Arts and the School of Education* (with Howard Mumford Jones and Francis Keppel). American Academy of Arts and Sciences, 1954.
14. *The Human Career: A Philosophy of Self-Transcendence.* New York: Harper & Bros., 1955.
15. *Professional Education as a Humane Study.* Kappa Delta Pi Lecture Series. New York: Macmillan Co., 1956.

16. *Change and Continuity in Civilization.* Felix Adler Lecture, 1957.
17. *The Cleavage between Intellectual and Spiritual Life.* New York: Myrin Institute, 1958.
18. *The Education of Nations: A Comparison in Historical Perspective.* Cambridge: Harvard University Press, 1961.
19. *Philosophy of Education.* New York: American Book Co., 1961 (rev. 1967).
20. *Education and the Idea of Mankind* (editor). New York: Harcourt, Brace & World, 1964 (Phoenix Book, University of Chicago Press, 1968).
21. *Education in Western Culture.* New York: Harcourt, Brace & World, 1965.
22. *A History of Religious Education. Documents and Interpretation.* New York: New York University Press, 1968.

Contributions to Symposiums, Yearbooks, and Collections

23. "German Problems of Selection." In *Conference on Examinations* (Eastbourne). Under the Auspices of the Carnegie Foundation. Edited by Paul Monroe. New York: Teachers College, Columbia University, 1931.
24. "Germany." In *Educational Yearbook of the International Institute*, pp. 339-61. Edited by I. L. Kandel. Teachers College, Columbia University, 1936.
25. *The Training of Secondary Teachers, Especially with Reference to English.* Report of a Joint Committee of the Faculty of Harvard College and the Graduate School of Education. Cambridge: Harvard University Press, 1942.
26. *Introduction to Universities, American, English, German,* by Abraham Flexner (rev. ed. edited by Robert Ulich). New York: Teachers College, Columbia University, 1968.
27. "On the Rise and Decline of Higher Education." In *Goals for American Education*, pp. 1-18. Ninth Symposium of the Conference of Science, Philosophy, and Religion. New York: Harper & Bros., 1950.
28. "Ethics and Education." In *Moral Principles of Education.* Edited by Ruth N. Anshen. New York: Harper & Bros., 1952.
29. "Freedom and Authority in Education." In *Freedom and Authority in Our Time.* Twelfth Symposium of the Conference of Science, Philosophy, and Religion. New York, 1953.
30. "Symbolism and the Education of Man." In *Symbols and Society.* Fourteenth Symposium of the Conference of Science, Religion, and Philosophy. New York, 1955.
31. "This is My Faith." In *This is My Faith; The Convictions of Representative Americans Today.* Edited by S. G. Cole. New York: Harper & Bros., 1956.

32. "The American University and Changing Philosophies of Education." In *Issues in University Education.* Edited by Charles Frankel. New York: Harper & Bros., 1959.
33. Preface to *The Idea of a University* by Karl Jaspers. Translated by H. A. T. Reiche and H. F. Vanderschmidt.
34. "The Educational Issue." In *Religion and the Public Schools* (with Paul A. Freund). The Burton Lecture and the Inglis Lecture, 1965. Cambridge: Harvard University Press, 1965.
35. "The Person and Organization." In *Issues in American Education.* Edited by Arthur M. Kroll (to be published in 1970).

Poetic Works

36. *Dich lieb' ich, Erde,* 1912.
37. *Mensch und Kosmos,* 1968.
38. *Das Grosse Geheimnis,* 1968.

The foregoing list omits numerous articles published in German literary and professional journals.

Part III

Robert Ulich: the Stoic as Educational Statesman

Jonathan Messerli

The impact of Robert Ulich on American education is neither easily identified nor assessed. More indirect than direct, and more interpretive and normative than programmatic, the nature and limits of his influence were conditioned by a personal history relatively distinct from the other subjects of this volume. Ulich's educational career spanned two world wars and extended into the period of social and technological upheavals which followed. In a period of crumbling institutions and mounting despair, Ulich survived and succeeded where lesser men capitulated to passing ideologies, retreated into an irresponsible cynicism, or simply permitted themselves to be pushed and shoved like passive pawns on a social and intellectual chessboard when the squares as well as the figures kept changing their colors and positions.

It is also noteworthy that unlike many of his educational contemporaries, Ulich has been able to look back upon his career with considerable personal satisfaction. This is striking because he suffered great tragedy and disappointments in his life. By comparing his life story with the other autobiographies presented here, one is aware of his relatively singular sense of gratification and fulfillment. All of the others had a more stable life, all achieved a more prominent public image, and all laid just claims to having contributed in concrete ways to the modification of American educational structure and practice.

Ulich's culminating sense of accomplishment, which grew out of a troubled career, poses an interesting problem for the biographer. As his early aspirations for himself and his country were dashed by the rise of Hitler and the destruction of many venerable German cultural institutions, he might well have reacted with a repugnance toward his own nation and embraced a synthetic chauvinism for his adopted land. But he neither succumbed to bitterness nor to the blind loyalty of a recent convert. Instead, he built a new career on this side of the Atlantic upon the ruins of the past. Never an adherent to a closed political, religious, or intellectual system, and ever seeking a degree of intellectual autonomy, Ulich managed to think and fend for himself in a world of social upheaval and military conflict. What one notes in his autobiography is a carefully fashioned fusion of detachment and involvement. Avoiding the complete immersion of himself within a movement of the moment but remaining at arm's length, Ulich also avoided the disappointment and disenchantment which follow when men's dreams become false ideologies. Yet his detachment was never more than arm's length, and he therefore was able to remain intellectually involved with the development of new trends in curriculum, teaching, and administration and to serve as a responsible commentator on them.

Herein is to be found the reason for his more intangible impact on American education, and herein also lies the explanation for his own sense of satisfaction where more programmatic men have found a degree of disillusion and disappointment. Despite his passionate participation in living, working, and politics, in the course of his life Ulich developed a disciplined stoical detachment from man and institutions and walked the thin line of responsible criticism, careful neither to become a devotee of a passing movement or cause on the one side nor veer to the other by retreating into a scholarly asceticism. Detached, yet never alienated, he pursued an intellectual and professional course which eschewed dogmatic certainties and sought, in Clyde Kluckholhn's felicitous phrase, "conditional absolutes" appropriate to educational philosophies and practices. To give in to the temptation to step to either side was to court personal and professional oblivion, yet to follow the course he took required a special measure of wisdom, fortitude, and resolution, and it conditioned the impact and set the limits of his contribution to American education.

I

Robert Ulich was a member of that great intellectual migration which came to this country between the two world wars. To mention some of the leaders in various fields of learning is to recognize their importance to our academic world. Einstein was only the most celebrated among a host of natural scientists; Paul Lazarsfeld became a leader among the social scientists; in theology and philosophy there was Paul Tillich; Werner Jaeger continued his unparalleled research on the antiquities; and in architecture and aesthetics, Mies van der Rohe and Walter Gropius established canons of beauty and function which would guide a host of younger architects and designers. All these individuals and countless others drew inspiration from the achievements of German culture with its proud legacies of Beethoven, Goethe, Kant, and Wundt. All were the unfortunate victims of its destruction and survived by emigrating to these shores, coming here in the hope of finding new homes and advancing their *Wissenschaft*. Among their ranks was Robert Ulich, recently counselor in charge of Saxon Universities and *Honorarprofessor* in the Philosophical Faculty of the Dresden Institute of Technology.

As his autobiography makes patently clear, by this time Ulich had already learned the technique of survival, which included the strategy of establishing a certain separation between himself and the institution within which he worked. To him, institutions were easily corrupted and destroyed. Within them the individual could survive only by maintaining a disciplined involvement tempered by a degree of deliberate detachment. In the gymnasium where he began his classical training and established the basis for his remarkable talents in languages, he was neither a robot nor a revolutionary although, for those teachers who bored him, he was a troublesome and unruly individual. In some of his earliest professional activities, including the establishment of libraries and institutions for adult education, he did not totally immerse himself in one or another movement. Then, as each of these gave way under the rise of nazism, Ulich managed to survive. He had witnessed the destruction of the trade union movement, the cynical manipulation of a comprehensive state system of elementary and secondary schools, the prostitution of great universities to political purposes, and the collapse of constitutional government. Yet Ulich survived all of these disasters physically and intellectually.

A teacher among laborers, he understood the value of learning to the working man; a scholar among bureaucrats, he easily saw beyond the suffocating dailyness of managerial routine; an educator and administrator among university scholars and scientists, he could appreciate the contributions of Marx, Freud, and Weber, yet also be aware of the dangers posed to the search for truth by the specialization and politicization of knowledge.

That he would continue to follow his particular version of detached involvement was soon evident upon his arrival in this country. After the demise of the German universities, one might have expected him to espouse the virtues of a defunct and destroyed German intellectualism and scholarship within the security of one of the academic departments of the Graduate School of Arts and Sciences at Harvard. Instead, as Francis Keppel has observed, Ulich "joined the Faculty of a School of Education well knowing that it was neither fashionable nor an easy road for a new citizen." [1] The past had taught him both the need for expanding man's existing body of knowledge and the application of this knowledge to human problems. Here, at Harvard, a professional school of education which could all too easily emphasize the application of knowledge at the expense of rigorous scholarship was to be his intellectual domain for the remainder of his career.

Once his acculturation began, Ulich neither joined those who espoused various versions of John Dewey's philosophy of progressivism nor did he become their reactionary detractor. Either were possible alternatives for an expatriate. By the 1930s, the disciples of Dewey had registered some impressive gains in their efforts to make the learner the focus of the educational process. If one is to believe the exposé of Joseph M. Rice, American schools at the turn of the century had become temples to rote learning and memorization where children as unwilling novitiates were forced to conform to mechanical schedules, superficial patriotic rituals, and endless textbook drill and recitation. Coming from the broadest plurality of ethnic and economic origins, they were indoctrinated into a WASP version of obedience, Americanism, and morality, and motivated towards a materialistic version of the ethic of success with its components of ambition, acquisitiveness, and Anglo-Saxon *chutz-*

1. Francis Keppel, "A Tribute to Robert Ulich," in *Liberal Traditions in Education,* ed. George Z. F. Bereday. (Cambridge: Harvard University Press 1958) p. xvii.

pah. The pedantic and mind-dulling assignments, the regimented discipline, and the endless hours of memorization bereft of any sense of appreciation, meaning, beauty, or virtue Ulich had himself experienced as a student. Knowing the possibility of the irretrievable waste of countless hours of childhood with its potential for creativity and imagination stifled, he could now join William A. Kilpatrick, George Counts, and John Childs, who were mounting an attack on this same travesty as it was perpetuated on American children. Other Europeans did, and there was even a growing number of converts to progressivism in Russia. Reading Dewey as if the scales were finally dropping from their eyes and observing the results of the Dalton plan, the Winnetka system, and the work at Gary, Indiana, they were certain that herein lay the patterns for educational reforms in their own countries.

As in Germany, similarly in the United States Ulich refused to become an uncritical devotee either of the status quo or of the more radical movements at work to upset it. Confident and secure within an intellectual and philosophical framework he painstakingly had fashioned for himself through years of self-critical mental endeavor, he did not require membership in a new institutional security. Thus, he did not join those in the vanguard of progressivism who believed they were ushering in a millenium of peace and social justice through their child-centered curriculums, psychological testing, and use of the schools for eradicating bigotry, racism, and economic exploitation. Instead, Ulich preferred to use his professorship at Harvard as a platform for commentary and criticism, supporting those achievements of public education which were committed to the ideal of an entire nation going to school and, at the same time, using his own keen intellectual judgment to examine the philosophy of instrumentalism and pragmatism, a philosophy which appeared to support public education but which to him lacked a sense of direction and failed to define and articulate its hierarchy of values. "The degree of one-sided, often wrongly interpreted 'Deweyism' in our schools and colleges of education," he warned, "is a bad sign of their vitality." [2] From Germany he had all too painfully learned that every social and intellectual movement contains within itself

2. Robert Ulich, "Unity or Confusion," *Journal of Education* 137 (January 1955), 3-4, 32.

the seeds of its own perversion and destruction if not held up to constant evaluation and criticism.

Frequently after 1940, he pointed to the futility of a philosophy of education which had no better expressed goals than "social efficiency," "meaningful learning," and "growth for its own sake." Such loose thinking, he believed, was the product of intellectually naive educators, uncertain of their goals but innocently believing that a basically harmonious society would result if the scientific method was applied to education and the restructuring of society. For the schools to accomplish their mission, an "ordering focus" was needed. In his *Fundamentals of Democratic Education* (1940), Ulich sounded a warning to those Progressivists assembling under the new banners of "life adjustment" and the "core curriculum." To them he wrote:

> The belief that we have no criteria for our actions but action and no criteria for our experiences but new experiences may well be suited, indeed, to the democratic way of life if we have nothing else in view than its willingness to adapt itself to changing situations and to learn from experimentation. But such a philosophy is incomplete; it does not tell us how and why and where in this continuous change we have the right to set up freedom, friendship, responsibility, beauty, and reason as regulating principles just as necessary for a democracy as change and experiment.[3]

Unwilling to use the educational jargon of the Progressivists, Ulich was taken to task for his "confusion" and "vagueness." More serious in their eyes was the fact that as an educator he had committed the unforgivable sin of having attacked their inner tribal council and questioned their holy writings. For this he was made to pay a price. He was ostracized from important national educational commissions and committees then in their control. Unperturbed, he continued to teach, lecture, and write in a similar vein in the years which followed. In the last chapter of his *History of Educational Thought* (1945), he departed long enough from his conventional treatment of Plato, Luther, Erasmus, and Pestalozzi to declare that the quality of instruction in the public schools had declined to the point where "a principal reexamination of the theory in practice

3. *Fundamentals of Democratic Education* (New York: American Book Co. 1940), p. 129.

in education is more necessary than ever."[4] But nowhere did he make this claim more emphatic and prophetic than in his *Crisis and Hope in American Education* (1951). "With our continual propaganda for prolonged schooling, without thinking what kind it shall be, Ulich wrote, "we force many young people to march to a melody they do not like to a goal they will never reach."[5] By the early 1950s, others would join in their attack upon a progressivism which previously had died intellectually and spiritually and was now undergoing institutional and corporeal decay. Arthur Bestor began jousting with the "copper-riveted educational bureaucracy"; Albert Lynd uncovered all sorts of subversive ideas in Dewey's writings and therefore concluded that public education could be no good; and Admiral Hyman Rickover discovered that the Swiss schools were superior to ours, even if their navy was not. In the rising chorus of criticism, Ulich might have auditioned for a solo part, smug in the knowledge that since his earlier strictures had not been heeded, schoolmen had brought down a justifiable public wrath upon their heads.

Instead, he saw these latter-day attackers as pseudointellectuals, equally as misinformed as the hapless objects of their scorn and vituperation. Urging a "return to the essentials," these critics, Ulich thought, all too often presented a narrow reactionary point of view, easily palatable to a growing body of nervous middle-class parents worrying that their offspring would not be accepted by the "college of their choice." To such anxiety, the "quest for intellectual excellence" became an inspirational touchstone and promised the ready solution to a reformation of the schools. Homework came back in vogue, especially assignments in English, mathematics, and science, and teachers were increasingly judged on how well their charges performed on college entrance examinations. As Ulich had been perceptive enough to note the dubious goal of making the schools the vehicle for a vaguely defined and ambiguous social efficiency, he could be equally sharp in his criticism of those who wished to harness them to selfish parental interests or some national defense purposes.

4. *History of Education Thought* (New York: American Book Co., 1945).

5. *Crisis and Hope in American Education* (Boston: Beacon Press, 1951).

II

A similar combination of detachment and involvement can be noted in Ulich's intellectual style. For all the gains he recognized stemming from the expansion of the social and behavioral sciences with their sophisticated theories and empirical research techniques, he could also regret the loss of men with a capability for comprehending broad human problems in their totality. The new generation of scholars, Ulich believed, would be more narrow, if more precise, proverbially knowing more and more about less. Conversely, some of these younger scholars criticized him for his inability to utilize new analytic techniques and conceptual models from the social sciences. Although his *Education of the Nations* (1961) was studded with rewarding insights into such men as Luther, Franklin, and Jefferson and filled with the wise generalizations of a man of the broadest intellectual experiences, it was also scored for its lack of a systematic method of inquiry. Upon reviewing the book, A. H. Halsey noted Ulich's "urbanity and felicity of style," and then he went on to say that "without the discipline of sociological theory we are left only with respect for his sagacity, without certainty of our knowledge."[6] In a day when a new generation of students would read Daniel Moynihan, David Riesman, and Daniel Bell, Ulich's scholarship would appear too eclectic, metaphysical, and heuristic.

In his autobiography, Ulich has noted his debt to Marx as well as to Weber and Durkheim. Early in his career he had also been a fairly thoroughgoing student of Hegel and Kant. Although he frequently followed a mode of Hegelian thought and sometimes remarked to his classes in an offhand manner that the only way really to think was dialectically, he never became a convinced Hegelian, even as he was not a Freudian or a Marxist. But there was more here than an informed and skillful eclecticism. Ulich believed that the scholar must go beyond intellectual systems, religious creeds, and political institutions. Utilizing all of these, he must nevertheless transcend them and seek understandings and values which are not ego-bound but the result of the highest quality of rational

6. E.g., see his review in the *Harvard Educational Review* 32 (1962): 227-28.

thought. In general style and metaphysics, he was probably as close to Alfred North Whitehead as to anyone. But where Whitehead based his philosophical writings on mathematics and logic, Ulich leaned more heavily on history and his knowledge of the classics.

To those seeking a narrow analytic precision in their prose, Ulich's writings about the quest for transcendence seemed murky and vague. With some justification, his critics chided him for the ambiguity and evanescent quality of such terms as the "totality of creation," the "All-Embracing," the "cosmos," and the "Great Life." There was, then, the shortest of distances between profound generalization and inflated pontifications and platitudes. Seeking the "ineffable" in his writings, Ulich was in constant danger of moving from the one to the other. With some reason, the intellectual response to his books was mixed. One reviewer of his *The Human Career* claimed it contained "much wisdom and is . . . rich and broad in its learning," noting accurately that Ulich never remained "quietly within himself, but reaches or goes intellectually beyond himself into unknown spheres of reality." [7] Similarly, Philip Phenix described the book as "inspiring and inspired . . . philosophy in the grand style—comprehensive in scope, catholic in outlook, adventurous in spirit." [8] In sharp contrast, Boyd H. Bode found in *Crisis and Hope in American Education* a plethora of "ex cathedra pronouncements" and a dearth of empirical analysis.[9] For both the more analytically oriented philosophers and progressive educators seeking a popular and easily grasped justification for their efforts, Ulich was proposing pseudoanswers for pseudoquestions.

III

This detachment as educational scholar and statesman was also evident in Ulich the teacher. After World War II, some of the faculty in the Yard viewed the Harvard School of Education as an embarrassing intellectual blemish on the proud escutcheon of the university which proudly claimed the virtue of *Veritas*. By the late

7. John E. Smith, *Christian Century* 72 (1955): 535.

8. Philip Phenix, *Journal of Philosophy* 52 (1955): 243-45.

9. Boyd H. Bode, *New Republic* 126 (February 18, 1952): 19.

1950s, especially due to the talented leadership of Francis Keppel, a transformation was underway. Tough-minded researchers and experienced practitioners had been recruited to the faculty, and the corridors of old Lawrence Hall, where William James had once lectured on psychology and pedagogy, began to vibrate with a new intellectual élan. The work of John Carroll in linguistics, Israel Scheffler in analytic philosophy, and John Whiting in anthropology all pointed to the rewards awaiting those who followed a disciplinary approach to the study of educational problems. More programmatically minded men also came to the fore. Judson Shaplin in team teaching, Fletcher Watson in science education, and Herold Hunt in school administration— all worked out training programs for the preparation of a new breed of teachers and administrators which would soon be emulated elsewhere. Within these winds of change, Ulich moved about on his own scholarly course, cognizant and appreciative of the efforts of his new colleagues. At times he also was critical of their ideas and endeavors, but at no time could he have been considered central to Keppel's efforts to gain the role of national leadership for the school of education.

One also sensed at that time an almost paranoid effort on the part of the education faculty to give professional deference to their arts and science counterparts across Kirkland Road. Educational opinions emanating from professors in philosophy, social relations, and science often were listened to with far more reverence and credence than deserved, and their conceptual contributions to the development of such new departures as the MAT program and the modified mathematics and science curricula were overrated at the time. All of these deferential efforts for rapprochement coming from the inhabitants of Lawrence Hall, Ulich, himself a member of the Department of History of Science and Learning and the Divinity School, viewed with a tinge of misgiving and considerable bemusement. Enjoying both the friendship and scholarly respect of such Harvard giants as Arthur Meier Schlesinger, Paul Tillich, Werner Jaeger, Pitirim Sorokin, and Harry Wolfson, he also understood that preeminence in one field of scholarship did not necessarily qualify a man as an infallible seer in the area of teacher training and educational research.

Although the trend in Lawrence Hall was toward greater

emphasis on the social and behavioral sciences, aided and abetted by Keppel's deft grantsmanship with the Office of Education and the Ford Foundation, Ulich continued to attract a steady stream of able doctoral students. Known at Harvard as "Ulich students," the appellation usually remained with them throughout their careers. Yet they never became his "disciples." Ulich's impact on them was real but not easily defined. Demands he made upon them, but he never exploited them. Instead, they would agree that they had studied with a man of infinite empathy and understanding who somehow brought out the best in them as he held them to high academic standards.

What they later accomplished, then, was their own even though they never forgot their indebtedness to him. Neither apologists nor implementers of Ulich's ideas (as the students of Dewey, Kilpatrick, and Skinner became of theirs) they did share a kind of pragmatic idealism. In their teaching and writing they would replicate no tightly knit system of metaphysics, no monolithic interpretation of educational history, no one methodology of research. Simply to mention their names is to recognize their diversity as activists and thinkers, administrators and scholars, teachers and writers: James Allen, Richard Boyd Ballou, George Z. F. Bereday, Frederick Ellis, Andreas Kazamias, Frederick Lilge, Solomon Lipp, Paul Nash, Henry Perkinson, Theodore Sizer, and Ernest Stabler. How much Ulich attracted students with exceptional talents and how much his influence helped them to become leaders in their respective fields is a moot question. The fact remains that in his teaching career at Harvard, Ulich worked with a group of students who went on to serve American education in many capacities, yet each bore in some way his own idiosyncratic version of Ulich's reverence for intellectual concerns and his commitment to serve others.

IV

If there is, then, some unifying theme which draws together Ulich's experiences on two continents, it is to be found in his ability to be involved within his culture while at the same time remaining detached from it. It was a disciplined detachment which saved him from a self-defeating cynicism during the rise and fall of the Third Reich. Detachment also enabled him to survive personal tragedy, particularly the death of his second wife, Elsa Brandstrom, a truly saintly woman whose memory is still revered in Harvard Square and abroad for her efforts to help German war orphans and newly arrived immigrants to this country. If his aspirations for classical scholarship and his education efforts for the trade unions were dashed, this did not destroy his hope for the future. Although he was a member both of a generation of Europeans who followed the false light of an anachronistic nationalism and a second generation of Americans who often seemed bent on material success to the exclusion of any more human goals, through his writing and teaching Ulich was a constant reminder to fallible men that they constantly must employ the means of reason to improve the quality of their lives. Neither a Sisyphean pessimist pushing an absurd burden uphill nor a Dionysian hedonist superficially sampling easily achieved pleasures, Ulich remained a Stoic, ever cognizant of man's duality—his rational potential and his tragic limitations.

To maintain this stoicism in the first half of the twentieth century required the strongest mental and spiritual fortitude. Ulich's sustenance came not from institutions, ideologies, or specific scholarly disciplines. Something of a *homo universalis,* Ulich remained true to his personal philosophy, attempting and succeeding in some measure to transcend all of these and seek his own manifestation of the "cosmos." With Nietszche, he could say, "I am not narrow enough for a system, not even my own system."

CHAPTER XII

Carleton Wolsey Washburne

Part I

An Autobiographical Sketch

Background

I was born in Chicago on December 2, 1889, the second of four children neatly spaced two years apart. My older brother, Norman, would undoubtedly have rated high in the genius class if I.Q.'s had been invented then, but he died at the age of ten. My sister, Dorothea, whom I adored from the beginning, is still living, the widow of Herman Stegeman, once director of athletics and dean of men at the University of Georgia. The youngest of us, John, had a brilliant career as a professor of educational psychology at Syracuse University cut off by a fatal heart attack when he was forty-seven years old.

Our father, George Foote Washburne, M.D., was a tall, handsome man, thoroughly professional, a competent physician and surgeon, especially skilled in obstetrics. He was a warmly loving and expressive father, much loved by all us children. He was a man of physical and moral courage. His ancestors had resided almost exclusively in the province and state of New York from the first part of the seventeenth century. His mother was a Wolsey distantly related to the cardinal.

But father's influence on us children was subtle and not readily defined. His first medical practice was with mother's father; he then branched off on his own in semisuburban Kenwood and developed a flourishing practice. This, however, he sold at the time of Norman's death to join the Klondike gold rush as surgeon to a mining company. Mother took us three children to her parents' home on the West Side. So we saw little or nothing of father from the time I was eight until I was eleven. Mother was the dominant factor in our lives, always.

Mother was born in Northampton, Massachusetts, shortly after her maternal grandfather, a physician, moved his family to his sanatorium there. Her ancestry was similar to father's and in one case, identical. But her father, R. N. Foster, M.D., was born in Canada, son of a British colonel.

It is of mother that I must speak in some detail, since her influence on my thought, feelings, and career was by far the greatest single influence in my life.

Mother was a rather tall, handsome woman, brown-eyed, enthusiastic, intensely vivid—a dramatic personality—who was dominant in any gathering or social group. She had a beautiful, well-trained, contralto voice which stood her well when she lectured in those days before microphones were invented. She was always deeply interested in public affairs, national and international. But her most profound interest, from childhood until her death at the age of eighty, was in philosophy and religion.

Yet, above all, and interwoven with all her activities, she was a mother. Her love and companionship gave her children the interests and aspirations that lasted throughout their lives. Her first writing—and most of it subsequently—was in the field of child study; so were her lectures. Her most effective political work, when I was six years old, was in lobbying to successful enactment the first law to provide state support for day school public education for deaf children. Her first editorial work was editing Colonel Parker's magazine, *The Course of Study*, which later became the *Elementary School Journal.* She shared all her activities with us children, making us a part of her life. She was a dramatic and fascinating storyteller and could make her activities come alive to us.

Her quite unorthodox and liberal religion was made intensely real to us, and she made essentials of philosophy meaningful by putting them into our terms. For example, it has been said that, when I was about three years old and was being reproved for some naughtiness, she said to me, "Carleton, what can you do?" I answered proudly, "Anysing I like!" "Except what?" she persisted. My head dropped and I meekly answered, "Bozzer ozer peoples." This was typical of the way she instilled abstract philosophic principles into us children. She was paraphrasing, in this instance, John Stuart Mills's statement, "The only part of the conduct of any one, for which he is amenable to society, is that which concerns others. In that which concerns himself, his independence is, of right, absolute. Over himself, over his own body and mind, the individual is sovereign."

Mother's interest in philosophy and religion stemmed from that of her parents, especially her father, who later greatly influenced my own thinking and interests, first through mother and later by direct contact when I lived with him during my second and third years of high school and when, after my marriage, he visited us summers a month at a time.

Her father, R. N. Foster, was a successful Chicago physician by profession, a scholar and philosopher by avocation. As a young man he had taught Latin, Greek, and Hebrew in an Ohio academy. He met his future father-in-law (who was also a physician) through their mutual interest in Swedenborg, and he fell in love with the daughter. That resulted in his deciding to study medicine. He financed his medical studies by translating several volumes of Swedenborg's works from Latin into English for J. B. Lippincott and Company. On completion of his studies he began medical practice in Chicago and continued it for over fifty years.

But he never forsook his interest in languages and philosophy. He taught me what very little Greek I learned and interested me in Hebrew as I tried to decipher Hebrew signs in the neighborhood where some of his patients lived. It was through him that I read my first philosophic work—Swedenborg's *Divine Love and Wisdom.* My own lifelong interest in philosophy and religion and in the origins of words came directly from Grandpa Foster.

To go back a step: When father returned from the Klondike in 1901, his health was temporarily broken from his hardships and he was almost penniless, the company he was with having gone bankrupt. He could not resume practice of medicine in Chicago, so he moved with mother and us children to Elkhart, Indiana. Patients were slow in coming to him; so mother took over most of the support of the family by writing and editorial work. To economize, we bought (on easy payments) a seven-acre farm on the outskirts of Elkhart. I took care of the cow, milking her twice a day, and curried and fed father's horse.

We raised pigs and chickens (my brother and sister were responsible for them), and we raised most of our vegetables and some fruit, as well as grew alfalfa for hay for the horse and cow. My farm experience stands out strongly in my memories of the past and doubtless contributed to my sense of responsibility all through my subsequent life.

Because the high school in Elkhart to which I went on my bicycle daily was not very good and to help the family financially, Grandpa Foster invited me to earn my board and keep with him in Chicago, doing household chores before school and driving him out to make his calls after I got home. So my second and third years were at the John Marshall High School in Chicago. By the time I was ready for the senior year, my family had moved to Elgin, where father opened a sanitorium and mother edited the *Mothers' Magazine*, published in that city. I graduated from the Elgin high school in 1908.

Education

After high school (where I took every possible course in the sciences) I entered the University of Chicago, where I was a "premedic" for two years. Then I studied a year at Hahnemann Medical College in Chicago and finally at Stanford University, where I graduated in physiology. By that time I had decided definitely not to become a physician—but *what* I was to do was still uncertain.

FIRST EXPERIENCE

Having no vocational training or experience, immediately after my graduation from college I had to find some way of making a living. I took a job under a corporation lawyer, William A. Wotherspoon, a California promoter who was afire with social ideals; a visionary, enthusiastic, in many ways astute and clever, but a poor judge of people. He had taken as a partner in an enterprise to finance his social scheme a man who, shortly after I went to work in his office, absconded to Mexico with all the funds.

Meanwhile I had met, fallen in love with, and married Heluiz Bigelow Chandler. She was a beautiful young art student, keenly alive, with a broad range of interests, who had come recently from Philadelphia to California with a friend of her mother's to "seek her fortune." When Will Wotherspoon's organization folded, both she and I began looking for a job—any kind of job that would pay us enough to live.

After nearly three months of vain search and living (very meagerly) on borrowed money, I happened to see a sign on an office building in Los Angeles reading "Teachers' Agency." I had never thought of becoming a teacher, but since I had to do something and was trained for nothing, I thought it worthwhile to find out what the agency might have to offer; so I went in. I learned that in those days in California anyone with a bachelor's degree could be certificated for teaching in rural elementary schools or small towns. I paid my dollar registration fee and within a month found myself the "principal" of a two-room rural school in La Puente District of Los Angeles County, four miles from El Monte. I was to teach grades 4, 5, 6, 7, and 8. The other teacher taught the first three grades. She was a graduate of a two-year normal school and was trained in traditional methods of managing and instructing large groups of young children. The school had eighty children, of whom thirty-five were in my group of grades.

I made all sorts of mistakes. But I had always been fond of children, had told them stories and taken them on hikes while I was in high school and college. I had gone to school under Colonel Parker's faculty three years in the early grades and had learned many of his and John Dewey's ideas from my mother, who knew both men well. I therefore did some things that were sound. Not being hampered by tradition, training, or close supervision, I experimented with various means of giving the children educational experiences and training—a school garden, dramatizations, a school library, sex education—and of providing for individual differences.

The next year I was offered a job as teacher of the "special room" for "misfits" in Tulare, in the San Joaquin Valley of California, at a salary of one thousand dollars a year—a hundred dollars more than I got at La Puente. During the summer before going to Tulare, I directed a municipal playground in Hollywood.

In Tulare I found myself with a class of seventeen children who could not get along in the regular classes—some with low learning ability, a taciturn Indian, a boy with a cleft palate and split lip unable to talk intelligibly, several older boys with high enough intelligence but serious behavior problems, and so on, children ranging from school grades 3 to 8. I was given carte blanche with only one proviso—the school board had granted only one year for the special room and I was to have the children ready to go back to regular grades at the end of that year. I was also to teach departmental courses in arithmetic to the regular seventh and eighth grades while another teacher was assigned to take charge of my special room for an hour each day. And I was to direct the playground for the entire school.

Naturally, I individualized the instruction of the children in my special room. And even in my two arithmetic classes I found the range of ability of the children spread through at least four grades and gave individual assignments to fit each child's readiness, as far as I could gauge it. But the superintendent found that all the seventh- and eighth-grade children were at different points in the textbook and said to me, "Washburne, you are a very young man, and you have a lot to learn; you should follow the course of study for the seventh and eighth grades."

On the playground I found considerable athletic ability among the older boys in my special room. I capitalized on this and developed a football team (Rugby) which became the champion of the San Joaquin Valley and which took up the energy of my behavior problem boys. And I tried all sorts of experiments in teaching my special class. Soliciting the local merchants from door to door for funds, I arranged to take my boy with a cleft palate to San Francisco for an operation by a plastic surgeon, enabling him to learn to talk. At the end of the year I had fitted the children to go on with the regular grades.

SAN FRANCISCO STATE NORMAL SCHOOL

But I was again without a job—and I had a wife and baby to support. The superintendent, however, did me one good turn for which I shall be eternally grateful; he gave me a pamphlet by Frederic Burk, President of the San Francisco State Normal School; the pamphlet was called "Lockstep Schooling and a Remedy." I wrote a long letter to Burk telling him what I had been trying to do, asking him how one became a normal school instructor and where I could find a job where I would be free to individualize instruction.

It took Burk nearly a month to reply briefly on a postal card that he was too busy to write at the time but I might hear from him later. Disappointed, I kept trying for other jobs, without any luck. But I got a summer job in Oakland directing a municipal playground.

Then one day that summer, 1914, came a phone call from Burk, asking me to see him. I asked my wife to supervise the playground that day, leaving the baby in charge of some of the older girls. I found Burk to be a middle-aged, rather fat, bald man with shaggy eyebrows, an engaging smile, an excellent sense of humor, and a remarkably keen mind. He warned me that he had no vacancy, but said he found my letter interesting and would like to have my ideas about preparing students to teach science in the elementary schools.

This was the first of several interviews with Burk. Each time he assigned me to a new task and when I submitted my ideas he unfailingly found the weak spots in my suggestions. While he was ruthless in his criticisms, I saw that he was generally right, and I was able to blunt his barbs by touching his sense of humor and joining him in his hearty laughs. I liked him, and it was evidently mutual.

In August (1914) I went to my fourth or fifth interview. I had not landed any job and the summer playground was about to close. Burk asked, "What are you going to do this next year?" "I'm going to teach here," I replied. "But I told you at the beginning that I had no vacancy," he said. I answered, "I know it, but this is where I belong." "Hmm," he said, looking over his spectacles at me from under his bushy eyebrows. He led me across the hall to a cubbyhole of an office under the stairs, with barely room for my desk and chair. "This will be your office," he said. "Your salary will be $1440 a year. We begin next week."

I took the ferry back to Oakland, my heart singing. I shouted across the playground to my wife, "I've got a job! And it's not teaching, but teaching teachers to teach, at $1440 a year!"

My Career—The Main Line

Then began five years of strenuous work, rigorous training, and productive activity.

After three months of apprenticeship in arithmetic under Miss Mary Ward (a superb teacher), I was assigned to work out the curriculum and plans for the physical sciences.

At the end of my second year I, for the first time, seriously considered my future career—what I really wanted to do in the long run. I privately made a list of my strong and weak points, those that were ingrained in my personality and presumably unchangeable, and those which I might reasonably expect to improve or eliminate. I did this with objectivity and candidness and did not even show the list to my wife. It was immediately evident to me that teaching and training teachers used more of my strong points and was hampered by fewer of my indelible weak ones than any other vocation that I could think of. Then and there I decided on my career.

I immediately began work on my doctorate across the Bay at the University of California in Berkeley, taking courses in the evenings, Saturdays, and summers. I tied in the work I was doing at the normal school with the term papers for my courses and wrote a dissertation entitled "A Science Curriculum Based on Research." For my minor I chose anatomy, transferring the credits from my medical training that were considered graduate work and had not been applicable, therefore, for my bachelor's degree. I completed my doctorate in the record time of two years—the first person, I believe, to get the Ed.D. degree from the University of California.

One day toward the end of my fourth year at the normal school, Burk came into my office and asked, "How would you like to be the superintendent of a small school system where you could carry out some of the ideas we have here?" I jumped up and said it was exactly what I wanted. He just said, "Hmm," and walked away. Hearing no more from him, I got worried as a month went by. Was he merely trying me out to see if I really wanted to remain on his faculty—my appointment was for only a year at a time? So I went to his office and asked him directly whether he had a real position in mind.

He said, "Oh yes, it is real enough. A member of a school board, named Yeomans, in a suburb of Chicago, has read some of my stuff; we've had quite a correspondence. He says they are disappointed with their superintendent and want me to recommend someone to take the place. You are a very young man and Winnetka is a very small place; so if you fail it won't make a very big splash. I guess I'll recommend you."

WINNETKA

The result was that I went to Winnetka, a residential suburb of Chicago, for interviews that summer, but I didn't begin my superintendency there until the following spring. Then, early in May 1919, I launched into my career. The accompanying time chart shows the sequence of my activities.

As the new, inexperienced, twenty-nine-year-old superintendent of schools, I began meeting regularly with my teachers in small groups—all first-grade teachers on alternate Tuesday afternoons after classes were dismissed; alternate Wednesdays, all second-grade teachers; all third-grade teachers Thursday afternoons; and in the alternate weeks, the fourth-, fifth-, and sixth-grade teachers on a similar schedule. Mondays and Fridays I met with the seventh- and eighth-grade (later, junior high school) teachers by departments. The groups consisted of five to seven teachers each during the first year, and, as the faculty grew, never more than twelve. There were also dinner meetings with the four principals one evening a month, lasting until midnight or longer. Advisers in special fields—art, music, playground, etc.—met with me as needed, usually one afternoon a month.

Through these meetings, which continued most of the time for the next twenty-four years, I came to know every member of the faculty closely and well, to know their problems, and to learn from them.

Most of the teachers had had more specific training than I. They knew all their children and their reactions; so they taught me more than I taught them. Half the faculty were leaving at the end of that first year; so I was able to fill out the staff with enthusiastic, young teachers of my own choosing. To counteract the gross inequities in the salaries I found, I immediately established, first, a minimum salary, then a salary scale based on training and experience and sufficiently high to prevent a large turnover and to attract good recruits.

In the grade meetings we plunged right into the problems of curriculum and standards. What did each teacher expect her children to know and be able to do at the end of a year? How far were her expectations being met? What were the minimal essentials needed in all subjects, and how many of the children could really achieve these by the end of a year?

Following Burk's technique of forcing, by Socratic questions, clear and explicit thinking and planning, we all began to see the need for diagnostic testing of each child's knowledge and skill, and for intelligence testing to determine each child's potential capacity and stage of mental growth. Burk had wisely, during my last two years in San Francisco, assigned me to give the course in educational psychology and to give intelligence tests to all children in the training school. As we in Winnetka prepared and administered diagnostic tests of achievement, and as we administered group intelligence tests, we became fully aware of the wide range that existed in each grade-room among the individual children—a range of at least four years or grades. The absurdity of requiring equal learning by all these children became manifest. It was then that I told the teachers of the self-instruction bulletins which were made and used by Burk's faculty to adapt the work to individual difference.

To my surprise and delight, the teachers asked me at the end of that first year whether they might stay on a week after school closed and prepare such self-instruction materials for use the next year, and whether I could arrange to have the materials mimeographed. The school board agreed, but suggested that schools be closed two days early to let the teachers get started on their plan and lose only three days of their vacation. My secretary—a girl of eighteen, Jessie Knox—willingly agreed to type and duplicate the resulting materials. Jessie had never cut a stencil nor run a mimeograph; so I taught her. Her quick intelligence, amazing memory, and willingness to overwork, plus her remarkable disposition, endeared her to all of us, and she stayed on for my entire twenty-four years and then with six of my successors.

Thus were born our first self-instruction textbooks—in arithmetic. A commercial publisher, years later, told me that these were the beginning of "workbooks," which he was the first to publish and to which he gave the name of "workbooks."

Anyhow, crude as our materials were at first, they made it possible for a teacher with thirty to forty children in a classroom to allow each child to work at his own pace on assignments which, as nearly as we could estimate, were fitted to his individual capacity.

The need for self-correction material became obvious; so the children were given correction books through which they could correct their daily work. To check on the children's work, we devised diagnostic tests to be administered by the teacher when a child was ready. And to keep track of each child's progress we devised "goal cards" on which were entered the dates of the successive tests of a child's progress. (This program was first fully described in the Twenty-fourth Yearbook of the National Society for the Study of Education.) The improvement and extension of such self-instruction materials and diagnostic tests were continued in grade meetings and by special committees for twenty-four years and to a lesser extent has continued ever since.

RESEARCH

It was primarily in these small group meetings that we almost immediately felt the need for scientific research to throw light on our problems. Whenever we found no published or only inadequate research in a field we were investigating in the remaking of our curriculum, we set about doing the research ourselves. We did this evenings, weekends, and summers, with no extra pay and purely voluntarily. And we published our research whenever our results seemed to be of general interest, using the *Elementary School Journal*, the *Journal of Educational Research*, NSSE yearbooks, and such other professional and lay periodicals as *School and Society* and *Parents' Magazine* as outlets.

Early in the game I discovered that one primary teacher, Mabel Vogel (later Mrs. Morphett), was unusually assiduous and thorough. In time, I persuaded an indulgent school board to let me release her from teaching so she could give full time to research. And I encouraged her to take work in statistics at the University of Chicago under Professor Karl Holzinger. Thereafter Holzinger was our prime consultant whenever we ran into statistical difficulties.

In an article in the *Journal of Educational Research* (entitled "One Year of Winnetka Research"), Mabel Vogel and I described briefly some twenty-three projects on which we were working in Winnetka at the time (1927). These ranged from some of purely local interest to the first stages of research which involved, ultimately, schools in about five hundred cities, such as the work in arithmetic for the Committee of Seven and the work on children's reading in which we had the help of the American Library Association and Carnegie Corporation. The arithmetic project of the Committee of Seven, centering in Winnetka, is described in chapter 13 of the Twenty-ninth Yearbook of the National Society of Education, Part II, and the work on grade placement of children's books is described in full in *The Winnetka Graded Booklist* and in the third edition of *The Right Book for the Right Child*.

The little above-noted 1927 article in the *Journal of Educational Research* described the types of problems with which we were wrestling all through my superintendency. Most of the problems came to light in grade meetings and were first tackled by small groups of classroom teachers. Mabel Vogel did the statistical work and kept the research organized. I planned the research, supervised it, and, when necessary, raised money for it.

It is clear that the research was never for the sake of research per se. It was, rather, always to help us solve real problems that confronted us. We tried to do so in as scientific a manner as possible.

Publishing all results that were of general interest resulted in wide publicity. Many articles were translated into foreign languages, and the work of the Winnetka schools became known in educational circles throughout the world.

GROUP AND CREATIVE ACTIVITIES

From the beginning, I recognized the importance of group attitudes of children and of social responsibility and creative activities. But first we had to clear the way for mastery of the tool subjects by eliminating the waste time inherent in the class lockstep system. Our early work was therefore in developing the techniques and materials for individual instruction. It was this for which we were, and still largely are, known.

It was about 1926 that I found Frances Presler. At first she taught in a third grade, but I soon found that she was doing an outstanding job with group and creative activities and I released her from regular grade work, making her an adviser in group and creative activities for the whole system of elementary schools. (We called all supervisors and specialists "advisors" in their fields to prevent their function from having any authoritarian implication.)

It was Frances Presler who developed the philosophy and techniques of group and creative activities. Our individual work had cleared first a third and later a half of the school day for such activities. Soon it was evident that one person could not meet the demand of the teachers for help in all three elementary schools; so Myrtle Craddock and Florice Tanner, both of whom were art advisers and had shown conspicuous ability in developing creative activity in children, were assigned to Frances Presler and learned to add their specialties to hers. Each took responsibility for one of the three elementary schools in turn so that the special strength of each could sooner or later be available to all three schools. Social studies and sometimes literature formed the base of most group projects.

For a description of these activities, see my *Living Philosophy of Education.* Other parts and aspects of our work in Winnetka are described in some detail in other parts of that book. These are briefly noted in the following paragraphs:

Sex education. We introduced this informally in the lower grades, then as part of the study of physiology in fifth or sixth grade, and as a part of biology, which was required in the junior high school.

Nursery schools in all schools. In the junior high school, assistance in the nursery school was part of the required course in family living, the nursery school serving as a laboratory. I induced Rose Alschuler to volunteer to help me organize nursery schools in all Winnetka schools, and she supervised them for years.

Mental hygiene. With much stimulus from Frances Dummer (later Mrs. Logan), we gradually established a department of educational counsel (a child guidance clinic) and every teacher was trained in mental hygiene.

The Graduate Teachers College of Winnetka. This was organized cooperatively by Flora Cooke of the Francis Parker School in Chicago, Perry Smith of the North Shore Country Day School in Winnetka, and me for the Winnetka public schools. Frances Murray served as dean and main spring of the venture as long as it lasted, until several years after I left Winnetka.[1]

In the Graduate Teachers College we took a small group of carefully selected graduates of liberal arts colleges who had not had educational training but who had the interest and personality to make excellent teachers of nursery schools, elementary grades, or junior or senior high schools. To accredit the degree of M.Ed., we organized a national society for intern-teacher education with several eastern schools that were, like us, giving apprenticeship training. As an accrediting body we appointed such outstanding men as Francis Spaulding and Ralph W. Tyler as an accrediting team.

Each candidate spent some time at every level, from nursery school through senior high school, as an observer, then specialized at the appropriate level in doing apprentice-teaching under one of our best qualified teachers in Francis Parker School, North Shore Country Day, New Trier Township High School, or in the Winnetka public schools, teaching all day, first under supervision, then gradually, with full responsibility for the class.

Seminars took place late afternoons and every evening. These were conducted by specialists who were working every day in our regular schools. For instance, educational psychology was under our school psychologist; psychiatry and mental hygiene were taught by our school psychiatrist; Flora Cooke, Perry Smith, and I took turns in conducting the seminar in educational philosophy, and so on. The work was eminently practical throughout the one or two years and led to the granting of the degree of master of education when we felt that the student was really ready to go out and teach. We picked some of the best students to teach in our own schools. Others rose to important positions in other schools in the United States and abroad.

Active participation of parents. It was essential that I have the backing and understanding of parents in all our work. Through

1. This college, though never a full-fledged institution, attracted able students and placed them in good jobs during the approximate five years of its existence (Editor).

innumerable P.T.A. meetings I kept the parents informed as to our activities and the reason for them and answered their numerous questions. I kept in close touch with them in small and large meetings and learned much from them.

Essential, too, was the cooperation and backing of the board of education. I was fortunate in having remarkably fine and intelligent members of the board all through my twenty-four years in Winnetka. Those who were somewhat dubious about some of our educational ventures and theories still backed me because they had confidence in my business ability—I always balanced my budget and lived within it.

Crow Island School. This elementary school in Winnetka was built by Eliel and Eero Saarinen and Lawrence Perkins, with numerous suggestions by our teachers, custodians, supervisors, principals, and me. The profusion of ideas flowing from our highly articulate staff nearly drove the architects "crazy." But the school became internationally known and many years later was called by the *Architectural Forum* the prototype of modern elementary school buildings in the United States.

Because the school was the product of the thinking and experience of the teachers who were to use it, as well as of first-rate architects, it was, and still is, highly functional as well as beautiful.

During these twenty-four years in Winnetka, not only was I publishing and lecturing, but members of the faculty were also spreading widely an understanding of what we were doing. Marion Carswell, principal of the Hubbard Woods School in Winnetka, for example, gave a summer demonstration at Teachers College, Columbia University; spent two or three years helping the International School in Geneva, Switzerland, adapt some of our techniques; and lectured frequently in the United States. Several teachers took turns teaching in the American School in Tokyo; another taught at the American College in Beirut; others gave summer demonstrations in various colleges and universities in this country. And I taught in various American universities nearly every summer.

ITALY

Then, after a training period in the summer of 1943 in Charlottesville, Virginia, the army asked me to accept a commission to take part in the Allied military government. My assignment was to Italy, first as a regional director of education, later as national director. My job was to reopen schools and universities and rid them of fascism and Fascists. I began in Sicily and moved on soon to Naples. There I met Dr. Gabriella Rombo, who was teaching English at the University of Naples. I persuaded her to tutor me in Italian three evenings a week during intervals free of bombing by German and Fascist Italian planes. I felt that my self-taught Italian, in which I was increasingly fluent, was very faulty. I was right, and she helped me greatly. But in practicing my speech I told her of my daily problems and activities and she proved not only interested but so well informed and helpful that I induced her to accept a position in the Allied commission as my special assistant. She proved invaluable and helped me there and later in the United States Information Service in Milan after the war. From Naples we moved on to Rome when it was "liberated," and Rome remained our headquarters until the war ended.

From the beginning in Sicily I started revising the elementary textbooks to cut out all Fascist propaganda, using a committee of Sicilian teachers to do the actual work under my supervision.

Printing, binding, and distributing the books involved great difficulty in war-torn Italy. We got a good quality of newsprint from the army; we confiscated binding thread from a cobbler's shop, got glue from the army quartermaster, took over printing establishments, and finally distributed the new books, by tens of thousands, in army trucks that were taking food to villages.

In Rome I appointed a committee of Italians to go through the great number of diversified secondary school textbooks and decide which were sufficiently innocuous to be retained and which were propagandistic and had to be eliminated.

In the Ministry of Education I appointed a committee to work under my supervision in preparing new "programs" or courses of study.

I had a team of British and American education officers who helped me with various parts of this job and who, especially, went out into the villages which the combat troops had "liberated" and opened up schools with non-Fascist teachers in army tents, church sacristies, movie houses, or wherever space could be found—school buildings were either bombed out or occupied as barracks by Italian or Allied troops.

Meanwhile, I had been promoted to the rank of lieutenant colonel under the Allied commission which had replaced the Allied military government. I acted as minister of education for the parts of Italy that had been liberated until gradually the army moved north and we turned the southern part of Italy over to the new Italian government. During my second year in Italy Professor Guido de Ruggiero, formerly president of the University of Rome, was the government's minister of public instruction, and he and I worked closely together and became fast friends. He advised me with respect to the parts of Italy I controlled, and I advised him in regard to the parts we successively turned over to the Italian government.

Those were three strenuous years. I had made many friends in Italy and the Italian Ministry asked our State Department to send me back when the war terminated.

As soon as I was separated from the army, in 1946, I was assigned by the State Department to return to Italy as Director of the United States Information Service for North Italy, with headquarters in Milan and branches in Genoa, Turin, and Padua. My wife went back with me, learned Italian, and helped me greatly in my necessary social contacts.

Besides my officially assigned duties—distribution of films, getting out newspaper publicity, helping in the Marshall Plan, running the USIS library, organizing the main office and the branches with an Italian staff, etc.—I "bootlegged" educational work into my regular duties. With the help of the Ministry of Public Instruction I selected ten teachers to go to Switzerland for a year of training under Professor Jean Piaget and to return to Italy to spread what they learned, and I got money to support them from my mother's old friend (and mine), Mrs. Emmons Blaine. Piaget was so impressed by this American support of Italian teachers to be trained by a Swiss educator that he persuaded the Swiss government to match Mrs. Blaine's gift.

I also got the Boy Scouts and Girl Scouts started again—they had been abolished by Mussolini—and through the British and American organizations got funds to give training to key leaders.

And of course I did considerable lecturing and some writing. (I could lecture in Italian quite understandably, but for publication I wrote in English and had my work translated.)

In the summer of 1948 I left the State Department and my wife and I returned to the United States. I looked for a teaching position, having resigned from Winnetka a year after I went to Italy on a leave of absence. Temporarily, I accepted an offer as educational reconstruction specialist for Unesco, in its New York office.

BROOKLYN COLLEGE

By midwinter 1949 I accepted a position at Brooklyn College which later became part of the City University of New York. I was to be director of teacher education and director of the graduate division and was elected chairman of the Department of Education.

At Brooklyn College I first divided the rather large education department (about fifty members then) into small groups of not more than twelve persons each, called "policy groups", and asked them to do some daydreaming. If they were not bound by state restrictions or city requirements, what would they consider to be the best possible education for teachers for each level of children's maturity?

The next year, having discerned some degree of consensus among the groups, who were kept informed of each other's "dreams," I reorganized the groups so that each would contain faculty members who had special knowledge of each of the various fields—early childhood, elementary grades, secondary education, history, philosophy, sociology, and psychology. In these groups we reworked the earlier speculative ideas. I kept in close touch with the groups, meeting fortnightly with all the group chairmen, helping them to synthesize their thinking and summarize it so that they could report back to their respective groups the thinking of all others.

This resulted in a proposed program consisting of an introductory course at the end of the second year of college, two parallel courses in the psychology and sociology of education, and a senior year of methods and practice teaching. The introductory course (abandoned after I left Brooklyn ten years later) was the same for all students. It was based on rather intensive supervised observation in nursery schools, youth-serving agencies, housing developments, scouting and camps, Y's, and our child guidance clinic. The two junior-year courses separated the students going into secondary education from those who were to deal with younger children and both were based on actual participation in the work of the agencies. The senior-year course in methods and practice teaching, lasting a year, was taught by our faculty members who supervised the practice teaching and who related the methods being taught to the daily work of the students in the schools of the New York area.

We postponed history and philosophy of education and education for world understanding to the fifth-year master's program, when these courses would have more meaning to the students. The whole program was accepted unanimously by the department and later, after a struggle, accepted by the faculty council of the college as a whole.

Shortly before my arrival in Brooklyn, a child guidance clinic had been established and was being organized by Professor Samuel Goldberg as a laboratory for teacher training. I capitalized on this and gave it the fullest possible support as it developed. But we lacked a comparable laboratory for early childhood education. It took two or three years, cooperation from the departments of home economics and psychology, and the support of President Harry Gideonse to wangle the necessary space and to find a topnotch director (Dr. Rebecca Shuey). But it became, with its nursery school, a vital part of our teacher education.

Without a department of evaluation and research we had to act in the dark. So one of my first acts at Brooklyn was to find, with the help of my many friends across the country, a director of evaluation and research. I found Dr. Louis Heil who, with several assistants, still fills that position, not only for the Department of Education but for the entire college.

Back in Winnetka I had done some research without much success on evaluating teacher effectiveness. But after working with Heil two or three years, I saw some hope of finding objective measures. He suggested that an adaptation of the Manifest Interest Schedule, a type of personality test, could be applied to the teachers and that the Brooklyn College Test of Children's Feelings could be applied to the children. After several years of work and a grant from the U.S. Office of Education, we got definitive data indicating that certain determinable types of teachers were effective in teaching certain subjects to equally definable kinds of children. We published a summary of this investigation in several professional journals and reported on it at the American Educational Research Association annual meeting.

While serving as director of teacher education, I was also director of the Graduate Division of Brooklyn College. As such, I was aided and advised by the graduate committee of the college faculty council, which met with me regularly every two weeks. For those students who were going to be teachers, we worked out a full general program; for other graduate students, we saw to it that the programs met scholarship standards and had some degree of coherence and overall plan.

Once a month I met with the corresponding directors of the graduate divisions of the three other municipal colleges. We four attempted to coordinate the graduate work of the four colleges which were parts of what was later called the City University of New York.

MICHIGAN STATE UNIVERSITY

In 1960, having reached the age of compulsory retirement, I moved to Okemos, Michigan, a suburb of East Lansing. When Dean Clifford Erickson of the College of Education at Michigan State University found that I was going to live nearby, he invited me to join his faculty as "distinguished professor," full or part time. Several of my old friends had accepted similar posts at M.S.U.—Ernest Melby, George Counts, and Floyd Reeves, among others—and I was happy to do so on a part-time basis. For several years I taught graduate courses on and off campus and acted as a consultant. And I did a little lecturing in other universities. But more and more I left institutional life and devoted myself to my home and writing.

Experiences Interwoven with Main Career

FOREIGN EXPERIENCES

A lifelong interest in cultures, customs, and ideas beyond those with which I had grown up gave me a lasting urge to travel. My wife shared this urge and shared all my foreign experiences.

We began in 1922-23, with a four-month leave from Winnetka, studying European experimental schools. This was reported in *New Schools in the Old World*. It was on that trip that I first learned of the New Education Fellowship (now called the World Education Fellowship), for it was that organization which gave me my leads as to what schools and educators I was to visit in Europe.

After participating in a New Education Fellowship Conference in Locarno, we made our first trip (1927) to the USSR. Immediately after my last lecture at Locarno, we flew to Berlin to join the unofficial trade union delegation to Russia, I to be their specialist in elementary and secondary schools. A group of us uncommitted specialists were to go wherever we liked, in connection with our studies, as guests of the Russian trade unions. We reported without censorship in our book *Soviet Russia in the Second Decade*.

In 1931, again on leave from Winnetka, I spent nine months on a worldwide study of the aims of education as conceived by leaders whose thoughts were likely to influence the education of the future in Asia and Europe. On our return to America we conducted similar interviews with American educators. The whole study was described in my book *Remakers of Mankind*.

During the summers of 1932 and 1936 I again took part in world conferences of the New Education Fellowship in Nice and Cheltenham, respectively, and in 1940 in Mexico. Each time we spent part of the summer traveling widely.

In the school year 1941-42 the Julius Rosenwald Fund asked me to direct a survey of the elementary and secondary schools of Louisiana under a commission appointed by the state legislature of that state. Geographically, this was not foreign travel, but Louisiana was terra incognita to me, its legal system, customs, and traditions reflecting those of Spain and France rather than those of Great Britain, like the rest of the states of the Union. Having done considerable reading on the subject during the preceding summer, I took a six-month leave from Winnetka and started work in September in the state capitol at Baton Rouge. I was expected to report back to Winnetka once a month for school board meetings and for conferences with my associate superintendent, Rae Logan, who was acting superintendent in my absence.

I spent the first few weeks in Louisiana getting the names of leaders in each community representing business, the professions, labor, agriculture, and women's organizations. I met with a number of such groups, then organized a team of northern educators, Negro and white, to help me. Together we organized "policy groups" throughout the state.

There were, ultimately, about fifty of us on the professional staff and about two thousand local citizens in "policy groups." The full report was published in mimeographed form in five large volumes and summarized by me in the book *Louisiana Looks at Its Schools.*

In 1942, under a State Department grant, I made a study of the problems of elementary and secondary education in five South American countries, reporting the results to the Department of State. On this trip we were accompanied by our son, just out of high school.

This trip, made while once more on leave of absence from Winnetka, was followed by the Italian experiences, 1943-1949, previously described.

In the summer of 1949, a few months after I went to Brooklyn College, my wife and I, joined by James Heming of England, made up a team for a lecture tour of Australia for the Australian section of the New Education Fellowship. We spoke in each of the state capitals, the national capital, and several small communities, and gave radio talks and newspaper interviews as well.

Except for a few days in the Fiji Islands on the way back from Australia and a two-week holiday in the Bahamas a few years later, we did not travel again outside our country until 1958.

In 1958 I used a sabbatical semester from Brooklyn College to go to Cambodia. We went under a State Department contract with the Unitarian Service Committee and the Cambodian government, I to act as a consultant in the establishment of Cambodia's first training school for rural elementary teachers. On the way home we spent the summer in Greece and Italy.

On retiring from Brooklyn College in 1960, I accepted an invitation from the University of Natal to participate in an international educational conference in Durban, celebrating the fiftieth anniversary of the university. Following this conference, I lectured in various parts of Natal and Transvaal. Then, taking a freighter for Spain, we had the chance to visit briefly the countries along the east coast of Africa. After six weeks in Spain and Portugal, we sailed for our new home in Okemos, Michigan.

We had a fun visit of a few weeks in 1963 to the Canary Islands to celebrate our golden wedding anniversary. This completed our foreign travel.

WRITING, LECTURES, AND ORGANIZATIONS

As shown in the accompanying bibliography, I wrote continuously during my whole career, sharing my studies, research, experiences, and thoughts with both lay and professional readers. Similarly, I lectured extensively in the United States and in many other countries. And I taught most summers in various American universities.

Naturally, I have been a member of many organizations, both professional and general. In most of them I have done little more than pay dues or attend occasional meetings, but a few should be mentioned:

I contributed chapters to several yearbooks of the National Society for the Study of Education. I reported almost annually to the American Educational Research Association. For about twenty years I was chairman of the Committee of Seven of the Northern Illinois Conference on Supervision.

The two organizations in which I took major responsibility were the Progressive Education Association (president 1937-41) and the New Education Fellowship (international president about 1948-56). After the demise of the Progressive Education Association in the early 1950s, I organized and headed the United States section of the New Education Fellowship.

PHILOSOPHY AND RELIGION

I cannot terminate this condensed autobiographical sketch without speaking of the very real part played in my life by what may be called its spiritual base. My mother's vital, mystical, and erudite studies and her experiences influenced me from the beginning, as her father's had influenced her and, later, me. His scholarly knowledge of philosophy, his deep concern with religion, and his interest in the philosophy and religion of India became potent elements in my own thoughts and feelings.

I refrained from joining any church until middle life, for I rebelled against the blanket acceptance of any dogma or creed. But in the 1930s I joined the Society of Friends (Quakers). They had no official creed, no authoritative dogma, and stressed the responsibility of every individual to follow his own "inner light." I found the long periods of silent meditation and worship refreshing. And I was so much in sympathy with the way the Quakers put their religion to work in the Friends Service Committee that I became active in the regional groups of that organization, both in the New York area and later in Michigan.

In my most recent book, *Windows to Understanding,* I have expressed my own philosophy of life and my religious thoughts, immanent in all my thinking and actions.

In Retrospect

As I look back over the years, my life has been remarkably full and rich. I have no real regrets—my mistakes have taught me valuable lessons. I am, however, sorry that I have sometimes inadvertently hurt some persons in my drive toward the attainment of my goals.

The confidence of my family and friends has always buoyed up my morale and strengthened my resolutions. But the prime movers for all my activities have been my ideals and aspirations, founded on my philosophy of life.

My wife's love and companionship, her sensitivity, intuition, and inherent wisdom, have interwoven inextricably with my life. Our three fine children and their spouses, loving and beloved, our twelve grandchildren and the spouses of several of them, and our budding crop of great grandchildren give us joy and fulfillment. We have many wonderful friends, a modest but beautiful home, basically good health, and reasonable economic security. What more can one ask in retirement?

A BIOGRAPHICAL SUMMARY

Carleton Wolsey Washburne. Born December 2, 1889, in Chicago, Illinois; died November 27, 1968, Lansing, Michigan.

Family. Married Heluiz Chandler, September 15, 1912. Children: Margaret Joan, Beatrice, Chandler.

Education. Public schools of Chicago, Elkhart, (Indiana), and Elgin, Illinois; University of Chicago (2 years); Stanford University, A.B., 1912; University of California (Berkeley), Ed.D., 1916.

Occupational history. Taught in public schools, California, 1912-14; instructor of science teaching, San Francisco State College, 1914-19; superintendent of schools, Winnetka, Illinois, 1919-43; war service, 1943-45; director, U.S. Information Service in Italy, 1946-48; educational specialist, Unesco, 1948-49; director of teacher education and director of Graduate Division, Brooklyn College, 1949-60; distinguished professor, College of Education, Michigan State University, 1961-68.

Memberships. Progressive Education Association (president, 1939-43); International New Education Fellowship (president, 1947-56); National Society for the Study of Education (chairman of yearbook Committee); American Educational Research Association (past vice-president).

Awards. Received Grande Bene Merito, University of Rome, 1945; Knight Officer, Order of Crown of Italy, 1946; Legion of Merit, 1946; Chevalier de Monisaraphon (Cambodia), 1958.

Part II

Selected Publications of

Carleton Wolsey Washburne

Books

1. *The Story of the Earth* (with Heluiz Chandler Washburne). New York: Century Co., 1916.
2. *Common Science.* Yonkers-on-Hudson, N.Y.: World Book Co., 1920.
3. *Individual Speller.* Yonkers-on-Hudson, N.Y.: World Book Co., 1924.
4. *Adapting the Schools to Individual Differences.* Twenty-fourth Yearbook of the National Society for the Study of Education, Part II, (under direction of Carleton W. Washburne). Bloomington, Ill.: Public School Publishing Co., 1925.
5. *New Schools in the Old World* (with Myron W. Stearns). New York: John Day Co., 1926. (foreign editions and translations: Turkey, 1931; China, 1931).
6. *A Survey of the Winnetka Public Schools* (with William Scott Gray and Mabel Vogel). Bloomington, Ill.: Public School Publishing Co., 1926.
7. *Winnetka Graded Book List* (with Mabel Vogel). Chicago: American Library Association, 1926. Reprinted as *What Children Like to Read,* Chicago: Rand McNally Co., 1926.
8. *Winnetka Individual Reading Material* (with Olivia Youngquist). Includes *My Reading Book, My Sound Book, My Other Reading Book.* Chicago: Rand McNally Co., 1926-1930.
9. *Soviet Russia in the Second Decade* (with Stuart Chase et al.). New York: John Day Co., 1928.
10. *Washburne Individual Arithmetic Series* (with teachers of Winnetka Public Schools). Yonkers-on-Hudson, N.Y.: World Book Co., 1927-30.
11. *Better Schools* (with Myron M. Stearns). New York: John Day Co., 1928 (foreign editions: Spain, 1931; Chile, 1930).
12. *Winnetka Speed Practice and Tests in Arithmetic* (with Vivian Weedon). Winnetka, Ill.: Winnetka Individual Materials, 1930.

13. *Adjusting the School to the Child.* Yonkers-on-Hudson, N.Y.: World Book Co., 1932 (foreign editions and translations: Iraq, 1929; Poland, 1934; China, 1936; Denmark, 1937; Italy, 1952; Argentina, 1959).
14. *Remakers of Mankind.* New York: John Day Co., 1932.
15. *The Story of Earth and Sky* (with Heluiz Washburne and Frederick Reed). New York: Century Co., 1933; Junior Literary Guild, 1933; Appleton-Century Co., 1935.
16. *The Right Book for the Right Child* (with Mary S. Wilkinson and Vivian Weedon). New York: John Day Co., 1933 (2d ed., 1936; 3d ed., rev., 1942).
17. *Child Development and the Curriculum.* Thirty-eighth Yearbook of the National Society for the Study of Education, Part I (Carleton W. Washburne, Chairman of the Yearbook Committee). Bloomington, Ill.: Public School Publishing Co., 1939.
18. *A Living Philosophy of Education.* New York: John Day Co., 1940 (foreign editions and translations: Finland, 1948; Japan, 1956; Italy, 1957).
19. *Winnetka Language Series,* including *Functional Grammar* (with teachers of Winnetka Public Schools). Winnetka, Ill.: Winnetka Educational Press, 1941 et ante.
20. *Louisiana Looks at Its Schools.* "Summary," vol. I of *Louisiana Educational Survey.* Baton Rouge: Louisiana Educational Survey Commission, 1942.
21. *Functional Arithmetic Series* (with teachers of Winnetka Public Schools). Winnetka, Ill.: Winnetka Educational Press, 1943.
22. *What is Progressive Education?* New York: John Day Co., 1953 (Foreign editions and translations: Great Britain [*Schools Aren't What They Were*], 1953; Italy, 1953; Japan, 1954; India, 1957; Greece, 1961).
23. *The World's Good: Education for World Mindedness.* New York: John Day Co., 1954. (foreign editions and translations: Japan, 1956: Italy, 1965; Argentina, 1967).
24. *La Formazione dell' Insegnante negli Stati Uniti.* Translation from French in *Revue Internationale de Psychopedagogie.* Florence: La Nuova Italia, 1958.
25. *Winnetka: The History and Significance of an Educational Experiment* (with Sidney P. Marland, Jr.). Englewood Cliffs, N.J.: Prentice-Hall, 1963. (foreign editions and translations: Pt. I, Italy, 1960; Pt. I, Argentina, 1962).
26. *Windows to Understanding: Thoughts on Science, Man and God.* New York: Carleton Press, 1968.

Articles and Brochures

27. "A Classified Scale for Measuring Intelligence." *Journal of Educational Psychology* 10 (1919): 309-22.
28. "The Formal Discipline Problem: Three Lines of Attack." *Sierra Educational News* 14 (1918): 392-95.
29. "Breaking the Lock Step in Our Schools." *School and Society* 8 (1918): 391-402.
30. "The Individual System in Winnetka." *Elementary School Journal* 21 (1921): 52-68.
31. "Can Public Schools Be Fitted to the Individual Pupils?" *Proceedings of the Illinois State Teachers' Association,* 1920.
32. "A Democratized School System." *American School Board Journal* 62 (March 1921): 42-43.
33. "Educational Measurement as a Key to Individual Instruction and Promotions." *Journal of Educational Research* (1922): 195-206.
34. "The Winnetka Social-Science Investigation" (with Louise Mohr). *Elementary School Journal* 23 (1923): 267-75.
35. "Building A Fact Course in History and Geography." *The Social Studies in Elementary and Secondary School,* pp. 99-110. Twenty-Second Yearbook of the National Society for the Study of Education, Part II. Bloomington, Ill.: Public School Publishing Co., 1923. "Basic Facts Needed in History and Geography," ibid., pp. 216-33.
36. "A Spelling Curriculum Based on Research." *Elementary School Journal* 23 (1923): 751-62.
37. "Progressive Tendencies in European Education." U.S. Bureau of Education Bulletin 1923, No. 27. Washington: Government Printing Office, 1923.
38. "The Attainments of Gifted Children under Individual Instruction." *Report of the Society's Committee on the Education of Gifted Children,* pp. 247-61. Twenty-Third Yearbook of the National Society for the Study of Education, Pt. I. Bloomington, Ill.: Public School Publishing Co., 1924.
39. "The Winnetka System." *Progressive Education* 1 (1924): 11-12.
40. "Organizing Public Schools for Research." *Journal of Educational Research* 10 (1924): 364-68.
41. "Social and Individual Work." *Progressive Education* 2 (1925): 146-48.
42. "Sex Education in School." *Intelligent Parenthood: Proceedings,* Chicago Association for Child Study and Parent Education, Chicago, March 4-6, 1926.
43. "Measurable Differences in Books Suitable for Different Grades." *Elementary English Review* 3 (1926): 113-14.
44. "Winnetka—An Educational Laboratory." *New Era* (London) 7 (1926): 115-20.

45. "The Philosophy of the Winnetka Curriculum." *Curriculum-Making: Past and Present*, pp. 219-28. Twenty-sixth Yearbook of the National Society for the Study of Education, Pt. I. Bloomington, Ill.: Public School Publishing Co., 1926.
46. "Freedom by Individual Mastery." *New Era* (London) 8 (1927): 126-28.
47. "An experimental Study of Various Graphic, Tabular, and Textual Methods of Presenting Quantitative Material." *Journal of Educational Psychology* 18 (1927): 361-76, 465-76.
48. "The Public School and the Parent." *Child Study* 5 (March 1928): 9-10.
49. "When Should We Teach Arithmetic?" *Elementary School Journal* 28 (May 1928): 659-65.
50. "Character in Two Dimensions." *Religious Education* 23 (October 1928): 721-29.
51. "Punishments Recommended for School Offenses: A Reply" (with Frances Drummer). *Elementary School Journal* 29 (1929): 774-86.
52. "Individual Guidance as It Is Applied in a Village School System" (with Marion Carswell). *Nation's Schools* 4 (December 1929): 23-28.
53. "The Grade Placement of Arithmetic Topics." *Report of the Society's Committee on Arithmetic*, pp. 641-70. Twenty-Ninth Yearbook of the National Society for the Study of Education, Part II. Bloomington: Public School Publishing Co., 1930.
54. "The Contribution of Preschool Education to a Public School System" (with Alschuler). *Journal of Home Economics* 22 (1930): 721-25.
55. "When Should Children Begin to Read?" (with Mabel Vogel Morphett). *Elementary School Journal* 31 (1931): 496-503.
56. "Arithmetic Grade-Placement Investigation of the Committee of Seven." *Educational Research Bulletin* 11 (November 1932): 396-401.
57. "The Graduate Teachers College of Winnetka" (brochure). Winnetka: The College, 1932.
58. "A New Venture in Teacher Training." *Nation's Schools* 14 (August 1934): 41-43.
59. "The Educator's Response" in "The School's Response to the Challenge of Childhood." *Mental Hygiene* 19 (January 1935): 47-58.
60. "The Values, Limitations, and Applications of the Findings of the Committee of Seven." *Journal of Educational Research* 29 (1936): 694-707.
61. "Science and the Free Personality." (summary of an address given at the World Conference on New Education, Cheltenham, England, August 4, 1936). *School and Society* 44 (1936): 734-36.
62. "Functional Arithmetic." *Educational Method* 16 (1937): 167-70.

63. "The Work of the Committee of Seven on Grade-Placement in Arithmetic." *Child Development and the Curriculum*, pp. 299-324. Thirty-eighth Yearbook of the National Society for the Study of Education, Pt. I. Bloomington, Ill.: Public School Publishing Co., 1939.
64. "South American Education." *Journal of the National Education Association* 32 (1943): 97-98.
65. "Education under the Allied Military Government in Italy." *Educational* Record 26 (1945): 261-72.
66. "Towards Democratic Living in the Schools." *New Horizons in Education*, Sydney, N.S.W., Autumn 1948.
67. "Children's Communities: A Challenge, a Need, and an Opportunity." *Pi Lamda Theta Journal* 29 (1951): 229-36.
68. "A New Policy"—Some Needed Revisions." *Progressive Education* 29 (1952): 126-28.
69. "The New Education and World Mindedness." *Jewish Forum* (London), December 1952.
70. "Toward a New Statement of Policy for the A.E.F." *Progressive Education* 30 (1953): 70-71.
71. "Art in the Life of a School." *New Era* (London) 35 (1954): 29-31.
72. "The New Teacher Education Program at Brooklyn College." *School and Society* 79 (1954): 88-91.
73. "The Universality of Human Rights." *Phi Delta Kappan* 35 (1954): 306-8, 311.
74. "Democratic Planning for Teacher Education." *Educational Leadership* 13 (December 1955): 176-87.
75. "Education and the World Community." Programs and Projects for International Understanding, American Association of Colleges for Teacher Education, Washington, 1956.
76. "Education Today for the 21st Century." *Childhood Education* 33 (1957): 341-43.
77. "What Characteristics of Teachers Affect Children's Growth?" (with Louis M. Heil). *School Review* 68 (1960): 420-28.

Part III

Carleton Wolsey Washburne: A Biographical Essay

PATRICIA ALBJERG GRAHAM

Carleton Washburne exemplified the Progressive education movement. To read his autobiography is to learn of the shifting emphases of the dominant educational movement of his time.

Those characteristics of Washburne's life which make him a prototype of the Progressive educator of the twentieth century include his social and geographical origins, the course of his professional career, his political and philosophical views, and his endorsement of specific educational programs. Thus, the journey from a midwestern birthplace to graduate training in the new discipline of "education"; the post as a superintendent of schools in a wealthy suburb; the ultimate appointment to a faculty of and administrative position in a school of education; the commitment to political liberalism and the resultant tensions with radicals in the thirties and conservatives in the late forties and fifties; the eschewing of rigorous and systematic philosophy in favor of an amorphous belief in democracy—all are symptomatic of, even if not universally present in, that generation of men and women who dominated Progressive education.

Washburne's principal prominence came from his work as superintendent of schools in Winnetka, Illinois, from 1919 to 1943. During this time Winnetka was probably the best known "Progressive" school system in the United States. His success there was substantially attributable to his administrative skill in implementing the vision he had brought with him to Winnetka. The setting was ideally receptive to Washburne's new ideas. The population of Winnetka was largely affluent, many of the men originally from the East and accustomed to private preparatory schools. Then part of a new breed soon to engulf America, the upper-middle-class suburban commuter, these men wanted to establish schools in their prestigious community on a par with the excellent private schools they had known in New England. Such groups are generally more receptive to novel educational practices than any other.

In the second decade of the twentieth century, education was a topic of considerable interest to many knowledgeable Americans. Criticism abounded in the periodicals they read of the inadequacies of many schools and particularly of the "academic lockstep" which forced all children to progress through schools at the same rate. The graduate schools of education at major universities were just beginning to assume important roles in shaping educational views, and the old normal schools were being transformed in name, if not in fact, to state teachers colleges. Combined with these developments was the new interest in individualism, stimulated by the increasingly widespread acquaintance with Freudianism among the business, professional, and literary communities. Winnetka was a community in which many of these strands converged. When Edward Yeomans, a pump manufacturer with a considerable avocational interest in education and a member of the Winnetka School Board, sought recommendations for a new superintendent, he turned to Frederic Burk, whose lineage as a Progressive educator was pure. Formerly a student at Clark University under G. Stanley Hall, who is often called the "father of the child study movement," Burk had imbibed early the doctrine of individual differences and developed and modified it while president of San Francisco Normal School. One of Burk's most promising young staff members in 1919 was Carleton Washburne, whose heritage of Progressive education was as pristine as Burk's. Washburne's mother, whose pervasive influence her son acknowledges in his autobiography, had been a good friend of Francis W. Parker, whom many Progressive educators considered their intellectual progenitor. Mrs. Washburne had sent her son to Parker's laboratory school where he had studied under one of Parker's most gifted teachers and disciples, Flora J. Cooke, who herself was well known in Progressive education circles. It would be difficult to find in 1919 a man whose credentials as a prospective Progressive educator were in better order than Carleton Washburne's.

The environment at Winnetka for Washburne was ideal, but many men have gone to favorable locations and not become nationally and internationally known. Washburne was able at Winnetka to develop a very simple idea, namely, assisting each student to learn at his own rate, into a scheme that became known as the Winnetka Plan, almost as well known as the more stringently arranged Dalton Plan, which also received wide publicity in the 1920s. The educational program in grades 1 to 8 at Winnetka emphasized such means for individualizing instruction as workbooks, then a novelty in American schoolrooms, diagnostic tests, and various other means of assessing pupils' progress. An effort was made throughout most of Washburne's tenure at Winnetka to permit each student to wend his way through the various elementary school subjects at his own rate. Washburne also involved the members of the faculty in a variety of meetings in small groups, a procedure he followed throughout his administrative career.

In the twenties Winnetka became the paradigm Progressive school system. As Washburne's substantial bibliography attests, many articles appeared explaining the apparently successful procedures in the North Shore Chicago suburb. Soon it became a training ground for Progressive educators. When the Bronxville, New York, school system, similar socioeconomically to Winnetka, looked for a superintendent, a Winnetka assistant superintendent was selected, Willard W. Beatty, who also became a leader in the Progressive education movement and preceded Washburne as president of the Progressive Education Association. In 1946, after Washburne had resigned as superintendent, another administrator active in the Progressive education movement became superintendent, Harold G. Shane. Shane became one of the vocal members of the Progressive Education Association in the late forties who urged a less radical posture for the PEA in its role as the apparent spokesman for Progressive educators.

As Washburne recounts in his autobiography, he resigned his position as superintendent of schools at Winnetka after he entered the army in 1943. During the three preceding years he had spent relatively little time there, supervising a study of schools in Louisiana in 1941, traveling to South America in 1942, and going to Italy as part of his army service in 1943. After the war he continued his work in Italy with the United States Information Service. Returning to the United States, he accepted a primarily administrative position at Brooklyn College in 1949. By the late forties and early fifties, about the only realm in which a committed Progressive educator could find sympathetic associates was a school of education in a university, and not surprisingly a great many former school principals and school superintendents sought refuge there. Among those former school teachers and administrators who joined schools of education faculties were Frederick Redefer and Alice V. Keliher (New York University), Wilford M. Aikin (Ohio State University), Harold G. Shane (Northwestern University and Indiana University), and, of course, Washburne.

In both major parts of his career, his twenty-four years as Winnetka superintendent of schools and his eleven years as director of teacher education and of the Graduate Division of Education at Brooklyn College, Carleton Washburne occupied positions characteristic of, although more prestigious than those held by, other Progressive educators of his generation. In his other activities and beliefs he was also true to the mythical "ideal" Progressive educator. It was his diversity and incessant activity, both in his jobs and in his writing, that gave Washburne such a position of prominence.

One of the recurrent themes in Washburne's activities is his concern for education in other countries. He began his foreign travel in 1922 with the support of the Winnetka Board of Education, who believed a visit to Europe to see schools was so important that his salary should be paid in full for the three months he was abroad. He also arranged for the U.S. Office of Education to give him a general introduction and to publish his impressions of European education when he returned. Finally, the Illinois superintendent of public instruction agreed to make him his official representative while visiting the European schools. This was the beginning of Washburne's extensive involvement in international education and is illustrative of Washburne's wisdom in avoiding the parochialism that affected so many American educators. With his customary adroitness at making the most of his opportunities, he became acquainted, in the leisurely shipboard life while returning from Europe, with an American journalist, Myron Stearns, who collaborated with him on his survey of European schools and, later, on several articles and a book on American schools.

Another shipboard friendship led to his next major European trip, a visit in 1927 to the USSR as an American guest of the Soviet trade unions to view and appraise Soviet schools. The original American invitee in education was George S. Counts, but Counts graciously accepted Washburne into the delegation. Washburne never waxed quite as ecstatic as some of his colleagues about the Soviet experiment, a reticence he exploited in the early 1930s when he was instrumental in delaying publication of Counts's *A Call to the Teachers of the Nation*, a report of the Progressive Education Association's Committee on Economic and Social Problems. Subsequent trips took Washburne around the world in 1931, to South America in 1942. to Australia in 1949, to Cambodia in 1958, and to South Africa in 1960. On the later visits he usually tied his trip to activities of the New Education Fellowship (now the World Education Fellowship), the international organization committed to promulgating Progressive education. The Progressive Education Association became the American affiliate in 1932 after Washburne's and Harold Rugg's lobbying in the late twenties and early thirties with both the international and the American groups. Washburne served as president of both the PEA and, later, of the NEF.

Like so many Progressive educators, Washburne's interest in foreign schools in the late twenties centered on the Soviet Union. John Dewey, George S. Counts, and William Heard Kilpatrick were among the others who traveled in the USSR in the halcyon twenties and early thirties when Progressive education was explicit national policy there. But Washburne's interest persisted through the thirties, forties, and fifties to include many other countries. Although he does not belong strictly in the intercultural relations wing of the Progressive education movement, in this area, as in so many others, Washburne touched base.

In addition to his work in the United States and his international activities, Carleton Washburne exemplified the attitude of many Progressive educators in the manner in which he accepted the necessity of a philosophy for Progressive education and in the willingness with which he undertook the task of devising one. By the late thirties the Progressive education movement was beginning to lose favor among the foundations and to be beset by serious internal friction. At such a time, groups naturally enough search for a unifying statement of philosophy. The Progressive Education Association attempted unsuccessfully to produce such a testament from 1938 to 1941. Washburne triumphed where the PEA committee floundered, publishing in 1940 *A Living Philosophy of Education.* In keeping with the mores of Progressive education, the work satisfied only the loosest definition of "philosophy," one that Washburne set forth in his introduction: "Whenever, in the course of any activity whatsoever, we stop to consider as explicitly as we can *what* it is that we are doing, *how* we are doing it, and *why*, that act of considering is philosophy." This volume of 576 pages includes five parts: "The Child as a Person," "The Child as an Individual," "The Child and the Means of Social Relationships," "The Child an Integral Part of an Organic Society," and "Democratic School Administration." He frankly admitted that the work was based much more upon his experience, and in particular his experience at Winnetka, than it was upon reading and reflection. "The selection, recombination, and assimilation are guided not by mere analysis and thought but by work with living children and with live teachers of living children, in a struggling, groping, living society." Ideological hairsplitting was not for him. Here was progressivism's action philosophy.

In his recollections and assessments of his life, Washburne notes that he was always an avid reader. The first category of books he listed was novels and "biographies of persons I admire." Secondly, he reported his interest in books and articles on most aspects of science. Finally, he added, "And selected books on religion and philosophy have had important influence on my thinking." His last book, *Windows to Understanding*, expressed his general religious and philosophic thinking.

Washburne's willingness to combine his religious and philosophic thoughts can also be seen in his decision in his forties to join a religious group. His choice, the Society of Friends, again was consistent with his emphasis upon good works. He reported that the activities of the American Friends Service Committee "in behalf of humanity regardless of race or creed impressed me so strongly that I wanted to help it." He also liked the "complete democracy" of the Friends' meetings. Having been reared in the Swedenborgian tradition, Washburne may have found in the Quakers a fragment of the earlier mysticism in the "inner light" which was missing from other religious groups emphasizing good works, such as the Unitarians and the Ethical Culture Society.

Finally, in his political views Washburne stood in the mainstream of the Progressive tradition. Staunchly calling himself a "liberal," he nonetheless repeatedly found himself at odds with the greater radicalism of some of his fellow Progressive educators. He managed relatively better, as liberals often do, with the more conservative constituency of his board of education in Winnetka, where his fiscal and administrative soundness (he always lived within the appropriated school budget) sustained him. In the early thirties, he tangled with George S. Counts on the role of the teacher in leading a movement to reform American society along less capitalistic and more cooperative lines. Later, in the forties, he opposed Theodore Brameld's proposal to have the PEA (then the American Education Fellowship) adopt policies that would again move the organization into the position of urging a general social reform for the nation. Despite his membership in SANE, the Americans for Democratic Action, American Civil Liberties Union, and the United World Federalists, Washburne remained primarily interested in children and schools, not just in America but throughout the world. He was simply less interested in education as a force in society or in the society itself. He professed great commitment to democracy as an educational as well as a political philosophy, but he was much more concerned about its application in educational matters than in political ones. The intense and even acrimonious disagreements over what position Progressive educators should take on these questions was one significant factor in the ultimate collapse of the movement.

One anomaly persists in viewing Carleton Washburne as a prototype of Progressive educators. How could anyone who scarcely mentions John Dewey in his autobiography possibly be representative of the Progressive education movement? Washburne illustrates how pervasive and diverse the Progressive education movement was. Washburne was never identified with the Teachers College establishment in education or even the major midwestern one at the University of Chicago. Despite his enormous list of publications,

Washburne was principally an activist in education, not a theorist. Furthermore, he was not particularly interested in questions of social philosophy or philosophy of education, even though he did write one book on the latter. After Dewey left the University of Chicago in 1904, he became more interested in larger educational questions than simply what was the best way to teach a child arithmetic. Washburne remained concerned with the concrete problems of devices to make children learn more easily and, later, of how to train teachers to teach more effectively. The ideological questions he left to others, and, he observed, their ruminations on the subject were not his favorite reading material. For precisely these reasons Washburne did exemplify the Progressive education movement. The hordes of summer school students who crowded into the classrooms at Teachers College were on the whole more interested in Washburne's workbooks than in Dewey's dialectics.

CHAPTER XIII

Concluding Comments

PAUL WOODRING AND ROBERT L. MCCAUL

Part I

On the Origins and Nature of Educational Leadership

PAUL WOODRING

The men and the woman whose autobiographies appear in this yearbook were born during the last decade of the nineteenth century or the first year or two of the present century. This was about the end of the period of the closing frontier when, as Dewey warned in *School and Society*, the schools were failing to respond to the new challenges presented by urbanization, industrialism, and an extended period of compulsory schooling.

They reached maturity and entered upon their careers during the heyday of progressive education when educators were making a valiant effort to adapt the schools to the new demands placed upon them. Their professional careers spanned the period from World War I to the 1960s. They responded vigorously, but in various ways, to the changes in the world and the schools about them during this period, and the fact that their stories appear in this volume suggests that they responded more vigorously and more effectively than most educators. In one way or another they rose above obscurity and made their voices heard and their influence felt. It seems logical to ask how they differ from other, less conspicuous educators—whether their emergence reflects chance factors or was the result of exceptional talent, exceptional preparation, exceptional motivation, unique psychological traits, or some combination of these.

Although positive conclusions regarding the preparation and experiences most conducive to leadership cannot safely be drawn from so small a number of cases, some negative conclusions are possible. These autobiographies make it evident that neither professional degrees in education nor classroom teaching experience at the elementary or secondary levels is essential to leadership in education, or at any rate neither was essential during the first half of the twentieth century.

Carr, Counts, and Strang took their Ph.D.'s in education while Washburne was the recipient of the first Ed.D. granted by the University of California. But Ulich wrote his doctoral thesis on an obscure German poet (Scherenberg) and Shuster's doctorate is also in literature. Conant was a chemist, while Stoddard and Pressey were psychologists before becoming educators. Brubacher took a law degree before entering Teachers College as a graduate student in educational administration. Gates does not clearly indicate whether his doctorate is in education or psychology, but the members of his committee—Woodworth, Poffenberger, Cattell, and Thorndike—were psychologists. It should be remembered, however, that education and psychology were more closely related fifty years ago than they are today and that in some universities education, psychology, and philosophy were taught in the same department.

Five of the eleven individuals included in our list had some elementary or secondary teaching experience before becoming college teachers. Counts taught briefly in a Kansas high school where he was also principal. Carr began his teaching career in a California junior high school while Washburne taught grades 4 through 8 in a two-room school near Los Angeles. Strang taught home economics to seventh- and eighth-grade girls in a slum area of New York for three years. Ulich began as a teacher of German literature in a gymnasium which was considered a secondary school though the age of the students he taught, and the level of the courses, were similar to our first two years of college.

All the others went directly from graduate school into college teaching: Stoddard at Iowa, Pressey at Indiana, Brubacher at Dartmouth, Shuster at Notre Dame, Gates at Teachers College, and Conant at Harvard. Some of these—notably Stoddard, Pressey, and

Gates—later worked closely with younger students as a part of their research work, but none had classroom teaching experience at the lower levels.

Although these leaders come from a wide variety of social backgrounds, all fall within the middle-class range. None of the families was wealthy or was likely to be found listed in the Social Register, but neither can any of them properly be called "disadvantaged." Stoddard's father owned a "modest insurance business." Washburne's was a physician, Pressey's was a Congregational minister, while Brubacher's was a school superintendent who later became a college president. Ulich's father "went into business" though many of his ancestors were university graduates and some were ministers. Strang and Counts grew up on farms but their fathers were farm owners rather than sharecroppers or farm laborers. Gates's father, "after sampling several occupations," worked for a lumber company. Carr and Shuster do not mention their fathers' vocations but Carr says, ". . . our family struggled with serious economic difficulties—never actual want but always required to seek added income and to avoid nonessential expenses." Shuster grew up in a small town in Wisconsin though both his grandfathers were farmers.

A researcher might inquire into the fact that none of these individuals, except possibly Strang, spent much of his childhood in a large city, despite the fact that at least one fourth of all Americans lived in such cities at the time they were children. It is notable, too, that only one woman appears on the list, and no Negroes—a fact that reflects the restrictions placed on opportunities for leadership during the first half of the twentieth century.

The autobiographies offer some clues to the psychological traits essential to leadership, but in the absence of quantifiable data and a control group the clues are not easily interpreted. It may reasonably be assumed that they possessed intelligence of a high order but we have no evidence regarding their I.Q.'s or other test scores as children—when the Stanford Binet was published in 1916, most of them were already adults.

Some other evidence of early ability is available. Gates learned to read soon after his third birthday and some of the others could read before they entered school. Counts completed four elementary grades in two years. Pressey, who attended a school that did not permit acceleration, speaks of ". . . being taught what I already knew, or could learn in a third the time." Everything on Stoddard's report card through elementary and high school fell between 96 and 100. Strang "became absorbed in Macaulay's *History of England*" while in grade school. The headmaster of Dresden Royal Gymnasium recognized Ulich's scholarly potential and singled him out for special attention.

Some of the group might be called "late bloomers," which may only mean that they found elementary school work too easy to be stimulating. Shuster says, ". . . I belatedly took an interest in my studies and was adjudged a bright boy," but he was reading *Harper's* at the age of nine or ten. Conant says, "Before I became consumed by a desire to master chemistry, my grades were about C plus or B minus," but his talent for scientific studies was evident at an early age.

All these individuals, including the administrators, have been prolific writers, the authors of books as well as numerous journal articles. It seems safe to say that an educator cannot hope to achieve leadership on the national level without reaching a large audience through his publications. All seem to have been highly motivated, but some place great emphasis on the importance of hard work in their autobiographies while others make no mention of it. Strang repeatedly comments on the fact that her work has been her entire life, precluding much opportunity for recreation or social life, but some of the others have managed to enjoy a wide variety of experiences in no way connected with their work as educators. Some of their careers appear to have been carefully planned while others became educators only after they achieved success in other fields and became leaders by responding to new challenges as they presented themselves.

The motivation of several of these individuals includes dissatisfaction with the schools they attended as children and a strong conviction that the schools could be and ought to be better. Pressey says, "Now, at the age of eighty, I am still battling long-continuing gross faults in our schools which first irked me as a boy in the grades." Ulich says, "Despite all gratitude for my classical education, I have become increasingly convinced that it was a pedagogical scandal," and of his secondary school teachers, "Only a very few taught me more than just plain surface knowledge."

Most of these leaders were vigorous critics of some aspects of the nation's educational system—indeed it may probably be said that criticism of existing institutions and practices is the first step toward leadership in any institution, art, or profession. Pressey was critical of the practice of requiring all children to spend the same amount of time in elementary and secondary schools, regardless of their ability. Stoddard was critical of the misuses and misinterpretation of intelligence test scores in the schools. Conant was critical of conventional programs for the education of teachers. Washburne was critical of both conventional teaching techniques and the conventional curriculum. Gates saw a need for drastic reforms in the teaching of reading. Counts was eager to change the society as well as the schools. All of them demanded changes in the schools and had the courage to face the counterattacks that must be expected by those who challenge the status quo.

Some warnings are appropriate for younger men and women who aspire to positions of leadership in American education and look to these autobiographies for guidance. Though some of the personal qualities that make for leadership may remain constant, the activities in which leaders engage may alter as institutions evolve, the culture changes, and new problems emerge. The schools, the culture, and the problems facing us are vastly different today than they were during the first half of the twentieth century and will be still different at the dawn of the twenty-first. The leaders of the future will be those educators who recognize the differences and respond effectively to the new challenges.

Part II

Autobiography in American Educational History

ROBERT L. MCCAUL

On the Location of the Autobiographers in American Educational History

Although the place of these eminent educators in the history of their times has been suggested at the beginning of the chapter, it may prove helpful to try to locate them rather more specifically in the long sweep of American educational history. One simple and convenient way of providing a context for them would be to sketch out in bold, stark strokes an impressionistic design showing some of the chief trends in American educational thought and practice during the last century and a half. Not all trends would appear in the design, only those relevant to the careers of the eleven leaders.

For this purpose certain trends or movements in American education over the last hundred and fifty years may be cast into sequences of change, each sequence consisting of three phases. In educational philosophy the trend has been from realism, to pragmatism, to existential and analytic philosophies. In history of education the trend has been from intellectual, to institutional, to social histories. In comparative education the trend has been from reportorial, to institutional-historical, to sociological studies.[1] In educational research and evaluation the trend has been from subjective, direct-experience, direct-observational approaches, to objective, tests-and-measurements, quantitative methods, to eclectic assessment procedures combining features of the previous two phases. In learning theory the trend has been from faculty psychology, to connectionistic S-R bond psychologies, to more holistic psychologies. In school governance the trend has been from localism, to amalgama-

1. I owe to my friend and colleague, Philip J. Foster, this characterization of the trend in comparative education.

tion and consolidation, and now seemingly to the beginnings of a swing back to localism of a sort. In school administration the trend has been from empiricism and autocracy, to efficiency and democracy, to theoretical formulations of the administrator's role and functions and the behaviors proper to those formulations. In mission of the school the trend has been from confidence in the school's power to change the child, to confidence in the school's power to change society, to doubts about the school's power to change either the child or society. In view of the learner (employing the nature vis-a-vis nurture paradigm) the trend has been from weight on nurture, to weight on nature, to weight on nurture. In instruction and curriculum the trend has been from subject-matter centered, to child-centered, to academic-discipline centered.

If this design is entertainable as an approximate representation of certain changes occurring in American education since 1820, it will be seen that the transition from first to second phases began roughly around 1895 and the transition from second to third phases around 1940 or 1950. Clearly these were changes that, by and large, were not initiated by the leaders in this yearbook. The generation previous to them—the generation of Dewey, Thorndike, Judd, Kandel, Terman, and Cubberley—was responsible for the changes from first to second phases. The generations after them or members of their generation who, for one reason or another, are not included in this yearbook were responsible for the changes from second to third phases. The eleven eminent educators here, with the possible exception of George D. Stoddard, did not set in motion forces destroying old orthodoxies and ushering in new ones. They did not revolutionize old fields of study as did those scholars who put theoretical foundations under educational administration. They did not create new fields of educational study like educational psychology or human development. Mostly they elaborated, applied, and improved, frequently with extraordinary brilliance and inventiveness, the ideas, techniques, and structures they had inherited from their predecessors.

Gates, Pressey, and Strang were beneficiaries of Thorndike's contributions to learning theory and to research and evaluation methodology; Counts was a legatee of Dewey's social reconstructionism and Washburne of Dewey's progressivism. Brubacher wrote educational philosophy in the pre-Deweyan and Deweyan modes and educational history in the pre-Cubberley and Cubberley veins. Conant's proposals were intended to improve existing educational structures, not transform or eradicate them. Carr joined an NEA organization that had been opened up to the generality of classroom teachers by the efforts of Ella Flagg Young and Margaret A. Haley in the famous election in Boston in 1910. He conducted the affairs of the NEA and the World Organization of the Teaching Profession in accordance with what might be called a nineteenth-century American "common school" ideology of collegiality and consensus. His writing and editing for the Educational Policies Commission were in the spirit of reaffirming the traditional values of American democracy and American public education in times of economic and military travail.

Shuster, Stoddard, and, to a certain extent, Ulich did advocate ideas and hold positions running counter to the orthodoxies of their times. Shuster tried to bring back to teacher training and the urban university the culture and standards of the Renaissance *studia humanitatis.* Ulich, though following familiar paths in educational history and comparative education, did try to infuse into American educational thinking, dominated by pragmatism, some of the philosophy and concerns of German idealism. But neither man, so far as can be discerned from the short perspective afforded by the year 1971, was able to initiate movements of a phase one to a phase two magnitude or of a phase two to a phase three. The case may be different with George Stoddard. His research and that of his colleagues, Beth L. Wellman and Harold M. Skeels, at the Iowa Child Welfare Research Station, showing dramatic increases and decreases in the I.Q.'s of children under enriched and deprived environmental conditions did lead, perhaps, to a trend from a "nature" emphasis to a "nurture" emphasis in our "view of the child." The Iowa data and the Iowa conclusions, widely disseminated by the Thirty-ninth Yearbook of the NSSE,[2] provoked questions about the doctrines that had been in vogue since the publication of Terman's *Measurement of Intelligence* in 1916—questions about the adequacy of the definitions of

2. *Intelligence: Its Nature and Nurture,* Thirty-Ninth Yearbook of the National Society for the Study of Education, Parts I and II (Bloomington, Ill., Public School Publishing Co., 1940). See also Stoddard's *The Meaning of Intelligence* (New York: Macmillan Co., 1943).

intelligence prevalent in the second, third, and fourth decades of the century, about the validity of highly verbal tests purporting to measure intelligence, about the alleged fixity of the I.Q., and about the persuasiveness of the supposition that academic potential is, on the whole, genetically determined.[3] The response to such questions as these, in time, moved American education toward a new environmentalism, becoming dominant in the 1950s and 1960s and likely to remain so in the seventies.

To aver that these leaders, with the exception of Stoddard, did not initiate great movements and changes in American educational thought and practice is not to diminish their achievements. Their ingenuity and vigor in developing and improving the ideas and structures produced by the previous generation of educators gave strength and richness to the second phase in the sequences of change that have been epitomized here, and made the period from 1920 to 1955 an exceptionally fruitful epoch in American educational history.

On the Uses of Autobiography and Biography

In writing their autobiographies and in permitting biographical essays to be written about them, these eleven leaders have performed a service—in some cases their last—for the profession to which they have devoted their lives. The intellectual and attitudinal estate they are leaving to their professional successors has now been enlarged by one more bequest.

Autobiographies and biographies such as these may have the value of providing us with:

1. An intimate revelation of the thoughts, hopes, successes, and failures of interesting human beings and of the philosophies that sustained them through the vicissitudes of their lives and careers.
2. An analysis of the experiences of persons of great ability and knowledge who faced certain perennial and important educational problems and devised solutions that may be adapted to the needs of other educators facing similar problems.

3. Lewis M. Terman, *The Measurement of Intelligence* (Boston: Houghton Mifflin Co., 1916). See p. 68 for his statement on the constancy of the I.Q. and pp. 91-92 for his belief in racial (genetic) differences in general intelligence.

3. Evidence on how and why the teaching profession and education as a societal institution have developed some characteristics and not others.

4. Evidence on how and why certain academic disciplines and fields of study in education have developed along some lines and not along others.

5. Testimonial materials that may aid the historian in reconstructing and interpreting the American past.

6. A body of data for studying the psychology of human behavior and the means by which eminence is won and leadership attained and exercised in American society.

7. An array of career models available for emulation by persons already in the profession, preparing for the profession, or wondering whether to enter it.

8. A series of depictions of human beings with whom the reader may identify and so escape from the provincialism and exclusiveness of his own ego and milieu and thereby expand his own sympathies and tolerances and extend the range of his own conceptions and assumptions.

CONSTITUTION AND BY-LAWS OF THE NATIONAL SOCIETY FOR THE STUDY OF EDUCATION

(As adopted May, 1944, and amended June, 1945, February, 1949, September, 1962 and February, 1968)

Article I

NAME

The name of this corporation shall be "The National Society for the Study of Education," an Illinois corporation not for profit.

Article II

PURPOSES

Its purposes are to carry on the investigation of educational problems, to publish the results of same, and to promote their discussion.

The corporation also has such powers as are now, or may hereafter be, granted by the General Not For Profit Corporation Act of the State of Illinois.

Article III

OFFICES

The corporation shall have and continuously maintain in this state a registered office and a registered agent whose office is identical with such registered office, and may have other offices within or without the State of Illinois as the Board of Directors may from time to time determine.

Article IV

MEMBERSHIP

Section 1. *Classes.* There shall be two classes of members—active and honorary. The qualifications and rights of the members of such classes shall be as follows:

(*a*) Any person who is desirous of promoting the purposes of this corporation is eligible to active membership and shall become such on payment of dues as prescribed.

(*b*) Active members shall be entitled to vote, to participate in discussion, and, subject to the conditions set forth in Article V, to hold office.

(*c*) Honorary members shall be entitled to all the privileges of active members, with the exception of voting and holding office, and shall be exempt from the payment of dues. A person may be elected to honorary membership by vote of the active members of the corporation on nomination by the Board of Directors.

(*d*) Any active member of the Society may, at any time after reaching the age of sixty, become a life member on payment of the aggregate amount of the regular annual dues for the period of life expectancy, as determined by standard actuarial tables, such membership to entitle the member to receive all yearbooks and to enjoy all other privileges of active membership in the Society for the lifetime of the member.

Section 2. *Termination of Membership.*

(*a*) The Board of Directors by affirmative vote of two-thirds of the members of the Board may suspend or expel a member for cause after appropriate hearing.

(*b*) Termination of membership for nonpayment of dues shall become effective as provided in Article XIV.

Section 3. *Reinstatement.* The Board of Directors may by the affirmation vote of two-thirds of the members of the Board reinstate a former member whose membership was previously terminated for cause other than nonpayment of dues.

Section 4. *Transfer of Membership.* Membership in this corporation is not transferable or assignable.

Article V

BOARD OF DIRECTORS

Section 1. *General Powers.* The business and affairs of the corporation shall be managed by its Board of Directors. It shall appoint the Chairman and Vice-Chairman of the Board of Directors, the Secretary-Treasurer, and Members of the Council. It may appoint a member to fill any vacancy on the Board until such vacancy shall have been filled by election as provided in Section 3 of this Article.

Section 2. *Number, Tenure, and Qualifications.* The Board of Directors shall consist of seven members, namely, six to be elected by the members of the corporation, and the Secretary-Treasurer to be the seventh member. Only active members who have contributed to the Yearbook shall be eligible for election to serve as directors. A member who has been elected for a full term of three years as director and has not attended at least two-thirds of the meetings duly called and held during that term shall not be eligible for election again before the fifth annual election after the expiration of the term for which he was first elected. No member who has been elected for two full terms as director in immediate succession shall be elected a director for a term next succeeding. This provision shall not apply to the Secretary-Treasurer who is appointed by the Board of Directors. Each director shall hold office for the term for which he is elected or appointed and until his successor shall have been selected and qualified. Directors need not be residents of Illinois.

Section 3. *Election.*

(*a*) The directors named in the Articles of Incorporation shall hold office until their successors shall have been duly selected and shall have qualified. Thereafter, two directors shall be elected annually to serve three years, beginning March first after their election. If, at the time of any annual election, a vacancy exists in the Board of Directors, a director shall be elected at such election to fill such vacancy.

(*b*) Elections of directors shall be held by ballots sent by United States mail as follows: A nominating ballot together with a list of members eligible to be directors shall be mailed by the Secretary-Treasurer to all active members of the corporation in October. From such list, the active members shall nominate on such ballot one eligible member for each of the two regular terms and for any vacancy to be filled and return such ballots to the office of the Secretary-Treasurer within twenty-one days after said date of mailing by the Secretary-Treasurer. The Secretary-Treasurer shall prepare an election ballot and place thereon in alphabetical order the names of persons equal to three times the number of offices to be filled, these persons to be those who received the highest number of votes on the nominating ballot, provided, however, that not more than one person connected with a given institution or agency shall be named on such final ballot, the person so named to be the one receiving the highest vote on the nominating ballot. Such election ballot shall be mailed by the Secretary-Treasurer to all active members in November next succeeding. The active members shall vote thereon for one member for each such office. Election ballots must be in the office of the Secretary-Treasurer within twenty-one days after the said date of mailing by the Secretary-Treasurer. The ballots shall be counted by the Secretary-Treasurer, or by an election committee, if any, appointed by the Board. The two members receiving the highest number of votes shall be declared elected for the regular term and the member or members receiving the next highest number of votes shall be declared elected for any vacancy or vacancies to be filled.

Section 4. *Regular Meetings.* A regular annual meeting of the Board of Directors shall be held, without other notice than this by-law, at the same place and as nearly as possible on the same date as the annual meeting of the corporation. The Board of Directors may provide the time and place, either within or without the State of Illinois, for the holding of additional regular meetings of the Board.

Section 5. *Special Meetings.* Special meetings of the Board of Directors may be called by or at the request of the Chairman or a majority of the directors. Such special meetings shall be held at the office of the corporation unless a majority of the directors agree upon a different place for such meetings.

Section 6. *Notice.* Notice of any special meeting of the Board of Directors shall be given at least fifteen days previously thereto by written notice delivered personally or mailed to each director at his business address, or by telegram. If mailed, such notice shall be deemed to be delivered when deposited in the United States mail in a sealed envelope so addressed, with postage thereon prepaid. If notice be given by telegram, such notice shall be deemed to be delivered when the telegram is delivered to the telegraph company. Any director may waive notice of any meeting. The attendance of a director at any meeting shall constitute a waiver of notice of such meeting, except where a director attends a meeting for the express purpose of objecting to the transaction of any business because the meeting is not lawfully called or convened. Neither the business to be transacted at, nor the purpose of, any regular or special meeting of the Board need be specified in the notice or waiver of notice of such meeting.

Section 7. *Quorum.* A majority of the Board of Directors shall constitute a quorum for the transaction of business at any meeting of the Board, provided, that if less than a majority of the directors are present at said meeting, a majority of the directors present may adjourn the meeting from time to time without further notice.

Section 8. *Manner of Acting.* The act of the majority of the directors present at a meeting at which a quorum is present shall be the act of the Board of Directors, except where otherwise provided by law or by these by-laws.

Article VI

THE COUNCIL

Section 1. *Appointment.* The Council shall consist of the Board of Directors, the Chairmen of the corporation's Yearbook and Research Committees, and such other active members of the corporation as the Board of Directors may appoint.

Section 2. *Duties.* The duties of the Council shall be to further the objects of the corporation by assisting the Board of Directors in planning and carrying forward the educational undertakings of the corporation.

Article VII

OFFICERS

Section 1. *Officers.* The officers of the corporation shall be a Chairman of the Board of Directors, a Vice-Chairman of the Board of Directors, and a Secretary-Treasurer. The Board of Directors, by resolution, may create additional offices. Any two or more offices may be held by the same person, except the offices of Chairman and Secretary-Treasurer.

Section 2. *Election and Term of Office.* The officers of the corporation shall be elected annually by the Board of Directors at the annual regular meeting of the Board of Directors, provided, however, that the Secretary-Treasurer may be elected for a term longer than one year. If the election of officers shall not be held at such meeting, such election shall be held as soon thereafter as conveniently may be. Vacancies may be filled or new offices created and filled at any meeting of the Board of Directors. Each officer shall hold office until his successor shall have been duly elected and shall have qualified or until his death or until he shall resign or shall have been removed in the manner hereinafter provided.

Section 3. *Removal.* Any officer or agent elected or appointed by the Board of Directors may be removed by the Board of Directors whenever in its judgment the best interests of the corporation would be served thereby, but such removal shall be without prejudice to the contract rights, if any, of the person so removed.

Section 4. *Chairman of the Board of Directors.* The Chairman of the Board of Directors shall be the principal officer of the corporation. He shall preside at all meetings of the members of the Board of Directors, shall perform all duties incident to the office of chairman of the Board of Directors and such other duties as may be prescribed by the Board of Directors from time to time.

Section 5. *Vice-Chairman of the Board of Directors.* In the absence of the Chairman of the Board of Directors or in the event of his inability or refusal to act, the Vice-Chairman of the Board of Directors shall perform the duties of the Chairman of the Board of Directors, and when so acting, shall have all the powers of and be subject to all the restrictions upon the Chairman of the Board of Directors. Any Vice-Chairman of the Board of Directors shall perform such other duties as from time to time may be assigned to him by the Board of Directors.

Section 6. *Secretary-Treasurer.* The Secretary-Treasurer shall be the managing executive officer of the corporation. He shall: (*a*) keep the minutes of the meetings of the members and of the Board of Directors in one or more books provided for that purpose; (*b*) see that all notices are duly given in accordance with the provisions of these by-laws or as required by law; (*c*) be custodian of the corporate records and of the seal of the corporation and see that the seal of the corporation is affixed to all documents, the execution of which on behalf of the corporation under its seal is duly authorized in accordance with the provisions of these by-laws; (*d*) keep a register of the postoffice address of each member as furnished to the secretary-treasurer by such member; (*e*) in general perform all duties incident to the office of secretary and such other duties as from time to time may be assigned to him by the Chairman of the Board of Directors or by the Board of Directors. He shall also: (1) have charge and custody of and be responsible for all funds and securities of the corporation; receive and give receipts for moneys due and payable to the corporation from any source whatsoever, and deposit all such moneys in the name of the corporation in such banks, trust companies or other depositories as shall be selected in accordance with the provisions of Article XI of these by-laws; (2) in general perform all the duties incident to the office of Treasurer and such other duties as from time to time may be assigned to him by the Chairman of the Board of Directors or by the Board of Directors. The Secretary-Treasurer shall give a bond for the faithful discharge of his duties in such sum and with such surety or sureties as the Board of Directors shall determine, said bond to be placed in the custody of the Chairman of the Board of Directors.

Article VIII

COMMITTEES

The Board of Directors, by appropriate resolution duly passed, may create and appoint such committees for such purposes and periods of time as it may deem advisable.

Article IX

PUBLICATIONS

Section 1. The corporation shall publish *The Yearbook of the National Society for the Study of Education*, such supplements thereto, and such other materials as the Board of Directors may provide for.

Section 2. *Names of Members.* The names of the active and honorary members shall be printed in the Yearbook or, at the direction of the Board of Directors, may be published in a special list.

Article X

ANNUAL MEETINGS

The corporation shall hold its annual meetings at the time and place of the Annual Meeting of the American Association of School Administrators of the National Education Association. Other meetings may be held when authorized by the corporation or by the Board of Directors.

Article XI

CONTRACTS, CHECKS, DEPOSITS, AND GIFTS

Section 1. *Contracts.* The Board of Directors may authorize any officer or officers, agent or agents of the corporation, in addition to the officers so authorized by these by-laws to enter into any contract or execute and deliver any instrument in the name of and on behalf of the corporation and such authority may be general or confined to specific instances.

Section. 2. *Checks, drafts, etc.* All checks, drafts, or other orders for the payment of money, notes, or other evidences of indebtedness issued in the name of the corporation, shall be signed by such officer or officers, agent or agents of the corporation and in such manner as shall from time to time be determined by resolution of the Board of Directors. In the absence of such determination of the Board of Directors, such instruments shall be signed by the Secretary-Treasurer.

Section 3. *Deposits.* All funds of the corporation shall be deposited from time to time to the credit of the corporation in such banks, trust companies, or other depositories as the Board of Directors may select.

Section 4. *Gifts.* The Board of Directors may accept on behalf of the corporation any contribution, gift, bequest, or device for the general purposes or for any special purpose of the corporation.

Section 5. *Dissolution.* In case of dissolution of the National Society for the Study of Education (incorporated under the GENERAL NOT FOR PROFIT CORPORATION ACT of the State of Illinois), the Board of Directors shall, after paying or making provision for the payment of all liabilities of the Corporation, dispose of all assets of the Corporation to such organization or organizations organized and operated exclusively for charitable, educational, or scientific purposes as shall at the time qualify as an exempt organization or organizations under Section 561 (C) (3) of the Internal Revenue Code of 1954 (or the corresponding provision of any future United States Internal Revenue Law), as the Board of Directors shall determine.

Article XII

BOOKS AND RECORDS

The corporation shall keep correct and complete books and records of account and shall also keep minutes of the proceedings of its members, Board of Directors, and committees having any of the authority of the Board of Directors, and shall keep at the registered or principal office a record giving the names and addresses of the members entitled to vote. All books and records of the corporation may be inspected by any member or his agent or attorney for any proper purpose at any reasonable time.

Article XIII

FISCAL YEAR

The fiscal year of the corporation shall begin on the first day of July in each year and end on the last day of June of the following year.

Article XIV

DUES

Section 1. *Annual Dues.* The annual dues for active members of the Society shall be determined by vote of the Board of Directors at a regular meeting duly called and held.

Section 2. *Election Fee.* An election fee of $1.00 shall be paid in advance by each applicant for active membership.

Section 3. *Payment of Dues.* Dues for each calendar year shall be payable in advance on or before the first day of January of that year. Notice of dues for the ensuing year shall be mailed to members at the time set for mailing the primary ballots.

Section 4. *Default and Termination of Membership.* Annual membership shall terminate automatically for those members whose dues remain unpaid after the first day of January of each year. Members so in default will be reinstated on payment of the annual dues plus a reinstatement fee of fifty cents.

Article XV

SEAL

The Board of Directors shall provide a corporate seal which shall be in the form of a circle and shall have inscribed thereon the name of the corporation and the words "Corporate Seal, Illinois."

Article XVI

WAIVER OF NOTICE

Whenever any notice whatever is required to be given under the provision of the General Not For Profit Corporation Act of Illinois or under the provisions of the Articles of Incorporation or the by-laws of the corporation, a waiver thereof in writing signed by the person or persons entitled to such notice, whether before or after the time stated therein, shall be deemed equivalent to the giving of such notice.

Article XVII

AMENDMENTS

Section 1. *Amendments by Directors.* The constitution and by-laws may be altered or amended at any meeting of the Board of Directors duly called and held, provided that affirmative vote of at least five directors shall be required for such action.

Section 2. *Amendments by Members.* By petition of twenty-five or more active members duly filed with the Secretary-Treasurer, a proposal to amend the constitution and by-laws shall be submitted to all active members by United States mail together with ballots on which the members shall vote for or against the proposal. Such ballots shall be returned by United States mail to the office of the Secretary-Treasurer within twenty-one days after date of mailing of the proposal and ballots by the Secretary-Treasurer. The Secretary-Treasurer or a committee appointed by the Board of Directors for that purpose shall count the ballots and advise the members of the result. A vote in favor of such proposal by two-thirds of the members voting thereon shall be required for adoption of such amendment.

MINUTES OF THE ANNUAL MEETING OF THE SOCIETY

The 1970 annual meeting of the Society was held in the American Room of the Traymore Hotel in Atlantic City at 2:30 P.M., Sunday, February 15, with Ralph W. Tyler presiding and with some three hundred members and friends present.

The annual meeting has often been devoted to presentations of Parts I and II of the yearbook. However, as in recent years, only one part (*Linguistics in School Programs*) was presented at the annual meeting, and the other volume (*Mathematics Education*) was presented at a subsequent meeting of the Society. The second meeting was held in Minneapolis.

The programs of both meetings follow:

PROGRAM OF THE ATLANTIC CITY MEETING

Joint Meeting of the National Society for the Study of Education and the American Association of School Administrators

Sunday, February 15, 2:30 P.M.
American Room, Traymore Hotel

Presiding: Ralph W. Tyler, Director Emeritus, Center for Advanced Study in the Behavioral Sciences; Chairman of the Board of Directors of the National Society

Presentation of

Linguistics in School Programs

(Part II of the Society's Sixty-ninth Yearbook)

Introducing the Yearbook

Albert H. Marckwardt, Professor of English and Linguistics, Princeton University

Critique of the Yearbook

W. Nelson Francis, Professor of Linguistics, Brown University
John B. Davis, General Superintendent of Schools, Minneapolis

Informal Discussion

Mr. Tyler, Mr. Marckwardt, Mr. Francis, Mr. Davis, and audience

PROGRAM OF THE MINNEAPOLIS MEETING

Joint Meeting of the National Society for the Study of Education and the American Educational Research Association

Tuesday, March 3, 10:20 A.M.
Iowa-Dakota Room, Leamington Hotel

Presiding: Robert J. Havighurst, Professor of Education, University of Chicago; Chairman of the Board of Directors of the National Society

Presentation of

Mathematics Education

(Part I of the Society's Sixty-ninth Yearbook)

Discussion of the Yearbook

Edward G. Begle, Director, School Mathematics Study Group, Stanford University

Critique of the Yearbook

Dr. Richard Shumway for F. Joe Crosswhite, Associate Professor of Mathematics Education, Ohio State University

Informal Discussion

Mr. Havighurst, Mr. Begle, Mr. Shumway, and audience

SYNOPSIS OF THE PROCEEDINGS OF THE BOARD OF DIRECTORS OF THE SOCIETY FOR 1970

I. Meeting of February 15, 1970

The Board of Directors met at 9:00 A.M. on February 15 in Haddon Hall (Atlantic City) with the following members present: Messrs. N. L. Gage, Robert J. Havighurst, Harold G. Shane, Ralph W. Tyler (Chairman), and Herman G. Richey (Secretary).

1. The Secretary reported that the November-December balloting had resulted in the election of John I. Goodlad and the reelection of Ralph W. Tyler, each for a term of three years beginning March 1, 1970.

2. The Board regretfully accepted the resignation of Ruth Strang and appointed Edgar Dale to complete Miss Strang's term ending March 1, 1971.

3. Officers of the Board of Directors for the year beginning March 1, 1970, were elected as follows: Robert J. Havighurst, Chairman; N. L. Gage, Vice-Chairman.

4. The Secretary-Treasurer presented reports as follows: "Report of the Treasurer, 1968-69; Receipts and Disbursements and Statement of Cash and Securities"; "Verified Membership Count, 1937-69"; and "Sales, 1968-69, and Inventory, October 1969."

5. It was voted to present the Seventieth Yearbook, Part I (*Curriculum: Prospect and Retrospect*) at the AASA meeting in Atlantic City (February 1971) and also at the ASCD meeting in St. Louis (March 1971). It was also voted to present *Leaders in American Education* at the annual meeting of the History of Education Society (sponsored by the AACTE) in February 1971.

6. Mr. Tyler discussed the possible need for the Society to plan new directions for the seventies. The discussion centered on (a) ways of involving more young members in the formulation of policy and (2) possible changes in publication policies. Mr. Havighurst presented a memorandum, "Future Developments in NSSE—Proposals." Discussion of the subject and of the memorandum was deferred to the March meeting of the Board.

7. Progress reports were presented for the following authorized yearbooks: *Curriculum: Retrospect and Prospect*, *Leaders in American Education*, *Educational Philosophy*, and *Learning in Early Childhood.*

8. Proposals for yearbooks on the following topics were presented and discussed: Modification of Teacher Behavior, Organizational and Structural Changes in Education, Educational Sociology, Communications, and Elementary Education. Action on the proposals was deferred to the March meeting.

II. Meeting of March 4, 1970

The Board of Directors met on March 4, at 9:00 A.M. in the Leamington Hotel (Minneapolis) with all members present: Messrs. Edgar Dale, N. L. Gage, John I. Goodlad, Robert J. Havighurst, Harold G. Shane, Ralph W. Tyler, and Herman G. Richey (Secretary).

1. Mr. Havighurst reported at length upon the problems encountered in obtaining a proposal and a committee chairman in the field of educational sociology.

2. Mr. Shane suggested that consideration be given to bringing out a yearbook, one part to deal with elementary education, the second part to deal with secondary education. Mr. Shane was asked to prepare a memorandum on elementary education and Mr. Havighurst was asked to explore further the need for and the possibility of preparing a volume on secondary education.

3. The proposal for a yearbook, *Behavior Modification in Education,* was approved and Professor Carl E. Thoresen was appointed chairman of the yearbook committee.

4. Other topics for proposed yearbooks were discussed: Teacher Education, Communications, Instruction, Financing, and Goals and Practices.

5. After a long discussion on the future of the Society—the possibility of placing more young people in positions of leadership, possible changes or extensions in our publication program, and other activities—Mr. Havighurst offered to draw up a short questionnaire for the examination of the Board and for circulation to a sample of the membership. Further discussion was postponed until after the response to the questionnaire could be examined.

III. Meeting of July 9-11, 1970

The Board of Directors met at 7:30 P.M. on July 9, at 9:00 A.M. on July 10, and at 9:30 A.M. on July 11 in the Hilton Hotel (Chicago) with the following members present: Messrs. Edgar Dale, N. L. Gage, John I. Goodlad, Robert J. Havighurst (Chairman), Harold G. Shane, Ralph W. Tyler, and Herman G. Richey (Secretary).

1. The Secretary-Treasurer summarized briefly the membership report (July 1970) and the financial report for the fiscal year ending June 30, 1970.

2. Progress on all authorized yearbooks was reported: *Leaders in American Education* (1971); *The Curriculum: Retrospect and Prospect* (1971); *Philosophy of Education* (1972); *Early Childhood Education* (1972); *Behavior Modification in Education* (1973). It was noted that a second volume for publication in February 1973 had not been authorized.

3. It was generally agreed that a yearbook on educational sociology

should be prepared if Mr. Havighurst proved successful in negotiations that were underway. Mr. Havighurst was authorized to approve the proposal for the Society.

4. Mr. Gage described his efforts to obtain a proposal on the field of communications. It was voted that Mr. Gage should arrange a meeting at which proponents of somewhat different approaches would be present along with Mr. Gage and Mr. Havighurst. It was urged that a proposal be prepared before the February meeting.

5. It was voted that Mr. Shane and Mr. Goodlad should develop a proposal for a yearbook on elementary education before the February meeting.

6. Mr. Havighurst was requested to develop his ideas for a yearbook on secondary education and to prepare a memorandum for presentation at the February meeting.

7. Other topics discussed were (a) Educational Psychology (b) Humanities and the Arts (c) Nature and Nurture Issues. and (d) Goals and Practices.

8. Mr. Havighurst described and discussed activities in connection with the polling of a sample of the membership concerning future directions of the Society. After discussion of the report, the Board voted (a) to arrange for a feasibility study of the proposed tape-recording, monograph, and other suggested projects, (b) to ask the chairman to appoint a project committee consisting of one board member and a number of members of the Society to conduct the study, (c) to appoint a project director on a part-time basis, (d) to support the feasibility study for one year; and (e) to study the report, sample tapes, etc., as soon as they were available. It was further agreed that Mr. Havighurst should approach Kenneth J. Rehage with a view to obtaining a part of his time to direct the study. Mr. Rehage accepted the invitation and was present at the last session of the board's meeting. It was further agreed that the feasibility study might be extended to cover the calendar year of 1971.

9. The Board voted to increase the regular annual dues from seven to eight dollars. The entrance fee of one dollar and the late payment fee of fifty cents were retained. First-year memberships (including the entrance fee) for graduate students was raised to seven dollars.

REPORT OF THE TREASURER OF THE SOCIETY

1969-70

Receipts and Disbursements

Receipts:	
Membership Dues	$ 38,014.40
Sale of yearbooks	61,566.54
Interest and dividends	4,610.42
Miscellaneous and transfer	857.40
Total	$105,048.76
Disbursements:	
Yearbooks:	
Manufacturing	$ 46,788.35
Reprinting	24,259.33
Preparation	3,614.06
Meetings of Board and Society	2,691.04
Secretary's Office:	
Editorial, secretarial, and clerical	24,240.06
Supplies	3,289.70
Equipment	62.63
Telephone	190.18
Miscellaneous:	
Bank charges (adjusted)	48.28
Refunds and transfers (commercial orders)	676.92
Other	65.95
Total	$105,926.50
Excess disbursements over receipts	$ 877.74
Checking account, July 1, 1969	3,376.09
Checking account, June 30, 1970	2,498.35

STATEMENT OF CASH AND SECURITIES

As of June 30, 1970

Cash:	
University National Bank, Chicago, Ill.	
Checking account	$ 2,498.35
Savings account	2,522.79

Savings and Loan Certificates:

Chicago Federal Savings & Loan Association	10,000.00
Home Federal Savings & Loan Association	10,000.00
Telegraph Savings & Loan Association	10,000.00

U.S. Government Securities:

U.S. Government Bonds (H) dated March 1, 1967	15,000.00
U.S. Treasury Notes ($15,000, 7¾%, 1973)	15,043.33

Bonds:

American Telephone & Telegraph ($21,000, 4⅜%, 1985)	14,679.42

Stock:

First National Bank of Boston, 38 shares, capital stock	1,063.97

Investment Fund:

Balance	275.23
Total assets	$ 81,083.09

Charges Against Current Assets

Annual dues paid for 1971	141.50
Life membership fund	8,000.00
Reprinting (on order, chargeable to 1969/70)	10,000.00
Total	$ 18,141.50
Unencumbered assets	$ 62,941.59

Reinvestment of Funds

Transfers:

Hyde Park Bank to Investment Fund	$ 15,000.00
Hyde Park Federal S & L to Investment Fund	15,000.00
Total transferred	$ 30,000.00

Purchases:

American T & T, $21,000, 4⅜%, 1985	14,679.42
U.S. Treasury Notes, $15,000, 7¾%, 1973	15,043.33
Total purchase	29,722.75
Bank charge	2.02
Total	$ 29,724.77
Balance in Investment Fund	$ 275.23

MEMBERS OF THE NATIONAL SOCIETY FOR THE STUDY OF EDUCATION

[This list includes all persons enrolled November 1, 1969, whether for 1969 or 1970. An asterisk (*) indicates Life Members of the Society.]

Aarestad, Amanda B., 1887 Gilmore Ave., Winona, Minn.
Aaron, Ira Edward, Col. of Educ., University of Georgia, Athens, Ga.
Aarons, Marjorie, 8 Mary Anna Drive, Fitchburg, Mass.
Abbott, Frank C., Colorado Comm. on Higher Education, Denver, Colo.
Abbott, Samuel Lee, Jr., Plymouth State College, Plymouth, N.H.
Abel, Frederick P., Western Illinois University, Macomb, Ill.
Abel, Harold, Pres., Castleton State Col., Castleton, Vt.
Abelson, Harold H., Sch. of Educ., City University, New York, N.Y.
Ables, Jack B., East Aurora Jr. High School, East Aurora, N.Y.
Abraham, Willard, Arizona State University, Temple, Ariz.
Abrahamson, David A., 131 Livingston St., Brooklyn, N.Y.
Abrahamson, Edward, Prin., Flower Hill School, Huntington, N.Y.
Abrahamson, Stephen, Sch. of Med., Univ. of So. Calif., Los Angeles, Calif.
Abramowitz, Mortimer J., 345 Lakeville Rd., Great Neck, N.Y.
Accetta, M. A., 2053 Swallow Hill Road, Pittsburgh, Pa.
Achilles, Charles M., Box 317 B, Rt. #1, Geneva, N.Y.
Ackerlund, George C., Southern Illinois Univ., Edwardsville, Ill.
Ackerman, Judy E., 407C Mason Farm Rd., Chapel Hill, N.C.
Ackerman, Thomas J., Univ. of Florida, Gainesville, Fla.
Ackley, James F., 1150 S. Pasadena Rd., Pasadena, Calif.
Adachi, Mitsuo, 5623 Halepa Pl., Honolulu, Hawaii
Adair, Mary R., Asst. Prof. of Spec. Educ., University Park, Pa.
Adams, Don, University of Pittsburgh, Pittsburgh, Pa.
Adams, Ernest L., Florida State Univ., Tallahassee, Fla.
Adams, Gary, 312 ½ E. Grandview Ave., Sierra Madre, Calif.
Adams, Gloria, 5550 Fieldston Rd., Bronx, N.Y.
Adams, James A., Asst. Supt., Saginaw, Mich.
Adams, Mrs. Ruth R., Sch. of Educ., New York City College, New York, N.Y.
Adatto, Albert, 228—165th Ave., N.E., Bellevue, Wash.
Adelberg, Arthur J., Supt. of Schls., Elmburst, Ill.
* Adell, James C., 16723 Fernway Rd., Shaker Heights, Ohio
Aden, Robert C., Middle Tennessee St. Univ., Murfreesboro, Tenn.
Adler, Mrs. Leona K., 101 Central Park W., New York, N.Y.
Adolphsen, Louis J., Hinsdale Senior High School, Hinsdale, Ill.
Ahrendt, Kenneth M., 2166 Dollarton Hwy., North Vancouver, B.C., Canada
Aichele, Douglas R., Oklahoma State Univ., Stillwater, Okla.
Ahrnsbrak, Henry C., 425 Berwyn Dr., Madison, Wis.
Aiken, Warren R., 2323 Farleigh Road, Columbus, Ohio
Airasian, Peter W., Cath. Educ. Res. Cent., Boston Col., Chestnut Hill, Mass.
Akemann, Mrs. Rhea, Marion Community Schools, Marion, Ind.
Akins, Harold S., 1300 High St., Wichita, Kans.
Alagna, Agostino A., 478 W. 26th St., Chicago, Ill.
Alberg, Gary L., 1990 Lakeaires Blvd., White Bear Lake, Minn.
Albrecht, Milton C., State Univ. of New York, Buffalo, N.Y.
Albright, Frank S., 1 N. Campus Drive, Canton, Mo.

Alcock, Wayne T., Dillond Univ., New Orleans, La.
Alessi, Samuel J., 99 Gordon St., Williamsville, N.Y.
Alexander, Burton F., Petersburg High School, Petersburg, Va.
Alexander, Elenora, Rm. 234, 1300 Capital Ave., Houston, Texas
Alexander, William M., Col. of Educ., Univ. of Florida, Gainesville, Fla.
Alkin, Marvin C., University of California, Los Angeles, Calif.
Allen, Annabelle, 286 Main St., New Canaan, Conn.
Allen, David, 8437 Truxton Ave., Los Angeles, Calif.
Allen, D. Ian, Simon Fraser University, Burnaby 2, B.C., Canada
Allen, Dwight W., Sch. of Educ., Univ. of Mass., Amherst, Mass.
Allen, Graham, Coburg Teachers College, Coburg, Melbourne, Australia
Allen, Harold Don, Nova Scotia Tchrs. Col., Nova Scotia, Canada
Allen, Mrs. Irene A., R.F.D. 1, Swanton, Vt.
Allen, James Robert, 1249 Lake Ave., Fort Wayne, Ind.
Allen, Jayne, 5706 Delwood Dr., Austin, Tex.
Allen, John E., 306 Arbour Dr., Newark, Del.
Allen, Ross L., State Univ. College, Cortland, N.Y.
Allen, Sylvia D., P.O. Box 14, Woodbridge, Va.
Allen, Warren G., State Teachers College, Minot, N.Dak.
Allender, Jerome S., 528 W. Sedgwick, Philadelphia, Pa.
Allison, John J., 200 Bloomfield Ave., West Hartford, Conn.
Allman, Reva White, Alabama State College, Montgomery, Ala.
Alm, Richard S., Dept. of Educ., University of Hawaii, Honolulu, Hawaii
Almen, Rev. Dr. Louis, 231 Madison Ave., New York, N.Y.
Almcrantz, Mrs. Georgia, 402 Brown Circle, Knox, Ind.
Almroth, Frank S., 20 Hilltop Ter., Wayne, N.J.
Alonso, Angel O., Ministry of Education, Madrid, Spain
Alper, Arthur E., Col. of Educ., Univ. of Ga., Athens, Ga.
Al-Rubaiy, Abdul Amir, Kent State University, Kent, Ohio
Alt, Pauline M., Central Connecticut State College, New Britain, Conn.
Althaus, Rosemary, Sch. of Educ., Winthrop College, Rock Hill, S.C.
Altman, Harold, 12006 Stanwood Dr., Los Angeles, Calif.
Altman, Herbert H., 832 Ocean Ave., Brooklyn, N.Y.
Amacher, Mrs. Walter, 7471 Mudbrook St., N.W., Massillon, Ohio
Ambrose, Edna V., 2124 N.E. 7th Ter., Gainesville, Fla.
Amershek, Kathleen, Col. of Educ., Univ. of Maryland, College Park, Md.
Ames, John L., 7 Laura Lane, E. Setauket, N.Y.
Amioka, Shiro, University of Hawaii, Honolulu, Hawaii
Ammon, Paul R., Sch. of Educ., Univ. of California, Berkeley, Calif.
Anastasiow, Nicholas J., Univ. School, By Pass #46, Bloomington, Ind.
Anders, Mrs. Elizabeth M., 3601 Palm Dr., Riviera Beach, Fla.
Anderson, Donald G., Oakland Public Schls., 1025 Second Ave., Oakland, Calif.
Anderson, Arnold G., 3700 Ross, Avdallas, Tex.
Anderson, Doyle R., 1731 Anthony Dr., St. Joseph, Mich.
Anderson, Edmond C., Sequoyah Junior High School, Dallas, Tex.
Anderson, Ernest M., Kansas State Col., Pittsburg, Kan.
Anderson, G. Lester, Pa. State Univ., University Park, Pa.
Anderson, Harold, 1531 W. Mourilaine, Ft. Collins, Colo.
*Anderson, Howard R., Houghton Mifflin Co., Boston, Mass.
Anderson, Isabel C., Sch. of Educ., Temple University, Philadelphia, Pa.
Anderson, J. Paul, Col. of Educ., Univ. of Maryland, College Park, Md.
Anderson, James Wendell, St. Cloud State Col., St. Cloud, Minn.
Anderson, Kenneth E., Sch. of Educ., Univ. of Kansas, Lawrence, Kans.
Anderson, Lester W., Sch. of Educ., Univ. of Michigan, Ann Arbor, Mich.
Anderson, Linnea M., 2103 S. Franklin, Apt. D, Kirksville, Mo.
Anderson, Philip S., Wisconsin State University, River Falls, Wis.
Anderson, Robert Henry, Grad. Sch. of Educ., Harvard Univ., Cambridge, Mass.
Anderson, Robert T., Col. of Educ., Univ. of Alabama, University, Ala.
Anderson, Ruth, 2569—7th Ave., Apt. 24 I, New York, N.Y.
Anderson, Stuart A., Sangamon State Univ., Springfield, Ill.
Anderson, Vernon E., Col. of Educ., University of Maryland, College Park, Md.

Anderson, W. Harold, 908 W. Main St., Waupun, Wis.
Anderson, William J., P.O. Box 288, Georgetown, Tex.
Andree, R. G., Southern Illinois University, Edwardsville, Ill.
Andregg, Neal B., 2553 Richmond Hill Rd., Augusta, Ga.
Andrews, Clay S., Dept. of Educ., San Jose State College, San Jose, Calif.
Andrews, Richard L., 2402-156th Ave., S.E., Bellevue, Wash.
Andrews, Sam D., Bowling Green State University, Bowling Green, Ohio
Andrews, Stella F., 544 Washington Ave., Pleasantville, N.Y.
Andrisek, John R., 119 Meadow Dr., Berea, Ohio
Angelini, Arrigo L., University of Sao Paulo, Sao Paulo, Brazil
Angell, George W., State University College, Plattsburg, N.Y.
Angelo, Rev. Mark V., St. Bonaventure Univ., St. Bonaventure, N.Y.
Angle, Philip H., Central Bucks School, Doylestown, Pa.
*Annis, Helen W., 6711 Conway Ave., Takoma Park, Md.
Ansara, Alice, Manter Hall Sch., Cambridge, Mass.
Ansel, James O., Western Michigan University, Kalamazoo, Mich.
Anselm, Karl R., 10516 Rampart Ave., Cupertino, Calif.
Anthony, Sally M., San Diego State Col., San Diego, Calif.
Antoine, Tamlin C., P.O. Box 1647, Taipei, Taiwan, Rep. of China
Anton, Anne S., 12435 Debby St., North Hollywood, Calif.
Antonelli, Luiz K., Queens College, Flushing, N.Y.
Apel, J. Dale, Kansas State Univ., Manhattan, Kans.
Apple, Joe A., San Diego State College, San Diego, Calif.
Apple, Michael W., Sch. of Educ., Univ. of Wis., Madison, Wis.
Appleton, David, Supt. of Schools, Pine St., North Conway, N.H.
Aquila, Frank D., Prin., E. Jr. High Sch., East Liverpool, Ohio
Arcarese, Lawrence C., State Univ. Col. of Arts & Sci., Plattsburgh, N.Y.
Archer, Marguerite P., 330 Overhill Dr., Chambersburg, Pa.
Archer, Philip, 192 Frank St., Schenectady, N.Y.
Arends, Wade B., 439 Wildwood, Park Forest, Ill.
Armistead, Roy B., 9234 Queenston Dr., St. Louis, Mo.
Armstrong, Betty W., Univ. of Cincinnati, Cincinnati, Ohio
Armstrong, Mrs. Carmen L., R.F.D. No. 2, 5 Points Rd., Sycamore, Ill.
Armstrong, Mrs. Jenny R., Univ. of Wisconsin, Madison, Wis.
Armstrong, J. Niel, Sch. of Educ., Agric. & Tech. College, Greensboro, N.C.
Arnaud, E. E., Our Lady of the Lake College, San Antonio, Tex.
* Arnesen, Arthur E., 35 Hillside Drive, Salt Lake City, Utah
Arnoff, Melvin, 4325 Groveland Rd., University Heights, Ohio
Arnold, Gala, 740 "J" Ave., Coronado, Calif.
Arnold, Marshall, 301 S. Water St., Henderson, Ky.
Arnold, Phyllis D., 628 Patterson Ave., San Antonio, Tex.
Arnold, Shirley L., 54 Kehr St., Buffalo, N.Y.
Arnsdorf, Val E., Sch. of Educ., Univ. of Delaware, Newark, Del.
Arnstein, George E., 2500 Virginia Ave. N.W., Washington, D.C.
Aromi, Eugene J., Univ. of So. Alabama, Mobile, Ala.
Arthur, Douglas C., Petaluma City Schools, Petaluma, Calif.
Arveson, Raymond G., 3178 Oakes Drive, Hayward, Calif.
Arvin, Charles L., Crawfordsville Community Schools, Crawfordsville, Ind.
Ashburn, Arnold G., Sch. Adm. Bldg., 3700 Ross Ave., Dallas, Tex.
Ashe, Robert W., Dept. of Educ., Arizona State University, Tempe, Ariz.
Asher, William, Dept. of Educ., Purdue Univ., Lafayette, Ind.
Ashley, Rubelle, 1504 Glenway Dr., Toledo, Ohio
Askins, Billy E., Box 4234, Texas Tech. College, Lubbock, Tex.
Aspridy, Chrisoula, 2986 Lyell Rd., Rochester, N.Y.
Atkins, Thurston A., Teachers Col., Columbia Univ., New York, N.Y.
Atkinson, Gene, Col. of Educ., Univ. of Houston, Houston, Tex.
Atkinson, William N., Jackson Junior College, Jackson, Mich.
Aubin, Albert E., Sch. of Educ., Univ. of California, Los Angeles, Calif.
Auble, Donavon, Western Col. for Women, Oxford, Ohio
Aubry, A. J., L. B. Landry School, New Orleans, La.
Auer, B. F., Prin., Westgate Jr. High Sch., East Liverpool, Ohio

Ause, Orval L., Federal Ways Schs., Federal Way, Wash.
Austin, David B., Richmond College, Staten Island, New York
Austin, Martha Lou, Univ. of South Florida, Tampa, Fla.
Austin, Mary C., Col. of Educ., Univ. of Hawaii, Honolulu, Hawaii
Austin, Roy S., State University College, Potsdam, N.Y.
Ausubel, David P., City University of New York, New York, N.Y.
Avant, Dorothea B., 8637 S. Michigan Ave., Chicago, Ill.
Avegno, T. Sylvia, 907 Castle Pt. Terrace, Hoboken, N.J.
Avella, Anthony A., Adm. Bldg., 195 Virginia St., Hillside, N.J.
Avinger, W. H., Abilene Christian College, Abilene, Texas
Ayer, Joseph C., 4200 Manchester Road, Middletown, Ohio
Azzarelli, Joseph J., New York University, Washington Sq., New York, N.Y.

Babcock, William E., 131 W. Nittany Ave., State College, Pa.
Babel, John Jr., 10927 Conestoga Ct., Cincinnati, Ohio
Bach, Jacob O., Southern Illinois University, Carbondale, Ill.
Bachman, Ralph V., South High School, Salt Lake City, Utah
Backus, Thomas A., 570—115th Ave., Treasure Island, Fla.
Bacon, Walter E., 1360 Touhy Ave., Chicago, Ill.
Bacon, William P., Sch. of Educ., Univ. of the Pacific, Stockton, Calif.
Bacsalmasi, Stephen, York Cent. Dist. H.S. Brd., Richmond Hill, Ont., Canada
Baer, Campion, Capuchin Sem. of St. Mary, Crown Point, Ind.
Bahlke, Susan J., 2101 Philo Road, Urbana, Ill.
Bahn, Lorene A., 2843 Lomita Circle, Springfield, Mo.
Bahner, Joel H., Box 9177, APO, New York, N.Y.
Bahner, John M., 5335 Far Hills Ave., Dayton, Ohio
Bahrenburg, Erma M., 27 Ninth St., Carle Place, L.I., N.Y.
Baich, Henry, University of Portland, Portland, Ore.
Bailer, Joseph R., Dept. of Educ., Western Maryland College, Westminster, Md.
Bailey, Lucile, 119 E. University Dr., Tempe, Arizona
Bajek, Robert S., 3830 S. Scoville, Berwyn, Ill.
Bajwa, Ranjit Singh, 2235 Georgetown Blvd., Ann Arbor, Mich.
Baker, Charles, Box 271, Weidman, Mich.
Baker, Earlene, 43 Barnes St., Providence, R.I.
Baker, Eugene H., 1402 N. Harvard, Arlington Hghts., Ill.
Baker, Harry J., 2241 Q Via Puerta, Laguna Hills, Calif.
Baker, I. D., Greenville College, Greenville, Ill.
Baker, John E., Col. of Educ. & Nurs., Univ. of Vermont, Burlington, Vt.
Baker, Judith M., IDEA, 5335 Far Hills Ave., St. 300, Dayton, Ohio
Baker, Lillian Mrs. 20257 Allentown Dr., Woodland Hills, Calif.
Baker, Rebecca, Southern Illinois University, Carbondale, Ill.
Baker, Robert C., Bemidji State College, Bemidji, Minn.
Baker, Robert E., Sch. of Educ., George Washington Univ., Washington, D.C.
Baker, William E., 11247 Dempsey Ave., Granada Hills, Calif.
Baldauf, R., 122 Forest Ave., Oak Park, Ill.
Baldwin, Alan L., Redwood City Sch. Dist., Redwood City, Calif.
Baldwin, Rollin, 924 West End Ave., New York, N.Y.
Balian, Arthur, 6804 W. Dickinson St., Milwaukee, Wis.
Ball, George G., Univ. of Northern Iowa, Cedar Falls, Iowa
Ballantine, Francis A., San Diego State College, San Diego, Calif.
Ballantine, Harden Parke, 303 W. 2nd St., Bloomington, Ind.
Ballou, Stephen V., Div. of Educ., Fresno State College, Fresno, Calif.
Balmer, Louise E., 619 Hibbard Dr., Chapel Hill, N.C.
Balzer, David M., Col. of Educ., University of Toledo, Toledo, Ohio
Banathy, Bela A., Monterey Peninsula Col., Monterey, Calif.
Bank, Adrianne, 4949 Ethel Ave., Sherman Oaks, Calif.
Banner, Carolyn Ann, 821 S.W. Blvd., Jefferson City, Mo.
Bany, Mary, 411 N. Third St., Alhambra, Calif.
Baratta, Anthony N., Sch. of Educ., Fordham University, New York, N.Y.
Barbaree, Frank, P.O. Box 547, Jackson, Ala.
Barbe, Walter B., 803 Church St., Honesdale, Pa.

Barber, Grant W., 1251 Shipman St., Birmingham, Mich.
Barber, Richard L., Col. of Arts & Sci., Univ. of Louisville, Louisville, Ky.
Barclay, Doris, 5151 State College Dr., Los Angeles, Calif.
Bard, George, 430 Silver Oaks Dr., Kent, Ohio
Barden, Michael W., Univ. of Rhode Island, Kingston, R.I.
Bardsley, Frederick G., 4 Eldorado Road, Chelmsford, Mass.
Barkley, Margaret V., Arizona State University, Tempe, Ariz.
Barlow, Melvin L., Sch. of Educ., Univ. of California, Los Angeles, Calif.
Barnard, W. Robert, Evans Chem. Lab., 88 W. 18th Ave., Columbus, Ohio
Barnes, Cyrus W., Beachlake, Pa.
Barnes, Fred P., Col. of Educ., University of Illinois, Urbana, Ill.
Barnes, O. Dennis, 263 Elmwood Ter., Rochester N.Y.
Barney, Angelo T., 818 Black Rd., Joliet, Ill.
Baron, Bruce G., Temple Univ., Philadelphia, Pa.
Barr, Charlotte A., Chicago State College, Chicago, Ill.
Barr, Dixon A., Sch. of Educ., East. Kentucky State Col., Richmond, Ky.
Barratt, Thomas K., Edinboro State Col., Edinboro, Pa.
Barrett, George M., Biscoe, N.C.
Barron, Donald, Huntington Station, N.Y.
Barron, Richard F., Syracuse Univ., Syracuse, N.Y.
Barros, Raymond, S.J. Santiago, Chile
Barron, William E., University of Texas, Austin, Tex.
Barry, Florence G., 5956 Race Ave., Chicago, Ill.
Bartel, Fred C., 856 Ivy St., Frankfort, Ky.
Bartelt, Kenneth C., 205 E. 10th St., Muscatine, Iowa
Barter, Alice K., 8547 W. 102nd St., Palos Hills, Ill.
Bartlett, Fernand E., Upstate Med. Center, Syracuse, N.Y.
Bartlett, Robert C., 2105 S. 23rd Ave., Broadview, Ill.
Barton, Carl L., Superintendent, Community Cons. Sch. Dist. 70, Freeburg, Ill.
Barton, George E., Jr., 1010 Short St., New Orleans, La.
Bartoo, Eugene, 34 Ellis Ave., Springville, N.Y.
Bastian, Janis Sue, 3333 Terrace, Terre Haute, Ind.
Batha, Robert, Chester Junior-Senior High School, Chester, Calif.
Batinich, Mary Ellen, 9215 S. Troy Ave., Chicago, Ill.
Batten, James W., Box 2455, East. Carolina College, Greenville, N.C.
Battle, John A., 11 Jones St., New Hyde Park, N.Y.
Battles, John J., 12 Ellis Ave., Ossining, N.Y.
Bauer, Norman J., 28 Westview Crescent, Geneseo, N.Y.
Bauman, Reemt R., Col. of Educ., Univ. of Toledo, Toledo, Ohio
Baumgartner, Reuben A., Senior High School, Freeport, Ill.
Baumgartner, Rolla W., 7500 Air Base Group, A P O, N.Y. 09218
Bausch, Cameron F., 234 Easterly Parkway, State College, Pa.
Bauthues, Donald J., 219 5th Ave., N.E. No. 29, Puyallup, Wash.
Baxel, George H., 1776 Raritan Rd., Scotch Plains, N.J.
Baxter, Eugenia, 629 Fourth St., Monongahela, Pa.
Baxter, Marlin B., Moline Public Schools, 1619 Eleventh Ave., Moline, Ill.
Bazik, A. Mathew, 477 Agyle Ave., Elmhust, Ill.
Beach, Lowell W., 3606 Univ. H.S., Univ. of Michigan, Ann Arbor, Mich.
Beach, Mary L., 101 Butternut Lane, Columbia, S.C.
Beall, David C., Dir., Pupil Personnel Serv., Mentor, Ohio
Beamer, George C., North Texas State College, Denton, Tex.
Beamer, Rufus W., Virginia Polytechnic Inst., Blacksburg, Va.
Bear, David E., 12 Ramona Pl., Godfrey, Ill.
Beard, Richard L., 1812 Meadowbrook Hgts. Rd., Charlottesville, Va.
Beaton, Daniel W., 225 Vista Del Parque, Hollywood Riviera, Calif.
Beattie, George W., P.O. Box 100, Aptos, Calif.
Beatty, Charles J., 13011 Bellevue St., Beltsville, Md.
Beatty, Walcott H., 209 Kensington Way, San Francisco, Calif.
Beaty, Edgar, Middle Tennessee State Univ., Murfreesboro, Tenn.
Beaubier, Edward Wm., 5631 El Parque St., Long Beach, Calif.
Beauchamp, George A., Sch. of Educ., Northwestern University, Evanston, Ill.

Beauchamp, Marian Z., 107 Century Drive, Syracuse, N.Y.
Beaumont, Urville J., Tenney High School, Methuen, Mass.
Bebb, Randall R., Univ. of No. Iowa, Cedar Falls, Iowa
Bebell, Clifford S., Southern Colorado State Col., Pueblo, Colo.
Bechtel, E. J., Rt. 1, Valparaiso, Ind.
Beck, Hubert Park, Sch. of Educ., City College, 523 W. 121st St., New York, N.Y.
Beck, John M., 5832 Stony Island Ave., Chicago, Ill.
Beck, Norman W., Supt., Monroe County Schls., Waterloo, Ill.
Beck, Robert H., 233 Burton Hall, University of Minnesota, Minneapolis, Minn.
Becker, Harry A., Superintendent of Schools, Norwalk, Conn.
Becker, Millie A., 7637 S. Loomis Blvd., Chicago, Ill.
Bedell, Ralph, Dept. of Educ., Univ. of Missouri, Columbia, Mo.
Beebe, Nelson, Jr., Pennsville Memorial High School, Pennsville, N.J.
Beeching, Robert B., 1461 W. Shaw, Fresno, Calif.
Beery, John R., Sch. of Educ., University of Miami, Coral Gables, Fla.
Behnke, Donald J., 60 Everit Ave., Hewlett, N.Y.
*Behrens, Minnie S., Pomeroy, Iowa
Beighley, Archie F., Dept. of Educ., Winona State Col., Winona, Minn.
Beitler, Roger T., 2676 Walnut Blvd., Ashtabula, Ohio
Belcastro, Frank P., Univ. of San Diego, San Diego, Calif.
Belcher, Eddie W., Louisville Public Schls., 506 W. Hill St., Louisville, Ky.
Belgum, Loretta E., San Francisco State College, San Francisco, Calif.
Bell, Harrison B., Silver-Burdett Co., Morristown, N.J.
Bell, Keith A., 22906—72 Pl., W., Mountlake Terrace, Wash.
Bell, Mary Anne. 118 N. Mozart St., Chicago, Ill.
Bell, Mildred, Harding College, Searcy, Ark.
Bell, Robert M., 2819 W. Sherwin Ave., Chicago, Ill.
Bell, Robert W., Wells Lane, Stony Brook, N.Y.
Bell, Wilmer V., 702 Kingston Rd., Baltimore, Md.
Bellack, Arno A., Tchrs. Col., Columbia University, New York, N.Y.
Belland, John C., Ohio State Univ., Columbus, Ohio
Belville, Donald H., 5925 Holly Glen Drive, Toledo, Ohio
Bemis, James Richard, 5243 Tango Ave., Yorba Linda, Calif.
Benben, John S., 7 Victoria Rd., Ardsley, N.Y.
Benda, Harold, Educ. Dept., West Chester State College, West Chester, Pa.
Bender, Coleman, Emerson College, Boston, Mass.
Bender, Kenneth R., University of Mississippi, University, Miss.
Bender, Martin L., 384 Prospect Ave., Hackensack, N.J.
Bender, Ralph E., Ohio State University, Columbus, Ohio
Benito, Sabado S., Rust College, Holly Springs, Miss.
Bennett, Kelly R., 1413 S. Almansor St., Alhambra, Calif.
Bennett, Dale E., Col. of Educ., Univ. of Ill., Urbana, Ill.
Bennett, Lloyd M., Texas Woman's University, Denton, Tex.
Bennett, Robert N., Greene Central School, Greene, N.Y.
Bennett, Roger V., 6736 Melrose Drive, McLean, Va.
Bennett, William R., Mt. Vernon Nazarene Col., Mt. Vernon, Ohio
Bennie, William A., Univ. of Texas, Austin, Tex.
Benson, Paul A., 1705 Campus Road, Toledo, Ohio
Bentley, Caryl B., Lake Nebagamon, Wis.
Bentley, Harold, Northern Essex Community Col., Haverhill, Mass.
Bentley, Mrs. Harriett P., 2985 Wooster Rd., Rocky River, Ohio
Bentley, Robert, 1535 Walton Ave., Bronx, N.Y.
Benvenuto, Arthur, 158 Garden Pkwy., Henrietta, N.Y.
Benz, Marion H., S-4493 So. Buffalo St., Orchard Park, N.Y.
Berg, Arthur D., Music Consult., Dearborn Pub. Schools, Dearborn, Mich.
Berg, Dorothy D., 5924 N. Forest Glen Ave., Chicago, Ill.
Berg, Selmer H., 1216 Running Springs Rd., Walnut Creek, Calif.
Berger, Allen, University of Alberta, Edmonton, Alba., Canada
Bergeson, Clarence O., State University College, Geneseo, N.Y.
Bergeson, John S., Western Michigan Univ., Kalamazoo, Mich.
Berke, Norman D., California State Col., Los Angeles, Calif.

Berkihiser, Frances, Evangel College, Springfield, Mo.
Berkowitz, Edward, 2 Loretta Dr., Syosset, L.I., N.Y.
Berkowitz, Howard, State University College, Oneonta, N.Y.
Berlin, Pearl, University of Massachusetts, Amherst, Mass.
Berlin, Robert S., 383 Grand St., New York, N.Y.
Bernal, Leslie C., 10 Ditson Pl., Methuen, Mass.
Bernard, Donald H., 1741 S.W. 37th Pl., Gainesville, Fla.
Bernard, Harold W., 1985 S.W. Warwick Ave., Portland, Oreg.
Bernd, John M., 824 Ellis St., Stevens Point, Wis.
Bernert, Roman A., S.J., Marquette Univ., Milwaukee, Wis.
Bernhoft, Otto L., Prin., South H.S., Fargo, N.D.
Berning, Norbert J., 204 W. Sunset Pl., DeKalb, Ill.
Bernstein, Abbot A., 104 Edwards Rd., Clifton, N.J.
Bertness, Henry J., 2909 N. 29th St., Tacoma, Wash.
Bertolaet, Frederick W., Univ. of Mich., Ann Arbor, Mich.
Bertrand, John R., Berry College, Mt. Berry, Ga.
Besselsen, Gilbert, 2242 Elliott S.E., Grand Rapids, Mich.
Bettelheim, Bruno 1365 E. 60th St., Chicago, Ill.
Betts, Emmett A., Sch. of Educ., University of Miami, Coral Gables, Fla.
Beynon, Robert P., Devel. & Resch., Bowling Green Univ., Bowling Green, Ohio
Bezanson, Clyde O., 2410 Hillside Rd., White Bear Lake, Minn.
Bibb, Walter C., RFD 2, Arlington, Vt.
Bickert, Roderick N., Supt. of Schools, Mason City, Iowa
Bidwell, Wilma W., 1400 Washington Ave., Albany, N.Y.
Biggy, Mary Virginia, 16 Park Ln., Concord, Mass.
Biles, Raymond, Baylor University, Waco, Tex.
Billups, Mrs. Clairene B., 2409 Tidewater Dr., Norfolk, Va.
Binford, George H., Central H.S., Charlotte Courthouse, Va.
Binford, Linwood T., J. Andrew Bowler School, Richmond, Va.
Bingham, William C., Rutgers University, New Brunswick, N.J.
Binkley, Marvin Edward, 1000 Noelton Ln., Nashville, Tenn.
Birch, Jack W., 2704 C.L., Univ. of Pittsburgh, Pittsburgh, Pa.
Bird, Barbara R., 541 Sligh Blvd., N.E., Grand Rapids, Mich.
Bird, Charles A., 23 Fraser Pl., Hastings on Hudson, N.Y.
Birdsell, Don F., Supt. of Schools, Wheaton, Ill.
Bishop, Clifford L., Univ. of Northern Iowa, Cedar Falls, Iowa
Bishop, Martha D., Dept. of Educ., Winthrop College, Rock Hill, S.C.
Bissell, Norman E., 1183 Ironstone Dr., Cincinnati, Ohio
Bizinkauskas, 424 North Cary St., Brockton, Mass.
Bjork, Alton J., Dept. of Educ., Illinois State University, Normal, Ill.
Black, Donald B., Univ. of Calgary, Calgary 44, Alberta, Canada
Black, Hugh C., Dept. of Educ., Univ. of California, Davis, Calif.
Black, John C., Lincoln Elem. Sch., Chicago Heights, Ill.
Black, Mrs. Marian W., Sch. of Educ., Florida State Univ., Tallahassee, Fla.
Black, Millard H., 10031 Vecino Lane, La Habra, Calif.
Blackledge, Mrs. Helen V., Southern Heights Sch., Fort Wayne, Ind.
Blackman, Charles A., 1962 Pawnee Trail, Okemos, Mich.
Blackshear, John S., 3933 Wisteria Ln., S.W., Atlanta, Georgia
Blackwell Leslie, Western Wash. State Col., Bellingham, Wash.
Blackwell, Lewis F., Jr., Box 1026, University, Ala.
Blackwell, Sara, N.Y. State Col. of H.E., Cornell Univ., Ithaca, N.Y.
Blaine, Russell K., 1816 Park Ave., S.E., Cedar Rapids, Iowa
Blake, Duane L., Colorado State Univ., Fort Collins, Colo.
Blakely, Richard F., Iona College, New Rochelle, N.Y.
Blanchard, Walter J., Rhode Island Col., Warwick, R.I.
Blanco, Carlomagno J., Univ. of Toledo, Toledo, Ohio
Blankenship, A. H., Educational Research Council, Cleveland, Ohio
Blanton, Roy R., Jr., Appalachian St. Univ., Boone, N.C.
Blaser, John W., Wahtonka High School, The Dalles, Ore.
Blessington, John P., Whitby School, Greenwich, Conn.
Bleyer, John F., Seton Hill Col., Greensburg, Pa.

Blezien, Stephen S., 5762 N. Kercheval, Chicago, Ill.
Bliesmer, Emery P., Read. Ctr., Pennsylvania State Univ., University Park, Pa.
Bligh, Harold F., 81 Lincoln Ave., Ardsley, N.Y.
Blocher, R. Banks, 411 N. Sixth St., Vincennes, Ind.
Block, Elaine C., Hunter College, New York, N.Y.
Blomenberg, Gilbert, 345 North 2nd St., Seward, Nebr.
Blomgren, Glen H., Fresno State College, Fresno, Calif.
Blommers, Paul, East Hall, State University of Iowa, Iowa City, Iowa
Bloom, Herbert C., 3481 Sheridan Ave., Miami Beach, Fla.
Blough, John A., 2840 Proctor Drive, Columbus, Ohio
Blum, Mrs. Joanne L., Point Park Junior College, Pittsburgh, Pa.
Blythe, L. Ross, 108 Green Acres, Valparaiso, Ind.
Boario, Dora A., 422 Third St., Leechburg, Pa.
Bock, R. Darrell, Dept. of Educ., Univ. of Chicago, Chicago, Ill.
Boeck, Clarence H., Univ. of Minnesota, Minneapolis, Minn.
Boeck, Marjorie A., 3747 15th Ave., N.E., Seattle, Wash.
Boeck, Robert W., 4090 Geddes Rd., Ann Arbor, Mich.
Boenig, Robert W., State Univ. Col., Fredonia, N.Y.
Boersma, Nancy, 7 Keller Lane, Dobbs Ferry, N.Y.
Boger, D. L., Morehouse College, Atlanta, Ga.
Boggess, Violet F., 2445 New Milford Rd., Atwater, Ohio
Bogle, Frank P., Superintendent of Schools, Millville, N.J.
Boisclair, Cecile, University of Montreal, Montreal, Que., Canada
Boldt, Frederick J., Chula Vista Schls., Bonita, Calif.
Bolin, Phyllis W., 5721 N.W. 12th Ct., Fort Lauderdale, Fla.
Bolton, Dale L., Dept. of Educ., Univ. of Washington, Seattle, Wash.
Bond, Barbara, Univ. of South Carolina, Columbia, S.C.
Bond, George W., 3 Julia Ave., New Paltz, N.Y.
Bond, Horace M., Sch. of Educ., Atlanta University, Atlanta, Ga.
Bonk, Edward C., North Texas University, Denton, Tex.
Booker, Ann, 849 E. 215th St., Bronx, N.Y.
*Booker, Ivan A., N.E.A. Mem. Div., 1201 Sixteenth St., N.W., Washington, D.C.
Boos, William A., 1515 Bryndon Rd., Glenview, Ill.
Booth, Delores C., 6604 Tremont St., Oakland, Calif.
Borders, Frances R., 3617 Raymond St., Chevy Chase, Md.
Borg, Robert L., Scott Hall, University of Minnesota, Minneapolis, Minn.
Borg, Walter R., 342 Mangrove Way, Walnut Greek, Calif.
Bortz, A. G., Lansing Sch. Bd. of Educ. (MSU), Lansing, Mich.
Bosch, Albert C., 500 W. 235th St., New York, N.Y.
Bosch, Gerald, 228 Ellen Ave., State College, Pa.
Bosco, J. Anthony, S.U.N.Y., 1400 Western Ave., Albany, N.Y.
Bossard, Grace, Route 3, Box 6, Seaford, Del.
Bossier, Antonia M., 1661 No. Roman St., New Orleans, La.
Bost, William A., 1330 Church St., Bethlehem, Pa.
Bouchard, John B., State Univ. Col., Fredonia, N.Y.
Boula, James A., 316 S. 2nd St., Springfield, Ill.
Boulac, Brian Michael, University of Notre Dame, Notre Dame, Ind.
Bouseman, John W., Cent. Y.M.C.A. Comm. Col., Chicago, Ill.
Bovee, Corlan D., Lewis-Cass Elem. Sch., Livonia, Mich.
Bowen, James J., 619 S. Russell St., Monterey Park, Calif.
Bowers, A. Eugene, Fayette County Schools, Fayetteville, Ga.
Bowers, Norman D., Sch. of Educ., Northwestern Univ., Evanston, Ill.
Bowers, Victor L., Southwest Texas State College, San Marcos, Tex.
Bowman, Howard A., Box 3307, Terminal Annex, Los Angeles, Calif.
Bowman, Orrin H., 66 Creekview Drive, Rochester, N.Y.
Boyajy, Robert J., 10 North Drive, Livingston, N.J.
Boyd, Richard A., 367 Trumbull S.E., Warren, Ohio
Boyd, Robert D., Dept. of Educ., Univ. of Wisconsin, Madison, Wis.
Boyd, Robert M., Col. of Educ., Ohio University, Athens, Ohio
Boyer, James B., Univ. of Houston, Houston, Tex.
Boyer, Judith, Watterson Towers, Normal, Ill.

Boykin, Leander L., Florida A. & M. University, Tallahassee, Fla.
Boyle, Marcella (Mrs. James G.), 43 Hazen Ct., Wayne, N.J.
Boyle, William J., 620 W. Clairmont Ave., Eau Claire, Wis.
Boynton, Paul M., 1183 Farmington Ave., W. Hartford, Conn.
Bozzelli, Albert, 70 Park Ave., West Caldwell, N.J.
Braam, L. S., Sch. of Educ., Syracuse University, Syracuse, N.Y.
Bracewell, George, Southern Illinois University, Carbondale, Ill.
Brackbill, A. L., Jr., Millersville State College, Millersville, Pa.
Bradford, James L., 1692 Northwest Blvd., Columbus, Ohio
Bradford, H. Frank, Northern Arizona Univ., Flagstaff, Ariz.
Bradley, Mrs. Howard R., 2147 Blue Hills Rd., Manhattan, Kans.
Bradley, Martha W., East Tennessee State Univ., Johnson City, Tenn.
Bradtmueller, Weldon G., Northern Ill. Univ., DeKalb, Ill.
Brady, Florence A., 15A Troy Drive, Springfield, N.J.
Brady, Francis X., Elmira College, Elmira, N.Y.
Brady, John C., Bemidji State College, Bemidji, Minn.
Brain, George B., Col. of Educ., Washington State Univ., Pullman, Wash.
Brainard, Lois, San Jose State College, San Jose, Calif.
Bramwell, John R., Univ. of Oregon, Eugene, Oreg.
Brandinger, Mrs. Alice, 19 Carnation Pl., Trenton, N.J.
Brandt, Willard J., University of Wisconsin-Milwaukee, Milwaukee, Wis.
Brannon, Phyllis J., 4778 Washtenaw, B-3, Ann Arbor, Mich.
Brantley, Mabel, 623 N. First St., DeKalb, Ill.
Braswell, Robert H., 1618 Stonehill Pl., Rock Hill, S.C.
Brauer, Walter L., Washington H.S., Milwaukee, Wis.
Braun, Frank R., Col. of Educ., University of Minnesota, Minneapolis, Minn.
Braun, Frederick G., Col. of Educ., Univ. of Hawaii, Honolulu, Hawaii
Braun, Gertrude E., West Conn. State Col., Danbury, Conn.
Braun, Irma D., 228 Ocean Blvd., Atlantic Highlands, N.J.
Braun, Mary Ann R., 709 S. Race St., Urbana, Ill.
Braun, Ray H., 101 N. McCullough St., Urbana, Ill.
Bravo, Anna, 32 Beach Hill St., Ft. Salonga, N.Y.
Bredesen, Dorothy A., 644 "D" St., N.E., Washington, D.C.
Breeding, Clifford C., 2708 Bridal Wreath Ln., Dallas, Tex.
Bregman, Sydell, 17 Bodnarik Rd., Edison, N.J.
Breihan, Edna, 1512 Briggs St., Lockport, Ill.
Brenner, Anton, East. Mich. Univ., Ypsilanti, Mich.
Brereton, Matthew J., 22 Oakland Ter., Newark, N.J.
Bresina, Bertha M., 8308 E. Highland Ave., Scottsdale, Ariz.
Breslin, Frederick D., Glassboro State College, Glassboro, N.J.
Bretsch, Howard S., Sch. of Ed., Univ. of Rochester, Rochester, N.Y.
Bretz, Frank H., 345 Overbrook Ave., Glassboro, N.J.
Brewster, Maurice A., Jr., Memorial Univ., St. John's Newfoundland
Brewton, Raymond E., Supt. of County Schools, Palo Pinto, Tex.
Brickman, William W., University of Pennsylvania, Philadelphia, Pa.
Bridgers, Raymond B., R.D. 2, Broadway Rd., Oswego, N.Y.
Bridges, C. M., Col. of Educ., University of Florida, Gainesville, Fla.
Bridges, Lonnie H., Box 10194, Southern University, Baton Rouge, La.
Bridges, Raymond H., Box 10194, Southern University, Baton Rouge, La.
Bridgham, Robert G., Sch. of Ed., Stanford Univ., Palo Alto, Calif.
Briggs, Larry A., 218 Cumberland Dr., Flint, Mich.
Briggs, Joseph M., 1710½ Cherry St., Fremont, Ohio
Bright, George W., Sutton Hall 5C, Austin, Tex.
Bright, John H., 628 Cuesta Ave., San Mateo, Calif.
* Bright, Orville T., 516½ Prospect Ave., Lake Bluff, Ill.
Brill, Donald M., 5420 Maher Ave., Madison, Wis.
Brim, Burl J., Southern Oregon Col., Ashland, Oreg.
Brimhall, Mrs. Alice, 111 Monticello Ave., Piedmont, Calif.
Briner, Conrad, 1221 Cambridge Ave., Claremont, Calif.
Bring, Curtis R., 12th Ave., Greeley, Colo.
Brink, William G., Sch. of Educ., Northwestern University, Evanston, Ill.

Brinkman, J. Warren, Kansas State Tchrs. College, Emporia, Kans.
Brinkmann, E. H., So. Illinois Univ., Edwardsville, Ill.
Brinkmeier, Oria A., 2384 Valentine, St. Paul, Minn.
Briscoe, Laurel A., 1520 Cedar Ridge Dr., N.E., Albuquerque, N.Mex.
Brish, William M., Supt., Washington Co. Schools, Hagerstown, Md.
*Bristow, William H., 70 Exeter St., Forest Hills, N.Y.
Britt, Laurence V., S.J., John Carroll Univ., Cleveland, Ohio
Brittain, Clay V., 1810 Panda Ln., McLean, Va.
Britton, Edward C., Sacramento State Col., Sacramento, Calif.
Britton, Gwyneth E., Oregon State Univ., Corvallis, Oreg.
Broadbent, Frank W., 6401 Allison Ave., Des Moines, Iowa
Brody, Erness B., Rutgers Univ., New Brunswick, N.J.
Brody, Seymour, 38 Burnett Terr., Maplewood, N.J.
Broening, Angela M., 3700 N. Charles St., Baltimore, Md.
Bromwich, Rose M., 13507 Hart St., Van Nuys, Calif.
Bronson, Homer D., Chico State College, Chico, Calif.
Bronson, Moses L., 290 Ninth Ave., New York, N.Y.
Brookins, Jack E., 1323 Bayview, North Bend, Ore.
Brooks, Robert L., North Texas State Univ., Winona, Tex.
Brother Adelbert James, Manhattan College, New York, N.Y.
Brother Charles Roe, F.S.C., 1515 Jackson, River Forest, Ill.
Brother Cosmas Herlihy, St. Francis College, Brooklyn, N.Y.
Brother Joseph Brusnahan, F.S.C., 650 E. Parkway So., Memphis, Tenn.
Brother Leo Gilskey, 414 N. Forest Ave., Oak Park, Ill.
Brother Leonard Coutney, St. Mary's College, Winona, Minn.
Brother Stephen Walsh, St. Edward's University, Austin, Tex.
Brother U. Cassian, St. Mary's Col., St. Mary's, Calif.
Brottman, Marvin C., University of Chicago, Chicago, Ill.
Brousseau, Sandy E., 43 Carlos Ct., Walnut Creek, Calif.
Brown, Aaron, 1468 President St., Brooklyn, N.Y.
Brown, Bob, Southwestern State Col., Weatherford, Okla.
Brown, Bryon B., Baylor Univ., Waco, Tex.
Brown, Carol L., 1701 W. Pensacola, Apt. 121, Tallahassee, Fla.
Brown, Carol S., 2634 Roseland, East Lansing, Mich.
Brown, Chester J., Col. of Educ., University of Arizona, Tucson, Ariz.
Brown, Cynthiana Ellen, 6644 Wildlife Rd., Malibu, Calif.
Brown, Douglas H., Pine Wood Dr., Contoocook, N.H.
Brown, Douglas M., Superintendent of Schools, Shorewood, Wis.
Brown, Mrs. Edith Farley, 133 Lynd St., Blossburg, Pa.
Brown, Francis A., 133 Lynd St., Blossburg, Pa.
Brown, George W., Superintendent of Schools, Webster Groves, Mo.
Brown, Gerald W., California State College, Hayward, Calif.
Brown, Gertrude E., 2835 Milan St., New Orleans, La.
Brown, Gordon L., 1012 Darrow Ave., Evanston, Ill.
Brown, Howard L., Schl. Admin. Center, 49 E. College Ave., Springfield, Ohio
Brown, Jeremy, Castleton State Col., Castleton, Vt.
Brown, Kenneth B., University of Missouri, Columbia, Mo.
Brown, Kenneth R., California Tchrs. Assn., 1705 Murchison Dr., Burlingame, Calif.
Brown, Lawrence D., Sch. of Educ., Indiana University, Bloomington, Ind.
Brown, Marion R., 404 Riverside Dr., New York, N.Y.
Brown, Mrs. Marjorie D., 4455 West 64th St., Los Angeles, Calif.
Brown, Marjorie M., University of Minnesota, St. Paul, Minn.
Brown, Mildred L., McGill University, Montreal, Canada
Brown, Pauline, 25800 Hillary St., Hayward, Calif.
Brown, Perry, Lock Haven State College, Lock Haven, Pa.
Brown, Robert H., Dillard H.S., Fort Lauderdale, Fla.
Brown, Robert M., Jr., 17913 Elm St., Fountain Valley, Calif.
Brown, Robert S., 702 N. Grandview, Stillwater, Okla.
Brown, Roy A., State Univ. of New York, Oneonta, N.Y.
Brown, Ruby J., 412 Steward Ave., Jackson, Mich.

Brown, Sara M., So. Connecticut State Col., New Haven, Conn.
Brown, Thomas J., Hofstra Univ., Hempstead, N.Y.
Brown, Virginia H., 1 Lafayette Plaisance, Detroit, Mich.
Brown, Warren M., Supt. of Schools, Ferguson, Mo.
Brownell, Samuel M., Yale Univ. & Univ. of Conn., New Haven, Conn.
Brownell, William A., 701 Spruce St., Berkeley, Calif.
Browning, Roy W., Topeka Public Schools, Topeka, Kans.
Brownlee, Geraldine D., 6937 S. Crandon Ave., Chicago, Ill.
Brownstein, Jewell, Dept. of Educ., Univ. of Louisville, Louisville, Ky.
Browy, Marjorie J., California State College, Los Angeles, Calif.
Broz, Joseph R., 3402 Clarendon Rd., Cleveland, Ohio
Brubaker, Leonard A., 409 Marian Ave., Normal, Ill.
Bruce, William C., 9205 Jackson Park Blvd., Wauwatosa, Wis.
Bruchak, Edward, 1115 Benning St., Durham, N.C.
Bruininks, Robert H., Univ. of Minnesota, Minneapolis, Minn.
Brumbaugh, W. Donald, University of Utah, Salt Lake City, Utah
Brunelle, Paul E., Supt., Winthrop, Maine
Brunetti, Frank A., 36 C. Escondido Village, Stanford, Calif.
Bruning, Charles R., University of Minnesota, Minneapolis, Minn.
Brunk, Jason W., Col. of Educ., Ohio Univ., Athens, Ohio
Brunner, Edward F., 847 El Prado, Lake City, Fla.
Bruno, Gordon A., Darien H.S., Darien, Conn.
Brunson, Mrs. Dewitt, P.O. Box 484, Orangeburg, S.C.
Brunsvold, Perley O., Mankato State Col., Mankato, Minn.
Bryan, Ray J., 220 Curtiss Hall, Iowa State Univ., Ames, Iowa
Bryant, B. Carleton, 810 Clear Lake Ave., West Palm Beach, Fla.
Bryant, Ira B., Kashmere Gardens High Sch., Houston, Tex.
Brydegaard, Marguerite, San Diego State Col., San Diego, Calif.
Bryner, James R., 185 Salisbury Dr., Saskatoon, Sask., Canada
Buchanan, Alfred K., 80 Grove St., Plantsville, Conn.
Buchanan, M. Marcia, Campus View House, 526 Bloomington, Ind.
Buchanan, Paul G., 61 Rosemary St., Buffalo, N.Y.
Buck, James E., Oregon College of Educ., Monmouth, Oreg.
Buckley, Richard Dale, Sch. of Educ., Wisconsin State University, Oshkosh, Wis.
Buckner, John D., 4246 W. North Market St., St. Louis, Mo.
Buckner, William N., 2643—15th St., N.W., Washington, D.C.
Budd, Mrs. Edith M., 3227 Parker Ave., West Palm Beach, Fla.
Buelke, John A., Western Michigan University, Kalamazoo, Mich.
Bulla, Helen M., Asst. Prin., Waterford Twsp. H.S., Pontiac, Mich.
Bullock, Portia C., 408 Tea St., N.W., Washington, D.C.
Bullock, William J., Superintendent of Schools, Kannapolis, N.C.
Bunda, Mary Anne, 301 W. Green, Champaign, Ill.
Bunger, Marianne, Alaska Methodist University, Anchorage, Alaska
Bunker, James G., Supt., Novato Unified Sch. Dist., Novato, Calif.
Bunnell, Robert A., Ford Foundation, 320 E. 43rd St., New York, N.Y.
Bunning, Madeline, Univ. of the Pacific, Stockton, Calif.
Buol, Mary Steudler, 91 Ten Acre Rd., New Britain, Conn.
Burch, Charles H., 1803 McDonald Dr., Champaign, Ill.
Burch, Mary J., 1123 Old Hillsborough Rd., RFD 4, Chapel Hill, N.C.
Burchett, Betty M., 531 Eigemann Hall, Bloomington, Ind.
Burdick, Alger E., St. Col. of Arkansas, Conway, Ark.
Burdick, Richard L., Educ. Dept., Carroll College, Waukesha, Wis.
Burford, Thomas E., Wayne St., Univ., Detroit, Mich.
Burg, Mrs. Mary, 2259 Wolfangle Rd., Cincinnati, Ohio
Burgdorf, Otto P., 36-12—210th St., Bayside, N.Y.
Burgess, Clara, 609 W. 147th St., New York, N.Y.
Burke, Carolyn L., 52 Portage, Highland Park, Mich.
Burke, Doyle K., Newport Spec. Sch. Dist., Newport, Ark.
Burke, Eileen M., 48 Bayberry Rd., Trenton, N.J.
• Burke, Gladys, 244 Outlook, Youngstown, Ohio
Burke, Henry R., 197 Ridgewood Ave., Glen Ridge, N.J.

Burke, Paul J., 1 Lookout Pl., Ardsley, N.Y.
Burke, Thomas O., 424 Bayberry Dr., Plantation, Fla.
Burke, Thomas S., 3171 W. 83rd St., Chicago, Ill.
Burkett, Lowell A., 1510 H. St. N.W., Washington, D.C.
Burks, Herbert M., Jr., 122 Kensington Rd., E. Lansing, Mich.
Burks, John B., Jersey City State College, Jersey City, N.J.
Burlingame, Dean R., 4109 Tripoli Dr., Corpus Christi, Tex.
Burns, Constance M., University of Bridgeport, Bridgeport, Conn.
Burns, Cranford H., Box 1549, Mobile, Ala.
Burns, Doris, 20 W. 86th St., New York, N.Y.
Burns, Gerald, Florida State Univ., Tallahassee, Fla.
Burns, James W., 2115 Waite Ave., Kalamazoo, Mich.
Burr, Elbert W., Monsanto Chemical Co., Lindbergh and Olive, St. Louis, Mo.
Burrell, E. William, Continental Drive, Middletown, R.I.
Burrough, Rudolph V., 526 Kirby, Shreveport, La.
Burrows, Alvina Treut, 117 Nassau Ave., Manhasset, N.Y.
Bursuk, Laura, 11 Harbor Lane, Glen Head, L.I., N.Y.
Burt, Lucile, Lincoln School, 338 Forest Ave., Fond du Lac, Wis.
Burton, Jane, R.R. #3, North Manchester, Ind.
Bushnell, Allan C., 309 South St., New Providence, N.J.
Buswell, Guy T., 1836 Thousand Oaks Blvd., Berkeley, Calif.
Buswell, Harrie R., 1316 N. Duff, Ames, Iowa
Butler, Mrs. B. LaConyea, Spelman College, Atlanta, Ga.
Butler, Joseph, 3847 Carrollton Ave., Indianapolis, Ind.
Butler, Laurence, 630 Leonard St., Ashland, Oreg.
Butler, Lester G., 468 E. Lincoln Ave., Columbus, Ohio
Butler, Marjorie, Div. of Ed., State Univ. Col., New Paltz, N.Y.
Butler, Paul W., 721 Australian Ave., W. Palm Beach, Fla.
Butler, Thomas M., 1428 W. Riverview St., Decatur, Ill.
Butts, David P., University of Texas, Austin, Tex.
Butts, Franklin A., 50 Delafield St., Poughkeepsie, N.Y.
Butts, Gordon K., Southern Illinois University, Carbondale, Ill.
Butts, R. Freeman, Tchrs. Col., Columbia University, New York, N.Y.
Buyse, R., Sch. of Educ., University of Louvain, Tournai, Belgium
Buzash, Gabriel A., Glassboro State Col., Glassboro, N.J.
Byers, Joe L., Michigan State Univ., East Lansing, Mich.
Byram, Harold M., Sch. of Educ., Michigan State Univ., East Lansing, Mich.
Byrne, John, Dist. Supt., Chicago Board of Education, Chicago, Ill.
Byrne, Richard Hill, Col. of Educ., Univ. of Maryland, College Park, Md.

Caccavo, Emil, 123 Willow St., Roslyn Heights, N.Y.
Cacha, Frances B., Pace College, New York, N.Y.
Cady, Henry L., Ohio State University, Columbus, Ohio
Cafiero, Albert J., Supt., Oradell Pub. Schools, Oradell, N.J.
Cafone, Harold C., Dept. of Educ., Oakland Univ., Rochester, Mich.
Cahan, Mrs. Ruth, 1916 Overland Ave., Los Angeles, Calif.
Cahraman, Thomas P., 35550 Bella Vista Dr., Yucaipa, Calif.
Cain, E. J., University of Nevada, Reno, Nev.
Cain, Lee C., Georgia Southern Branch, Statesboro, Ga.
Cain, Ralph W., Sutton Hall, University of Texas, Austin, Tex.
Calabrese, Vincent, 416 Sixth St., Palisades Park, N.J.
Caldwell, Cleon C., 2917 Noble Ave., Bakersfield, Calif.
Caldwell, Herbert M., 2568 St. Andrews Drive, Glendale, Calif.
Calfee, Robert, Stanford University, Stanford, Calif.
Califf, Stanley N., Chapman College, Orange, Calif.
Calip, Rev. Osmundo A., St. John's University, Jamaica, N.Y.
Call, Mrs. Ardell, Utah Education Association, Salt Lake City, Utah
Callahan, William T., 131 Jericho Turnpike, Jericho, N.Y.
Callan, John H., McQuaid Hall, Seton Hall Univ., South Orange, N.J.
Callas, Eliza E., 7080 Oregon Ave., N.W., Washington, D.C.
Callaway, A. Byron, Col. of Educ., Univ. of Georgia, Athens, Ga.
Calmes, Robert E., 5216 Mission Hill Dr., Tucson, Ariz.

Calvert, Lloyd, Supt. of Schools, Windsor, Conn.
Calvin, Thomas H., State Educ. Dept., State Univ. of N.Y., Albany, N.Y.
Cameron, Don C., 350 E. 700 S., St. George, Utah
Campanella, Alfred J., 589 Bogert Rd., River Edge, N.J.
Campbell, Clyde M., Michigan State University, East Lansing, Mich.
Campbell, E. G., Col. of Educ., Univ. of Maryland, College Park, Md.
Campbell, Roald F., Ohio State Univ., Columbus, Ohio
Campbell, Ronald T., 23644 Edward, Dearborn, Mich.
Canar, Donald A., Central YMCA Schls., 211 W. Wacker Dr., Chicago, Ill.
Candoli, Italo C., 315 Bryant Ave., Worthington, Ohio
Canfield, John M., Superintendent of Schools, West Plains, Mo.
Cannizzo, Florence, 6 Runyon Rd., Clifton, N.J.
Cannon, Wendell, Univ. of So. California, Los Angeles, Calif.
Cantlon, R. Jerry, Illinois State University, Normal, Ill.
Capehart, Bertis E., 120 Squire Hill Rd., Upper Montclair, N.J.
Capocy, John S., 4628 Seeley St., Downers Grove, Ill.
Cappa, Dan, California State Col., Los Angeles, Calif.
Cappelluzzo, Emma M., University of Massachusetts, Amherst, Mass.
Capps, Barbara, Maxwell Terrace, Bloomington, Ind.
Capps, Lelon R., Bailey Hall, University of Kansas, Lawrence, Kans.
Capri, Walter P., 2339 Chateau Way, Livermore, Calif.
Carder, W. Ray, Hillsboro High School, Hillsboro, Oreg.
Cardina, Philip J., Box 269, R.D. 2, Farmingdale, N.J.
Cardinale, Anthony, Dir., Dependents Educ., Dept. of Defense, Washington, D.C.
Cardinelli, C. F., Northern Arizona Univ., Flagstaff, Ariz.
Cardozo, Joseph A., Box 9958, Baton Rouge, La.
Cardwell, Robert H., Tyson Junior High School, Knoxville, Tenn.
Carey, Clarence B., Dir., Jones Commercial H.S., Chicago, Ill.
Carey, Jess Wendell, Park College, Parkville, Mo.
Carey, Justin P., 105 Lyncroft Rd., New Rochelle, N.Y.
Carlin, James B., Reading Center, Murray St. Univ., Murray, Ky.
Carlin, Irving, Setauket, N.Y.
Carline, Donald E., 365 Seminole, Boulder, Colo.
Carlisle, John C., Col. of Educ., Utah State Univ., Logan, Utah
Carlson, Alma Jane, 81 Manito Ave., Oakland, N.J.
Carlson, Mrs. Evelyn F., 6899 N. Wildwood, Chicago, Ill.
Carlson, Mrs. Ruth K., 1718 LeRoy Ave., Berkeley, Calif.
Carlson, Thorsten R., 5120 Montecito Ave., Santa Rosa, Calif.
Carlson, Wesley, Humboldt Comm. Sch. Dist., Humboldt, Iowa
Carmen, Inez O., 815 N. Keystone, Chicago, Ill.
Carmichael, John H., Essex County Col., Newark, N.J.
Carne, Vernon E., 1383 Dorothy Dr., Decatur, Ga.
Carnochan, John L., Jr., Route 5, Frederick, Md.
Carpenter, Aaron C., P.O. Box 387, Grambling, La.
Carpenter, Don A., 43 S. 4th East, Salt Lake City, Utah
Carpenter, James L., 206 S. 19th Ave., Maywood, Ill.
Carpenter, N. H., Superintendent, City Schools, Elkin, N.C.
Carr, Carolyn Jane, 1409 N. Walnut Grove Ave., Rosemead, Calif.
Carr, Julian W., 1410 Terrace Drive, St. Paul, Minn.
Carriere, Robert H., 57 Theroux Dr., Chicopee, Mass.
Carrington, Joel A., Univ. of Maryland, College Park, Md.
Carroll, Clifford, Gonzaga University, Spokane, Wash.
Carroll, John B., Educational Testing Service, Princeton, N.J.
Carruth, Edwin Ronald, University of Southern Mississippi, McComb, Miss.
Carsello, Carmen J., University of Illinois Circle Campus, Chicago, Ill.
Carstater, Eugene D., Bur. of Naval Personnel, Washington, D.C.
Carter, Burdellis L., 6437 Lupine Dr., Indianapolis, Ind.
Carter, Harold D., Sch. of Educ., University of California, Berkeley, Calif.
Carter, James S., North High School, Phoenix, Ariz.
Carter, Dr. Lamore J., Grambling Col., Grambling, La.
Carter, Margaret Ann, 1310 Berlin Turnpike, Weathersfield, Conn.

Carter, Richard C., Box E, Glendale, Oreg.
Carter, Sims, 214 Spalding Dr., Beverly Hills, Calif.
Carter, Susan C., 10634 Eggleston Ave., Chicago, Ill.
Carter, Thomas D., Alamo Hgts. Indep. Sch. Dist., San Antonio, Tex.
Carter, Vincent, San Jose State College, San Jose, Calif.
Cartwright, William H., Duke University, Durham, N.C.
Caruso, Charles F., 739 Devier Rd., Piscataway, N.J.
Caruso, George E., Town Hall, 333 Washington St., Brookline, Mass.
Caselli, Robert E., 1614 S. Phillips Ave., Sioux Falls, S.Dak.
Casey, John J., 197 Nebraska Ave., Hamilton Square, N.J.
Casey, Neal E., 7607 Kirwin Lane, San Jose, Calif.
* Cash, Christine B., Arkansas Baptist College, Little Rock, Ark.
Caskey, Helen C., Tchrs. Col., University of Cincinnati, Cincinnati, Ohio
Cassidy, Rosalind, University of California, 405 Hilgard Ave., Los Angeles, Calif.
Castaneda, Alberta M., U. of Texas, Austin, Tex.
Castrale, Remo, Supt. of Schools, Johnston City, Ill.
Catrambone, Anthony Ronald, 106 S. Landis Ave., Vineland, N.J.
Caughran, Alex M., 93 N. Main St., Orono, Me.
Caulfield, Patrick J., Dept. of Educ., St. Peter's College, Jersey City, N.J.
Cawein, Paul E., 2032 Belmont Rd., N.W., Apt. 600, Washington, D.C.
Cawrse, Robert C., 26927 Osborn Rd., Bayvillage, Ohio
* Cayco, Florentino, President, Arellano University, Manila, Philippines
Cecco, Mrs. Josephine L., Springfield College, Springfield, Mass.
Cecil, Eddie D., Div. of Educ., Benedict College, Columbia, S.C.
Center, Benjamin, 1653 Roseview Drive, Columbus, Ohio
Center, William R., Western Carolina Univ., Cullowhee, N.C.
Cestero, Marie, 790 Riverside Dr., New York, N.Y.
Chaffee, Pamila, 8920 Canby Ave., Northridge, Calif.
Chall, Jeanne, Grad. Sch. of Educ., Harvard University, Cambridge, Mass.
Champagne, R. P., Holy Savior Central High School, Lockport, La.
Chandler, Herbert E., 1304 Fairlane, Lawrence, Kans.
Chang, Alvin K., 3642 S. Court St., Palo Alto, Calif.
* Chang, Jen-chi, 323 Arpieka Ave., St. Augustine, Fla.
Chang, Lynette Y. C., St. Cloud Tchrs. Col., St. Cloud, Minn.
Channell, W. R., Argentine High School, Kansas City, Kans.
Chansky, Norman M., Temple University, Philadelphia, Pa.
Chao, Sankey C., 154 Redwood Ave., Wayne, N.J.
Chaplin, Charles C., 707 E. New York Ave., Brooklyn, N.Y.
Charles, Ramon L, 448 N.W. 39th St., Topeka, Kans.
Charlton, Huey E., 3785 Wisteria Lane, S.W., Atlanta, Ga.
Charters, Alexander N., Syracuse University, Syracuse, N.Y.
Chase, Francis S., Dept. of Educ., Univ. of Chicago, Chicago, Ill.
Chase, Naomi C., University of Minnesota, Minneapolis, Minn.
Chasnoff, Robert, Newark State College, Union, N.J.
Chatwin, Jerry, 1134 Calle Allmendro, Thousand Oaks, Calif.
Chavez, Phillip G., 1148 Navajo, Barstow, Calif.
Chay, Josephine S., 1669 Makuakane Place, Honolulu, Hawaii
Cheatham, Alflorence, Dist. Supt., Dist. 19, Chicago, Ill.
Cheers, Arlynne Lake, Grambling College, Grambling, La.
Chen, Kuan-Yu, Central Conn. St. Col., New Britain, Conn.
Chern, Mrs. Nona E., 492 Concord Rd., Broomall, Pa.
Chevat, Edith, 143-26, 232d St., Laurelton, N.Y.
Chiavaro, John, Newfane Cent. Sch., Newfane, N.Y.
Chidekel, Samuel J., Madison Sch., Chicago, Ill.
Chidester, Charles B., 8646 Linden St., Munster, Ind.
Childs, James N., Lincoln Elem. Sch., Rt. 4, Riverwood, Minn.
Childs, Vernon C., 1514 South 14th St., Manitowoc, Wis.
Chipley, Donald R., Univ. of Georgia, Athens, Ga.
Christensen, Viktor Albert, 5130 Leon Court, Riverside, Calif.
Christenson, Bernice M., 5045 Alta Canyada Rd., La Canada, Calif.
Christina, Robert J., 3445 S. Adams Rd., Pontiac, Mich.

Christine, Ray O., Arizona State University, Tempe, Ariz.
Chuck, Harry C., 265 Kanoelam Dr., Hilo, Hawaii
Chudler, Albert A., Intern. Sch. of Kuala Lumpur, Kuala Lumpur, Malaysia
Chung, Yong Hwan, Dept. of Educ., Wiley College, Marshall, Tex.
Churchill, Donald W., Bemidji State College, Bemidji, Minn.
Cianciolo, Patricia J., Michigan State University, East Lansing, Mich.
Cicchelli, Jerry J., Prin., Oradell Public School, Oradell, N.J.
Ciccoricco, Edward A., Rt. 32, North New Paltz, N.Y.
Ciklamini, Joseph, 921 Carnegie Ave., Plainfield, N.J.
Ciminillo, Lewis, Col. of Educ., Indiana University, Bloomington, Ind.
Cioffi, Joseph M., 652 Doriskill Ct., River Vale, N.J.
Clague, W. Donald, La Verne Col., La Verne, Calif.
Clanin, Edgar E., 309 Highland Dr., West Lafayette, Ind.
Clare, Mrs. Elizabeth Rae, 949 N. Alfred St., Los Angeles, Calif.
Clark, Angeline, 493 Pittsfield Drive, Worthington, Ohio
Clark, Charles W., P.O. Box 254, Rogue River, Oreg.
Clark, David L., 1243 Matlock Rd., Bloomington, Ind.
Clark, Elmer J., Col. of Educ., Southern Illinois Univ., Carbondale, Ill.
Clark, Franklin B., Dist. Supt. of Schools, Athens, N.Y.
Clark, H. Robert, 430 No. Michigan Ave., Chicago, Ill.
Clark, John F., 4338 Via Largo, Cypress, Calif.
Clark, Leonard H., 240 Van Nostrand Ave., Jersey City, N.J.
Clark, Lewis F., 355 Durham Ave., Eugene, Oreg.
Clark, Maurice P., Supt. of Schools, Western Springs, Ill.
Clark, Michael C., Arizona State Univ., Temple, Ariz.
Clark, Moses, Alabama State College, Montgomery, Ala.
Clark, Richard M., State University of N.Y., Albany, N.Y.
Clark, Richard McCallum, Schl. of Educ., S.U.N.Y., Albany, N.Y.
Clark, Sidney L., 855 Bronson Rd., Fairfield, Conn.
Clark, Woodrow Wilson, 101 W. Leake St., Clinton, Miss.
Clarke, Juno-Ann, San Francisco State Col., San Francisco, Calif.
Clarke, Stanley C. T., 11615—78th Ave., Edmonton, Alba., Canada
Classon, Miss Marion E., 19 Nantes Rd., Parsippany, N.J.
Claxton, Norman L., So. Junior High Schl., Bloomfield, N.J.
Claybrook, Dorothy, 913 N. 12th Ave., Humboldt, Tenn.
Clayton, Thomas E., #2 Road West, Manlius, N.Y.
Clegg, Ambrose A., Jr., 8304 SE 62nd St., Mercer Island, Wash.
Cleland, Donald L., Sch. of Educ., Univ. of Pittsburgh, Pittsburgh, Pa.
Clifford, Mrs. Miriam, 2535 Sevier St., Durham, N.C.
Clift, Virgil A., Sch. of Educ., New York University, New York, N.Y.
Cline, Marion, Jr., Univ. of Texas, El Paso, Tex.
Clinton, Robert Jr., Western Texas Col., Synder, Tex.
Clopper, Elizabeth, Brd. of Educ., Anne Arundel Cnty., Annapolis, Md.
Clouthier, Raymond P., St. Norbert College, West DePere, Wis.
Clymer, Theodore W., 4312 Via Glorieta, Santa Barbara, Calif.
Cobb, Beatrice M., Cambell Shore Rd., Gray, Maine
Cobb, Joseph L., 2706 Baynard Blvd., Wilmington, Del.
Cobban, Margaret R., 9 William St., Stamford, Conn.
Coblentz, Dwight O., 615 N. School St., Normal, Ill.
Cobley, Herbert F., Superintendent of Schools, Nazareth, Pa.
Cobun, Frank E., State University College, New Paltz, N.Y.
Cochi, Oscar R., 471 Manse Ln., Rochester, N.Y.
Cochran, Alton W., Supt. of Schools, Charlestown, Ind.
Cochran, John R., Kalamazoo Public Schools, 1220 Howard St., Kalamazoo, Mich.
Cochran, Russell T., 16552 Nearview Dr., Saugus, Calif.
Code, Allen L., 208 S. Third St., Seneca, S.C.
Coen, Alban Wasson, II, Central Michigan University, Mt. Pleasant, Mich.
Coffee, James M., 5903 Woodside Drive, Jacksonville, Fla.
Coffey, Thomas F., 5900 N. Glenwood Ave., Chicago, Ill.
Coffey, Warren C., 7416 East Parkway, Sacramento, Calif.
Coffman, Phillip, 4618 Secor, Toledo, Ohio

Cogswell, Mark E., Northern State College, Aberdeen, S.Dak.
Cohen, Edward G., 558 E. Parr Ave., Long Beach, N.Y.
Cohen, George, 83 Summit Rd., South Spring Valley, N.Y.
Cohen, Hyman Z., 744 Henry Rd., Far Rockaway, N.Y.
Cohen, Jerome, 403 E. 80th Terr., Kansas City, Mo.
Cohen, Samuel J., 9 Coventry Rd., Syosset, N.Y.
Cohler, Milton J., 3450 N. Lake Shore Drive, Chicago, Ill.
Coker, William F., Portland Sr. High Sch., Portland, Tenn.
Colbath, Edwin H., 97-16 118th St., Richmond Hill, N.Y.
Colburn, A. B., Cascade Senior High School, Everett, Wash.
Colclazar, Gloria L., 7319 Capps, Reseda, Calif.
*Cole, Glenn A., University of Arkansas, Fayetteville, Ark.
Cole, James C., 1946 Mira Flores, Turlock, Calif.
Cole, James E., University of Utah, Salt Lake City, Utah
Coleman, Alwin B., Univ. of Cincinnati, Cincinnati, Ohio
Coleman, Mary Elisabeth, University of Pennsylvania, Philadelphia, Pa.
Colla, Frances S., 49 Regina St., Trumbull, Conn.
Collier, Mrs. Anna K., 903 Fourth St., Liverpool, N.Y.
Collier, Calhoun C., Michigan State University, East Lansing, Mich.
Collier, Richard E., 4822 Eades St., Rockville, Md.
Collings, Miller R., 9201 W. Outer Dr., Detroit, Mich.
Collins, Carol M., 425 E. Fourth St., Hinsdale, Ill.
Collins, F. Ethel, Box 536, Presidential Way, Guilderland, N.Y.
Collins, Helen C., 1203 Gilpin Ave., Wilmington, Del.
Collins, Mary Lucille, Beaubien Sch., 5025 N. Laramie Ave., Chicago, Ill.
Collins, Paul W., R. #5, Box 221C, Ocala, Fla.
Collins, Mrs. Ray, 3101 W. Carson, Torrance, Calif.
Collins, Ted, 1023 Oakdale St., West Covina, Calif.
Collison, Sidney B., 410 New London Road, Newark, Del.
Colman, John E., C.M., Sch. of Educ., St. John's University, Jamaica, N.Y.
Combs, W. E., Florida A. & M. University, Tallahassee, Fla.
Comer, J. M., Box 820, Rt. 2, Collinsville, Ill.
Conan, Mrs. Beatrice, 2063—74th St., Brooklyn, N.Y.
Conaway, John O., 431 S. Brown, Terre Haute, Ind.
Congreve, Willard J., 807 S. 6th St.W., Newton, Iowa
Conley, Jack, Prin., Elementary School, Culver City, Calif.
Conley, William H., Sacred Heart University, Bridgeport, Conn.
Conner, John W., University High School, Univ. of Iowa, Iowa City, Ia.
Conner, Orval, 305 E. McGuffey Hall, Miami U., Oxford, Ohio
Connor, William H., Washington Univ. Grad. Inst. of Education, St. Louis, Mo.
Conry, Rev. Thomas P., S.J., John Carroll Univ., Cleveland, Ohio
Conte, Anthony F., 1000 Spruce St., Trenton, N.J.
Converse, David T., State Univ. Col., Buffalo, N.Y.
Conway, Marie M., Jefferson Court No. 31, 4925 Saul St., Philadelphia, Pa.
Cook, William J., 385 Winnetka Ave., Winnetka, Ill.
Cool, Dwight W., 6840 W. 32nd Pl., Wheat Ridge, Colo.
Cooley, Max L., Box 44, Newton, Utah
Cooley, Robert L., Supt., Dunkirk Public Schools, Dunkirk, N.Y.
Cooling, Elizabeth, 600 Mt. Pleasant Ave., Providence, R.I.
Cooper, Bernice L., Baldwin Hall, Univ. of Georgia, Athens, Ga.
Cooper, Dian Annise, 500 E. 33rd St., Chicago, Ill.
Cooper, George H., 8946 Bennett Ave., Chicago, Ill.
Cooper, David J., 408 Riverside Ave, Muncie, Ind.
Cooper, John H., 63 Lucero St., Thousand Oaks, Calif.
Cooper, Joyce, University of Florida, Gainesville, Fla.
Cooper, Shawn, Psychology Dept., Brown Univ., Providence, R.I.
Cooper, Thelma, 55 Knolls Crescent-(9k), Riverdale, N.Y.
Cooperman, Saul, Box 147B, Skillman, N.J.
Coplein, Leonard E., Haddon Township Bd. of Educ., Westmont, N.J.
Corbin, Joseph W., 2700 Warwick Lane, Modesto, Calif.
Cordasco, Francesco M., Montclair State Col., Upper Montclair, N.J.

Corley, Clifford L., Oregon College of Education, Monmouth, Oreg.
Corman, Bernard R., 705-11025—82nd Ave., Edmonton, Alba., Canada
Cornell, Francis G., 7 Holland Ave., White Plains, N.Y.
Cornish, Robert L., Arkansas University, Fayetteville, Ark.
Corona, Bert C., 426 Locust St., Modesto, Calif.
Cortage, Cecelia, 2053 Illinois Ave., Santa Rosa, Calif.
Cory, N. Durward, 908 W. North St., Muncie, Ind.
Cosentino, Bruno, 6 Glenside Dr., New City, N.Y.
Cosper, Cecil, Box 107, West. Carolina Univ., Cullowhee, N.C.
Coster, John K., North Carolina State University, Raleigh, N.C.
Cotter, Katharine C., Boston Col., Chestnut Hill, Mass.
Cotton, Janie West, Univ. of Minn., Minneapolis, Minn.
Cottone, Sebastian Charles, School Planning Dept., Philadelphia, Pa.
Couche, Martha E., Rust College, Holly Springs, Miss.
Coughlan, Robert J., Sch. of Educ., Northwestern Univ., Evanston, Ill.
Coulter, Myron L., Sch. of Educ., West. Michigan Univ., Kalamazoo, Mich.
Courtney, Robert W., Box 198, Middlebush, N.J.
Covert, Warren O., Western Illinois University, Macomb, Ill.
Cowan, Persis H., 333 W. California, Pasadena, Calif.
Coward, Gertrude O., Charlotte-Mecklenburg Bd. of Educ., Charlotte, N.C.
Cowgill, Robt. G., Col. of Educ., Fla. Tech. Univ., Orlando Park, Fla.
Cowles, Clifton V., Jr., Div. of Music, Ark. St. Univ., State College, Ark.
Cowles, James D., 104 Leon Drive, Williamsburg Va.
Cowles, Milly, Sch. of Educ., Univ. of South Carolina, Columbia, S.C.
Cox, David H., New Trier H.S. West, Northfield, Ill.
Cox, Edwin A., Superintendent of Schools, North Parade, Stratford, Conn.
Cox, Hugh F., 17012 Grovemont St., Santa Ana, Calif.
Cox, John A., 735 N. Allen St., State College, Pa.
Cox, Marjorie L., Punahou School, Honolulu, Hawaii
Cox, Robert A., University of Pittsburgh, Pittsburgh, Pa.
* Craig, Gerald S., 8 Paseo Redondo, Tucson, Ariz.
Craig, James C., 9403 Crosby Rd., Silver Spring, Md.
Craig, Jimmie M., 11512 Fuerte Farms Rd., El Cajon, Calif.
Craig, Robert C., Michigan State University, East Lansing, Mich.
Crane, Donald C., 67 Payson Lane, Piscataway, N.J.
Crarey, Hugh W., 9150 S. Cregier Ave., Chicago, Ill.
Craton, Edward J., 1777 Glenwood Ct., Bakersfield, Calif.
Craver, Samuel Mock, 717 E. Thach Ave., Auburn, Ala.
Crawford, Dorothy M., 212 W. Washington St., Ottawa, Ill.
Crawford, Leslie W., Ohio Univ., Athens, Ohio
Crawford, T. James, Sch. of Business, Indiana University, Bloomington, Ind.
Creel, Kenneth E., Hemingway, S.C.
Creason, Frank M., 75342 W. 100th, Shawnee Mission, Kans.
Creighton, Samuel L., 1517 Secor Rd. #134, Toledo, Ohio
Cresci, Gerald D., State Dept. of Educ., Sacramento, Calif.
Crescimbeni, Joseph, Jacksonville University, Jacksonville, Fla.
Crespy, H. Victor, 94 Broad St., Freehold, N.J.
Creswell, Mrs. Rowena C., 305 Montclair Ave., So., College Station, Tex.
Crews, Alton C., Rt. 1, Due West Road, Marietta, Ga.
Crews, Roy L., Aurora College, Aurora, Ill.
Crim, Kenneth, 15 N. Main St., Dayton, Ohio
Criscuolo, Nicholas P., Read. Spec., Pub. Schools, New Haven, Conn.
Crocker, Richard F., Jr., Superintendent of Schools, Caribou, Maine
Crolley, Donald L., Supt. of Schs., Lancaster, S.C.
Cromartie, Sue W., Col. of Educ., University of Georgia, Athens, Ga.
Crombe, William A., 1087 Webster Rd., Webster, N.Y.
Cron, Celeste Maia, 801 Gull Ave., San Mateo, Calif.
Cronin, Kevin W., 401 No. Michigan, Chicago, Ill.
Cronin, Rev. Robert E., 3245 Rio St., Apt. 811, Falls Church, Va.
Crook, Robert B., Queens Col., Flushing, N.Y.
Crooks, Judith, 128 N. Carolina Ave. SE, Washington, D.C.

Cross, Donald A., Bathurst Tchrs. Col., Bathurst, N.S.W., Australia
Crossland, Mrs. Kathryn M., 3326 Pinafore Drive, Durham, N.C.
Crossley, J. K., 44 Eglinton Ave. W., Toronto 310, Ontario, Canada
Crosson, Robert Henry, 2747 West 35th Ave., Denver, Colo.
*Crow, Lester D., 5300 Washington St., Hollywood, Fla.
Crowley, Mary C., 7 Boone Lane, Dearborn, Mich.
Crowley, Robert J., 7 Charles St., Hamilton, N.Y.
Cruckson, Fred A., 72 S. Portland St., Fond du Lac, Wis.
Crum, Clyde E., Div. of Educ., San Diego State College, San Diego, Calif.
Culbertson, Jack A., Ohio State University, Columbus, Ohio
Cumbee, Carroll F., Apt. D-4, Trojan Arms Apt., Troy, Ala.
Cummings, C. Thomas, Canajoharie Cent. Sch. Canajoharie, N.Y.
Cummings, Mabel Anna, 6044 Linden St., Brooklyn, N.Y.
Cummings, Joseph K., 1871 Woodside Dr., Salt Lake City, Utah
Cummings, Susan N., Arizona State University, Tempe, Ariz.
Cummins, Lester L., 3512 S. 263rd St., Kent, Wash.
Cunningham, Calvin, 853 E. Dempster Ave., Memphis, Tenn.
Cunningham, Donald J., Indiana University, Bloomington, Ind.
Cunningham, George S., 4 Glenwood St., Orono, Me.
Cunningham, Luvern L., Dean of Educ., Ohio State Univ., Columbus, Ohio
Cunningham, Myron, Col. of Educ., University of Florida, Gainesville, Fla.
Cupp, Gene R., 1704 N. Park Ave., Canton, Ohio
Currey, Ralph B., State Dept. of Education, Charleston, W.Va.
Currie, Robert J., Col. of Educ., University of Idaho, Moscow, Idaho
Currier, Mrs. Lynor O., 1925 Harwood Rd., Annapolis, Md.
Currier, Robt. L., Pennsbury Sch. Dist., Fallsington, Pa.
Curry, John F., Box 6765, North Texas State College, Denton, Tex.
Curry, Laura June, Deerfield Dr., Norfolk, Va.
Curtin, James T., 4140 Lindell Blvd., St. Louis, Mo.
Curtin, John T., 21761 Mauer Dr., St. Clair Shores, Mich.
Curtis, E. Louise, Macalester College, St. Paul, Minn.
Curtis, Francis H., Univ. of Scranton, Scranton, Pa.
Curtis, James P., University of Alabama, University, Ala.
Curtis, Theodore, Warwick School Dept., Warwick, R.I.
Cusick, Ralph, 6721 N. Newgard, Chicago, Ill.

Daddazio, Arthur H., 41 Brady Ave., Newburgh, N.Y.
Daeufer, Carl Joseph, 3425 S.W. 2nd Ave., Gainesville, Fla.
D'Agostino, Nicholas E., Wolcott High School, Wolcott, Conn.
Dahl, John A., California State College, Los Angeles, Calif.
Dahlberg E. John Jr., 720 Kirby St., Boise, Idaho
Daines, Delva, 2124 N. 220 East, Provo, Utah
Dale, Arbie Myron, Sch. of Commerce, New York University, New York, N.Y.
Dale, Edgar, Sch. of Educ., Ohio State University, Columbus, Ohio
D'Alessio, Theodore, 10 Gaston St., W. Orange, N.J.
Dal Santo, John, Northern Illinois Univ., De Kalb, Ill.
Daly, Edmund B., 1839 N. Richmond St., Chicago, Ill.
Daly, Francis M., Jr., Eastern Michigan University, Ypsilanti, Mich.
Dandoy, Maxine A., Fresno State College, Fresno, Calif.
Daniel, George T., N. 319 Locust Rd., Spokane, Wash.
Daniel, Dr. Kathryn B., 83 Nob Hill, Columbia, S.C.
Daniels, Paul R., 520 "N" St. S.W., Apt. S-131, Washington, D.C.
Danielson, Paul J., Col. of Educ., University of Arizona, Tucson, Ariz.
Danzy, Richard L., Woodlawn Experimental Schls., 7420 Ingleside, Chicago, Ill.
Darcy, Natalie T., Dept. of Educ., Brooklyn College, Brooklyn, N.Y.
Darling, Dennis E., 501 N. Clarendon, Kalamazoo, Mich.
Darm, Adam E., State Col. at Long Beach, Long Beach, Calif.
Darr, George F., 155 Rodeo Rd., Glendora, Calif.
Darrow, Helen F., Western Washington State Col., Bellingham, Wash.
D'Ascoli, Louis N., 5 Hughes Ter., Yonkers, N.Y.
Daubek, Gerald G., Univ. of Kentucky Ext., Fort Knox, Ky.

Davenport, William R., Campbellsville College, Campbellsville, Ky.
Davey, Mrs. Elizabeth P., 5748 Harper Ave., Chicago, Ill.
Davidson, Edmonia W., Howard Univ., Washington, D.C.
Davidson, Mrs. Evelyn K., Dept. of Educ., Kent State University, Kent, Ohio
Davidson, Terrence R., University of Michigan, Ann Arbor, Mich.
Davies, Daniel R., Croft Consult. Serv., Tucson, Ariz.
Davies, Don, Office of Educ., Washington, D.C.
Davies, J. Leonard, Bur. of Educ. Resch., Univ. of Iowa, Iowa City, Iowa
Davies, Lillian S., Illinois State University, Normal, Ill.
Davis, Ann E., 525 N.W. Armstrong Way, Corvallis, Oreg.
Davis, Curtis, 1605 Park Ave., San Jose, Calif.
Davis, David Carson, 1045 E St., Apt. 4, Lincoln, Nebr.
Davis, Donald, 3316 Edgemere Ave. N.E., Minneapolis, Minn.
Davis, Donald Jack, P.O. Box 11504, St. Louis, Mo.
Davis, Dwight E., 6726 S. Washington Ave., Lansing, Mich.
Davis, Dwight M., 505 Glenview Dr., Des Moines, Iowa
Davis, Mrs. Eldred D., Knoxville College, Knoxville, Tenn.
Davis, Frederick B., 3700 Walnut St., Philadelphia, Pa.
Davis, Guy C., Trinidad State Junior College, Trinidad, Colo.
Davis, Harold S., 760 Mix Ave., Hamden, Conn.
Davis, Hazel Grubbs, Queens Col., City Univ. of N.Y., Flushing, N.Y.
Davis, J. Clark, Col. of Educ., University of Nevada, Reno, Nev.
Davis, J. Sanford, Box 646, Madison, Conn.
Davis, Marianna W., 156 Aberdeen Ave., Columbia, S.C.
Davis, Milton J., 725 West 18th St., North Chicago, Ill.
Davis, O. L., Jr., Col. of Educ., Univ. of Texas, Austin, Tex.
Davis, Paul Ford, Morehead State Univ., Morehead, Ky.
Davis, Ron W., 223 Hillcrest Cir., Chapel Hill, N.C.
Davis, Ruby T., 1003 Eigenmann, Bloomington, Ind.
Davison, Dewitt C., University of Toledo, Toledo, Ohio
Davoren, David, Superintendent of Schools, Milford, Mass.
Dawkins, Sue, P.O. Box 1972, Detroit, Mich.
Dawson, Kenneth E., P.O. Box 31, Lawrenceville, Va.
Dawson, W. Read, Baylor University, Waco, Tex.
Day, James F., Dept. of Educ., Univ. of Texas, El Paso, Tex.
Day, Marjorie S., 7626 Stetson Ave., Los Angeles, Calif.
Deady, John E., Supt. of Schools, Springfield, Mass.
Dease, E. Richard, 413 Lorraine Rd., Wheaton, Ill.
DeBernardis, Amo, 6049 S. W. Luradel, Portland, Oreg.
Debin, Louis, 83-37—247th St., Bellerose, N.Y.
Decker, Joel T., Florida State Univ., Tallahassee, Fla.
Deever, Merwin, Col. of Educ., Arizona State University, Tempe, Ariz.
DeGrow, Gerald S., 509 Stanton St., Port Huron, Mich.
Dejnozka, Edward L., 5801 N. Paradise Rd., Flagstaff, Ariz.
Della Penta, A. H., Superintendent of Schools, Lodi, N.J.
Deller, W. McGregor, Superintendent of Schools, Fairport, N.Y.
Dellinger, Harry V., Box 1002, Southern Station, Hattiesburg, Miss.
Delmonaco, Thomas M., 44 Lanewood Ave., Framingham Centre, Mass.
Delon, Floyd G., Univ. of Missouri, Columbia, Mo.
DeLong, Arthur R., Grand Valley State College, Allendale, Mich.
Demerio, William D., Baldwinsville, N.Y.
De Milia, Lorraine, 222 Babcock St., Brookline, Mass.
Demming, John A., Bldg. S-502, 6th St., N., West Palm Beach, Fla.
DeMoraes, Maria P. Tito, WHO Reg. Off., 8 Scherfigsvej, Copenhagen, Denmark
Dempsey, Richard A., P.O. Box 1167, Darien, Conn.
Denemark, George W., University of Kentucky, Lexington, Ky.
De Nio, James, 25 Dunrovin Lane, Rochester, N.Y.
Denman, Milton H., Stonegate Elem. Sch., Oklahoma City, Okla.
Denning, Mrs. Bernadine, 5057 Woodward, Rm. 1338, Detroit, Mich.
Dennis, Donald Albert, 19533 Haynes St., Reseda, Calif.
Dennis, Ronald T., Northwestern State College, Natchitoches, La.

Denny, Robert R., Des Moines Pub. Schls., Des Moines, Iowa
Denova, Charles C., 420 N. Prospect, Redondo Beach, Calif.
Denson, Lucille D., 6 Town Garden Dr., Liverpool, N.Y.
De Ortega, Eneida Santizo, Calle Real 6101, Betania-Panama, Rep. of Panama
DePaul, Frank J., 2727 North Long Ave., Chicago, Ill.
Derby, Orlo Lee, State Univ. Col., Brockport, N.Y.
DeRidder, Lawrence M., Col. of Educ., Univ. of Tennessee, Knoxville, Tenn.
DeSantis, Joseph P., 204 Orchard St., Dowagiac, Mich.
Desimowich, Donald M., Route 3, Box 30, Hartland, Wis.
Desjarlais, Lionel P., 1684 Rhodes Ct., Ottawa 8, Ont., Canada
DeStefano, Anthony J., 48 Lenox Ave., Hicksville, N.Y.
Detrick, Frederick M., 10 Sheldon Rd., Pemberton, N.J.
Dettre, John Richard, Univ. of New Mexico, Albuquerque, N. Mex.
Detwiller, Harry G., George Washington Univ., Washington, D.C.
Deutschman, Mrs. Marilyn L., 201 St. Pauls Ave., Jersey City, N.J.
De Vaughn, J. E., Georgia State College, Atlanta, Ga.
DeVault, M. Vere, University of Wisconsin, Madison, Wis.
De Velez, Esther Arvelo, Univ. of Puerto Rico, Rio Piedras, P.R.
Devenport, Claude Nelson, 94 Forest Hills Dr., Eureka, Mo.
Devor, John W., 6860 Montezuma Rd., San Diego, Calif.
De Vries, Ted, 600 Coffee Tree Lane, Evansville, Ind.
Deyell, J. Douglas, 1354 Leighton Rd., Peterborough, Ont., Canada
Dickens, Hugh L., Wm. Carey College, Hattiesburg, Miss.
Dickey, Otis M., 18933 Greenwald Dr., Southfield, Mich.
Dickmeyer, Mrs. K. H., 200 8th Ave., S.E., Fairfax, Minn.
Dickson, Richard, 3C Yale Rd., Storrs, Conn.
*Diederich, A. F., St. Norbert College, West DePere, Wis.
Diederich, Paul B., Educ. Testing Serv., Princeton, N.J.
Diefenderfer, Omie T., 828 Third St., Fullerton, Pa.
Diehl, T. Handley, Miami University, Oxford, Ohio
Diener, Russell E., 1034 Novara St., San Diego, Calif.
Dierzen, Mrs. Verda, Comm. Consol. Sch. Dist., Woodstock, Ill.
Dieterle, Louise E., Illinois State Univ., Normal, Ill.
Dietz, Elisabeth H., 1093 Northern Blvd., Baldwin, N.Y.
Di Giacinto, Rose D., 68 Pilgrim Ave., Yonkers, N.Y.
DiGiammarino, Frank, Lexington Public Schools, Lexington, Mass.
DiLeonarde, Joseph H., 6309 N. Cicero Ave., Chicago, Ill.
DiLieto, Ray Marie, 4 Bayberry Lane, Westport, Conn.
Dillehay, James A., Bowling Green State Univ., Bowling Green, Ohio
Dillman, Duane H., 139 Pelham Rd., Philadelphia, Pa.
Dillman, Dr. Beryl, Pasadena Col., Pasadena, Calif.
Dillon, Jesse D., Jr., 850 Cranbrook Dr., Liftwood Estates, Wilmington, Del.
DiLuglio, Domenic R., 1849 Warwick Ave., Warwick, R.I.
Dimitroff, Lillian, 1525 Brummel St., Evanston, Ill.
Dimond, Ray A., Jr., 4034 E. Cambridge, Phoenix, Ariz.
Dimond, Stanley E., 2012 Shadford Rd., Ann Arbor, Mich.
Di Muccio, Virginia, Hanford Elem. Schl., Hanford, Calif.
DiNardo, V. James, Massachusetts State College, Bridgewater, Mass.
Di Pasquale, Vincent C., 705 19th Ave., So. Fargo, N. Dak.
Disberger, Jay, Box 268, Haven, Kans
Disko, Michael, 16 Briarwood Dr., Athens, Ohio
Distin, Leslie, Supt. of Schls., Johnson City, N.Y.
Dittmer, Daniel G., 1647 Francis Hammond Pkwy., Alexandria, Va.
Dittmer, Jane E., Kouts High School, Kouts, Ind.
Dixon, Glendora M., 3969 Dakota Rd., S.E., Salem, Oreg.
Dixon, James E., 27146 Elias St., Saugus, Calif.
Dixon, James T., 13 Lake Rd., Huntington Station, L.I., N.Y.
Dixon, M. Ted, Dept. of Educ., San Diego Co., San Diego, Calif.
Dixon, W. Robert, University of Michigan, Ann Arbor, Mich.
Dodd, John M., Eastern Montana College, Billings, Mont.
Dodds, A. Gordon, Superintendent of Schools, Edwardsville, Ill.

Dodge, Norman B., 523 S. Oneida Way, Denver, Colo.
Dodson, Dan W., New York University, Washington Sq., New York, N.Y.
Dodson, Edwin S., Col. of Educ., University of Nevada, Reno, Nev.
Dohemann, H. Warren, San Francisco State Col., San Francisco, Calif.
Doherty, Benton H., 403 Washington, Park Ridge, Ill.
Dohmann, C. William, Loyola University, Los Angeles, Calif.
Doll, Ronald C., 17 Rossmore Ter., Livingston, N.J.
Domian, O. E., 6801 Olympia, Golden Valley, Minn.
Donahoe, Thomas J., 74 Fallston St., Springfield, Mass.
Donatelli, Rosemary V., Loyola University, Chicago, Ill.
Donnelly, Peter J., Jersey City State Col., Jersey City, N.J.
Donnersberger, Anne, 2309 W. 91st St., Chicago, Ill.
Donoghue, Mildred R., California State College, Fullerton, Calif.
Donovan, David, 6095 Harkson, E. Lansing, Mich.
Doody, Louise E., 191 Dedham St., Newton Highlands, Mass.
Doria, Helen D., 3144 Ridge Rd., Highland, Ind.
Dorricott, H. J., Western State College, Gunnison, Colo.
Doss, Jesse Paul, 12631 Fletcher Dr., Garden Grove, Calif.
Dotson, John M., 154 Jones Dr., Pocatello, Idaho
Douglass, Harl R., Col. of Educ., University of Colorado, Boulder, Colo.
Douglass, Malcolm P., Claremont Grad. Sch., Claremont, Calif.
Dow, John A., 2597 W. Calimyrna, Fresno, Calif.
Downey, Richard D., Evergreen Terrace 173-7, Carbondale, Ill.
Downing, Carl, Central State Col., Edmond, Okla.
Doyle, Andrew McCormick, 1106 Bellerive Blvd., St. Louis, Mo.
Doyle, David W., 75 Koenig Rd., Tonawanda, N.Y.
Doyle, E. A., Jesuit High School, New Orleans, La.
Doyle, James Francis, 1751 Noble Drive, N.E., Atlanta, Ga.
Doyle, Jean, 511 E. High St., Lexington, Ky.
Doyle, Walter, University of Notre Dame, Notre Dame, Ind.
Drachler, Norman, Detroit Pub. Schs., Detroit, Mich.
Drag, Francis L., 1440 Butler Ave., Los Angeles, Calif.
Drag, Mrs. Lillian K., 1100 Glendon Ave., Los Angeles, Calif.
Dragositz, Anna, Educational Testing Service, Princeton, N.J.
Drake, Thelbert L., Univ. of Connecticut, Storrs, Conn.
Drechsel, Lionel C., 2009 Fillmore, Ogden, Utah
*Dreikurs, Rudolph, 6 N. Michigan Ave., Chicago, Ill.
Dreisbach, Dodson E., Gibraltar, Pa.
Dressel, Paul L., Michigan State University, East Lansing, Mich.
Drew, Alfred S., Purdue University, Lafayette, Ind.
Drew, Robert E., Community Unit School Dist. 303, St. Charles, Ill.
Drexel, Karl O., 1005 Escobar St., Martinez, Calif.
Driscoll, Eleanor D., 64 Calkins Rd., Rochester, N.Y.
Driver, Cecil E., Vandenberg Elem. School, APO, New York, N.Y.
Dropkin, Stanley, Queens College, Flushing, N.Y.
Drummond, Harold D., Univ. of New Mexico, Albuquerque, N.Mex.
Drummond, William H., 623 S. Decatur, Olympia, Wash.
DuBois, Helen, Medical Center, Maple Ave. Ext., Glen Cove, N.Y.
Ducanis, Alex J., 230 N. Craig, Apt. 703, Pittsburgh, Pa.
Ducharme, Raymond A., Jr., Smith Col., Northhampton, Mass.
Duckers, Robert L., 601 W. Central Rd., Mt. Prospect, Ill.
Dudley, James, Col. of Educ., Univ. of Maryland, College Park, Md.
Duff, Franklin L., Bur. of Instr. Res., Univ. of Illinois, Urbana, Ill.
Duffett, John W., 341 Bellefield Ave., Pittsburgh, Pa.
Duffey, Robert V., 9225 Limestone Pl., College Park, Md.
Dufford, William C.. Box 1345, Sumter, S.C.
Duffy, Gerald G., 357 Michigan St. Univ., E. Lansing, Mich.
Duke, Ralph L., Sch. of Educ., University of Delaware, Newark, Del.
Dumler, Marvin J., Concordia Teachers College, River Forest, Ill.
Dunbar, Donald A., Mt. Lebanon Sch. Dist., Pittsburgh, Pa.
Duncan, Ernest R., Sch. of Educ., Rutgers Univ., New Brunswick, N.J.

Duncan, J. A., Agric. Hall, University of Wisconsin, Madison, Wis.
Duncan, William B., Miami Edison Senior High School, Miami, Fla.
Dunham, Ralph E., 2113 White Oaks Dr., Alexandria, Va.
Dunkel, Harold B., Dept. of Educ., University of Chicago, Chicago, Ill.
Dunkeld, Colin G., 8105 S.W. 61st Ave., Portland, Oreg.
Dunkle, Maurice Albert, Superintendent, Calvert Co. Schls., Prince Frederick, Md.
Dunlap, William H., Hempfield Area Schl. Dist., Greensburg, Pa.
Dunsky, Elmer S., 14830 S. Van Ness, Gardena, Calif.
Dunnell, John P., 1004 Wenonah, Oak Park, Ill.
Dunning, Frances E., 125 Owre Hall, Univ. of Minnesota, Minneapolis, Minn.
Durant, Adrian J., Jr., 1115 Holiday Park Dr., Champaign, Ill.
Durante, Spencer E., 425 Dayton Towers Dr., Dayton, Ohio
Durflinger, Glenn W., 5665 Cielo Ave., Goleta, Calif.
Durkee, Frank M., Box 911, Harrisburg, Pa.
Durost, Walter N., RFD # 2, Box 120, Dover, N.H.
Durr, William K., Col. of Educ., Michigan State Univ., East Lansing, Mich.
Durrell, Donald D., Boston University, 332 Bay State Rd., Boston, Mass.
Dussault, Gilles, 2390 Nerre Beauchamin, Sillery, P.Q., Quebec
Duthler, B. Thomas, 1330 Western Dr., Grand Rapids, Mich.
Dutro, Richard F., Lakewood Public Schools, Lakewood, Ohio
Dutton, Wilbur H., 1913 Greenfield Ave., Los Angeles, Calif.
DuVall, Lloyd A., 30 Mountain Rise, Fairport, N.Y.
Dwyer, Roy E., P.O. Box 343, Thonotasassa, Fla.
Dyer, Frank E., Supt., Delano Jt. Union High School, Delano, Calif.
Dygert, Marian, 1930 Sylvan Ave., Grand Rapids, Mich.
Dyke, Elwood E., Southport Elem. Sch., 723—76th St., Kenosha, Wis.
Dykes, Mrs. Alma, 9755 Cincinnati-Columbus Rd., Cincinnati, Ohio
Dyson, Ernest, Colonial Sch. Dist., Plymouth Meeting, Pa.
Dyson, R. E., 202 Northlawn Ave., East Lansing, Mich.
Dziuban, Charles D., 5573 N. Semoran Blvd., Winter Park, Fla.

Eaddy, Edward Allen, Box 347, Williston, S.C.
Earles, Lucius C., Jr., 123 Peabody St., N.W., Washington, D.C.
Eash, Maurice J., Univ. of Ill. (Circle Campus), Chicago, Ill.
Easterly, Ambrose, Harper Col. Library, Palatine, Ill.
Eastman, Kermit L., Dist. Admin. Bldg., 13th Av. & 7th St.S., St. Cloud, Minn.
Eaton, Albert G., Saybrook School, Ashtabula, Ohio
Eaton, Edward J., 64 Pine Tree Lane, Rochester, N.Y.
Ebel, Robert L., Michigan State University, East Lansing, Mich.
Eberle, August William, Indiana Univ., Bloomington, Ind.
Eberman, Paul W., 1801 John F. Kennedy Blvd., Philadelphia, Pa.
Eboch, Sidney C., Dept. of Educ., Ohio State Univ., Columbus, Ohio
Echevarris, Major Ramon L., Inter. Amer. University, APO, New York, N.Y.
Eckert, Edwin K., Supt., Lutheran Schools, Chicago, Ill.
Eckert, Ruth E., Col. of Educ., University of Minnesota, Minneapolis, Minn.
Eckhardt, John W., 2600 Elm St., Bakersfield, Calif.
Eddins, William N., P.O. Box 9036, Crestline Heights Br., Birmingham, Ala.
Edelmann, Anne M., 7614 Garden Rd., Cheltenham, Pa.
Edelstein, David S., Connecticut State College, Yonkers, N.Y.
Eden, Donald F., Adams State College, Alamosa, Colo.
Edinger, Lois V., University of North Carolina, Greensboro, N.C.
Edmundson, W. Dean, Detroit Public Schls., 12021 Evanston, Detroit, Mich.
Edson, William H., 206 Burton Hall, Univ. of Minnesota, Minneapolis, Minn.
Edstrom, A. E., Senior High School, 1001 State Hwy., Hopkins, Minn.
Edwards, Andrew S., Georgia Southern College, Statesboro, Ga.
Edwards, Arthur U., Eastern Illinois University, Charleston, Ill.
Edwards, Carlos R., Boys High School, Brooklyn, N.Y.
Edwards, Charles, Illinois State Univ., Normal, Ill.
Edwards, Gerald F., 3075 - 14 Ave., Marion, Iowa
Edwards, Joseph O., Jr., 251 - 13th St., Arcata, Calif.

Edwards, T. Bentley, Sch. of Educ., Univ. of California, Berkeley, Calif.
Egelston, Elwood, Jr., Illinois State University, Normal, Ill.
Egge, Donald E., 325 N.E. 10th St., Newport, Oreg.
Eggerding, Roland F., Lutheran High School, South, St. Louis, Mo.
Eherenman, William C., Wisconsin State University, Platteville, Wis.
Ehlers, Henry J., Duluth Branch, University of Minnesota, Duluth, Minn.
Ehrlich, Emanuel, 92 Joyce Rd., East Chester, N.Y.
Ehrmann, Jeanne S., Box 104, Poestenkill, N.Y.
Eibler, Herbert J., University of Michigan, Ann Arbor, Mich.
Eicher, Charles E., 936 N. Summit, Madison, S. Dak.
Eichholz, G. C., Educ. Research, Inc., Tampa, Fla.
Eikaas, Alf T., Kjolsdalen, Nordfjord, Norway
Einolf, W. L., Birchrunville, Pa.
Eisele, James E., University of Georgia, Athens, Ga.
Eisenstein, Herbert S., Pennsylvania State University, Middletown, Pa.
Eiserer, Paul E., Tchrs. Col., Columbia University, New York, N.Y.
Eisner, Elliot W., Stanford University, Stanford, Calif.
Eiszler, Charles F., Jr., 714 Superior Ave., N.W., Cleveland, Ohio
Elder, Rachel A., Tolman Hall, University of California, Berkeley, Calif.
Elie, Marie-Therese, 2920 Boulevard Rosemont, Montreal 36, Quebec, Canada
Elkins, Keith E., Washington University, St. Louis, Mo.
Elland, A. H., Hutchinson Junior College, 1300 Plum Hutchinson, Kans.
Elle, Martin J., Southern Oregon College, Ashland, Oreg.
Ellenburg, Fred C., Rt. #1, Grove Lakes, Statesboro, Ga.
Ellerbrook, Louis William, Box 4628, S.F.A. Sta., Nacogdoches, Tex.
Ellery, Marilynne, Ohio Northern University, Ada, Ohio
Elliott, Arthur H., Simon Fraser University, Burnaby 2, B.C., Canada
Elliott, David L., University of Illinois, Urbana, Ill.
Ellis, Mrs. Celia Diamond, 1125 S. LaJolla Ave., Los Angeles, Calif.
Ellis, Frederick E., Western Washington State Col., Bellingham, Wash.
Ellis, Gerald W., 1215 Waukegan Rd., Glenview, Ill.
Ellis, G. W., Drew Junior High School, 1055 N.W. 52nd St., Miami, Fla.
Ellis, John F., Simon Fraser University, Burnaby, B.C., Canada
Ellis, Joseph R., Northern Illinois University, DeKalb, Ill.
Ellis, Robert L., 1125 S. LaJolla Ave., Los Angeles, Calif.
Ellison, Alfred, New York University, Washington Sq., New York, N.Y.
Ellison, F. Robert, 1354 Laurel St., Casper, Wyo.
Ellison, Jack L., Francis W. Parker Sch., Chicago, Ill.
Ellner, Carolyn Lipton, 426 S. McCadden Pl., Los Angeles, Calif.
Ellson, Douglas G., Indiana University, Bloomington, Ind.
Ellwein, Mrs. Ileane, 2905 S. Jefferson St., Sioux Falls, S. Dak.
Elstein, Arthur J., Olin Health Center, MSU, E. Lansing, Mich.
Emans, Robert, 29 W. Woodruff Ave., Columbus, Ohio
Emery, Harriet E., 15200 McLain Ave., Allen Park, Mich.
Emeson, David L., 210 - 5th Ave. N.E., Independence, Iowa
Emmet, Thomas A., P.O. Box 52, Detroit, Mich.
Emmons, Jean F., Evanston Township H.S., Evanston, Ill.
Ende, Russell S., Northern Illinois University, DeKalb, Ill.
Endres, Mary P., Purdue University, Lafayette, Ind.
Endres, Richard J., 707 Salisbury Rd., Columbus, Ohio
Engelhardt, Jack E., 1500 Maywood Ave., Ann Arbor, Mich.
Engelhardt, Nickolaus L., Jr., Purdy Station, N.Y.
Engler, David, McGraw-Hill Book Co., New York, N.Y.
English, John W., Superintendent of Schools, Southfield, Mich.
English, Marvin D., National College of Education, Evanston, Ill.
Enoch, June E., Manchester College, North Manchester, Ind.
Entwisle, Doris, Johns Hopkins University, Baltimore, Md.
Eraut, Michael R., University of Sussex, Brighton, Sussex, England
Erbe, Wesley A., Col. of Educ., Univ. of Iowa, Iowa City, Iowa

Erdman, Robert L., Univ. of Utah, Salt Lake City, Utah
Erickson, Harley E., University of North Iowa, Cedar Falls, Iowa
Erickson, L. W., Sch. of Educ., Univ. of California, Los Angeles, Calif.
Erickson, Ralph J., Virginia Union University, Richmond, Va.
Erickson, Wayne C., 266 Orrin St., Winona, Minn.
Eriksen, Aase, 3700 Walnut St., Philadelphia, Pa.
Ernst, Susan C., 500 S. Grammercy Place, Los Angeles, Calif.
Ersted, Ruth, State Department of Education, St. Paul, Minn.
Ervin, John B., 5933 Enright St., St. Louis, Mo.
Ervin, William B., 1 Midland Pl., Newark, N.J.
Erxleben, Arnold C., 157 Bemis Dr., Seward, Nebr.
Erzen, Richard G., 931 Bartlett Terr., Libertyville, Ill.
Eson, Morris E., State University of New York, Albany, N.Y.
Esparo, Louis J., Michigan State Univ., East Lansing, Mich.
Essig, Lester Clay, Jr., Utah State University, Logan, Utah
Estes, Kenneth A., 1722 Woodhurst Ave., Bowling Green, Ky.
Estes, Sidney H., Urban Lab. in Educ., Atlanta, Ga.
Estvan, Frank J., Col. of Educ., Wayne State Univ., Detroit, Mich.
Etheridge, Robert F., Miami University, Oxford, Ohio
Etscovitz, Lionel P., 408 Penwyn Rd., Wynnewood, Pa.
Ettinger, Mrs. Bernadette C., 474 Brooklyn Blvd., Brightwaters, L.I., N.Y.
Eurich, Alvin C., Acad. for Educ. Dev., 437 Madison Ave., New York, N.Y.
Evans, Bruce M., Lubbock Christian Col., Lubbock, Texas
Evans, Edgar Ernest, Alabama State College, Montgomery, Ala.
Evans, Harley, Jr., 35952 Matoma Dr., Eastlake, Ohio
Evans, J. Bernard, 3163 Warrington Rd., Shaker Heights, Ohio
Evans Joyce S., 5807 Trailridge Circle, Austin, Tex.
Evans, Orlynn R., F-15 So. Campus Court, Lafayette, Ind.
Evans, Ralph F., Fresno State College, Fresno, Calif.
Evans, Rupert N., Col. of Educ., Univ. of Illinois, Urbana, Ill.
Evans, Warren D., 34 E. Winding Rd., Mechanicsburg, Pa.
Eve, Arthur W., Schl. of Educ., Univ. of Mass., Amherst, Mass.
Evenson, Warren L., 1528 S. Douglas St., Springfield, Ill.
Evertts, Eldonna L., N.C.T.E., Champaign, Ill.
• Ewigleben, Mrs. Muriel, 3727 Weisser Park Ave., Ft. Wayne, Ind.
Eyster, Elvin S., Dept. of Bus. Educ., Indiana Univ., Bloomington, Ind.

Facok, John, Tchrs. Col., Columbia Univ., New York, N.Y.
Fadden, Joseph A., Marywood College, Scranton, Pa.
Faddis, Mrs. Gabrielle J., Col. of Educ., Temple University, Philadelphia, Pa.
Failor, Harvey A., 13800 Ford Road, Dearborn, Mich.
Fair, Jean E., Wayne State University, Detroit, Mich.
Fairbanks, Gar, Supt. of Schools, Rocky Hill, Conn.
Falk, Alma M., 1330 New Hampshire Ave., N.W., Washington, D.C.
Fallon, Berlie J., Dept. of Educ., Texas Technological Col., Lubbock, Tex.
Fanslow, W. V., R.F.D. 3, Amherst, Mass.
Farabaugh, Martin P., Edinboro St. Col., Edinboro, Pa.
Farber, Bernard E., Brady Elementary School, Detroit, Mich.
Farber, Irvin J., 10823 Kelvin Ave., Philadelphia, Pa.
Fargen, J. Jerome, Catherine Spalding College, Louisville, Ky.
Faricy, William H., Michigan State Univ., East Lansing, Mich.
Farley, Gilbert J., Belmont Abbey Col., Belmont, N.C.
Farmer, Geraldine, University of Alberta, Edmonton, Alba., Canada
Farmerie, Samuel A., RR. 1, New Wilmington, Pa.
Farrell, Anne B., 342-74th St., Brooklyn, N.Y.
Farrell, Joseph L., 109 Cornell Ave., Hawthorne, N.J.
Farris, Dan C., R.D. 3, Box 140, Jersey Shore, Pa.
Farris, Marjorie, Appalachian St. Univ., Boone, N.C.
Fasan, Walter R., 3401 West 65th Pl., Chicago, Ill.
Faust, Claire Edward, 206 Floral Ave., Mankato, Minn.

Fawcett, Claude W., Sch. of Educ., Univ. of California, Los Angeles, Calif.
Fawley, Paul C., Dept. of Educ., University of Utah, Salt Lake City, Utah
Fay, Leo C., Sch. of Educ., Indiana University, Bloomington, Ind.
Fay, Robert S., Schl. of Educ., Boston Univ., Boston, Mass.
Fearn, Leif, San Diego State Col., San Diego, Calif.
Fee, Edward M., Bok Technical High School, Philadelphia, Pa.
Feely, Robert W., 10117 Albany Ave., Evergreen Park, Ill.
Feingold, S. Norman, 1640 Rhode Island Ave., N.W., Washington, D.C.
Feldman, David, Univ. of Minnesota, Minneapolis, Minn.
Felsenthal, Mrs. Norman, 422 Waldron Ave., West Lafayette, Ind.
Feltner, Bill D., Inst. of Higher Educ., Univ. of Georgia, Athens, Ga.
Fenderson, Julia K., Culver City Unified Schools, Culver City, Calif.
Fennema, Elizabeth H., 121 N. Allen, Madison, Wis.
Fenollosa, George M., Houghton Mifflin Co., 110 Tremont St., Boston, Mass.
Fenske, Arthur S., 435 Liberty St., Belmont, Wis.
Fenstermacher, G.D., Univ. of California, Los Angeles, Calif.
Feringer, F. R., Western Washington State College, Bellingham, Wash.
Ferris, Donald, 1316 N. Salisbury St., West Lafayette, Ind.
Ferris, Francis X, Spencerport, N.Y.
Ferry, Richard E., 236 Delmar, Decatur, Ill.
Fesperman, Mrs. Kathleen C., Newberry College, Newberry, S.C.
Feuerbach, F. Kenneth, Hammond High School, Hammond, Ind.
Feuers, Mrs. Stelle, Pierce College, Woodland Hills, Calif.
Ficek, Daniel E., R. 1, Box 3, River Falls, Wis.
Fiedler, E. L., Superintendent of Schools, Abilene, Kans.
Field, Robert L., 1506 Jackson St., Oshkosh, Wis.
Fields, Ralph R., Tchrs. Col., Columbia University, New York, N.Y.
Fielstra, Clarence, Sch. of Educ., Univ. of California, Los Angeles, Calif.
Fielstra, Helen, San Fernando Valley State College, Northridge, Calif.
Fieman, Marvin E., 305 S. Arnaz Dr., Los Angeles, Calif.
Figurel, J. Allen, Indiana University, N.W. Campus, Gary, Ind.
Filbeck, Orval, Abilene Christian College, Abilene, Tex.
Fillbrandt, James R., 4005 El Dorado, Bakersfield, Calif.
Fillmer, Henry T., University of Florida, Gainesville, Fla.
Filosa, Mary G., 32 Ross Hall Blvd., No., Piscataway, N.J.
Fina, Robert P., 2625 Chew St., Allentown, Pa.
Finch, F. H., Col. of Educ., Univ. of Illinois, Urbana, Ill.
Finder, Morris, State University of N.Y., Albany, N.Y.
Findlay, Stephen W., Delbarton School, Morristown, N.J.
Findley, Dale, 1639 S. Sixth St., Terre Haute, Ind.
Findley, Warren G., Col. of Educ., University of Georgia, Athens, Ga.
Findley, William H., Jr., 111 Curtiss Pkwy., Miami Springs, Fla.
Fink, Abel K., State University College, 1300 Elmwood Ave., Buffalo, N.Y.
Fink, Herbert J., Tuley High School, 1313 N. Claremont Ave., Chicago, Ill.
Fink, Martin B., 3713 Merridan Dr., Concord, Calif.
Finstein, Milton W., Div. of Educ., Indiana Univ., Gary, Ind.
Finster, Virginia, 2203 Mocking Bird Drive, Baytown, Tex.
Finucan, J. Thomas, Assumption High School, Wisconsin Rapids, Wis.
Firth, Gerald R., University of Alabama, Tuscaloosa, Ala.
Fischer, John H., Tchrs. Col., Columbia University, New York, N.Y.
Fischler, Abraham S., 5000 Taylor St., Ft. Lauderdale, Fla.
Fischoff, Ephraim, Marathon Co. Campus, Univ. of Wis., Wausau Wis.
Fish, Lawrence D., NWREL, 710 S.W. 2nd Ave., Portland, Oreg.
Fishback, Woodson W., Southern Illinois University, Carbondale, Ill.
Fishco, Daniel T., Southern Ill. University, Carbondale, Ill.
Fishell, Kenneth N., Syracuse University, Syracuse, N.Y.
Fisher, Betty G., 49 E. College Ave., Springfield, Ohio
Fisher, Carol M., R.R. # 2, 5747 Detrick-Jordan Rd., Springfield, Ohio
Fisher, George, Ohio State University, Columbus, Ohio
Fisher, Ijourie Stocks, Miami-Dade Junior College, Miami, Fla.

Fisher, Lawrence A., Univ. of Calgary, Calgary Alberta, Canada
Fisher, Robert D., 4930 Sharon Ave., Columbus, Ohio
* Fisher, Mrs. Welthy H., Literacy Village, P.O. Singar Nagar, Lucknow, U.P., India
Fishler, Edward, 72 Hedgerow Lane, Commack, L.I., N.Y.
Fisk, Robert S., State University of New York, Buffalo, N.Y.
Fitzgerald, William F., 5835 Kimbark Ave., Chicago, Ill.
Fitzpatrick, E. D., Illinois State University, Normal, Ill.
Flak, J.H.E., Mitchell C.A.E., Bathurst NSW, Australia
Flagg, E. Alma, 44 Stengel Ave., Newark, N.J.
Flanagan, John C., P.O. Box 1113, Palo Alto, Calif.
Fleck, Henrietta, H.E. Dept., New York Univ., Washington Sq., New York, N.Y.
Fleckles, David E., San Jose Unified Schl. Dist., San Jose, Calif.
Fleming, Elyse S., Western Reserve University, Cleveland, Ohio
Fleming, Harold D., 2020 Birchmont Dr., Bemidji, Minn.
Fleming, Robert S., Virginia Commonwealth Univ., Richmond, Va.
Fletcher, Ruby J., University of Utah, Salt Lake City, Utah
Fliegel, Norris E., 98 Riverside Dr., New York, N.Y.
Fligor, R. J., Southern Illinois University, Carbondale, Ill.
Flint, Jack M., Kansas City Community Junior College, Kansas City, Kans.
Flodin, Raymond, P.O. Box 213, 24 W. Spring St., Oxford, Ohio
Flores, Vetal, 2818 Southland Blvd., San Angelo, Tex.
Flower, George E., Ontario Inst. for Studies in Educ., Toronto, Ont., Canada
Flowers, Anne, Box 3231, Columbia, S.C.
Flusche, Rev. Ernest A., P.O. Box 507. Oklahoma City, Okla.
Flug, Eugene R. F., Stout State University, Menomonie, Wis.
Fluitt, John L., Col. of Educ., Louisiana State Univ., New Orleans, La.
Flynn, John H., 5501 Arvada St., Torrance, Calif.
Flynn, Veronica, 2021 N. Western Ave., Los Angeles, Calif.
Fochs, John S., 1732 Wauwatosa Ave., Wauwatosa, Wis.
Focht, James R., Educ. Dept., Salisbury State Col., Salisbury, Md.
Fogg, William E., Long Beach State College, Long Beach, Calif.
Foley, Robert L., 2901 S. Parkway, Chicago, Ill.
Fonacier, Andres M., Laoag, Ilocos Norte, Philippines
Foord, James, University of Manchester, Manchester, England
Foran, Mary Ellen, 6301 N. Sheridan Rd., Chicago, Ill.
Foran, William L., 1007 Alberta, Oceanside, Calif.
Forbes, Beverly A., Univ. of Washington, Renton, Wash.
Force, Dewey G., Jr., Pattee Hall, Univ. of Minnesota, Minneapolis, Minn.
Ford, Gervais W., San Jose State College, San Jose, Calif.
Ford, Harry J., 19009 E. Badillo St., Covina, Calif.
Ford, John, 315 Ashbourne Rd., Elkins Park, Pa.
Ford, Luther L., P.O. Box 805, Grambling, La.
Ford, Roxana R., Sch. of Home Econ., Univ. of Minnesota, St. Paul, Minn.
Forer, Ruth K., 6013 Greenbush Ave., Van Nuys, Calif.
Foresi, Joseph, Jr., 29-C Hasbrouck Apt., Ithaca, N.Y.
Forgnone, Charles, Univ. of Florida, Gainesville, Fla.
Forrester, Carl M., Lake Park H.S., 6 N. 600 Medina Rd., Roselle, Ill.
Fortress, Lillian F., P.S. 102, 315 E. 113th St., New York, N.Y.
Fosback, Alta B., P.O. Box 443, Carlton, Oreg.
Foshay, Arthur W., Tchrs. Col., Columbia University, New York, N.Y.
Fossett, Barbara, Box 323, Churchville, N.Y.
Fossieck, Theodore H., The Milne Sch., State Univ. of New York, Albany, N.Y.
Foster, E. M., Fresno State Col., 4021 Mt. Vernon Ave., Bakersfield, Calif.
Foster, Garrett R., Florida State Univ., Tallahassee, Fla.
Fournier, Rev. Edmond A., 241 Pearson Ave., Ferndale, Mich.
Fowler, William, Ontario Inst. for Stud. in Educ., Toronto, Ont., Canada
Fowler, Wilton R., Jr., 1120 Forest Oaks, Hurst, Tex.
Fowlkes, John Guy, 204 Educ. Bldg., Univ. of Wisconsin, Madison, Wis.
Fox, Clinton, Goddard Jr. H.S., Glendora, Calif.

Fox, Frederich, S.J., Canisius Col., Buffalo, N.Y.
Fox, Marion W., 3200 Atlantic Ave., Atlantic City, N.J.
Fox, Willard, Ohio Sch. Board Assoc., Columbus, Ohio
Fox, Robert S., 102 Univ. Sch., University of Michigan, Ann Arbor, Mich.
Frain, Thomas J., 1931 Brunswick Ave., Trenton, N.J.
France, Harold S., Memorial Schl., Grant Ave., Maywood, N.J.
Francis, Ida L., Public Schools, Somerville, N.J.
Francis, Rodney I., 16 London Dr., W. Wollongong, N.S.W., Australia
Frandsen, Arden N., Utah State University, Logan, Utah
Franer, William J., Supt. of Schools, Cincinnati, Ohio
Frankland, Elizabeth M., 512 Algoma Blvd., Oshkosh, Wis.
Franklin, Arthur J., Univ. of So. Louisiana, Lafayette, La.
Franklin, Ruby Holden, Roosevelt University, 430 S. Michigan Ave., Chicago, Ill.
Franson, Arthur H., 50 N. Spring, LaGrange, Ill.
Franz, Evelyn B., Dept. of Educ., Trenton State College, Trenton, N.J.
Franz, Vivian, 410 Sandra Dr., Oxford, Ohio
Franzblau, Daniel M., 525 Sandra Dr., Oxford, Ohio
Franzen, William L., Col. of Educ., Univ. of Toledo, Toledo, Ohio
Frase, H. Weldon, 1635 Hutchinson, S.E., Grand Rapids, Mich.
Fraser, Hugh W., 502 Browncroft Blvd., Rochester, N.Y.
Fraser, Rosemary, Miami University, Oxford, Ohio
Fratelli, Mrs. Anthony, 67 Wood Rd., Centereach, N.Y.
Frater, Dorothy, 59 Normandy Ave., Truro, Nova Scotia, Canada
Frazier, Andrew J., 303 Biddle Ave., Harrison, Ohio
Fred, Bernhart G., 108 McCormick Dr., DeKalb, Ill.
Frederick, William C., Shoreline School District, Seattle, Wash.
Fredman, Norman, 76-07 168th St., Flushing, N.Y.
Fredrick, James R., Arizona State College, Flagstaff, Ariz.
Freeberg, Howard, 207 Sixth Ave. East, West Fargo, N.Dak.
Freeman, Daniel M., R.D. 1, W. Springfield, Pa.
Freeman, Donald, 831 Crown Blvd., East Lansing, Mich.
Freeman, Julia H., 347 W. 145th St., New York, N.Y.
Freeman, Kenneth H., 3308 59th St., Lubbock, Tex.
Freeman, Robert P., 406 Hollywood Ave., Hampton, Va.
Freeman, Ruges Richmond, Jr., 8027 Bennett Ave., St. Louis, Mo.
Freeman, William F., Florida State Univ., Tallahassee, Fla.
Fremont, Herbert, Queens College, Flushing, N.Y.
French, Henry P., 2 Bedford Way, Pittsford, N.Y.
French, William M., Muhlenberg College, Allentown, Pa.
Fretwell, Elbert K., Jr., Pres., State Univ. Col., Buffalo, N.Y.
Freund, Evelyn, 5954 Guilford, Detroit, Mich.
Frick, Herman L., Florida State University, Tallahassee, Fla.
Frick, Ralph, 4016 Stoneview Circle, Stone Mountain, Ga.
Fridlund, John V., 414 N. Elm St., Itasca, Ill.
Frieberg, Carter N., Loyola University, 820 N. Michigan Ave., Chicago, Ill.
Friederichs, Lloyd, Lynwood H.S., Lynwood, Calif.
Friedhoff, Walter H., Illinois State University, Normal, Ill.
Friedrich, Kurt, San Diego State College, San Diego, Calif.
Frisk, Jack L., Supt. of Schools, Yakima, Wash.
Frizzell, Lois, 1031 Chula Vista Rd., Tucson, Ariz.
Froehlich, Gustave J., Bur. of Inst. Res., Univ. of Illinois, Urbana, Ill.
Froling, Raymond S., Nether Providence Sch. Dist., Wallingford, Pa.
Frye, Richard M., Purdue University, Lafayette, Ind.
Fryer, Thomas W., Jr., Miami-Dade Junior College, Miami, Fla.
Fuchs, Sarel P., 810 East Lake Ave., Baltimore, Md.
Fuglaar, Ollie B., Louisiana State University, Baton Rouge, La.
Full, Harold, 870 United Nations Plaza, New York, N.Y.
Fullagar, William A., Box 40, Mendon, N.Y.
Fuller, R. Buckminster, Southern Illinois University, Carbondale, Ill.

Fullerton, Craig K., 2712 North 52nd St., Omaha, Nebr.
Funderburk, Earl C., Fairfax County Schools, Fairfax, Va.
Furey, Mary Z., 7926 Jackson Rd., Alexandria, Va.
Furlow, Mrs. Florine D., 2968 Collier Dr., N.W., Atlanta, Ga.
Furner, Beatrice, University of Iowa, Iowa City, Iowa
Furst, Philip W., 47 W. Water St., Lock Haven, Pa.
Futch, Olivia, Woman's College, Furman University, Greenville, S.C.

Gadell, Sandra, Wright State Univ., Dayton, Ohio
Gaetano, Mary Ann, 2648 Eaton Rd., University Hts., Ohio
Gage, George J., Univ. of California, Los, Angeles, Calif.
Gage, N. L., Sch. of Educ., Stanford University, Stanford, Calif.
Gaines, Berthera E., 4208 S. Galvez St., New Orleans, La.
Gaines, John C., State University of Tennessee, Nashville, Tenn.
Gaiter, Worrell G., Florida A. & M. University, Tallahassee, Fla.
Galbreath, Dorothy J., 3001 King Dr., Chicago, Ill.
Gale, Ann V., 403 Jackson Ave., Glencoe, Ill.
Gale, Frederick, 20820 River Rd., Haney, B.C., Canada
Gallegos, Arnold M., Washington State Univ., Pullman, Wash.
Gallicchio, Francis A., 325 College Ave., Mt. Pleasant, Pa.
Galloway, Geraldine, 111 Northwest Tenth St., Fairfield, Ill.
Gaman, Vivian C., Yeshiva Univ., New York, N.Y.
Gambert, Charles A., 24 Bennett Village Terr., Buffalo, N.Y.
Gambino, Vincent, Dept. of Educ., Roosevelt University, Chicago, Ill.
Gamelin, Francis C., 2359 - 29th St., Rock Island, Ill.
Gandy, Frances C., 2597 Avery Ave., Memphis, Tenn.
Gandy, Thomas W., Berry Col., Mt. Berry, Ga.
Gannon, John T., 1504 S. Broadway, Emmetsburg, Iowa
Gans, Leo, 4300 West 62nd St., Indianapolis, Ind.
Gansberg, Lucille, 2255-C Goodrich St., Sacramento, Calif.
Gantz, Ralph M., Superintendent of Schools, New Britain, Conn.
Garbe, Lester, 2110 W. Marne Ave., Milwaukee, Wis.
Garbee, Frederick E., 465 W. Avenue 44, Los Angeles, Calif.
Garbel, Marianne, 6732 Crandon Ave., Chicago, Ill.
Garber, Leonard, State Dept. of Educ., Hartford, Conn.
Garber, M. Delott, Central Connecticut State College, New Britain, Conn.
Gardiner, Robert J., Asst. Prin., Bakersfield H.S., Bakersfield, Calif.
Gardner, Harrison, 1007 Ravinia, West Lafayette, Ind.
Garetto, Lawrence A., 5162 Walnut Ave., Chino, Calif.
Garfinkel, Alan, Dept. of Educ., Okla. St. Univ., Stillwater, Okla.
Garin, Mrs. Bail W., 1625 E. Prine Rd., Tucson, Ariz.
Garinger, Elmer H., 2625 Briarcliff Pl., Charlotte, N.C.
Garland, Colden B., 1569 Elmwood Ave., Rochester, N.Y.
Garlich, Melvin O., 2223 Robincrest Ln., Glenview, Ill.
Garoutte, Bill Charles, Univ. of California Medical Center, San Francisco, Calif.
Garrett, Charles G., 2130 Tarpon Road, Naples, Fla.
Garrison, Harry L., 4802 E. Mercer Way, Mercer Island, Wash.
Garrity, William J., Jr., 45 Gaynos Dr., Bridgeport, Conn.
Gartrell, Callie, P.O. Box 33, Cheboygan, Mich.
Garvey, Reba, 12700 Fairhill Rd., Cleveland, Ohio
Gaston, Don, Couns., New Rochelle High School, New Rochelle, N.Y.
*Gates, Arthur I., Tchrs. Col., Columbia University, New York, N.Y.
Gates, James O., Jr., Northwest Missouri St. Col., Maryvillle, Mo.
Gatewood, Thomas, 605 Redbud Hill Apts., Bloomington, Ind.
Gaudette, R. Dean, Eastern Washington St. Col., Cheney, Wash.
Gauerke, Warren E., 316 Merriweather Rd., Grosse Pointe Farms, Mich.
Gauvey, Ralph E., Roger Williams Jr. Col., Providence, R.I.
Gavin, Ann M., 617 Broad St., Bldg. 10 #9, East Weymouth, Mass.
Gavin, Joseph M., Sch. Dist. of Philadelphia, Philadelphia, Pa.
Gayheart, S. Jack, 315 S. Locust St., Apt. 4, Oxford, Ohio
Gaynor, Alan K., 358 Alex. Colony East, Columbus, Ohio

Gayo, Francisco, Box 526, Eigenmann Hall, Bloomington, Ind.
Gazelle, Hazel N., 60 N. Auburn Ave., Sierra Madre, Calif.
Geckler, Jack W., Asst. Supt., Oak Ridge Schools, Oak Ridge, Tenn.
Geer, Owen C., P.O. Box 2398, Dhahran, Saudi Arabia
Geeslin, Robt. H., Avalon Estates, Thomasville, Ga.
Geigle, Ralph C., Superintendent of Schools, Reading, Pa.
Geiken, Lloyd A., Prin., Shorewood High School, Shorewood, Wis.
Geiss, Doris T., 107 Beverwyck Dr., Guilderland, N.Y.
Geitgey, Richard, 1026 Menlo Circle, Ashland, Ohio
Gelerinter, Alfred, Sch. Psych., Rochester City Schools, Rochester, N.Y.
Geller, Joshua S., 16 Andrea Lane, Avon, Conn.
Geng, George, Glassboro State College, Glassboro, N.J.
Gentry, George H., Box 663, Baytown, Tex.
George, Howard A., Northwest Missouri State College, Maryville, Mo.
Georgiades, William, Univ. of Southern California, Los Angeles, Calif.
Georgiady, Nicholas P., 110 W. Bull Run Dr., Oxford, Ohio
Gephart, Woodrow W., Supt. of Schools, Jefferson, Ohio
Geraty, T. S., 7422 Hancock Ave., Takoma Park, Md.
Gerber, Wayne J., Bethel College, Mishawaka, Ind.
Gerlach, Vernon S., Arizona State University, Tempe, Ariz.
Gerletti, John D., 1901 Mission St., South Pasadena, Calif.
Gerlock, D. E., Dept. of Educ., Valdosta State College. Valdosta, Ga.
Gernert, Herbert F., 3361 Lindberg Ave., Allentown, Pa.
Gerut, Ronald B., 9636 N. Kenton Ave., Skokie, Ill.
Gesinsky, William J., 6690 Broadside Rd., Independence, Ohio
Gesler, Harriet L., 70 Agnes Dr., Manchester, Conn.
Gest, Viola S., 915 E. Weinert St., Seguin, Tex.
Gettys, Helen C., Missouri Western Col., St. Joseph, Mo.
Getz, Howard G., Westbrook Addn., Morton, Ill.
Getzels, J. W., Dept. of Educ., University of Chicago, Chicago, Ill.
Geyer, John J., Sch. of Educ., Rutgers Univ., New Brunswick, N.J.
Ghalib, Hanna, P. O. Box 4638, Beirut, Lebanon
Gialas, George J., 1150 Wayland Ave., Cornwells Heights, Pa.
Gibbons, Constance M., 74 Franklin Ave., Oakville, Conn.
Gibbs, Edward Delmar, Univ. of Puget Sound, Tacoma, Wash.
Gibbs, Edward, III, 1145 Clinton Ter., South Plainfield, N.J.
Gibbs, Gloria Stanley, 501 East 32nd St., Chicago, Ill.
Gibbs, John Donald, 1147 S. Ash St., Moses Lake, Wash.
Gibbs, Wesley, Superintendent, Dist. No. 68, 9300 N. Kenton, Skokie, Ill.
Gibert, James M., Randolph-Macon Woman's Col., Lynchburg, Va.
Gibson, Charles H., Eastern Kentucky Univ., Richmond, Ky.
Gibson, Mrs. Kathryn Snell, Prairie View A & M College, Prairie View, Tex.
Gibson, R. Oliver, State University of New York, Buffalo, N.Y.
Giddis, W. James, 229 Greenwood Ave., Holland, Mich.
Giesecke, G. Ernst, Sangamon State Univ., Springfield, Ill.
Giesy, John P., 1017 Blanchard, Flint, Mich.
Gilbert, Daniel, 8446 Major, Morton Grove, Ill.
Gilbert, Mrs. Doris Wilcox, 1044 Euclid Ave., Berkeley, Calif.
Gilbert, Harry B., Dept. of Educ., Fordham University, Bronx, N.Y.
Gilbert, Jerome H., 815 Ashbury, El Cerrito, Calif.
Gilbert, John H., Dept. of Educ., Monmouth College, West Long Branch, N.J.
Gilbert, William B., Onondaga Central School, Nedrow, N.Y.
Giles, LeRoy H., University of Dubuque, Dubuque, Iowa
Gili, Joe P., Salem H.S., Salem, Ind.
Gilk, Edwin John, P.O. Box 642, Columbia Falls, Mont.
Gilkey, Richard W., 5516 S.W. Seymour St., Portland, Oreg.
Gill, Kenneth F., Supt. of Schools, Wheeling, Ill.
Gill, Margaret, Mills College, Oakland, Calif.
Gillespie, John H., Lenape Reg. Sch. Dist., Medford, N.J.
Gillette, B. Frank, Superintendent of Schools, Los Gatos, Calif.

Gilliom, Bonnie, 2495 Haverford Rd., Columbus, Ohio
Gillis, Ruby, 6300 Grand River Ave., Detroit, Mich.
Gilmore, Douglas M., Central Michigan Univ., Mt. Pleasant, Mich.
Gingerich, Julia B., 1408 Lewis, Des Moines, Iowa
Giroux, Robert J., Clarke Col., Dubuque, Iowa
Gittler, Joseph B., Yeshiva Univ., New York, N.Y.
Glaess, Herman L., Concordia Teachers College, Seward, Nebr.
Glaser, Donald P., California Teachers Assoc., Burlingame, Calif.
Glaser, Robert, Res. & Dev. Cent., Univ. of Pittsburgh, Pittsburgh, Pa.
Glasow, Ogden L., P.O. Box 143, Macomb, Ill.
Glass, Olive Jewell, 3910 Latimer St., Dallas, Tex.
Glass, Ruth S., 775 Riverside Dr., New York, N.Y.
Glassman, Milton, 529 Silver Oaks Dr., Kent, Ohio
Glendenning, Donald E., 6 Johnson Ave., Charlottetown, P.E.I., Canada
Glicken, Irwin J., Chicago State Col., Chicago, Ill.
Glock, Marvin D., Stone Hall, Cornell University, Ithaca, N.Y.
Glogau, Arthur H., Oregon College of Education, Monmouth, Oreg.
Glover, George T., Prin., Columbus Sch., Oklahoma City, Okla.
Glover, Robert H., Mutual Plaza, Durham, N.C.
Glovinsky, Sanford J., The ASSIST Center, Wayne, Mich.
Glynn, Richard L., Supt. of Schs., Johannesburg, Mich.
Gobetz, Wallace, 540 East 22nd St., Brooklyn, N.Y.
Goble, Robert I., McGuffey No. 301, Miami University, Oxford, Ohio
Godfrey, Mary E., Pennsylvania State University, University Park, Pa.
Goebel, E. J., Supt., Archdiocese of Milwaukee, Milwaukee, Wis.
Goff, Robert J., Univ. of Massachusetts, Amherst, Mass.
Gold, Charles E., 1418 E. Colton Ave., Redlands, Calif.
Gold, Lewis L., Indiana Univ. of Pennsylvania, Indiana, Pa.
Gold, Milton J., Hunter College, New York, N.Y.
Goldberg, Miriam L., Tchrs. Col., Columbia University, New York, N.Y.
Goldberg, Nathan, 75-47—196th St., Flushing, N.Y.
Goldhammer, Keith, 2929 Highland Way, Corvallis, Oreg.
Goldman, Bert A., Sch. of Educ., Univ. of North Carolina, Greensboro, N.C.
Goldman, Harvey, Col. of Educ., Univ. of Maryland, College Park, Md.
Goldman, Samuel, Sch. of Educ., Syracuse University, Syracuse, N.Y.
Goldner, Ralph H., Sch. of Educ., New York University, New York, N.Y.
Goldstein, Herbert, Yeshiva University, 55 Fifth Ave., New York, N.Y.
Goldstein, Sanford G., 115 Woodgate Terr., Rochester, N.Y.
Goltry, Thomas K., Box 572, Springfield, S. Dak.
Gomes, Lawrence A., Jr., 4 Vincent Ave., Belmont, Mass.
Gonzalez, Alice M., University of Puerto Rico, Rio Piedras, Puerto Rico
Goo, Frederick J. K., c/o Bur. of Indian Affairs Sch., Barrow, Alaska
Good, Warren R., 1604 Stony Run Dr., Northwood, Wilmington, Del.
Goodell, Jerome L., Asst. Prin., Carl Sandburg H.S., Glendora, Calif.
Goodlad, John I., Sch. of Educ., Univ. of California, Los Angeles, Calif.
Goodman, John O., University of Connecticut, Storrs, Conn.
Goodman, Kenneth S., Wayne State Univ., Detroit, Mich.
Goodpaster, Robert L., University of Kentucky-Ashland Center, Ashland, Ky.
Goodside, Samuel, 504 Beach 139th St., Belle Harbor, L.I., N.Y.
Goodwin, Margaret J., 1412 Winfield Rd., Bloomington, Ind.
Goodwin, Dr. William L., 7332 Panorama Dr., Boulder, Colo.
Googins, Duane G., 2964—116th Ave., N.W., Coon Rapids, Minn.
Goolsby, Thomas M., Res. and Dev. Cen., Univ. of Georgia, Athens, Ga.
Goossen, Carl V., 108 Burton Hall, Univ. of Minnesota, Minneapolis, Minn.
Gordon, Irving, 1635 Harvard St., Washington, D.C.
Gordon, Mrs. Vineta H., Box 156, Christiansted, St. Croix, V.I.
Gordon, Ted E., 317 N. Lucerne, Los Angeles, Calif.
Gordon, William M., Sch. of Educ., Miami University, Oxford, Ohio
Gore, Jeffrey B., 5795-A N. Meadows Blvd., Columbus, Ohio
Gorham, Marion, Elem. Prin., Emerson School, Concord, Mass.

Gorman, William J., 219-40—93rd Ave., Queens Village, N.Y.
Gormley, Charles L., Dept. of Educ., Alabama College, Montevallo, Ala.
Gorn, Janice L., 60 E. 12th St., New York, N.Y.
Gorth, William P., 15 Brae Burn Rd., S. Deerfield, Mass.
Gorton, Harry B., 224 Orange St., Northumberland, Pa.
Gorton, Robert G., 309 South St., New Providence, N.J.
Gott, John W., 3060 Quail, Lakewood, Colo.
Gottenid, Allan J., Comm. on Educ., ELCT, P.O. Box 412, Arusha, Tanzania
Gotts, Ernest A., U. of Texas, Austin, Tex.
Goudreault, Fernand, Mott Academic Ctr., Olivet Col., Olivet, Mich.
Gough, Jessie P., LaGrange College, LaGrange, Ga.
Gould, Norman M., Supt., Madera County Schools, Madera, Calif.
Gow, James S., 4519 Middle Rd., Allison Park, Pa.
Gowan, John Curtis, San Fernando Valley State Col., Northridge, Calif.
Gowin, Dixie B., Stone Hall, Cornell Univ., Ithaca, N.Y.
Graber, Eldon W., Freeman Jr. College, Freeman, S. Dak.
Grabowski, A. A., 2512 Southport Ave., Chicago, Ill.
Graef, Ardelle, 1232 S. Dewey St., Eau Claire, Wis.
Graff, Orin B., Col. of Educ., University of Tennessee, Knoxville, Tenn.
Graham, Audrey R., Lib., Col. of St. Rose, Albany, N.Y.
Grahm, Milton L., Cambridge School of Business, Boston, Mass.
Granskog, Dorothy, Knox Col., Galesburg, Ill.
Grant, Eugene B., Northern Illinois University, DeKalb, Ill.
Grant, Geraldine R., 701 Locust Ave., Long Beach, Calif.
Grant, Sydney R., Florida State Univ., Tallahassee, Fla.
* Grant, Wayman R. F., Booker T. Washington Junior High School, Mobile, Ala.
Grau, R. T., Clinton Public Schls., Box 110, Clinton, Iowa
Graven, John P., 2800 Lake Shore Dr., Chicago, Ill.
Graves, Jack A., P.O. Box 671, Turlock, Calif.
Graves, Linwood D., 115 Leathers Circle, N.W., Atlanta, Ga.
Graves, William, 907 Poplar Rd., Starkville, Miss.
Gray, George T., c/o 303 N. Hillcrest Dr. S.W., Marietta, Ga.
Gray, Mary Jane, Loyola University, 820 N. Michigan, Chicago, Ill.
Gray, Ronald F., Canadian Nazarene Col., Winnipeg, Manitoba, Canada
Gray, William, Univ. of Dayton, Dayton, Ohio
Graybeal, William S., 1700 Fox Run Ct., Vienna, Va.
Graye, Mytrolene L., 25 W. 132nd St., New York, N.Y.
Grayson, William H., Jr., 21-71—34th Ave., Long Island City, N.Y.
Green, Donald Ross, 680 Dry Creek Rd., Monterey, Calif.
Green, Gertrude B., 100 W. Hickory Grove Rd., Bloomfield Hills, Mich.
Green, John A., Central Washington St. Col., Ellensburg, Wash.
Green, Mrs. Martha, 1929 Northwest Seventh Ln., Gainesville, Fla.
Green, Ronald F., Sch. of Educ., Indiana Univ., Bloomington, Ind.
Greenberg, Gilda M., University of Tennessee, Nashville, Tenn.
Greenberg, Mrs. Judith W., Sch. of Educ., City College, New York, N.Y.
Greene, Bert I., 1111 Grant St., Ypsilanti, Mich.
Greene, Charles E., P.O. Box 185, East Side Sta., Santa Cruz, Calif.
Greene, Frank P., 707 Sumner Ave., Syracuse, N.Y.
Greene, Mrs. Maxine, 1080—5th Ave., New York, N.Y.
Greene, Mrs. Minnie S., 1121 Chestnut St., San Marcos, Tex.
Greenfield, Curtis O., 345 W. Windsor Ave., Phoenix, Ariz.
Greenlaw, Marilyn, Michigan St. Univ., East Lansing, Mich.
Greenman, Margaret H., P.O. Box 56, Goreville, Ill.
Greenwood, Edward D., Menninger Clinic, Box 829, Topeka, Kans.
Greer, Evelyn, Fayette County Schls., 400 Lafayette Dr., Lexington, Ky.
Greer, Peter, High School, Ipswich, Mass.
Gregg, Russell T., Sch. of Educ., University of Wisconsin, Madison, Wis.
Greif, Ivo P., Illinois State University, Normal, Ill.
Greivell, Richard H., P.O. Box 7078, Agat, Guam
Grenda, Ted T., Box 189, Stone Ridge, N.Y.

Grennell, Robert L., State University College, Fredonia, N.Y.
Gress, James R., 4728 Arbor Dr., Rolling Meadows, Ill.
Griffin, Gary A., 1255 New Hampshire Ave., N.W., Washington, D.C.
Griffin, William S., Dept. of Educ., Univ. of Chicago, Chicago, Ill.
Griffiths, Daniel E., 54 Clarendon Rd., Scarsdale, N.Y.
Griffiths, John A., Superintendent of Schools, Monongahela, Pa.
Griffiths, Ruth, Massachusetts State College, Worcester, Mass.
Grimes, Wellington V., 4 Liberty Sq., Boston, Mass.
* Grizzell, E. Duncan, 640 Maxwelton Ct., Lexington, Ky.
Grobman, Hulda, Juniper Lane, Piscataway, N.J.
Groff, Warren H., 721 Highland Ave., Jenkintown, Pa.
Gromacki, Chester P., 1000 N. Lemon St., Fullerton, Calif.
Gronlund, Norman E., Col. of Educ., University of Illinois, Urbana, Ill.
Grose, Robert F., Amherst College, Amherst, Mass.
Gross, Lydia E., State Col., Lock Haven, Pa.
Gross, Neal, Grad. Sch. of Educ., Harvard University, Cambridge, Mass.
Grossman, Ruth H., Sch. of Educ., City College of N.Y., New York, N.Y.
Grossnickle, Foster E., 1116 Melbourne Ave., Melbourne, Fla.
Grosswald, Jules, 21st St. and the Parkway, Philadelphia, Pa.
Grover, Burton L., Western Washington St. Col., Bellingham, Wash.
Groves, Ramsey M., Colorado St. Univ., Ft. Collins, Colo.
Groves, Vernon T., Olivet Nazarene College, Kankakee, Ill.
Gruber, Frederick C., Grad. Sch. of Educ., Univ. of Pa., Philadelphia, Pa.
Grudell, Regina C., 45 Chadwick Rd., Teaneck, N.J.
Guba, Egon G., NISEC, Indiana Univ., Bloomington, Ind.
Guckenheimer, S. N., Heath Area Vocational School, Heath, Ohio
Guditus, Charles W., Schl. of Educ., Lehigh Univ., Bethlehem, Pa.
Guilbault, Georges, Box 160, Ste. Anne, Man., Canada
Guild, Joann, 6139 Flores Ave., Los Angeles, Calif.
Guilford, Jerome O., 705 Searles Rd., Toledo, Ohio
Gullan, Ann Mary, Quincy Col., Quincy, Ill.
Gunn, Jack G., Rt. 2, Box 514, State Blvd. Ext., Meridian, Miss.
Gunther, John F., 3 Cek Ct., Sayville, L.I., N.Y.
Guss, Carolyn, Indiana Univ., Bloomington, Ind.
Gustafson, A. M., Alice Vail Junior High Sch., 5350 E. 16th St., Tucson, Ariz.
Gustafson, Alma L., 1211 North 5th St., East Grand Forks, Minn.
Gutcher, G. Dale, Colo. St. Univ., Fort Collins, Colo.
Gwynn, J. Minor, 514 North St., Chapel Hill, N.C.
Gyuro, Steven J., 2300 Edgevale Rd., Columbus, Ohio

Haage, Catherine M., College of New Rochelle, New Rochelle, N.Y.
Haas, Richard J., Jr., 119 Stubbs Dr., Trotwood, Ohio
Haberman, Martin, Dept. of Educ., Univ. of Wisconsin, Milwaukee, Wis.
Hack, Walter G., Ohio State University, Columbus, Ohio
Hacking, Eleanor, 34 Hamlet St., Fairhaven, Mass.
Hackmann, Jane, 326 N. 49th Street, Belleville, Ill.
Hackney, Ben H., Jr., 4618 Walker Rd., Charlotte, N.C.
Haddad, Fred, GRC, Bloomington, Ind.
Hadden, John F., Rt. # 2, Cranbury, N.J.
Haddock, Thomas T., 7232 N. 12th Ave., Phoenix, Ariz.
Haenn, Joseph F., 212 Birch St., Park Forest, Ill.
Haffner, Hyman, 6229 Nicholson St., Pittsburgh, Pa.
Hagen, Donald E., 13028 Root Rd., Columbia Station, Ohio
Hagen, Elizabeth, Tchrs. Col., Columbia University, New York, N.Y.
Hager, Walter E., 4625 S. Chelsea Ln., Bethesda, Md.
Haggerson, Nelson L., 132 W. Balboa Dr., Tempe, Ariz.
Hagglund, Oliver C., Gustavus Adolphus College, St. Peter, Minn.
Hagstrom, Ellis A., 30 Kristen Ct., Cheshire, Conn.
Hahn, Albert R., Veterans' Administration Hospital, Phoenix, Ariz.
Hahn, L. Donald, Western Illinois University, Macomb, Ill.

Haight, Wilbur T., 314 S. DuPont Blvd., Milford, Del.
Haimowitz, Clement, Box 134, Hillsboro Rd., Belle Mead, N.Y.
Hale, Gifford G., Sch. of Educ., Florida State University, Tallahassee, Fla.
Hale, R. Nelson, State Teachers College, Slippery Rock, Pa.
Hales, Russell G., University of Utah, Salt Lake City, Utah
Haley, Elizabeth M., 843 Marshall Dr., Palo Alto, Calif.
Hall, J. Floyd, 420 N. Pleasantburg Dr., Greenville, S.C.
Hall, James A., 24 Crescent Rd., Port Washington, N.Y.
Hall, John E., Jackson State College, Jackson, Miss.
Hall, John W., 14 Church St., Canton, N.Y.
Hall, Joseph I., 3333 Elston Ave., Chicago, Ill.
Hall, Keith A., Pennsylvania State Univ., University Park, Pa.
Hall, Morris E., Box 343, SFA Station, Nacogdoches, Tex.
Hall, Robert H., Gulf Coast Junior College, Panama City, Fla.
Hall, Ronald D., U.S. Rep., Univ. of the Americas, New York, N.Y.
Hall, Walter J., Jr., Haverford Senior High School, Havertown, Pa.
Hall, William Frank, 125 E. Lincoln St., Phoenix, Ariz.
Hall, William P., 19300 Watkins Mill Road, Gaithersburg, Md.
Hallenbeck, Edwin F., Roger Williams Col., Bristol, R.I.
Hallgren, Ragnar F., Box 297, R.D. 1, Mount Joy, Pa.
Halliday, Laura A., 479 Youngwood Dr., Stroudsburg, Pa.
Halligan, W. W., Jr., Converse College, Spartanburg, S.C.
Halliwell, Joseph W., 17 Mary Drive, Woodcliff Lake, N.J.
Halpern, Aaron, Clifton Senior High School, Clifton, N.J.
Hamann, H. A., 2000 Harrison St., Glenview, Ill.
Hamblen, Charles P., The Norwich Free Academy, Norwich, Conn.
Hamilton, Gene E., Sunny Hollow Elem. Schl., Minneapolis, Minn.
Hamilton, H. J., 7 Highgate, Box 42, Buffalo, N.Y.
Hamilton, Herbert M., Banta Apts., F-108, Bloomington, Ind.
Hamilton, Lester L., Charleston Cnty. Schl. Dist., Charleston, S.C.
Hammel, John A., 1275 Cook Rd., Grosse Pointe Woods, Mich.
Hammer, Eugene L., Dept. of Educ., Wilkes College, Wilkes-Barre, Pa.
Hammer, Viola, Redwood City Schools, Redwood City, Calif.
Hammock, Robert C., Grad. Schl. of Educ., Univ. of Pa., Philadelphia, Pa.
Hammond, Granville S., New Delhi, Dept. of State, Washington, D.C.
Hampton, Bill R., Ferguson Florissant Schl. Dist., Ferguson, Mo.
Hancock, Emily, Florida Southern College, Lakeland, Fla.
Handle, Christa, 1 Berlin 12, Ruschev Str., Germany
Handley, W. Harold, Granite School District, Salt Lake City, Utah
Hanigan, Levin B., Superintendent, Echobrook School, Mountainside, N.J.
Hanisits, Richard M., 8623 S. Kilpatrick Ave., Chicago, Ill.
Hanitchak, John J., Sch. of Educ., Indiana Univ., Bloomington, Ind.
Hanna, Alvis N., Prin., John Tyler School, Tyler, Tex.
Hanna, Paul R., Dept. of Educ., Stanford Univ., Stanford, Calif.
Hannemann, Charles E., 5820 S.W. 51st Terr., Miami, Fla.
Hannifin, Mrs. Blanche B., 5259 Strohm Ave., North Hollywood, Calif.
Hannon, Elizabeth F., 1432 S. Crescent Ave., Park Ridge, Ill.
Hannon, Joseph P., 1001 Cranford, Greeley, Colo.
Hansen, Dorothy Gregg, 722 Ivanhoe Rd., Tallahassee, Fla.
Hansen, Douglas E., Hillsdale Col., Hillsdale, Mich.
Hansen, G. G., Superintendent of County Schools, Aurora, Nebr.
Hansen, Helge E., 15735 Andover Dr., Dearborn, Mich.
Hansen, Maxine M., Wis. State Univ., Whitewater, Wis.
Hansen, R. G., 2075 St. Johns Ave., Highland Park, Ill.
Hansen, Robt. E., Cherry Hill Pk. Sch., Cherry Hill, N.J.
Hanson, Donald L., 1513 W. 18th St., Cedar Falls, Iowa
Hanson, Eddie, Jr., Rt. No. 1, Box 1432, Auburn, Calif.
Hanson Ellis G., 13224 Pine Ridge Rd., Burnsville, Minn.
Hanson, Ellis G., 3810 Bel Aire Rd., Des Moines, Iowa
Hanson, Gordon C., Wichita State Univ., Wichita, Kans.

Hanson, Ralph A., 1505 North La Brea, Inglewood, Calif.
Hanson, Wesley L., 3021 Washburn Pl., Minneapolis, Minn.
Hanuska, Julius P., 550 Edith Ave., Johnstown, Pa.
Harckham, Laura D., 240 New Hempstead Rd., New City, N.Y.
Harding, James, Prin., Dunbar Elementary School, Dickinson, Tex.
Harding, Lowry W., Arps Hall, Ohio State University, Columbus, Ohio
Harding, Merle D., 421 Irving St., Beatrice, Nebr.
Hardt, Annanelle, Ariz. St. Univ., Tempe, Ariz.
Hardy, J. Garrick, Alabama State College, Montgomery, Ala.
Hargett, Earl F., 111 W. Brookwood Dr., Valdosta, Ga.
Harlow, James G., Pres., West Virginia Univ., Morgantown, W.Va.
Harmon, Ruth E., 1720 Commonwealth Ave., West Newton, Mass.
Harmon, Adelaide T., York Col., Carle Place, N.Y.
Harnack, Robert S., Sch. of Educ., State Univ. Col., Buffalo, N.Y.
Harner, Robert W., Rt. 2, Box 288C, Rigrish Rd., Sciotoville, Ohio
Harootunian, Berj, Sch. of Educ., Syracuse Univ., Syracuse, N.Y.
Harper, Ray G., Michigan State Univ., East Lansing, Mich.
Harrington, Edmund Ross, 309 Ave. E., Redondo Beach, Calif.
Harrington, Johns H., 1515 Greenbriar Rd., Glendale, Calif.
Harris, Albert J., 35 Rockwood Pl., New Rochelle, N.Y.
Harris, Ben M., 325 Sutton Hall, University of Texas, Austin, Tex.
Harris, C. W., P.O. Box 1510, Deland, Fla.
*Harris, Claude C., 501 S. 30th St., Muskogee, Okla.
Harris, Eugene, Capitol Area Vocational School, Baton Rouge, La.
Harris, Fred E., Univ. of Evansville, Evansville, Ind.
Harris, James M., 3045 E. Buckingham, Fresno, Calif.
Harris, Janet D., 130 Boylston St., Chestnut Hill, Mass.
Harris, Larry A., Dept. of Educ., Univ. of N. Dak., Grand Forks, N. Dak.
Harris, Lewis E., 6800 High St., Worthington, Ohio
Harris, Raymond P., 15 Westerly Lane, Thornwood, N.Y.
Harris, Robert B., 2834 Gladiolus Ln., Dallas, Tex.
Harris, Theodore L., Dept. of Educ., Univ. of Puget Sound, Tacoma, Wash.
Harrison, C. Barker, Univ. of Mississippi, University, Miss.
Harrison, Edward N., Rev., 494 Bath, Long Beach, N.J.
Harrison, James P., 200 S. Providence Rd., Wallingford, Pa.
Harry, David P., Jr., 1659 Compton Rd., Cleveland Heights, Ohio
Harsanyi, Mrs. Audrey, Pennsylvania State University, University Park, Pa.
Harshbarger, Lawrence H., Educ. Dept., Ball State Univ., Muncie, Ind.
Harste, Jerome C., Univ. of Minnesota, Minneapolis, Minn.
Hart, Mary A., 4 Esternay Lane, Pittsford, N.Y.
Hart, Ruth M. R., 1100 Douglas Ave., Minneapolis, Minn.
Harthern, Alvis T., Univ. of Montevallo, Montevallo, Ala.
Harting, Roger D., 4711 Orchard Ln., Columbia, Mo.
Hartley, James R., Univ. Extn., University of California, Riverside, Calif.
Hartsell, Horace C., Univ. of Texas, Dental Branch, Houston, Tex.
Hartsig, Barbara A., California State College, Fullerton, Calif.
Hartung, Maurice L., Dept. of Educ., University of Chicago, Chicago, Ill.
Harvey, Jasper, 1122 Colorado, 1205, Austin, Tex.
Harvey, Valerien, Univ. Laval, Quebec, Canada
Harwell, John Earl, Nicholls State Col., Thibodaux, La.
Hasenpflug, Thomas R., 600 Hunt Rd., Jamestown, N.Y.
Haskew, Laurence D., Col. of Educ., University of Texas, Austin, Tex.
Haskins, Esther N., Box 4798, Carmel, Calif.
Hassel, Carl W., Supt. of Schs., Upper Marlboro, Maryland
Hastie, W. Reid, 2114-65th Pl., Lubbock, Tex.
Hastings, Glen R., Dept. of Educ., State Col. of Iowa, Cedar Falls, Iowa
Hastings, J. Thomas, Educ. Bldg., University of Illinois, Urbana, Ill.
Hatashita, Elizabeth S., 6510 Cielo Drive, San Diego, Calif.
Hatch, Terrance E., Col. of Educ., Utah State University, Logan, Utah
Hatfield, Donald M., Dept. of Educ., University of California, Berkeley, Calif.

Hauer, Nelson A., Louisiana State University, Baton Rouge, La.
Haupt, Leonard R., 2801 Glenview Rd., Glenview, Ill.
Hauptfuehrer, Helen, 159 Norris Gym, Univ. of Minn., Minneapolis, Minn.
Hauschild, Mrs. J. R., 20528 Rhoda St., Woodland Hills, Calif.
Hauser, Raymond A., 1564 Oceanaire Dr., San Luis Obispo, Calif.
Havens, Betty J., 3033 N. Cramer St., Milwaukee, Wis.
* Havighurst, Robert J., Dept. of Educ., University of Chicago, Chicago, Ill.
Hawkins, Brennan C., 370 Richmond Lane, Crystal Lake, Ill.
Hawkins, Edwin L., Horace Mann High School, Little Rock, Ark.
Hawkins, Lee E., 322 S. Jordan, Bloomington, Ind.
Hawkinson, Mabel J., 11 Gregory St., Oswego, N.Y.
Hawley, Leslie R., 94 Walden Dr., RFD #1, Lakeview, Erie Co., N.Y.
Haws, J. C., Brd. of Educ. Office, Cnty. Court Hse., Brigham City, Utah
Hayden, Alice H., Miller Hall, University of Washington, Seattle, Wash.
Hayden, James R., 166 William St., New Bedford, Mass.
Hayden, Mary Lee Griffith, 3449 Longview Ave., Bloomington, Ind.
Hayes, Allen P., 757 McKinley Ave., Auburn, Ala.
Hayes, Gordon M., Consult., State Dept. of Educ., Sacramento, Calif.
Hayes, Hathia, 460 Morton Ave., Athens, Ga.
Hayes, Paul C., 405 Woodland, Wadsworth, Ohio
Hayes, Robert B., Dept. of Pub. Instr., Harrisburg, Pa.
Haynes, Hubert Ray, 108 E. Tilden Dr., Brownsburg, Ind.
Hays, Albert Z., Abilene Christian College, Abilene, Tex.
Hays, Harry N., Supv. Prin., West Branch Area Sch. Dist., Morrisdale, Pa.
Hays, Warren S., 3218 N. Reno Ave., Tucson, Ariz.
Hayward, W. George, 357A Dorchester Dr., Lakewood, N.J.
Hazell, Joseph W., 486 Montecito Dr., Corte Madre, Calif.
Hazleton, Edward W., Bogan High School, Chicago, Ill.
Headd, Pearl Walker, Tuskegee Institute, Ala.
Headley, Quentin, Univ. of Delaware, Newark, Del.
Headley, Ross A., 80 Hauppauge Dr., Commack, N.Y.
Headspeth, Dorothy, Hine Library, State Off. Bldg., Hartford, Conn.
Heagney, Genevieve, Towson State Col., Baltimore, Md.
Heald, James Euden, 450 W. Lincoln Hwy., De Kalb, Ill.
Healy, Madelyn, 91 Park Place, Kearney, N.J.
Healy, Winston, Jr., Punahou Schl., 1601 Punahou St., Honolulu, Hawaii
Heathers, Glen, University of Pittsburgh, Pittsburgh, Pa.
Heavenridge, Glen G., 5844 Gilman St., Garden City, Mich.
Hebeler, Jean R., University of Maryland, College Park, Md.
Hecht, Scotte J., Rt.1 Box 43A, Moscow, Idaho
Heck, Theodore, St. Meinrad Seminary, St. Meinrad, Ind.
Hedden, George W., 1435 Twinridge Rd., Santa Barbara, Calif.
Hedges, William D., 5454 Beacon, Pittsburgh, Pa.
Heding, Howard W., Col. of Educ., Univ. of Missouri, Columbia, Mo.
Heger, Herbert K., 3017 Stanford Dr., Lexington, Ky.
Hegman, M. Marian, 332 South Ave., Medina, N.Y.
Heimann, Therese M., 2330 W. Lapham St., Milwaukee, Wis.
Heimberger, Mary J., Falk Lab Sch., Univ. of Pittsburgh, Pittsburgh, Pa.
Hein, William J., Mills College, Oakland, Calif.
Heintz, Kenneth G., Stout State Univ., Menomonie, Wis.
Heinz, John A., California State Polytechnic College, San Luis Obispo, Calif.
Heise, Margaret A., 5361 Princeton Ave., Westminster, Calif.
Heisler, Florence, Dept. of Educ., Brooklyn College, Brooklyn, N.Y.
Heist, Paul H., 4606 Tolman Hall, Univ. of California, Berkeley, Calif.
Held, John T., 426 College Ave., Gettysburg, Pa.
Heller, Melvin P., Dept. of Educ., Loyola University, Chicago, Ill.
Hellerich, Mahlon H., 1112 Highland Ave., Bethlehem, Pa.
* Helms, W. T., 1109 Roosevelt Ave., Richmond, Calif.
Helsep, Thomas R., 2700 Dorp Lane, Morristown, Pa.

Helser, David C., 2738 Dover Dr., Troy, Mich.
Helwig, Carl, Old Dominion Univ., Norfolk, Va.
Heming, Hilton P., 12 Leonard Ave., Plattsburgh, N.Y.
Hemink, Lyle H., 4134 Trailing Dr., Williamsville, N.Y.
Hencley, Stephen P., 1505 Indian Hills Dr., Salt Lake City, Utah
Hendee, Dr. Raymond, 400 S. Western, Park Ridge, Ill.
Henderson, John R., P.O. Box 995, Shannon, Ga.
Henderson, Robert A., Col. of Educ., University of Illinois, Urbana, Ill.
Hendon, Mrs. Betty, 4975 Judy Lynn, Memphis, Tenn.
Hendrick, Irving G., University of California, Riverside, Calif.
Hendrickson, A.D., Univ. of Minnesota at Duluth, Duluth, Minn.
Hendrix, Holbert H., Nevada Southern Univ., Las Vegas, Nev.
Hendrix, Jon R., 835 N. Rensselaer, Griffith, Ind.
Hengesbach, Robert W., 7886 Munson Rd., Mentor, Ohio
Hengoed, James, Boston University, Boston, Mass.
Henle, R.J., Pres., Georgetown Univ., Washington, D.C.
Henry, Bailey Ray, Supt. of Schools, Farmington, Mo.
Henry, George H., Alison Hall, Univ. of Delaware, Newark, Del.
Henry, M. Daniel, 114 E. Berkshire Ave., Linwood, N.J.
Henson, Kenneth T., Indiana State Univ., Terre Haute. Ind.
Hephner, Thomas A., Ohio State University, Columbus, Ohio
Herber, Harold L., 7020 Highland Rd., Fayetteville, N.Y.
Herbst, Leonard A., 3550 Crestmoor Dr., San Bruno, Calif.
Herge, Henry C., 12 South Dr., East Brunswick, N.J.
Herget, George H., 2619 N.W. 11th Ave., Gainesville, Fla.
Herman, James A., 4325 Virgusell Circle, Carmichael, Calif.
Herman, Wayne L., Jr., Col. of Educ., Univ. of Maryland, College Park, Md.
Hermanowicz, Henry J., Illinois State University, Normal, Ill.
Herr, Ross, 3452 W. Drummond Pl., Chicago, Ill.
Herring, W.C., P.O. Box 30, Baynton, Tex.
Herrington, Mrs. Evelyn F., Texas A. & I. Univ., Kingsville, Tex.
Herrmann, D. J., College of William and Mary, Williamsburg, Va.
Herrscher, Barton R., RELCV- Mutual Plaza, Durham, N.C.
Hershberger, James K., 215 N. Whiteoak St., Kutztown, Pa.
Hershey, Gerald L., Sch. of Bus., Indiana University, Bloomington, Ind.
Hershfield, Mrs. Joseph, 75 Pleasant St., Methuen, Mass.
Hertwick, Keith, Indiana Univ., Bloomington, Ind.
* Hertzler, Silas, 1618 So. 8th St., Goshen, Ind.
Herz, Mort, 1864 Pattiz Ave., Long Beach, Calif.
Hesla, Orden E., Mankato State College, Mankato, Minn.
Heslep. Thomas R., 2700 Dorp Lane, Norristown, Pa.
Hess, Clarke F., Marshall College, Huntington, W.Va.
Hess, Glenn C., 44 W. Wheeling St., Washington, Pa.
Hesse, Alexander N., 90 Salisbury Ave., Garden City, L.I., N.Y.
Hetrick, Dr. J. B., Dept. of Educ., Edinboro State Col., Edinboro, Pa.
Hettinger, George B., 436 W. Pioneer Trail, Aurora, Colo.
Hetzel, Walter L., Superintendent of Schools, Ames, Iowa
Heuer, Josephine C., 8444 Edna St., St. Louis, Mo.
Heusner, William W., Michigan State University, East Lansing, Mich.
Hiberman, I.A., South Carroll H.S., Sykesville, Md.
Hickey, Bernard, 7 Digren Rd., Natick, Mass.
Hickey, Howard, Michigan State University, East Lansing, Mich.
Hickman, Lauren C., Nation's Schools, Chicago, Ill.
Hickner, Marybelle R., Stout State Univ., Menomonie, Wis.
Hicks, Mrs. Aline Black, 812 Lexington St., Norfolk, Va.
Hicks, Samuel I., Ohio University, Athens, Ohio
Hicks, William R., Southern University, Baton Rouge, La.
Hidy, Mrs. Elizabeth Willson, Box 287, Gila Bend, Ariz.
Hiebert, Nobel C., Supt. of Schs., Ramsey, N.J.

Hieronymus, Albert N., East Hall, State Univ. of Iowa, Iowa City, Iowa
Hiers, Mrs. Turner M., 1501 S.E. 15th St., Ft. Lauderdale, Fla.
Higdon, Claude J. 859 S. Plymouth Blvd., Los Angeles, Calif.
Higgins, F. Edward, 9524 S. Keeler Ave., Oak Lawn, Ill.
Highbarger, Mrs. Claire, 1045 N. Quentin Rd., Palatine, Ill.
Hightower, Emory A., 14 W. 64th St., New York, N.Y.
Hilgard, Ernest R., Dept. of Psych., Stanford University, Stanford, Calif.
Hill, Alberta D., White Hall, W.S.U., Pullman, Wash.
Hill, Charles E. 529 Fifth St., S.W., Rochester, Minn.
Hill, Mrs. Cecilia, 2008 Veteran Ave., Los Angeles, Calif.
Hill, George E., Dept. of Educ., Ohio University, Athens, Ohio
Hill, Joseph K., Downstate Medical Center, Brooklyn, N.Y.
Hill, Katherine E., Press 23, New York Univ., Washington Sq., New York, N.Y.
Hill, Norman J., 49 S. Lake Ave., Bergen, N.Y.
Hill, Richard, 2206 Haddington Road, St. Paul, Minn.
Hill, Suzanne D., Louisiana State University, New Orleans, La.
Hillerich, Robert L., 950 Huber Lane, Glenview, Ill.
Hillson, Maurie, 1208 Emerson Ave., Teaneck, N.J.
Himes, Jack E., 6718 Callaghan Rd. #202, San Antonio, Tex.
Hinds, Charles F., Murray State University Library, Murray, Ky.
Hinds, Jena, Grinnell Col., Grinnell, Iowa
Hinds, Lillian Ruth, 13855 Superior Rd., Cleveland, Ohio
Hindsman, Edwin, S.W. Educ. Dev. Corp., Commodore Perry Hotel, Austin, Tex.
Hineline, Edna C., Fac. of Educ., Macdonald College, Quebec, Canada
Hines, Vynce A., 1220 S.W. Ninth Rd., Gainesville, Fla.
Hinkle, Dennis E., Col. of Educ., Univ. of Toledo, Toledo, Ohio
Hinkle, Michael D., R.R. 6, Evergreen Dr., Crawfordsville, Ind.
Hintz, Edward R., Westwood Heights Schools, Flint, Mich.
Hipkins, Wendell C., 724-9th St., Washington, D.C.
Hirsch, Mrs. Gloria T., 13121 Addison St., Sherman Oaks, Calif.
Hirshorn, Raymond D., Ministry of Educ., Tegucigalpa, Honduras
Hirst, Wilma E., 3458 Green Valley Rd., Cheyenne, Wyo.
Hitchcock, Catharine, 1837 E. Erie Ave., Lorain, Ohio
Hites, Christopher, 302 Portola Rd., Portola Valley, Calif.
Hitt, Harold H., 4206 Sylvan Oaks, San Antonio, Tex.
Hittinger, Martha S., 12417 E. Beverly Dr., Whittier, Calif.
Hittle, David R., 201 S. 16th St., Escanaba, Mich.
Ho, Thomas C. K., 72 Distler Ave., West Caldwell, N.J.
Ho, Wai Ching, Educ. Research Council, Rockefeller Bldg., Cleveland, Ohio
Hoagland, Robert M., 627 Houseman, La Canada, Calif.
Hobbie, Katherine E., State University College, Oneonta, N.Y.
Hobbs, Billy S., White House High School, White House, Tenn.
Hobbs, Earl W., Renton Sch. Dist., 1525 Fourth Ave., N., Renton, Wash.
Hobson, J. Victor, Jr., Off. of Educ., Palau Dist., Koror, Palau, Caroline Is.
Hochstetler, Ruth, 225 S. Nichols, Muncie, Ind.
Hock, Louise E., Sch. of Educ., New York Univ., New York, N.Y.
Hockwalt, Ronald W., 1563 Hobert Dr., Camarillo, Calif.
Hodge, Harry F., P.O. Box 940, State University, Ark.
Hodge, William Carey, McKendree College, Lebanon, Ill.
Hodges, David Julian, 185 Hall St., Apt. 507, Brooklyn, N.Y.
Hodges, James G., 3856 Kenard Court, Columbus, Ohio
Hodges, Lawrence W., University of Montana, Missoula, Mont.
Hodges, Richard E., Grad. Sch. of Educ., Univ. of Chicago, Chicago, Ill.
Hodges, Ruth Hall, Morris Brown College, Atlanta, Ga.
Hodgins, George W., Paramus High School, Paramus, N.J.
Hodnett, Ruth Germann, Scott, Foresman & Co., Chicago, Ill.
Hoeffner, Karl, Prin., Wm. Hawley Atwell Junior High School, Dallas, Tex.
Hoekstra, S. Robert, RR 1, Box 77H, Grayslake, Ill.
Hoerauf, William E., 19990 Beaufait, Harper Woods, Mich.
Hoffman, Carl B., Abington Sch. Dist., Abington, Pa.

Hofstrand, John M., 1731 Sweetbriar Dr., San Jose, Calif.
Hogan, John C., 840 Twelfth St., Santa Monica, Calif.
Hohl, George W., Superintendent of Schools, Waterloo, Iowa
Holda, Frederick W., 26 Hampden Rd., Monson, Mass.
*Holden, A. John, Jr., RD 1, Montpelier, Vt.
Holliday, Jay N., 10224 N. Wellen Ln., Spokane, Wash.
Hollis, Loye Y., Col. of Educ., University of Houston, Houston, Tex.
Holloway, George E., Jr., 64 Main St., Pittsfield, N.H.
Holm, Joy A., 424 W. Union, Edwardsville, Ill.
Holman, W. Earl, Jackson High School, 544 Wildwood Ave., Jackson, Mich.
Holmes, Augusta, 250 W. 154th, New York, N.Y.
Holmes, Daniel L., P.O. Box 331, North Reading, Mass.
Holmes, Emma E., 17621 E. 17th St., Tustin, Calif.
Holmquist, Emily, Indiana Univ. School of Nursing, Indianapolis, Ind.
Holt, Charles C., 807 S. 1st St., Maywood, Ill.
Holton, Samuel M., University of North Carolina, Chapel Hill, N.C.
Homer, Francis R., 4800 Conshohocken Ave., Philadelphia, Pa.
Honel, Milton F., 167 E. Jackson, Elmhurst, Ill.
Honeychuck, Joseph M., 2808 Parker Ave., Silver Spring, Md.
Hood, Edwin M., 19 Seneca Ave., White Plains, N.Y.
Hood, Evans C., Superintendent of Schools, Palestine, Tex.
Hood, W. R., 2627—29th St., S.W., Calgary, Alba., Canada
Hook, Edward N., 100 Madrid Plaza. Mesa, Arizona
Hooker, Clifford P., University of Minnesota, Minneapolis, Minn.
Hooper, George J., 3631 S. Yorktown, Tulsa, Okla.
Hoops, Robert C., 76 Branch Ave., Red Bank, N.J.
Hoover, Erna B., Tennessee A. & I. State Univ., Nashville, Tenn.
Hoover, Louis H., 2304 Tenth Ave. So., Broadview, Ill.
Hopkins, Everett P., 1520 Pinecrest Rd., Durham, N.C.
Hopkins, Theresa, 226 N. Buchanan, Edwardsville, Ill.
Hopmann, Robert P., Concordia Teachers College, River Forest, Ill.
Horn, Ernest W., Indiana University, Bloomington, Ind.
Horn, Margaret, Concordia College, St. Paul, Minn.
Horn, Thomas D., Sutton Hall, University of Texas, Austin, Tex.
Hornback, Mrs. May, Rt. 1, Old Sauk Rd., Middleton, Wis.
Hornbeck, William J., 3335 Wood Terr., Los Angeles, Calif.
Hornburg, Mabel C., 118 Champlain Ave., Ticonderoga, N.Y.
Hornick, Sandra Jo, 1937 Courtland Drive, Kent, Ohio
Horning, Leora N., 10 Gramercy Pl., 7110 Old Post Rd., Lincoln, Neb.
Horns, Virginia, 1934 A Shades Cliff Terr., Birmingham, Ala.
Horrocks, John E., Ohio State University, Columbus, Ohio
Horvat, John, Schl. of Educ., Indiana U., Bloomington, Ind.
Hosford, Marion H., Trenton State College, Trenton, N.J.
Hoskins, Charles W., 503 Sioux Lane, San Jose, Calif.
Hoskins, Glen C., Dept. of Educ., Southern Methodist Univ., Dallas, Tex.
Houck, William R., 550 Dauphin, P.O. Box 129, Mobile, Ala.
Hough, John M., Jr., Mars Hill College, Mars Hill, N.C.
Hough, Robert E., Arthur L. Johnson Regional High School, Clark, N.J.
Houghton, John J., Superintendent of Schools, Ferndale, Mich.
Houlahan, F. J., Catholic University of America, Washington, D.C.
Houle, Cyril O., Dept. of Educ., University of Chicago, Chicago, Ill.
Householder, Daniel L., Sch. of Tech., Purdue University, Lafayette, Ind.
Houston, James J., Jr., Patterson State Col., Wayne, N.J.
Houston, John, Superintendent of Schools, Medford, Mass.
Houston, W. Robert, Col. of Educ., Mich. State University, East Lansing, Mich.
Houts, Earl, Westminster College, New Wilmington, Pa.
Hovet, Kenneth O., University of Maryland, College Park, Md.
Howard, Alexander H., Jr., Central Washington State Col., Ellensburg, Wash.
Howard, Daniel D., Pestalozzi-Froebel Tchrs. College, Chicago, Ill.
Howard, Elizabeth Z., Col. of Educ., Univ. of Rochester, Rochester, N.Y.

Howard, Glenn W., Queens College, Flushing, N.Y.
Howard, Herbert, P.O. Box 162, Taylor St., Roscoe, N.Y.
Howd, M. Curtis, 200 Winthrop Rd., Muncie, Ind.
Howe, Robert W., Assoc. Prof., Ohio State University, Columbus, Ohio
Howe, Walter A., 6840 Eastern Ave., N.W., Washington, D.C.
Howlett, Dorn, R.D. 1, Edinboro, Pa.
Howsam, Robert B., University of Houston, Houston, Tex.
Hoye, Almon G., Marshall Univ. H.S., Minneapolis, Minn.
Hoyle, Anne M., 3900 Hamilton St., L-103, Hyattsville, Md.
Hoyle, Dorothy, Temple University, Philadelphia, Pa.
Hoyt, Cyril J., Burton Hall, Univ. of Minnesota, Minneapolis, Minn.
Hrabi, James S., Dept. of Educ., 10820—98th Ave., Edmonton, Alba., Canada
Hrynyk, Nicholas P., 11010—142nd St., Edmonton, Alba., Canada
Hubbard, Ben, Illinois State University, Normal, Ill.
Huber, H. Ronald, 315 W. State St., Doylestown, Pa.
Hubert, Frank W. R., Texas A. & M. Univ., College Station, Tex.
Huck, Charlotte S., Ohio State University, Columbus, Ohio
Huckins, Wesley, 2309 Randy Drive, Kettering, Ohio
Hudson, Bertha J., 7251 S. Euclid Ave., Chicago, Ill.
Hudson, Bruce M., 2892 Robb Circle, Lakewood, Colo.
Hudson, Douglas, 3981 Greenmont Drive, Warren, Ohio
Hudson, L. P., 1225 Oakwood St., Bedfort, Va.
Hudson, Robert I., University of Manitoba, Winnipeg, Manitoba, Canada
Hudson, Wilburn, Cordova High School, Cordova, Ala.
Huebner, Dwayne E., Tchrs. Col., Columbia University, New York, N.Y.
Huebner, Mildred H., So. Connecticut State Col., New Haven, Conn.
Huehn, Kermith S., Superintendent of County Schools, Eldora, Iowa
Huelsman, Charles B., Jr., 74 S. Roosevelt Rd., Columbus, Ohio
Huff, Jack F., 9030 Glorieta Ct., Elk Grove, Calif.
Hug, John W., RD 1 Box 97, Mill Run, Pa.
Hughes, Carolyn Sue, R.R. 2, Newton Falls, Ohio
Hughes, John, 534 Michigan Ave., Evanston, Ill.
Hughes, Larry W., 4046 Towanda Trail, Knoxville, Tenn.
Hughes, McDonald, 1732—32nd Ave., Tuscaloosa, Ala.
Hughes, Thomas G., Ventura College, Ventura, Calif.
Hughes, Thomas M., 990 Brower Rd., Memphis, Tenn.
Hughes, Vergil H., San Jose State College, San Jose, Calif.
Hughes, Msgr. William A., Supt., Diocese of Youngstown, Youngstown, Ohio
Hughson, Arthur, 131 East 21st St., Brooklyn, N.Y.
Hulbert, Dolores S., 16301 Lassen St., Sepulveda, Calif.
Hull, J. H., Supt. of Schools, Torrance, Calif.
Hult, Esther M., Dept. of Educ., State College of Iowa, Cedar Falls, Iowa
Humelsine, Martha, Roberts Wesleyan College, North Chili, N.Y.
Humphrey, Charles F., 6001 Berkeley Dr., Berkeley, Mo.
Humphrey, G. C., 316 Fraser Dr. East, Mesa, Ariz.
Humphries, Jack W., Sam Houston St. Univ., Huntsville, Tex.
Hunkins, Francis P., University of Washington, Seattle, Wash.
Hunsicker, C. L., Mansfield State College, Mansfield, Pa.
Hunt, Herold C., Grad. Sch. of Educ., Harvard University, Cambridge, Mass.
Hunt, Ruth, Educ. Dept., Loyola Univ., Chicago, Ill.
Hunter, Eugenia, Woman's Col., Univ. of North Carolina, Greensboro, N.C.
Hunter, James Jamison, Jr., 6240 Cresthaven Dr., La Mesa, Calif.
Hunter, Robert W., Grambling College, Grambling, La.
*Huntington, Albert H., 2535 Kentland Dr., St. Louis, Mo.
Huntington, John F., Miami Univ., Oxford, Ohio
Hupper, Richard D., 765 Depot Rd., Gurnee, Ill.
Hurd, Blair E., 8015 South Lake Circle, Loomis, Calif.
Hurd, Paul DeH., Sch. of Educ., Stanford University, Stanford, Calif.
Hurt, E. L., Jr., Gragg Junior High School, Memphis, Tenn.
Hurt, Mary Lee, Div. of Voc. & Tech. Educ., Washington, D.C.

Husen, Peter M., Univ. of Tennessee, Knoxville, Tenn.
Husmann, John L., 256 Ash St., Crystal Lake, Ill.
Huss, Francis C., 4655 Parker Rd., Florissant, Mo.
Husson, Chesley H., Husson College, 157 Park St., Bangor, Maine
Husted, Inez M., P.O. Box 1165, Kingston, Pa.
Husted, Vernon L., Supt., Armstrong Twp. High School, Armstrong, Ill.
Hutchison, James M., 26904 Grayslake Rd., Palos Verdes Peninsula, Calif.
Hutson, Percival W., University of Pittsburgh, Pittsburgh, Pa.
Hutto, Jerome A., Los Angeles State College, Los Angeles, Calif.
Hutton, Dr. Duane E., 6 Seneca St., Sudney, N.Y.
Hyde, Sandra, 8113 Dawson Drive, S.E., Warren, Ohio
Hyder, Charles M., Univ. of Chattanooga, Chattanooga, Tenn.
Hyer, Anna L., 7613 Wiley Dr., Lorton, Va.
Hyman, Ronald Terry, 15 Oakbrook Pl., Somerset, N.J.
Hyram, George H., 4092 Fieldstone Dr., Florissant, Mo.

Iannacone, George, Supt. of Schools, Palisades Park, N.J.
Iannaccone, Laurence, Linstead Court, Weston, Ont., Canada
Igo, Robert V., Pennsylvania State University, University Park, Pa.
Ihrman, Donald L., Superintendent of Schools, Holland, Mich.
Ilowit, Roy, C. W. Post College, Greenvale, L.I., N.Y.
Imbriano, Louis A., Revere Public Schools, Revere, Mass.
Imhoff, Myrtle M., 5151 State Col. Blvd., Los Angeles, Calif.
Imison, Kenneth, Mitchell CAE, Bathurst, NSW, Australia
Imura, Harry S., University of California, Berkeley, Calif.
Inabnit, Darrell J., Sacramento State College, Sacramento, Calif.
Ingebritson, Kasper I., 2790 Sunny Grove Ave., Arcata, Calif.
Ingram, Margaret H., East Carolina College, Greenville, N.C.
Ingrelli, Anthony V., University of Wisconsin-Milwaukee, Milwaukee, Wis.
Ingve, Cheryl S., 1907 S. Milledge, Athens, Ga.
Ingwerson, Don, 1580 Yarrow St., Lakewood, Colo.
Inskeep, James E., Jr., San Diego State College, San Diego, Calif.
Ireland, Robert Stanton, Old Orchard Lane, Boxborough, Mass.
Irizarry, Casandra Rivera de, 1628 Arenida Central, Caparra Terr., P.R.
Isaacs, Ann F., 8080 Springvalley Dr., Cincinnati, Ohio
Isacksen, Roy O., Hazel Pk. Jr. H.S., 1140 White Bear Ave., St. Paul, Minn.
Isert, Rev. Louis F., 1540 E. Glenn, Tucson, Ariz.
Isler, Norman P., Fac. of Educ., Univ. of Manitoba, Winnipeg, Man., Can.
Ives, Josephine Piekarz, New York University, New York, N.Y.
Ivie, Claude M., Div. of Curric., State Dept. of Educ., Atlanta, Ga.
Israel, Benjamin L., 29 Woodmere Blvd., Woodmere, N.Y.
Ivins, Wilson H., Col. of Educ., Univ. of New Mexico, Albuquerque, N.Mex.
Izard, John F., 9 Abelia Court, Bundoora, Vic. 3083, Australia
Izzo, Raymond J., 12 Girard Rd., Winchester, Mass.

Jacklin, William T., 411 E. 17th St., Lombard, Ill.
Jackson, Bryant H., Illinois State University, Normal, Ill.
Jackson, Jo Ann, Brownong Business Col., Alberquerque, N. Mex.
Jackson, Joyce, Sch. of Educ., Wisconsin St. Univ., Oshkosh, Wis.
Jackson, Philip W., Dept. of Educ., Univ. of Chicago, Chicago, Ill.
Jackson, Ronald B., 5 Gibson Rd., Lexington, Mass.
Jackson, Thomas A., Florida A. & M. Univ., Tallahassee, Fla.
Jacobs, J., 26141 Schoolcraft Rd., Detroit, Mich.
Jacobs, John F., Southern Illinois Univ., Carbondale, Ill.
Jacobs, Judith E., Richmond Col., (CUNY) Jackson Hghts., N.Y.
Jacobs, Robert, American Embassy, APO San Francisco, Calif.
Jaeger, Alan Warren, 10220 Dale Dr., San Jose, Calif.
Jaeger, Herman F., Box 10, Grandview, Wash.
Jeffarian, Sara, 251 Waltham St., Lexington, Mass.

James, C. Rodney, 38 B. Bord du Lac, Pointe Claire, Quebec, Canada
James, Carl A., Superintendent of Schools, Emporia, Kans.
James, Jo Nell, P.O. Box 425, Compti, La.
* James, Preston E., Dept. of Geog., Syracuse University, Syracuse, N.Y.
James, Ronald G., 230 E. Eagle St., Findlay, Ohio
James, W. Raymond, 9 Bugbee Rd., Oneonta, N.Y.
Jameson, Sanford C., 625 Colfax St., Evanston, Ill.
Jamison, W. Thomas, Appalachian State Univ., Boone, N.C.
Jansen, Udo H., Tchrs. Col., Univ. of Nebraska, Lincoln, Nebr.
*Jansen, William, 900 Palmer Rd., Bronxville, N.Y.
Jansic, Anthony F., Educ. Clinic, City College of New York, New York, N.Y.
Jardine, Alex, 2105—19th Ave., Greeley, Colo.
Jarvie, Lawrence L., Pres., Fashion Inst. of Tech., New York, N.Y.
Jarvis, Mrs. Elizabeth O., Bayview House, R.R. 2, Hamilton, Ont., Canada
Jarvis, Galen M., 1147 White St., Des Plaines, Ill.
Jashni, Reza, 4748 La Villa Marina, Marina del Rey, Calif.
Jason, Hilliard, Col. of Med., Michigan State Univ., East Lansing, Mich.
Jaspen, Nathan, New York University, New York, N.Y.
Jeffers, Jay W., 931 Franklin Ave., Las Vegas, Nev.
Jeffries, Thomas S., Sch. of Educ., Univ. of Louisville, Louisville, Ky.
Jelinek, James J., Col. of Educ., Arizona State University, Tempe, Ariz.
Jellins, Miriam H., 2849 Dale Creek Dr., N.W., Atlanta, Ga.
Jenkins, Clara Barnes, St. Paul's College, Lawrenceville, Va.
Jenkins, Ernest W., 811 W. 2nd St., Pittsburgh, Kans.
Jenkins, James J., University of Minnesota, Minneapolis, Minn.
Jenkins, Jerry A., 1400 W. Maple Ave., Downers Grove, Ill.
Jenkins, John M., Univ. of Miami, Coral Gables, Fla.
Jenkins, Offa Lou, Marshall University, Huntington, W.Va.
Jenkins, Walter D., Clark County Sch. Dist., Las Vegas, Nev.
Jensen, Arthur R., University of California, Berkeley, Calif.
Jensen, Esther M., University of Wisconsin, Milwaukee, Wis.
Jensen, Grant W., Kern Jt. Union H.S. Dist., Bakersfield, Calif.
Jenson, Dean, Bowling Green State University, Bowling Green, Ohio
Jenson, T. J., 1024 Lyn Rd., Bowling Green, Ohio
Jess, C. Donald, Superintendent of Schools, Bergenfield, N.J.
Jetton, Clyde T., 720 Amherst, Abilene, Tex.
Jewell, R. Ewart, Superintendent of Schools, 547 Wall St., Bend, Oreg.
Jewett, Mary Jane, 9 Lincoln Place, New Platz, N.Y.
Jex, Frank B., Dept. of Educ. Psych., Univ. of Utah, Salt Lake City, Utah
Jiboku, Simon O., 7-15 South Campus Ct., W. Lafayette, Ind.
Jinks, Elsie H., 1597 Lochmoor Blvd., Grosse Pointe Woods, Mich.
Jobe, (Robinson), Helen M., 3710 Gulf of Mex., Sarasota, Fla.
Johns, Edward B., Dept. of P.E., University of California, Los Angeles, Calif.
Johns, Jerry L., Northern Illinois Univ., De Kalb, Ill.
Johnsen, E. Peter, 1618 W. 28 Terrace, Lawrence, Kans.
Johnson, Mrs. Andrew L., 101 E. 14th Ave., Apt. L, Columbus, Ohio
Johnson, B. Lamar, Sch. of Educ., Univ. of California, Los Angeles, Calif.
Johnson, Claudine, 112-39—175th St., Jamaica, N.Y.
Johnson, Dale A., 1318 Gibbs Ave., St. Paul Minn.
Johnson, Dale L., Dept. of Psych., University of Houston, Houston, Tex.
Johnson, Mrs. Dorothea N., 317 Whitman Blvd., Elyria, Ohio
Johnson, Dorothy E., Calumet Campus, Purdue Univ., Hammond, Ind.
Johnson, Douglas, Jr., 707 E. 14th St., Panama City, Fla.
Johnson, Douglas A., 341 Claydon Way, Sacramento, Calif.
Johnson, Einar O., 3254 48th Ave. South, Minneapolis, Minn.
Johnson, Eleanor M., Box 360, Middletown, Conn.
Johnson, Eugene L., Howard Payne Col., Brownwood, Tex.
Johnson, Frank R., Brd. of Educ., Granville Ave., Margate City, N.J.
Johnson, G. Orville, Col. of Educ., Ohio State University, Columbus, Ohio
Johnson, George L., Lincoln University of Missouri, Jefferson City, Mo.

Johnson, Harry C., Duluth Branch, Univ. of Minnesota, Duluth, Minn.
Johnson, Homer M., 301 Acalanes Dr., Apt. 57, Sunnyvale, Calif.
Johnson, Irwin T., Univ. of Wisconsin, Milwaukee, Wis.
Johnson, Jerry G., Asst. Supt. of Schls., Alexander County, McClure, Ill.
Johnson, J. O., Central Jr. H.S., Rochester, Minn.
Johnson, Joan C., 5222 Western Ave., Davenport, Iowa
Johnson, John L., Adm. Bldg., Syracuse Univ., Syracuse, N.Y.
Johnson, Leonard E., Prin., Bugbee Sch., West Hartford, Conn.
Johnson, Lois V., California State Col., Los Angeles, Calif.
Johnson, Margaret E., Alpine School District, American Fork, Utah
Johnson, Mrs. Marjorie Seddon, 61 Grove Ave., Flourtown, Pa.
Johnson, Olive Lucille, 1925 Thornwood Ave., Wilmette, Ill.
Johnson, Paul E., Livonia Public Schools, Livonia, Mich.
Johnson, Paul O., Salem H.S., Geremonty Dr., Salem, N.H.
Johnson, Philip E., 53 Front St., Bath, Maine
Johnson, Robert L., 9333 W. Lincoln Ave., West Allis, Wis.
Johnson, Robert Leonard, 2500 South 118th St., West Allis, Wis.
Johnson, Roger E., 218 Park Ridge Ave., Temple Terrace, Fla.
* Johnson, Roy Ivan, 2333 Southwest Eighth Dr., Gainesville, Fla.
Johnson, Russell H., Corvallis Sch. Dist., Corvallis, Ore.
Johnson, Simon O., 2001 S.W. 5th Pl., Ocala, Fla.
Johnson, Theodore D., 5236 N. Bernard St., Chicago, Ill.
Johnson, Walter F., Col. of Educ., Michigan State Univ., East Lansing, Mich.
Johnson, Walter R., Libertyville High School, Libertyville, Ill.
Johnson, William H., Colorado State Univ., Fort Collins, Colo.
Johnston, Aaron M., Col. of Educ., Univ. of Tennessee, Knoxville, Tenn.
Johnston, Edgar G., 2301 Vinewood Ave., Ann Arbor, Mich.
Johnston, Lillian B., 538 W. Vernon Ave., Phoenix, Ariz.
Johnston, William R., 1241 Satinwood Lane, Whitewater, Wis.
Jones, Annie Lee, University of North Carolina, Chapel Hill, N.C.
Jones, Cloyzelle, Wayne State Univ., Detroit, Mich.
Jones, Clyde A., University of Connecticut, Storrs, Conn.
Jones, Daisy M., Sch. of Educ., Arizona State University, Tempe, Ariz.
Jones, Dilys M., 305 Roxbury Rd., Shippensburg, Pa.
Jones, Donald W., 508 W. North St., Muncie, Ind.
Jones, Earl, Tex. A&M Univ. Bldg., College Station, Tex.
Jones, Harvey E., 104 Lee Avenue, Tahlequah, Okla.
Jones, Henry W., Western Washington State College, Bellingham, Wash.
Jones, Howard Robert, State University of Iowa, Iowa City, Iowa
Jones, Jack J., Fontana Unified Sch. Dist., Fontana, Calif.
Jones, Joseph F., Michigan Christian Col., Rochester, Mich.
Jones, John E., University of Oregon, Eugene, Oreg.
Jones, Kenneth G., State University College, Oswego, N.Y.
Jones, Lloyd M., 30 Leahey Ave., South Hadley, Mass.
Jones, Nevin, Prin., Model School, Box 67, Shannon, Ga.
Jones, Richard N., Carroll Rd., Monkton, Md.
Jones, Richard V., Jr., Stanislaus State College, Turlock, Calif.
Jones, Robert William, Lincoln Community High School, Lincoln, Ill.
Jones, Roger H., 216 Bell Court East, Lexington, Ky.
Jones, Ruth G., 3938 Walnut Ave., Lynwood, Calif.
Jones, Vyron Lloyd, 5901 S. Wahoo Dr., Terre Haute, Ind.
Jones, Wendell P., Sch. of Educ., Univ. of California, Los Angeles, Calif.
Jones, William E., California State College, Hayward, Calif.
Joneson, Della, 1040 State St., Ottawa, Ill.
Jongsma, Eugene A., 2639 E. Second St., Bloomington, Ind.
Jonsson, Harold, Div. of Educ., San Francisco State Col., San Francisco, Calif.
Jordan, A. B., 5811 Riverview Blvd., St. Louis, Mo.
Jordan, Benjamin W., Educ. Bldg., Wayne State Univ., Detroit, Mich.
Jordan, Diana, 19200 Roseland, Euclid, Ohio
Jordan, Ralph J., 192 Clark St., Brockport, N.Y.

Joynt, Denis, University of Papua and New Guinea, Boroko, Papua
Joseph, Kenneth E., FBI Training Div., Washington, D.C.
Joselyn, Edwin G., 4068 Hampshire Ave., N., Minneapolis, Minn.
Juan, K. C., President's Office; Lingnan Col., Hong Kong
Judenfriend, Harold, Dept. of Spec. Educ., 695 Park Ave., New York, N.Y.
Julstrom, Eva, 7647 Colfax Ave., Chicago, Ill.
June, Elmer D., 619 Bamford Rd., Cherry Hill, N.J.
Jung, Raymond K., 11116 Vanalden Ave., Northridge, Calif.
Junge, Charlotte W., Col. of Educ., Wayne University, Detroit, Mich.
Junker, Margaret, 9138 S. Claremont Ave., Chicago, Ill.
Jurjevich, J. C., Jr., 1844 74th Ave., Elmwood Park, Ill.
Justman, Joseph, Lincoln Center, New York, N.Y.
Juvancic, William A., Eli Whitney Elem. Sch., Chicago, Ill.

* Kaar, Mrs. Galeta M., 7050 Ridge Ave., Chicago, Ill.
Kabrud, Margaret J., Univ. of North Dakota, Ellendale Cent., Ellendale, N.Dak.
Kacik, Terrence D., Rt. 18, Cedar Hill Rd., Pottstown, Pa.
Kaffer, Roger L., St. Charles Borromeo Seminary, Lockport, Ill.
Kahler, Carol, 221 N. Grand Blvd., St. Louis, Mo.
Kahn, Albert S., Sch. of Educ., Boston University, Boston, Mass.
Kahrs, Mary V., Mankato State College, Mankato, Minn.
Kairies, Eugene B., Jr., 947- 17th Ave. S.E. Minneapolis, Minn.
Kaler, Charles A., 48 Elm Street, Potsdam, New York
Kalina, David L., P.O. Box 134, Shenorock, N.Y.
Kalish, Thomas F., 813 Walworth, Kingsford, Mich.
Kallenbach, W. Warren, San Jose State College, San Jose, Calif.
Kamil, Irving, 885 Bolton Ave., Bronx, N.Y.
Kandyba, Bernard S., 9403 N. Parkside Dr., Des Plaines, Ill.
Kane, Dermott P., 1300 West 97 Pl., Chicago, Ill.
Kane, Elmer R., 7530 Maryland Ave., Clayton, Mo.
Kantor, Bernard R., 117 S. Poinsettia Pl., Los Angeles, Calif.
Kaplan, Bernard A., Dept. of Educ., 225 W. State St., Trenton, N.J.
Kaplan, Lawrence, Rutgers Univ., St. Univ. of N.J., New Brunswick, N.J.
Karlin, Robert, Dept. of Educ., Queens College, Flushing, N.Y.
Karlsen, Bjorn, 7252 Bennett Valley Rd., Santa Rosa, Calif.
Karr, Johnston T., 300 W. 59th Ave., Merrillville, Ind.
Kasdon, Lawrence M., 13 W. 13th St., New York, N.Y.
Kass, Corrine E., 5801 Camino Esplendora, Tucson, Ariz.
Kata, Joseph J., Redbank Valley Joint Schools, New Bethlehem, Pa.
Katenkamp, Theodore W., Jr., 9128 Bengal Rd., Randallstown, Md.
Katser, Arthur D., Col. of Educ., Univ. of Houston, Houston, Tex.
Katz, Joseph, University of British Columbia, Vancouver, B.C., Canada
Kauffman, Merle M., Col. of Educ., Bradley University, Peoria, Ill.
Kaufman, Martin, 5610 Shoalwood Ave., Austin, Tex.
Kaulfers, Walter V., University of Illinois, Urbana, Ill.
Kavanaugh, J. Keith, 1639 So. Maple Ave., Berwyn, Ill.
Kay, Patricia M., City Univ. of New York, New York, N.Y.
Kean, John M., Univ. of Wisconsin, Madison, Wis.
Keane, John M., 3558 W. 147th St., Midlothian, Ill.
Kearl, Jennie W., State Department of Education, Salt Lake City, Utah
Kearney, Rev. George G., 15785A Foothills Rd., Morgan Hill, Calif.
Keating, Frederic, 25 Lucile Dr., Sayville, N.Y.
Keck, Winston B., Westfield State College, Westfield, Mass.
Keefer, Daryle E., Southern Illinois University, Carbondale, Ill.
Keesling, James W., 1521 Yale St., Santa Monica, Calif.
Kehas, Chris D., Claremont Graduate School, Claremont, Calif.
Keislar, Evan R., University of California, Los Angeles, Calif.
Keithley, Perry G., 3354 Ken Lake Dr., Olympia, Wash.
Keleher, Gregory C., Rev., St. Anselm's Col., Manchester, N.H.
*Keliher, Alice V., Box 307, Peterborough, N.H.

Kelleher, William J., Hirsch High School, Chicago, Ill.
* Keller, Franklin J., 333 E. Mosholu Pkwy., New York, N.Y.
Keller, Floyd E., Ind. Sch. Dist. 834, Stillwater, Minn.
Keller, Robert J., Col. of Educ., Univ. of Minnesota, Minneapolis, Minn.
Kelley, Claude, West Virginia University, Morgantown, W. Va.
Kelley, H. Paul, University of Texas, Austin, Tex.
Kelley, Robert, S.U.N.Y. at Albany, 1400 Washington Ave., Albany, N.Y.
Kelley, William F., S.J., Creighton Univ., Omaha, Nebr.
Kelly, Dean, 175 Tamarack Dr., Berea, Ohio
Kelly, Edward J., 2109 Buena Vista Dr., Greeley, Colo.
Kelly, Edward L., East 103 Orion Dr., Pullman, Wash.
Kelly, James A., 101 Borromeo Ave., Placentia, Calif.
Kelly, John W., 27 Earle Pl., New Rochelle, N.Y.
Kelly, Preston W., CBS Publishing, 383 Madison Ave., New York, N.Y.
Kelly, Shaun, Jr., P.O. Box 83, Dublin, N.H.
Kelly, Warde, Educ. Dept., St. Francis Col., Ft. Wayne, Ind.
Kelly, William F., University of Rhode Island, Kingston, R.I.
Kelsey, Roger R., Educ. Annex, University of Maryland, College Park, Md.
Kemp, John S., Univ. of Illinois, Urbana, Ill.
Kemper, Lawrence B., 4837 Oakwood Lane, La Canada, Calif.
Kennedy, Anna Helen, 101 N. Grand Ave., Pasadena, Calif.
Kennedy, Clephane A., Benjamin Franklin University, Washington, D.C.
Kennedy, Larry D., Dept. of Educ., Illinois St. Univ., Normal, Ill.
Kenney, Helen J., Dept. of Educ., Northeastern Univ., Boston, Mass.
Kenny, Joan M., 114-1155 Cromwell, Bronx, N.Y.
Kentner, Harold M., Rochester Institute of Technology, Rochester, N.Y.
Kephart, Ruby Grey, 1807 Milton, Lima, Ohio
Kepner, Henry S., Jr., University School, Iowa City, Iowa
Kerns, LeRoy, Lab. Sch., Colorado State College, Greeley, Colo.
Kerr, Everett F., Superintendent of Schools, Blue Island, Ill.
Kerr, Margaret, 7558 Drexel Dr., University City, Mo.
Kerr, R. D., 113 Hill Hall, Univ. of Missouri, Columbia, Mo.
Keske, Eldora E., 2329 Chalet Gardens Rd., Madison, Wis.
Kessler Clifton L., 4008 Edgerock Drive, Austin, Tex.
Kettle, John E., Bauder Fashion Col., Miami, Fla.
Kherlopian, Richard H., Univ. of South Carolina, Columbia, S.C.
Khouri, John W., Superintendent of Schools, Bethlehem, Pa.
Kicklighter, Ray S., Resch. Physicist, Eastman Kodak, Rochester, N.Y.
Kidder, Frederick E., Univ. of P.R., San Juan, Puerto Rico
Kidder, William W., 216 Walton Ave., South Orange, N.J.
Kilbourn, Mrs. Robert W., 4902 Argyle St., Dearborn, Mich.
Kilburn, H. Parley, Evening Div., Bakersfield College, Bakersfield, Calif.
Kilpatrick, Arnold R., Pres., Northwestern State Col., Natchitoches, La.
Kilpatrick, Joel Fred, Western Carolina College, Cullowhee, N.C.
Kimberly, Mrs. Marian, 33 Southern Way, Princeton, N.J.
Kimble, Raymond L., Wichita State Univ., Wichita, Kans.
Kimpston, Richard M., Univ. of Minnesota, Minneapolis, Minn.
Kincheloe, James B., University of Kentucky, Lexington, Ky.
Kindy, Harold G., 110 Bleecker St., New York, N.Y.
King, A. Richard, Univ. of Victoria, Victoria, B.C., Canada
King, Charles T., Millburn Twp. Pub. Schls., Millburn, N.J.
King, Mrs. June, Box 39, Prince Frederick, Md.
King, Kent H., 103 Thayer Ave., Mankato, Minn.
King, Lloyd H., Sch. of Educ., Univ. of the Pacific, Stockton, Calif.
King, Louise M., Univ. of Portland, Milwaukee, Oreg.
King, Robert N., 15 Quade St., Glens Falls, N.Y.
King, Thomas C., Sch. of Educ., University of Miami, Coral Gables, Fla.
Kingsley, Iva Marie, Box 157, Bellmont Rur. Sta., Flagstaff, Ariz.
Kinkade, Jerry B., R.R. #2, Eldorado, Ill.
Kinsellar, Frances M., Rye St., Broad Brook, Conn.

*Kinsman, Kephas A., 2177-0 Via Puerta, Laguna Hills, Calif.
Kinzer, John R., 5756 East 6th St., Tucson, Ariz.
Kirby, Inabell T., 2002 E. Main St., Decatur, Ill.
Kirchhaefer, Esther, Illinois State University, Normal, Ill.
Kirchman, Mrs. Rose, Jamaica High School, Jamaica, N.Y.
Kirk, Samuel A., Col. of Educ., Univ. of Arizona, Tucson, Ariz.
Kirkland, Eleanor R., 8707 Mohawk Way, Fair Oaks, Calif.
Kirkland, J. Bryant, North Carolina State College, Raleigh, N.C.
Kirkman, Ralph E., R. #4, Murfreesboro, Tenn.
Kirkwood, James J., Ball State Univ., Muncie, Ind.
Kirsch, Victor, Commack Public Schools, Commack, N.Y.
Kirshman, H.S., P.O. 2338, Jackson, Miss.
Kise, Leonard, Northern Illinois Univ., DeKalb, Ill.
Kiser, Chester, State University of New York, Buffalo, N.Y.
Kissinger, Doris C., 34 Roosevelt St., Glen Head, L.I., N.Y.
* Kitch, Donald E., 520 Messina Hall, Sacramento, Calif.
Kitson, Elizabeth W. P., 9411 Jamaica Dr., Miami, Fla.
Kittell, Jack E., Col. of Educ., University of Washington, Seattle, Wash.
Kittleson, Howard, Kansas St. Univ., Manhattan, Kans.
Kitts, Harry W., Dept. of Agric. Educ., Univ. of Minn., St. Paul, Minn.
Kizer, George A., Iowa State Univ., Ames, Iowa
Kjarsgaard, Donald R., 3600 Lakeway Dr., Bellingham, Wash.
Klahn, Richard P., Des Moines Indep. Comm. Sch. Dist., Des Moines, Iowa
Klausmeier, Herbert J., Sch. of Educ., University of Wisconsin, Madison, Wis.
Kleffner, John H., Assoc. Supt. of Cath. Schools, Oklahoma City, Okla.
Klein, Howard A., Col. of Educ., Univ. of Sask., Saskatoon, Sask., Canada
Klein, M. Francis, 928-23rd St., Santa Monica, Calif.
Klein, Margrete, 2026 Lincoln St., Evanston, Ill.
Klein, Philip, 1520 Spruce St., Philadelphia, Pa.
Klein, Richard K., Department of Public Instruction, Bismarck, N.Dak.
Kleis, Russell J., Michigan State University, East Lansing, Mich.
Klevean, Albert, Peace Corps, c/o U.S. Embassy, Seoul, Korea
Kleyensteuber, Carl J., Northland College, Ashland, Wis.
Klinckmann, Evelyn, San Francisco Col. for Women, San Francisco, Calif.
Kline, Charles E., Purdue University, Lafayette, Ind.
Kline, Robert D., 3712 Mt. Ranier Dr., Alberquerque, N. Mex.
Kling, Martin, Grad. Sch. of Educ., Rutgers State Univ., New Brunswick, N.J.
Klingstedt, Joe Lars, 5411 40th St., Lubbock, Tex.
Klohr, Paul R., 420 Walhalla Rd., Columbus, Ohio
Klopf, Gordon J., Bank Street Col. of Educ., New York, N.Y.
Klopfer, Leopold E., University of Pittsburgh, Pittsburgh, Pa.
Knape, Clifford S., 1024 North 18-A St., Waco, Tex.
Knapp, Frederick C., 272 Rochelle Park, Tonawanda, N.Y.
Knapp, Thomas R., Univ. of Rochester, Rochester, N.Y.
Knapp, William D., 6800 Schoolway, Greendale, Wis.
Knauer, Thomas E., 1410 Central Ave., Deerfield, Ill.
Knepp, A. Christine, 634 Cedar Dr., Cortland, Ohio
Knight, Octavia B., North Carolina Cent. Univ., Durham, N.C.
Knight, Reginald R., 4338 Heather Rd., Long Beach, Calif.
Knolle, Lawrence M., 208 Dewey St., Pittsburgh, Pa.
Knope, Mrs. Perle, Madison Public Schools, Madison, Wis.
Knorr, Amy Jean, University of Arizona, Tucson, Ariz.
Knowlden, Gayle E., 3003 Laurel Ave., Manhattan Beach, Calif.
Knox, Carl S., 2017 Louisiana St., Lawrence, Kans.
Knox, Stanley C., St. Cloud State College, St. Cloud, Minn.
Koch, Mrs. Sylvia L., 539 N. Highland Ave., Los Angeles, Calif.
Koehler, Everette E., The King's College, Briarcliff Manor, N.Y.
Koehring, Dorothy, Univ. of N. Iowa Field Serv., Cedar Falls, Iowa
Koenig, Vernon H., 11878 Ridgecrest Dr., Riverside, Calif.
Koeppe, Richard P., Asst. Supt., Denver Public Schools, Denver, Colo.

Koerber, Walter F., Scarborough Board of Education, Scarborough, Ont., Canada
Koerner, Warren A., 4608 West 106th St., Oak Lawn, Ill.
Koester, George A., San Diego State College, San Diego, Calif.
Koff, Robert H., Sch. of Educ., Stanford Univ., Stanford, Calif.
Kohake, Cletus, St. Benedict's Col. Library, Atchison, Kans.
Kohler, Lewis T., 7659 Whitsett Ave., N. Hollywood, Calif.
Kohlmann, Eleanor L., 169 MacKay Hall, Iowa State University, Ames, Iowa
Kohn, Martin, 35 West 92nd St., New York, N.Y.
Kokras, Nocolaos, Elia-Gonnon, Parissa, Greece
Kolakowski, Donald, 5719 S. Kimbark Ave., Chicago, Ill.
Kollar, Theodore H., Paterson Cath. Reg. H.S., Paterson, N.J.
Konishi, Walter K., San Jose State College, San Jose, Calif.
Konrad, Abram G., Tabor College, Hillsboro, Kans.
Konsh, Adeline, 7 East 14th St., New York, N.Y.
Konstantinos, K. K., Lenape Regional High School, Medford, N.J.
Kontos, George, 3921 West Park, Poscoe, Wash.
Koontz, David, West Virginia State College, Institute, W. Va.
Koos, Leonard V., Route 2, Newago, Mich.
Kopan, Andrew T., 1228 Ashland Ave., River Forest, Ill.
Kopel, David, Chicago St. Col. 6800 Stewart Ave., Chicago, Ill.
Koppenhaver, Albert H., Calif. State Col., Long Beach, Calif.
Korach, Steven, 500 Martin Rd., Lackawanna, N.Y.
Korella, Lynell, 6212 Lewis Dr., S.W., Calgary, 10, Alberta, Canada
Korntheuer, Gerhard A., St. Johns College, Winfield, Kan.
Kovach, Gaza, Pocahontas High School, Pocahontas, Va.
Kowitz, George T., Dept. of Educ. Psych., Univ. of Oklahoma, Norman, Okla.
Koyanagi, Elliot Y., 2630 Dekist St., Bloomington, Ind.
Kozma, Ernest J., 8081 Worthington Park Dr., Strongsville, Ohio
Krafft, Larry J., 739 Roslyn St., Glenside, Pa.
Kraft, Milton Edward, Earlham College, Richmond, Ind.
Kramer, William A., 3558 S. Jefferson Ave., St. Louis, Mo.
Kraus, Howard F., 512 Alameda de las Pulgas, Belmont, Calif.
Kraus, Philip E., 40 E. 84 St., New York, N.Y.
Krause, Frank H., Ball State Univ., Muncie, Ind.
Kravetz, Sol, 11545 Duque Dr., Studio City, Calif.
Kravitz, Jerry, 986 Van Buren St., Baldwin, N.Y.
Kreinheder, Adeline E., Muhlenberg Col., Allentown, Pa.
Kreismer, Clifford R., Clara E. Coleman Sch., 100 Pinelynn Rd., Glen Rock, N.J.
Kreitlow, Burton W., Route #1, Mazonmanie, Wis.
Kress, Roy A., 800 Moredon Rd., Meadowbrook, Pa.
Kretschmer, Joseph C., 1178c Sanborn Pl., Columbus, Ohio
Krich, Percy, Dept. of Educ., Queens College, Flushing, N.Y.
Krippner, Stanley C., Dept. of Psychiatry, Maimonides Hosp., Brooklyn, N.Y.
Krolikowski, W. P., Loyola University, Chicago, Ill.
Kroman, Nathan, University of Saskatchewan, Saskatoon, Sask., Canada
Kropp, John P., 12455 Russell Ave., Chino, Calif.
Krueger, Louise W., 1520 Laburnum Ave., Chico, Calif.
Krug, Edward, Dept. of Educ., University of Wisconsin, Madison, Wis.
Kruse, Mary L., 1200 E. Glenoaks Blvd., Glendale, Calif.
Krzesinski, Daniel J., 801 Tinkham, Attica, N.Y.
Krull, R. Pratt, Editor, "Instructor" Magazine, Dansville, N.Y.
Kruszynski, Eugene S., San Francisco State College, San Francisco, Calif.
Kubalek, Josef, Usenory 198, O Praha-Zapad, C S S R, Czech.
Kubik, Edmund J., 9741 S. Leavitt St., Chicago, Ill.
Kucera, Geoffrey, Col. of Educ., Univ. of Hawaii, Honolulu, Hawaii
Kuhn, Donald K., 8520 Mackenzie Rd., St. Louis, Mo.
Kuhn, Joseph A., 99 Buffalo Ave., Long Beach, N.Y.
Kuhnen, Mrs. Mildred, 2106 Park Ave., Chico, Calif.
Kulberg, Janet M., 149 Cedar St., Bangor, Maine
Kullman, N. E., Jr., 153 Murray Ave., Delmar, N.Y.

Kumpf, Carl H., Superintendent of Schools, Clark, N.J.
Kunimoto, Mrs. Tadako, 734—16th Ave., Honolulu, Hawaii
Kuntz, Allen H., 72 Lombardy St., Lancaster, N.Y.
Kunzler, William J., 34 Overbrook Dr., Kirksville, Mo.
Kupfer, Robert E., 1701 E. Capitol Dr., Shorewood, Wis.
Kusler, Gerald E., E. Lansing High Schl., E. Lansing, Mich.
Kusnik, Cornell J., 7400 Augusta St., River Forest, Ill.
Kvaraceus, William C., Clark University, Worcester, Mass.
Kwasnaza, Miriam, 10 Kingsbridge Rd., Somerset, N.J.
Kyle, Helen F., Rhode Island College, Providence, R.I.
Kysilka, Marcella L., Univ. of Tex., Austin, Tex.

Labatte, Henry, 40 College St., Toronto, Ontario, Canada
LaBay, Michael J., 4008 Rochester Road, San Diego, Calif.
Lacey, Archie L., 7330-14th St., Washington, D.C.
Lache, Sheldon I., The Henrietta Szold Inst., Jerusalem, Israel
Lacivita, James, 2515 Olive, Arlington Heights, Ill.
Lackey, Kenneth E., 6304 N. Askew, Kansas City, Mo.
Ladd, Edward T., Emory University, Atlanta, Ga.
Ladd, Eleanor M., Col. of Educ., University of Georgia, Athens, Ga.
Ladd, Paul, Wooster High School, Wooster, Ohio
LaDue, Donald C., Elem. Educ. Dept., Temple University, Philadelphia, Pa.
LaFauci, Horatio M., 871 Commonwealth Ave., Boston, Mass.
Lafferty, Charles W., Supt. of Schools, Fairbanks, Alaska
Lafferty, Henry M., East Texas State Univ., Commerce, Tex.
LaForce, Charles L., 426 Malden Ave., LaGrange Park, Ill.
Lafranchi, W. E., Stabley Library, State College, Indiana, Pa.
LaGrone, Herbert F., Sch. of Educ., Texas Christian Univ., Fort Worth, Tex.
Lahaderne, Henrietta M., IDEA, 1100 Glendon Ave., Los Angeles, Calif.
Laird, Albert W., Western Ky. Univ., Bowling Green, Ky.
Lake, Doris S., State Univ. Col., Oneonta, N.Y.
Lake, K., 151 N. Craig St., Pittsburgh, Pa.
Lambert, Pierre D., Sch. of Educ., Boston College, Chestnut Hill, Mass.
Lambert, Roger H., 1409 H Spartan Village, E. Lansing, Mich.
Lambert, Ronald T., University of Minnesota, Minneapolis, Minn.
Lambright, Gale, Univ. of Texas, Austin, Tex.
Lampard, Dorothy M., Univ. of Letherbridge, Letherbridge, Alba., Canada
Lampshire, Richard H., Drake University, Des Moines, Iowa
Landry, Clarence D., 1142 Jackson St., Beloit, Wis.
Lane, Frank T., USAID, Rio de Janiero/SUN, APO New York, NY.
Lane, Mrs. Mary B., 10 Lundy's Lane, San Mateo, Calif.
Lane, Vera J., P.O. Box 44064-Louisiana St. Dept. of Educ., Baton Rouge, La.
Lang, Mrs. Pauline R., Southern Connecticut State Col., New Haven, Conn.
Lange, Paul W., 2304 Linden Dr., Valparaiso, Ind.
Lange, Phil C., Tchrs. Col., Columbia University, New York, N.Y.
Langeveld, M. J., Prins Hendriklaan 6, Bilthoven, Holland
Langland, Lois E., 4021 Olive Hill Dr., Claremont, Calif.
Langley, Elizabeth M., 4937 W. Wellington Ave., Chicago, Ill.
Langley, Lorita, 137 East Woodworth, Roselle, Ill.
Langman, Muriel P., 2111 Delafield Dr., Ann Arbor, Mich.
Langston, Genevieve R., Eureka College, Eureka, Ill.
Langston, Roderick G., 1451 S. Loma Verde St., Monterey Park, Calif.
Lanham, Frank W., Wayne St. Univ., Detroit, Mich.
Lanier, Ruby, Route No. 2, Box 619, Hickory, N.C.
Lanning, Frank W., Northern Illinois University, DeKalb, Ill.
Lano, Richard L., University of California, Los Angeles, Calif.
Lansing, Marvin G., 122 Mappa St., Eau Claire, Wis.
Lansu, Walter J., 5724 W. Lindenhurst, Los Angeles, Calif.
Lantz, James S., 413 Burr Oak St., Albion, Mich.
Lantz, Ralph G., Box 278, Warrington, Pa.

La Plant, James, 1054 Ironstone, Cincinnati, Ohio
Lapp, Diane, 26 Waverly, Brighton, Mass.
Larkins, William J., 32000 Chagrin Blvd., Cleveland, Ohio
Larmee, Roy A., Cntr. for Educ. Admn., Ohio State Univ., Columbus, Ohio
Larsen, Arthur Hoff, Illinois State University, Normal, Ill.
Larson, Eleanore E., Col. of Educ., Univ. of Rochester, Rochester, N.Y.
Larson, L. C., Audio-Visual Center, Indiana University, Bloomington, Ind.
Larson, Shirley G., Univ. of Minn. St. Paul, Minn.
Larson, Vera M., 13601 N.E. Fremont St., Portland, Oreg.
Lashingter, Donald R., Syracuse Univ., Syracuse, N.Y.
Laska, John, Sutton Hall, Univ. of Texas, Austin, Tex.
Lassanske, Paul A., 4389 Hodgson Rd., St. Paul, Minn.
Lathrop, Irvin T., California State College, Long Beach, Calif.
Lattimer, Everett C., Magee Rd., Glenmont, N.Y.
Laub, Beatrice K., 6414 N. Mozart, Chicago, Ill.
Laudico, Minerva G., Centro Escolar University, Manila, Philippines
Lauria, Joseph L., 6401 Shoup Ave., Canoga Park, Calif.
Laurier, Blaise V., Les Clercs de Saint-Viateur, Montreal, Quebec, Canada
Lavenburg, F. M., Public Schls., 155 Broad St., Bloomfield, N.J.
Laverty, John A., 5944 S. Washtenaw Ave., Chicago, Ill.
Lawhead, Victor B., Ball State University, Muncie, Ind.
Lawler, Marcella R., Tchrs. Col., Columbia University, New York, N.Y.
Lawrence, Richard E., Univ. of New Mexico, Albuquerque, N.Mex.
Lawrence, Ruth E., 627 Grove St., Denton, Tex.
Lawrie, Jack D., 1274 Duane Rd., Chattanooga, Tenn.
Lawson, James R., 1719 Haslett Rd., E. Lansing, Mich.
Lazar, Alfred L., Schl. of Educ., Calif. St. Col. at Long Beach, Long Beach, Calif.
Lazow, Alfred, 2631 W. Berwyn Ave., Chicago, Ill.
Leavitt, Jerome E., Col. of Educ., Univ. of Arizona, Tucson, Ariz.
Lebofsky, Arthur E., Rd. #1, Box 814, June Rd., Chester, N.Y.
Lee, Annabel, Univ. of Puget Sound, Tacoma, Wash.
Lee, Della, Asst. Prin., Public School, Bronx, N.Y.
Lee, Ernest C., Prin., Beaufort H.S., Beaufort, Victoria, Australia
Lee, Howard D., Atwater School, Shorewood, Wis.
Lee, J. Murray, Southern Illinois University, Carbondale, Ill.
Lee, James Michael, University of Notre Dame, Notre Dame, Ind.
Lee, John J., Col. of Educ., Wayne State University, Detroit, Mich.
Lee, William B., U.S.D.E.S.E.A., APO New York, N.Y.
Lee, William C., Fairleigh Dickinson University, Rutherford, N.J.
Leeds, Donald S., 923 Lincoln St., Superior, Wis.
Leese, Joseph, State Univ. Col., Albany, N.Y.
Lefever, David Welty, Sch. of Educ., Univ. of California, Los Angeles, Calif.
* Lefforge, Roxy, 1945 Fruit St., Huntington, Ind.
Lehman, Lloyd W., 926 Ferdinand, Forest Park, Ill.
Lehmann, Irvin J., Michigan State University, East Lansing, Mich.
Lehmkuhl, Carlton B., 4 Wilogreen Rd., Natick, Mass.
Lehsten, Nelson G., Sch. of Educ., Univ. of Michigan, Ann Arbor, Mich.
Leib, Joseph A., 240 Sinclair Pl., Westfield, N.J.
Leibert, Robert E., 1005 W. Gregory Ave., Kansas City, Mo.
Leibik, Leon J., 204 Dodge Ave., Evanston, Ill.
Leigh, Robert K., Box 2501, University, Ala.
Leitch, John J., Jr., Admin. Off., Wheeler Rd., Central Islip, N.Y.
Lembo, John M., 117 Victoria Rd., Millersville, Pa.
Lennon, Lawrence J., Univ. of Scranton, Scranton, Pa.
Leonard, Lloyd L., Dept. of Educ., Northern Illinois Univ., DeKalb, Ill.
Leonard, William P., Temple Univ., Philadelphia, Pa.
Lepera, Alfred G., 254 Franklin St., Newton, Mass.
LePere, Jean M., Michigan State University, East Lansing, Mich.
Lepore, Albert R., 2614 Lancaster Rd., Hayward, Calif.
Lesniak, Robert J., 314 W. Oak St., Palmyra, Pa.

Leverson, Leonard O., 201 W. Newhall Ave., Waukesha, Wis.
Levin, Alvin I., 12336 Addison St., North Hollywood, Calif.
Levin, J. Joseph, 221 N. Cuyler Ave., Oak Park, Ill.
Levine, Daniel U., Sch. of Educ., Univ. of Missouri, Kansas City, Mo.
Levine, Elliot, 92-29 Lamont Ave., Elmhurst, N.Y.
Levine, Murray, 74 Colonial Circle, Buffalo, N.Y.
Levine, Stanley L., 1627 Anita Ln., Newport Beach, Calif.
Levinson, Leo, Clarkston Sch. Dist. No. 1, New City, N.Y.
Levit, Martin, Sch. of Educ., University of Missouri, Kansas City, Mo.
Levy, Nathalie, 506 Mississippi Ave., Bogalusa, La.
Lewis, Arthur J., Col. of Educ., Univ. of Fla., Gainesville, Fla.
Lewis, Edward R., 5293 Greenridge Rd., Castro Valley, Calif.
Lewis, Elizabeth V., P.O. Box 1833, University, Ala.
Lewis, Eva P., 2131 52nd St. 227, Dallas, Tex.
Lewis, J. Lamar, 1218 N. Adams St., Tallahasse, Fla.
Lewis, Maurice S., Col. of Educ., Arizona State University, Tempe, Ariz.
Lewis, P. Helen, 17 E. 14th Ave., Columbus, Ohio
Lewis, Philip, 6900 S. Crandon Ave., Chicago, Ill.
Lewis, Robert, 915 N. Union St., Natchez, Miss.
Lewis, Roland B., Eastern Washington State College, Cheney, Wash.
Lewis, William, Millikin Univ. Library, Decatur, Ill.
Libby, David, 3671 Sea Robin, St. Petersburg, Fla.
Licata, William, State Univ. Col., Buffalo, N.Y.
Licthy, E. A., Illinois State University, Normal, Ill.
Lieberman, Ann, 13040 Hartland St., North Hollywood, Calif.
Lieberman, Marcus, 5835 Kimbark Ave., Chicago, Ill.
Lien, Ronald L., Mankato State College, Mankato, Minn.
Lietwiler, Helena K., 5907 Aberdeen Rd., Bethesda, Md.
Liggett, Donald R., Grinnell College, Grinnell, Ia.
Liggitt, William A., 703 St. Marks Ave., Westheld, N.J.
Light, Alfred B., 17 Webster, Glens Falls, N.Y.
Light, Judy A., 5930 Howe St., Pittsburgh, Pa.
Lighthall, Frederick, Dept. of Educ., Univ. of Chicago, Chicago, Ill.
Ligon, Mary Gilbert, Hofstra College, Hempstead, N.Y.
Liljeblad, Maynard T., 766 Sheelin, Glendora, Calif.
Lim Jit Poh, 208C Keng Lee Rd., Singapore, Rep. of Singapore
*Lincoln, Edward A., Thompson St., Halifax, Mass.
Lind, Arthur E., 4702 W. Yellowstone, Kennewich, Wash.
Lind, Marshall L., P.O. Box 557, Kodiak, Alaska
Lindberg, Lucile, Queens College, Flushing, N.Y.
Lindbloom, Dwight, 1636 Hewitt St., St. Paul, Minn.
Lindeman, Richard H., Tchrs. Col., Columbia University, New York, N.Y.
Lindemer, George Charles, Seton Hall University, South Orange, N.J.
Linder, J.B., Rt. 5, Box 142, Orangeburg, S.C.
Lindgren, Henry C., 1975-15th Ave., San Francisco, Calif.
Lindly, Charles, 809 South St., Rapid City, S. Dak.
Lindman, Mrs. Margaret R., Prin., College Hill School, Skokie, Ill.
Lindvall, C. Mauritz, Sch. of Educ., University of Pittsburgh, Pittsburgh, Pa.
Linehan, Mrs. Louise W., 4 Bolton Pl., Fair Lawn, N.J.
Linn, Frank J., S.E. Mo. State College, Cape Girardeau, Mo.
Linscott, John S., Supt. of Schs., Roselle Park, N.J.
Linson, Marvin G., 933 Fulton St., Aurora, Colo.
Linstrum, Dick, 2156 Sierra Way, San Luis Obispo, Calif.
Linville, William J., 203 Hudson Ave., Terre Haute, Ind.
Lipham, James M., Univ. of Wis., Madison, Wis.
Lipscomb, William A., Box 249, Eureka, Nev.
Lissovoy, Vladimir de, Pennsylvania State Univ., University Park, Pa.
Litherland, Bennett H., 2705-34th St., Rock Island, Ill.
Litin, Mrs. Annette, 5302 N. Granite Reef Rd., Scottsdale, Ariz.
Litsinger, Dolores A., San Fernando Valley State College, Northridge, Calif.

Little, J. Kenneth, Bascom Hall, University of Wisconsin, Madison, Wis.
Little, Sara, Presbyterian Sch. of Christian Education, Richmond, Va.
Litton, H. John, Jr., Crystal Sprgs Dr., Rt. 4, Falcon Ranche, Lexington, S.C.
Litzky, Leo, 11 Pomona Ave., Newark, N.J.
Livingston, Thomas B., Box 4060, Texas Tech. Station, Lubbock, Tex.
Livo, Mrs. Norma J., 11960 W. 22nd Pl., Denver, Colo.
Llewellyn, Ardelle A., San Francisco State College, San Francisco, Calif.
Lloyd, Florence M., St. Francis Col., Ft. Wayne, Ind.
* Lloyd, Francis V., 222 Pleasant St., South Yarmouth, Mass.
Lloyd-Jones, Esther M., 430 West 116th St., New York, N.Y.
Loadman, William, 2511 E. 2nd St., Bloomington, Ind.
Lobdell, Lawrence O., Springfield Coll., Springfield, Mass.
Locke, William W., 1317 Pine St., Kingsport, Tenn.
Lockett, B. T., 1848 Tiger Flowers Dr., N.W., Atlanta, Ga.
Lockett, Mortimer W., 904 Cumberland Dr., Woodbridge, Va.
Loewe, Melanie, 3052 Parkside, Chicago, Ill.
Lofgren, Marie Luise S., 5068 Cocoa Palm Way, Fair Oaks, Calif.
Logan, Lillian May, Brandon Univ., Brandon, Manitoba, Canada
Logdeser, Mrs. Thomas, 11616 Woodview Blvd., Parma Heights, Ohio
Lohman, Maurice A., Tchrs. Col., Columbia University, New York, N.Y.
Lohse, Arnold W., 3595 Stillwater Rd., St. Paul, Minn.
Lola, Justita O., Bicol Teachers College, Legaspi, Albay, Philippines
Lomax, James L., 808 S. Loombs, Valdosta, Ga.
Lombari, Dorothy K., 4503 Sherwood Forest N., Columbus, Ohio
Long, Isabelle, 4343 Harriet Ave., S., Minneapolis, Minn.
Longsdorf, Homer, 413 Leslie, Lansing, Mich.
Lonsdale, Mrs. Maxine deLappe, 1405 Campbell Lane, Sacramento, Calif.
Lonsdale, Richard C., 220 Palmer Ave., North Tarrytown, N.Y.
Longstreet, Wilma S., Col. of Educ., Univ. of Illinois, Urbana, Ill.
Looby, Thomas F., 241 S. Ocean Ave., Patchogue, N.Y.
Loomis, Arthur K., 917 W. Bonita Ave., Claremont, Calif.
Loomis, William G., 684 Illinois Ave., N. E., Salem, Oreg.
Loop, Alfred B., P.O. Box 896, Bellingham, Wash.
Loree, M. Ray, Box 742, University of Alabama, University, Ala.
Lorenz, Donald W., Concordia H. S., Portland, Oreg.
Loudon, Mrs. Mary Lou, 1408 Stephens Ave., Baton Rouge, La.
Loughlin, Leo J., 257 Rolfe Rd., DeKalb, Ill.
Loughrea, Mildred K., 659 City Hall, St. Paul, Minn.
Love, Virginia H., 1515 W. Washington, Sherman, Tex.
Lovely, Edward C., Trumbull High School, Trumbull, Conn.
Lowe, A. J., University of South Florida, Tampa, Fla.
Lowe, Mary G., Dept. of H.E., University of Utah, Salt Lake City, Utah
Lowe, R. N., Sch. of Educ., University of Oregon, Eugene, Oreg.
Lowe, William T., 328 Hopeman, University of Rochester, Rochester, N.Y.
Lowery, Zeb A., Rutherford County Schools, Rutherford, N.C.
Lowes, Ruth, 2004 Seventh Ave., Canyon, Tex.
Lowey, Warren G., Box 64, Setauket, L.I., N.Y.
Lows, Raymond L., Southern Illinois Univ., Carbondale, Ill.
Lowther, Malcolm A., Sch. of Educ., Univ. of Michigan, Ann Arbor, Mich.
Lowther, William L., Supt. of Schools, Boonton, N.J.
Lubell, Richard M., 2 Stoddard Pl., Brooklyn, N.Y.
Lubin, Harry, Supt. of Schools, Bellmawr, N.J.
Lucas, J. H., 2006 Fayetteville St., Durham, N.C.
Lucas, Robert E., Fort Morgan High School, Fort Morgan, Colo.
Lucash, Benjamin, 9801 Montour St., Philadelphia, Pa.
Lucietto, Lena, 5835 Kimbark Ave., Chicago, Ill.
Lucio, William H., Sch. of Educ., University of California, Los Angeles, Calif.
Lucito, Leonard J., Rt. 2, Woodbury, Ga.
Luddeke, Nancy, 848 Yorkhaven Rd., Cincinnati, Ohio
Ludeman, Ruth, Augsburg College, Minneapolis, Minn.

Luetkemeyer, Joseph F., 7002 St. Annes Ave., Lanham, Md.
Luhmann, Philip, 1407 E. 54th St., Chicago, Ill.
Luker, Arno Henry, Colorado State College, Greeley, Colo.
Lundblad, Helen A., 2815 N. Dunn, Bloomington, Ind.
Lundin, Stephen C., 3405 N. Cleveland #5, St. Paul, Minn.
Lunney, Gerald H., L. I. Univ., Greenvale, N.Y.
Lyman, Francis J., Washington Schl., 735 Washington Rd., Pittsburgh, Pa.
Lynch, Florence M., 8338 S. Kedvale Ave., Chicago, Ill.
Lynch, John C., DePaul University, Chicago, Ill.
Lynch, Patrick D., Pa. State Univ., University Park, Pa.
Lyons, Mrs. Cora E., P.O. Box 133, Amboy, Ill.
Lyons, John H., 17 Colton Rd., Somers, Conn.
Lyons, Paul R., 300-11 Diamond Village, Gainesville, Fla.

Maag, Raymond E., 122 W. Franklin Ave., Minneapolis, Minn.
Mabon, Thomas, Rev., 1406 12th Ave., Altoona, Pa.
Macagnoni, Virginia, Univ. of Georgia, Athens, Ga.
MacArthur, Austin J., Schl. Three, 230 Joralemon St., Belleville, N.Y.
MacConnell, John C., Muhlenberg College, Allentown, Pa.
Macdonald, Leland S., 5609—19th St., N., Arlington, Va.
MacGown, Paul C., 3128 N. Ash St., Spokane, Wash.
* MacKay, James L., 3737 Fredericksburg Rd., San Antonio, Tex.
MacKay, Vera A., Col. of Educ., Univ. of British Columbia, Vancouver, B.C.
MacKay, William R., 124 Underhill Rd., Bellingham, Wash.
Mackenzie, Donald M., White House, Park College, Parkville, Mo.
MacKenzie, Elbridge G., Anderson College, Anderson, Ind.
Mackenzie, Gordon N., Tchrs. Col., Columbia University, New York, N.Y.
Mackintosh, Helen K., 215 Wolfe St., Alexandria, Va.
MacLean, Effie, Saskatoon Pub. Sch. Brd., Saskatoon, Sask., Canada
MacLeay, Ian A., P.O. Box 560, Lennoxville, Quebec, Canada
MacLeod, James J., 6300 Grand River, Detroit, Mich.
MacMillan, Robert W., Univ. of R.I., Kingston, R.I.
MacNaughton, Elizabeth A., 2990 Richmond Ave., Houston, Tex.
MacRae, Douglas G., Fulton County Board of Educ., Atlanta, Ga.
Maddox, Mrs. Clifford R., 525 Enid Ave., Dayton, Ohio
Maddox, Joe W., St. Bernard Col., St. Bernard, Ala.
Madeja, Stanley S., 6838 Pershing Ave., University City, Mo.
Mader, Charles E., Univ. of Ill.-Chicago Circle, Chicago, Ill.
Madonna, Shirley M., 47-27 215 St., Bayside, N.Y.
Madore, Normand William, Illinois State University, Normal, Ill.
Magann, Douglas P., 60 W. Salisbury Dr., Wilmington, Del.
Magary, James F., Sch. of Educ., Univ. of So. California, Los Angeles, Calif.
Maggart, Zelda, 6109 Rogers, Alberquerque, N. Mex.
Maginnis, Maria, 20522 Parthenia St., Canoga Park, Calif.
Magoon, Thomas M., 1316 Canyon Rd., Silver Spring, Md.
Magram, P. Theodore, 88 E. Mohawk St., Oswego, N.Y.
Mahan, James, 3280 Warrington Rd., Cleveland, Ohio
Mahar, Robert J., Col. of Educ., Temple University, Philadelphia, Pa.
Maher, Alan E., Unqua School, Massapequa, N.Y.
Maher, Trafford P., St. Louis University, 15 N. Grand Blvd., St. Louis, Mo.
Mahler, Clarence A., Chico St. Col., Chico, Calif.
Mahon, Bruce R., Mount Royal Junior College, Calgary 2, Alba., Canada
Mailey, James H., Supt. of Schools, Midland, Tex.
Mailliard, Mrs. Margaret E., 221 E. 49th St., Chicago, Ill.
Mains, Mrs. Susie T., 29 West St., Barre, Vt.
Major, Joseph M., 770 Nita Ave., Canoga Pk., Calif.
Major, Suzanne T., 233 Woodland, Highland Park, Ill.
Malafouris, John P., 19948 Great Oak Circle, Mt. Clemens, Mich.
Mallet, Jeanette, 11 Peabody Ter., 1601, Cambridge, Mass.

Maloof, Mitchell, 63 Main St., Williamstown, Mass.
Mandel, E. Jules, 20918 Calimali Rd., Woodland Hills, Calif.
Mangum, G.C., P.O. Box 399, Darlington, S.C.
Manley, Francis J., Frontier Central Sch., Bay View Rd., Hamburg, N.Y.
Mann, Edward L., Jr., P.O. Box 188, Great Barrington, Mass.
Mann, James W., Roosevelt University, Chicago, Ill.
Mann, Sidney J., 703 S. Main St., Horseheads, N.Y.
Mann, Mrs. Thelma T., 949 Hunakai St., Honolulu, Hawaii
Mann, Vernal S., Box 266, State College, Miss.
Manning, Doris E., University of Arizona, Tucson, Ariz.
Mannos, Nicholas T., Niles Twp. High School West, Skokie, Ill.
Manoil, Adolph, Sch. of Educ., Boston University, Boston, Mass.
Manone, Carl, 34 Kirkline Ave., Hellertown, Pa.
Manuel, Herschel T., University of Texas, Austin, Tex.
Mapel, Seldon, 1208 Kathryn St., Hurst, Tex.
Marazzi, Maureen, 10 Plaza St., Brooklyn, N.Y.
Marburger, Carl L., Dept. of Educ., 225 W. State St., Trenton, N.J.
Marc-Aurele, Paul, 455, 80 Rue Est, Charlesbourg, Quebec 7, Canada
Marchie, Howard E., 26 Norman St., Springfield, Mass.
Marconnit, George D., 7432 Woodland Way, St. Louis, Mo.
Marcum, Laverne, Idaho State Univ., Pocatello. Idaho
Marcus, Marie, Louisiana State University, New Orleans, La.
Margarones, John J., 210 College St., Lewiston, Maine
Margolis, Henry, 2030 S. Taylor Rd., Cleveland Heights, Ohio
Mark, Arthur, 6 Cross Brook Ln., Westport, Conn.
Marks, Claude H., Univ. of Tex., Austin, Tex.
Marks, Merle B., University of So. California, Los Angeles, Calif.
Marks, Ralph M., 309 Lime Dr., Nokomis, Fla.
Marksberry, Mary Lee, Sch. of Educ., Univ. of Missouri, Kansas City, Mo.
Marksheffel, Ned D., Oregon State University, Corvallis, Oreg.
Markus, Frank 1420 Heights Blvd., Winona, Minn.
Marquand, Richard L., Michigan State Univ., East Lansing, Mich.
Marquardt, Robert L., Thiokol Chemical Corp., Ogden, Utah
Marquis, Francis N., 4712 Elzo Lane, Kettering, Ohio
Marquis, R. L., Jr., Box 5282, North Texas Sta., Denton, Tex.
Marsden, W. Ware, Okla. St. Univ., Zuck Addition, Stillwater, Okla.
Marsh, Mrs. Augusta B., 252 Bronner St., Prichard, Ala.
Marshall, Beth, 1325 S. Orange, Fullerton, Calif.
Marshall, Daniel W., Filene Center, Tufts University, Medford, Mass.
Marshall, Robert D., Naperville Public Schs., Naperville, Ill.
Marshall, Thomas O., 17 Mill Rd., Durham, N.H.
Marshall, Wayne P., 704 East 36th St., Kearney, Nebr.
Marso, Ronald N., Bowling Green State Univ., Bowling Green, Ohio
Marston, Mrs. Marjorie, 860 Lake Shore Dr., Chicago, Ill.
Martin, C. Keith, Col. of Educ., Univ. of Md., College Park, Md.
Martin, Edwin D., 2341 Quenby, Houston, Tex.
Martin, Jackson J., 509 Irene Pl., Cheney, Wash.
Martin, Jeanette V., P.O. Box 3462, Univ. Pk., N. Mex.
Martin, Josephine W., 1403 Haynsworth Rd., Columbia, S.C.
Martin, Kathryn J., 2208 Fairhill Ave., Glenside, Pa.
Martin, Mavis D., SWCEL, 117 Richmond, N.E., Albuquerque, N.Mex.
Martin, R. Lee, State Univ. Col., Oswego, N.Y.
Martin, Robert M., University of Hawaii, Honolulu, Hawaii
Martin, Ruth G., 206 Parkview Dr., Marietta, Ga.
Martin, William R., 320 N.W. 19th Ave., Fort Lauderdale, Fla.
Martini, Miss Angiolina A., 1555 Oxford St., Berkeley, Calif.
Martinson, John S., 7 Rustic Lane, S.W., Tacoma, Wash.
Martire, Harriette A., St. Joseph College, West Hartford, Conn.
Martorana, Sabastian V., State University of New York, Albany, N.Y.
Marx, George L., Col. of Educ., University of Maryland, College Park, Md.

Marzolf, Stanley S., Illinois State University, Normal, Ill.
Marzullo, Santo P., 764 Furman Rd., Fairport, N.Y.
Mascetta, Joseph A., 124 S. Central Ave., Canonsburg, Pa.
Masem, Paul W., University of South Carolina, Columbia, S.C.
Masia, Bertram B., Dept. of Educ., Western Reserve Univ., Cleveland, Ohio
Masiko, Peter, Miami-Dade Junior College, Miami, Fla.
Mason, John M., Michigan State University, East Lansing, Mich.
Masoner, Paul H., University of Pittsburgh, Pittsburgh, Pa.
Massey, William J., 4906 Roland Ave., Baltimore, Md.
Massialas, Byron G., University of Michigan, Ann Arbor, Mich.
Massingill, Richard A., 15905 Harrison, Livonia, Mich.
Mathiott, James E., 3165 Ramona, Palo Alto, Calif.
Mathis, Claude, Sch. of Educ., Northwestern University, Evanston, Ill.
Matovich, Mike, 4332 Ivy St., East Chicago, Ind.
Matteson, Harold S., Univ. of Wisconsin, Madison, Wis.
Matthew, Eunice Sophia, 340 Riverside Dr., New York, N.Y.
Matthews, James W., Star Rt. 3, McGrath Rd., Fairbanks, Alaska
Matthews, William P., 1114 N. Centennial, High Point, N.C.
Mattila, Ruth Hughes, P.O. Box 872, Las Vegas, N.Mex.
Mattke, W.J., Centennial Schs., Circle Pines, Minn.
Mattox, Daniel V., Jr., Schl. of Educ., Ind. Univ. of Pa., Indiana, Pa.
Matzner, G. C., Eastern Illinois University, Charleston, Ill.
Maucker, James W., Univ. of Northern Iowa, Cedar Falls, Iowa
Mauk, Gertrude, Box 312, Garden City, Mich.
Maurer, Marion V., 148 Ann St., Apt. 23, Clarendon Hills, Ill.
Maurer, Robert L., California State Polytechnic College, Pomona, Calif.
Mauth, Leslie J., Ball State University, Muncie, Ind.
Maw, Wallace H., Sch. of Educ., University of Delaware, Newark, Del.
Mawter, Paul T., Wollongong Teachers Col., Wollongong, N.S.W., Australia
Max, Robert H., 95 Montvale Ave., Montvale, N.J.
Maxcy, Horace P., Pond Rd., RFD 1, Oakland, Maine
Maxwell, Celia H., 112 Mulberry Ct., Martinsville, Va.
Maxwell, Ida E., 9 Chester Creek Rd., Cheyney, Pa.
May, Charles R., 431 S. 55th St., Lincoln, Nebr.
May, John B., State Teachers College, Salisbury, Md.
May, Robert E., Emerson Vocational High School, Buffalo, N.Y.
Mayer, Lewis F., 4275 W. 196th St., Fairview Park, Ohio
Mayer, Richard A., 600 S. La Grange Rd., La Grange, Ill.
Mayhew, Lewis B., 945 Valdez Pl., Stanford, Calif.
Maynard, Glenn, Kent State University, Kent, Ohio
Mayo, Samuel T., Sch. of Educ., Loyola University, Chicago, Ill.
Mayor, John R., AAAS, 1515 Massachusetts Ave., N.W., Washington, D.C.
Mazyck, Harold E., Jr., 2007 Chelsea Lane, Greensboro, N.C.
McAllister, David, Kathmandu, State Dept., Washington, D.C.
McArthur, L. C., Jr., Drawer 1180, Sumter, S.C.
McAuliffe, M. Eileen, 5649 N. Kolmar Ave., Chicago, Ill.
McBirney, Ruth, Boise St., Col. Library, Boise, Idaho
McBride, James H., 1246 Riverside Drive, Huron, Ohio
McBride, Ralph, Supt., Buckley-Loda Unit #8, Loda, Ill.
McBride, Richard L., 3221 Ave. S., Birmingham, Ala.
McBride, William B., Ohio State University, Columbus, Ohio
McBurney, Mrs. Doris, 1641 West 105th St., Chicago, Ill.
McCahon, David M., 2300 Pittock St., Pittsburgh, Pa.
McCaig, Thomas E., 3447 W. Pierce Ave., Chicago, Ill.
McCain, Paul M., Arkansas College, Batesville, Ark.
McCall, Charlotte L., 433 Atherton, University Park, Pa.
McCann, Lewis E., 18637 San Fernando Mission Blvd., Northridge, Calif.
McCann, Thomas W., 19 Jeffery Pl., Trumbull, Conn.
McCarthy, Joseph F. X., 641 Forest Ave., Larchmont, N.Y.
McCarthy, Joseph J., 9531 S. Kostner, Oak Lawn, Ill.

McCartney, Hilda, 2916 Redwood Ave., Costa Mesa, Calif.
McCarty, Henry R., 206 Ebony Ave., Imperial Beach, Calif.
McCaslin, James J., 5916 N. Crittenden, Indianapolis, Ind.
McCaul, Robert L., Col. of Educ., University of Chicago, Chicago, Ill.
McClanahan, L. D., 86 W. State St., Athens, Ohio
McCleary, Lloyd E., University of Illinois, Urbana, Ill.
McClellan, James E., 70 Greentree Dr., Doylestown, Pa.
McClintock, Eugene, Kaskaskia College, Shattuc Rd., Centralia, Ill.
McClure, L. Morris, Col. of Educ., Univ. of Maryland, College Park, Md.
McClure, Nancy, Col. of Educ., Univ. of Kentucky, Lexington, Ky.
McClure, Robert M., NEA, 1201 16th St., Washington, D.C.
McClurkin, W. D., Peabody College, Nashville, Tenn.
McClusky, Howard Yale, Elem. Sch., University of Michigan, Ann Arbor, Mich.
McCollum, Elinor C., 619 Ridge Ave., Evanston, Ill.
McCollum, Robert E., Col. of Educ., Temple Univ., Philadelphia, Pa.
McConnell, Emma, Vassar College, Poughkeepsie, N.Y.
McConnell, Gaither, Cen. for Tchr. Educ., Tulane Univ., New Orleans, La.
McConnell, Thomas R., Center for Study of Higher Educ., Berkeley, Calif.
McCook, T. Joseph, 1408 W. Friendly Ave., Greensboro, N.C.
McCormick, Felix J., Tchrs. Col., Columbia University, New York, N.Y.
McCormick, Robert W., Ohio State University, Columbus, Ohio
McCowan, Richard J., 2466 W. Oakfield Dr., Grand Island, N.Y.
McCoy, Karen, 4704 W. 62nd St., Edina, Minn.
McCoy, Noel H., 1905 Sabine, Apt. 102, Austin, Tex.
McCracken, Oliver, Jr., Superintendent of Schools, Skokie, Ill.
McCuaig, Susannah, Col. of Educ., U. of Maryland, College Park, Md.
McCue, Robert E., 2308 N. Hazelwood Ave., Davenport, Iowa
McCuen, John T., 1340 Loretta Dr., Glendale, Calif.
McCullough, Constance M., 80 Vincente Rd., Berkeley, Calif.
McCuskey, Dorothy, Western Michigan University, Kalamazoo, Mich.
McCutcheon, Nancy Sue, Sch. of Educ., Univ. of South Carolina, Columbia, S.C.
McDaniel, Ernest D., Educ. Resch. Cent., Purdue Univ., Lafayette, Ind.
McDaniel, Marjorie C., Indiana State University, Terre Haute, Ind.
McDaniels, Garry L., 8830 Piney Branch Rd., Silver Spring, Md.
McDavit, H. W., South Orange-Maplewood Public Schools, South Orange, N.J.
McDiarmid, Garnet Leo, 102 Bloor St. West, Toronto, Ont., Canada
McDonald, Donald, Texas Technological College, Lubbock, Tex.
McDonald, Louis R., 3921 N. Keenland Ave., Peoria, Ill.
McDonough, Fred J., McKinley Schl., 65 Yeaman St., Revere, Mass.
McDonough, Robert K., 2090 E. Tremont Ave., Bronx, N.Y.
McDougle, Larry G., 522 Center St., Findlay, Ohio
McDowell, John B., 11 Blvd. of Allies, Pittsburgh, Pa.
McElhinney, James, 3816 Brook Dr., Muncie, Ind.
McEwen, Gordon B., 13602 E. Walnut, Whittier, Calif.
McFadden, Edward C., Hofstra Univ., Hempstead, N.Y.
McFarland, John W., Sch. of Educ., Univ. of Texas, El Paso, Tex.
McFarren, G. Allen, 11 Willow Lane Ct., Tonawanda, N.Y.
McFeaters, Margaret M., 608 Brown's Lane, Pittsburgh, Pa.
McGary, Carroll R., 125 Stroudwater St., Westbrook, Maine
McGary, Harry E., 8643 Kilby Rd., R.R. 4, Harrison, Ohio
McGavern, John H., University of Hartford, Hartford, Conn.
McGee, Ralph G., 1526 Washington Ave., Wilmette, Ill.
McGee, Robert T., Asst. Supt. Pennsbury School Dist., Fallsington, Pa.
McGeoch, Dorothy M., Tchrs. Col., Columbia University, New York, N.Y.
McGinnis, Frederick A., Wilberforce University, P.O. Box 22, Wilberforce, Ohio
McGinnis, James H., Knoxville College, Knoxville, Tenn.
McGlasson, Maurice A., Sch. of Educ., Indiana University, Bloomington, Ind.
McGrath, J. H., Dept. of Ed. Admin., Illinois State Univ., Normal, Ill.
McGrath, John W., Superintendent of Schools, Belmont, Mass.
McGraw, Mrs. Robert, 108 Grannis Rd., Orange, Conn.

McGroarty, Rosemary, Queens College Teacher Corps, Flushing, N.Y.
McGuire, George K., 7211 Merrill Ave., Chicago, Ill.
McGuire, Christine, 901 S. Wolcott, Chicago, Ill.
McHale, Edward G., 703 S. Main St., Horseheads, N.Y.
McHugh, Michael, Rev., Supt. of Dioc. Schs., Jefferson City, Mo.
McHugh, Walter J., California State College, Hayward, Calif.
McInerney, George K., 88-19—211th St., Jamaica, N.Y.
McIntyre, Margaret, George Washington Univ., Washington, D.C.
McKay, Jean W., Board of Education, Manassas, Va.
McKee, Paul J., 3106 Elmwood Ave. Apt. 10, Rochester, N.Y.
McKelpin, Joseph P., 3269 Pamlico Dr., Atlanta, Ga.
McKelvey, Troy V., State Univ. of N.Y. at Buffalo, N.Y.
McKenna, Charles D., Sch. Dist. of the City of Ladue, St. Louis, Mo.
McKenna, John J., Supt. of Schs., Madison, N.J.
McKenney, James L., Grad. Sch. of Business, Harvard Univ., Boston, Mass.
McKenzie, Robert M., 2031 Poyntz, Manhattan, Kans.
McKercher, Mrs. Berneth N., 1600 Dryden Rd., Metamora, Mich.
McKinney, Carolyn, 3540 Merrick Crt. Lexington, Ky.
McKinney, Edward C., 439 Loveman. Worthington, Ohio
McKinney, Lorella A., State Univ. Col., New Paltz, N.Y.
McKnight, Eloise, Dept. of Educ., St. Univ. Col., New Paltz, N.Y.
McKnight, Philip C., 250 No. Terrace Dr., Wichita, Kans.
McKown, George W., 2603 S. Forest Ave., Palatine, Ill.
McKoy, Judith B., Hunter College, New York, N.Y.
McKune, Esther J., State Univ. Col., Oneonta, N.Y.
McLain, William T., P.O. Box 86, Newark, Del.
McLaughlin, Eleanor T., Albion College, Albion, Mich.
McLaughlin, Frances, Ida Moffett Sch. of Nursing, Birmingham, Ala.
McLaughlin, Kenneth F., 871 N. Madison, Arlington, Va.
McLaughlin, Mary Ann, 212H-4400 Okemos Rd., Okemos, Mich.
McLaughlin, Rita E., 126 University Rd., Brookline, Mass.
McLees, Martha P., 829 Lucas St., Rock Hill, S.C.
McLellan, Keith A., 113 Heaslip St., Wollongong 2500, N.S.W., Australia
McLendon, Jonathan C., Col. of Educ., Univ. of Georgia, Athens, Ga.
McLevie, San Diego State Col., San Diego, Calif.
McMahan, John Julia, Keene State College, Keene, New Hampshire
McMahon, Ometra, 3924 Springfield Dr., Memphis, Tenn.
McMaster, Blanche E., 102 Hull St., Bristol, Conn.
McMillen, Leland A., Winona St. Col., Winona, Minn.
McMurray, Monte C., 633 S. Oak St., Inglewood, Calif.
McNally, Harold J., 7132 N. Crossway Rd., Fox Point, Wis.
McNeff, Marie O., Dir. of Elem Educ., Wayzata, Minn.
McNeill, Charles A., Sch. of Educ., University of S.C., Columbia, S.C.
McNinch, George H., Univ. of Southern Mississippi, Hattiesburg, Miss.
McNutt, C. R., 116 Ridge Rd., Woodbridge, Va.
McPhee, Roderick F., Punahou Schl., Honolulu, Hawaii
McPherson, Virgil L., Adams State College, Alamosa, Colo.
• McPherson, W. N., Darke County Superintendent of Schools, Greenville, Ohio
McSwain, E. T., University of North Carolina, Greensboro, N.C.
McSweeney, Maryellen, Mich. St. Univ., E. Lansing, Mich.
McTeer, Blanche R., 803 Lafayette St., Beaufort, S.C.
McWilliams, Elma A., William Carey College, Hattiesburg, Miss.
• Mead, Arthur R., 1719 N.W. 6th Ave., Gainesville, Fla.
Meade, David W., 722 W. 5th, Red Wing, Minn.
Meaders, O. Donald, Col. of Educ., Michigan State Univ., East Lansing, Mich.
Mease, Clyde D., Superintendent of Schools, Humboldt, Iowa
Mecklenburger, James A., 715 E. 8th Street, Bloomington, Ind.
Medeiros, Joseph V., Superintendent of Schools, New London, Conn.
Medler, Byron W., Sch. of Educ., No. Texas St. Univ., Denton, Tex.
Mednick, Martha T., 6428 Bannockburre Dr., Bethesda, Md.

Medsker, Nancy D., 125-147th Ave., Bellevue, Wash.
Medved, A. A., Cherry Lawn School, Darien, Conn.
Meeks, Heber J., 757 S. Russell, Monterey Park, Ill.
Meer, Samuel J., 631 Lafayette Ave., Mt. Vernon, N.Y.
Meese, Mrs. K., 3402 N. Meadowcraft Ave., Pittsburgh, Pa.
Megiveron, Gene Erwin, 3170 Angelus Dr., Pontiac, Mich.
Megonegal, E. Russell, 464 Granite Ter., Springfield, Pa.
Mehrens, William, Michigan State Univ., East Lansing, Mich.
Meier, Frederick A., State Col. at Salem, Salem, Mass.
Meier, Paralee B., Rt. 2, Box 467K, Chico, Calif.
Meier, Willard H., Dept. of Educ., La Sierra Col., Riverside, Calif.
Meinke, Dean L., Col. of Educ., University of Toledo, Toledo, Ohio
Melberg, Merritt E., 1222 W. 22nd St., Cedar Falls, Iowa
Melbo, Irving R., University of Southern California, Los Angeles, Calif.
Melby, Ernest O., Michigan State University, East Lansing, Mich.
Mellott, Malcolm E., Col. of Educ., Temple University, Philadelphia, Pa.
Mellott, Virginia T., 335 E. Granville Rd., Worthington, Ohio
Melnick, Curtis C., Supt., Dist. 14, Chicago Public Schls., Chicago, Ill.
Melnik, Amelia, Col. of Educ., University of Arizona, Tucson, Ariz.
Melton, Arthur W., Dept. of Psychol., Univ. of Michigan, Ann Arbor, Mich.
Melville, William G., Wisconsin State Univ., Platteville, Wis.
Melvin, Keith L., Peru State College, Peru, Nebr.
Mendel, Mrs. Dolores M., Paterson State College, Wayne, N.J.
• Mendoza, Romulo Y., 17 Iba, Sta. Mesa Heights, Quezon City, Philippines
Menge, Joseph W., Wayne University, Detroit, Mich.
Menosky, Dorothy, Wayne St. Univ., Detroit, Mich.
Merchant, Vasant V., 308 W. Forest Ave., Flagstaff, Ariz.
Meredith, Cameron W., Southern Illinois Univ., Edwardsville, Ill.
Merenda, Peter F., 258 Negansett Ave., Warwick, R.I.
Merideth, Howard V., Central Sch. Dist. No. 2, Syosset, L.I., N.Y.
Merigis, Harry, Eastern Illinois University, Charleston, Ill.
Merkhofer, Beatrice E., Chicago State College, Chicago, Ill.
Merryman, Edward P., Ball State Univ., Muncie, Ind.
Merryman, John E., Col. of Educ., Indiana University, Indiana, Pa.
Mersand, Joseph, Jamaica High Sch., 168th St. and Gothic Dr., Jamaica, N.Y.
Merwin, Jack C., Col. of Educ., Univ. of Minn., Minneapolis, Minn.
Mestdagh, William A., 1640 Vernier Rd., Grosse Pointe Woods, Mich.
Metcalfe, William W., 6816 Wooddale Ave., Edina, Minn.
Metfessel, Newton S., Univ. of Southern California, Los Angeles, Calif.
Meyer, Ammon B., Route 1, Fredericksburg, Pa.
Meyer, Lorraine V., 2940 N. 124th St., Apt. #4, Wauwatosa, Wis.
Meyer, Mrs. Marie, Douglass Col., Rutgers Univ., New Brunswick, N.J.
Meyer, Roy C., 2059 N. Hamline Ave., St. Paul, Minn.
Meyer, Warren G., 5829 Portland Ave., So., Minneapolis, Minn.
Meyer, William T., Adams State College, Alamosa, Colo.
Meyerhoff, Herman, 5400 E. Pomona Blvd., Los Angeles, Calif.
Meyers, Max B., 324 E. 59th St., Brooklyn, N.Y.
Meyers, Russell W., 5835 Kimbark Ave., Chicago, Ill.
Michael, Calvin B., Col. of Educ., East. Mich., Univ., Ypsilanti, Mich.
Michael, Lloyd S., Evanston Township High School, Evanston, Ill.
Michael, William B., Sch. of Educ., Univ. of So. California, Los Angeles, Calif.
Michaelis, John U., Sch. of Educ., Univ. of California, Berkeley, Calif.
Michaels, Melvin L., Teaneck H.S., Teaneck, N.J.
Micheels, William J., Stout State University, Menomonie, Wis.
Mickelsen, John K., 106 Jackson Dr., Liverpool, N.Y.
Mickelson, John M., Sch. of Educ., Temple University, Philadelphia, Pa.
Middledorf, Carl W., St. Peter's Lutheran School, East Detroit, Mich.
Middleton, Caryl A., State Col. of Iowa, Cedar Falls, Iowa

Midjaas, Carl L., 12408 Via Catherina, Grand Blanc, Mich.
Migdail, Sherry, 7301 Connecticut Ave., Chevy Chase, Md.
Milchus, Norman J., 20504 Williamsburg Rd., Dearborn Heights, Mich.
Miles, F. Mike, 424 Oakland Ave., Iowa City, Iowa
Miller, Allen R., South St., Springfield, S. Dak.
Miller, Arthur L., 5625 Rosa Ave., St. Louis, Mo.
Miller, Benjamin, 251 Ft. Washington Ave., New York, N.Y.
Miller, C. Earl, Jr., 157 Eldridge Ave., Mill Valley, Calif.
Miller, Carroll H., Dept. of Educ., Northern Illinois Univ., DeKalb, Ill.
Miller, Carroll L., Howard University, Washington, D.C.
Miller, Edward John, 621 E. Meda, Glendora, Calif.
Miller, Eliza Beth, Catskill High School, Catskill, N.Y.
Miller, Ethel B., 337 Kishwaukee Dr., Sycamore, Ill.
Miller, G. Dean, State Dept. of Educ., St. Paul, Minn.
Miller, G. Harold, 1600 N. Morris, Gastonia, N.C.
Miller, George E., Univ. of Illinois Col. of Medicine, Chicago, Ill.
Miller, George R., University of Pittsburgh, Pittsburgh, Pa.
Miller, Harold E., Eastern Mennonite Col., Harrisonburg, Va.
Miller, Henry, Sch. of Educ., City College of New York, New York, N.Y.
Miller, Herbert R., Univ. of Southern Calif., Los Angeles, Calif.
Miller, Holbert M., 1026 Washington St., Iowa City, Iowa
Miller, Howard G., North Carolina State College, Raleigh, N.C.
Miller, Ingrid O., Edina-Morningside Senior High School, Edina, Minn.
Miller, Ira E., Eastern Mennonite College, Harrisonburg, Va.
Miller, Jacob W., Brooke Rd., Savbrooke Park, Pottstown, Pa.
Miller, Jack W., Peabody Col., Nashville, Tenn.
Miller, Leon F., Northwest Missouri State College, Maryville, Mo.
Miller, Lyle L., Col. of Educ., University of Wyoming, Laramie, Wyo.
Miller, Mrs. Marian B., Dept. of Pub. Instr., Dover, Del.
Miller, N. A., Jr., Watauga High School, Boone, N.C.
Miller, Norman N., Superintendent of Schools, Tyrone, Pa.
Miller, Olimpia V., Fordham Univ., Redding, Conn.
Miller, Paul A., 1011 Granden Ridge Dr., Cincinnati, Ohio
Miller, Richard I., Baldwin Wallace Col., Berea, Ohio
Miller, Robert F., 7106 Farralone Ave., Canoga Park, Calif.
Miller, Ross, West Georgia College, Carrollton, Ga.
Miller, Texton R., North Carolina State University, Raleigh, N.C.
Milling, Euleas, 231 Spring St., N.W., Concord, N.C.
Mills, Boyd C., Eastern Washington State Col., Cheney, Wash.
Mills, Donna M., 530 Taft Place, Gary, Ind.
Mills, Editha B., Univ. of Georgia, Athens, Ga.
Mills, Forrest L., Racine Public Library, Racine, Wis.
Mills, Henry C., Provost, St. John's Univ., Jamaica, N.Y.
Mills, Patricia, Miami University, Oxford, Ohio
Mills, Ruth I., Concord College, Athens, W.Va.
Mills, William H., Sch. of Educ., Univ. of Michigan, Ann Arbor, Mich.
Milner, Ernest J., Sch. of Educ., Syracuse University, Syracuse, N.Y.
Millsop, Lillian A., 1324 Stanton St., Sharon, Pa.
Milstein, Mike, SUNY, Foster Hall, Buffalo, N.Y.
Mimaki, James M., 11224 Huston St., North Hollywood, Calif.
Mims, Samuel, Bethany Bible College, Santa Cruz, Calif.
Mincy, Homer F., 100 Wildwood Dr., Oak Ridge, Tenn.
Miniclier, Gordon E., 1965 Laurel Ave., St. Paul, Minn.
Mininberg, Elliot I., 7-13 Washington Square, New York, N.Y.
Minkoff, Sol., 601 N. Eastwood, Mt. Prospect, Ill.
Minnis, Roy B., 7889 E. Kenyon Ave., Denver, Colo.
Mirenda, Joseph J., 1627 N. Humboldt Ave., Milwaukee, Wis.
Mitby, Norman P., 211 N. Carroll St., Madison, Wis.
Mitchell, Addie S., Dept. of Eng., Morehouse College, Atlanta, Ga.
Mitchell, Donald P., 5166 Tilden St., N.W., Washington, D.C.

Mitchell, Guy Clifford, Sch. of Educ., Baylor University, Waco, Tex.
Mitchell, Virginia L., Indiana State Univ., Terre Haute, Ind.
Mitzel, Harold E., 928 S. Sparks St., State College, Pa.
Miyasato, Albert H., 297 Puiwa Rd., Honolulu, Hawaii
Moberly, William J., 5035 Garsden Ave., Charter Oak, Calif.
Moe, Alden J.. Univ. of Minnesota, Minneapolis, Minn.
Moffatt, Maurice P., 210 Valencia Blvd., Largo, Fla.
Mohr, Raymond E., 2050 S. 108th St., Milwaukee, Wis.
Molenkamp, Alice, 5 Homeside Lane, White Plains, N.Y.
Mollohan, Hugh, Crestline H.S., Crestline, Ohio
Molloy, Eugene J., Superintendent, Catholic Schools, Brooklyn, N.Y.
Monell, Ira H., 2714 Augusta Blvd., Chicago, Ill.
Monfort, Jay B., 20109 Chavoya Dr., Cupertino, Calif.
Monke, Mrs. Edgar W., High Point High School, Beltsville, Md.
Monnin, Lloyd N., 4733 W. National Rd., Springfield, Ohio
Monroe, Bruce Perry, 640 Sea Breeze Dr., Seal Beach, Calif.
Monroe, Mrs. Helen V., 1253 Lake Breeze, Oshkosh, Wis.
Montor, Karel, 732 Cottonwood Dr., Severna Park, Md.
Monts, Elizabeth A., Home Ec. Dept., Univ. of Wisconsin, Madison, Wis.
Moody, Lamar, 1100 Bridle Park Rd., Rt. 3, Box 303, Starkville, Miss.
Moore, Barry E., 103 William Dr., Normal, Ill.
Moore, Harold E., Col. of Educ., Arizona State University, Tempe, Ariz.
Moore, Robert Ezra, 20 Tapia Dr., San Francisco, Calif.
Moore, William J., 372 High St., Richmond, Ky.
Moorefield, Thomas E., Off. of Educ., 400 Maryland Ave., Washington, D.C.
Moorhead, Sylvester A., Sch. of Educ., Univ. of Mississippi, University, Miss.
Moran, Beatrice, 418 Tulip Tree, Bloomington, Ind.
Moray, Joseph, San Francisco State College, San Francisco, Calif.
Morden, Frederick P., 4708 Queensbury Rd., Riverdale, Md.
Morehouse, Charles O., 601 S. Howard St., Kimball, Nebr.
Moreland, Kenneth O., 107 William Dr., Normal, Ill.
Moretz, Elmo E., Grad. Sch. of Educ., Eastern Kentucky Univ., Richmond, Ky.
Morford, John A., John Carroll University, Cleveland, Ohio
Morgan, Donald L., 20 Graham Ave., Brookeville, Pa.
Morgan, Lorraine Lee, 6909 Meade St., Pittsburgh, Pa.
Morgan, Muriel, Newark State College, Union, N.J.
Morgan, Roland R., Superintendent, Mooresville City Schls., Mooresville, N.C.
Morgenstern, Anne, 2037 Oliver Way, Merrick, L.I., N.Y.
Moriarty, Thomas E., 1100 Crestview Dr., Vermillion, So. Dak.
Moriconi, R. J., 1121 Lavendar Lane, Modesto, Calif.
Morley, Franklin P., 101 Arthur Ave., Webster Groves, Mo.
Morris, Carl E., The Western Col., Oxford, Ohio
Morris, Earl W., Rt. 5, East Lake Drive, Edwardsville, Ill.
Morris, George L., 1245 S. 40th St., Lincoln, Neb.
Morris, Gregory A., 811 Maple St., West Mifflin, Pa.
Morris, James L., 675 Omar Circle, Yellow Springs, Ohio
Morris, James Vaughn, 603 E. Matson Run Pky., Wilmington, Del.
Morris, Rev. John E., Diocesan Schls., Paterson, N.J.
Morris, M. B., 1133 Westridge, Abilene, Tex.
Morris, Mrs. Marjorie S., 16225 Moorpark, Encino, Calif.
Morris, William Alfred, Eastern Kentucky Univ., Richmond, Ky.
Morris, William P., 6445 Lake Mere Ct., San Diego, Calif.
Morrison, D. A., East York Bd. of Educ., Toronto, Ont., Canada
* Morrison, J. Cayce, 580 North Bank Ln., Lake Forest, Ill.
Morrison, Leger R., 16 Brown St., Warren, R.I.
Morrissey, Madeline M., 65 Court St., Brooklyn, N.Y.
Morrow, Richard G., 502 State St., Madison, Wis.
Morrow, Robert O., Dept. of Psych., State College of Ark., Conway, Ark.
Morrow, Howard 8501 S. Victoria, Oklahoma City, Okla.
Morse, Richard N., 2690 Warden St., San Diego, Calif.

Morse, William C., 2010 Penncraft Ct., Ann Arbor, Mich.
Morton, R. Clark, 210 Drummond St., Warrensburg, Mo.
Mosbo, Alvin O., Univ. of Northern Colorado, Greeley, Colo.
Moser, Robert P., 316 Master Hall, Univ. of Wis., Madison, Wis.
Moser, William G., 95 Concord Rd., Chester, Pa.
Moses, Mrs. Ida O., 2431 Aubry St., New Orleans, La.
Moses, Elizabeth, 7483 Countrybrook Dr., Indianapolis, Ind.
Mosher, Frank Kenneth, Sadaquada Apt., Whitesboro, N.Y.
Moss, Theodore C., 88 Sixth Ave., Oswego, N.Y.
Mother C. Welch, San Francisco College for Women, San Francisco, Calif.
Mother Margaret Burke, Barat Col. of the Sacred Heart, Lake Forest, Ill.
Mother Mary Aimee Rossi, San Diego Col. for Women, San Diego, Calif.
Mother Mary Dennis, Rosemont College, Rosemont, Pa.
Mother Rose Alice, 2675 Larpenteur Ave. East, St. Paul, Minn.
Motyka, Agnes L., 6311 Utah Ave., N.W., Washington, D.C.
Muck, Mrs. Ruth E. S., 1091 Stony Point Rd., Grand Island, N.Y.
Muck, Webster C., Bethel Col., St. Paul, Minn.
Muckenhirn, Erma F., Dept. of Educ., East. Mich. Univ., Ypsilanti, Mich.
Muellen, T. K., 3606 Spruell Dr., Silver Spring, Md.
Mueller, Richard J., Northern Illinois University, DeKalb, Ill.
Mueller, Siegfried G., 5429 Sawyer, Chicago, Ill.
Mueller, Van D., Col. of Educ., Univ. of Minn., Minneapolis, Minn.
Muldoon, Kathleen, Indiana Univ., Bloomington, Ind.
Mullen, Norman, Superintendent of Schools, Woodsville, N.H.
Muller, Philippe H., University of Neuchatel, Neuchatel, Switzerland
Mulligan, Joseph P., 320 Cooper, Piscataway, N.J.
Mulliner, John H., 645 Abbotsford Rd., Kenilworth, Ill.
Mullins, John W., Super. of Schs., Newport, Ark.
Mullins, Robert A., RFD 2, South Side, Rt. 23, Onenta, N.Y.
Mumford, Kennedy A., 14845 Robinson St., Miami, Fla.
Muns, Arthur C., Northern Illinois Univ., DeKalb, Ill.
Munshaw, Carroll, 555 Byron St., Plymouth, Mich.
Murdick, Olin J., Superintendent, Diocesan Schools, Saginaw, Mich.
Murdock, Mrs. Ruth, Andrews University, Berrien Springs, Mich.
Murfin, Don L., Prin., South H.S., Bakersfield, Calif.
Murphy, Anne P., 480 S. Jersey St., Denver, Colo.
Murphy, Daniel A., Seton Hall University, South Orange, N.J.
Murphy, Dennis, St. Mary's Col., Winona, Minn.
Murphy, Forrest W., 201 S. Hickory St., Aberdeen, Miss.
Murphy, John E., Clifton H. S., 333 Colfax Ave., Clifton, N.J.
Murphy, Kenneth B., Jersey City State Col., Jersey City, N.J.
Murphy, Loretta M., 415 Larkin Ave., Joliet, Ill.
Murphy, William F., 37 High St., Milford, Mass.
Murray, Joseph A., Jr., Cranston School Dept., Cranston, R.I.
Musgrave, Ray S., Univ. of Southern Mississippi, Hattiesburg, Miss.
Musick, James E., Dist. Off. of Educ., Saipan, Marina Is.
Muston, Ray Allen, Univ. of Iowa, Iowa City, Iowa
Myer, Marshall E., Col. of Educ., Univ. of Tenn., Knoxville, Tenn.
Myers, Allen D., Eastern Michigan Univ., Ypsilanti, Mich.
Myers, Donald A., 1100 Glendon Ave., Los Angeles, Calif.
Myers, Donald W., State Univ. Coll., Brockport, N.Y.
Myers, Garry C., Ed., *Highlights for Children*, Honesdale, Pa.

Nacke, Phil L., 16 Providence St., New Providence, N.J.
Nadler, Leonard, George Washington Univ., Washington, D.C.
Nafziger, Mary K., Goshen College, Goshen, Ind.
Nagel, Wilma I., Dept. of Educ., Univ. of Rhode Island, Kingston, R.I.
Nagy, Richard, North Junior High School, Bloomfield, N.J.
Nahshon, Samuel, Hebrew Teachers College, Brookline, Mass.
Nairus, John P., Cleveland Public Schools, Cleveland, Ohio

Nakamura, Richard J., 530 W. Malibu Dr., Tempe, Ariz.
Nakashima, Mitsugi, P.O. Box 155, Kaumakani, Kanai, Hawaii
Nally, Thomas P., University of Rhode Island, Kingston, R.I.
Nance, Mrs. Afton D., 3416 Land Pk. Dr., Sacramento, Calif.
Narkis, William F., 1046 S. 22nd Ave., Bellwood, Ill.
Nash, Philip C., 3336 Sycamore Pl., Carmel, Calif.
Naslund, Robert A., Sch. of Educ., Univ. of So. California, Los Angeles, Calif.
Nason, Doris E., University of Connecticut, Storrs, Conn.
Nasser, Sheffield T., 6801 Pennywell Dr., Nashville, Tenn.
Nattress, LeRoy W., 430 N. Mich. Ave., Chicago, Ill.
Nault, William H., Field Enterprises Educational Corp., Chicago, Ill.
Naus, Grant H., 374 "D" Ave., Coronado, Calif.
Naylor, Marilyn, 233 W. Cascade, River Falls, Wis.
Neale, Daniel C., Col. of Educ., University of Minnesota, Minneapolis, Minn.
Nearhoff, Orrin, 2745 Bennett Ave., Des Moines, Iowa
Nearing, Mrs. Jewell, 9050 S. Parnell, Chicago, Ill.
Nebel, Dale, Univ. of Northern Colorado, Greeley, Colo.
Nelson, Avis, 4618 Russell Ave., No. Minneapolis, Minn.
Nelson, Carl B., New York State University College, Cortland, N.Y.
Nelson, Clifford L., Univ. of Maryland, College Park, Md.
Nelson, Edith I., 380 Claremont Ave., Montclair, N.J.
Nelson, Florence A., Univ. of South Carolina, 825 Sumter St., Columbia, S.C.
Nelson, Jack L., State Univ. Col., Buffalo, N.Y.
Nelson, Janice Ann, 8350 Olentangy River Rd., Worthington, Ohio
Nelson, John M., Dept. of Educ., Purdue University, Lafayette, Ind.
Nelson, Kenneth G., Shore Acres, Dunkirk, N.Y.
Nelson, Lois Ney, 7 Lakeview Dr., Daly City, Calif.
Nelson, Orville W., Stout State College, Menomonie, Wis.
Nelson Owen N., 1806 Adams St., La Crosse, Wis.
Nelson, Quentin D., 5050 N. Mozart St., Chicago, Ill.
Nelson, Sylvia, 415 W. 8th St., Topeka, Kans.
Nelson, Torlef, University of Hawaii, Honolulu, Hawaii
Nelum, J. Nathaniel, Div. of Educ., Bishop College, Dallas, Tex.
Nemzek, Claude L., Educ. Dept., Univ. of Detroit, Detroit, Mich.
Nesbitt, William O., University of Houston, Houston, Tex.
Nesi. Carmella, 906 Peace St., Pelham Manor, N.Y.
Neufeld, Evelyn M., 708 Brentwood Dr., San Jose, Calif.
Neuman, Donald B., Univ. of Wis. Milwaukee, Milwaukee, Wis.
Neuner, Elsie Flint, 2 Atlas Place, Mt. Vernon, N.Y.
Nevala, Leo R., 6901 N. Ironwood Ln., Milwaukee, Wis.
Neville, Richard F., Col. of Educ., University of Maryland, College Park, Md.
Nevin, Mrs. Virginia L., 418 Franklin St., Fayetteville, N.Y.
Newark, Eleanor, 1408 Terrace Blvd., New Hyde Park, N.Y.
Newburn, H. K., Col. of Educ., Arizona State University, Tempe, Ariz.
Newbury, David N., Curric Cood., H.P. Sch. Dist., Hazel Park, Mich.
Newcomer, Charles A., Lock Haven State Col., Lock Haven, Pa.
Newman, Herbert M., Educ. Dept., Brooklyn College, Brooklyn, N.Y.
Newman, Wilfred, West High School, Rochester, N.Y.
Newsom, Herman A., P.O. Box 5243, North Texas Station, Denton, Tex.
Newton, Kathryn L., 42 13th Ave., Columbus, Ohio
Newton, W. L., Florida State University, Tallahassee, Fla.
Nicely, Robert F., 137 Autumn Dr., Trafford, Pa.
Nicholas, William T., 2205 Monte Vista Ave., Modesto, Calif.
Nichols, David L., University of Maine, Orono, Me.
Nichols, Edith J., 2655 Littleton Rd., El Cajon, Calif.
Nichols, Lyle A., Newport Senior H.S., Bellevue, Wash.
Nichols, Richard J., 1209 Maple Hill Rd., Scotch Plains, N.J.
Nicholson, Jon M., 312 Nevada, Northfield, Minn.
Nicholson, Lawrence E., Psych. Dept., Harris Tchrs. Col., St. Louis, Mo.
Nicholson, Robert A., Anderson Col., Anderson, Ind.

Nicholson, Sarah Alice, 1009 E. Hatton St., Pensacola, Fla.
Nicklas, Martin, Jefferson Jr. H. S., Pittsburgh, Pa.
Nicolari, Richard F., Willis Schl., Ansonia, Conn.
Nicoletti, Donald, 200 Thurber St., Syracuse, N.Y.
Niehaus, Philip C., Sch. of Educ., Duquesne University, Pittsburgh, Pa.
Nielsen, Jack, Col. of Educ., Univ. of Iowa, Iowa City, Iowa
Niemeyer, John H., Bank Street College of Education, New York, N.Y.
Niland, William P., 417 Candleberry Rd., Walnut Creek, Calif.
Nixon, Clifford L., 756 Westmont Rd., Santa Barbara, Calif.
Nixon, John Erskine, Sch. of Educ., Stanford University, Stanford, Calif.
Noar, Gertrude, 500 E. 77th St., New York, N.Y.
Nolde, Randall L., 312 E. Main, Barrington, Ill.
Noll, Frances E., 1810 Taylor St., N.W., Washington, D.C.
Noll, Victor H., Col. of Educ., Michigan State Univ., East Lansing, Mich.
Noon, Elizabeth F., F. A. Owen Publishing Co., Dansville, N.Y.
Norcross, Claude E., 2120 W. Newman Pkwy., Peoria, Ill.
Norman, Ralph Paul, 18395 Clemison Ave., Saratoga, Calif.
Norman, Robert H., 315—4th Ave., N.W., Faribault, Minn.
Norris, Mrs. Dorothy G., 1907 Dumaine St., New Orleans, La.
Norris, Ralph C., 112-116—11th St., Des Moines, Iowa
North, Stewart D., Univ. of Houston, Houston, Tex.
Northey, Ethel M., 1309 Orange St., Muscatine, Iowa
Northrup, Sunbeam Ann, 1816 Queens Lane, Arlington, Va.
Norton, Chauncey E., 31 Decker Rd., R.D. 1, Newfield, N.J.
Norton, Frank Edgar, Jr., 225 Fairway Dr., Wharton, Tex.
Norton, Robert E., Univ. of Arkansas, Fayetteville, Ark.
Nothem, Al H., St. Bonaventure Univ., St. Bonaventure, N.Y.
Novak, Benjamin J., Frankford High School, Philadelphia, Pa.
Novotney, Jerrold M., 18282 Yellow Wood, Irvine, Calif.
Now, Herbert O., State Dept. of Educ., Findlay, Ohio
Nutter, H. E., Norman Hall, University of Florida, Gainesville, Fla.
•Nutterville, Catherine, 1101 Third St., S.W., Washington, D.C.
Nutting, William C., 4653 Fortuna Way, Salt Lake City, Utah
Nuzum, Lawrence H., Marshall University, Huntington, W.Va.
Nye, Robert E., Sch. of Music, University of Oregon, Eugene, Oreg.
Nygaard, Joseph M., Butler University, Indianapolis, Ind.
Nystrand, Raphael O., Ohio State Univ., Columbus, Ohio

Oakland, Thomas D., 2702 Greenlawn Pkwy., Austin, Tex.
Oaks, Ruth E., B-104 Haverford Villa, Haverford, Pa.
Oberholtzer, Kenneth E., 752 El Cerro Blvd., Danville, Calif.
Obourn, L. C., Superintendent of Schools, East Rochester, N.Y.
O'Brien, Cyril C., P.O. Box 666, Edmonton, Alba., Canada
Ochitwa, Orest P., 408 Campus View House, Bloomington, Ind.
O'Connor, John D., Maple Park, Ill.
O'Connor, Mrs. Marguerite O., Maple Park, Ill.
O'Donnell, Lewis B., State University of New York, Oswego, N.Y.
Oehring, Esther A., Southern Oregon College, Ashland, Oreg.
Oen, Urban T., 1948 Marlboro Lane, Joliet, Ill.
O'Fallon, O. K., Sch. of Educ., Kansas State University, Manhattan, Kans.
O'Farrell, John J., Loyola University, 7101 W. 80th St., Los Angeles, Calif.
O'Hare, Mary Rita, 212 Hollywood Ave., Tuckahoe, N.Y.
O'Hearn, George T., 202 Warren Ct., Green Bay, Wis.
Ohlsen, Merle M., Indiana State Univ., Terre Haute, Ind.
Ohs, Phyllis D., 727 Crestline, Kamloops, B. C., Canada
• Ojeman, Ralph H., Educ. Research Council, Rockefeller Bldg., Cleveland, Ohio
O'Kane, Robert M., 306 Nut Bush Circle, Jamestown, N.C.
O'Keefe, Kathleen, 4615 Langdrum Ln., Chevy Chase, Md.
Okula, Frederick S., 90 Mattatuck Rd., Bristol, Conn.

*Oldham, Mrs. Birdie V., 621 W. 2nd St., Lakeland, Fla.
Oldman, Kenneth R., Case West. Reserve Univ., Chagrin Falls, Ohio
O'Leary, Francis V., 5480 S. Cornell Ave., Chicago, Ill.
Olicker, Isidore I., 85-17—143rd St., Jamaica, N.Y.
Olivas, Romeo A., 412 Brookview Ct., Oxford, Ohio
Oliver, Tommy, Willard School, Ada, Okla.
Ollenburger, Alvin, 2613 Jean Duluth Rd., Duluth, Minn.
Olmsted, M. D., State University College, Oneonta, N.Y.
Olphert, Warwick B., Univ. of New England, Armidale, N.S.W., Australia
Olsen, Clarence R., The Univ. of Conn., Storrs, Conn.
Olsen, David E., 7866 Mulberry Rd., Chesterland, Ohio
Olsen, Eugene A., Univ. of Hartford, West Hartford, Conn.
Olsen, Hans C., Jr., University of Missouri, St. Louis, Mo.
Olson, Boyd E., P.O. Box 226, Singapore, Rep. of Singapore
Olson, David R., OISE, 252 Bloor St., Toronto, Ontario, Can.
Olson, Gerald Victor, 8610 W. 19th St., Phoenix, Ariz.
Olson, George H., Florida State Univ., Tallahassee, Fla.
Olson, LeRoy C., 329 Nichols Ave., McDaniels Crest, Wilmington, Del.
Olson, Manley E., Col. of Educ., Univ. of Minnesota, Minneapolis, Minn.
Olson, R. A., Ball State University, Muncie, Ind.
Olson, Richard F., Vice-pres., Xicom, Inc., R.F.D. 1, Tuxedo, N.Y.
*Olson, Willard C., Sch. of Educ., University of Michigan, Ann Arbor, Mich.
Olson, William L., 1945 Sharondale Ave., St. Paul, Minn.
O'Malley, Mrs. Martha R., 44 Glenview Dr., Belleville, Ill.
O'Mara, J. Francis, 29 Snowling Rd., Uxbridge, Mass.
O'Neill, John H., 1039 W. Vine St., Springfield, Ill.
O'Neill, John J., Boston State College, Boston, Mass.
O'Neill, Patrick J., Superintendent, Diocesan Schools, Fall River, Mass.
O'Piela, Joan M., Res. & Dev., Detroit Pub. Schools, Detroit, Mich.
Oppenheimer, E. H., 3760 N. Pine Grove, Chicago, Ill.
Oppleman, Dan L., Box 8208 Univ. Station, Reno, Nevada
Ore, Malvern L., 9331 Ridgeland, Chicago, Ill.
Ore, Stanley H., Jr., 2221 Emmers Dr., Appleton, Wis.
O'Reilly, Robert C., University of Nebraska at Omaha, Omaha, Nebr.
Orlovich, Joseph, 206 Reed St., Joliet, Ill.
Orr, Charles W., 137 Oakmont Circle, Durham, N.C.
Orr, Louise, 925 Crockett St., Amarillo, Tex.
Orton, Don A., Lesley College, Cambridge, Mass.
Orton, Kenneth D., Tchrs, Col., University of Nebraska, Lincoln, Nebr.
Osborn, Wayland W., 2701 Hickman Rd., Des Moines, Iowa
Osibov, Henry, University of Oregon, Eugene, Oreg.
Ostler, Ruth-Ellen, 115 A Wellington, Albany, N.Y.
Ostwalt, Jay H., P.O. Box 387, Davidson, N.C.
Osuch, A. E., 6636 N. Odell, Chicago, Ill.
Oswalt, William W., Jr., 9 Berger St., Emmaus, Pa.
Otomo, Aiko, 780 Amana St., Honolulu, Hawaii
O'Toole, James J., Cleveland Hghts. High Schl., Cleveland Heights, Ohio
O'Toole, Jeanne M., 9636 Oakley Ave., Chicago, Ill.
Ott, Elizabeth, 4615 Laurel Canyon Dr., Austin, Tex.
Otto, Henry J., University of Texas, Austin, Tex.
Otts, John, University of South Carolina, Columbia, S.C.
Overfield, Ruth, State Educ. Bldg., 721 Capitol Ave., Sacramento, Calif.
*Overstreet, George Thomas, 811 S. Frances St., Terrell, Tex.
Oxman, Mrs. Wendy, Fordham Univ., Sch. of Educ., Englewood, N.J.
Owings, Ralph S., Univ. of Southern Mississippi, Hattiesburg, Miss.

Pace, C. Robert, Sch. of Educ., University of California, Los Angeles, Calif.
Pacheco, Angel M., 420 Sand Creek Rd., Albany, N.Y.
Pacheco, Edmundo, Calle Simon Planas, Caracas, Venezuela, S.A.
Padgett, Robert L., 614 Plum St., Vienna, Va.

Page, Ellis B., Bur. of Educ. Res., Univ. of Connecticut, Storrs, Conn.
Pagel, Betty Lou, 304 E. 5th Ave., Cheyenne, Wyo.
Palisi, Anthony T., 25 Crescent, Maplewood, N.J.
Palisi, Marino A., 300 Woodland Ave., Point Pleasant Beach, N.J.
Palladino, Joseph R., State College, Framingham, Mass.
Pallesen, Lorraine Sysel, 2727 Royal Ct., Lincoln, Nebr.
Palliser, Guy C., P.O. Box 30-632, Lower Hutt, New Zealand
Palmatier, Robert A., Jr., Col. of Educ., U. of Georgia, Athens, Ga.
Palmer, Albert, San Joaquin Delta College, Stockton, Calif.
Palmer, Anne M. H., 22277 Cass Ave., Woodland Hills, Calif.
Palmer, Dale H., Univ. of Washington, Seattle, Wash.
Palmer, J. Denton, 33961 Clark Lane, Yucaipa, Calif.
Palmer, John C., Tufts University, Medford, Mass.
Paltridge, James G., 2651 Cactus Ave., Santa Rosa, Calif.
Panas, Michael C., 4825 Kentfield 200, Stockton, Calif.
Panos, Robert J., 900 W. Minnehaha Pkwy., Minneapolis, Minn.
Papanek, Ernst, 1 West 64th St., New York, N.Y.
Papke, Ross R., Wisconsin State Univ., Richland Center, Wis.
Paradis, Edward E., Univ. of Minn., Minneapolis, Minn.
Pardini, Aldo, Burlingame H.S., Burlingame, Calif.
Parelius, Allen M., St. Louis University, St. Louis, Mo.
Paris, John A., 75 Pueblo Circle, Henrietta, N.Y.
Parisho, Eugenia B., Lab. School, Univ. of North. Iowa, Cedar Falls, Iowa
Park, Mary Frances, Educ. Dept., Sam Houston State Col., Huntsville, Tex.
Park, Maxwell G., 3 Susan Lane, Lexington Pk., Md.
Parker, Don H., Emlimar, Big Sur, Calif.
Parker, Emma W., Cath. Univ. of Amer., Washington, D.C.
Parker, Jack F., University of Oklahoma, Norman, Okla.
Parker, James R., 210 Thornbrook Rd., DeKalb, Ill.
Parker, Jesse J., Louisiana State University, Baton Rouge, La.
Parker, Mrs. Lilla C., Box 464-A, Donnan Road, Macon, Ga.
Parker, Richard H., 7964 Middlesex Rd., Mentor, Ohio
Parker, Samuel D., St. Bernard Col., St. Bernard, Ala.
Parker, Virjean, W. Va. Univ., Morgantown, W. Va.
Parkinson, Daniel S., 409 W. Vine St., Oxford, Ohio
Parr, Kenneth Earl, East Burke, Vt.
Parrett, Betty J., 3024 South Shore Dr., Albany, Oreg.
Parry, O. Meredith, 329 S. Lindbergh Ave., York, Pa.
Parsey, John M., 305 Droste Circle, East Lansing, Mich.
Parsley, Kenneth M., 214 St. Ives Dr., Severna Park, Md.
Parsons, Brooks A., Superintendent of Schools, Norwood, Ohio
Parsons, David R., Wollongong Tchr. Col., Wollongong, NSW, Australia
Parsons, James C., Alaska Methodist Univ., Anchorage, Alaska
Pascoe, David D., LaMesa Spring Valley Sch. Dist., LaMesa, Calif.
Passalacqua, Benedict J., 21030 Beaconsfield, St. Clair, Mich.
Passow, Aaron Harry, Teachers College, Columbia University, New York, N.Y.
Paster, Julius, 867 Barbara Dr., Teaneck, N.J.
Patch, Robert B., 4 Carleton Dr., Glens Falls, N.Y.
Pate, Mildred, 1806 East 6th St., Greenville, N.C.
Paterson, John J., 377 Lawnview Dr., Morgantown, W.Va.
Paton, William, Superintendent of Schools, Oconomowoc, Wis.
Patrick, Edward M., 1040 N. Pleasant St., Amherst, Mass.
Patrick, Robert B., R.D., Petersburg, Pa. 16665
Patrick, T. L., Tulane Univ., New Orleans, La.
Patten, W. George, 2250 W. Roosevelt Blvd., Milwaukee, Wis.
Patterson, Gordon E., New Mexico Highlands Univ., Las Vegas, N.Mex.
Patterson, Harold D., 3736 Crestbrook Rd., Birmingham, Ala.
Patton, Earl D., Superintendent of Schools, Culver City, Calif.
Patton, Violet S., 6306 Regal Rd., Louisville, Ky.
Patty, Delbert L., 1412B Anthony St., Columbia, Mo.

Paul, Marvin S., 4750 W. Glenlake Ave., Chicago, Ill.
Paul, Warren I., 3424 Dickens Ave., Manhattan, Kans.
Paulson, Casper F., Jr., Oregon College of Education, Monmouth, Oreg.
Pautz, Wilmer A., Wisconsin State University, Eau Claire, Wis.
Pavan, Barbara, 6 Wessex Rd., Newton Centre, Mass.
Paxson, Robert C., Troy State College, Troy, Ala.
Paxton, Mrs. J. Hall, 1405 Pine St., Apt. 606, St. Louis, Mo.
Payne, David L., 131 Juanita St., Columbus, Miss.
Payne, LaVeta M., P.O. Box 591, Pierson and Suhrie Dr., Collegedale, Tenn.
Payne, William V., Virginia St. Col., Petersburg, Va.
Paynovich, Nicholas, 932 E. 7th St., Tucson, Ariz.
Payzant, Thomas W., 30 Glenn Circle, Philadelphia, Pa.
Paziotopoulos, James A., 9345 S. Crawford Ave., Evergreen Pk., Ill.
Pearson, Frank, Miles Col., Birmingham, Ala.
Pearson, Guelda, 8907 Lemont Rd., Downers Grove, Ill.
Pearson, James R., Dade Co. Public Schools, Miami, Fla.
Pearson, Lois, State University College, Buffalo, N.Y.
Peccolo, Charles M., 2840 Nevada St., Manhattan, Kans.
Peck, Austin, State Univ. Col., Potsdam, N.Y.
Peckenpaugh, Donald H., 6 So. 36th Ave. East, Duluth, Minn.
Peddicord, Paul W., Univ. of Southern Miss., Hattiesburg, Miss.
Pederson, Arne K., Pacific Lutheran University, Tacoma, Wash.
Pederson, Clara A., Dept. of Educ., Univ. of North Dakota, Grand Forks, N.Dak.
Peirce, Leonard D., Olympia Public Schools, Olympia, Wash.
Pell, Sarah W., Kodiak Comm. Col., Naval Base, Kodiak, Alaska
Pella, Milton O., Wisconsin High School, Univ. of Wisconsin, Madison, Wis.
Pellegrin, Lionel, 945 E. River Oaks Dr., Baton Rouge, La.
Pellett, Vernon L., Texas A & M Univ., College Station, Tex.
Pelton, Frank M., Dept. of Educ., Univ. of Rhode Island, Kingston, R.I.
Peltz, Seamen, 6650 S. Ellis Ave., Chicago, Ill.
Pendarvis, S. T., McNeese State College, Lake Charles, La.
Penn, Floy L., 2675 Strathmore Lane, Bethel Park, Pa.
Penniman, Blanche L., Bergenfield High School, Bergenfield, N.J.
Pentecost, Percy M., 540 Coconut St., Satellite Beach, Fla.
Perdew, Philip W., Sch. of Educ., University of Denver, Denver, Colo.
Perez-Febles, Kathleen, 536 N. Brandywine, Schenectady, N.Y.
Perkins, Frederick D., Alto High School, Alto, La.
Perry, Clarence R., Shady Lane, Dover, Mass.
Perry, Harold J., 1040 Park Ave., West Highland Park, Ill.
Perry, James Olden, 3602 S. MacGregor Way, Houston, Tex.
Perry, T. Edward, Chagrin River Rd., Gates Mills, Ohio
Perryman, Lucile C., 330 Third Ave., New York, N.Y.
Persing, Thomas E., Wyomissing Area Schls., Wyomissing, Pa.
Pescosolido, John R., Central Connecticut State College, New Britain, Conn.
Peters, Donald L., Pennsylvania St. Univ., University Park, Pa.
Peters, Jon S., 41705 Covington, Fremont, Calif.
Petersen, Anne C., 5748 S. Blackstone, Chicago, Ill.
Petersen, Clarence E., 7500 Hudson St., Redwood City, Calif.
Petersen, Dorothy G., Trenton State College, Trenton, N.J.
Petersen, Dwain F., 108 E. Glencrest Dr., Mankato, Minn.
Peterson, Barbara A., 38 Crest Road West, Rolling Hills, Calif.
Peterson, Bernadine H., University of Wisconsin, Madison, Wis.
Peterson, Donald W., 4708—25th Ave., Rock Island, Ill.
Peterson, Donovan, Amer. Embassy, Tegucigueka, Honduras, Central Amer.
Peterson, Douglas W., 1402 Henry St., Ann Arbor, Mich.
Peterson, J. Vincent, 2910 S. Woodmont, South Bend, Ind.
Peterson, Mrs. Leona, 341 Poplar Ave., Elmhurst, Ill.
Peterson, Miriam E., 5422 Wayne Ave., Chicago, Ill.
Pethick, Wayne M., 6136 Northwest Hwy., Chicago, Ill.
Petor, Andrew P., 728 Hulton Rd., Oakmont, Pa.

Petrequin, Gaynor, 3905 S.E. 91st Ave., Portland, Oreg.
Pett, Dennis W., 4228 Saratoga Drive, Bloomington, Ind.
Pettersch, Carl A., 200 Southern Blvd., Danbury, Conn.
Pettiss, J. O., Dept. of Educ., Louisiana State University, Baton Rouge, La.
Petty, Mary Clare, Col. of Educ., University of Oklahoma, Norman, Okla.
Petty, Michael A., Palpa 2440/Capital Federal, Argentina
Petty, Olan L., Box 6906, Col. Sta., Duke University, Durham, N.C.
Petty, Walter T., Sch. of Educ., State Univ. of New York, Buffalo, N.Y.
Pewitt, Edith M., North Texas State Univ., Denton, Tex.
Pezzoli, Jean A., 1139 9th Ave., Honolulu, Hawaii
Pezzullo, Thomas J., 268 Greenville Ave., Johnston, R.I.
Pfeifer, Michael F. CM, 2233 N. Kenmore, Chicago, Ill.
Pfost, H. Philip, Univ. of South Florida, Tampa, Fla.
Phay, John E., Bur. of Educ. Res., University of Mississippi, University, Miss.
Phelan, William F., 201 Sunrise Hwy., Patchogue, N.Y.
Phelps, H. Vaughn, 8727 Shamrock Rd., Omaha, Nebr.
Phelps, Harold R., Illinois State University, Normal, Ill.
Phelps, Roger P., 718 Barnes Ave., Baldwin, L.I., N.Y.
Phelts, Alejandro, Tehuantepac 247, Mexico D.F., Mexico
Phillips, Cecil K., University of Northern Iowa, Cedar Falls, Iowa
Phillips, Don O., 1158 S. Harris Ave., Columbus, Ohio
Phillips, James A., Jr., Col. of Educ., Kent State University, Kent, Ohio
Phillips, James E., 1446 E. Maryland Ave., St. Paul, Minn.
Phillips, Paul, Supt. of Schools, 520 W. Palmer St., Morrisville, Pa.
Phillips, Richard C., Univ. of North Carolina, Chapel Hill, N.C.
Phillips, Thomas Arthur, 1536 S. Sixth St., Terre Haute, Ind.
Philp, William A., 440 Williams Ave., Natchitoches, La.
Phleger, John V., Superintendent of Schools, Geneseo, Ill.
Phoenix, William D., 8561 Holmes Rd., Kansas City, Mo.
Piche, Gene L., Univ. of Minnesota, Minneapolis, Minn.
Pickett, Paul C., Upper Iowa University, Fayette, Iowa
Pickett, Vernon R., 2411 Brookland Ave., N.E., Cedar Rapids, Iowa
Pickrel, Glenn E., Supt. of Schools, Dists. 58 and 99, Downers Grove, Ill.
Pierce, Arthur N., Supt. of Schools, Hanover, N.H.
Pierce, Raymond K., Rt. 463 & Vine St., Lansdale, Pa.
Pierce, Truman M., Sch. of Educ., Auburn University, Auburn, Ala.
Pierce, Walter D., Illinois State Univ., Normal, Ill.
Pierleoni, Robert G., 21 Nova Ln., Rochester, N.Y.
Piggush, Kenneth J., 324 Sauganash, Park Forest, Ill.
Pike, Earl O., Jr., 2194 16th Ave. W., Eugene, Oreg.
Pikunas, Justin, Psych. Dept., University of Detroit, Detroit, Mich.
Piland, Joseph C., Bronk Road, Plainfield, Ill.
Pinkham, Mrs. Rossalie G., Southern Connecticut State College, New Haven, Conn.
Pins, Arnulf M., 345 E. 46th St., New York, N.Y.
Pirtle, Ivyl, Palm Beach Curric. Lab., West Palm Beach, Fla.
Pitman, John C., 3501 Manford Dr., Durham, N.C.
Pittman, Dewitt Kennieth, 6700 Monroe Rd., Charlotte, N.C.
Piucci, Virginio, Rhode Island Col., Providence, R.I.
Platt, William J., 4 Ave. du Pres. Kennedy, Paris, France
Pletcher, James D., 1 Brookview Dr., Plattsburgh, N.Y.
Pletcher, Paul R., Jr., 3001 Floravista Ct., Riverside, Calif.
Plimpton, Blair, Superintendent of Schools, 400 S. Western Ave., Park Ridge, Ill.
Pliska, Stanley Robert, 1041 S. Lexan Cr., Norfolk, Va.
Plumb, Valworth R., University of Minnesota, Duluth Branch, Duluth, Minn.
Plunkett, Irma M., 612 Ridge Rd., Cedar Grove, N.J.
Poche, Margaret Una, 3861 Virgil Blvd., New Orleans, La.
Pocket, Delmar B., 738 Cherokee Court, Murfeesboro, Tenn.
Poehler, W. A., Concordia College, St. Paul, Minn.
Pogue, E. Graham, Ball State University, Muncie, Ind.
Pohek, Marguerite V., 13 Coolidge Ave., Glen Head, N.Y.

Pohlmann, Neil A., Bowling Green State University, Bowling Green, Ohio
Poindexter, Robert C., 9740 S. 50th Ct., Oaklawn, Ill.
Pole, E. John, Ball State University, Muncie, Ind.
Polglase, Robert J., 5 Upper Warren Way, Warren, N.J.
Pollach, Samuel, California State College, Long Beach, Calif.
Pollack, Allan, 3534 Thurmond St., Columbia, S. C.
Pollard, William, Jr., P.O. Box 407, Mill Shoals, Ill.
Pollert, Irene E., 700 N. Alabama, Indianapolis, Ind.
Polley, Warren P., 1133 S. Main St., Antioch, Ill.
Pollock, Marion B., Calif. State Col. L.B., So. Pasadena, Calif.
Polmantier, Paul C., University of Missouri, Columbia, Mo.
Pond, Millard Z., Superintendent of Schools, Dist. No. 4, Eugene, Oreg.
Pool, Harbison, Oberlin Col., Oberlin, Ohio
Poole, Albert E., 214 N. Washington Cir., Lake Forest, Ill.
Pope, Allen, 1407 Missoula Ave., Helena, Mont.
Pope, Madaline, Rt. 3, Box 544, Courtland, Ohio
Popper, Samuel H., Burton Hall, University of Minnesota, Minneapolis, Minn.
Portee, Richard C., 2941 Michigan, Chicago, Ill.
Porter, Donald A., Douglas Regional Col., New Westminster, B.C., Can.
Porter, E. Jane, Univ. of Delaware, Newark, Del.
Porter, LeRoy E., 560 Hayannis Dr., Sunnyvale, Calif.
Porter, R. H., The Steck Co., P.O. Box 2028, Austin, Tex.
Porter, Willis P., Sch. of Educ., Indiana University, Bloomington, Ind.
Posch, Peter, Bauernfeldgasse 7/1 A-1190, Wien, Europe
Potell, Herbert, New Utrecht High School, Brooklyn, N.Y.
Potts, John F., Voorhees Junior College, Denmark, S.C.
Poulter, James R., Superintendent of Schools, Anamosa, Iowa
Pounds, Ralph L., Tchrs. Col., University of Cincinnati, Cincinnati, Ohio
Powell, Mrs. Ruth Marie, 1601 Lock Rd., Nashville, Tenn.
Powers, Francis P., State College, Fitchburg, Mass.
Powers, Fred R., 619 Cleveland Ave., Amherst, Ohio
Powers, Philander, Ventura College, 4667 Telegraph Rd., Ventura, Calif.
Powers, Thomas E., Univ., of Maryland, Baltimore, Md.
Pozdal, Marvin D., 3700 Rolliston Rd., Shaker Heights, Ohio
Prasch, John, 8224 S. Hazelwood Dr., Lincoln, Nebr.
Pratt, Anna M., 105 Colton Ave., San Carlos, Calif.
Pravalpruk, Kowit, 230 Cedar St., East Lansing, Mich.
Preil, Joseph J., 189 Shelley Ave., Elizabeth, N.J.
Prentice, Justus A., 61 Parrott Rd., West Nyack, N.Y.
Preseren, Herman J., Wake Forest College, Winston-Salem, N.C.
Pressman, Florence, 3080 Broadway, New York, N.Y.
Preston, Albert P., Prin., Washington High School, Norfolk, Va.
Prestwood, Elwood L., 426 Righters Mill Rd., Gladwyne, Pa.
Pricco, Ernest, Melrose Park School, Melrose Park, Ill.
Price, Fred A., 237 S. Cook Ave., Trenton, N.J.
Price, Louis E., University of New Mexico, Albuquerque, N.Mex.
Price, Randel K., University of Missouri, Columbia, Mo.
Price, Robert Diddams, 7819 Pinemeadow Lane, Cincinnati, Ohio
Price, Robert R., Agric. Hall, Oklahoma State Univ., Stillwater, Okla.
Price, Uberto, Appalachian State College, Boone, N.C.
Pridgen, Mrs. Ennie Mae, 1507 Russell St., Charlotte, N.C.
Priestley, Mabel, Directorate, USDESEA, APO, New York, N.Y.
Prince, Mrs. Virginia Faye, P.O. Box 4015, St. Louis, Mo.
Pritchard, Efton O., Marysville H.S., Marysville, Calif.
Pritchard, James T., 2333 5th Ave., New York, N.Y.
Pritzkau, Philo T., Univ. of Conn., Storrs, Conn.
Procunier, Robert W., 999 Kedzie Ave., Flossmoor, Ill.
Prokop, Manfred F., Univ. of Alberta, Edmonton, Alberta, Canada
Prokop, Polly, Rt. 1, Archer Ave., Lemont, Ill.

Propsting, Mrs. M., 44 Henrietta St., Waverley, N.S.W., Australia
Protheroe, Donald W., Univ. of Conn., Storrs, Conn.
Prutzman, Stuart E., 135 Alum St., Lehighton, Pa.
Pryor, Guy C., Our Lady of the Lake Col., San Antonio, Tex.
Przewlocki, Lester E., Supt. of Schools, Dist. No. 4, Addison, Ill.
Puckett, Allen, 306 Beechwood Lane, Indianapolis, Ind.
Pugmire, Dorothy Jean, 468 E. Fourth St. No., Logan, Utah
Purdy, Ralph D., 927 Silyoer Lane, Oxford, Ohio
Puryear, Royal W., Fla. Memorial Col., Miami, Fla.
Putnam, John F., Office of Education, Dept. of H.E.W., Washington, D.C.

Quall, Alvin B., Whitworth College, Spokane, Wash.
Quanbeck, Martin, Augsburg College, Minneapolis, Minn.
Quaranta, Joseph J., 3198 Kenney Rd., Columbus, Ohio
Quatraro, John A., 25 Harrison Ave., Delmar, N.Y.
Queen, Bernard, Marshall University, Huntington, W.Va.
Queen, Larry Preston, 169 Honeysuckle Lane, Huntington, W. Va.
Queensland, Kenneth, Supt. of Schools, Blue Earth, Minn.
Quick, Henry E., 293 Main St., Box 279, Oswego, Tioga County, N.Y.
Quick, Maryalice, 806 Grand Ave., Rochester, N.Y.
Quick, Otho J., Northern Illinos University, DeKalb, Ill.
Quilling, Joan I., Univ. of Missouri, Columbia, Mo.
Quinn, Villa H., State Department of Education, Augusta, Maine
Quintero, Angel G., Secretary of Education, Rio Piedras, Puerto Rico
Quish, Bernard A., 4343 W. Wrightwood Ave., Chicago, Ill.

Rabin, Bernard, Bowling Green State University, Bowling Green, Ohio
Rachford, George R., Col. of Grad. Studies, Univ. of Omaha, Omaha, Nebr.
Rackauskas, John A., 6558 S. Rockwell St., Chicago, Ill.
Racky, Donald J., Lane Technical High School, Chicago, Ill.
Radcliffe, David H., 516 N. Jackson St., Danville, Ill.
Radebaugh, Byron F., Northern Illinois University, DeKalb, Ill.
Rademaker, Dean B., Superintendent of Schools, Virginia, Ill.
Rader, William D., 240 Laurel Ave., Wilmette, Ill.
Rafalides, Madeline B., Jersey City State College, Jersey City, N.J.
Raffone, Alexander M., Woodbridge Public Schools, Woodbridge, Conn.
Ragan, William Burk, University of Oklahoma, Norman, Okla.
Ragsdale, Ted R., Southern Ill. Univ., Carbondale, Ill.
Rahn, James E., Concordia Academy, St. Paul, Minn.
Railsback, C.E., Sch. Dist. 102, La Grange Pk., Ill.
Railton, Esther P., California State Col., Hayward, Calif.
Raine, Douglas, Rt. 6, Box 296, Tucson, Ariz.
Rakow, Ernest A., Cath. Educ. Research Ctr., Boston Col., Chestnut Hill, Mass.
Ramer, Earl M., University of Tennessee, Knoxville, Tenn.
Ramey, Mrs. Beatrix B., Dept. of Educ., Appalachian State Univ., Boone, N.C.
Ramig, Clifford L., 11859 Canfield Ct., Cincinnati, Ohio
Ramirez, Judith, UCLA, Moore Hall, 244, Los Angeles, Calif.
Ramos, Rafael E., P.O. Box 371, APO, New York
Ramsay, James G., 2 Washington Square Village, New York, N.Y.
Ramsey, Imogene, 257 Sunset Ave., Richmond, Ky.
Randall, Edwin H., Western State College, Gunnison, Colo.
Randhawa, B. Randy, Univ. of Saskatchewan, Saskatoon, Canada
Rank, Ben, 1721 Brook Ave. S.E., Minneapolis, Minn.
Rankin, Earl F., 1225 Colonial Dr., Lexington, Ky.
Rankin, Eugene L., Walnut Grove Trl. Ct., Bloomington, Ind.
Rankin, Marjorie E., Drexel Inst. of Tech., Philadelphia, Pa.
Rankine, Frederick C., 548 Squires St., Fredericton, New Brunswick, Canada
Rapp, Gene E., 408 Del Oro Ave., Davis, Calif.
Rappaport, David, 2747 Coyle Ave., Chicago, Ill.
Rasmussen, Elmer M., Dana College, Blair, Nebr.

Rasmussen, L. V., 514 Vinnedge Ride, Tallahassee, Fla.
Ratekin, Ned, University of Northern Iowa, Cedar Falls, Iowa
Rathbone, Charles, Syracuse Univ., Syracuse, N.Y.
Rausch, Richard G., Hut Hill Rd., Bridgewater, Conn.
Ray, Rolland, State University of Iowa, Iowa City, Iowa
Raybern, Judith A., 1634 N. Norfolk St., Speedway, Ind.
Razik, Taher A., State University of New York, Buffalo, N.Y.
Rea, Robert E., 8001 National Bridge St., St. Louis, Mo.
Reavis, Peyton, 125 E. Prince Rd., Tucson, Ariz.
Reddin, Estoy, Dept. of Educ., Lehigh University, Bethlehem, Pa.
* Reddy, Anne L., P.O. Box 64, Runnymede, Bluffton, S.C.
Rediger, Milo A., Taylor University, Upland, Ind.
Reed, John L., 122 White St., Saratoga Springs, N.Y.
Reese, Clyde, State College of Arkansas, Conway, Ark.
Reeve, Roscoe E., U. of N.C., Chapel Hill, N.C.
Reeves, Emily D., Centre College of Kentucky, Danville, Ky.
Reeves, Glenn D., Saginaw Public Schools, Saginaw, Tex.
Reeves, Louis H., 905 Thorndale Drive, Ottawa, Ont., Canada
Regier, Margaret, Roosevelt Univ., 430 S. Michigan Ave., Chicago, Ill.
Rehage, Kenneth J., Dept. of Educ., University of Chicago, Chicago, Ill.
Reichert, Conrad A., Andrews Univ., Berrien Springs, Mich.
Reid, Clarence E., Jr., 8740 Skyview, Beaumont, Tex.
Reid, Leon L., Rt. 2, Box 221, McDonald, Pa.
Reilley, Albert G., 28 Long Ave., Framingham, Mass.
Reilly, Vincent E., 100 Hillside Rd., Greenville, Del.
Reiner, Kenneth L., Box 495, Jos, Nigeria
Reiner, William B., Hunter College, 695 Park Ave., New York, N.Y.
*Reinhardt, Emma, Pittsfield, Ill.
Reinking, Wayne W., 1105 St. Louis, Edwardsville, Ill.
Reinstein, Barry J., Univ. of South Carolina, Columbia, S.C.
Reisboard, Richard J., 7476 Brockton Rd., Philadelphia, Pa.
Reisman, Diana J., 223 N. Highland Ave., Merion Station, Pa.
Reiss, William, 22905-108th Ave., West Edmonds, Wash.
Reiter, Anne, 155 West 68th St., New York, N.Y.
Reitz, Donald J., Loyola College, 4501 N. Charles St., Baltimore, Md.
Reitz, Louis M., Rev., 711 Maiden Choice Ln., Baltimore, Md.
Relic, Peter D., 60 Wilson Rd., Bedford, Mass.
Reller, Theodore L., Sch. of Educ., Univ. of California, Berkeley, Calif.
Rempel, Peter J., Rte. 1, P.O. Box 977, Sequim, Wash.
Renard, John N., Oxnard Evening High School, Oxnard, Calif.
Renfrow, O.W., 3600 Union Rd., Cheek Towaga, N.Y.
Rennels, Max R., Illinois State Univ., Normal, Ill.
Renouf, Edna M., 116 Yale Square, Swarthmore. Pa.
Rentsch, George J., 80 Main St. W., Rochester, N.Y.
Replogle, V. L., Metcalf School, Normal, Ill.
Reschly, Daniel J., 725 E. 19th Ave., Eugene, Oreg.
Restaino, Lillian, Fordham Univ. at Lincoln Center, New York, N.Y.
Reuter, George S., P.O. Box 56, New Madrid, Mo.
Revie, Virgil A., California State Col., Long Beach, Calif.
Rex, Ronald G., Michigan State University, East Lansing, Mich.
Reyna, L. J., 227 Beacon St., Boston, Mass.
Reynolds, James Walton, Box 7998, University of Texas, Austin, Tex.
Reynolds, Lee, 113 Woodland Dr., Boone, N.C.
Reynolds, M. C., University of Minnesota, Minneapolis, Minn.
Rhoads, Philip A., 3908 Klausmier Rd., Baltimore, Md.
Rhodes, Gladys L., State University College, Geneseo, N.Y.
Rhodes, Patricia Hertert, Rt. 2, Box 343, Sonora, Calif.
Ricciardi, Richard S., Dept. of Education, 100 Reef Rd., Fairfield, Conn.
Rice, David, Indiana State University, Evansville, Ind.
Rice, Dick C., Univ. of Maine, Farmington, Maine

Rice, Ernest T., R.D. 1, 38 Crestmont Dr., Shippenville, Pa.
Rice, Eric D., 759 W. Hwy. 80, El Centro, Calif.
Rice, James A., University of Houston, Houston, Tex.
Rice, John E., Jenkintown Sch. Dist., Jenkintown, Pa.
Rice, Robert K., 4820 Campanile Dr., San Diego, Calif.
Rice, Roy C., Arizona State University, Tempe, Ariz.
Rice, Theodore D., 17158 Hubbell, Detroit, Mich.
Richard J. Walter, 114 Pleasant St., Fitchburg, Mass.
Richards Eugene R., 8912 S. McVickers, Oaklawn, Ill.
Richards H.L., P.O. Box 326, Grambling, La.
Richards, James J., 2400 Hudson Ter., Fort Lee, N.J.
Richardson, Canute M., Paine College, Augusta, Ga.
Richardson, Edwin W., 1800 Grand Ave., Des Moines, Iowa
Richardson, Orvin T., Ball State University, Muncie, Ind.
Richardson, Thomas H., 852 Valley Rd., Upper Montclair, N.J.
Richardson, William R., University of North Carolina, Chapel Hill, N.C.
Richey, Herman G., Dept. of Educ., University of Chicago, Chicago, Ill.
Richey, Robert W., Sch. of Educ., Indiana University, Bloomington, Ind.
Richmond, George S., Crestview Village, 30th & Frederick, St. Joseph, Mo.
Richter, Charles O., Public Schools, 7 Whiting Lane, West Hartford, Conn.
Riedel, Mark T., 210 S. Edgewood, LaGrange, Ill.
Riehm, Carl L., 7402 Fenwood Ct., Manassas, Va.
Riese, Harlan C., 511 North Ave., East, Missoula, Mont.
*Riethmiller, M. Gordon, 7088 Beeman Rd., Chelsea, Mich.
Riggle, Earl L., 180 Highland Dr., New Concord, Ohio
Riggs, William J., 716 Clover Ct., Cheney, Wash.
Rikkola, V. John, Horace Mann Training Schl., Salem, Mass.
Riley, Garland G., 115 Kishwaukee Lane, DeKalb, Ill.
Ringler, Leonore, New York Univ., New York, N.Y.
Ringler, Mrs. Norma, 3721 Lytle Rd., Shaker Heights, Ohio
Rinsland, Roland Del, 100 W. 73rd St., New York, N.Y.
Riordan, Eugene, Queen of Apostles College, Dedham, Mass.
Rios, Noel J., R.R. 2, Mohegan Ave., Mohegan Lake, N.Y.
Ripper, Eleanor S., Geneva College, Beaver Falls, Pa.
Ripple, Richard E., Stone Hall, Cornell University, Ithaca, N.Y.
Risinger, Robert G., Col. of Educ., University of Maryland, College Park, Md.
Risk, Thomas M., 622 Gilbert Ave., Eau Claire, Wis.
Ritchie, Harold L., Superintendent of Schools, West Paterson, N.J.
Ritter, William E., 2910 E. State St., Sharon, Pa.
Rittschoff, Louis W., 240 Kenwood Dr., Thiensville, Wis.
Rivard, Thomas L., Superintendent of Schools, Chelmsford, Mass.
Rivlin, Harry N., 302 Broadway, New York, N.Y.
Roaden, Arliss, Dept. of Education, Ohio State University, Columbus, Ohio
Roan, John D., 153 Marlin Dr., Naples, Fla.
Roark, Bill, 11211 N. 32nd Pl., Phoenix, Ariz.
Robards, Shirley N., 2301 E. 2nd St., Bloomington, Ind.
Robarts, James R., Florida State University, Tallahassee, Fla.
Robbins, Edward L., 7346 Shamrock Dr., Indianapolis, Ind.
Robbins, Edward T., 602 Larkwood Dr., San Antonio, Tex.
Robbins, Jerry H., Sch. of Educ., Univ. of Miss., Oxford, Miss.
Robeck, Mildred C., 452 Venado Dr., Santa Barbara, Calif.
Roberson, James A., 2925 S. Perkins Rd., Memphis, Tenn.
Roberts, A. Douglas, OISE, 102 Bloor St., Toronto, Ontario, Can.
Roberts, Dodd Edward, University of Maine, Orono, Maine
Roberts, Maurice, 920 Tanglewood Dr., Cary, N.C.
Roberts, R. Ray, 3309 Rocky Mount Rd., Fairfax, Va.
Robertson, Anne McK., Tchrs. Col., Columbia University, New York, N.Y.
Robertson, Jean E., University of Alberta, Edmonton, Alba., Canada
Robertson, Robert L., 315 East Main St., Springfield, Ky.

Robinson, Alice, Rt. 1, Box 16A, Frederick, Md.
Robinson, Cliff, Chico State College, Chico, Calif.
Robinson, H. Alan, Hofstra Univ., Hempstead, L.I., N.Y.
Robinson, Herbert B., California State Col., Long Beach, Calif.
Robinson, Lucille T., 603 Buena Vista, Redlands, Calif.
Robinson, Phil C., 1367 Joliet Pl., Detroit, Mich.
Robinson, Richard C., 175 Talmadge, Athens, Ga.
Robinson, Robert S., Jr., Eastern Michigan Univ., Ypsilanti, Mich.
Robinson, Russell D., Univ. of Wis.-Milwaukee, Milwaukee, Wis.
Robinson, Walter J., Northwestern State College, Natchitoches, La.
Robinson, Walter K., New England College, Henniker, N.H.
Robison, William L., 4132 Thalia Dr., Virginia Beach, Va.
Roche, Lawrence A., Duquesne University, Pittsburgh, Pa.
Rochfort, George B., Jr., RFD #1, Cedar Point Rd., Durham, N.H.
Rockwell, Perry J., Jr., Wisconsin State Univ., Platteville, Wis.
Roden, Aubrey H., State Univ. of New York, Buffalo, N.Y.
Rodgers, John O., 4115 Honeycomb Cir., Austin, Tex.
Rodgers, Margaret, Lamar State College of Technology, Beaumont, Tex.
Rodgers, Maria A., Bauder Fashion Col., Miami, Fla.
Rodgers, Paul R., 255 W. Vermont St., Villa Park, Ill.
Rodney, Clare, Long Beach State College, Long Beach, Calif.
Roe, Anne, 5151 E. Holmes St., Tucson, Ariz.
Roelke, Patricia L., Emory Univ., Atlanta, Ga.
Roenigk, Elsie Mae, 121 Oak Ridge Dr., Butler, Pa.
Roeper, George A., City and Country School, Bloomfield Hills, Mich.
Roff, Mrs. Rosella Zuber, 4410 S. 148th St., Seattle, Wash.
Rogers, Harold L., 29 Sunny Plain Ave., Weymouth, Mass.
Rogers, Martha E., Div. of Nurse Educ., N.Y.U., New York, N.Y.
Rogers, Virgil M., 3810 Birchwood Rd., Falls Church, Va.
Rogowski, Richard A., 2421 Pearsall Pkwy., Waukegan, Ill.
Rohan, William, E. G. Foreman High School, Chicago, Ill.
Rolfe, Howard C., 5160 Atherton, Long Beach, Calif.
Rolleta, Vincent M., 35 Clearview Dr., Spencerport, N.Y.
Rollins, William B., Jr., 7772 Otto St., Downey, Calif.
Romano, Louis, Michigan State University, East Lansing, Mich.
Romano, Louis A., 227—65th St., West New York, N.J.
Rome, Samuel, 9852 Cerritos Ave., Anaheim, Calif.
Romoser, Richard C., 2580 Westmoor Rd., Rocky River, Ohio
Rondinella, Orestes R., 48 Sheridan Ave., West Orange, N.J.
Ronshausen, Nina L., 413 S. Henderson, Bloomington, Ind.
Roose, Jack L., Ulster County Boces, New Paltz, N.Y.
Root, Edward L., Maryland Fellow-Univ. of Md., Cumberland, Md.
Rorison, Margaret L., University of S.C., Columbia, S.C.
Rosamilia, M. T., 183 Union Ave., Belleville, N.J.
Rose, Gale W., Schl. of Educ., N.Y. Univ., New York, N.Y.
Rose, Mrs. Ruth R., 908 S.W. 18th Ct., Fort Lauderdale, Fla.
Rosen, Carl L., 1165 Falstaff Dr., Roswell, Ga.
Rosen, Sidney, Col. of Educ., University of Illinois, Urbana, Ill.
Rosenbach, John H., 1400 Washington Ave., Albany, N.Y.
Rosenbaum, Wyatt I., 325 Bristol Rd., Webster Groves, Mo.
Rosenberg, Arthur I., 147-03 10th Ave., Whitestone, N.Y.
Rosenberg, Donald A., Supt., Lutheran Schools, Wausau, Wis.
Rosenberg, Max, 5057 Woodward Ave., Detroit, Mich.
Rosenberger, Russell S., Dept. of Educ., Gettysburg Col., Gettysburg, Pa.
Rosenbluh, Benjamin J., Central High School, Bridgeport, Conn.
Rosenblum, Beth W., 2185 LeMoine Ave., Ft. Lee, N.J.
Rosenthal, Alan G., 18 Homeside Lane, White Plains, N.Y.
Rosenthal, Alice M., S.U.N.Y., Buffalo, N.Y.
Rosenthal, Lester, 94 Stirling Ave., Freeport, N.Y.
Rosenthal, Samuel, 5213 N. Moody Ave., Chicago, Ill.

Rosenthal, Yonia, 2713 Circle Dr., Durham, N.C.
Rosenzweig, Celia, 6239 N. Leavitt St., Chicago, Ill.
Roser, Nancy Lee, 1222 Algarita, Austin, Tex.
Rosewell, Paul T., Iowa State Univ., Ames, Iowa
Rosin, Bill, Box 2096, Eastern New Mexico Univ., Portales, N.Mex.
Ross, Mrs. Alice M., 1446 Wilbraham Rd., Springfield, Mass.
Ross, Robert D., Auburn Community College, Auburn, N.Y.
Rossi, Mary Jean, University of Miami, Miami, Fla.
Rossien, Saul, c/o Thailand Desk, Peace Corps, Washington, D.C.
Rossmiller, Richard A., 5806 Cable Ave., Madison, Wis.
Rost, Nellie May, Indiana Univ., Bloomington, Ind.
Roth, Mrs. Frances, 21598 Ellacott Pkwy., Cleveland, Ohio
Roth, Lois H., 5209 Brentwood Dr., Lacey, Wash.
Rothenberg, William, Jr., 1 S. Broadway, Hastings-on-Hudson, N.Y.
Rothenberger, Otis J., 1517 Pennsylvania St., Allentown, Pa.
Rothstein, Jerome H., San Francisco State College, San Francisco, Calif.
Rothwell, Angus B., Coord. Council for Higher Educ., Madison, Wis.
Roueche, John E., RELCV—Mutual Plaza, Durham, N.C.
Rousseau, Joseph, P.O. Box 340, Wabush, Newfoundland and Labrador, Canada
Rousseve, Numa Joseph, Xavier University, New Orleans, La.
Row, Howard E., State Dept. of Pub. Instr., Dover, Del.
Rowley, Judge Kernan, Morris Brown College, Atlanta, Ga.
Rozendaal, Julia, University of North. Iowa, Cedar Falls, Iowa
Rozran, Andrea Rice, 4248 N. Hazel, Chicago, Ill.
Rubadeau, Duane O., Algoma Col., Sault St., Marie, Canada
Rubeck, Patricia, 800 Parkway, Bloomington, Ind.
Rubeck, Robert F., 1182 Sanborn Pl., Columbus, Ohio
Rucinski, Philip R., Wisconsin State Univ., Oshkosh, Wis.
Rucker, Chauncy N., Rockridge Apts., Baxter Rd., Storrs, Conn.
Rudman, Herbert C., Col. of Educ., Michigan State Univ., East Lansing, Mich.
Rueff, Charles M., Jr., 626 S. Sixth St., McComb, Miss.
Ruggles, Stanford D., 96 Lochatong Rd., Trenton, N.J.
Rummel, J. Francis, Sch. of Educ., Univ. of Montana, Missoula, Mont.
Rumpf, Edwin L., 1805 Rupert St., McLean, Va.
Runbeck, Junet E., Bethel College, St. Paul, Minn.
Runyan, Charles S., Marshall University, Huntington, W.Va.
Ruoff, Herman J., 7208 Warwick Dr., Washington, D.C.
Rusch, Reuben R., State University of New York, Albany, N.Y.
Rusche, Philip J., 118 Edgemere Rd., W. Roxbury, Mass.
Russel, John H., Col. of Educ., Univ. of Toledo, Toledo, Ohio
Russell, David L., Dept. of Psych., Ohio University, Athens, Ohio
Russell, Elder H., P.O. Box 4313, Phoenix, Ariz.
Russell, Irene, Lock Haven State College, Lock Haven, Pa.
* Russell, John Dale, R.R. 10, Russell Rd., Bloomington, Ind.
Russell, William J., Pelham Memorial High School, Pelham, N.Y.
Russo, Anthony J., 51 Wabun Ave., Providence, R.I.
Rutherford, William L., 1812 Cedar Ridge Dr., Austin, Tex.
Rutledge, James A., Univ. of Nebraska, Lincoln, Neb.
Ryan, Carl J., 220 W. Liberty St., Cincinnati, Ohio
Ryan, Kevin, Univ. of Chicago, Chicago, Ill.
Ryan, Maria, 629 Wyckshire Ct., Fairburn, Ohio
Rzepka, Louis, S.U.N.Y., College at Cortland, Cortland, N.Y.

Sack, Saul, Grad. Sch. of Educ., Univ. of Pennsylvania, Philadelphia, Pa.
Safford, George R., 3640 Scenic Dr., Redding, Calif.
Sage, Daniel D., Syracuse University, Syracuse, N.Y.
Sager, Kenneth, Lawrence University, Appleton, Wis.
Salett, Stanley J., 225 W. State St., Trenton, N.J.
Salinger, Herbert E., 1273 Sylvaner, St. Helena, Calif.
Salisbury, C. Jackson, 410 Conshohocken St. Rd., Narberth, Pa.

Sallee, Mrs. Mozelle T., 4401 North Ave., Richmond, Va.
Salmon, Hanford A., 310 Stratford St., Syracuse, N.Y.
Salmons, George B., State College, Plymouth, N.H.
* Salser, G Alden, 516 E. Estelle, Wichita, Kans.
Salten, David G., 41 Park Ave., New York, N.Y.
Saltzman, Irving J., Dept. of Psych., Indiana Univ., Bloomington, Ind.
Sam, Norman H., Lehigh University, Bethlehem, Pa.
Samlin, John R., 840 Cheryl Lane, Kankakee, Ill.
Sample, William J., 3022 Cedarbrook Court, Vineland, N.J.
Samson, Gordon E., Cleveland State University, Cleveland, Ohio
Sanchez, Manuel, 4641 S. Lawler, Chicago, Ill.
Sand, Ole, Natl. Educ. Assn., 1201 Sixteenth St., N.W., Washington, D.C.
Sandel, Lenore, 33 Sherman Avenue, Rockville Centre, N.Y.
Sander, Paul J., 2828 E. Weldon Ave., Phoenix, Ariz.
Sanders, Mrs. Ruby, P.O. Box 1956, Waco, Tex.
Sanderson, Marjorie, Sch. of Nursing, Univ. of S.C., Columbia, S.C.
Sandilos, Peter C., Superintendent of Schools, West Long Branch, N.J.
Sandow, Lyn A., Grolier Incorporated, New York, N.Y.
Sands, Miss Billie L., Michigan State Univ., East Lansing, Mich.
Sanford, Wayne A., Winona State Col., Winona, Minn.
Sangster, Cecil Henry, 1248 Cross Cres. S.W., Calgary, Alba., Canada
Santigian, M. Marty, 4596 E. Fredora, Fresno, Calif.
Sapiro, Marion E., 4561 Round Top Drive, Los Angeles, Calif.
Sardo, Arlene A., Cedarwood Blvd., Baldwinsville, N.Y.
Sartain, Harry W., Falk Lab. Schls., Univ. of Pittsburgh, Pittsburgh, Pa.
Satterlee, Ward, St. University Col., Potsdam, N.Y.
Saterlie, Mary E., 1710 Kurtz Avenue, Lutherville, Md.
Saunders, Margaret C., 701 Wheeling Ave., Muncie, Ind.
Sause, Edwin F., Educ. Res. Coun., Rockefeller Bldg., Cleveland, Ohio
Sause, Edwin F., Jr., 484 Cary Avenue, Staten Island, N.Y.
Sauter, Joyce H., 1041 Catalpa Road, Arcadia, Calif.
Sauvain, Walter H., Dept. of Educ., Bucknell Univ., Lewisburg, Pa.
Savage, Kent B., Fairview Senior High School, Berkeley, Mo.
Savage, Mary E., 114 Middleton Pl., Bronxville, N.Y.
Sax, Gilbert, University of Washington, Seattle, Wash.
Saxe, Richard W., Univ. of Toledo, Toledo, Ohio
Saylor, Charles F., 535 Kathryn St., New Wilmington, Pa.
Schall, William E., 419 Main St., Fredonia, N.Y.
Scanlan, William J., Highland Park Sr. High School, St. Paul, Minn.
Scanlon, Kathryn I., Fordham Univ., Lincoln Center Campus, New York, N.Y.
Scarnato, Samuel A., P.O. Box 869, Wilmington, Del.
Schaadt, Mrs. Lucy G., Cedar Crest College, Allentown, Pa.
Schaefer, Alan E., 900 Crestfield Ave., Libertyville, Ill.
Schaeffer, Norma C., 10700 S. Hamlin, Chicago, Ill.
Schaibly, Colon L., Waukegan Township High School, Waukegan, Ill.
Schall, William C., 419 Main St., Fredonia, N.Y.
Schasteen, Joyce W., 2500 Spruce St., Bakersfield, Calif.
Schauerman, Sam, Jr., 22806 Eriel Ave., Torrance, Calif.
Schell, Very Rev. Joseph O., John Carroll Univ., Cleveland, Ohio
Schell, Leo M., Col. of Educ., Kansas State Univ., Manhattan, Kans.
Schenke, Lahron H., 301 Chamberlin Dr., Charleston, Ill.
Scherer, Frank H., Rutgers University, New Brunswick, N.J.
Schieser, Hans, DePaul Univ., Chicago, Ill.
Schiller, Clarke E., 863 Garland Dr., Palo Alto, Calif.
Schiller, Leroy, Mankato State College, Mankato, Minn.
Schilling, Paul M., Superintendent of Schools, LaGrange Park, Ill.
Schleif, Mabel E., 110 Forest Ave., Vermillion, S. Dak.
Schlessinger, Fred R., 1399 LaRochelle Dr., Columbus, Ohio
Schlosser, Alvin, 144-15 41st Ave., Flushing, N.Y.
Schmidt, Florence M., 5925 Canterbury Dr., Culver City, Calif.
Schmidt, L. G. H., J. J. Cahill Mem. Sch., Mascot, N.S.W., Australia

Schmidt, Ralph L. W., 568 Magnolia Wood Dr., Baton Rouge, La.
Schmidt, William S., County Superintendent of Schools, Upper Marlboro, Md.
Schnabel, Robert V., 6902 S. Calhoun St., Fort Wayne, Ind.
Schnee, Ronald G., 1413 N. 23rd St., Lawton, Okla.
Schneider, Albert A., Superintendent of Schools, Albuquerque, N.Mex.
Schneider, Arthur J., Webster Cent. School, Webster, N.Y.
Schneider, Byron J., 3416 Humboldt Ave. So., Minneapolis, Minn.
Schneider, Erwin H., Univ. of Iowa, Iowa City, Iowa
Schneider, Raymond C., University of Washington, Seattle, Wash.
Schneider, Samuel, 150 W. End Ave., New York, N.Y.
Schnell, Fred, 2724 Highland Terrace, Sheboygan, Wis.
Schnell, Rodolph L., Univ. of Calgary, Calgary, Alba., Canada
Schnepf, Virginia, 718 Normal Ave., Normal, Ill.
Schneyer, J. Wesley, 7454 Ruskin Rd., Philadelphia, Pa.
Schnitzen, Joseph P., University of Houston, Houston, Tex.
Schoeller, Arthur W., 8626 W. Lawrence Ave., Milwaukee, Wis.
Scholl, Paul A., Univ. of Connecticut, Storrs, Conn.
Schollmeyer, Fred C., Dade County Public Schools, Miami, Fla.
Schooler, Virgil E., 209 S. Hillsdale Dr., Bloomington, Ind.
Schooling, Herbert W., Col. of Educ., Univ. of Missouri, Columbia, Mo.
Schor, Theodore, 149 N. Fifth Ave., Highland Park, N.J.
Schorow, Mitchell, 50 N. Medical Dr., Salt Lake City, Utah
Schott, Marion S., Central Missouri State College, Warrensburg, Mo.
Schowe, Ben M., Jr., 500 Morse Rd., Columbus, Ohio
Schreiber, Daniel, 7 Peter Cooper Rd., New York, N.Y.
Schroeder, Carl N., 39 Othoridge Rd., Lutherville, Md.
Schroeder, Howard H., Mankato St. Col., Mankato, Minn.
Schroeder, Marie L., 3125 N. Spangler St., Philadelphia, Pa.
Schroeder, W. P., State Polytechnic College, San Luis Obispo, Calif.
Schrof, Walter J., 912 Arrowhead Dr., Oxford, Ohio
Schubert, Leland, Central Nat. Bank Bldg., Cleveland, Ohio
Schuller, Charles F., Michigan State University, East Lansing, Mich.
Schulte, Emerita S., Dept. of English, Ball St. Univ., Muncie, Ind.
Shultz, Kenneth M., 847 New England Ave., Centerville, Ohio
Schumacher, Henry A., Univ. of Pittsburgh, Pittsburgh, Pa.
Schumann, Victor, 1537 Cedar Lane, Waukesha, Wis.
Schwanholt, Dana B., Valparaiso University, Valparaiso, Ind.
Schwartz, Alfred, Drake University, Des Moines, Iowa
Schwartz, Judy I., 175-20 Wexford Ter., Jamaica, N.Y.
Schwartz, Melvin, 9 Stonegate Rd., Ossining, N.Y.
Schwartz, William, 467 W. Cross St., Westbury, L.I., N.Y.
Schwartz, William P., 273 Ave. P., Brooklyn, N.Y.
Schwarz, Peggy M., 25 Cornell St., Scarsdale, N.Y.
Schwarzenberger, Alfred J., Sault Sainte Marie, Mich.
Schwebel, Milton, Sch. of Educ., New York University, New York, N.Y.
Schweitzer, Thomas F., 89-19 218 St., Queens Village, L.I., N.Y.
Schwyhart, Keith, Earlham College, Richmond, Ind.
Scian, Marie J., 305 Elm St., Westford, N.J.
Sciranka, Paul G., 1129 Via Alamosa, Alameda, Calif.
Scobey, Mary-Margaret, San Francisco State College, San Francisco, Calif.
Scofield, Alice Gill, San Jose State College, San Jose, Calif.
Scofield, J. Woodleigh, 4 Fontlee Lane, Fontana, Calif.
Scoggins, James A., 1912 E. Gadsden St., Pensacola, Fla.
Scott, Guy, 3815 Cutler Ave., Visalia, Calif.
Scott, Hugh M., Royal Victoria Hospital, Montreal, P.Q., Canada
Scott, Loren L., Idaho State University, Pocatello, Idaho
Scott, Robert C., Drawer 829, Florence, S.C.
Scott, Ruth E., 69 Paladin Ave., Sault Ste. Marie, Ontario, Canada
Scott, Thomas B., University of Tennessee, Knoxville, Tenn.
Scott, Waldo I., 14-16 Franklin Ave., Port Washington, N.Y.

Scribner, Jay D., University of California, Los Angeles, Calif.
Scritchfield, Floyd C., Univ. of Nev., Las Vegas, Nev.
Seagoe, May V., Sch. of Educ., University of California, Los Angeles, Calif.
Searles, Warren B., Queens Col., Flushing, N.Y.
Sears, Jesse B., 40 Tevis Pl., Palo Alto, Calif.
*Seay, Maurice F., W. Mich. Univ., Kalamazoo, Mich.
Sebaly, A. L., Western Michigan Universty, Kalamazoo, Mich.
Sebolt, Alberta P., Resource Learning Lab-Title 111, Sturbridge, Mass.
See, Harold W., Col. of Educ., Univ. of Bridgeport, Bridgeport, Conn.
Seelye, Margaret R., P.O. Box 37, Bourbonnais, Ill.
Segal, Marilyn, The Pre-School, Hollywood, Fla.
Seidman, Eric, University of Maryland, College Park, Md.
Seifert, George G., Bowling Green State Univ., Bowling Green, Ohio
Seitz, Robert, Ball St. Univ., Muncie, Ind.
Selden, Edward H., Dept. of Psych., Wisconsin State Univ., River Falls, Wis.
Sellery, Austin Roy, 5021 Rolling Hills Pl., El Cavon, Calif.
Seltzer, Richard W., 639 Redlion Rd., Huntingdon Valley, Pa.
Selzer, Edwin, 67-30 167th St., Flushing, N.Y.
Semmel, Melvyn I., University of Michigan, Ann Arbor, Mich.
Semple, Stuart W. 1603 Larch St., Halifax, N.S., Canada
Semrow, Joseph J., North Central Association, Chicago, Ill.
Sentman, Everett E., United Educators, Inc., Lake Bluff, Ill.
Setze, Leonard A., Northeastern Ill. St. Col., Chicago, Ill.
Severino, D. Alexander, Alisal H.S., Salinas, Calif.
Severson, John E., 11 Chalon Cir., Salinas, Calif.
Seyfarth, John T., P.O. Box 1348, Charleston, W. Va.
Seyfert, Warren C., 5607 Gloster Rd., Washington, D.C.
Sgan, Arnold D., 213 Purefoy Rd., Chapel Hill, N.C.
Shaddick, Bryan A., 200 E. 4th St., Jamestown, N.Y.
Shafer, Robert E., Arizona State University, Tempe, Ariz.
Shafran, Lillian, 711 E. 11th St., New York, N.Y.
Shane, Estelle, 12250 Richwood Dr., Los Angeles, Calif.
Shane, Harold G., Sch. of Educ., Indiana University, Bloomington, Ind.
Shane, James, 5941 Fuller Ct., Riverside, Calif.
Shank, Lloyd L., Superintendent of Schools, Arkansas City, Kans.
Shankman, Florence, Temple University, Philadelphia, Pa.
Shankman, Sheila, 244 Riverside Dr., New York, N.Y.
Shapiro, Benjamin, Rutgers Univ., New Brunswick, N.J.
Shaplin, Judson T., Washington University, St. Louis, Mo.
Sharlow, John F., East. Connecticut St. Col., Willimantic, Conn.
Sharp, George M., Lakewood Terr., New Milford, Conn.
Shaw, Frances. 4717 Central Ave., Indianapolis, Ind.
Shaw, Nancy E., 129 Gunson St., East Lansing, Mich.
*Shaw, M. Luelle, Box 264, Young Harris Col., Young Harris, Ga.
Shaw, Robert C., Superintendent of Schools, Columbia, Mo.
Shea, James, 59 Old Farm Road, Levittown, N.Y.
Shear, Twyla M., Pennsylvania, St. Univ., University Pk., Pa.
Sheehan, Donald J., State Univ. Col., Plattsburgh, N.Y.
Sheely, Richard L., Lancaster City Schools, Lancaster, Ohio
Sheldon, Muriel Inez, Los Angeles City Board of Educ., Los Angeles, Calif.
Sheldon, William Denley, 508 University Pl., Syracuse, N.Y.
Shelley, Florence D., 415 Madison Ave., New York, N.Y.
Shelton, Nollie W., 328 Blowing Rock Rd., Boone, N.C.
Shepard, Loraine V., Antioch Col., Yellow Springs, Ohio
Shepard, Samuel, Jr., Supt. of Schs., East Chicago, Ill.
Shepard, Stanley, 353 Summit Ave., St. Paul, Minn.
Sheppard, Lawrence E., 1322 S. 58th St., Richmond, Calif.
Sherer, Harry, 385 Ocean Blvd., Long Beach, Calif.
Sheridan, Alton, NEA, 1201 Sixteenth St., N.W., Washington, D.C.
Sheridan, William C., 333 Washington St., Brookline, Mass.

Sherk, John K., Univ. of Missouri, Kansas City, Mo.
Sherk, John K., Jr., 6112 Summit St., Kansas City, Mo.
Sherrill, Joyce, 7805 San Rafael Dr., Buena Park, Calif.
Sherman, C. A., 121 Bauman Ave., Pittsburgh, Pa.
Sherman, Mrs. Helene, 350 Central Park West, New York, N.Y.
Sherwood, Virgil, Radford College, Radford, Va.
Sherwyn, Fred, State Dept. of Educ., Cupertino, Calif.
Shier, John B., 200 Elm High Dr., Edgerton, Wis.
Shimel, W. A., Univ. Ext., Univ. of Wis., Rhinelander, Wis.
Shinol, Julian W., 2405 Bird Dr., Wesleyville, Pa.
Shnayer, Sidney W., Chico State College, Chico, Calif.
Shoemaker, A. T., Box 584, Vidalia, La.
Shohen, Samuel S., 229 Friends Lane, Westbury, L.I., N.Y.
Sholund, Milford, Gospel Light Press, 725 E. Colorado, Glendale, Calif.
Shope, Nathaniel H., Appalachian State Univ., Boone, N.C.
Shores, J. Harlan, University of Illinois, Urbana, Ill.
Short, Edmund C., University of Toledo, Toledo, Ohio
Short, Robert Allen, 15510—112th St., Bothell, Wash.
Showkeir, James R., 1126 Tollgate Dr., Oxford, Ohio
Shroff, Piroja, California Col. of Arts & Crafts, Oakland, Calif.
Shulman, Lee S., Col. of Educ., Michigan State Univ., East Lansing, Mich.
* Shuman, Elsie, 805 S. Florence St., Kirksville, Mo.
* Sias, A. B., Route 3, Box 459B, Orlando, Fla.
Sidden, Curtis A., P.O. Box 385, Pickens, S.C.
Siddiqui, F.A., 109 Gainesboro St., Boston, Mass.
Siegel, Martin, 130 Crane Circle, New Providence, N.J.
Siegner, C. Vernon, Peru State College, Box 75, Peru, Nebr.
Sieving, Eldor C., Concordia Teachers College, River Forest, Ill.
Siewers, Karl, 2301 Estes Ave., Chicago, Ill.
Silberman, Charles E., Fortune-Time/Life Bldg., New York, N.Y.
Silva, J. Winston, California State Dept. of Educ., Sacramento, Calif.
Silvaroli, Nicholas J., Arizona State University, Tempe, Ariz.
Silver, Nettie, 83-80 118th St., Kew Gardens, N.Y.
Silver, Rona, 47 Burroughs Way, Maplewood, N.J.
Silvern, Leonard C., Educ. & Trng. Consults. Co., Los Angeles, Calif.
Silverman, William, 5110 S. Kenwood Ave., Chicago, Ill.
Simmons, M. Lindsay, 1 Lexington Dr., Urbana, Ill.
Simmons, Muriel H., 304—22nd Ave. North, Nashville, Tenn.
Simmons, Patricia C., 4420 Myrtle Ave., Long Beach, Calif.
Simmons, Robert M., 4703 Fox Rest Dr., Richmond, Va.
Simmons, Virginia Lee, Indianapolis Public Schools, Indianapolis, Ind.
Simms, Naomi, 333 College Ct., Kent, Ohio
Simon, Dan, Superintendent of Schools, East Chicago, Ind.
Simon, Herman, 3510 Bergenline Ave., Union City, N.J.
Simon, Murray, Rockland Community Coll., Suffern, N.Y.
Simons, Herbert D., 969 Hilldale Rd., Berkeley, Calif.
Simpkins, Katherine W., P.O. Box 88, Chesapeake, Ohio
Simpson, Mrs. Anne E., Bethel Park Senior High School, Bethel Park, Pa.
Simpson, Dorothy C., Mahopac H.S., Mahopac, N.Y.
Simpson, Mrs. Elizabeth A., 5627 Blackstone Ave., Chicago, Ill.
Simpson, Frederick W., University of Tulsa, Tulsa, Okla.
Simpson, Mrs. Hazel D., Col. of Educ., University of Georgia, Athens, Ga.
Simpson, Raymond J., San Francisco State College, San Francisco, Calif.
Sims, Harold W., 9423 Harvard Ave., Chicago, Ill.
Sims, Stephen B., Leonia Public Schools, Leonia, N.J.
Sincock, William R., Allegheny College, Meadville, Pa.
Singe, Anthony L., 1138 McQuade Ave., Utica, N.Y.
Singer, Harry, Univ. of California, Riverside, Calif.
Singletary, James D., 10307 Conover Dr., Silver Spring, Md.
Singleton, Ira C., Silver Burdett Co., Morristown, N.J.

Singleton, John, University of Pittsburgh, Pittsburgh, Pa.
Singleton, Stanton J., Col. of Educ., University of Georgia, Athens, Ga.
Sipay, Edward R., 16 Belmonte Lane, Elnora, N.Y.
Sipe, H. Craig, State Univ. of New York, Albany, N.Y.
Sirchio, Joseph J., Chicago Voc. H.S., Chicago, Ill.
Sires, Ely, 9245 N. Waverly Dr., Milwaukee, Wis.
Sister Alice Huber SSJ, Mt. St. Joseph Col., Buffalo, N.Y.
Sister Allene Derganz, 1050 S. Lumpkin St., Athens, Ga.
Sister Ann Mary Gullan, Mount Senario College, Ladysmith, Wis.
Sister Dorothy Marie Riordan, College of St. Elizabeth, Convent Station, N.J.
Sister Eileen Marie Cronin, Col. of the Holy Names, Oakland, Calif.
Sister Elaine Weber, 4927 N. Claremont, Chicago, Ill.
Sister Fides Huber, College of St. Catherine, St. Paul, Minn.
Sister Gabrielle Henning, Nazareth Col., Nazareth, Mich.
Sister James Claudia, Siena Heights College, Adrian, Mich.
Sister James Edward, Brescia College, Owensboro, Ky.
Sister John Vianney Coyle, St. Francis Convent, Graymoor, Garrison, N.Y.
Sister Julia Ford, 444 Centre St., Milton, Mass.
Sister Laurina Kaiser, Mount Mary Col., Yankton, S. Dak.
Sister Margaret Mary, R.S.M., Gwynedd-Mercy College, Gwynedd Valley, Pa.
Sister Marie Claudia, Barry College, Miami Shores, Fla.
Sister Marie Gabrielle, Annhurst Col., Woodstock, Conn.
Sister Marilyn Hofer, Marian Col., Indianapolis, Ind.
Sister Mary Agnes Hennessey, Mount Mercy College, Cedar Rapids, Iowa
Sister Mary Albertus, Mount St. Vincent Univ., Halifax, Canada
Sister Mary Ann Fox, 4501 S. Arlington, Ft. Wayne, Ind.
Sister M. Arilda, St. Francis Col., Ft. Wayne, Ind.
Sister Mary Basil, Good Counsel College, White Plains, N.Y.
Sister Mary Berding, Edgecliff Col., Cincinnati, Ohio
Sister Mary Bernice, Our Lady of the Elms, Akron, Ohio
Sister Mary Bonita, The Felician Col., Chicago, Ill.
Sister M. Brideen Long, Holy Family Col., Manitowoc, Wis.
Sister M. Camille Kliebhan, Cardinal Stritch College, Milwaukee, Wis.
Sister Mary Charles, Molloy Catholic College for Women, Rockville Centre, N.Y.
Sister Mary Edward, Clarke Col., Dubuque, Iowa
Sister M. Christopher, 5801 Smith Ave., Baltimore, Md.
Sister Mary Chrysostom, College of Our Lady of the Elms, Chicopee, Mass.
Sister Mary Clarissa, Dominican College of Blauvelt, Blauvelt, N.Y.
Sister Mary David, College of St. Benedict, St. Joseph, Minn.
Sister Mary de Lourdes, Saint Joseph College, West Hartford, Conn.
Sister Mary Dorothy, Queen of Apostles Col. Library, Harrimon, N.Y.
Sister M. Edith Brotz, Marian Col., Fond du Lac, Wis.
Sister M. Edwina Bogel, Hilbert Col., Hamburg, N.Y.
Sister Mary Fidelia, Immaculata College, Bartlett, Ill.
Sister Mary Fidelma, Marylhurst College, Marylhurst, Oreg.
Sister M. Francis Regis, 444 Centre St., Milton, Mass.
Sister Mary Gabrieline, Marygrove College, Detroit, Mich.
Sister Mary Gabrielle, Nazareth College, Nazareth, Mich.
Sister M. Gregory, Marymount Col., Palo Verdes Estates, Calif.
Sister M. Harriet Sanborn, Aquinas College, Grand Rapids, Mich.
Sister Mary Helen, Dominican Col., Racine, Wis.
Sister Mary Hugh, Fontbonne College, St. Louis, Mo.
Sister M. Iona Taylor, Assumption Grotto Convent, Detroit, Mich.
Sister Mary Irmina Saelinger, Villa Madonna College, Covington, Ky.
Sister Mary Joanne, Marycrest College, Davenport, Iowa
Sister Mary Judith, Dept. of Educ., Briar Cliff College, Sioux City, Iowa
Sister Mary Lawrence, Mary Manse College, Toledo, Ohio
Sister Mary Leo, Immaculata College, Immaculata, Pa.

Sister M. Loyola, Russell Col., 2500 Adeline Dr., Burlingame, Calif.
Sister M. Luke Reiland, 6501 Almeda Rd., Houston, Tex.
Sister M. Margarita, Rosary College, River Forest, Ill.
Sister Mary Martin, Mercyhurst Col. Library, Erie, Pa.
Sister Mary Mercita, St. Mary College, Xavier, Kans.
Sister M. Nora Barber, Mt. Mary Col., Milwaukee, Wis.
Sister Mary Paul, Mt. Mercy College, Pittsburgh, Pa.
Sister Mary Priscilla, Notre Dame College, Cleveland, Ohio
Sister Mary Stephanie, Mt. St. Mary College, Hooksett, N.Y.
Sister Mary Theodine Sebold, Viterbo College, La Crosse, Wis.
Sister Mary Verona, Notre Dame Col., Cleveland, Ohio
Sister Mary Vianney, St. Xavier College, 103rd and Central Park, Chicago, Ill.
Sister Mary Warin, Notre Dame of Dallas, Irving, Tex.
Sister Mildred Clare, Nazareth College, Nazareth, Ky.
Sister Miriam Richard, St. James Convent, Elkins Park, Pa.
Sister Muriel Hogan, Ottumwa Heights College, Ottumwa, Iowa
Sister Regina Clare, Mt. St. Mary's College, Los Angeles, Calif.
Sister Rita Corkery, 5600 Washington Blvd., Chicago, Ill.
Sister Rita Donahue, Notre Dame College, Staten Island, N.Y.
Sister Rita Mercille, St. Mary's Col., Notre Dame, Ind.
Sister Rose Matthew, Marygrove College, Detroit, Mich.
Sister Rosemarie Julie, Educ. Dept., College of Notre Dame, Belmont, Calif.
Sister Rosemary Hufker, Notre Dame Col., St. Louis, Mo.
Skaggs, Darcy A., 3699 N. Holly Ave., Baldwin Park, Calif.
Skalski, John M., Sch. of Educ., Fordham University, New York, N.Y.
Skarzinski, Jo., 205 Virginia Ave., Pittsburgh, Pa.
Skatzes, D. H., Box 125, Old Washington, Ohio
Skeel, Dorothy J., Indiana Univ., Bloomington, Ind.
Skilton, John E., 793 Sycamore, Dr., Southhampton, Pa.
Skinner, Richard C., Clarion State College, Clarion, Pa.
Skinner, Vincent P., Univ. of Maine at Farmington, Farmington, Maine
Skinner, William S., Arizona State University, Scottsdale, Ariz.
Skogsberg, Alfred H., Bloomfield Junior High School, Bloomfield, N.J.
Skrocki, Patricia M., 409 Espanola Ave., Parchment, Mich.
Slan, A.A., Illinois State Univ., Normal, Ill.
Sletten, Vernon, Sch. of Educ., Univ. of Montana, Missoula, Mont.
Sliepcevich, Elena M., 2000 N. St. N.W. #301, Washington, D.C.
Sligo, Joseph R., 102 N. Lancaster St., Athens, Ohio
Slocum, Terry S., Jane Stenson Schl., Skokie, Ill.
Slocum, Thomas J., 11 S. Cagwin, Joliet, Ill.
*Smallenberg, Harry W., Supt. of Schools, L. A. Co., L.A., Calif.
Smart, Barbara C., 1550-1 Spartan Vil., E. Lansing, Mich.
Smart, Margaret E., Univ. of Southern California, Los Angeles, Calif.
Smedstad, Alton O., Superintendent, Elem. Schools, Hillsboro, Oreg.
Smelser, Rex H., 501 Broad St., Lake Charles, La.
Smith, Aaron A., 530 W. McClellan, Flint, Mich.
Smith, Alice P., 2977 Elmhurst, Detroit, Mich.
Smith, Alvin H., St. Andrews Presbyterian College, Laurinburg, N.C.
Smith, Anne M., 3401 N. Columbus Blvd., Tucson, Ariz.
Smith, Ara K., 609 Lafayette St., Michigan City, Ind.
Smith, B. Othanel, Col. of Educ., University of Illinois, Urbana, Ill.
Smith, Burnell R., 650 S. 15th St., Marion, Iowa
Smith, C. Klein, 1200 E. Fairmount Ave., Milwaukee, Wis.
Smith, Calvert H., 8813 S. Eggleston, Chicago, Ill.
Smith, Calvin M., Jr., Columbus Public Schls., Columbus, Ohio
Smith, Cleovis C., 4801 Tremont St., Dallas, Tex.
Smith, Clodus R., 9203 St. Andrews Pl., College Park, Md.
Smith, David C., Michigan State University, East Lansing, Mich.
Smith, Earl P., 122 Sims Road, Syracuse, N.Y.
Smith, E. Brooks, Wayne State University, Detroit, Mich.

Smith, Edward C., 990 Grove St., Evanston, Ill.
Smith, Emmitt D., Box 745, West Texas Station, Canyon, Tex.
Smith, Garmon B., Furman Univ., Greenville, S.C.
Smith, Gary F., 2951 Ramble Rd., Bloomington, Ind.
Smith, Gary R., 3514 Arrowvale Dr., Orchard Lake, Mich.
Smith, Gerald R., 411 Audubon Dr., Bloomington, Ind.
Smith, Hannis S., State Office Annex, 117 University Ave., St. Paul, Minn.
Smith, Harry E., The Har Schl., Princeton, N.J.
Smith, Hester M., 910 Wegman Rd., Rochester, N.Y.
Smith, Hilda C., Dept. of Educ., Loyola University, New Orleans, La.
Smith, James B., 221 S. Missouri, Belleville, Ill.
Smith, James J., Jr., New York Urban League, Albany, N.Y.
Smith, James O., 684 Van Ave., Shelbyville, Ind.
Smith, John W., 10001 Princeton Ave., Chicago, Ill.
Smith, Joseph M., 83 Apple Hill, Wethersfield, Conn.
Smith, Kenneth E., Grad. Sch. of Educ., Univ. of Chicago, Chicago, Ill.
Smith, Lawrence J., Central Michigan University, Mt. Pleasant, Mich.
Smith, Leslie F., 705 N. Killingsworth, Portland, Oreg.
Smith, Lewis B., University of Idaho, Moscow, Idaho
Smith, Lloyd N., Dept. of Educ., Indiana State University, Terre Haute, Ind.
Smith, Mark H., 682 Riverview Dr., Columbus, Ohio
Smith, Mary Alice, State College, Lock Haven, Pa.
Smith, Melvin, 1057 N. 7th, Rochelle, Ill.
Smith, Melvin, Lockport Twp. H.S., Lockport, Ill.
Smith, Menrie M., Rte. 4, Hamilton, Ala.
Smith, Nila Banton, 800 W. First St., Los Angeles, Calif.
Smith, Paul E., P.O. Box 11, Boulder, Colo.
Smith, Paul M., 104 Coral Sea Circle, China Lake, Calif.
Smith, Philip John, Box 63, Post Office, South Perth, W. Australia
Smith Richard N., 4214-43rd St., Des Moines, Iowa
Smith, Robert L., The Sidwell Friends Schl., Washington, D.C.
Smith, Robert M., Pennsylvania State Univ., University Park, Pa.
Smith, Russell F. W., 9 Bursley Pl., White Plains, N.Y.
Smith, Sisera, 115 South 54th St., Philadelphia, Pa.
*Smith, Stephen E., East Texas Baptist College, Marshall, Tex.
Smith, W. Holmes, El Camino Col., Torrance, Calif.
Smolens, Richard, 69 Wooleys, Great Neck, N.Y.
Snearline, Paul A., 815 Market St., Lewisburg, Pa.
Snider, Donald A., 2680 Fayette, Mountain View, Calif.
Snider, Glenn R., Col. of Educ., University of Oklahoma, Norman, Okla.
Snider, Hervon Leroy, Sch. of Educ., University of Idaho, Moscow, Idaho
Sniderman, Sam M., Ann Arbor Brd of Educ., 1220 Wells, Ann Arbor, Mich.
Snyder, Agnes, 50 Central Ter., Clifton Park, Wilmington, Del.
Snyder, Darl E., 1425 Madison. Tifton, Ga.
Snyder, Helen I., 1020 W. Beaver Ave., State College, Pa.
Snyder, Jerome R., 1114 Mogford St., Midland, Tex.
Snyder, Marjorie Sims, Col. of Educ., Indiana St. Univ., Terre Haute, Ind.
Snyder, Robert D., Superintendent of Schools, Wayzata, Minn.
Snyder, Robert E., 4658 Crystal Dr., Columbia, S.C.
Snyder, Ruth C., 110 Laurelton Rd., Rochester, N.Y.
Soares, Anthony T., 290 Lawrence Rd., Trumbull, Conn.
Sobel, Morton J., State Educ. Dept., Albany, N.Y.
Sobin, Gloria A., 370 Seymour Ave., Derby, Conn.
Soeberg, Dorothy D., 4034 Calle Ariana, Cyprus Shore, San Clemente, Calif.
Sokol, John N., 455 Park Ave., Leonia, N.J.
Solomon, Benjamin, Indust. Rela. Cntr., Univ. of Chicago, Chicago, Ill.
Solomon, Ruth H., 91 N. Allen St., Albany, N.Y.
Somers, Mary Louise, Sch. of SSA, Univ. of Chicago, Chicago, Ill.
Sommer, Maynard E., 1348 Romona Dr., Camarillo, Calif.
Sommers, George, 575 Pincrest Dr., Rantoul, Ill.

Sommers, Wesley S., 820 Sixth St., Menomonie, Wis.
Sonntag, Ida May, 5101 Norwich Rd., Toledo, Ohio
Sonstegard, Manford A., Southern Illinois Univ., Edwardsville, Ill.
Sorbo, Paul J., Jr., Board of Education, Windsor, Conn.
Sorensen, Edwin, P.O. Box 210, Northport, N.Y.
Sorenson, A. Garth, Moore Hall, University of California, Los Angeles, Calif.
Sorenson, Helmer E., Okla. St. Univ., Stillwater, Okla.
Sorenson, Mrs. Virginia, 105 N. Division Ave., Grand Rapids, Mich.
Sosulski, Michael C., 530 Carriage Dr., West Chicago, Ill.
Sotelo, Gloria, 1235 Boynton Ave., Bronx, N.Y.
Soucy, Leo A., Dist. Supt. of Schools, Auburn, N.Y.
Southall, Maycie K., Box 867, Peabody Col., Nashville, Tenn.
Sowards, George W., Florida State Univ., Tallahassee, Fla.
Spaulding, Robert L., Duke University, Durham, N.C.
Spaulding, Seth J., UNESCO, Place de Fontenory, Paris VII, France
Spear, William G., 7233 W. Lunt Ave., Chicago, Ill.
Spears, Louise, Eigenmann Center, Univ. of Ind., Bloomington, Ind.
Spears, Sol, El Marino School, Culver City, Calif.
Speciale, Anna Gloria, 120 Soundview Ave., Plains, N.Y.
Speer, Hugh W., University of Missouri, Kansas City, Mo.
Speicher, A. Dean, 8008 Kennedy Ave., Highland, Ind.
Speier, Peter, 327 Hill St., Athens, Ga.
Speights, Mrs. R. M., Limestone College, Gaffney, S.C.
Spence, Joseph R., Mankato St., Col., Mankato, Minn.
Spence, Ralph B., 355 Beechwood Dr., Athens, Ga.
Spencer, Doris U., Johnson State College, Johnson, Vt.
Spencer, Edward M., Fresno State College, Fresno, Calif.
Spencer, Elizabeth F., Ball State University, Muncie, Ind.
Spencer, James E., P.O. Box 813, Danville, Calif.
Sperber, Robert I., 21 Lowell Rd., Brookline, Mass.
Spielman, Lester A., 2970 N. Lake Shore Dr., Chicago, Ill.
Spigle, Irving S., Park Forest Pub. Schools, Park Forest, Ill.
Spinks, Sam, Hattiesburg Pub. Schs., Hattiesburg, Miss.
Spinner, Arnold, New York University, New York, N.Y.
Spinola, A. R., Superintendent, Denville School Dist. No. 1, Denville, N.J.
Spiro, Mrs. David (Molly), 68 Vernon Dr., Pittsburgh, Pa.
Springman, John H., 1215 Waukegan Rd., Glenview, Ill.
Sprung, Hilda, Shelter Rock Sch., Manhasset, N.Y.
Squire, James R., Ginn & Co., Boston, Mass.
Stacy, Don, Baylor Univ., Box 115,Waco, Tex.
Stadthaus, Alice, 6499 Kenview Dr., Cincinnati, Ohio
Staggs, Jack, Sam Houston State Col., Huntsville, Tex.
Stahl, Albert F., 20345 Westpointe Ct., Southfield, Mich.
Stahlecker, Lotar V., Kent State University, Kent, Ohio
Stahly, Harold L., 8343 Manchester Dr., Grand Blanc, Mich.
Staidl, Doris J., 535 Moorland Rd., Madison, Wis.
Staiger, Ralph C., 701 Dallam Rd., Newark, Del.
Staiger, Roger P., Dept. of Chem., Ursinus College, Collegeville, Pa.
Stalnaker, John M., 569 Briar Lane, Northfield, Ill.
Stancato, Frank A., 7182 Bellevue Dr., Mt. Pleasant, Mich.
Stang, Genevieve E., 730 First St., Apt. H, Bowling Green, Ohio
Stanley, Calvin, Texas Southern University, Houston, Tex.
Stansbury, George W. Jr., Georgia State Univ., Atlanta, Ga.
Stanton, Hy, 8340 S.W. 131st St., Miami, Fla.
Stanton, William A., Purdue University, Lafeyette, Ind.
Starner, Norman Dean, Wyalusing Valley Joint High School, Wyalusing, Pa.
Starnes, Thomas A., Atlanta Public Schools, Atlanta, Ga.
Starr, Fay H., M. W. Regional Educ. Lab., St. Ann, Ill.
Starr, W. Gene, 6192 Trinette Ave., Garden Grove, Calif.
Stathopulos, Peter H., 1027 Valley Forge, Devon, Pa.

Statler, Charles R., Univ. of South Carolina, Columbia, S.C.
Stauffer, Arthur L., Jr., State Univ. Col., Fredonia, N.Y.
Stauffer, Russell G., c/o Sandford Schs., Hockessin, Del.
Staven, LaVier L., 1304 MacArthur Rd., Hays, Kans.
Steadman, E. R., 277 Columbia, Elmhurst, Ill.
Steege, Barbara, Concordia Theological Sem. Libr., Springfield, Ill.
Steele, Joe Milan, 1016 W. William St., Champaign, Ill.
Steele, Lani, 37 Ozone Ave., Venice, Calif.
Steele, Lysle Hugh, P.O. Box 914, Beloit, Wis.
Steele, Marilyn H., 510 Mott Foundation Bldg., Flint, Mich.
Steensma, Geraldine J., Covenant Col., Lookout Mountain, Tenn.
Steer, Donald R., University of Michigan, Ann Arbor, Mich.
Steeves, Frank L., Dept. of Educ., Marquette Univ., Milwaukee, Wis.
Steffen, Robert, Syracuse Univ., Syracuse, N.Y.
Steg, Doreen E., 1616 Hepburn Dr., Villanova, Pa.
Stegall, Alma Lirline, Virginia State College, Petersburg, Va.
Steger, Robert I., Rt. 2, Rhinelander, Wis.
Steimer, William M., 2112 Broad St., Durham, N.C.
Stein, Michael W., Western Jr. H.S., Greenwich, Conn.
Stein, Rita F., Ind. Schl. of Nursing, Indianapolis, Ind.
Steinberg, Paul M., Hebrew Union Col., New York, N.Y.
Steinberg, Warren L., 2737 Dunleer Pl., Los Angeles, Calif.
Steiner, Harry, 5 Belaire Dr., Roseland, N.J.
Steinhagen, Margaret J., 107 McKendree Ave., Annapolis, Md.
Steinhauer, Charlotte H., 1560—75th St., Downers Grove, Ill.
Steininger, Earl W., 535 West 5th St., Dubuque, Iowa
Stell, Samuel C., Robeson County Bd. of Educ., Lumberton, N.C.
Stephens, E. R., Univ. of Iowa, Iowa City, Iowa
Stephens, Kenton, Oak Park Schools, Oak Park, Ill.
Stephens, Thomas M., Ohio St. Univ., Columbus, Ohio
Stephenson, Alan R., 11227 Plymouth Ave., Cleveland, Ohio
Sterling, A. M., 1017 Garner Ave., Schenectady, N.Y.
Stern, Harold O., Oberlin Col., Oberlin, Ohio
Sterner, William S., Rutgers Univ., Newark, N.J.
Stetson, Ethel A., 47 Westchester Ave., North Babylon, N.Y.
Stevens, Humphrey, Northeastern Ill. St. Col., Chicago, Ill.
Stevens, J. H., 916 Carter Hill Rd., Montgomery, Ala.
Stevens, Robert L., 1040 N. Pleasant St., Amherst, Mass.
Stewart, Alan D., St. Educ. Dept., 480 Madison Ave., Albany, N.Y.
Stewart, Clinton E., Texarkana Col., Texarkana, Tex.
Stewart, James T., Delgado Institute, New Orleans, La.
Stewart, Lawrence H., University of California, Berkeley, Calif.
Stickler, W. Hugh, Florida State University, Tallahassee, Fla.
Stiemke, Eugenia A., Valparaiso University, Valparaiso, Ind.
Stier, Lealand D., P.O. Box 247, Saratoga, Calif.
Stiles, Grace E., Box 502, Farmington, Maine
Stirzaker, Norbert A., 766 Palmetto, Spartanburg, S.C.
Stitt, J. Howard, Northern Arizona University, Flagstaff, Ariz.
Stitt, Sam C., Superintendent of Schools, Ellinwood, Kans.
Stivers, Stephen N., 3731 University Way, N.E., Seattle, Wash.
Stoddard, George D., 434 E. 87th St., New York, N.Y.
Stoddart, Charles L., 6592 Powers Rd., Orchard Pk., N.Y.
Stofega, Michael E., 271 State St., Perth Amboy, N.J.
Stoffler, James A., Colorado State College, Greeley, Colo.
Stoia, George, 234 Conover Rd., Pittsburgh, Pa.
Stokes, Maurice S., Savannah State College, Savannah, Ga.
Stolee, Michael J., 6618 San Vincente Ave., Coral Gables, Fla.
Stolurow, Lawrence M., 110 Pleasant St., Lexington, Mass.
Stone, Curtis C., Kent State University, Kent, Ohio

Stone, Franklin D., Univ. of Iowa, Iowa City, Iowa
Stone, George P., Union College, Lincoln, Nebr.
Stone, Howard L., 1732 Wauwatosa Ave., Wauwatosa, Wis.
Stone, James C., University of California, Berkeley, Calif.
Stone, Paul T., Huntingdon College, Montgomery, Ala.
Stonehocker, D. Doyle, 1515 Oakdale St., Burlington, Iowa
Stoops, John A., Dept. of Educ., Lehigh University, Bethlehem, Pa.
Stordahl, Kalmer E., Northern Michigan Univ., Marquette, Mich.
Storen, Helen F., 114 Morningside Dr., New York, N.Y.
Storlie, Theodore R., 1400 W. Maple Ave., Downers Grove, Ill.
Storm, Jerome F., 2206 Westchester Blvd., Springfield, Ill.
Stottler, Richard H., University of Maryland, College Park, Md.
Stoutenburgh, W. H., Wissahickon Sch. Dist., Ambler, Pa.
Stoughton, Robert W., State Department of Education, Hartford, Conn.
Strahler, Violet R., 5340 Brendonwood Ln., Dayton, Ohio
Strain, Joe P., Ball State Univ., Muncie, Ind.
Strain, John P., Dept. of Educ., Texas Tech. Col., Lubbock, Tex.
Strain, Mrs. Sibyl M., 2236 Los Lunas St., Pasadena, Calif.
Strand, Richard H., Azusa Pacific Col., San Gabriel, Calif.
Strand, William H., Sch. of Educ., Stanford University, Stanford, Calif.
Strang, Ruth M., 1904 N. Jones Ave., Wantagh, L.I., New York
Strathairn, Pamela L., Women's Phy. Ed. Dept., Stanford Univ., Stanford, Calif.
Straub, Raymond R., Jr., 1120 S. Gay St., Phoenixville, Pa.
Strauss, John F., Jr., 14004-119th Ave. N.E., Kirkland, Wash.
Strawn, Aimee W., Chicago State Col., South, Chicago, Ill.
Strayer, George D., Jr. Col. of Educ., University of Washington, Seattle, Wash.
Strebel, Jane D., Bd. of Educ., 807 N.E. Broadway, Minneapolis, Minn.
Street, William Paul, Univ. of Kentucky, Lexington, Ky.
Streich, William H., Farmington Pub. Schools, Farmington, Conn.
Streitmatter, Kenneth D., State Office Bldg., Denver, Colo.
Strem, Bruce E., 109 Marykay Rd., Timonium, Md.
Streng, Alice, University of Wisconsin-Milwaukee, Milwaukee, Wis.
Strickland, C. G., Sch. of Educ., Baylor University, Waco, Tex.
Strickland, J. D., 3302 Conner Dr., Canyon, Tex.
Stringfellow, Mrs. Jackie R., 1833 Second St., S.E., Moultrie, Ga.
Strohbehn, Earl F., 12151 Mellowood Dr., Saratoga, Calif.
Strole, Lois E., R.R. No. 2, West Terre Haute, Ind.
Stromberg, Francis I., Oklahoma State University, Stillwater, Okla.
Strowbridge, Edwin D., Oregon State University, Corvallis, Oreg.
Stuart, Alden T., St. Andrews Rd., Southampton, N.Y.
Stuart, Chipman G., Col. of Educ., Univ. of Okla., Norman, Okla.
Stuber, George, Clayton School Dist., 7530 Maryland Ave., Clayton, Mo.
Studer, Harold, 2103 Market St., Harrisburg, Pa.
Stuenkel, Walter W., Concordia College, Milwaukee, Wis.
Stull, Lorren L., Arps Hall, Ohio St. Univ., Columbus, Ohio
Sturge, Harry H., 91 Victor St., Plainview, N.Y.
Stutzman, Carl R., Fresno State Col., Fresno, Calif.
Sudyk, James Edward, 830 Williams Way, Mountain View, Calif.
Suess, Alan R., M. Golden Labs., Purdue Univ., Lafayette, Ind.
Sugarman, Alan, Ramapo Cent. Sch. Dist. No. 2, Spring Valley, N.Y.
Suhd, Melvin, 8501 Tampa, Northridge, Calif.
Suhr, Virtus W., Northern Illinois University, DeKalb, Ill.
Suiter, Phil E., Chesapeake High School, Chesapeake, Ohio
Sullivan, Dorothy D., University of Maryland, College Park, Md.
Sullivan, Edmund V., 102 Bloor St., W., Toronto, Ont., Canada
Sullivan, Floyd W., 1015 Lena St., N.W., Atlanta, Ga.
Sullivan, Joanna, 21 N. Mountain Ave., Montclair, N.J.
Sullivan, Maurice, Miami Univ., Oxford, Ohio
Sullivan, John J., Roosevelt Sch. Dist., Phoenix, Ariz.

Sullivan, Mona Lee R., 1302 Brooklawn Rd., N.E., Atlanta, Ga.
Sullivan, Robert E., Notre Dame Col., Cotabato City, Philippines
Sullivan, Ruth E., 306 Bayswater, Salem Harbour, Andalusia, Pa.
Sundquist, Ralph R., Jr., Hartford Seminary Foundation, Hartford, Conn.
Sunzeri, Adeline V., 6142 Afton Pl., Hollywood, Calif.
Susskind, Edwin G., 150-14th St., Buffalo, N.Y.
Sutherland, Angus W., Public Schools, Detroit, Mich.
Sutherland, Jack W., San Jose State College, San Jose, Calif.
Sutherland, Margaret, Col. of Educ., University of California, Davis, Calif.
Sutton, Elizabeth W., 5628 Massachusetts, Washington, D.C.
Sutton, Kenneth R., Dept. of Educ., Univ. of N. Mex., Albuquerque, N. Mex.
Swain, R. Stanley, 1361 Xanadu, Aurora, Colo.
Swalm, James, Reading Center, Rutgers Univ., Piscataway, N.J.
Swann, Mrs. A. Ruth, 2713 Mapleton Ave., Norfolk, Va.
Swanson, Gordon I., Dept. of Agric. Educ., Univ. of Minnesota, St. Paul, Minn.
Swanson, Herbert L., El Camino Col., Torrance, Calif.
Swartout, Sherwin G., State Univ. Col., Brockport, N.Y.
Sweany, H. Paul, Michigan State University, East Lansing, Mich.
Sweeney, Christopher J., Youngstown St. Univ., Youngstown, Ohio
Swenson, Esther J., Box 1942, University, Ala.
Swertfeger, Floyd F., Route 3, Box 16, Farmville, Va.
Swindall, Wellington, Palmdale School, 3000 E. Wier Ave., Phoenix, Ariz.
Swindel, Mrs. Mabel A., Three Rivers Jr. Col., Poplar Bluff, Mo.
Syvinski, Henry B., Villanova University, Villanova, Pa.
Szabo, Robert J., 1868 W. North St., Bethlehem, Pa.

*Tag, Herbert G., Univ. of Conn., Storrs, Conn.
Tajima, Yuri, 1918 N. Bissell, Chicago, Ill.
Tallen, Rachel R., Psych. Dept., Indiana Univ., Bloomington, Ind.
Talley, T. Lavon, Oglethorpe Col., Atlanta, Ga.
*Tallman, Russell W., Jewell, Iowa
Tamashunas, Edward T., Central H.S., Bridgeport, Conn.
Tambe, Naren, Box 1393, Durham, N.C.
Tanck, Marlin L., 3748 N. Downer Ave., Milwaukee, Wis.
Tanenbaum, Bernard M., 3620 N. Pine Grove Ave., Chicago, Ill.
Tanner, B. William, 650 S. Detroit Ave., Toledo, Ohio
Tanner, Daniel, Rutgers University, New Brunswick, N.J.
Tarver, Klisby, E., 2175 Hebert St., Beaumont, Tex.
Taschow, Horst G., Univ. of Saskatchewan, Regina, Saskatchewan, Can.
Tate, Virginia, 2228 Eighth St. Cr., Charleston, Ill.
Tauber, Ann, 16401 Knollwood Dr., Granada Hills, Calif.
Taylor, Azella, 18 Vista Rd., Ellensburg, Wash.
Taylor, Barr, Murray State Col., Murray, Ky.
Taylor, George E., Supt. of Schs., Fairbanks, Alaska
Taylor, John M., 2409 Huffine Circle, Johnson City, Tenn.
Taylor, Kenneth I., Madison Public Schools, Madison, Wis.
Taylor, Marvin, Div. of Educ., Queens College, Flushing, N.Y.
Taylor, Marvin J., 4873 Far Hills Ave., Kellering, Ohio
Taylor, Mrs. Mary C., Box 164, Rt. No. 1, New Lenox, Ill.
Taylor, Peter A., Fac. of Educ., Univ. of Manitoba, Winnepeg, Man., Canada
Taylor, Robert E., 3759 Klondike Ave., Delaware, Ohio
Taylor, Wayne, 160 Kenberry, East Lansing, Mich.
Teare, Benjamin R., Jr., Carnegie-Mellon Univ., Schenley Park, Pa.
Tedeschi, Anthony, P.O. Box 216, Falls Village, Conn.
Telego, Gene, 7010 Salisbury Rd., Columbus, Ohio
Telford, Charles W., San Jose State College, San Jose, Calif.
Temp, George E., Educ. Test. Service, Berkeley, Calif.
Tempero, Howard E., Teachers Col., University of Nebraska, Lincoln, Nebr.
Temple, F. L., Box 2185, University, Ala.
Templin, Mildred C., Inst. of Child Welfare, Univ. of Minnesota, Minneapolis, Minn.

Tenny, John W., 239 E. 12 Mile Rd., Royal Oak, Mich.
Terlaje, Shirley A., P.O. Box 1719, Agana, Guam
Tetz, Henry E., Oregon College of Education, Monmouth, Oreg.
Theisen, Richard H., 2701 Chicago, Detroit, Mich.
Thelen, L. J., University of Massachusetts, Amherst, Mass.
Thevaos, Deno G., 575 Westview Ave., State College, Pa.
Thomann, Don F., Dept. of Educ., Ripon College, Ripon, Wis.
Thomas, David C., Ottawa Univ., Ottawa, Kans.
Thomas, Granville S., Superintendent of Schools, Salem, N.J.
Thomas, J. Alan, University of Chicago, Chicago, Ill.
Thomas, James E., Supt. of Schools, Bristol, Tenn.
Thomas, T. M. 71 Mencel Circle, Bridgeport, Conn.
Thomas, Wade F., Santa Monica City College, Santa Monica, Calif.
Thompson, Mrs. Alberta S., Dept. of H.E., Kent State Univ., Kent, Ohio
Thompson, Anton, Long Beach Public Schls., 715 Locust Ave., Long Beach, Calif.
Thompson, Barry B., Waco Independent School Dist., Waco, Tex.
Thompson, Bertha Boya, Western Col. for Women, Oxford, Ohio
Thompson, Charles H., Grad. Sch., Howard University, Washington, D.C.
Thompson, Elton N., Calif. State Col., San Bernadino, Calif.
Thompson, Franklin J., South Pasadena High School, South Pasadena, Calif.
Thompson, Fred R., Col. of Educ., Univ. of Maryland, College Park, Md.
Thompson, Gary, 406 Crescent Dr., Westerville, Ohio
Thompson, Helen M., Thompson Reading Clinic, Orange, Calif.
Thompson, James H., 35 Pleasantview Dr., Athens, Ohio
Thompson, John D., P.O. Drawer 877, Seminole Public Schools, Seminole, Tex.
Thompson, John F., 5408 Forest Lawn, McFarland, Wis.
Thompson, Lloyd R., 5018 N. Geer Rd., Turlock, Calif.
Thompson, Margaret M., San Fernando State Col., Northridge, Calif.
Thompson, O. E., University of California, Davis, Calif.
Thompson, Olive L., 1541 Iroquois Ave., Long Beach, Calif.
Thompson, Ralph H., Western Washington State Col., Bellingham, Wash.
Thompson, Ray, 923 Plum St., Durham, N.C.
Thompson, Mrs. Sheilah, 930 Whitchurch St., North Vancouver, B.C., Canada
Thoms, Denis, Campus View # 124, Bloomington, Ind.
Thomsen, Ronald W., Box 361, Sidney, Iowa
Thomson, Procter, Pitzer Hall, Claremont Men's College, Claremont, Calif.
Thomson, Scott C., 2508 Benvenue #204, Berkeley, Calif.
Thorn, Elizabeth, Provincial Teachers College, North Bay, Ont., Canada
Thorndike, Robert L., Tchrs. Col., Columbia University, New York, N.Y.
Thornsley, Jerome R., 764 Laurel Ave., Pomona, Calif.
Thornton, James W., Jr., San Jose State College, San Jose, Calif.
Throne, Elsie M., 306 Lincoln Ave., Avon-by-the-Sea, N.J.
Thurner, Ronald, University of Houston, Houston, Tex.
Thursby, Marilyn P., Box 13795, Univ. Sta., Gainesville, Fla.
Thyberg, Clifford S., 1717 W. Merced Ave., West Covina, Calif.
Tidwell, Robert E., 1602 Alaca Pl., Tuscaloosa, Ala.
Tiedeman, Herman R., Illinois State University, Normal, Ill.
Tielke, Elton F., Univ. Park Elem. Schl., Dallas, Tex.
Tiffany, Betty Jane, 305 E. Church St., Ridgecrest, Calif.
Tiffany, Burton C., Supt. of Schools, Chula Vista, Calif.
Tiitsman, Katrin, Hunter Col., CUNY, New York, N.Y.
Tikasingh, Ancel J., Sacramento St. Col., Sacramento, Calif.
Tillman, Rodney, George Washington University, Washington, D.C.
Timmons, F. Alan, 1700 Octavia St., San Francisco, Calif.
Tinari, Charles, Shackamaxon School, Scotch Plains, N.J.
Tingle, Mary J., Col. of Educ., University of Georgia, Athens, Ga.
Tink, Albert K., 18 Wendall Pl., DeKalb, Ill.
Tinker, Miles A., P.O. Box 3193, Santa Barbara, Calif.
Tinney, James J., Supt. of Schools, Rutland, Vt.

Tinsley, Drew, 3909 Roland Blvd., St. Louis, Mo.
Tipton, Elis May, 202 Coast Blvd., La Jolla, Calif.
Tira, Daniel E., Ohio St. Univ., Columbus, Ohio
Tittle, Carol K., 133 W. 94th St., New York, N.Y.
Todd, Edward S., Rochester Inst. of Tech., Rochester, N.Y.
Todd, G. Raymond, R.D. No. 3, Bethlehem, Pa.
Todd, Karen, 2402 Woodmere Dr., Cleveland Heights, Ohio
Todd, Neal F., 128 Main St., Ware, Mass.
Toepfer, Conrad F., Jr., State Univ. Col., Buffalo, N.Y.
Toepfer, Conrad S., SUNY at Buffalo, Buffalo, N.Y.
Toles, Caesar F., Bishop Junior College, 4527 Crozier St., Dallas, Tex.
Tolleson, Sherwell K., Box 146A, T.T.U., Cookeville, Tenn.
Tom, Chow Loy, Univ. of Denver, Denver, Colo.
Tomaszewski, Raymond J., 333 Richard Ter., S.E., Grand Rapids, Mich.
Tomacek, Carolyn L., 2518 W. 59th St., Chicago, Ill.
Tomita, Shiochi, Waller H.S., Chicago, Ill.
Toney, Jo Anne, Indiana St. Univ., Terre Haute, Ind.
Toops, Herbert A., 1430 Cambridge Blvd., Columbus, Ohio
Torchia, Joseph, Millersville State Col., Millersville, Pa.
Torkelson, Gerald M., 408 Miller, Univ. of Washington, Seattle, Wash.
Torrance, E. Paul, University of Georgia, Athens, Ga.
Torres, Leonard, 9892 Oma Pl., Garden Grove, Calif.
Tothill, Herbert, East. Michigan Univ., Ypsilanti, Mich.
Totten, W. Fred, Mott Sci. Bldg., 1401 E. Court St., Flint, Mich.
Tough, D.L., 15 Oakburn Crescent, Willowdale, Ontario, Can.
Toussaint, Isabella H., 1670 River Rd., Beaver, Pa.
Tovey, Duane R., 720 Cloute St., Ft. Atkinson, Wis.
Towe, Arthur, P.O. Box 100, Cheboygan, Mich.
Towers, Richard L., St. John's Univ., Jamaica, N.Y.
Towner, John C., 547 N. Dallas St., River Falls, Wis.
Tracy, Elaine M., St. Olaf College, Northfield, Minn.
Tracy, Neal H., University of North Carolina, Chapel Hill, N.C.
Traeger, Carl, 375 N. Eagle St., Oshkosh, Wis.
Traiber, Frank, USAID Mission, Guatemala, State Dept., Washington, D.C.
Tramondo, Anthony, White Plains High School, White Plains, N.Y.
Travelstead, Chester C., Col. of Educ., Univ. of New Mexico, Albuquerque, N.M.
Travers, John F., Boston College, Chestnut Hill, Mass.
Travers, Kenneth J., Col. of Educ., Univ. of Ill., Urbana, Ill.
Travis, Vaud A., Dept. of Educ., Northeastern State College, Tahlequa, Okla.
Travis, Vaud A., Jr., Central Piedmont Community Col., Charlotte, N.C.
Traxler, Arthur E., 6825 S.W. 59th St., Miami, Fla.
Treece, Marion B., Southern Illinois University, Carbondale, Ill.
Tremont, Joseph J., 22 Fletcher St., Ayer, Mass.
Trigg, Harold L., State Board of Educ., Greensboro, N.C.
Triggs, Frances, Mountain Home, N.C.
Trippe, Mathew J., 1824 Oak Creek Dr., Palo Alto, Calif.
Trout, Len L., 2000 Royal Dr., Reno, Nev.
Troyer, Maurice E., Syracuse Univ., Syracuse, N.Y.
Truckey, George R., 1424 Price Drive, Cape Girardeau, Mo.
Truher, Helen Burke, 245 Hillside Rd., South Pasadena, Calif.
Trumble, Verna J., 42 West St., Johnson City, N.Y.
Trump, J. Lloyd, Nat. Assoc. Sec. Sch. Prin., Washington, D.C.
Truncellito, Louis, 6129 Leesburg Pike, Falls Church, Va.
Trusty, Francis M., 8605 Wimbledon Dr., Knoxville, Tenn.
Tuchman, Maurice S., Hebrew Col., Brookline, Mass.
Tucker, Jan L., 3780 Starr King Circle, Palo Alto, Calif.
Tucker, Sylvia B., 30929 Rue Langlois, Palos Verdes, Pen, Calif.
Tupper, Frank B., 389 Congress St., Portland, Maine
Turansky, Isadore, Western Michigan University, Kalamazoo, Mich.
Turchan, Donald G., 516 Riley Rd., New Castle, Ind.

Turck, Merton J., Tennessee Tech. Univ., Cookeville, Tenn.
Turner, Delia F., 3310 Edgemont, Tucson, Ariz.
Turner, Harold E., Univ. of Missouri, St. Louis, Mo.
Turner, Mae D., 672 Warner Rd., Hubbard, Ohio
Turney, David T., Sch. of Educ., Indiana State Univ., Terre Haute, Ind.
Turnquist, Carl H., Detroit Pub. Schls., 5057 Woodward Ave., Detroit, Mich.
Turnure, James E., Univ. of Minnesota, Minneapolis, Minn.
Tuseth, Alice A., 6410—37th Ave. No., Minneapolis, Minn.
Tuttle, Edwin A., Jr., State Univ. Col., New Paltz, N.Y.
Twombly, John J., Cumberland Comm. Col., Vineland, N.J.
Tydings, R. N., Hobbs Municipal Schools, Hobbs, N. Mex.
Tyer, Harold L., 111 Chelsea Circle, Statesboro, Ga.
Tyler, Fred T., University of Victoria, Victoria, B.C., Canada
Tyler, I. Keith, Ohio State University, Columbus, Ohio
Tyler, Louise L., University of California, Los Angeles, Calif.
Tyler, Priscilla, Univ. of Missouri, Kansas City, Mo.
Tyler, Ralph W., 440 Davis Ct., San Francisco, Calif.
Tyler, Robert, Educ. Dept., Southwestern State College, Weatherford, Okla.
Tyrrell, Francis M., Immaculate Conception Seminary, Huntington, N.Y.
Tystad, Edna, Thoreau Public Schools, Thoreau, N.M.

Ubben, Gerald C., Univ. of Tennessee, Knoxville, Tenn.
Uhlir, Richard F., 800½ W. White St., Champaign, Ill.
Umansky, Harlan L., Emerson High School, Union City, N.J.
Umholtz, Mrs. Anne K., 292 N. Fifth Ave., Highland Park, N.J.
Umstattd, James G., Sutton Hall, University of Texas, Austin, Tex.
Underwood, Anna M., 1944 Howell Branch Rd., Winter Pk., Fla.
Underwood, Bertha M., Alabama State Col., Montgomery, Ala.
Underwood, Mrs. Frances A., 5900 Hilltop Rd., Pensacola, Fla.
Underwood, Helen B., School of Voc. Nurs., Napa, Calif.
Underwood, Mary H., 434 Prince St., Whitewater, Wis.
Underwood, William J., 304 Lakeview, Lee's Summit, Mo.
Unger, Mrs. Dorothy Holberg, 99 Lawton Rd., Riverside, Ill.
Unruh, Adolph, 151 N. Bemiston, Clayton, Mo.
Urdang, Miriam E., Queens College, Flushing, N.Y.
Usitalo, Richard J., 2015 Clairemont Cir., Olympia, Wash.
Utley, Quentin, 136 E.S. Temple, Salt Lake City, Utah

Vail, Edward O., Los Angeles City Schools, Los Angeles, Calif.
Vaccaro, Albert, 4271 Gemini Path, Liverpool, N.Y.
Valdez, Barbara M., Harmon Johnson Schl., Sacramento, Calif.
Van Auken, Robert A., Superintendent of Schools, North Olmsted, Ohio
Van Bruggen, John A., 1590 Innes St., N.E., Grand Rapids, Mich.
Vance, Douglas S., Mesa Public Schools, Mesa, Ariz.
Vandagrifft, Donna Jo, 2608 Eastgate Lane, Bloomington, Ind.
Van de Bogart, Carl R., 69 Maple St., W. Lebanon, N.H.
Vanderhoof, C. David, Superintendent of Schools, Little Silver, N.J.
Vander Horck, Karl J., 644 Leicester, Duluth, Minn.
Vander Linde, Louis F., 3344 Pall Dr., Warren, Mich.
VanderMeer, A. W., Pennsylvania St. Univ., University Pk., Pa.
Van de Roovaart, Elizabeth G., 203 East 113th St., Chicago, Ill.
Vanderpool, J. Alden, 1736 Escalante Way, Burlingame, Calif.
Vander Werf, Lester S., Long Island Univ., Brookville, N.Y.
Van Donegan, Richard D., Univ. of New Mexico, Alberquerque, N. Mex.
Van Every, Donald F., 19265 Linville Ave., Grosse Pointe Woods, Mich.
Van Hoy, Neal E., 8308 E. Clarendon Ave., Scottsdale, Ariz.
Van Istendal, Theodore G., Spartan Village, East Lansing, Mich.
Van Loo, Eleanor, South Macomb Com. College, Detroit, Mich.
Van Metre, Patricia D., 333 S. Alvernon, Tucson, Ariz.

Van Pelt, Jacob J., 721 N. Juanita St., LaHabra, Calif.
Van Wagenen, Marvin J., 1729 Irving Ave., South, Minneapolis, Minn.
Van Zanten, Mrs. Hazel, 4754 Curwood, S.E., Grand Rapids, Mich.
Varn, Guy L., Supt. of Schools, 1616 Richland St., Columbia, S.C.
Varner, Charles S., Supt. of Schools, Runnells, Iowa
Varner, Leo P., Bakersfield Cntr., Fresno State Col., Bakersfield, Calif.
Varty, Jonathan W., 149 Brixton Rd., Garden City, N.Y.
Vasey, Hamilton G., 346 Second Ave., S.W., Cedar Rapids, Iowa
Vaughan, W. Donald, R. D., Pipersville, Pa.
Vaughn, C. A., Jr., Howey Academy, Howey-in-the-Hills, Fla.
Vaught, Maxine H., 1415 Crestwood Dr., Fayetteville, Ark.
Vayhinger, Harold P., Ohio Northern Univ., Ada, Ohio
Veltman, Peter, 600 College Ave., Wheaton, Ill.
Vergiels, John M., Col. of Educ., Univ. of Nevada, Las Vegas, Nev.
Verill, John E., University of Minnesota, Duluth, Minn.
Vermillion, Edward F., 914 Maxwell Ter., Bloomington, Ind.
Verseput, Robert Frank, 8 South St., Dover, N.J.
Versteegh, Madge, 3528-38th St., Des Moines, Iowa
Vest, Thomas, Miami Univ., Oxford, Ohio
Vial, Lynda W., 6522 Pennsylvania Ave., Kansas City, Mo.
Vice, Billy J., Univ. of Kentucky, Lexington, Ky.
Vickery, Tom Rusk, 111 Berkeley Dr., Syracuse, N.Y.
Vigilante, Nicholas J., Frostburg St. Col., Frostburg, Md.
Vikner, Carl F., Gustavus Adolphus College, St. Peter, Minn.
Vinicombe, Harry W., Jr., 2445 Lyttonsville Rd., Silver Spring, Md.
Vint, Virginia H., P.O. Box 271, Bloomington, Ill.
Vlahakos, Irene J., Cent. Connecticut State Col., New Britain, Conn.
Vlcek, Charles, Central Washington State College, Ellensburg, Wash.
Voelker, Paul Henry, 552 N. Neville St., Pittsburgh, Pa.
Voigt, Harry R., St. Paul's College, Concordia, Mo.
Voigt, Virginia E., 9 East Clark Pl., South Orange, N.J.
Volante, William, 220 W. Jersey St., Elizabeth, N.J.
Vonk, Paul K., 5355 Timber Trail, N.E., Atlanta, Ga.
Von Redlich, Jean D., 3936 Clairmont Ave., Birmingham, Ala.
Vopni, Sylvia, Univ. of Washington, Col. of Educ., Seattle, Wash.
Voris, George A., R.D. No. 1, Goodyear Lake, Oneonta, N.Y.
Voss, Burton E., Univ. High Sch., University of Michigan, Ann Arbor, Mich.
Vroon, John W., 3700 Sutherland Ave., Knoxville, Tenn.

Wade, Durlyn, State Univ. Col., Geneseo, N.Y.
Wadsworth, Erwing W., Appalachian St. Univ., Boone, N.C.
Wagner, Carl, Supt. of Schs., Livonia, Mich.
Wagner, Jean, 722 Eigenmann, Bloomington, Ind.
Wagner, Robert W., Ohio State University, Columbus, Ohio
Wagstaff, Lonnie H., 2707 Sonata Dr., Columbus, Ohio
Wagstaff, Robert F., Box 541, LeClaire, Iowa
Waimon, Morton D., Illinois State University, Normal, Ill.
Waine, Sidney I., 34 Thomas Dr., Hauppauge, N.Y.
Wainscott, Carlton O., 3607 Fleetwood, Austin, Tex.
Walby, Grace S., 700 Elgin Ave., Winnipeg 4, Man., Canada
Waldau, Helen, 87 Matson Hill Rd., S. Glastonbury, Conn.
Waldron, James S., New Slocum Hgts. Syracuse, N.Y.
Waldron, Margaret L., Ayrshire, Iowa
Walker, Charles L., P.O. Box 114, Jonas Ridge, N.C.
Walker, Clare C., Univ. of Guam, Agana, Guam
Walker, Decker, Stanford Univ., Stanford, Calif.
Wall, G. S., Stout State University, Menomonie, Wis.
Wall, Harry V., 17013 Alwood St., West Covina, Calif.
Wall, Jessie S., Box 194, Univ. of So. Mississippi, Hattiesburg, Miss.
Wallace, Donald G., Col. of Educ., Drake University, Des Moines, Iowa

Wallace, James O., 1001 Howard St., San Antonio, Tex.
Wallace, Richard C., East. Reg. Inst. for Educ., Syracuse, N.Y.
Wallen, Norman E., San Francisco State Col., San Francisco, Calif.
Waller, Virginia P., Vance Co. Schls., Henderson, N.C.
Wallin, William H., 1765 Santa Anita, Las Vegas, Nev.
Walsh, John E., Educ. & Training Grp., Oak & Pawnee Sts., Scranton, Pa.
Walter, Raymond L., Box 265, Millbrook, Ala.
Walter, Robert B., 434 N. DelMar Ave., San Gabriel, Calif.
Walthew, John K., 4 Larkspur Lane, Trenton, N.J.
Walz, Garry R., 1718 Arbordale, Ann Arbor, Mich.
Wampler, W. Norman, Superintendent of Schools, Bellflower, Calif.
Ward, Byron J., 155 Park Way, Camillus, N.Y.
Ward, Charles A., 2525 Columbus, Waco, Tex.
Ward, George H., P.O. Box 15, Hauppauge, N.Y.
Ward, Ted, Michigan State University, East Lansing, Mich.
Ward, Virgil S., Sch. of Educ., University of Virginia, Charlottesville, Va.
Wardeberg, Helen L., Cornell University, Ithaca, New York
Warmbrod, J. Robert, Ohio St. Univ., Columbus, Ohio
Warner, Alvina C., 169 Horseshoe Dr., Kirkwood, Mo.
Warren, Alex M., R. D. #4, Comfort Road, Ithaca, N.Y.
Warren, John H., 425 W. Ormsby Ave., Louisville, Ky.
Warren, Mary Lou, 1334 Division St., Port Huron, Mich.
Warren, Robert A., 730 Santa Barbara, Kingsville, Tex.
Warshavsky, Mrs. Belle, 35 Cooper Dr., Great Neck, N.Y.
Warshavsky, Bernard, 910 West End Ave., New York, N.Y.
Wartenberg, Herbert, 8631 Patton Rd., Philadelphia, Pa.
Warwick, Raymond, Box 73, Delmont, N.J.
Warwick, Ronald P., 2222 Scottwood-Apt. 1, Toledo, Ohio
Wasem, G. Leighton, 50 Wedgewood Terr., Springfield, Ill.
Washington, Walter, Alcorn A & M Col., Larmon, Miss.
Wasserman, Mrs. Lillian, 1684 Meadow Lane, East Meadow, N.Y.
Wasson, Margaret, 3705 University Blvd., Dallas, Tex.
Waterman, David C., Indiana State University, Terre Haute, Ind.
Waterman, Floyd T., Univ. of Nebr. at Omaha, Omaha, Nebr.
Waters, E. Worthington, Morgan State College, Baltimore, Md.
Waters, Mrs. Emma B., 228 E. Valley Ave., Holly Springs, Miss.
Watkins, Ralph K., 702 Ingleside Dr., Columbia, Mo.
Watkins, Ray H., Dallas Baptist College, Dallas, Tex.
Watkins, W. O., Eastern New Mexico University, Portales, N.Mex.
Watkins, Yancey L., 803 N. 20th St., Murray, Ky.
Watson, Carlos M., Indiana State College, Terre Haute, Ind.
Watson, D. Gene, 5835 Kimbark Ave., Chicago, Ill.
Watson, David R., Highland Park, Ill.
Watson, John E., N. Z. Council for Educ. Res., Wellington, New Zealand
Watson, Norman E., Orange Coast College, Costa Mesa, Calif.
Watson, Paul E., Univ. of Pittsburgh, Pittsburgh, Pa.
Watson, William Crawford, 29 Woodstock Rd., Mt. Waverly, Victoria, Australia
Watt, Ralph W., 1206 Parker Ave., Hyattsville, Md.
Wattenberg, William W., 20220 Murray Hill, Detroit, Mich.
Watters, Velma V., 1365 Mozley Pl., S.W., Atlanta, Ga.
Watts, Mrs. Helen S., University of Dubuque, Dubuque, Iowa
Waxwood, Howard B., 303 Witherspoon St., Princeton, N.J.
Way, Gail W., 1232 Henderson St., Chicago, Ill.
Wayson, William W., 1330 President Dr., Columbus, Ohio
Weakley, Mrs. Mary L., 1426 Center St., Geneva, Ill.
Weaver, Gladys C., 4708 Tecumseh St., College Park, Md.
Weaver, David A., Southwest Baptist Col., Bolivar, Mo.
Webb, Anne K., 1402 W. Main St., Shelbyville, Ky.
Webb, Clark D., Brigham Young Univ., Provo, Utah

Webb, E. Sue, 216 West 5th St., Shawano, Wis.
Webb, Holmes, Dept. of Educ., Texas Tech. College, Lubbock, Tex.
Webb, Leland, Sutton Hall, Univ. of Texas, Austin, Tex.
Webber, Warren L., Music Dept., Cedarville College, Cedarville, Ohio
Weber, Clarence A., N. Eagleville Rd., Storrs, Conn.
Weber, Martha Gesling, Bowling Green State University, Bowling Green, Ohio
Weber, Wilford A., Syracuse University, Syracuse, N.Y.
Weber, William C., Signal Hill Schl. Dist. # 181, E. St. Louis, Ill.
Weddington, Rachel T., Queens College, 65-30 Kissena Blvd., Flushing, N.Y.
Weeks, Shirley, University of Hawaii, Honolulu, Hawaii
Weele, Jan C. Ter, Hanover Supv. Union # 22, Hanover, N.H.
*Wees, W. R., Ont. Inst. for Studies in Educ., Toronto, Ont., Can.
Weesner, Gary L., 619 Hendricks Court, Marion, Ind.
Wegrzyn, Helen A., 5240 W. Newport Ave., Chicago, Ill.
Wehner, Freda, Wisconsin State College, Oshkosh, Wis.
Wehrer, Charles S., John F. Kennedy Col., Wahoo, Neb.
Weigler, Diane L., 5733 S.W. Orchid Ct., Portland, Oreg.
Weiland, Mrs. Harry, 67-14 168th St., Flushing, N.Y.
Weilbaker, Charles R., Tchrs. Col., University of Cincinnati, Cincinnati, Ohio
Weiner, Robert I., 1208 Westshore Dr., Ashtabula, Ohio
Weinhold, John D., 1637 Meadow Lane, Seward, Nebr.
Weintraub, Samuel, Indiana University, Bloomington, Ind.
Weis, Harold P., 437—23rd Ave., Moline, Ill.
Weisbender, Leo F., 12792 Topaz St., Garden Grove, Calif.
Weisberg, Patricia H., 2370 N. Terrace Ave., Milwaukee, Wis.
Weischadle, David E., 6 Ribsam St., Trenton, N.J.
Weisiger, Louise P., 2722 Hillcrest Rd., Richmond, Va.
Weisman, Gerald, 407 E. Allens Lane, Philadelphia, Pa.
Weiss, Joel, 20 Bernard Ave., Apt. 4, Toronto, Ont., Canada
Weiss, M. Jerry, Jersey City State College, Jersey City, N.J.
Weissleder, Claudette P., 135 Belmont Ave., Jersey City, N.J.
Welcenbach, Frank J., Trombly School, Grosse Pointe, Mich.
Welch, Cornelius A., St. Bonaventure Univ., St. Bonaventure, N.Y.
Welch, Ronald C., Sch. of Educ., Indiana University, Bloomington, Ind.
Weldon, John J., RFD 2, New Era Rd., Carbondale, Ill.
Welker, Latney C., Jr., Univ. of So. Mississippi, Hattiesburg, Miss.
Weller, Harold, 4 Corsa St., Dix Hills, N.Y.
Welliver, Paul W., 229 S. Patterson St., State College, Pa.
Wells, Carl S., Box 485, Col. Sta., Hammond, La.
Wells, Robert S., Superintendent of Schools, Reading, Mass.
Weltner, William H., Colo. State Coll., McKee Hall #35, Greeley, Colo.
Welton, William B., Prospect Public Schools, Prospect, Conn.
Wendt, Paul R., Southern Illinois University, Carbondale, Ill.
Wenger, Roy E., Kent State University, Kent, Ohio
Wenner, Harry W., 40 Mills St., Morristown, N.J.
Wennstrom, Harold, 2922 W. 167th St., Torrance, Calif.
Wentz, Robert E., Penn-Harris-Madison Sch. Corp., Mishawaka, Ind.
Werley, Harriet, H., 1447 Hollywood, Grosse Pointe Woods, Mich.
Werstler, Richard E., Adrian College, Adrian, Mich.
Werth, Trostel G., 18549 S.E. Tibbetts Ct., Gresham, Oreg.
Wesley, Emory J., Henderson State Tchrs. Col., Arkadelphia, Ark.
Wesselman, Roy L., MSU-Macomb Teacher Educ. Ctr., Warren, Mich.
Wessler, Martin, F., 3558 S. Jefferson Ave., St. Louis, Mo.
Wesson, James B., Miami Univ., Oxford, Ohio
West, Charles K., 501 S. Westlawn, Champaign, Ill.
West, Edna, 648 Sunset Blvd., Baton Rouge, La.
West, Helene, Beverly Hills H.S., 310 S. Altmont Dr., Los Angeles, Calif.
West, Lorraine W., Fresno State College, Fresno, Calif.
West, William H., Supt., County Union Schls., Elizabeth, N.J.
Westbrooks, Sadye Wylena, 1433 Sharon St., N.W., Atlanta, Ga.

Westby-Gibson, Dorothy, San Francisco State College, San Francisco, Calif.
Westcott, William D., Swartley Rd., Hatfield, Pa.
Wetmore, Joseph N., Dept. of Educ., Ohio Wesleyan Univ., Delaware, Ohio
Wetzel, Rev. Chester M., 55 Elizabeth St., Hartford, Conn.
Wewer, William P., 1461 Wedgewood Dr., Anaheim, Calif.
Weyer, F. E., Dept. of Educ., Campbell College, Buies Creek, N.C.
Whalen, Thomas J., 33 Pearl St., Pittsfield, Mass.
Whaley, Charles, Kentucky Educ. Assn., 101 W. Walnut St., Louisville, Ky.
Whang, H. Henry, 2620 West Prospect, Milwaukee, Wis.
Wharton, William P., Allegheny College, Meadville, Pa.
•Wheat, Leonard B., Univ. of Missouri, St. Louis, Mo.
Wheelock, Warren H., Reading Clinic, Univ. of Missouri, Kansas City, Mo.
Whelan, Gerald J., Rev., Colegio St. George, Santiago, Chile
Whelan, William J., Wells High Schl., Des Plaines, Ill.
Whetton, Annette, 1810 N. Mitchell St., Phoenix, Ariz.
Whetton, Mrs. Betty B., 1810 N. Mitchell St., Phoenix, Ariz.
Whilt, Selma E., 24 Yorkshire Dr., Buffalo, N.Y.
Whitaker, Prevo L., Indiana University, Bloomington, Ind.
Whitcraft, Carol J., Box 8005 Univ. Sta., Austin, Tex.
White, Andrew W., Col. of Santa Fe, Cerrillos Rd., Santa Fe, N.Mex.
White, George L., Polk & Geary Sts., San Francisco, Calif.
White, Jack, Rt. 5, Parker Pl., Franklin, Tenn.
White, John C., Edison School, Mesa, Ariz.
White, Kenneth E., Dept. of Educ., Hamline Univ., St. Paul, Minn.
Whited, Frances M., 29 South Ave., Brockport, N.Y.
Whiteford, Emma B., 740 River Dr., St. Paul, Minn.
Whitehead, Willis A., 23351 Chagrin Blvd., Beachwood, Ohio
Whitman, Harold L., Columbus Col., Columbus, Ohio
Whitmer, Dana P., Superintendent of Schools, Pontiac, Mich.
Whitmore, Keith E., 396 Oakridge Drive, Rochester, N.Y.
Whitt, Robert L., Drake Univ., Des Moines, Iowa
Wicklund, Lee A., Idaho State Univ., Pocatello, Idaho
Wiebe, Elias H., Pacific College, Fresno, Calif.
Wiebe, Joel A., 315 S. Wilson Ave., Hillsboro, Kans.
•Wieden, Clifford, 31 Barton St., Presque Isle, Maine
Wiggin, Gladys A., Col. of Educ., Univ. of Maryland, College Park, Md.
Wiggins, Henry, Southern Univ., Baton Rouge, La.
Wiggins, Thomas W., Univ. of Oklahoma, Norman, Okla.
Wilber, Lora Ann, Stony Brook, L.I., N.Y.
Wilburn, D. Banks, Glenville State College, Glenville, W.Va.
Wile, Marcia, 4341 Baintree, University Hghts., Ohio
Wilhelms, Fred T., 1201-16th St., Washington, D.C.
Wilkerson, Doxey A., 34 Dock Rd., South Norwalk, Conn.
Wilkinson, Harold A., 7744 Sta. ACC, Abilene, Tex.
Wilkinson, Jack, Univ. of No. Iowa, Cedar Falls, Iowa
Wilks, Jerome, 33 Larkin St., Huntington Sta., N.Y.
Willard, Robert L., Utica College, Utica, N.Y.
Willey, Laurence V., Jr., 3001 Veazey Terrace, N.W., Washington, D.C.
Williams, Alfred H., 9712 Nova St., Pico Rivera, Calif.
Williams, Arloff L., 316½ W. Koenig St., Grand Island, Nebr.
Williams, Arthur E., Dillard Comprehensive High School, Fort Lauderdale, Fla.
Williams, Buford W., Southwest Texas State College, San Marcos, Tex.
Williams, Charles C., North Texas State College, Denton, Tex.
Williams, Clarence M., Col. of Educ., Univ. of Rochester, Rochester, N.Y.
Williams, Donald F., Emory Univ., Atlanta, Ga.
Williams, Douglas F., 404 Green St., Auburn, Ala.
•Williams, Fannie C., 3108 Tours St., New Orleans, La.
Williams, Fountie N., 505 Pennsylvania Ave., Clarksburg, W.Va.
Williams, Frances I., Lab. Sch., Indiana State Univ., Terre Haute, Ind.
Williams, Gloria M., Univ. of Minnesota, St. Paul, Minn.

Williams, Harold A., Flat Top, W.Va.
Williams, Herman, 40 Elmwood St., Tiffin, Ohio
Williams, Howard Y., Jr., 3464 Siems Ct., St. Paul, Minn.
Williams, Mrs. Lois, 200 North 18th St., Montebello, Calif.
Williams, Malcolm, Sch. of Educ., Tennessee A. & I. University, Nashville, Tenn.
Williams, Mary Jo, 7862 Melrose, Detroit, Mich.
Williams, Myrtle M., 4631 Annette St., New Orleans, La.
Williams, Richard H., 380 Moseley Rd., Hillsborough, Calif.
Williams, Major Thomas, 109 Porter St., Blackburg, Va.
Williams, W. Morris, 2301 East St., Washington, D.C.
Williams, Wilbur A., Eastern Michigan University, Ypsilanti, Mich.
Williams, William K., 2342 S. Glen Ave., Decatur, Ill.
Williamson, Jane, Pacific Lutheran University, Tacoma, Wash.
Willis, Henry H., 1102 Sixth Ave., Cleveland, Ohio
Wills, Benjamin G., 1145 Stenway Ave., Campbell, Calif.
Willsey, Alan D., SUNY College, Courtland, N.Y.
Wilson, Alan S., Hillyer Col., University of Hartford, Hartford, Conn.
Wilson, Alan T., Faircrest Sch., St. Francis, Wis.
Wilson, David A., 9125 Gross Pt. Rd., Skokie, Ill.
Wilson, David H., Seneca St., Interlaken, N.Y.
Wilson, Elizabeth, 3148 Que St., N.W., Washington, D.C.
Wilson, Frederick R., 1633 K., Spartan Village, East Lansing, Mich.
Wilson, George H., 430 S. Michigan, Chicago, Ill.
Wilson, Harold M., 3006 N. Trinidad St., Arlington, Va.
Wilson, Herbert B., University of Arizona, Tucson, Ariz.
Wilson, James W., 249 Harris Ave., Needham, Mass.
Wilson, James W., Univ. of Georgia, Athens, Ga.
Wilson, Jean Alice, 715 Tidball Ave., Grove City, Pa.
Wilson, John A. R., 2519 Chapala St., Santa Barbara, Calif.
Wilson, John L., 15800 N.W. 42nd Ave., Miami, Fla.
Wilson, Lois, N.Y. State Teachers Assn., Albany, N.Y
Wilson, Merle A., 2800—62nd St., Des Moines, Iowa
Wilson, Robert D., 1081 Gayley Ave., Los Angeles. Calif.
Wilson, Roy K., N.E.A., 1201—16th St., N.W., Washington, D.C.
Wilson, Roy R. Jr., 1014 Decker Dr., West Bend, Wis.
Wilson, William J., Jr., 1821 N.W. 27th Terr., Fort Lauderdale, Fla.
Wilson, Yolande M., Sch. of Educ., Univ. of Chicago, Chicago, Ill.
Wilstach, Mrs. Ilah M., 2127 N. Eastern Ave., Los Angeles, Calif.
Wiltse, Earl W., Northern Illinois Univ., DeKalb, Ill.
Windsor, John G., 4354 West 9th Ave., Vancouver, B.C., Canada
Winebrenner, Neil T., 3844 N. Morris Blvd., Shorewood, Wis.
Winfield, Kenneth, East Stroudsburg State Col., Stroudsburg, Pa.
Wing, Richard L., Directorate USDESEA, APO-09164
Wing, Sherman W., Superintendent of Schools, Provo, Utah
Wingerd, Harold H., Superintendent of Schools, West Chester, Pa.
Wingren, Ralf, River Lane, Santa Ana, Calif.
Winkley, Carol K., 125 Forsythe Ln., DeKalb, Ill.
Winkler, Neal K., P.O. Box 1084, Bloomington, Ind.
Winsor, George E., Wilmington College, Wilmington, Ohio
Winter, Nathan B., 3206 Sunnyside Drive, Rockford, Ill.
Wise, Harold L., Hecksville Public Schs., Hecksville, N.Y.
Wise, Joe, Eastern Kentucky St. Univ., Richmond, Ky.
Wise, Pauline, 928 Larchmont Crescent, Norfolk, Va.
Wisniewski, Virginia, 4623 Ostrom, Lakewood, Calif.
Witchel, Barbara M., 27 Myrtledale Rd., Scarsdale, N.Y.
Witherspoon, W. H., P.O. Box 527, Rockhill, S.C.
Witt, Carl P., 22900 Blythe St., Canoga Park, Calif.
Witt, Marquis G., Mjr., 5390 Mitchell Ave., Otis AFB, Mass.
Witt, Paul W. F., Michigan State Univ., East Lansing, Mich.
Witte, Cyril M., R. 2, Box 264, Mt. Airy, Md.

Witten, Charles H., University of South Carolina, Columbia, S.C.
Witter, Sanford C., 1900 W. County Rd., St. Paul, Minn.
Wittick, Mildred Letton, 300 Pompton Rd., Wayne, N.J.
Wittmer, Arthur E., 315 Park Ave. S., Rm. 1920, New York, N.Y.
Witty, Paul A., 5555 N. Sheridan Rd., Chicago, Ill.
Wixon, John L., 29080 Oxford Ave., The Knolls, Richmond, Calif.
Wochner, Raymond E., Arizona State University, Tempe, Ariz.
Woditsch, June, 6801 Maplewood, Sylvania, Ohio
Woerdehoff, Frank J., Dept. of Educ., Purdue University, Lafayette, Ind.
Woestehoff, Orville W., Oak Park Elementary Schls., Oak Park, Ill.
Wohlers, A. E., Ohio State University, Columbus, Ohio
Wolbrecht, Walter F., 316 Parkwood, Kirkwood, Mo.
Wold, Stanley G., 1924 Orchard Pl., Fort Collins, Colo.
Wolf, Dan B., Indiana Univ., Indianapolis, Ind.
Wolf, Helen S., 2035 Heather Terrace, Northfield, Ill.
Wolf, Ray O., Portland State College, Portland, Oreg.
Wolf, Vivian C., 8802-9th Ave., S.W., Seattle, Wash.
Wolf, William C., Jr., University of Massachusetts, Amherst, Mass.
Wolfe, Deborah P., Queens College, Flushing, N.Y.
Wolfe, Josephine B., Beaver Hill Apts., Jenkintown, Pa.
Wolfendon, Mrs. R., 25 S. Hazelton, B.C., Canada
Wolfson, Bernice J., 2121 E. Capitol Dr., #410, Milwaukee, Wis.
Wolinsky, Gloria F., 69-52 Groton St., Forest Hills, N.Y.
Womack, James, Board of Coop. Educ'l Serv., Huntington, N.Y.
Wong, William T. S., 1640 Paula Dr., Honolulu, Hawaii
Wood, C. Robert, 2608 Sherwood Lane, Austin, Tex.
Wood, Donald I., Dept. of Educ., Rice University, Houston, Tex.
Wood, George T., 3405 Longview, Bloomington, Ind.
Wood, Joseph E., 3 Tam-O-Shanter Way, S. Yarmouth, Mass.
Wood, Rebecca H., P.O. Box 3329, Lafayette, La.
Wood, W. Clement, Fort Hays Kansas State College, Hays, Kans.
Woodard, Nancy, 2732 Alnwick Rd., Bryn Athyn, Pa.
Woodburn, A. C., Alamogordo Public Schools, Alamogordo, N.Mex.
Woodburn, John H., Charles E. Woodward H.S., Rockville, Md.
Woodburn, Mary Jean, 507 E. Main St., Madison, Ind.
Woodbury, Tom, Livonia Pub. Schools, Livonia, Mich.
Woodhouse, David J., Brookside Apts., Chapel Hill, N.C.
Woodin, Ralph J., Ohio St. Univ., Columbus, Ohio
Woods, Joanne, Univ. of Southern Calif., Los Angeles, Calif.
Woods, Robert K., Div. of Elem. Jr. H.S. Educ., Platteville, Wis.
Woodson, C. C., 435 S. Liberty St., Spartanburg, S.C.
Woodward, Dorothy E., Williams Sch., Glendora, Calif.
Woodworth, Denny, Col. of Educ., Drake University, Des Moines, Iowa
Woodworth, William O., 999 Kedzie Ave., Flossmoor, Ill.
Woody, Roger I., 2006 Dew Ave., West Columbia, S.C.
Woolley, Dale C., 405 Hilgard Ave., Los Angeles, Calif.
Woolley, Joan, 4615 Via Corona, Torrance, Calif.
Woolson, Edith L., Box 203, Imperial, Calif.
Wootton, Nancy M., Alex. Hamilton Sch., Morristown, N.J.
Wootton, John W., 459 Lyons Rd., Liberty Corner, N.J.
Workman, Stanley, 149-07 Sanford Ave., Flushing, N.Y.
Wozencraft, Marian, Eastern Ill. Univ., Charleston, Ill.
Wray, Mabel Elizabeth, 224 Mower St., Worcester, Mass.
Wrenn, Michael P., 6642 Bosworth, Chicago, Ill.
Wright, Floyd K., 1432 Price Dr., Cape Girardeau, Mo.
Wright, John R., San Jose State College, San Jose, Calif.
Wright, Robert D., 1205 Cling Circle, Hanford, Calif.
Wright, Samuel Lee, 8919—91st Pl., Lanham, Md.
Wright, Walka C., 285 Franklin Rd., Englewood, N.J.
Wright, William H., Jr., 13542 E. Starbuck St., Whittier, Calif.

Wright, William J., 12093 Monter, Bridgeton, Mo.
Wrightstone, J. Wayne, 21 Hickory Rd., Summit, N.J.
Wronski, Stanley P., Col. of Educ., Michigan State Univ., East Lansing, Mich.
Wu, Julia Tu, Hunter Col., New York, N.Y.
Wunderlich, Kenneth W., 665 Wald Rd., New Braunfels, Tex.
Wuolle, Mrs. Ethel, P.O. Box 173, Pine City, Minn.
Wyatt, William K., 3406 Brookmeade, Memphis, Tenn.
Wyckoff, D. Campbell, Princeton Theological Seminary, Princeton, N.J.
Wyeth, E. R., 18111 Nordhoff St., Northridge, Calif.
Wyllie, Eugene D., Sch. of Bus., Indiana University, Bloomington, Ind.
Wynn, Willa T., 1122 N. St. Clair St., Pittsburgh, Pa.

Yamamoto, Kaoru, Col. of Educ., Penn. State Univ., University Park, Pa.
Yanis, Martin, 101 S. Second St., Harrisburg, Pa.
Yates, J. W., 223 Wham, Southern Illinois University, Carbondale, Ill.
Yauch, Wilbur A., Northern Illinois University, DeKalb, Ill.
Yeager, John L., LRDC, 160 No. Craig St., Pittsburgh, Pa.
Yeazell, Mary W., Virginia Univ., Morgantown, W. Va.
Yee, Albert H., Univ. of Wisconsin, Madison, Wis.
Ylinen, Gerald A., Gustavus Adolphus College, St. Peter, Minn.
Ylisto, Ingrid P., Eastern Michigan University, Ypsilanti, Mich.
Yochim, Louise Dunn, 9545 Drake, Evanston, Ill.
Yockey, Gay J., Box 46, Benton Ridge, Ohio
Yoder, Orville L., 3023 Stadium Dr., Columbus, Ohio
York, L. Jean, Univ. of Texas, Austin, Tex.
York, William, Bowling Green University, Bowling Green, Ohio
Young, Carol A., Doane College, Crete, Nebr.
Young, Charles R., 999 Green Bay Road, Glencoe, Ill.
Young, Harold L., Central Missouri State College, Warrensburg, Mo.
Young, J. E. M., Macdonald College Post Office, Quebec, Canada
Young, Jean A., Sonoma State College, Rohnert Park, Calif.
Young, John A., 35 Vincent Rd., Dedham, Mass.
Young, Michael A., 1022 Varsity Sq. West, Bowling Green, Ohio
Young, Paul A., Judson College, Elgin, Ill.
Young, Robert W., 68 E. Main St., Mendham, N.J.
* Young, William E., State Education Department, Albany, N.Y.
Young, W. H., 1150 N. Belsay Rd., Flint, Mich.
Young, William Howard, 1460 Tampa Ave., Dayton, Ohio
Youngblood, Chester E., 506 N. 6th St., Weatherford, Okla.
Younie, William J., Tchrs. Col., Columbia University, New York, N.Y.
Yuhas, Theodore Frank, Educ. Dept., Ball State University, Muncie, Ind.
Yunghans, Ernest E., Wartburg College, Waverly, Iowa

Zahorsky, Mrs. Metta, San Francisco State College, San Francisco, Calif.
Zak, Eugene, 7205 Beresford Ave., Parma, Ohio
Zambito, Stephen Charles, Eastern Michigan University, Ypsilanti, Mich.
Zambor, Ronald J., 75 Manalapan Rd., Spotswood, N.J.
Zari, Rosalie V., 1218 - 17th Ave., San Francisco, Calif.
Zatlukal, James M., 104 Pearl St., Liverpool, N.Y.
Zbornik, Joseph J., 3219 Clarence Ave., Berwyn, Ill.
Zdanowicz, Paul John, 10 Detson Pl., Methuen, Mass.
Zebrowski, Kenneth M., Decatur Sch., USNAF, Box 8, APO, N.Y.
Zeldin, David, Oriel Cottage, St. Mary's Rd., Mortimer, Berkshire, England
Zeller, William D., Dept. of Educ., Illinois State Univ., Normal, Ill.
Zelmer, A. C. Lynn, 305-12021 Jasper Ave., Edmonton, Alta., Can.
Zelnick, Joseph, 201 Marine St., Beach Haven, N.J.
Zepper, John T., Educ. Bldg., University of New Mexico, Albuquerque, N.Mex.
Ziebold, Edna B., 6401 Linda Vista Rd., San Diego, Calif.
Ziegler, Lorene E., Eastern Ill. Univ., Charleston, Ill.

Zieman, Orlyn A., Appleton Public Schools, Appleton, Wis.
Ziemba, Walter J., St. Mary's College, Orchard Lake, Mich.
Zierman, Raymond T., 606 Virginia St., Joliet, Ill.
Zim, Herbert S., Box 34, Tavernier, Fla.
Zimmerman, Gary E., Guilford Col., Greensboro, N.C.
Zimmerman, Herbert M., Roosevelt High School, Chicago, Ill.
Zimmerman, Howard, 9001 Stockdale, Bakersfield, Calif.
Zimmerman, William G., 28 Winthrop Rd., Hingham, Mass.
Zimnoch, Frances J., Meadowbrook Elem. Schl., East Meadow, L.I., N.Y.
Zintz, Miles V., 3028 Marble Ave., N.E. Albuquerque, N.Mex.
Ziobrowski, Stasia M., Sch. of Educ., New York Univ., New York, N.Y.
Zipper, Joseph H., 1569 West 41st St., Erie, Pa.
Zoepfel, Mary M., 1385 Ukiah Way, Upland, Calif.
Zunigha, Bennie Jean, Box 354, Ft. Wingate, N.Mex.
Zussman, Barbara, 3545 Mound View Ave., Studio City, Calif.
Zweig, Richard L., 9442 Rambler Dr., Huntington Beach, Calif.

INFORMATION CONCERNING THE NATIONAL SOCIETY FOR THE STUDY OF EDUCATION

1. PURPOSE. The purpose of the National Society is to promote the investigation and discussion of educational questions. To this end it holds an annual meeting and publishes a series of yearbooks.

2. ELIGIBILITY TO MEMBERSHIP. Any person who is interested in receiving its publications may become a member by sending to the Secretary-Treasurer information concerning name, title, and address, and a check for $9.00 (see Item 5), except that graduate students, on the recommendation of a faculty member, may become members by paying $7.00 for the first year of their membership. Dues for all subsequent years are the same as for other members (see Item 4).

Membership is not transferable; it is limited to individuals, and may not be held by libraries, schools, or other institutions, either directly or indirectly.

3. PERIOD OF MEMBERSHIP. Applicants for membership may not date their entrance back of the current calendar year, and all memberships terminate automatically on December 31, unless the dues for the ensuing year are paid as indicated in Item 6.

4. DUTIES AND PRIVILEGES OF MEMBERS. Members pay dues of $8.00 annually, receive a cloth-bound copy of each publication, are entitled to vote, to participate in discussion, and (under certain conditions) to hold office. The names of members are printed in the yearbooks.

Persons who are sixty years of age or above may become life members on payment of fee based on average life-expectancy of their age group. For information, apply to Secretary-Treasurer.

5. ENTRANCE FEE. New members are required the first year to pay, in addition to the dues, an entrance fee of one dollar.

6. PAYMENT OF DUES. Statements of dues are rendered in October for the following calendar year. Any member so notified whose dues remain unpaid on January 1 thereby loses his membership and can be reinstated only by paying a reinstatement fee of fifty cents.

School warrants and vouchers from institutions must be accompanied by definite information concerning the name and address of the person for whom membership fee is being paid. Statements of dues are rendered on our own form only. The Secretary's office cannot undertake to fill out special invoice forms of any sort or to affix notary's affidavit to statements or receipts.

Cancelled checks serve as receipts. Members desiring an additional receipt must enclose a stamped and addressed envelope therefor.

7. DISTRIBUTION OF YEARBOOKS TO MEMBERS. The yearbooks, ready prior to each February meeting, will be mailed from the office of the distributor, only to members whose dues for that year have been paid. Members who desire yearbooks prior to the current year must purchase them directly from the distributor (see Item 8).

8. COMMERCIAL SALES. The distribution of all yearbooks prior to the current year, and also of those of the current year not regularly mailed to members in exchange for their dues, is in the hands of the distributor, not of the Secretary. For such commercial sales, communicate directly with the University of Chicago Press, Chicago, Illinois 60637, which will gladly send a price list covering all the publications of this Society. This list is also printed in the yearbook.

9. YEARBOOKS. The yearbooks are issued about one month before the February meeting. They comprise from 600 to 800 pages annually. Unusual effort has been made to make them, on the one hand, of immediate practical value, and, on the other hand, representative of sound scholarship and scientific investigation.

10. MEETINGS. The annual meeting, at which the yearbooks are discussed, is held in February at the same time and place as the meeting of the American Association of School Administrators. Members will be notified of other meetings.

Applications for membership will be handled promptly at any time on receipt of name and address, together with check for $9.00 (or $8.50 for reinstatement). Applications entitle the new members to the yearbook slated for discussion during the calendar year the application is made.

5835 Kimbark Ave.
Chicago, Illinois 60637

HERMAN G. RICHEY, *Secretary-Treasurer*

PUBLICATIONS OF THE NATIONAL SOCIETY FOR THE STUDY OF EDUCATION

NOTICE: Many of the early Yearbooks of this series are now out of print. In the following list, those titles to which an asterisk is prefixed are not available for purchase.

POSTPAID PRICE

*First Yearbook, 1902, Part I—*Some Principles in the Teaching of History.* Lucy M. Salmon ....
*First Yearbook, 1902, Part II—*The Progress of Geography in the Schools.* W. M. Davis and H. M. Wilson..
*Second Yearbook, 1903, Part I—*The Course of Study in History in the Common School.* Isabel Lawrence, C. A. McMurry, Frank McMurry, E. C. Page, and E. J. Rice ....
*Second Yearbook, 1903, Part II—*The Relation of Theory to Practice in Education.* M. J. Holmes, J. A. Keith, and Levi Seeley..
*Third Yearbook, 1904, Part I—*The Relation of Theory to Practice in the Education of Teachers.* John Dewey, Sarah C. Brooks, F. M. McMurry, *et al.* ....
*Third Yearbook, 1904, Part II—*Nature Study.* W. S. Jackman..................
*Fourth Yearbook, 1905, Part I—*The Education and Training of Secondary Teachers.* E. C. Elliott, E. G. Dexter, M. J. Holmes, *et al.* ....
*Fourth Yearbook, 1905, Part II—*The Place of Vocational Subjects in the High-School Curriculum.* J. S. Brown, G. B. Morrison, and Ellen Richards...............
*Fifth Yearbook, 1906, Part I—*On the Teaching of English in Elementary and High Schools.* G. P. Brown and Emerson Davis..
*Fifth Yearbook, 1906, Part II—*The Certification of Teachers.* E. P. Cubberley......
*Sixth Yearbook, 1907, Part I—*Vocational Studies for College Entrance.* C. A. Herrick, H. W. Holmes, T. deLaguna, V. Prettyman, and W. J. S. Bryan.........
*Sixth Yearbook, 1907, Part II—*The Kindergarten and Its Relation to Elementary Education.* Ada Van Stone Harris, E. A. Kirkpatrick, Marie Kraus-Boelté, Patty S. Hill, Harriette M. Mills, and Nina Vandewalker..
*Seventh Yearbook, 1908, Part I—*The Relation of Superintendents and Principals to the Training and Professional Improvement of Their Teachers.* Charles D. Lowry
*Seventh Yearbook, 1908, Part II—*The Co-ordination of the Kindergarten and the Elementary School.* B. J. Gregory, Jennie B. Merrill, Bertha Payne, and Margaret Giddings ....
*Eighth Yearbook, 1909, Part I—*Education with Reference to Sex: Pathological, Economic, and Social Aspects.* C. R. Henderson..
*Eighth Yearbook, 1909, Part II—*Education with Reference to Sex: Agencies and Methods.* C. R. Henderson and Helen C. Putnam..
*Ninth Yearbook, 1910, Part I—*Health and Education.* T. D. Wood..............
*Ninth Yearbook, 1910, Part II—*The Nurse in Education.* T. D. Wood, *et al.*.......
*Tenth Yearbook, 1911, Part I—*The City School as a Community Center.* H. C. Leipziger, Sarah E. Hyre, R. D. Warden, C. Ward Crampton, E. W. Stitt, E. J. Ward, Mrs. E. C. Grice, and C. A. Perry..
*Tenth Yearbook, 1911, Part II—*The Rural School as a Community Center.* B. H. Crocheron, Jessie Field, F. W. Howe, E. C. Bishop, A. B. Graham, O. J. Kern, M. T. Scudder, and B. M. Davis..
*Eleventh Yearbook, 1912, Part I—*Industrial Education: Typical Experiments Described and Interpreted.* J. F. Barker, M. Bloomfield, B. W. Johnson, P. Johnson, L. M. Leavitt, G. A. Mirick, M. W. Murray, C. F. Perry, A. L. Safford, and H. B. Wilson ....
*Eleventh Yearbook, 1912, Part II—*Agricultural Education in Secondary Schools.* A. C. Monahan, R. W. Stimson, D. J. Crosby, W. H. French, H. F. Button, F. R. Crane, W. R. Hart, and G. F. Warren..
*Twelfth Yearbook, 1913, Part I—*The Supervision of City Schools.* Franklin Bobbitt, J. W. Hall, and J. D. Wolcott..
*Twelfth Yearbook, 1913, Part II—*The Supervision of Rural Schools.* A. C. Monahan, L. J. Hanifan, J. E. Warren, Wallace Lund, U. J. Hoffman, A. S. Cook, E. M. Rapp, Jackson Davis, and J. D. Wolcott..
*Thirteenth Yearbook, 1914, Part I—*Some Aspects of High-School Instruction and Administration.* H. C. Morrison, E. R. Breslich, W. A. Jessup, and L. D. Coffman..
*Thirteenth Yearbook, 1914, Part II—*Plans for Organizing School Surveys, with a Summary of Typical School Surveys.* Charles H. Judd and Henry L. Smith.....
*Fourteenth Yearbook, 1915, Part I—*Minimum Essentials in Elementary School Subjects—Standards and Current Practices.* H. B. Wilson, H. W. Holmes, F. E. Thompson, R. G. Jones, S. A. Courtis, W. S. Gray, F. N. Freeman, H. C. Pryor, J. F. Hosic, W. A. Jessup, and W. C. Bagley..
*Fourteenth Yearbook, 1915, Part II—*Methods for Measuring Teachers' Efficiency.* Arthur C. Boyce..
*Fifteenth Yearbook, 1916, Part I—*Standards and Tests for the Measurement of the Efficiency of Schools and School Systems.* G. D. Strayer, Bird T. Baldwin, B. R. Buckingham, F. W. Ballou, D. C. Bliss, H. G. Childs, S. A. Courtis, E. P. Cubberley, C. H. Judd, George Melcher, E. E. Oberholtzer, J. B. Sears, Daniel Starch, M. R. Trabue, and G. M. Whipple..

POSTPAID PRICE

*Fifteenth Yearbook, 1916, Part II—*The Relationship between Persistence in School and Home Conditions.* Charles E. Holley..

*Fifteenth Yearbook, 1916, Part III—*The Junior High School.* Aubrey A. Douglass..

*Sixteenth Yearbook, 1917, Part I—*Second Report of the Committee on Minimum Essentials in Elementary-School Subjects.* W. C. Bagley, W. W. Charters, F. N. Freeman, W. S. Gray, Ernest Horn, J. H. Hoskinson, W. S. Monroe, C. F. Munson, H. C. Pryor, L. W. Rapeer, G. M. Wilson, and H. B. Wilson............

*Sixteenth Yearbook, 1917, Part II—*The Efficiency of College Students as Conditioned by Age at Entrance and Size of High School.* B. F. Pittenger...............

*Seventeenth Yearbook, 1918, Part I—*Third Report of the Committee on Economy of Time in Education.* W. C. Bagley, B. B. Bassett, M. E. Branom, Alice Camerer, J. E. Dealey, C. A. Ellwood, E. B. Greene, A. B. Hart, J. F. Hosic, E. T. Housh, W. H. Mace, L. R. Marston, H. C. McKown, H. E. Mitchell, W. C. Reavis, D. Snedden, and H. B. Wilson..

*Seventeenth Yearbook, 1918, Part II—*The Measurement of Educational Products.* E. J. Ashbaugh, W. A. Averill, L. P. Ayers, F. W. Ballou, Edna Bryner, B. R. Buckingham, S. A. Courtis, M. E. Haggerty, C. H. Judd, George Melcher, W. S. Monroe, E. A. Nifenecker, and E. L. Thorndike.......................

*Eighteenth Yearbook, 1919, Part I—*The Professional Preparation of High-School Teachers.* G. N. Cade, S. S. Colvin, Charles Fordyce, H. H. Foster, T. S. Gosling, W. S. Gray, L. V. Koos, A. R. Mead, H. L. Miller, F. C. Whitcomb, and Clifford Woody ....

*Eighteenth Yearbook, 1919, Part II—*Fourth Report of Committee on Economy of Time in Education.* F. C. Ayer, F. N. Freeman, W. S. Gray, Ernest Horn, W. S. Monroe, and C. E. Seashore..

*Nineteenth Yearbook, 1920, Part I—*New Materials of Instruction.* Prepared by the Society's Committee on Materials of Instruction...........................

*Nineteenth Yearbook, 1920, Part II—*Classroom Problems in the Education of Gifted Children.* T. S. Henry..

*Twentieth Yearbook, 1921, Part I—*New Materials of Instruction.* Second Report by Society's Committee ....

*Twentieth Yearbook, 1921, Part II—*Report of the Society's Committee on Silent Reading.* M. A. Burgess, S. A. Courtis, C. E. Germane, W. S. Gray, H. A. Greene, Regina R. Heller, J. H. Hoover, J. A. O'Brien, J. L. Packer, Daniel Starch, W. W. Theisen, G. A. Yoakam, and representatives of other school systems............

*Twenty-first Yearbook, 1922, Parts I and II—*Intelligence Tests and Their Use,* Part I—*The Nature, History, and General Principles of Intelligence Testing.* E. L. Thorndike, S. S. Colvin, Harold Rugg, G. M. Whipple, Part II—*The Administrative Use of Intelligence Tests.* H. W. Holmes, W. K. Layton, Helen Davis, Agnes L. Rogers, Rudolf Pintner, M. R. Trabue, W. S. Miller, Bessie L. Gambrill, and others. The two parts are bound together..............................

*Twenty-second Yearbook, 1923, Part I—*English Composition: Its Aims, Methods and Measurements.* Earl Hudelson ....

*Twenty-second Yearbook, 1923, Part II—*The Social Studies in the Elementary and Secondary School.* A. S. Barr, J. J. Coss, Henry Harap, R. W. Hatch, H. C. Hill, Ernest Horn, C. H. Judd, L. C. Marshall, F. M. McMurry, Earle Rugg, H. O. Rugg, Emma Schweppe, Mabel Snedaker, and C. W. Washburne.............

*Twenty-third Yearbook, 1924, Part I—*The Education of Gifted Children.* Report of the Society's Committee. Guy M. Whipple, Chairman........................

*Twenty-third Yearbook, 1924, Part II—*Vocational Guidance and Vocational Education for Industries.* A. H. Edgerton and Others..............................

*Twenty-fourth Yearbook, 1925, Part I—*Report of the National Committee on Reading.* W. S. Gray, Chairman, F. W. Ballou, Rose L. Hardy, Ernest Horn, Francis Jenkins, S. A. Leonard, Estaline Wilson, and Laura Zirbes.......................

*Twenty-fourth Yearbook, 1925, Part II—*Adapting the Schools to Individual Differences.* Report of the Society's Committee. Carleton W. Washburn, Chairman....

*Twenty-fifth Yearbook, 1926, Part I—*The Present Status of Safety Education.* Report of the Society's Committee. Guy M. Whipple, Chairman.....................

*Twenty-fifth Yearbook, 1926, Part II—*Extra-Curricular Activities.* Report of the Society's Committee. Leonard V. Koos, Chairman..........................

*Twenty-sixth Yearbook, 1927, Part I—*Curriculum-making: Past and Present.* Report of the Society's Committee. Harold O. Rugg, Chairman.....................

*Twenty-sixth Yearbook, 1927, Part II—*The Foundations of Curriculum-making.* Prepared by individual members of the Society's Committee. Harold O. Rugg, Chairman

*Twenty-seventh Yearbook, 1928, Part I—*Nature and Nurture: Their Influence upon Intelligence.* Prepared by the Society's Committee. Lewis M. Terman, Chairman...

*Twenty-seventh Yearbook, 1928, Part II—*Nature and Nurture: Their Influence upon Achievement.* Prepared by the Society's Committee. Lewis M. Terman, Chairman.

Twenty-eighth Yearbook, 1929, Parts I and II—*Preschool and Parental Education.* Part I—*Organization and Development.* Part II—*Research and Method.* Prepared by the Society's Committee. Lois H. Meek, Chairman. Bound in one volume. Cloth $5.00

	POSTPAID PRICE
Twenty-ninth Yearbook, 1930, Parts I and II—*Report of the Society's Committee on Arithmetic*. Part I—*Some Aspects of Modern Thought on Arithmetic*. Part II—*Research in Arithmetic*. Prepared by the Society's Committee. F. B. Knight, Chairman. Bound in one volume. Cloth	$5.00
Thirtieth Yearbook, 1931, Part I—*The Status of Rural Education*. First Report of the Society's Committee on Rural Education. Orville G. Brim, Chairman. Cloth	2.50
Thirtieth Yearbook, 1931, Part II—*The Textbook in American Education*. Report of the Society's Committee on the Textbook. J. B. Edmonson, Chairman. Cloth	2.50
Paper	1.75
*Thirty-first Yearbook, 1932, Part I—*A Program for Teaching Science*. Prepared by the Society's Committee on the Teaching of Science. S. Ralph Powers, Chairman. Paper	
Thirty-first Yearbook, 1932, Part II—*Changes and Experiments in Liberal-Arts Education*. Prepared by Kathryn McHale, with numerous collaborators. Cloth	3.00
Thirty-second Yearbook, 1933—*The Teaching of Geography*. Prepared by the Society's Committee on the Teaching of Geography. A. E. Parkins, Chairman. Cloth	
Paper	3.75
Thirty-third Yearbook, 1934, Part I—*The Planning and Construction of School Buildings*. Prepared by the Society's Committee on School Buildings. N. L. Engelhardt, Chairman. Cloth	2.50
Thirty-third Yearbook, 1934, Part II—*The Activity Movement*. Prepared by the Society's Committee on the Activity Movement. Lois Coffey Mossman, Chairman. Cloth	3.00
Thirty-fourth Yearbook, 1935—*Educational Diagnosis*. Prepared by the Society's Committee on Educational Diagnosis. L. J. Brueckner, Chairman. Cloth	5.00
Paper	3.75
*Thirty-fifth Yearbook, 1936, Part I—*The Grouping of Pupils*. Prepared by the Society's Committee. W. W. Coxe, Chairman. Cloth	
*Thirty-fifth Yearbook, 1936, Part II—*Music Education*. Prepared by the Society's Committee. W. L. Uhl, Chairman. Cloth	
*Thirty-sixth Yearbook, 1937, Part I—*The Teaching of Reading*. Prepared by the Society's Committee. W. S. Gray, Chairman. Cloth	
*Thirty-sixth Yearbook, 1937, Part II—*International Understanding through the Public-School Curriculum*. Prepared by the Society's Committee. I. L. Kandel, Chairman. Paper	
*Thirty-seventh Yearbook, 1938, Part I—*Guidance in Educational Institutions*. Prepared by the Society's Committee. G. N. Kefauver, Chairman. Cloth	
*Thirty-seventh Yearbook, 1938, Part II—*The Scientific Movement in Education*. Prepared by the Society's Committee. F. N. Freeman, Chairman. Paper	
*Thirty-eighth Yearbook, 1939, Part I—*Child Development and the Curriculum*. Prepared by the Society's Committee. Carleton Washburne, Chairman. Paper	
Thirty-eighth Yearbook, 1939, Part II—*General Education in the American College*. Prepared by the Society's Committee. Alvin Eurich, Chairman. Cloth	4.00
Thirty-ninth Yearbook, 1940, Part I—*Intelligence: Its Nature and Nurture. Comparative and Critical Exposition*. Prepared by the Society's Committee. G. D. Stoddard, Chairman. Cloth	
Thirty-ninth Yearbook, 1940, Part II—*Intelligence: Its Nature and Nurture. Original Studies and Experiments*. Prepared by the Society's Committee. G. D. Stoddard, Chairman. Cloth	
*Fortieth Yearbook, 1941—*Art in American Life and Education*. Prepared by the Society's Committee. Thomas Munro, Chairman. Paper	
Forty-first Yearbook, 1942, Part I—*Philosophies of Education*. Prepared by the Society's Committee. John S. Brubacher, Chairman. Cloth	4.00
Paper	3.25
Forty-first Yearbook, 1942, Part II—*The Psychology of Learning*. Prepared by the Society's Committee. T. R. McConnell, Chairman. Cloth	4.50
Paper	3.75
Forty-second Yearbook, 1943, Part I—*Vocational Education*. Prepared by the Society's Committee. F. J. Keller, Chairman. Cloth	3.25
Paper	2.50
Forty-second Yearbook, 1943, Part II—*The Library in General Education*. Prepared by the Society's Committee. L. R. Wilson, Chairman. Cloth	4.00
Forty-third Yearbook, 1944, Part I—*Adolescence*. Prepared by the Society's Committee. Harold E. Jones, Chairman. Cloth	
Paper	3.25

POSTPAID PRICE

Forty-third Yearbook, 1944, Part II—*Teaching Language in the Elementary School.* Prepared by the Society's Committee. M. R. Trabue, Chairman. Cloth.......... $3.00

Forty-fourth Yearbook, 1945, Part I—*American Education in the Postwar Period: Curriculum Reconstruction.* Prepared by the Society's Committee. Ralph W. Tyler, Chairman. Paper 3.00

*Forty-fourth Yearbook, 1945, Part II—*American Education in the Postwar Period: Structural Reorganization.* Prepared by the Society's Committee. Bess Goodykoontz, Chairman. Paper 3.00

*Forty-fifth Yearbook, 1946, Part I—*The Measurement of Understanding.* Prepared by the Society's Committee. William A. Brownell, Chairman. Paper..........

Forty-fifth Yearbook, 1946, Part II—*Changing Conceptions in Educational Administration.* Prepared by the Society's Committee. Alonzo G. Grace, Chairman. Cloth. 4.50

*Forty-sixth Yearbook, 1947, Part I—*Science Education in American Schools.* Prepared by the Society's Committee. Victor H. Noll, Chairman. Paper..........

Forty-sixth Yearbook, 1947, Part II—*Early Childhood Education.* Prepared by the Society's Committee. N. Searle Light, Chairman. Cloth.......... 4.50
Paper 3.75

Forty-seventh Yearbook, 1948, Part I—*Juvenile Delinquency and the Schools.* Prepared by the Society's Committee. Ruth Strang, Chairman. Cloth.......... 4.50

Forty-seventh Yearbook, 1948, Part II—*Reading in the High School and College.* Prepared by the Society's Committee. William S. Gray, Chairman. Cloth.......... 4.50
Paper 3.75

Forty-eighth Yearbook, 1949, Part I—*Audio-visual Materials of Instruction.* Prepared by the Society's Committee. Stephen M. Corey, Chairman. Cloth.......... 4.50

Forty-eighth Yearbook, 1949, Part II—*Reading in the Elementary School.* Prepared by the Society's Committee. Arthur I. Gates, Chairman. Cloth.......... 4.50
Paper 3.75

Forty-ninth Yearbook, 1950, Part I—*Learning and Instruction.* Prepared by the Society's Committee. G. Lester Anderson, Chairman. Cloth..........
Paper 3.75

Forty-ninth Yearbook, 1950, Part II—*The Education of Exceptional Children.* Prepared by the Society's Committee. Samuel A. Kirk, Chairman. Cloth..........
Paper 3.75

Fiftieth Yearbook, 1951, Part I—*Graduate Study in Education.* Prepared by the Society's Board of Directors. Ralph W. Tyler, Chairman. Cloth.......... 4.50
Paper 3.75

Fiftieth Yearbook, 1951, Part II—*The Teaching of Arithmetic.* Prepared by the Society's Committee. G. T. Buswell, Chairman. Cloth.......... 4.50
Paper 3.75

Fifty-first Yearbook, 1952, Part I—*General Education.* Prepared by the Society's Committee. T. R. McConnell, Chairman. Cloth.......... 4.50
Paper 3.75

Fifty-first Yearbook, 1952, Part II—*Education in Rural Communities.* Prepared by the Society's Committee. Ruth Strang, Chairman. Cloth.......... 4.50
Paper 3.75

Fifty-second Yearbook, 1953, Part I—*Adapting the Secondary-School Program to the Needs of Youth.* Prepared by the Society's Committee. William G. Brink, Chairman. Cloth 4.50
Paper 3.75

Fifty-second Yearbook, 1953, Part II—*The Community School.* Prepared by the Society's Committee. Maurice F. Seay, Chairman. Cloth.......... 4.50
Paper 3.75

Fifty-third Yearbook, 1954, Part I—*Citizen Co-operation for Better Public Schools.* Prepared by the Society's Committee. Edgar L. Morphet, Chairman. Cloth.......... 4.50
Paper 3.75

Fifty-third Yearbook, 1954, Part II—*Mass Media and Education.* Prepared by the Society's Committee. Edgar Dale, Chairman. Cloth.......... 4.50
Paper 3.75

Fifty-fourth Yearbook, 1955, Part I—*Modern Philosophies and Education.* Prepared by the Society's Committee. John S. Brubacher, Chairman. Cloth.......... 4.50
Paper 3.75

Fifty-fourth Yearbook, 1955, Part II—*Mental Health in Modern Education.* Prepared by the Society's Committee. Paul A. Witty, Chairman. Cloth.......... 4.50
Paper 3.75

Fifty-fifth Yearbook, 1956, Part I—*The Public Junior College.* Prepared by the Society's Committee. B. Lamar Johnson, Chairman. Cloth..........
Paper ....

	POSTPAID PRICE
Fifty-fifth Yearbook, 1956, Part II—*Adult Reading.* Prepared by the Society's Committee. David H. Clift, Chairman. Cloth	$4.50
Paper	3.75
Fifty-sixth Yearbook, 1957, Part I—*In-service Education of Teachers, Supervisors, and Administrators.* Prepared by the Society's Committee. Stephen M. Corey, Chairman. Cloth	4.50
Paper	3.75
Fifty-sixth Yearbook, 1957, Part II—*Social Studies in the Elementary School.* Prepared by the Society's Committee. Ralph C. Preston, Chairman. Cloth	4.50
Paper	3.75
Fifty-seventh Yearbook, 1958, Part I—*Basic Concepts in Music Education.* Prepared by the Society's Committee. Thurber H. Madison, Chairman. Cloth	4.50
Paper	
Fifty-seventh Yearbook, 1958, Part II—*Education for the Gifted.* Prepared by the Society's Committee. Robert J. Havighurst, Chairman. Cloth	4.50
Paper	3.75
Fifty-seventh Yearbook, 1958, Part III—*The Integration of Educational Experiences.* Prepared by the Society's Committee. Paul L. Dressel, Chairman. Cloth	4.50
Fifty-eighth Yearbook, 1959, Part I—*Community Education: Principles and Practices from World-wide Experience.* Prepared by the Society's Committee. C. O. Arndt, Chairman. Cloth	4.50
Paper	3.75
Fifty-eighth Yearbook, 1959, Part II—*Personnel Services in Education.* Prepared by the Society's Committee. Melvene D. Hardee, Chairman. Cloth	4.50
Paper	3.75
Fifty-ninth Yearbook, 1960, Part I—*Rethinking Science Education.* Prepared by the Society's Committee. J. Darrell Barnard, Chairman. Cloth	4.50
Fifty-ninth Yearbook, 1960, Part II—*The Dynamics of Instructional Groups.* Prepared by the Society's Committee. Gale E. Jensen, Chairman. Cloth	4.50
Paper	3.75
Sixtieth Yearbook, 1961, Part I—*Development in and through Reading.* Prepared by the Society's Committee. Paul A. Witty, Chairman. Cloth	5.00
Paper	4.25
Sixtieth Yearbook, 1961, Part II—*Social Forces Influencing American Education.* Prepared by the Society's Committee. Ralph W. Tyler, Chairman. Cloth	4.50
Sixty-first Yearbook, 1962, Part I—*Individualizing Instruction.* Prepared by the Society's Committee. Fred T. Tyler, Chairman. Cloth	4.50
Sixty-first Yearbook, 1962, Part II—*Education for the Professions.* Prepared by the Society's Committee. G. Lester Anderson, Chairman. Cloth	4.50
Sixty-second Yearbook, 1963, Part I—*Child Psychology.* Prepared by the Society's Committee. Harold W. Stevenson, Editor. Cloth	6.50
Sixty-second Yearbook, 1963, Part II—*The Impact and Improvement of School Testing Programs.* Prepared by the Society's Committee. Warren G. Findley, Editor. Cloth	4.50
Sixty-third Yearbook, 1964, Part I—*Theories of Learning and Instruction.* Prepared by the Society's Committee. Ernest R. Hilgard, Editor. Cloth	5.50
Sixty-third Yearbook, 1964, Part II—*Behavioral Science and Educational Administration.* Prepared by the Society's Committee. Daniel E. Griffiths, Editor. Cloth	4.50
Sixty-fourth Yearbook, 1965, Part I—*Vocational Education.* Prepared by the Society's Committee. Melvin L. Barlow, Editor. Cloth	5.00
Sixty-fourth Yearbook, 1965, Part II—*Art Education.* Prepared by the Society's Committee. W. Reid Hastie, Editor. Cloth	5.00
Sixty-fifth Yearbook, 1966, Part I—*Social Deviancy among Youth.* Prepared by the Society's Committee. William W. Wattenberg, Editor. Cloth	5.50
Sixty-fifth Yearbook, 1966, Part II—*The Changing American School.* Prepared by the Society's Committee. John I. Goodlad, Editor. Cloth	5.00
Sixty-sixth Yearbook, 1967, Part I—*The Educationally Retarded and Disadvantaged.* Prepared by the Society's Committee. Paul A. Witty, Editor. Cloth	5.50
Sixty-sixth Yearbook, 1967, Part II—*Programed Instruction.* Prepared by the Society's Committee. Phil C. Lange, Editor. Cloth	5.00
Sixty-seventh Yearbook, 1968, Part I—*Metropolitanism: Its Challenge to Education.* Prepared by the Society's Committee. Robert J. Havighurst, Editor. Cloth	5.50
Sixty-seventh Yearbook, 1968, Part II—*Innovation and Change in Reading Instruction.* Prepared by the Society's Committee. Helen M. Robinson, Editor. Cloth	5.50
Sixty-eighth Yearbook, 1969, Part I—*The United States and International Education.* Prepared by the Society's Committee. Harold G. Shane, Editor. Cloth	5.50

	POSTPAID PRICE
Sixty-eighth Yearbook, 1969, Part II—*Educational Evaluation: New Roles, New Means.* Prepared by the Society's Committee. Ralph W. Tyler, Editor. Cloth....	$5.50
Sixty-ninth Yearbook, 1970, Part I—*Mathematics Education.* Prepared by the Society's Committee. Edward G. Begle, Editor. Cloth..............................	7.00
Sixty-ninth Yearbook, 1970, Part II—*Linguistics in School Programs.* Prepared by the Society's Committee. Albert H. Marckwardt, Editor. Cloth................	5.50
Seventieth Yearbook, 1971, Part I—*The Curriculum: Retrospect and Prospect.* Prepared by the Society's Committee. Robert M. McClure, Editor. Cloth............	5.50
Seventieth Yearbook, 1971, Part II—*Leaders in American Education.* Prepared by the Society's Committee. Robert J. Havighurst, Editor. Cloth.....................	6.50

Distributed by

THE UNIVERSITY OF CHICAGO PRESS, CHICAGO, ILLINOIS 60637

1971